MOSCOW VANGUARD ART

1922–1992

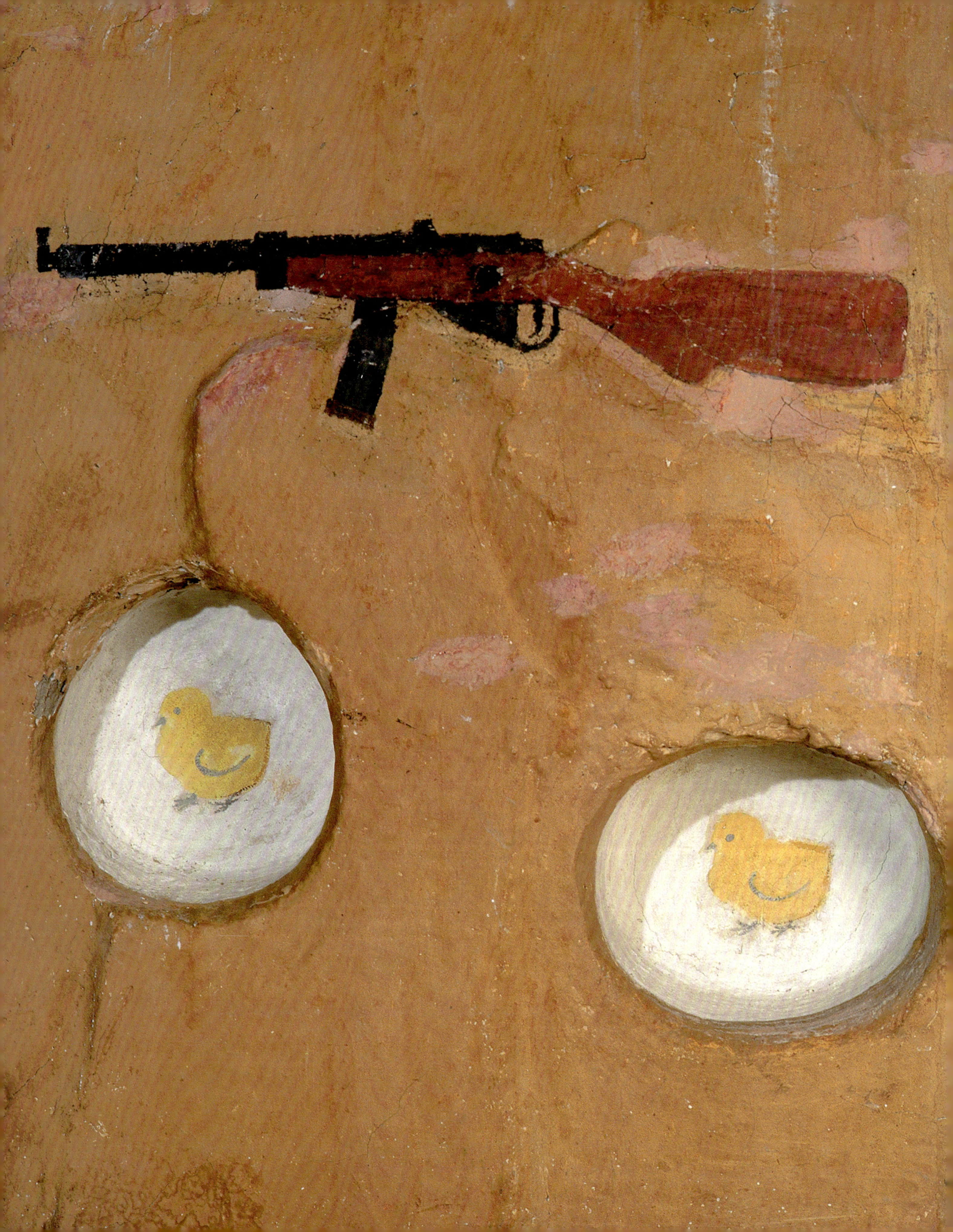

MOSCOW VANGUARD ART

1922–1992

Margarita Tupitsyn

YALE UNIVERSITY PRESS
LONDON AND NEW HAVEN

First published by Yale University Press 2017
302 Temple Street, P.O. Box 209040, New Haven CT 06520-9040
47 Bedford Square, London WC1B3 DP
yalebooks.com / yalebooks.co.uk

Library of Congress Control Number: 2016055763
ISBN 978-0-300-179750 HB

2021 2020 2019 2018 2017
10 9 8 7 6 5 4 3 2 1

Project editor and designer: Charlotte Grievson.
Jacket designer: Catherine Gaffney.
Copyeditor: Katharine Ridler.
Printed in China.

Front cover: Konstantin Zvezdochetov, *You Shall Know Us!* 1982. Private collection, Moscow.
Back cover: The Nest group, *Iron Curtain*, 1974, with Gennady Donskoi (left) and Mikhail Roshal.
Frontispiece: Ilya Kabakov, *Machine Gun and Chickens*, 1966 (detail of fig. 76).
Page vi: Gustav Klutis, illustration for the magazine *Young Guard*, 1924.

ACKNOWLEDGMENTS

I dedicate this book to the artists who dared to experiment in the most unlikely of sociocultural atmospheres.

During the many years of my work in the field of Soviet avant-garde and contemporary art, I have had the invaluable friendship and assistance of many people. I would like to thank all the Moscow artists who, for years, welcomed me in their studios, supplied productive conversations, and shared rare images that have greatly enriched this book. My correspondence with them, cited here, along with the discussions of some of my exhibitions organized in New York, undoubtedly reflect my direct involvement in this milieu. However, in order to construct an objective narrative, no traces of the memoir genre, or a favoring of better-known artists over lesser-known ones, can be found in this book.

My time in the doctorate program of the City University of New York (CUNY) Graduate Center, where I studied with the innovative art historians Rosalind Krauss and Linda Nochlin, taught me how to blend art history with criticism, and how to read discursively the past in the present, and vice versa. Because the CUNY program encouraged studies of contemporary art, I was able to initiate my project of turning postwar Moscow vanguard art into a field of art history. This book is the result of that long-term project, which has been immensely enhanced by the openness of perestroika, when I was able to visit Moscow for the first time since emigrating from the USSR in 1975.

Many colleagues have encouraged, assisted, and supported my research and projects in various ways. Thanks go to Manuel J. Borja-Villel, Ute Eskildsen, Michael Goven, the late Jeanette Ingberman, Phyllis Kind, Priska Pasquer, David Ross, Vicente Todoli, Stella Kesaeva, Margarida Veiga, Jo-Anne Birnie Danzker, Michael Buhrs, and Georg-W. Költzsch, who invited me to curate both historical and contemporary exhibitions. Elena Gasparova, Lidia Iovleva, Edvard Kulagin, Maria Tsantsanoglou, and the late Lilia Ukhtomskaia were extremely helpful with research and exhibition loans. Sabeth Buchmann, Maud Lavin, Christina Lodder, Roxana Marcoci, Vals Osborne, Brandon Taylor, Jyrki Siukonen, Vivian Endicott Barnett, Maria

Gough, John E. Bowlt, Charlotte Douglas, John Milner, and Sarah Wilson invited me to lecture in universities and museums or supported my various scholarly projects. I am grateful to the late Norton Dodge, who in 1981 asked me to be the Curator of the Contemporary Russian Art Center of America in New York, where I organized the first shows of Moscow Conceptualism and Sots Art. The Warhol Foundation Art Writers Grant generously supported the writing of this book. My deepest gratitude goes to Gillian Malpass at Yale University Press for her continuous support. I would like to thank Charlotte Grievson, who turned my manuscript into a handsome book. Finally, Victor Tupitsyn, a critic and theorist of Russian culture, and a seminal communication link between the Moscow and New York art worlds in the late 1970s and 1980s, has been my unfailing intellectual comrade. My hope for the endurance of vanguard culture rests with my daughter, the writer, critic, and video artist, Masha Tupitsyn.

NOTE TO READERS

This book uses a modified form of the Library of Congress system of transliteration. For readability, I omit diacritical marks from proper nouns and use "y" rather than "ii" or "yi" for the end of proper names, except in the titles of Russian texts in the references, where these endings and diacritical marks are retained. Also retained are Western spellings of well-known names such as Ilya Ehrenburg, Ilya Kabakov, and Sergei Eisenstein, and transliterations used in publications printed by the Russians.

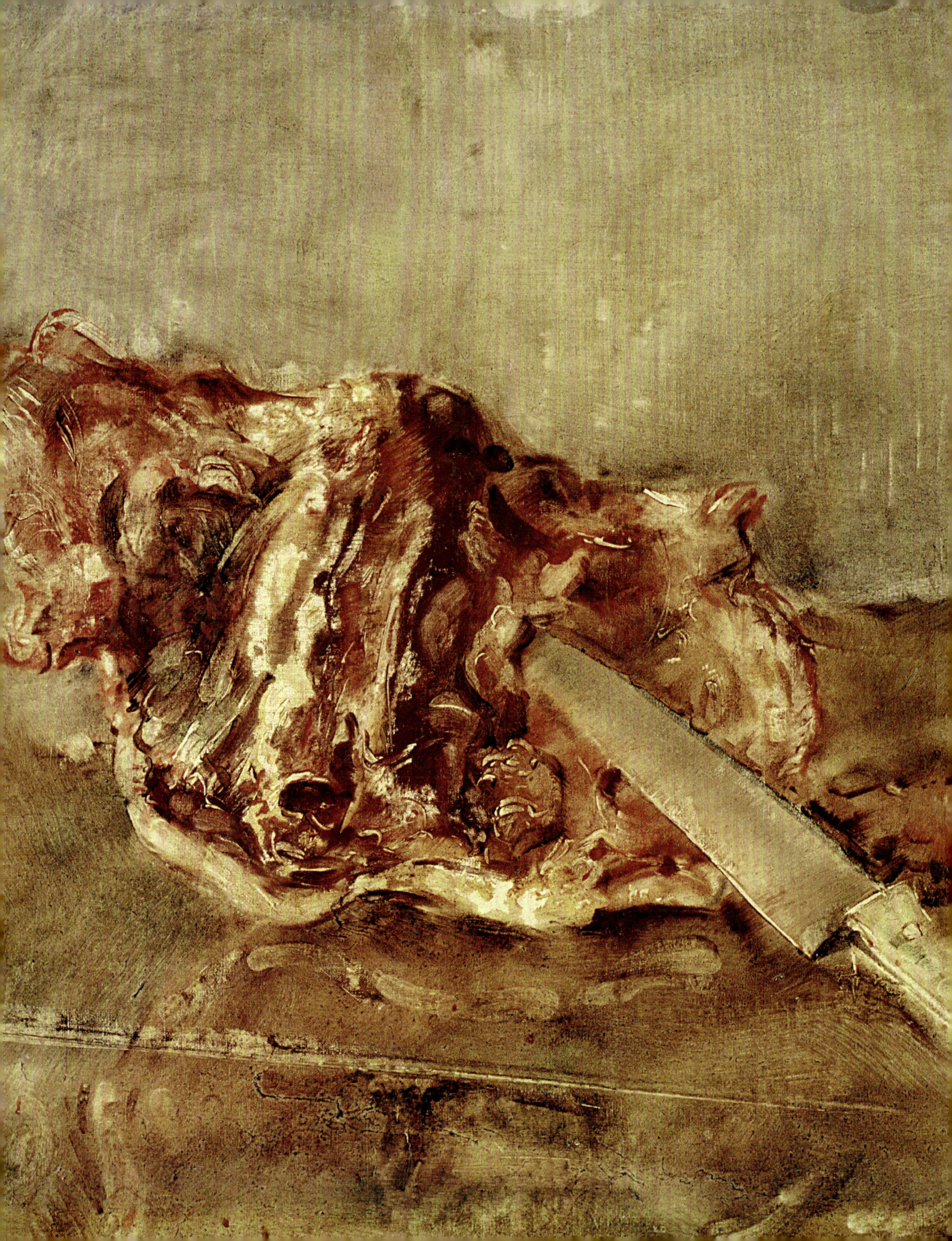

INTRODUCTION

Moscow is the heart of a creative sea.
Kaszimir Malevich, "Dead Stick,"
Anarchy no. 33, 1918.

It isn't new ideas but new places to put ideas.
Richard Foreman, *Book of Splendors: Part Two
(Book of Leaves) Action at a Distance,* 1976.

What does it mean to be a native agent in a foreign environment? To write about a culture whose context is not transparent and whose genealogy was never thoroughly evaluated or documented by its own country? These are questions that weighed heavily on the minds of a handful of specialists, who, during the cold war, embarked on the dissemination of twentieth-century Soviet art in the West. The canon has divided this art history into three periods: the internationally recognized historical avant-garde, the anti-modernist Socialist Realism, and the postwar counterculture (also referred to as unofficial or non-conformist art) that developed after Stalin's death. The purpose of this study is to consolidate Soviet-era artists who, regardless of fluctuating levels of state control, insisted on what the constructivist Gustav Klutsis in 1935 called "the right to an experiment."[1] To fight for this right increasingly felt like being in the barricades or in psychological warfare. The iconography of Konstantin Zvezdochetov's *You Shall Know Us!* (see overleaf) featuring a woman wearing a *budenovka,* a hat associated with the Red Army uniform of the Civil War, amply expresses this combative state of affairs in Soviet art.

My decision to focus on Moscow artists exclusively is determined by two things: their unflagging vanguardist (hence my choice to unite them under the term vanguard) and experimental mindset and my interest in the decisive role of milieu with its perpetual mechanism of conversing. To some degree this book aims at testing Clement Greenberg's 1955 pronouncement on Kasimir Malevich's paintings: "like almost all experiments in art, it failed

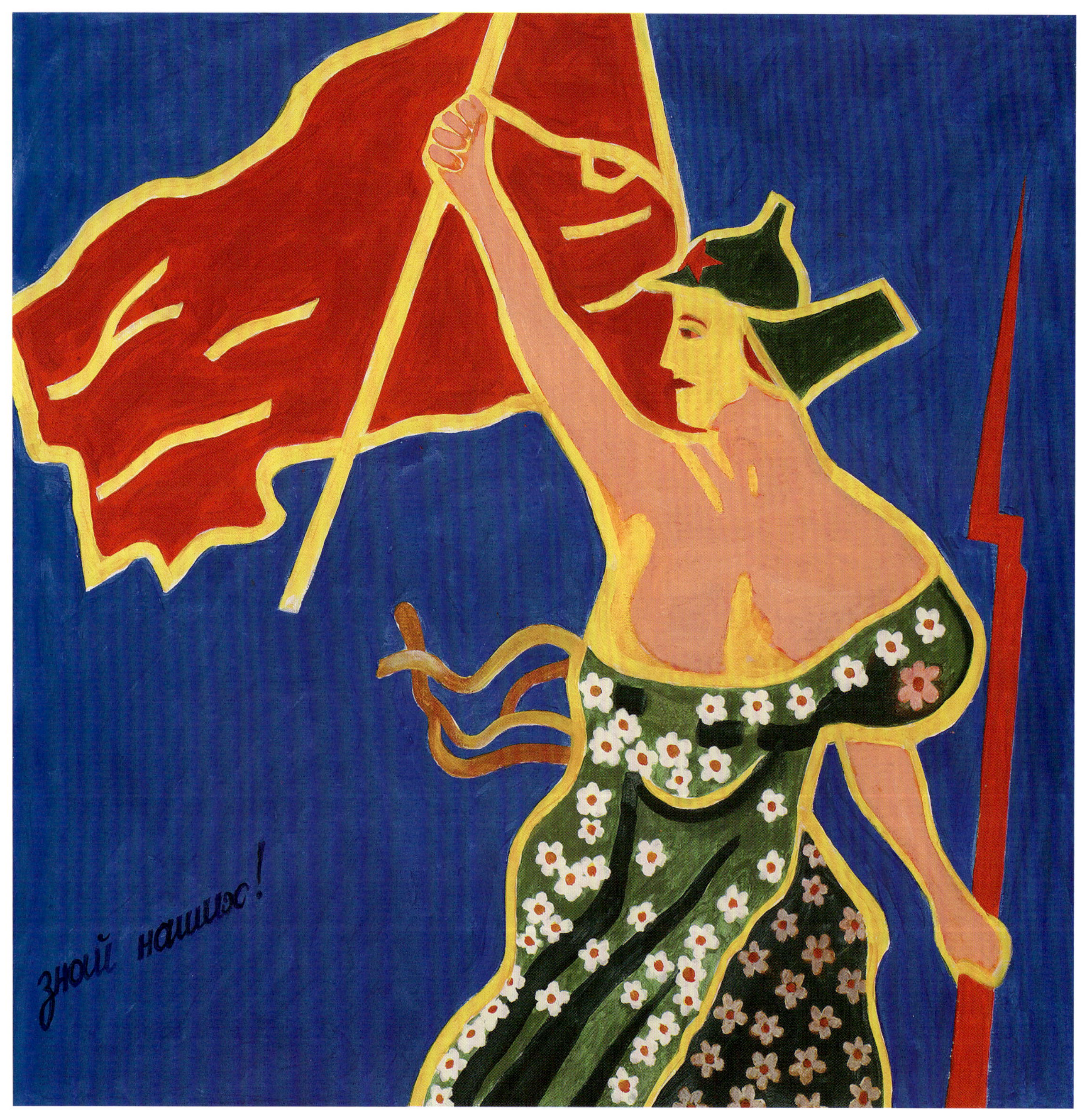

Konstantin Zvezdochetov, *You Shall Know Us!* 1982. Private collection, Moscow.

aesthetically."[2] At the time Greenberg wrote this, the concept of the aesthetic largely meant depoliticized art supported by galleries and museums, that is, the very thing that the artists discussed in this book had lacked. Another goal of this volume is to show how artists acted and created without twentieth-century Western support structures and within the space of overpoliticized reality. What were their theoretical and formal tenets and why and with what socio-cultural forces did they contend and which contended with them?

This study begins where Camilla Gray's seminal 1962 book, *The Great Experiment: Russian Art, 1863–1922* ended. The year 1922 was pivotal for Russian politics and culture alike. The civil war ended, the Soviet Union was established, and the New Economic Policy (NEP), a program of state capitalism that conflicted with the Bolshevik's socialist economic directives, was in its second year. That period was also a time when most avant-garde artists practiced nonobjective art because, they believed, it was "the revolutionary condition of form," in the words of Liubov Popova.[3] They held important administrative and educational offices and their exhibitions, both at home and abroad, were well funded. This mainstream position made the avant-garde milieu a target for disenfranchised and marginalized traditional realists who were prepared to consolidate their energies and make public their long-brewing discontent with avant-garde circles. Although most realists were on the side of the October Revolution, they did not adhere to the far-left rhetoric associated with avant-garde artists, romanticizing instead the academic values that the latter disparaged. Chapter One maps the trajectory of the clash between the two camps, their fight for state-supported culture, and ultimately for the right to determine the principles of proletarian art. I claim that it was in defense against such conditions that avant-garde artists and critics disengaged from nonobjective painting, and radicalized representational art by experimenting with graphic design, film, and photography.

Since perestroika, Camilla Gray's cut-off year for the avant-garde period has been significantly expanded, resulting in important studies of post-nonobjective practices that attested to the key role Russians played in the formation of theory and practice in the fields of the mass media. Along with this scholarly advancement, at the end of the cold war, Socialist Realism began to be elevated to the level of aesthetic and/or discursive practice. Worse still, a contagious ahistorical trend emerged: the claim that the avant-garde's intellectual elite was somehow to blame for Socialist Realism's authoritative platform. Igor Golomstock points out that Soviet anti-modernist and anti-formalist critics such as Mikhail Livshits linked German modernism to fascist culture in order to degrade the former. The best demonstration of the falsity of Livshits's claim is Herwarth Walden's daring and relentless rebuffing of it in the Soviet press, for which this prominent expert in the international avant-garde regularly wrote after escaping to the Soviet Union from Nazi Germany. As a result, he was disgraced and arrested. When the same approach is applied to the Soviet Union, Golomstock continues, it "grants the widest opportunity for all kinds of falsification and distortion, even of the Stalinist epoch itself."[4] Another approach that has surfaced in relation to the years after the avant-garde period is a revisionist reading of Socialist Realist works, which calls for its "positive or productive contributions…to the project of revolutionary art, to be distinguished from its negative aim of eliminating the avant-garde from that project."[5] Chapter Two is written in opposition to such attempts of endowing Socialist Realist works with a progressive status and against rehabilitation of artists who conformed to a one-style system. Instead I embark on an excavation of "a modernist retort,"[6] developed in a harsh anti-formalist environment and delivered by the left avant-gardists Valentina Kulagina, Malevich, Aleksandr Rodchenko, Nikolai Suetin, and Vladimir Tatlin. A reconstruction of their input in the preservation of Russian modernism is possible owing to the availability of letters and diaries rare for the Stalin period, for, "the nature of this culture precluded their very existence and are still missing today in most studies."[7] These documents give voice to the avant-garde beyond its established chronology, revealing how these artists rejected official realist dogma, challenged its key adherents, and sustained left and formalist convictions.

It is this kind of preservation of modernist thinking and practice, endured during the darkest periods of censorship in the Soviet capital, that permitted a fairly prompt emergence of the first generation of post-Stalin Moscow counterculture. For them, I invented a term – "dissident modernists" – in order to emphasize that regardless of how much these artists wanted to disassociate from what was perceived to be a political movement, the Soviet government and Westerners alike viewed them as such. Owing to this status, these artists were largely excluded from official media, and advanced without access to state museums or other institutional privileges. Chapter Three analyzes the resurgence of non-representational art in the unofficial circles of the late 1950s and 1960s. By then, the revolutionary specificity of nonobjective forms had lost its relevance, and concepts of abstraction, oriented toward individual rather than collective aspirations, had replaced it. Abstraction's function to resist conservative forms of art, however, remained intact. In this chapter, I give preference to the single works and movements that exemplify the advancement of classical modernist studio painting (Lydia Masterkova, Vladimir Nemukhin, and Vladimir Slepian), along with Movement, a collective whose members endeavored to bring abstract art out of the studios and into public spaces. The latter managed to install abstract sculpture in public spaces, unprecedented in the history of counterculture. Also considered are the artists Mikhail Chernyshov, Erik Bulatov, Ilya Kabakov, Vitaly Komar and Aleksandr Melamid, and Mikhail Roginsky, who gave abstract painting a conceptual angle and shared some tenets with American minimalists, such as the mechanical application of color, or what Malevich called "color realism," and the exploration of the abstractness of everyday objects. The discussion of this group of dissident modernists also initiates the deferred project of reconnecting the Moscow postwar vanguard with the historical local avant-garde. Until now, the latter's production has been cited primarily to give more historical weight to American Minimalism. Here I rely, wherever possible, on equally rare primary sources, avoiding both later artists' recollections and their citation by scholars who consider them useful. The radical socio-cultural changes that descended on Moscow vanguardists after the fall of the Soviet Union, and their preference to live and exhibit in the West, often tainted their perspectives on the Soviet period.

In Chapter Four I analyze the influence of the open-air *Bulldozer Exhibition* (organized in 1974 by dissident modernists on the outskirts of Moscow and brutally dispersed by the government) on the development of vanguard art. I claim that this radical event, as well as its follow-up, sanctioned by the government in Moscow's Izmailovsky Park, encouraged a younger generation of artists to value the *plein air* as a potent alternative site for production and display. In parks and country fields, artists, in the company of only a handful of viewers, escaped censorship, worked in collectives, and managed to invent new, primarily interactive art forms. They acted under the banner of the "dematerialization" of art objects in a country that had neither institutional demand nor the market for independent contemporary art. The pioneering late 1960s work of Francisco Infante and Nonna Goriunova, which predated this *plein air* trend, is discussed along with the late 1970s activities of the Red Star group and the Collective Actions Group.

Chapter Five returns to the art studio in order to trace both the origins and conceptual underpinnings of the Moscow paradigm of installation art. I argue that while in the West this medium originated as institutional critique (a critique mostly staged within those very institutions), in Moscow, installation art was a response to the protracted absence of institutional demand, critical appraisal, and audience. These voids created a feeling of captivity that Ivan Chuikov, Komar and Melamid, Igor Makarevich, and Vladimir Yankilevsky allegorized in their 1970s studio installations. Further, I claim that the accumulation of art works, and their constant rearrangement for private showings to a handful of visitors, turned artists' studios into both an interactive and restricted space. Kabakov's and Irina Nakhova's early 1980s studio installations offered paradigms for exiting these psychological and spatial constraints.

Chapter Six is dedicated to the conceptualists who challenged the political and aesthetic borders between East and West, long before the fall of the Soviet Union and the globalization of the art world. This includes Komar and Melamid's 1976 collaboration with the New York artist and critic Douglas Davis and the Nest group's neo-Dada proposals for global communication devices. Further, this chapter considers work produced by the Moscow vanguardists who immigrated and settled in New York City in the 1970s and early in the 1980s. I concentrate on Moscow artists' critical response to the cultural specificity and institutional exclusivity of the New York art world, arguing that Sots Art, a movement that originated in Moscow in 1972, was the most effective way to build visibility in a sea of early 1980s postmodern trends. Objects and performances by Vagrich Bakhchanian, Rimma Gerlovin, Valery Gerlovin, Komar and Melamid, Aleksandr Kosolapov, and Leonid Sokov are discussed in the framework of the first exhibitions of Conceptual and Sots Art organized in New York. I conclude *Moscow Vanguard Art* with a discussion of works and exhibitions made during the cultural emancipation of the Gorbachev era, similar to the period after the Revolution – except that in the earlier, the Soviet cultural system was in the process of being constructed, but in the later, dismantled. Both periods developed outside of the capitalist culture industry, proving to be highly experimental and antagonistic toward conformist, mediocre and conservative practices. As a result of perestroika's exhibition opportunities, installation art gained popularity, and neglected forms of production, such as photography, revived the camera as an experimental tool. A stream of exhibitions abroad prompted the authorities to permit hitherto underground artists to travel abroad. With this new mobility and global exposure, Moscow vanguardists' prolonged reliance on the support of the milieu, along with an adherence to collective creativity, began to crumble as quickly as the Union of Soviet Republics.

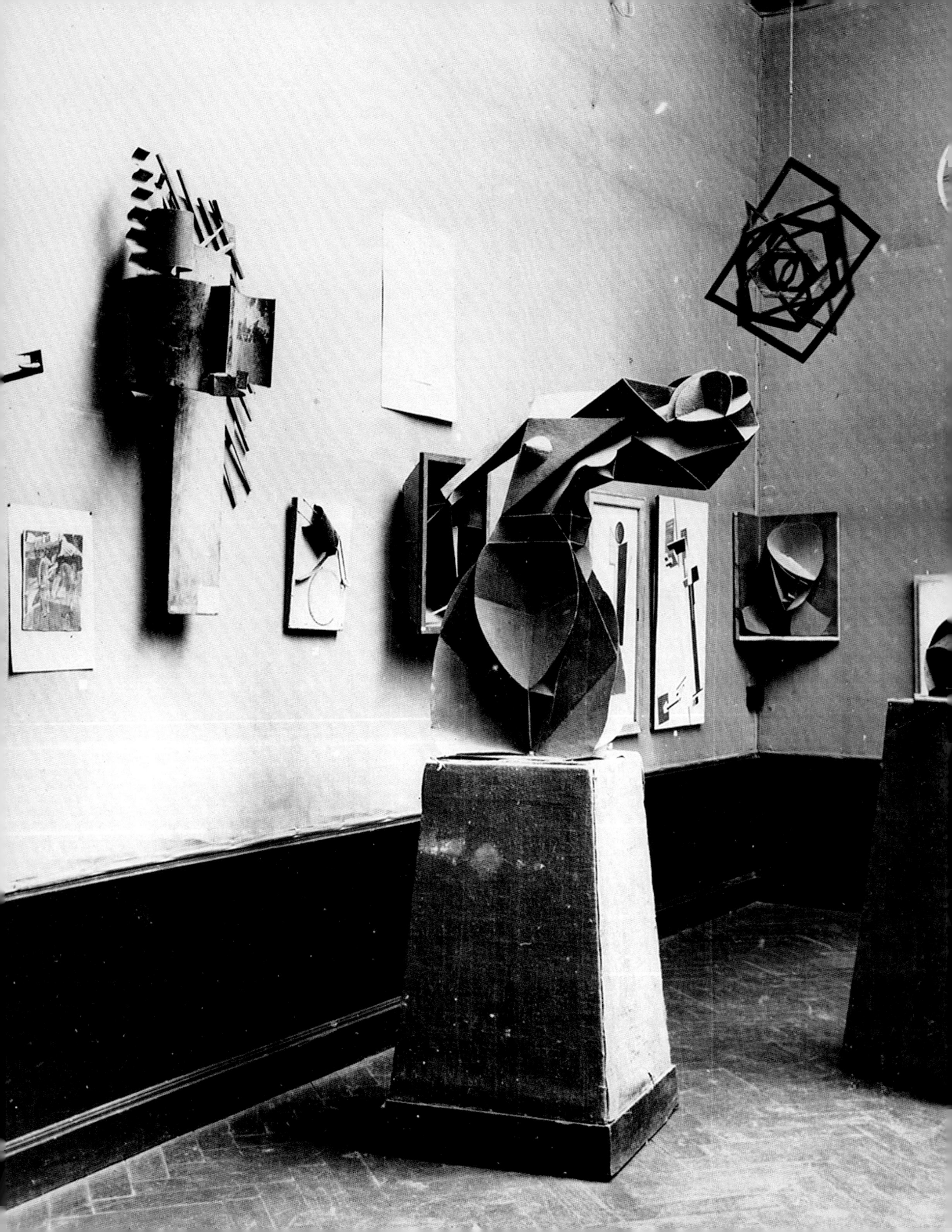

IN DEFENSE OF NONOBJECTIVE ART

Russia has given birth to its own art, and its name is nonobjectivity.

Aleksandr Rodchenko, 1918.

I don't think that nonobjective form is the final form: it is the revolutionary condition of form.

Liubov Popova, 1921.

During the year of the October Revolution, 1917, Evgeny Katsman, a recent graduate of the progressive Moscow Institute of Painting, Sculpture, and Architecture (MUZhVZ), demonstrated his portraiture skill on Kazimir Malevich, the founder of Suprematism and a key player in avant-garde circles (fig. 1). Katsman's portrait, however, was not a tribute to Malevich's status. Rather, it revealed an ironic coincidence: the two artists, who for the next two decades would serve as locomotives for adversarial paradigms of proletarian art, were married to the sisters Natalia and Sofia Rafalovich. It was at the sisters' dacha that Katsman rendered Malevich's portrait, emphasizing his haircut

with bangs combed to the left. He also shaded the left side of the sketch with a swirl of charcoal strokes. In these details, Katsman encoded his antipathy toward the leftist aspirations of the avant-garde milieu, an attitude he developed during his studies in MUZhVZ where he declined the futurists' invitation to join them.

An adamant nonobjectivist eager to liberate painting from its "electric connection with an object," and transform "reality and themes" into "ideal"[1] forms, Malevich could only think of Katsman's portrait as "mediocre."[2] By then, Malevich's *Black Square*, disputed even by his fellow nonobjectivists after it was shown in 1915 at *0,10: The Last Futurist Exhibition of Paintings*, had become a "revered sign"[3] for the system he termed "new painterly realism" (fig. 2).[4] His use of the word realism in relation to nonobjective art alerted first academicians and later steadfast realists like Katsman who recognized Malevich's ambition to eradicate canonical models of representation. *Black Square*, with its blunt eclipsing of all signs of fig-

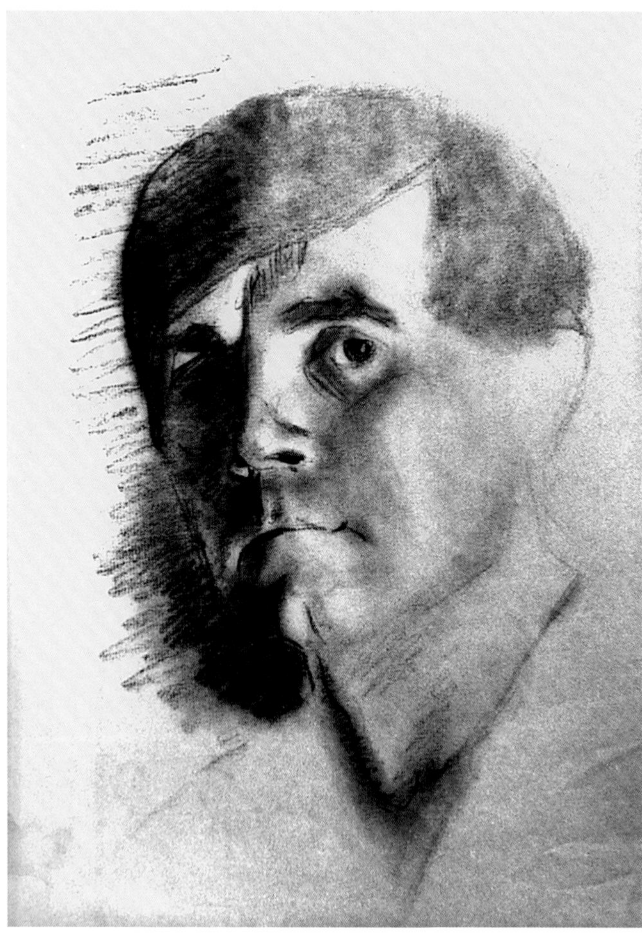

1 Evgeny Katsman, *Untitled (Malevich)*, 1917. Russian State Archive of Literature and Art, Moscow.

uration, along with the absence for the viewer of a reciprocal relationship with a painting, created the conditions for activating, to use Ernst Bloch's words, "the imaginative gaze of the utopian function."[5] In contrast to "bourgeois 'realism,'" "that gaze," Bloch continues, "is corrected by the only real realism that is the only one because it grasps the tendency of reality. It grasps the objectively real potentiality toward which the tendency strives. The real realism is at home in those qualities of reality that are utopian themselves; i.e., they contain future."[6] *Black Square* then became "the point of contact between dream and life," a springboard from "abstract utopia" to "concrete utopia." While admitting that it is "a paradoxical term," Bloch emphasized that concrete utopia "designates precisely the power and truth of Marxism,

which pushed the cloud in the dreams forward without extinguishing the fire of the dreams, but rather strengthened them through concreteness."[7] This fusion of utopianism and concreteness, embedded in nonobjective art, enabled its practitioners to envision it as a visual emblem for a new political reality.

The advancement of nonobjective artists along this path was precisely what made conservative realists like Katsman worry that they "had huge power," and that "in their hands was the management of art business all over the vast USSR."[8] In 1920 after the formation of several key avant-garde schools – the Institute of Artistic Culture (INKhUK), the Affirmers of the New Art (UNOVIS), and the Higher State Artistic and Technical Workshops (VKhUTEMAS) – Katsman moved his anti-avant-garde crusade out of the private space of the dacha he shared with Malevich. His first target was VKhUTEMAS where, together with a group of teachers and students, he filed a complaint to the Central Committee of the Communist Party of Bolsheviks (TSK RKP[b]) about "a preponderance in studios for the representatives of 'cubist and other perverse tendencies in art.'"[9] A seasoned combatant of the "smotherers of art,"[10] Malevich immediately recognized the damaging consequences of the VKhUTEMAS affair, informing his UNOVIS students that "the academics are pressing hard,"[11] and that he must therefore postpone his return to Vitebsk in order to participate in the committee – headed by the commissar of the People's Commissariat for Education (Narkom-pros), Anatoly Lunacharsky – for the change of VKhUTEMAS's curriculum. The fact that Lunacharsky invited Malevich to resolve the school's dispute suggested that, regardless of Lenin's demand to find "reliable anti-futurists"[12] after his visit to VKhUTEMAS on February 25, 1921, Lunacharsky continued to support avant-gardists (now also referred to as "left" artists), refusing to let the school fall into conservative hands.[13] Moreover, in his 1921 speech, delivered at the Third Congress of the Comintern, Lunacharsky explained that "reaching out to 'left' artists" was part of the "general politics of Narkompros," for it needed "to lean on a serious collective of a creative artistic force."[14] For him, the activities of "nonobjectivists-suprematists" were rooted in an anti-bourgeois position and thus fell into the realm of Marxist theory.

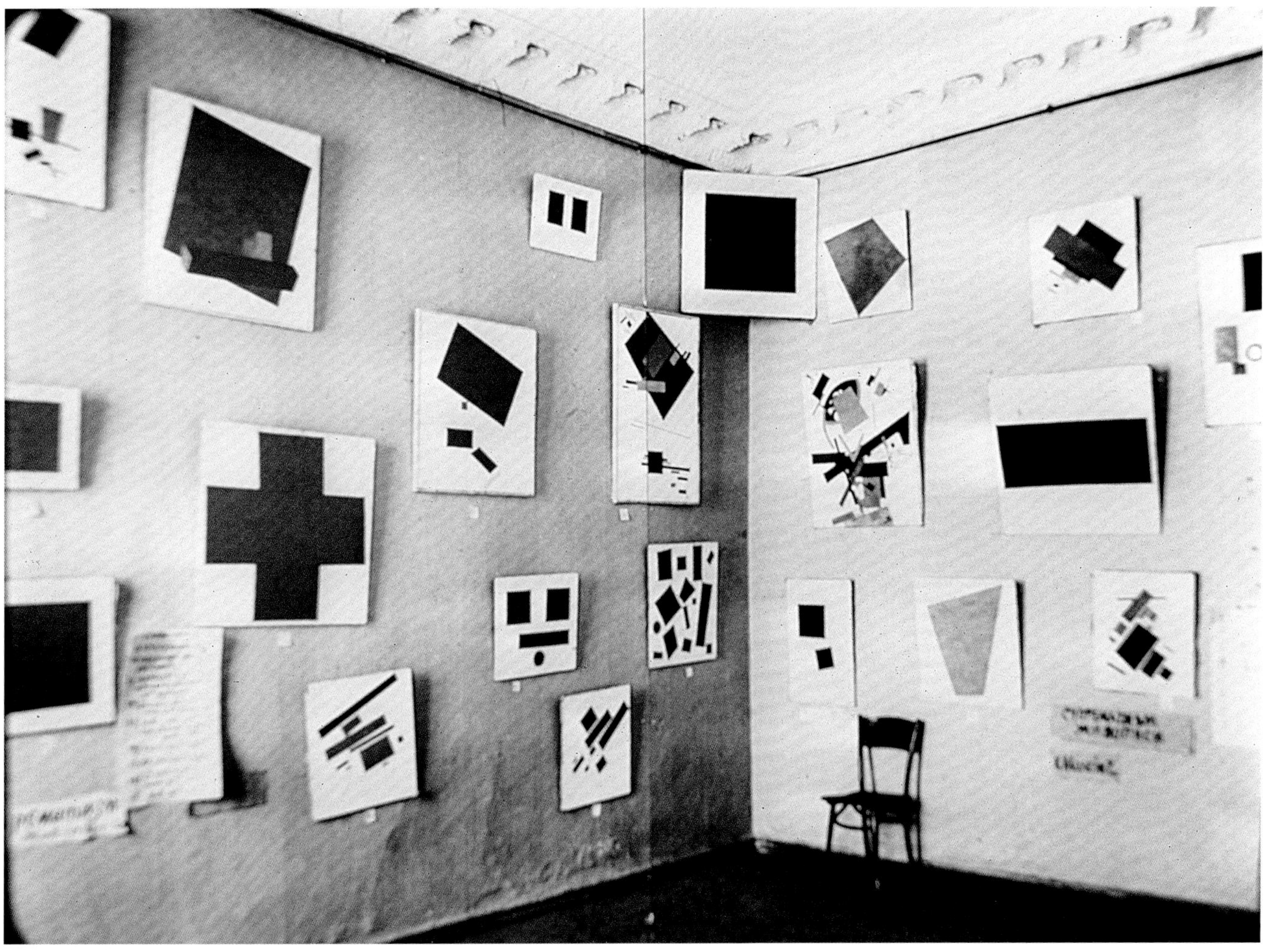

2 View of Kazimir Malevich's installation at *0,10: The Last Futurist Exhibition of Paintings*, 1915, St. Petersburg.

"Left" art[15] was "a laboratory or a kitchen into which it was necessary to descend from the stuffy air of academic and realist art that fell into decay and lost its soul."[16]

Lunacharsky's siding with the avant-garde was directly reflected in the ambitious project of organizing *The First Russian Exhibition* (Die Erste Russische Kunstausstellung) in Berlin in 1922, which Lenin's support ensured was generously funded.[17] Putting the artist David Shterenberg (a VKhUTEMAS professor, the head of the Department of Fine Arts [IZO] in Narkompros, and Katsman's active antagonist) in charge of the exhibition's coordination secured the inclusion of all major nonobjectivists. In the eyes of the Western public, this created the impression that nonobjective art was the favored style of the Bolshevik State (figs. 3, 4).[18] In Lunacharsky's opinion, the *First Russian Exhibition* "achieved a broader audience's sympathy toward Russia than would a series of diplomatic gestures."[19]

When it became evident to the conservative realists that they were not included in the *First Russian Exhibition*, they made a decision to unite into the Association of Artists of Revolutionary Russia (AKhRR),[20] nominating Katsman to be the group's "nonstop" secretary. Another trigger for AKhRR's formation was the 47th exhibition of the Peredvizhniki ("Wanderers" or "Itinerants") in 1922. AKhRR's association with this seminal nineteenth-century group (some of whose original members were still alive) was

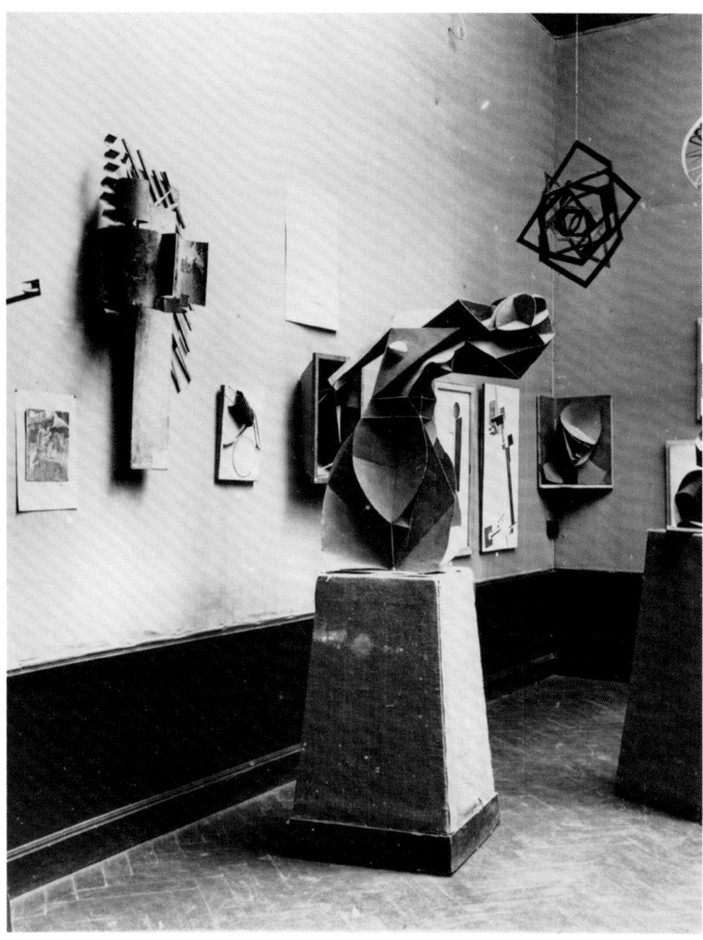

3 Installation view of *The First Russian Exhibition*, 1922, Berlin. Archives Nakov, Paris.

strategic but damaging for the Wanderers themselves, whose reputation of anti-academic, critical realism was firmly positioned at the dawn of Russian modernism. AKhRR's artists lacked their critical edge and favored the idealization and heroization of everyday life. In their social utopianism, the Wanderers were in fact much closer to the nonobjectivist program.[21]

The Wanderers' still undefined position in the Bolshevik state made them good material for constructing a genealogy for both "left" and "right" wings. This explains why the dispute, organized at the Central House of Enlightenment and Arts on the occasion of their exhibition, was so broadly attended. Katsman recalled that it "gathered key figures of all art movements and organizations…the headquarters of the so-called 'left' artists were fully represented. Present

were D.P. Shterenberg and O.M. Brik."[22] Katsman further noted that "the 'leftists,' how formalists were then called, even facilitated the opening of the Wanderers' exhibition, hoping once again to bury 'a corpse,' but they failed: the emerging AKhRR stopped them."[23] The dispute escalated after the poet and realist painter Pavel Radimov delivered a speech, "On the Meaning of Everyday Life in Art." Asserting that Soviet everyday life must be reflected realistically, Radimov directly infringed on the nonobjective interpretation of the same subject. In his turn Katsman accused Osip Brik of "trying to prove that small red and small black squares suit the Revolution most and that it does not need easel realist art."[24] In general, Brik, according to another of the debate's participants from TSK RKP(b), "was making a mistake by calling nonobjectivity the true art of the proletarian revolution."[25] Shterenberg joined Brik in "ridiculing" academic realism, which according to him, was an "ichthyosaurus," then added that it was "laughable to talk about realism, about this 'dead body,' when 'left' artists ha[d] won not only in the RSFSR [Russian Soviet Federative Socialist Republic] but all over the world."[26]

With Radimov and the realist Aleksandr Grigoriev (another participant in the dispute and a member of the Communist Party), Katsman sent a letter to TSK RKP(b), stating their readiness "to submit themselves to the Revolution" (five years after it took place), and asking the Party "to instruct artists how to work."[27] With this willingness voluntarily to submit to government control over aesthetic practices, AKhRR set a precedent for artistic conformity and servility that would plague the subsequent history of twentieth-century Russian art. In line with Lunacharsky's vision of the new artist as being "completely free of the outside,"[28] the Party's response to AKhRR's appeal did not provide any stylistic instructions. It did, however, advise artists to: "Go into working masses, study them, represent them, and they will prompt the direction of your activities. Go to the factories!"[29] This meant that AKhRR failed to receive the Party's blessing for usurping revolutionary identity and to "monopolize" the concept of "the revolutionary in art."[30] Yet AKhRR's coming to work places of the proletariat intending to depict their activities naturalistically was the first blow to the utopian project of nonobjectivists, who imagined the proletariat not as the subject of art but as its participatory force.

In the spring of 1922, AKhRR marked its entry into the Soviet cultural arena with the *Exhibition of Pictures by Artists of the Realist Direction in Aid of the Starving*. For this first show, the group "generated energetic agitation in support of AKhRR"[31] that resulted in a broader consolidation of realists, including some surviving Wanderers as well as the impressionist painter and popular MUZhVZ professor, Konstantin Korovin. In other words, at exactly the same time that the most radical factions of nonobjective artists either rejected or put aside easel painting, AKhRR, using the attachment of many artists to this medium, managed to consolidate many of them under its wing.

As if anticipating the Red Army elite's discontent with formalism, promulgated by their leader Leon Trotsky's article, "Formal School of Poetry and Marxism,"[32] AKhRR artists rushed to demonstrate their loyalty by organizing the *Exhibition of Studies, Sketches, Drawings and Graphics from Everyday Life of the Workers and Peasants' Red Army* (1922).[33] On this occasion, they issued a declaration that pledged "to provide a true picture of events and not abstract concoctions discrediting our Revolution in the face of the international proletariat."[34] A theoretically naïve text, it underscored the importance of content and called for "monumental forms in the style of heroic realism."[35] This appeal to heroic representations determined AKhRR's position toward the proletariat as a source of perpetual productivity (well exploited during Stalin's rule), and the reference to monumental forms betrayed AKhRR's aim to conquer public space that had been delegated to artists of the "left" wing after the Revolution. A review of this exhibition was, predictably, published in *Pravda*, and although the reviewer admitted to AKhRR's artistic weaknesses, he "welcomed" the group's "attempt to depict 'the revolutionary day' and give an actual picture of events, instead of abstract fantasies."[36] The reviewer drew parallels between AKhRR and the "art of the French Revolution era" in general, and Jacques-Louis David's "heroic portraits of the revolutionaries" in particular.[37] Such comparisons attempted to locate the

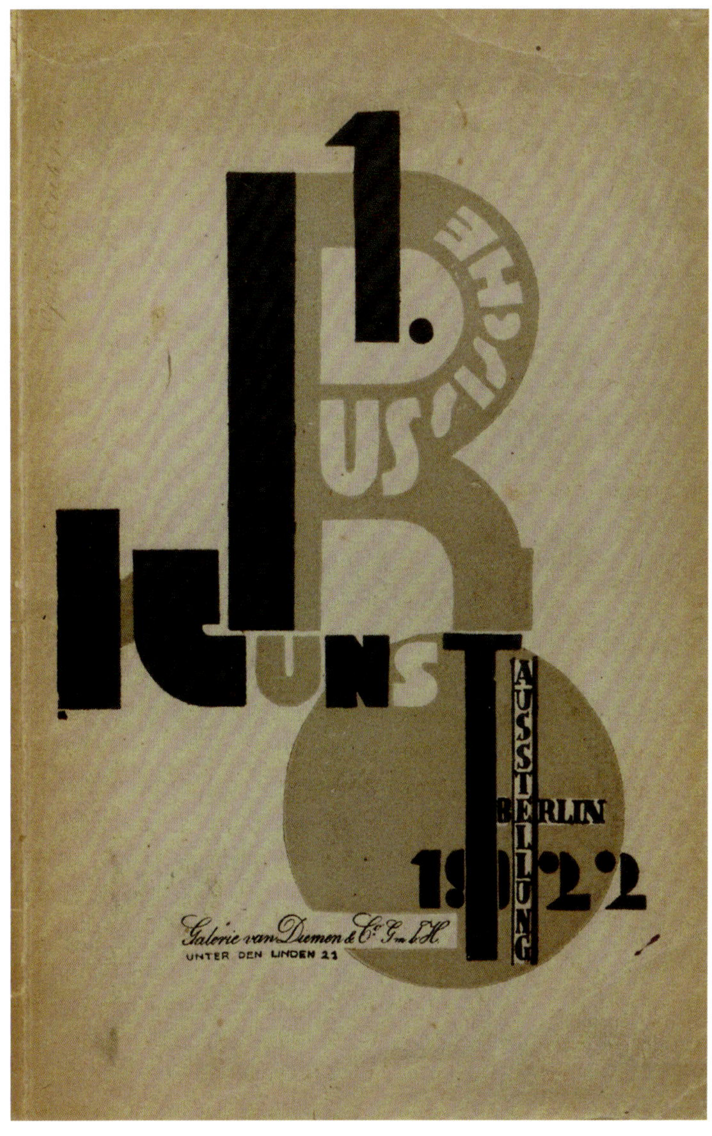

4   El Lissitzky, cover of the catalogue of *The First Russian Exhibition*, 1922, Berlin. State Mayakovsky Museum, Moscow.

premodernist roots of AKhRR's production. But, as with Katsman's claimed affinity with Wanderers, this genealogy was false given that David's "work was crucial in shaping the attitudes that led, ultimately, to twentieth-century abstract art."[38]

The reviewer's focus on the fact that David had run the French Academy undoubtedly stirred up AKhRR's interest in VKhUTEIN (Higher Art and Technical Institute), opened in 1922 in place of the Imperial Academy of Arts that had been abolished in 1917. The restructured Academy aspired to make modernism part of mainstream culture, and ultimately to "academicize" it. The institution was under the influence of "left" artists, including nonobjectivists like Malevich, Pavel Mansurov, and Mikhail Matiushin. In the eyes of the AKhRR's artists, this was a contradiction. For them, the Academy[39], by definition, had to elaborate on the existing realist traditions rather than involve itself in "futurist and Suprematist hysterics."[40] Katsman maintained that he decided to visit the Academy after he received a letter from its students asking for help to rebuild the Academy. "Until now, we have been studying cubes, nonobjective art, and other tricks,"[41] the letter stated. Before Katsman and Grigoriev arrived in Petrograd, the latter obtained permission from the local Party Committee to convene a general assembly at which both artists could lecture on AKhRR's activities. They also sent a letter to the Academy asking for a list of those students who were members of the Russian Communist Party (RKP) and Russian League of Communist Youth (RKSM).[42] Katsman claimed that "among [the Academy's] students there were many workers and peasants for whom the mysticism of cubes, planes, and other absurdities is physically repugnant…Professors who 'combine planes'…were scolding us in every way. Their enthusiastic followers amid the students were helping them. As usual for the art world of those times, a huge dispute was brewing."[43] Katsman's encounter with the poet and artist Igor Terentiev was particularly antagonistic. Like Katsman, Terentiev was willing to collaborate with the Communist Party and actively sought the support of the communist youth. This automatically positioned him not only as AKhRR's aesthetic adversary but as the group's rival in the political struggle for government support. Terentiev's letter to the poet Aleksei Kruchenykh, describing the dispute at the Academy, promised a brutal fight:

There were endless crowds of people. All students and almost all maestros. Malevich spoke academically. He "overturns" one "god" after another with my Marxist help, which is grasped with hunger. Malevich is the first class worker, and his "philosophy" is spoiled by polemics with all kinds of scum, but young people nevertheless prefer to study with

him because he is a master!…the opportunities for a collective work on a cultural front with the Communist Party are growing quite tangibly.[44]

His sense of the looming invasion of figuration forced Terentiev to talk about Malevich and his art in academic terms, emphasizing his technical mastery and popularity among students. His fusion of nonobjective art with Marxism and the Communist Party's agenda was aimed at the concretization of nonobjective forms discussed at the outset of this chapter.

Terentiev was not alone in his conviction that nonobjective art could be joined to reality. The literary critic Roman Jakobson insisted early on that "there was no chasm" in Malevich's "gradual transition from objective to nonobjective art…The issue was in the nonobjective approach to objectness and the object-oriented attitude toward a nonobjective thematic – to the thematic of planes, paint, and space."[45] In his summary of the left-wing trends, the critic Nikolai Chuzhak similarly noted that "an artist's striving…toward…nonobjectivity, precisely signifies a yearning for an object, dissatisfaction with 'a frozen moment' of a painting."[46] For Chuzhak this was a path "from illusion to an object (even though in relation to 'nonobjectiveness' this sounds paradoxical), from the art of 'a concept of a thing' to the 'thing as such.'"[47]

Nonobjectivists' claim of the inbuilt objectness (*predmetnost*) of their forms presented a strong case against a return to representation in a traditional format such as an easel painting. In 1919 Malevich's student, Gustav Klutsis, described his nonobjective canvas *Dynamic City* as a "picture-object" (*kartina-veshch*), building, like his teacher, a case for painting as a practice of rational and reactive "pictorial-professional shifts,"[48] with a staunch fidelity to nonobjective forms and an "attempt to construct out of 'style' an impersonal visual language" (fig. 5).[49] By 1922 the word *veshch* was applied to a variety of nonobjective production, including Aleksandr Rodchenko's "Spatial Objects" (Aleksei Gan's retitling of Rodchenko's *Spatial Constructions*) and Malevich's "Suprematist Object," dubbed as such by El Lissitzky in the magazine *Veshch-Gegenstand-Object*. Launched in Berlin in 1922, several months before the opening of the *First*

Russian Exhibition, Veshch printed a one-page illustration of Malevich's *Black Square* and *Black Circle* next to a photograph of a snowplowing train.[50] The editors annotated their juxtaposition as an equation between the "technical thing" (the train) and what they designated as "economy" (severe reductivism), or the "Suprematist thing." Commenting on this statement, the literary critic Viktor Pertsov concluded that in it: "1) the correct relationship of nonobjectivity with industry has been mapped, 2) industry is proposed not as a new subject of representation, but as methodology of constructivism."[51] Such reduction of the empirical world to "the zero of forms," implied the space of "geometric existence" or "the world as objectlessness."[52]

AKhRR's embarking upon the subject of everyday life was not accidental. It was shaped by the rivalry with the modernists' engagement with quotidian themes. As a nonobjective system of representation took over the modernist genealogy, "the relation of 'event' to form"[53] occurred through "the material advancement of *faktura*."[54] After the Revolution, nonobjective forms signified revolutionary consciousness, catapulting nonobjectivists into public space, and organizing nonobjective forms into a communicative system with new audiences. AKhRR's appearance threatened the trajectory of the relation between formal innovation and the radicalization of reality. To oppose this, Gan worked on building a bridge between anti-mimetic nonobjective forms and the filmmaker Dziga Vertov's newsreels; one example of this unlikely symbiosis was Rodchenko's use of *Spatial Constructions* for titles that demonstrated the possibility of nonobjective forms to enter and organize social space (fig. 6). The co-existence of nonobjective art with representational photography and cinema was the result of their common "fight against the unique, the original, the nonreplicable."[55] When Malevich unleashed in UNOVIS a free copying of his suprematist vocabulary, he revealed, to quote Krauss again, "the grids, the nested squares, the monochromes, the color fields — are themselves submitted to the mark of the multiple."[56]

Vertov's immaterial cine-forms disengaged aesthetics from the production of commodities (intensified with the inauguration of the NEP in 1921) and succeeded in documenting everyday life on a screen rather than on canvas, as in AKhRR's case. In Gan's view, expressed in his theoretical pamphlet *Long Live the Demonstration of Everyday Life!*, the new fusion of form and content was based on the conversion of "a tempestuous and incessant flow of people" into "an uninterrupted moving form of a never-ending content."[57] Ignoring such radical developments in representation, AKhRR's sixth exhibition, *Revolution, Everyday Life, and Labor* (January 31, 1924), only increased cultivation of easel painting. The show received funding from Narkompros and took place in the Museum of History in line with the group's desire to be anchored in the past. To the avant-garde community, this "smelled of the Academy"[58] (that is, the nineteenth-century one)and of the "room-museum *easelism*"[59] and it impelled Malevich, an inveterate anti-academic, to break his silence regarding AKhRR. In a brief but pointed text, he spoke about the group's "antagonism…toward nonobjective artists," argued that the two wings of Soviet art were too "diverse" to be "enemies,"[60] and distinguished between AKhRR's and the avant-garde's paradigms of everyday life. "The AKhRR artists are life-writers and portrayers of an event; the left artists are themselves creators of a different everyday life and participants in the revolutionary events," stated Malevich.[61] He allied the Revolution with modernism in their common goal to obliterate the existing political, economic, and cultural order. Malevich concluded that if at the heart of AKhRR's art lay "'representation,' in our case science and life themselves operate."[62]

This approach coincided with current definitions of the formal method and theorizations of the utopian function of art. In the first issue of *Lef* magazine in 1923, Brik argued that the formal method is not a manifestation of individual creativity, but an arsenal of techniques, or "scientific systems," that correspond to the social needs of a given epoch, and are available for mastery to the masses (fig. 7).[63] Each time, these "scientific systems" impregnate a form with revolutionary content. In the following year, the critic Boris Arvatov, also in *Lef*, responded to attacks on the avant-garde's utopianism, calling for the creation of experimental laboratories and an alliance with science.[64] Fantastic architecture (akin to suprematist

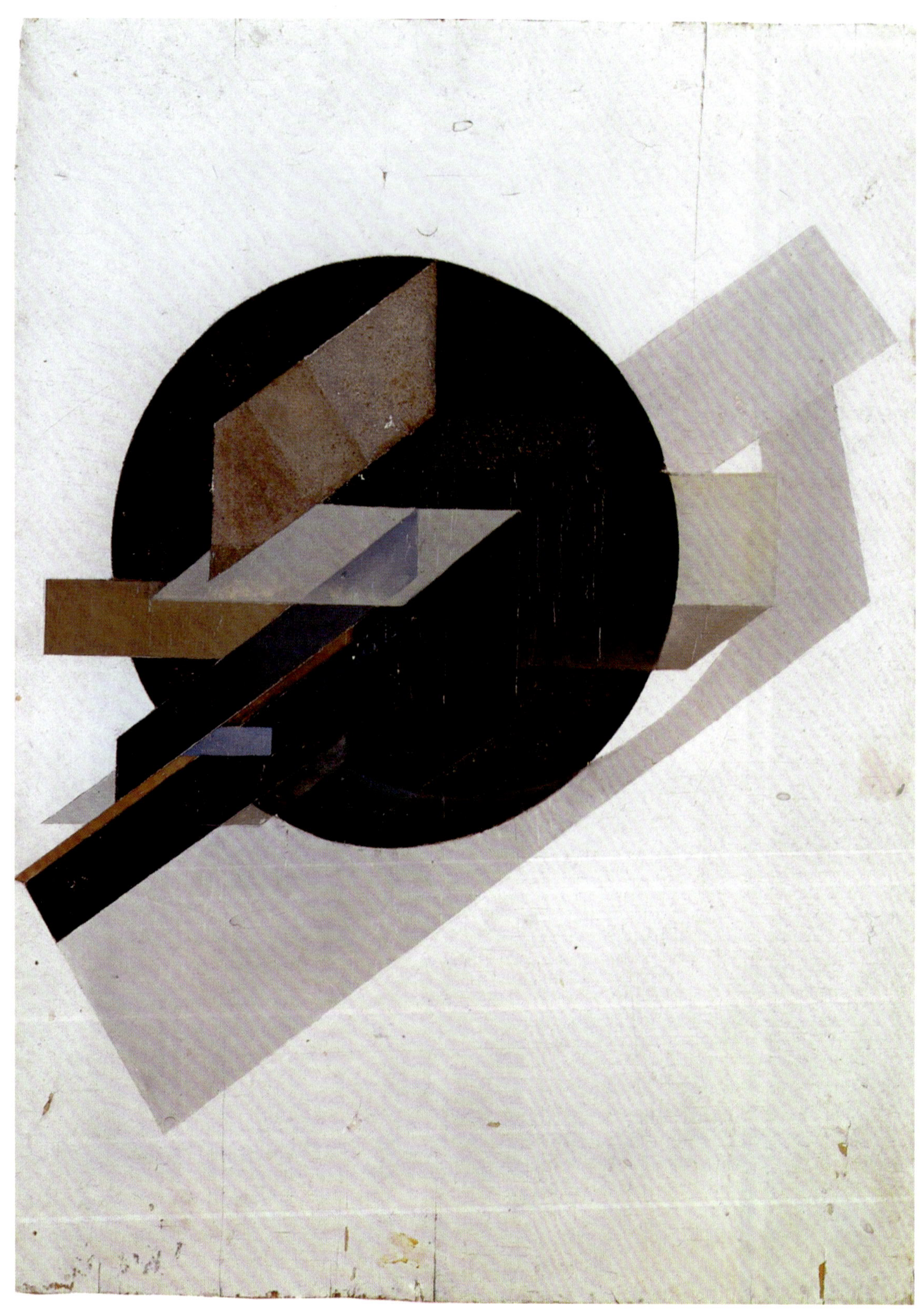

5   Gustav Klutsis, *Dynamic City*, 1919. State Museum of Contemporary Art, Costakis Collection, Thessaloniki.

architectural models) and photomontage or "ultra-representational art, executed by a machine, and tightly linked with the material everyday life of urban industrial workers" were his chosen examples for what he dubbed the "reified utopia."[65]

To consolidate "the dispersed *Lef* workers"[66] in order to challenge AKhRR, the first meeting of *Lef* workers was organized in January 1925. Among the participants were the critics Brik, Gan, and Chuzhak and the artists Rodchenko, Klutsis, Sergei Senkin, the poet Kruchenykh, and Vertov. Pertsov, who later edited the volume "Revision of the Left Front in Contemporary Russian Art" (1925) that included the meeting's proceedings, backed the left critics' (Brik, Gan, Terentiev) consensus that nonobjectivity and Suprematism had played a paramount role in the genealogy of left trends. Moreover, Pertsov identified "the starting point" of nonobjectivity in "Malevich's notorious 'black square,'" arguing that in it:

> we find an acute symptom of the decomposition of representation that landed today's left artists on a categorical assertion about the impossibility of easel art (of a painting) in our epoch…the task of nonobjective art is not to represent some kind of object. It is based on the assumption that the "content" of a painting is its painterly construction and that an object is just the ground for the construction of a painting…By deconstructing painting into its elements, Suprematism provided the unheard of culture of some of these elements. It has become an experimental laboratory for studying the distinctive problems of painting…It played the role of a kind of scientific research vestibule through which a production artist must logically walk today.[67]

Pertsov's positioning of Malevich as a precursor of production art offers a convincing argument against some Malevich scholars, who persistently have encased his art in a transcendental context.[68] It is also a strong reminder that most future constructivists and production artists, as well as key critics of these movements, had developed in Malevich's presence and in response to his formal radicalism. During the dispute, the participants sharply criticized AKhRR and called for the eradication of easel painting and for "a direct junc-

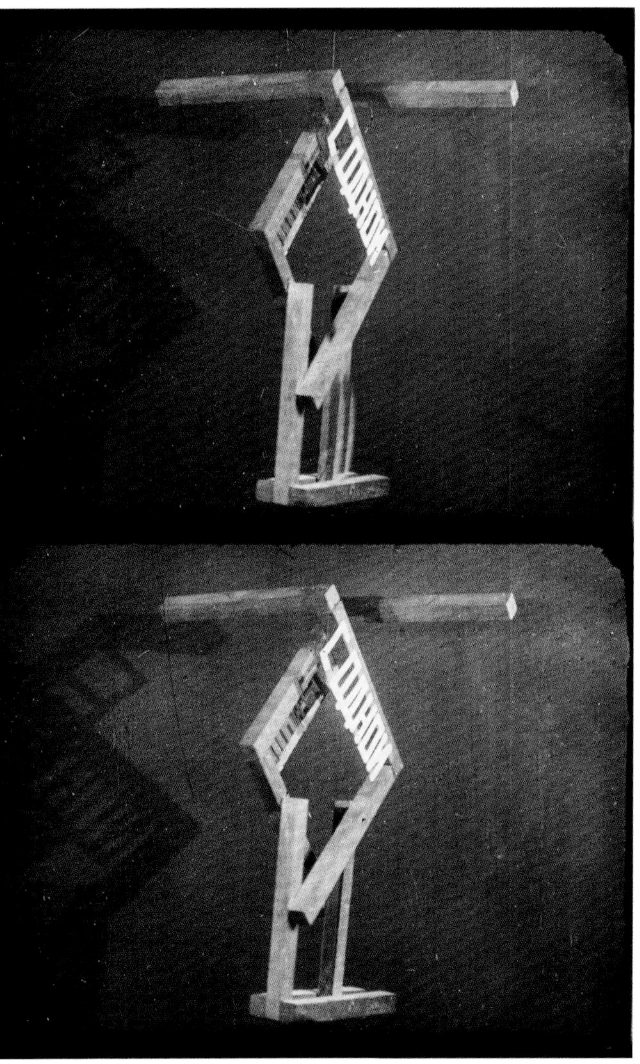

6   Stills from Dziga Vertov's film *Cine-truth*, 1922, with Aleksandr Rodchenko's *Spatial Constructions*.

tion with everyday life" as a way of ensuring "a maximum departure from the illusion of old art into real life."[69] In line with Gan's and Arvatov's intention to link nonobjectivity with mechanical media, Chuzhak came up with an expression, "*lef* photomontage" (already practiced by Malevich's students Klutsis and Senkin), hailing it as "a bridge from 'nonobjectivity' to the 'material,' from 'cognition' to 'construction,' from the illusion-symbolic…to the concrete-real" (figs. 8, 9).[70]

AKhRR's seventh exhibition, yet again called *Revolution, Everyday Life, and Labor,* opened at the

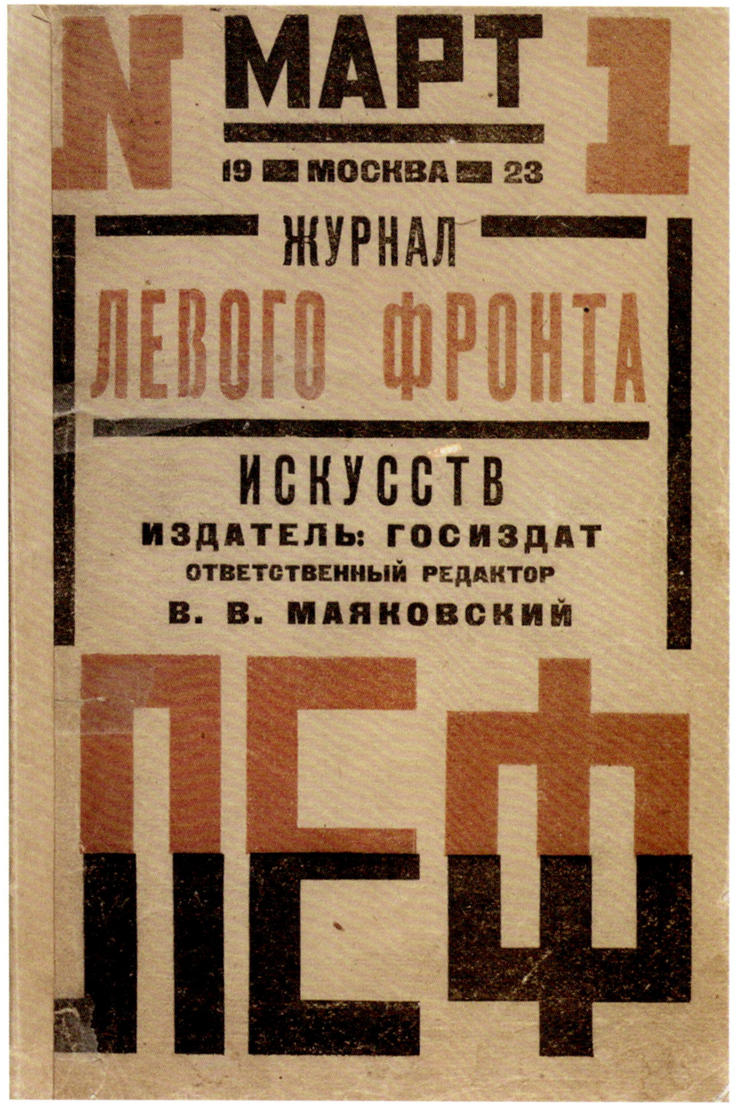

7   Aleksandr Rodchenko, cover of the magazine *Lef* no. 1, 1923. State Mayakovsky Museum, Moscow.

Pushkin State Museum of Fine Arts a few weeks after the January 1925 meeting of the *Lef* community took place (fig. 10). The AKhRR member Isaak Brodsky had provided an example of the infiltration of this prestigious venue (which housed important examples of classical art) by photographic realism, which staked its claim to high status as a chronicler of the Communist Party. Taking advantage of the topical subject matter, Brodsky managed to display there his long-labored canvas *The Solemn Opening of the Second Comintern Congress* (1920–4). This, like his later works (that were just as massive), depicted the meeting in Petrograd of the Party's founding fathers and numerous members, with the ambition of a master of history painting, but without a talent for monumental compositions, despite his studies at the Imperial Academy of Arts with Ilya Repin and extensive travels in Europe before the Revolution. The fact that Brodsky's outdated and clumsy work represented a key international Communist event angered some radical VKhUTEMAS students to such a degree that a barrier and guards were placed in front of Brodsky's exhibit.

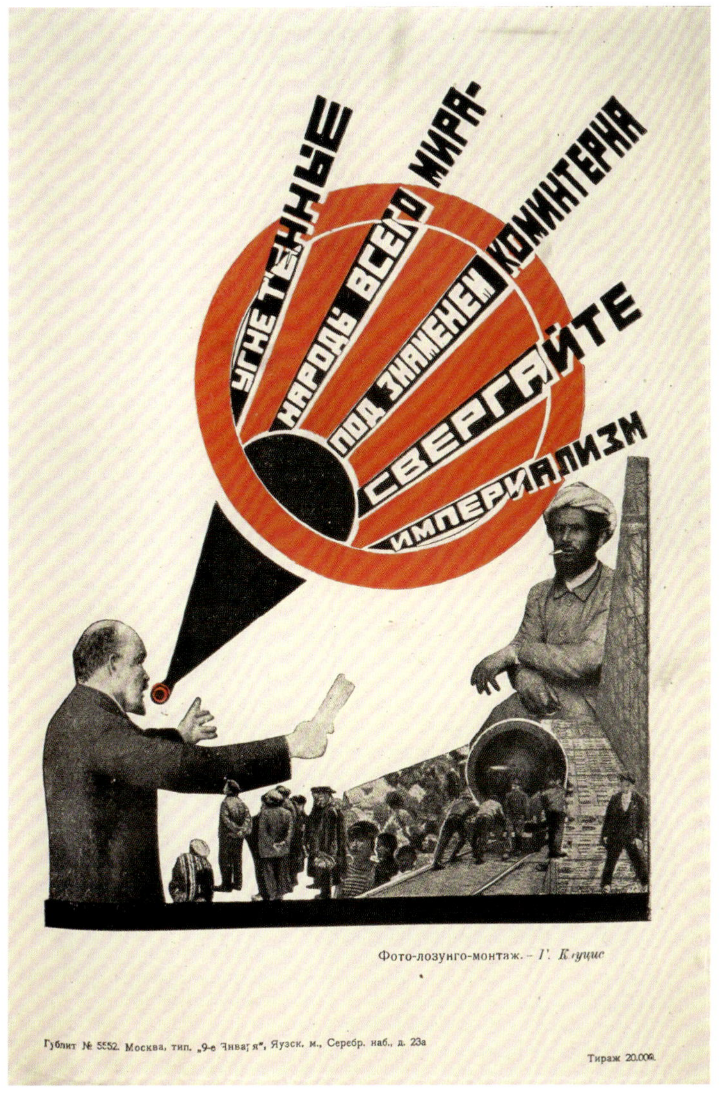

8   Gustav Klutsis, illustration for the magazine *Young Guard*, 1924.

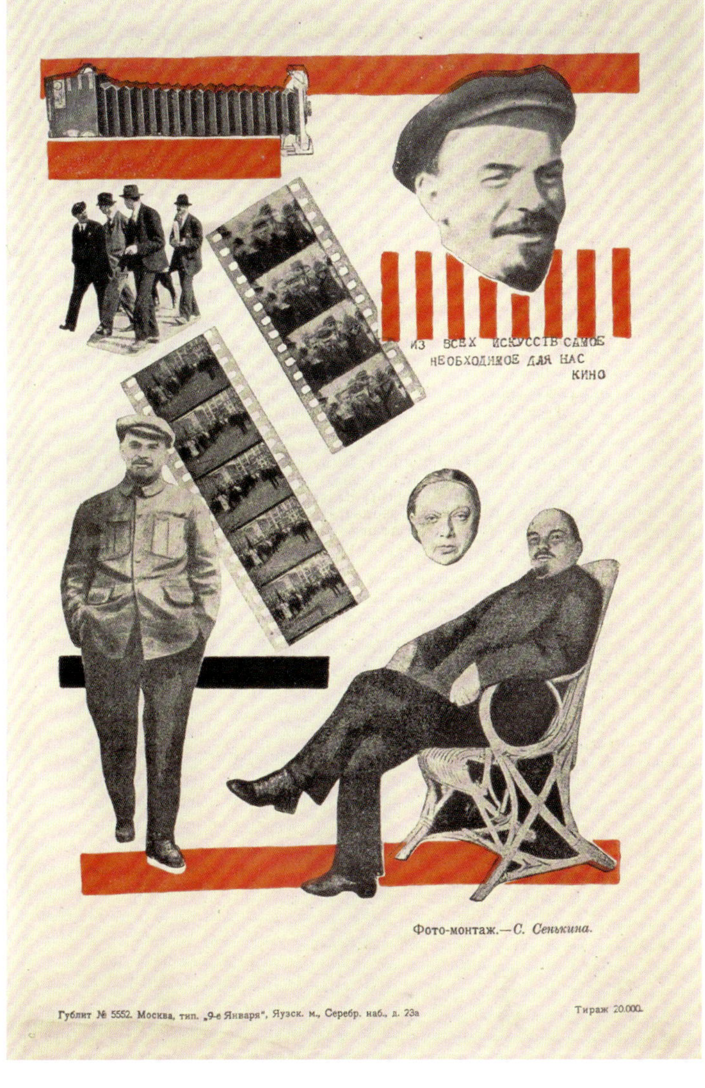

9   Sergei Senkin, illustration for the magazine *Young Guard*, 1924.

The outrage of the avant-garde youth could only encourage AKhRR, hungry for attention, to "occupy" the Pushkin State Museum of Fine Arts with their *Revolution, Everyday Life, and Labor* in the hope of receiving attention from the government that, by initially favoring left artists, had caused realists "to live poorly for the first five years after the Revolution."[71] Lunacharsky's attending the opening promised a reversal of AKhRR's fortune. Although his speech in the courtyard of the Pushkin State Museum of Fine Arts was "reserved,"[72] his review in the news-paper *Izvestia* (News) revealed the first signs of his softening toward the AKhRR milieu. As the commissar of education he was predictably impressed by the exhibition's large attendance that, regardless of the left's anti-painting campaigns, seemed to indicate some "interest of the masses in painting."[73] Lunacharsky called others' criticism of AKhRR "slanderous," but agreed that the group's first exhibitions were inferior, the palette "muddy", and the plots "uninteresting." He kept citing demeaning characterizations of AKhRR by other critics such as "adaptive," "obsequious," guilty of "sell-

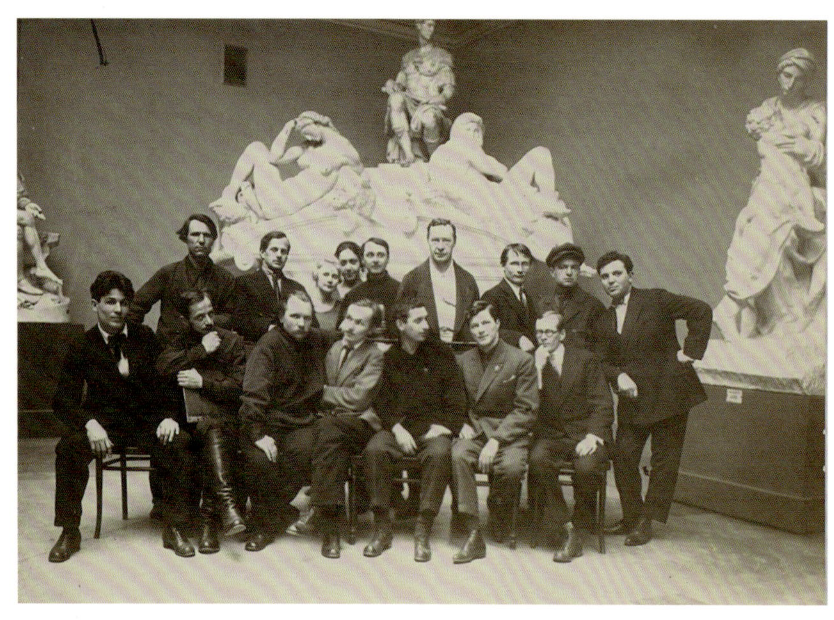

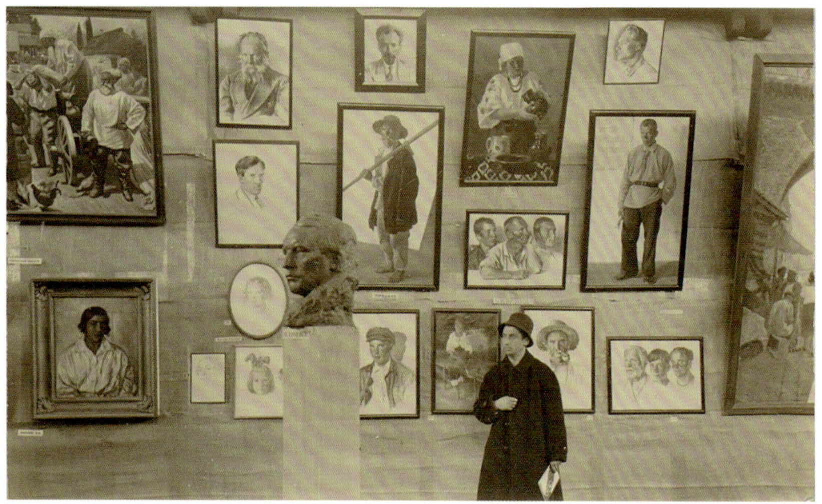

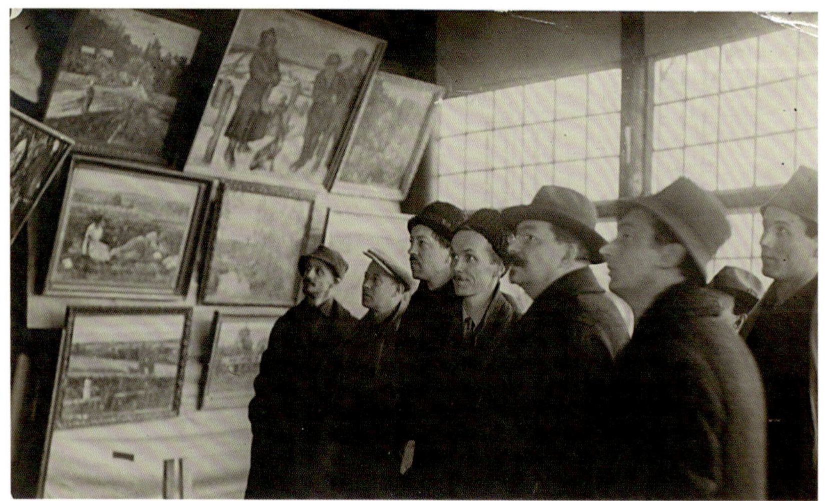

ing the brush of a pure painter for a mess of potage as a reward for a 'revolutionary hack job.'"[74] Lunacharsky summed up on a pessimistic note, concluding that the seventh AKhRR exhibition appealed to "the low public…corrupts the inexperienced masses…spoils the public's taste, and lowers its demands."[75] Such a harsh assortment of epithets exp-osed AKhRR's premise of pleasing unrefined army commanders rather than uplifting the proletariat.

As a result of living in Europe before the Revolution, Lunacharsky both knew and valued modernist painting. Consequently, he believed that past art movements must not be rejected but, rather, evaluated and utilized by proletarian culture. The AKhRR artists, who had been criticizing modernism, were undoubtedly aware of Lunacharsky's attitude toward French modernism, which explains their regular manifestations of allegiance to the "formal achievements of French art."[76] In order to expand its membership, AKhRR constantly lobbied those modernists who did not practice nonobjective art to join their exhibitions. Such politically motivated moves allowed critics like Lunacharsky to call the postimpressionist artists Abram Arkhipov and Ilia Mashkov "brilliant masters," adding, however, that their works lacked "a grand theme" and "a revolutionary plot."[77]

In the spring of 1926, the next massive AKhRR exhibition, *Life and Existence of the Peoples of the USSR*, opened in Moscow's Gorky Park in celebration of the government's multicultural policies (figs. 11, 12). The exhibition's "unprecedented funding"[78] automatically meant a reduction of subsidies promised to the already launched projects by left artists. For example, in a letter of July 1925 to the head of Narkompros's Science Department, Malevich described the direct impact of

10 AKhRR artists in the Pushkin State Museum of Fine Arts during their exhibition *Revolution, Everyday Life, and Labor*, 1925. Russian State Archive of Literature and Art, Moscow.

11 View of Evgeny Katsman's installation in *Life and Existence of the Peoples of the USSR*, 1926, Gorky Park, Moscow. Russian State Archive of Literature and Art, Moscow.

12 AKhRR artists with Anatoly Lunacharsky (second right) in *Life and Existence of the Peoples of the USSR*, 1926, Gorky Park, Moscow. Russian State Archive of Literature and Art, Moscow.

AKhRR's activities on the funding of the State Institute of Artistic Culture (GINKhUK).[79] According to him, the Institute was in a

sad state…although there is plenty of energy in myself and in all the workers of art culture, regardless of 6 rub[les] given to scientific expenses…if we continue receiving such sums of money, we would inscribe formulas on fences, and write theory on the walls of buildings; there is not yet a place for a practical worker in the USSR; so far everything is occupied by AKhR [*sic*] (the space of foreign currency).[80]

To make matters worse, GINKhUK's 1926 annual exhibition was harshly criticized in *Leningradskaia Pravda* (Leningrad Truth) for the use of the term the "order of nonobjectivists."[81] Their conclusion was that funding this "state monastery" was wasteful. Lunacharsky's speech at the opening of *Life and Existence of the Peoples of the USSR*, as before, stopped short of endowing AKhRR with any artistic significance. However, in his text for the exhibition catalogue, he withdrew his hitherto full support of the far-left artists. In defense of the government's backing of AKhRR, Lunacharsky accused the left artists of "looking down with contempt from above at 'the artistic bast-shoe' that has started playing a role. The representatives of the left 'Lef' and of the center-formalists see a huge sin in the Soviet government's interest in this 'bast-shoe' and in passing by the infamous works of art full of European mastery."[82] Yet, to keep some distance from AKhRR, and from endorsing the group's practices, Lunacharsky aligned himself with moderate "right wing formalists," who "rightly point out that some things in the achievements of European mastery, and thus in the mastery of our Europeanized artists, must be paid attention to by our young Soviet art."[83]

Lunacharsky's carrot and stick approach to AKhRR reflected the ongoing Party criticism of "intrigues" instigated by its administration and that it was "undermining the influence of the Party on art circles."[84] Grigoriev was specifically accused of "causing all Communists and non-party members to quarrel,"[85] and removed from office as the president on September

19, 1926. The reshuffle of AKhRR's ideologues and the moderation of their agitated partisanship promised to attract arts graduates and thus threatened the popularity of left artists among the young. Prematurely celebrating his victory, Katsman, when he met the poet and editor of *Lef* magazine, Vladimir Mayakovsky, at *Life and Existence of the Peoples of the USSR*, gave him a book with the following inscription: "To the conquered from the conqueror."[86] A recent debate, "We and Lefs," organized by AKhRR in the Polytechnic Museum, was attended by Mayakovsky along with the influential politician Nikolai Bukharin, Lunacharsky, Brik, Shterenberg, and Chuzhak, which gave the event undeserved attention.

This proved to be a beneficial encounter, prompting, I believe, Mayakovsky to revive *Lef* magazine. Renamed *Novyi Lef* (New Lef), the first issue crystallized key disagreements between AKhRR and avant-garde artists (fig. 13). In his first editor's note, Mayakovsky targeted mega-exhibitions such as AKhRR's, arguing that, "in the last few years the condition of culture in the realm of visual arts had become a swamp".[87] Also in the first issue, Arvatov argued against a return to painting that, to him, positioned workers in the role of consumers and reinstated bourgeois values and class structures. Lunacharsky's efforts to push AKhRR toward the canons of bourgeois "easelism" also resonated with Arvatov, who as early as 1922 made an important distinction between practicing nonobjective art in capitalist society and in a socialist one. Alluding, probably, to the current practices of UNOVIS and INKhUK, he spoke of a "nonobjective laboratory…that will become the very key point where the paths of art and science, practise and theory, merge. And here lies the cardinal difference between contemporary nonobjectivity and proletarian nonobjectivity (still to come)."[88] Arvatov continues:

> While the problems resolved by the former are posed quite subjectively…and depend ultimately on the personal desires of the individual artist, the comradely collaboration of artists and theoreticians in the proletarian laboratory will create an atmosphere in which each problem will emerge indispensably and objectively from practical and conscious premises….[nonobjectivity] is a direct step toward industrial art.[89]

In Arvatov's *Novyi Lef* article, "Why Easel Painting Did not Die," he drew a parallel between Soviet and Western realism: "When Picasso paints à la Ingres and primitive AKhRR vulgarize…Wanderers, the difference is only in mastery."[90] Arvatov explained the failure to realize large-scale nonobjective projects by the poor state of the economy, the absence of industrial development, and the activity of some new layers of consumers (petty bourgeois) who were not used to thinking beyond "'a little picture.'"[91] Following Gan, Arvatov assigned to cinema, photography, and photomontage the role of legitimate successors of nonobjective art and the sole alternative to AKhRR's *byt-kartina* (a picture of everyday life), a mere "substitute of a disorganized reality."[92] These mechanical media established rather than invented facts,[93] and "reflected everyday life and events more cheaply, faster, and more precisely than painters."[94] With a camera one is able to accumulate "trans-artistic plots," the material in Chuzhak's words for "ultra-realism," and in Arvatov's terminology "ultra-representational art," which is "mass-oriented, executed by a machine, and tightly linked with the material everyday life of urban industrial workers."[95] Such an original representational system would once and for all cut any ties with traditional methods of making art.

The end of the NEP-market economy and the inauguration of the first Five-Year Plan in 1928 empowered these cine-photo practices and provided left artists with another opportunity to fight for their model of realism. In the year of the Plan's inauguration, "the *lef* workers" consolidated into the October group, and AKhRR, in an effort to broaden its influence, dropped the word "Russia" from its name, calling itself AKhR (Association of Artists of the Revolution; for ease of reference, I shall use AKhRR throughout). Both associations almost simultaneously issued declarations that confirmed their long-established irreconcilable differences. October, with its concentration on collectively produced industrial arts, proclaimed its direct link to the "revolutionary industrial proletariat" as their sole audience. The political element of the class struggle that they injected into the realm of the arts demanded a complete separation from forms of art that were associated with "individualistic and commercial relationships."[96] In unison with the left critics discussed earlier, October members

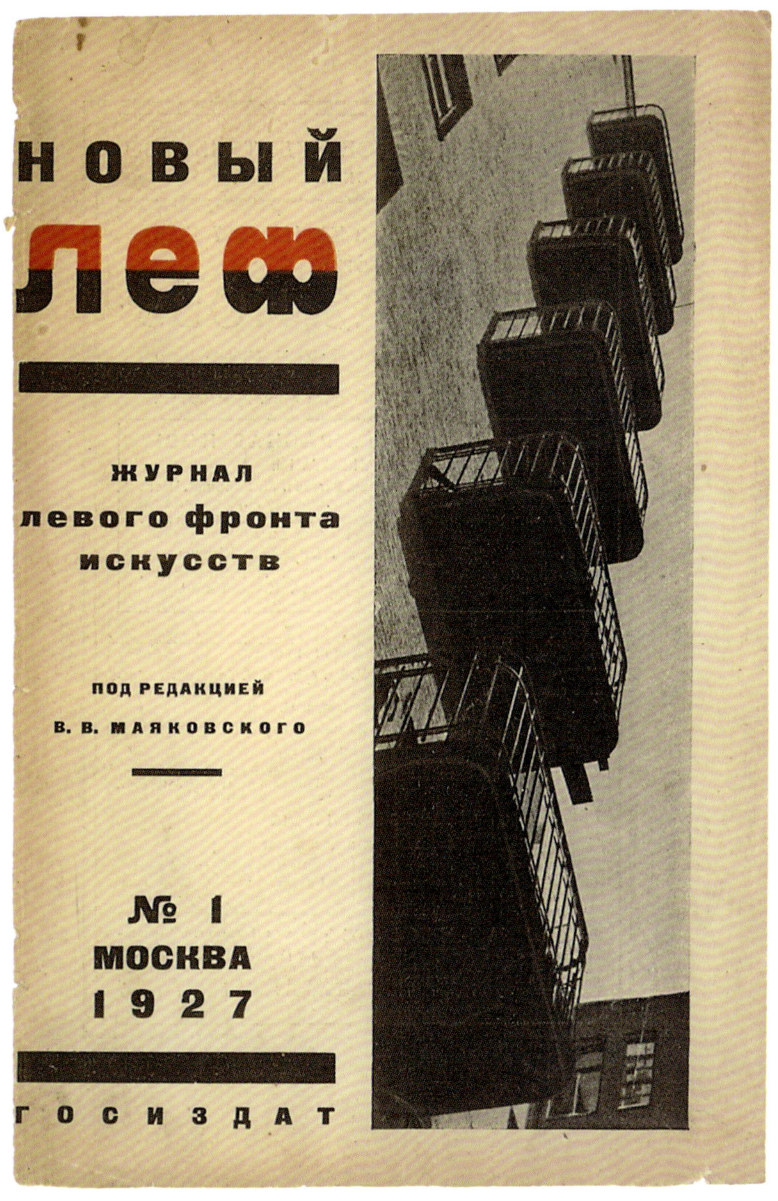

13   Aleksandr Rodchenko, cover of the magazine *Novyi Lef* no. 1, 1927.
State Mayakovsky Museum, Moscow.

insisted that mimetic representation was contaminated by the clichés of the bourgeois class, and thus could not take on the responsibility for developing the aesthetic consciousness of the new class of "the culturally under-developed proletariat."[97] In its turn, AKhRR's declaration continued to defend what October saw as a "fruitless copying of reality"[98] and the simplification of realistic forms so that they are "comprehensible to the broad masses of the workers."[99] In the declaration, AKhRR spoke briefly of the importance of "artistically designing everyday life" as well as the production of "articles of mass consumption."[100] This, however, came across as an artificial concern (undoubtedly made under the pressure of production art), for it stood in obvious conflict with AKhRR's definition of its future as an advance toward "a monumental style" and "the style of heroic realism."

To the left community, the most disturbing aspect of AKhRR's new declaration was their proposal to create "INTERNAKhR," and thus infringe on the leftists' central idea, which was internationalism. Accordingly, they convinced the Mexican artist Diego Rivera, a member of the October Group since 1928, to display his designs for a mural for the Central House of the Red Army in the tenth AKhRR exhibition, which opened on February 23, 1928 and was dedicated to the tenth anniversary of the Red Army.[101] Rivera's non-painting example of rigorous stylized figuration, energized by a Marxist negativity, became a formula of modernization for the group's influx of young artists from the Youth section of AKhRR (OMAKhRR, formed out of the students of VKhUTEIN). Adherence to Rivera's "wall painting" also satisfied left practitioners like Mayakovsky who believed that, unlike easel pictures, murals could qualify as a revolutionary medium.[102] Rivera's synthesizing of modernist and classical styles similarly fit Lunacharsky's earlier prescription for AKhRR that "art begins when an artist stylizes reality, that is sharpens it, gives it something of his own, makes it expressive to such a degree that it hits the viewer with an enormous force."[103] Armed with this contemporary medium, young AKhRR members spoke about the negative influence of photorealism and "Brodskyism" on AKhRR, and demanded Brodsky's as well as Katsman, Radimov, and Perelman's expulsion from the association. Katsman was even described as "a class enemy."[104] Although the membership of these artists who were well connected in the Politburo was salvaged,[105] AKhRR's last and eleventh exhibition, *Art into Masses* (which opened on June 2, 1929), demonstrated a shift toward a broader variety of media, including frescoes and applied arts. This was followed in March 1930 by AKhRR's debate, "Is Easel Painting Doomed to Die?"[106] which again demonstrated the limited agitational power of this medium to promote the government's industrial agenda. The result was sharply reduced subsidies for easel painters from all camps. Malevich amply expressed this state of affairs: "In Moscow, artists are groaning, there is no work, AKhR has no subsidies either. End, end, end to everyone."[107] This worry pushed Malevich into thinking of working in other media such as film,[108] and continuing with

the application of Suprematism in architecture that he had begun with the three-dimensional structures called *architektons* in 1923.

Such a move should have lessened Katsman's old rivalry with Malevich as well as AKhRR's overall competition with nonobjective painting. Yet, unexpectedly after Malevich's several successful exhibitions in Warsaw and Berlin in 1927, his interest in painting returned. Moreover, after living in Europe for several months, in an atmosphere of "fame pouring like rain,"[109] Malevich received equal appreciation upon his return home, specifically in Lunacharsky's review of his Berlin exhibition in which he presented Malevich as "our famous 'suprematist'…a great master" with "a talent, tenacity, and a system."[110] As if settling scores with Kandinsky for not returning to Russia after being delegated to Germany in 1922 by the Russian Academy of Artistic Sciences (RAKhN), Lunacharsky favors Malevich over Kandinsky as "a more steadfast" artist, particularly in the context of his "shift to hard and solid painting."[111] This was another indication that Lunacharsky was paying attention to what was happening in Europe. It also showed that his support of Russian modernists, whom he compared with "sophisticated Europeans such as Matisse and even Picasso,"[112] was unwavering.

Malevich's brief arrest upon his return suggested that in 1927 progressive and conservative factions existed in parallel, endorsing distinct cultural practices and giving conflicting orders. Malevich wanted to return to Europe to paint, but first he needed to raise money by selling his paintings on view in Berlin. Based on his correspondence with Western colleagues, it seems that three canvases were considered for purchase, including *Reaping Woman* (1911–12) and *Burial of a Peasant* (1911–12).[113] Malevich's admission that he preferred "to keep these works for himself" but was willing to part with them if "they bring a needed sum of money,"[114] may explain his decision to repeat these early themes and back-date them. Charlotte Douglas pointed out that in fact these paintings were not exact copies of earlier canvases, for Malevich "worked from memory or from small pencil sketches, thus leaving greater room for spontaneous, contemporary creativity."[115] Thus Malevich was not "embarrassingly…back-dat[ing]"[116] his peasant series, as she also had suggested. Rather, he was driven by the impulse (not unusual for the capitalist art market) to paint in the style favored by collectors. Moreover, Malevich's attitude toward the issue of originality had been far from traditional ever since he had subjected Suprematism to a collective appropriation and disseminated it by mechanical means. His making of the second *Black Square* around 1924 also indicated that he regarded copying his own works as a recontexualization and attainment of semantic variations in the ever-changing Soviet cultural and political climate. This is how, I believe, the formation of the second peasant series transpired. When Malevich failed to raise the money he needed to return to Europe, his replication of the first peasant series brought him to the point of no return with nonobjective painting. By then, his stocky and volumetric peasants with stylized faces had transformed into "flattened, geometricized, and ordered"[117] figures, which meant that in this updated format his Suprematist grid was resurfacing (see fig. 16). And although the new versions were representational, they still fulfilled the abstract grid's characteristics of being "antinatural, antimimetic, antireal,"[118] and thus were the very antitheses to AKhRR's mimetic renderings of Soviet peasants and workers. If the Suprematist grid was Malevich's choice of "an emblem of modernity," the gridded representations of the rural proletariat emblematized Stalin's violent modernization.

Judging from Malevich's letter to his wife written at the beginning of 1929, he felt positive about winning over AKhRR's "new campaign…against new tendencies…My line is prevailing and thus all their efforts will be in vain,"[119] he assertively remarked. By the end of the year he had triumphed with his retrospective at the State Tretiakov Gallery: the heavy presence of representational canvases presented a new challenge to AKhRR, for now they had to battle Malevich not within a structure of pure oppositions. This shift probably instigated a new wave of personal and institutional attacks from the conservative camps, including a search of Malevich's studio (located at the State Institute for Art History in Leningrad), with the confiscation of records and a second arrest, and the purging of Narkompros that resulted in Lunacharsky's dismissal. Feliks Kon, the Party functionary and the editor of several newspapers and magazines, was reported in the press as remarking that "Glaviskusstv [Chief Administration for Art Institutions at Narkompros] must decisively take AKhR under protection," after being nominated as its director.[120] This betrayed AKhRR's involvement in this new campaign.

With the completion of the first Five-Year Plan in 1932, the Soviet Union was no longer a fractured state. In contrast to its political and economic unity, the divide between the groups of diverse aesthetic persuasions only intensified. To end this irreconcilable situation, the Communist Party issued, on April 23, 1932, the Decree on the Reconstruction of Literary and Artistic Organizations, which dispersed all existing art groups.[121] An enormous exhibition, *Artists of the RSFSR of the Last 15 Years*, which opened in November 1932 in the Russian Museum with works numbering in their thousands,[122] put this order into effect. The catalogue had two introductions, one written by the left critic Nikolai Punin, and the other by the Impressionist artist and art historian Igor Grabar. Both contributors took the position of educated internationalists, emphasizing those groups of painters that absorbed the best traditions of European art (classical and modernist) in order "to express their attitude to Soviet reality within a more perfect standard."[123] The fact that some of these Europeanized artists had joined AKhRR allowed both critics to write of the association in more positive terms. Yet Punin mentioned that AKhRR had been "formed as an antithesis to the 'left art,'"[124] and Grabar, himself a figurative painter, replaced AKhRR's slogan of "Back to realism, forward to the masses," with "Back to realism, forward to painting."[125] He also signed his text "academician of painting," implying that many Soviet realists lacked academic mastery. Furthermore, Grabar's call for the unification of Soviet artists under the principles of the medium rather than those of ideology demonstrated his optimism about Soviet art's immediate future.

The inclusion in *Artists of the RSFSR* of the practitioners of nonobjective trends is a key factor in reconsidering when exactly nonobjective art vanished from the public eye. Moreover, Malevich's successful presentation of his works in a coherent installation testified to the success of the battle (by then carried

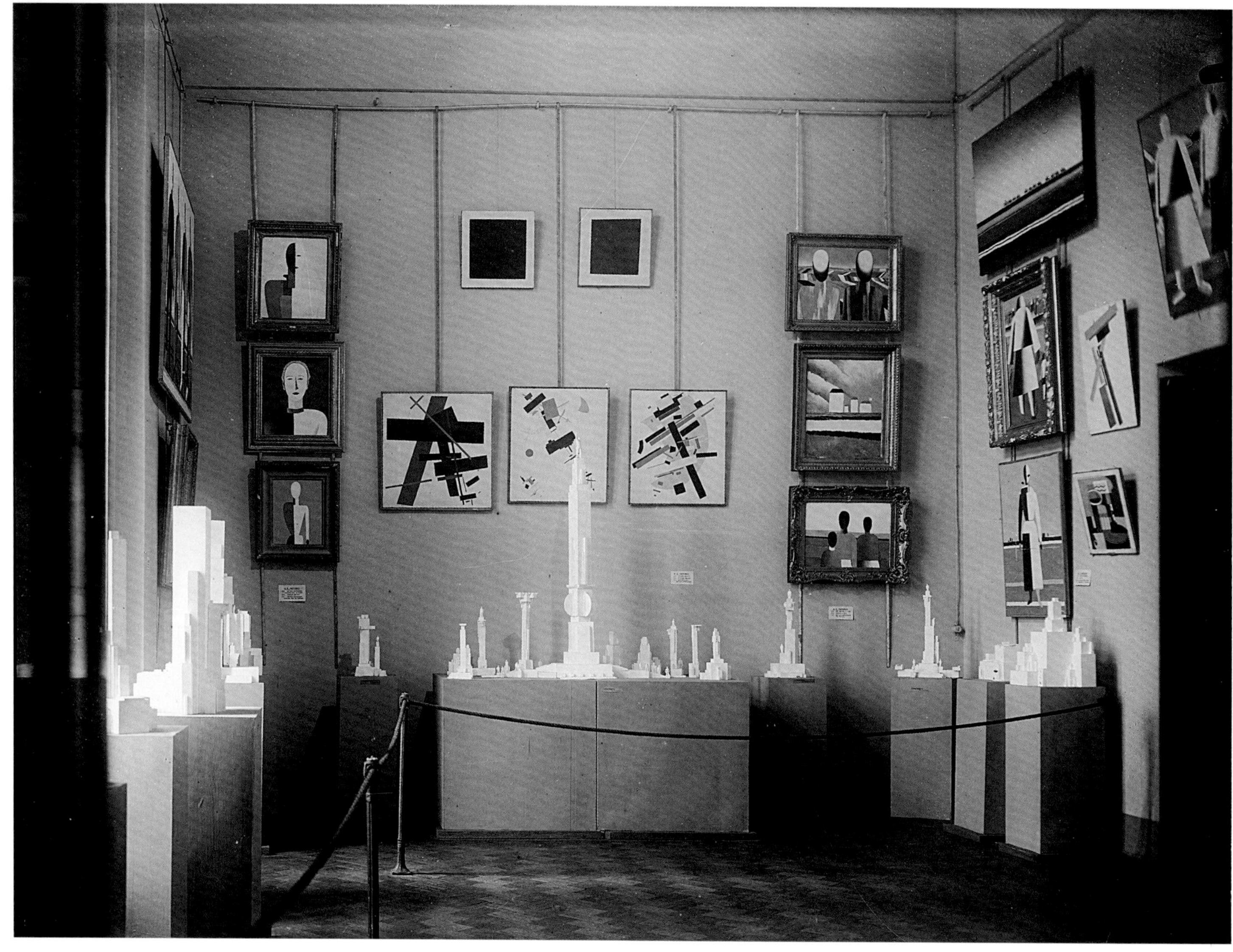

14   Malevich's works in *Artists of the RSFSR During the Last 15 Years*, 1932. State Russian Museum, Leningrad.

out by a small group of critics and museum administrators) against the monopolization of the art world by conservatives. Malevich, who unlike most other nonobjective artists was present during the installation, saved his exhibits by insisting that they would "not be submitted to a selection committee."[126] The result was a generous amount of works (thirty mentioned in the catalogue, but in reality probably more), including nonobjective and post-Suprematist paintings, *architektons*, and designs (fig. 14). Punin dubbed this assemblage of works the "suprematist room" and explained to visitors that "Suprematism is a particular tendency in contemporary Soviet art that played a significant role in the development of painting's forms as well as in contemporary architecture, applied arts, posters, and book covers."[127]

Malevich crowned his display with *Black Square*, this time not hung alone in the corner but in line with *Red Square*. The former, in Malevich's terms, being "a sign of economy" (reduction of forms) and the latter "a signal of Revolution," sent a message to those artists exhibiting nearby who were ready to endorse Socialist

Realism as an imperative language for revolutionary art. Nikolai Suetin, who was "one of [Malevich's] most reliable"[128] students, and with whom he shared the "suprematist room," intensified the impact of Malevich's emphasis on a square shape (which as early as 1919 the nonobjective artists considered to be a trademark of left identity), by making and exhibiting his own version of *Black Square*.[129] This was also consistent with Suetin's current assessment of Malevich's *Black Square* as "the phenomenon of Russian art that will turn out to be a world important event as it was to me. The square is akin to the Egyptian sphinx and is closely linked to the culture of icon painting," as he inscribed on one of his drawings in May 1933.[130] Suetin's endowing *Black Square* with utopian connotations, as well as (paradoxically for a radical artist) with the protective powers of a religious object, could have been prompted by the increasingly adversarial reception of nonobjective works in the Moscow venue of *Artists of the RSFSR*.[131] In *Izvestia*, Malevich and Suetin's installation was called the "cabinet of 'nonobjective art,'"[132] and its contents were classified as "the primary hotbed of formalism."[133] Malevich's summary of the Moscow reviews, including one by Bukharin, accentuated the "harsh attacks on" *Black Square* that Malevich described as "our end."[134]

While in this pessimistic state, Malevich met the sculptor and art historian Vladimir Pavlov who, Malevich reported to his family, "praises my works very much."[135] Shortly after, Malevich's anguish over the harsh critiques of *Black Square* with which his nonobjective art commenced was mirrored in his half-length portrait of Pavlov (fig. 15). Painted in a somber palette reflective of his mood and in an unusually conventional style, the canvas included a rendition of *Black Square* on the background wall. By placing it behind his new friend, Malevich was stating that he was appointing him to defend his legacy.[136] However, along with this personal trust, assigning *Black Square* the function of a representation

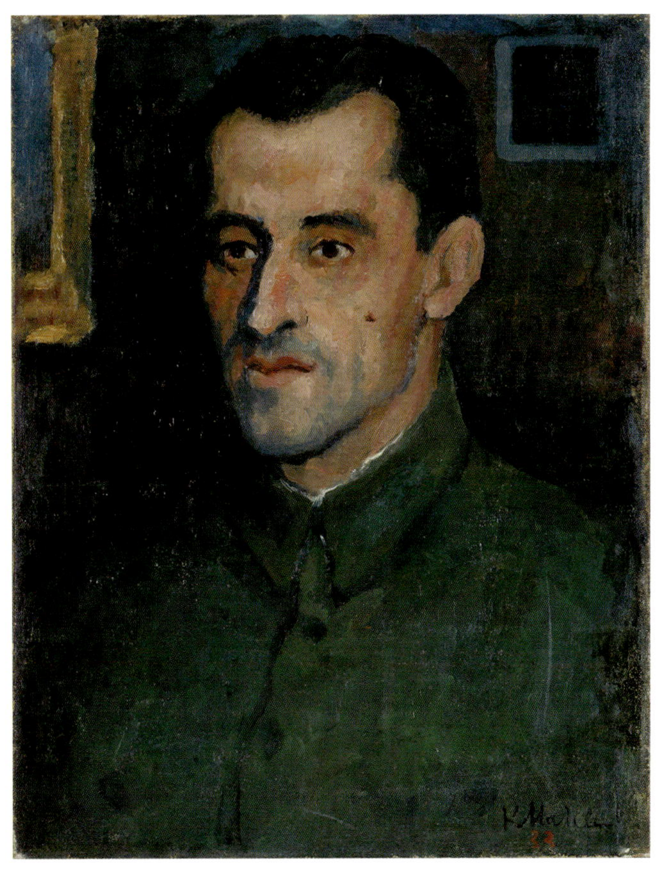

15 Kazimir Malevich, *V.A. Pavlov*, 1933. State Tretiakov Gallery, Moscow.

positioned it as a double signifier of nonobjective art's beginning and end. That metaphor was particularly appropriate in view of the fact that in the Moscow installation of *Artists of the RSFSR*, the room of "formalist tendencies" included, along with Malevich's exhibits, Vladimir Tatlin's *Board No. 1*, a counter-relief, and *Letatlin*. This reunion concluded the trajectory of paradigmatic shifts that Malevich and Tatlin had achieved in nonobjective art since they first triumphantly unveiled its two versions in the *0,10* exhibition of 1915.[137]

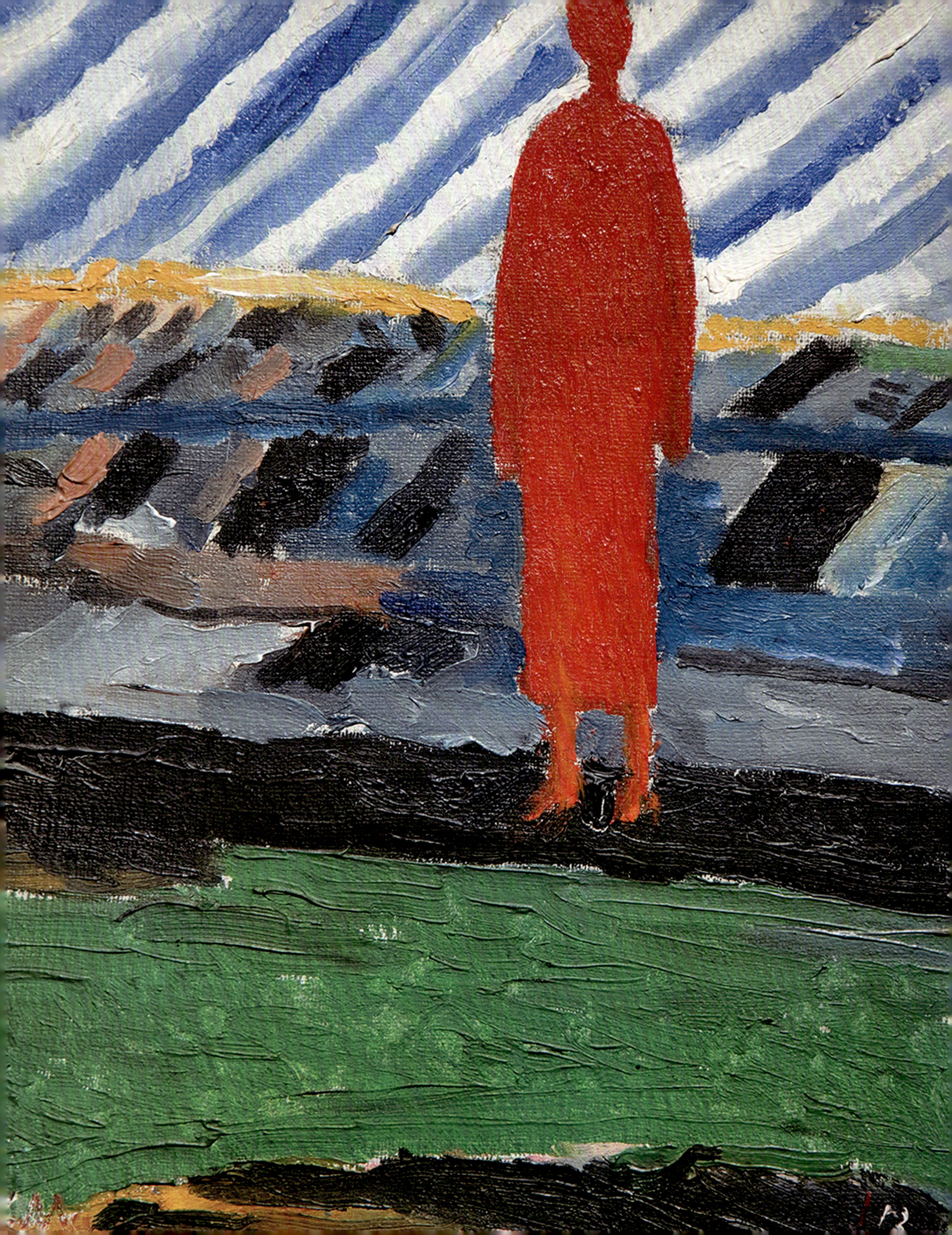

2

THE SPECTERS OF FORMALISM

Impressionism is the beginning of a great epoch. Of the new nonobjective painterly values.

Kazimir Malevich, 1934.

I read my diary of 1918 and 1920. Everything was just like it is now. Art isn't needed. Well, maybe now it's worse…The same hatred for formalists.

Aleksandr Rodchenko, 1943.

In the summer of 1933, a troika of former AKhRR members – Isaak Brodsky, Aleksandr Gerasimov, and Evgeny Katsman – paid a visit to Joseph Stalin, accompanied by their backer Kliment Voroshilov, the soon to be People's Commissar for Defense. As Katsman's diaries describe, the group arrived at Stalin's dacha with catalogues featuring their own as well as their aesthetic adversaries' work. Impressed by Stalin's grandeur and "sweet face with serene smile" (both reflected in Brodsky's portrait of Stalin executed the same year; State Museum and Exhibition Center ROSIZO, Moscow), the artists were convinced that the leader was "most capable of objectively seeing people and events."[1] Not easily seduced, Stalin criticized the realists' predilection for idealizing Politburo members – in particular, Marshal Voroshilov, whom Gerasimov and Katsman had courted and painted since the 1920s. In his 1933 representations of Voroshilov, Gerasimov, for example, promoted his status as the "favorite hero of the people,"[2] which did not please Stalin. So when the troika asked him if he would support the "organization of a commissariat of art," Stalin declined: "No, no. We do not need it. Let it develop freely, let no one disturb it. Your art business is free, but a commissariat would tie you up."[3] Stalin's admission that he knew neither the art of his guests nor that of the formalists illustrated that painting had no great importance for him.[4] This was partially the result of the triumphant role that printed media and documentary cinema had played in the propaganda of the first Five-Year Plan. In fact, Stalin would probably have agreed with the production artists' claim that painting was a residue of bourgeois society, and thus had no immediate value for the

OPPOSITE PAGE   Kazimir Malevich, *Red Figure*, 1928–32 (detail of fig. 17).

proletariat. Similarly, given Stalin's fascination with mass media and cinema, the troika's characterization of production artists (still living in the headquarters of the already closed VKhUTEMAS on Miasnitskaia Street) as those who "prepared freaks, and producers of books and posters" did not move him.

The year 1933 signified a new epoch for the Soviet art community. The first Five-Year Plan had been completed and its message effectively disseminated under the new concept of the artist as producer. With the inauguration of the second Five-Year Plan (1933–7), the government's demand for this particular artist type promised to continue, decreasing the chances of AKhRR's agenda monopolizing the visual arts. This explains why AKhRR early on joined forces with Army leaders, appealing to the highest authority, Stalin himself, during the preparation of the Moscow version of *Artists of the RSFSR of the Last 15 Years*. As a result, the exhibition was linked to the Seventeenth Congress of the All Russian Communist Party (Bolsheviks), or VKP(b), which opened in January 1934, an event symbolically dubbed "the congress of winners," which had a mandate to endorse the second Five-Year Plan. Reactionary camps of artists also managed to convince the committee to add some works to *Artists of the RSFSR* from the exhibition *Fifteen Years of the RKKA* (Workers' and Peasants' Red Army), which opened at Gorky Park on June 30. Although it included innovative designs dedicated to the subject of the Red Army, in their statement to the exhibition committee, *Artists of RSFSR* urged the Congress's delegates "to pay attention to the paintings taken from the art exhibition, *Fifteen Years of RKKA*,"[5] defining painting as "the center"[6] of the *Artists of RSFSR* exhibition. Hailing realism's growing popularity among Soviet artists with regard to left circles and formalists, the speech revealed the same rhetoric that the troika delivered to Stalin at his dacha. "The so-called formalists…are included to symbolize the past and to illustrate an ideological creative thinking that is unacceptable, alien and hostile for us, but the remnants of which are still found today among some groups of artists. A ruthless fight with them is the present task."[7]

The Moscow Regional Union of Soviet Artists (MOSSKh) became the forum for consolidating a more effective warfare against the left milieu. Although the Decree on the Reconstruction of Literary and Artistic Organizations did not dictate a single aesthetic dogma, it did make all Soviet artists flock together under the umbrella of a single organization, and introduced the concept of "official artist," while giving conservative forces more control over their aesthetic adversaries. After a decade of AKhRR's lobbying, the various decrees of the Party bureaucrats on culture could now be implemented within one organization. Aleksei Volter, AKhRR's founding member and chair of the jury of *Artists of RSFSR*, became MOSSKh's chair, and Shterenberg was assigned to be his first deputy. As before, Shterenberg was committed to safeguarding experimental art against those who would "affix a label of formalism [to an artist] only because he is not like everyone else." Furthermore, Shterenberg criticized the activities of partisan critics who "defend[ed] and propagat[ed] epigones,"[8] probably a reference to the anti-formalist writings of the critic Osip Beskin. The latter shared a hunger for gaining centralized control of cultural affairs with AKhRR, and by 1933 succeeded in occupying several key positions, including that of head of the critics' section of MOSSKh and editor of the two newly established art magazines, *Iskusstvo* (Art) and *Tvorchestvo* (Creativity). Just the names of these magazines undermined the anti-creativity and anti-art agenda of productivist artists whose broad alliance with the State Publishing House (IZOGIZ) was now being threatened with Volter becoming its chief editor. In order better to distribute his anti-formalist articles, Beskin quickly compiled them into a concise publication, *Formalism in Painting*, narrowing down his discussion of the medium to suit the chief concerns of the original AKhRR agenda. In addition to the artists such as Shterenberg who refused to succumb to academic realism, Beskin attacked Suprematists and Constructivists, naming the most visible participants of *Artists of the RSFSR*, Malevich, Suetin, and Kliun. Beskin called their art (in a reference to modernists often having their studios in attic rooms) a "mansard-anarchic 'revolt,'"[9] rooting left artists in the genealogy of modernism, and thus displaying an alliance with the right wing of AKhRR, who defined modernists as embodying an "anarcho-individualistic, postimpressionist revolt."[10]

As an early opponent of AKhRR, and one of the key theorists of formalism, Osip Brik disparaged Beskin's publication in the widely read *Literaturnaia gazeta* (Literary Gazette).[11] He opposed Beskin's focus on painting since the artists discussed were multimedia practitioners, and reminded Beskin that all of them were equal members of MOSSKh, and thus could not be labeled as "class enemies" and "corrupters" of young artists. Brik attacked Beskin's favoritism toward AKhRR, arguing that similar "debates and disputes" must be directed toward its artists "Bogorodsky, Katsman, and Perelman." Brik mocked Beskin's "illiterate" analysis of formalist art, and spoke of his irresponsible dispensing of "anti-Soviet attestations," the kind of unsubstantiated criticism that would later bring about the denunciations, isolation, and purges of the avant-garde milieu.

There was an immediate answer in *Pravda* (Truth) to Brik's bold retort, revealing AKhRR's habit of pushing their agenda through that Party mouthpiece, thus giving it an aura of government endorsement. Written by a little-known critic, S. Dinamov, the *Pravda* article condemned and reprimanded the activities of IZO Narkompros under the administrations of Shterenberg, Punin, and Brik, and praised Narkompros of the RSFSR, where Beskin served as a general artistic inspector.[12] Dinamov called Brik's text "suspicious" and slammed *Literaturnaia gazeta* for standing by formalists, whose practitioners were "turning the life of people and objects into schematized transrational signs." Dinamov equated formalism and "left art" with negative labels that he employed against anyone who deviated from AKhRR's "corpulent, healthy, and optimistic" style of painting. He claimed that Brik's text was "against Socialist Realism," using this term even before it was officially endorsed two months later at the First All-Union Congress of Soviet Writers (opened on August 17, 1934).

Thus was revealed the plan of ex-AKhRR artists to usurp the cultural doctrine of Socialist Realism and control its meaning through the alliance with Party ideologues such as Andrei Zhdanov. Like Voroshilov with visual art, Zhdanov had an ambition to interfere in literature, which, like cinema and mass media, was much closer to Stalin's interests. Although the Congress of Soviet Writers only defined literary Socialist Realism, Zhdanov's classification of it as truthfulness, and formalism as scholastic, resonates with Beskin and Dinamov's distinctions. In his speech, which revered Stalin's dubbing of Soviet writers as "engineers of human souls," Zhdanov insisted on the eradication of the avant-garde's utopian aspirations, and called for concentration on "real life."[13] Stalin's and Zhdanov's use of the expression "engineers of human souls" seems paradoxical coming from these materialists. The formalist critic Viktor Shklovsky explained this inconsistency by claiming that in fact it was the writer Iury Olesha who coined the phrase during a meeting with Stalin at Maxim Gorky's house in 1932. When asked to organize the Congress of Soviet Writers and assigned to give a major speech there, Zhdanov carelessly appropriated a formalist lexicon in an unmistakably alien way. For example, in his speech he incongruously appropriated Shklovsky's terminology, loathed by realists like Katsman,[14] from the seminal text "Art as Technique" (1917), in claiming that: "One cannot be an engineer of human souls without knowing the technique of literary work, and it must be noted that the technique of the writer's work possesses a large number of specific peculiarities."[15] The result was a gross misuse and reversal of Shklovsky's call to destroy clichés, complicate form, and prevent instant perception.[16]

In view of the harsh press and exhibition campaigns of 1933, the choice of only one artist – Igor Grabar – to speak on behalf of visual art at the Congress of Soviet Writers signaled a compromise. Grabar peppered his speech with productivist terminology, and accentuated Socialist Realism's literary origin, using generalizations and tautology. "Comrade writers, you depict life as you see it, understand it, and feel it, and we depict it in the same way. You use the method of Socialist Realism, and we too use this well-tested method – the best of all existing ones."[17] His statement confirmed the government's selection of literature, both "*belles lettres* and literary criticism,"[18] as the main field for controlling a population that was by then addicted to mass media and novels, printed in huge editions. This shook up Russian modernism's canonical and hitherto productive exchange between visual and literary culture, and made visual art supplementary to literary practices.

Unlike AKhRR's decision to paint Stalin, Grabar, the year before the Congress of Soviet Writers, had finished *Lenin in his Kremlin Office* (1933), a portrait painted in unnatural, even toxic, reds and violets, like early hand-colored photographs. Lenin's yellowish, depressed, and detached face recalls his appearance in photographs (concealed from the public for decades) that were taken while he was alive but much debilitated in Gorki, shortly before his death. Judging by this portrait, Grabar was not ready to "vacate" Lenin from the Kremlin, even though Stalin had already occupied his office. Yet Grabar's intuition, or the pressure from AKhRR's high-ranking supporters, compelled him to endorse portraiture as a primary Socialist Realist genre and a portrait of Stalin as its *sine qua non*.[19] The one Grabar presented to the Congress of Soviet Writers was by Pavel Malkov.

On the whole, Grabar was a typical representative of a modernist wing of Soviet figuration that was not seduced by nonobjective forms, had no zeal for perpetual experiment, and did not drop painting for the sake of mechanical media. His belief that "the task of a contemporary artist is to convey customs, ideas, and the face of our epoch as each individual artist feels and understands them"[20] anchored Grabar to early Modernism. As such, Grabar cared about and substantially contributed to collecting and preserving modern art from before and after the Revolution. This included the acquisition of left art for the State Tretiakov Gallery, on display until 1936, and managing the nationalization of Sergei Shchukin's and Ivan Morozov's collections of French modernism (which would otherwise have been sold to foreign states).

Grabar's influence helped curb AKhRR's disdain for heterodoxy before the Congress of Soviet Writers, and his speech there on behalf of "the entire army of the visual art front"[21] promised to hinder AKhRR's agitation for stylistic homogeneity in MOSSKh. The deferral of its dictatorship was possible because the visual parameters of Socialist Realism were left undetermined at the Congress of Soviet Writers, which was attended primarily by the literary community. As a result, the task was delegated to MOSSKh members and put into the hands of contending artists. This meant that the precise framework of Socialist Realist style depended on who held power in MOSSKh. In the beginning, Shterenberg shielded the left camp with monetary support,[22] whereas Sergei Gerasimov,[23] an impressionist and MOSSKh's head of painting, was sustaining a non-dogmatic model of Socialist Realism similar to the one Lunacharsky outlined shortly before he was removed from Narkompros. This was "an extensive program" that "include[d] many different methods – those we already possess and those we are still acquiring,"[24] wrote Lunacharsky. At this point, those MOSSKh members formally associated with AKhRR could be tamed through a sort of "impressionist fraternity" that had been formed at MUZhVZ, where many key MOSSKh players of all convictions had studied with impressionist painters like Abram Arkhipov (who in 1924 himself became an AKhRR member) and Konstantin Korovin. They had thus been "infected" to varying degrees with this key modernist movement. Even production artists could work with such a compromise for, as Linda Nochlin pointed out, "The 'instantaneity' of the Impressionists is 'contemporaneity' taken to its ultimate limits. "Now,' 'today,' 'the present,' had become 'this very moment,' 'this instant.' No doubt photography helped identify the contemporary as instantaneous."[25]

Thus during the second Five-Year Plan, Impressionism was crystallizing into a unifying approach that "would at once be convincingly truthful and unembellished, yet at the same time, create when appropriate, a sense of long-range value and importance."[26] Its depiction of current social and political events contested AKhRR's "heroic realism" that defied French and local modernism and thus inevitably led to the resurrection of academic readymade formulae, such as the "rhetoric of grandeur."[27]

It was then that Malevich decided to "recompose," as he put it the human figure (as in his cubo-futurist canvases of 1914–15), and formulate an allegorical image of a new class. One of the earliest works that marked Malevich's return to figuration has a description on the back of the canvas: "Prototype of a New Image/Problem/Color and Form/and/Content" (1928–32; fig. 16). With these words, Malevich posed the objectives of his new painterly program: to preserve color and form as primary elements, thus refusing to give up these key aspects of modernist painting. However, the mention of "Content" signals

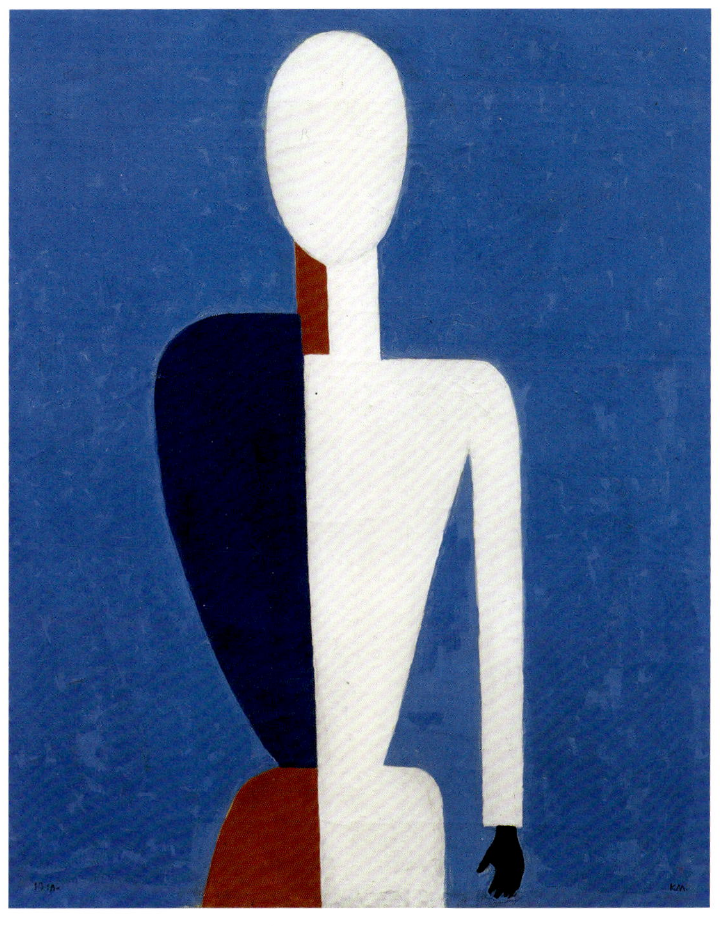

16 Kazimir Malevich, "Prototype of a New Image," 1928–32. State Russian Museum, St. Petersburg.

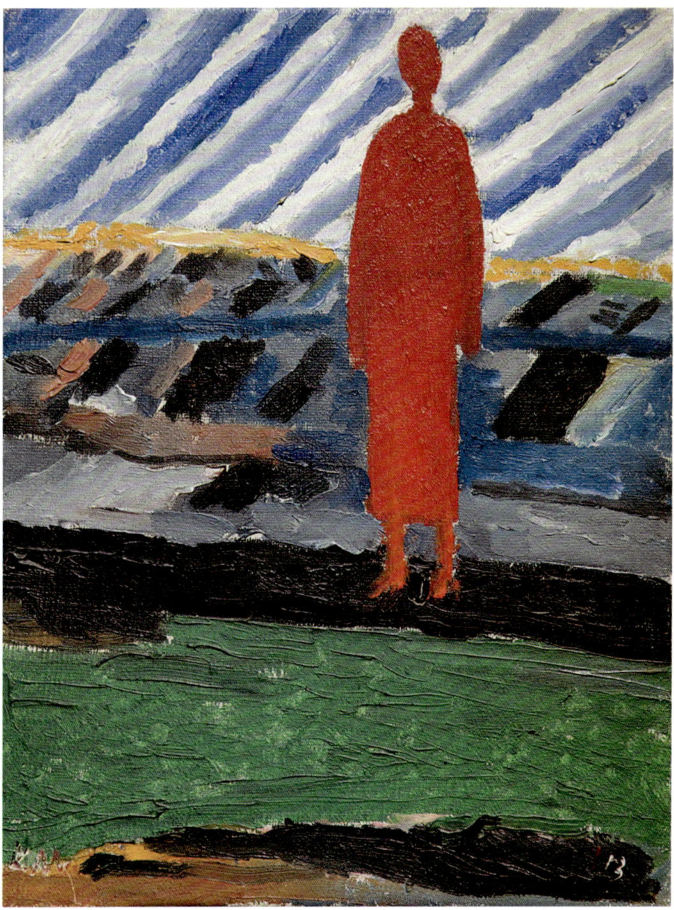

17 Kazimir Malevich, *Red Figure*, 1928–32. State Russian Museum, St. Petersburg.

Malevich's recognition of the end of the utopian content that had permeated his projects until the late 1920s. In its place, Malevich hoped to formulate a socialist content to counteract Socialist Realism. An extended series of single and group compositions with faceless characters and flatly painted bodies had moved to a more realistic portraiture, shifting from calculated to expressive brushwork (fig. 17). As before, while creating a new representational model, Malevich was creating the opposite of the one proposed by the realists' approach to the same subject matter, such as workers and peasants. A comparison with Katsman's canvases, executed during the same period, amply demonstrates this (fig. 18). If Malevich's image of the new man claimed universality, Katsman painted his figures with particular attention to individual features in painstaking detail and naturalistic accuracy, thus contradicting his training with the impressionists, Korovin and Sergei Maliutin. Oddly enough, Malevich's schematized figures are much more animated than Katsman's ordinary people, whose poses are overly controlled, and who seem to be artificially stuck in restricted spaces. There is a stony sensation to these pictures that uncannily connects them to Katsman's portraits of the dead Lenin and Sergei Kirov.

Malevich's first figurative series ended when he decided to give his figures a face, while maintaining his arbitrary palette and grafting of styles. And here, again, he acted circumspectly, only contradicting Katsman's groups of robotic male and female shock-workers with a humane old-guard worker placed against a cityscape rendered with loose brush-

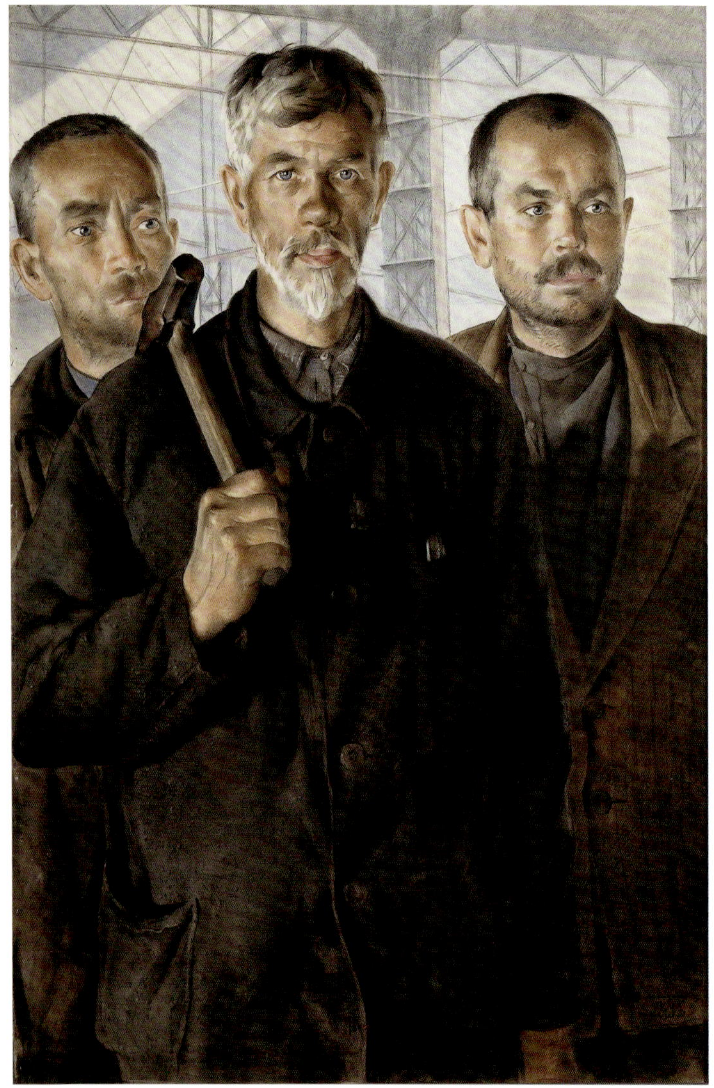

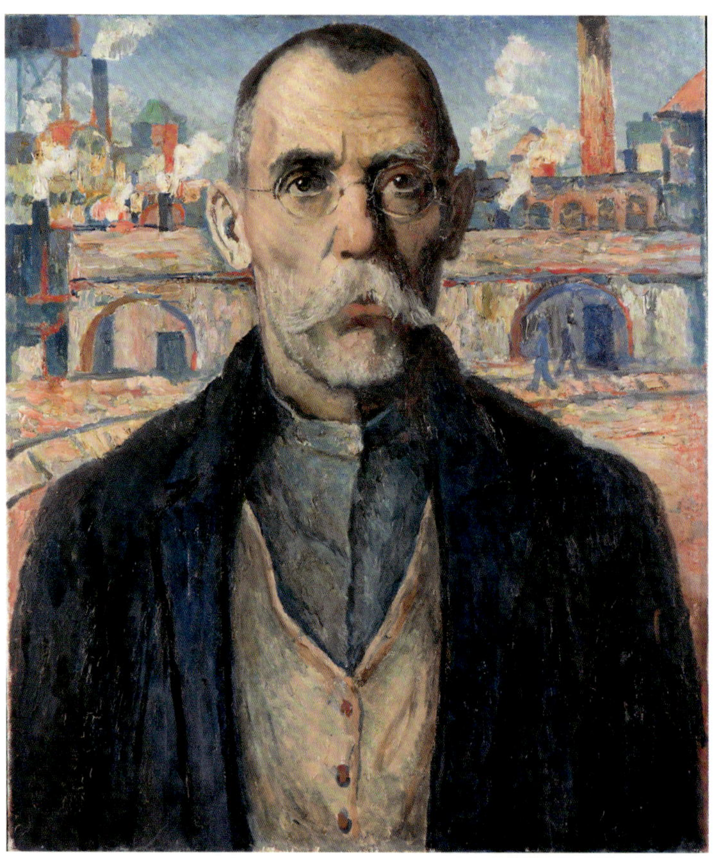

work and bright colors (fig. 19). The two artists' competition became increasingly personal when they both painted family portraits. Malevich's self-portrait and those of his wife and his daughter present them dressed in retro-costumes, making theatrical gestures, and in profile (unprecedented and atypical for him, but characteristic of Katsman) against a shallow monochrome space (figs. 20, 21). Katsman's 1933 family portrait follows his own formulae already worked out in the late 1920s in a preliminary study as well as in his well-known canvases such as *Lacemakers from Kaliazin* (figs. 22, 23).[28]

In the summer of 1934, less than two months before the Congress of Soviet Writers, and one year before

his death, Malevich in a letter to Kliun described his plan to unleash "a painterly attack on photo-realists or 'Leicists,'" agitating young artists to choose Impressionism over naturalism.[29] He took the Soviet realists' agenda beyond the local context by dubbing the AKhRR camp "epigones oriented at the English magazine *The Studio*," thus joining the anti-realism campaign led by the English critics Roger Fry and Clive Bell. Much like them, Malevich reacted to the growing criticism that abstract art was too complex and intellectual, and objected to the ascendency of "realist profanation."[30] Fry, whose 1928 *Self-portrait* is remarkably similar to Malevich's portrait of Pavlov (see fig. 15; both are painted in a somber palette and feature grid-like images in the background), argued that people side with realism because the formal purification of art forms removes art from "the ordinary man." Fry continued: "In proportion, as art becomes purer, the number of people to whom it appeals gets less. It cuts out all the romantic overtones of life, which are the usual bait by which men are induced to accept a work of art. It appeals only to aesthetic sensibility, and that in most men is comparatively weak."[31] Although for Fry, unlike Malevich, the path to abstraction was fueled by a belief in art for art's sake, his categorization of romanticism as a tool for mesmerizing the masses finds its echo in Zhdanov's call at the Congress of Soviet Writers for a new kind of romanticism, one that is detached from "utopian dreams,"[32] and hence from the modernist project altogether. In Malevich's instruction to fight against naturalism with Impressionism, he specifies Pierre-Auguste Renoir as a valuable example of "representational and genre painting."[33] In fact, some of Malevich's own portraits of 1933 and 1934 display the impact of Renoir's synthesis of classicism with the freedom of Impressionism, and reflect "values at once more timeless and more evanescent."[34] This was the moment when Malevich's journey from Impressionism to Suprematism made a u-turn.[35]

Like Malevich, Lunacharsky too praised Renoir in his introduction (published posthumously) to a translation of Ambroise Vollard's book on the Impressionist. Entitled "The Painter of Happiness," the essay associated Impressionism with an exuberant expression of pleasure, as had the Russian futurists. Lunacharsky defined Impressionism as a positivist art, calling Manet and Monet "the sons of science," for whom reality was "the result of [their] observation."[36] He contradicted Beskin's negative comment on the anarchic nature of French modernism, when he praised "the attic" life of Parisian artists. Overall, the arguments he made for Impressionism were meant to fit it into the norms of materialist society and into the humanistic rhetoric of Soviet ideology. To make a stronger argument for Renoirean realism, and thus securing it as an alternative to AKhRR's dry and dictatorial method, Lunacharsky expanded Renoir's significance beyond a single modernist style, stating that, "Renoir transcends the borders of Impressionism and joins the greatest masters of human painting." In conclusion, he observed that Renoir was unable to represent "grief" because he was "a man hungry for happiness who found a lot of it. He was a man depicting a lot of it. He was a man who gave it to people in some special airy coinage, which could appear false only to the coarsest bumpkin."[37] Had Lunacharsky attended the Congress of Soviet Writers, such would have been his prescription for the model of Soviet realism. And yet, in spite of his death several months before the Congress of Soviet Writers took place, Renoirean realism did become the creative paradigm of many MOSSKh artists who, explicitly or implicitly, resisted the looming dictate of Soviet academicism. Like Renoir and other French Impressionists, Soviet impressionists veiled public and private "grief" with a painterly happiness that was formally powerful enough to elude an accusation of false joy. The opportunity to practice this particular manifestation of subjective painting lasted until militant academicism triumphed by securing protection from the Academy of Arts of the USSR, established in Moscow in 1947.

In my analysis of the period between the Congress of Soviet Writers and the establishment of the Academy, I do not intend to discuss canonical Socialist Realist canvases and "the empty shell of its demagogic phraseology."[38] Imitative art, as Plato had warned, is "far from reality," and its Soviet form lacks what Martin Heidegger called "metaphysical thinking." Instead, I rely on primary sources (letters and diaries) that, as Igor Golomstock reminds us, are rare from this period, for "the repressive nature of this culture precluded their very existence and [they] are still missing today in most studies."[39] These sources allow the construction of another genealogy of this period, redefining its heroes and anti-heroes and documenting the moments of dissent in thinking and practices that hitherto were considered unfeasible under Stalin's dictatorial regime.

Malevich, Rodchenko, Gustav Klutsis, and Valentina Kulagina knew each other well. Rodchenko, Klutsis and Kulagina had been living on Miasnitskaia Street, in a building across the courtyard from VKhUTEMAS, the school where Rodchenko and Klutsis taught and Kulagina studied. They shared artistic trajectories: a transition from nonobjective art to graphic arts and

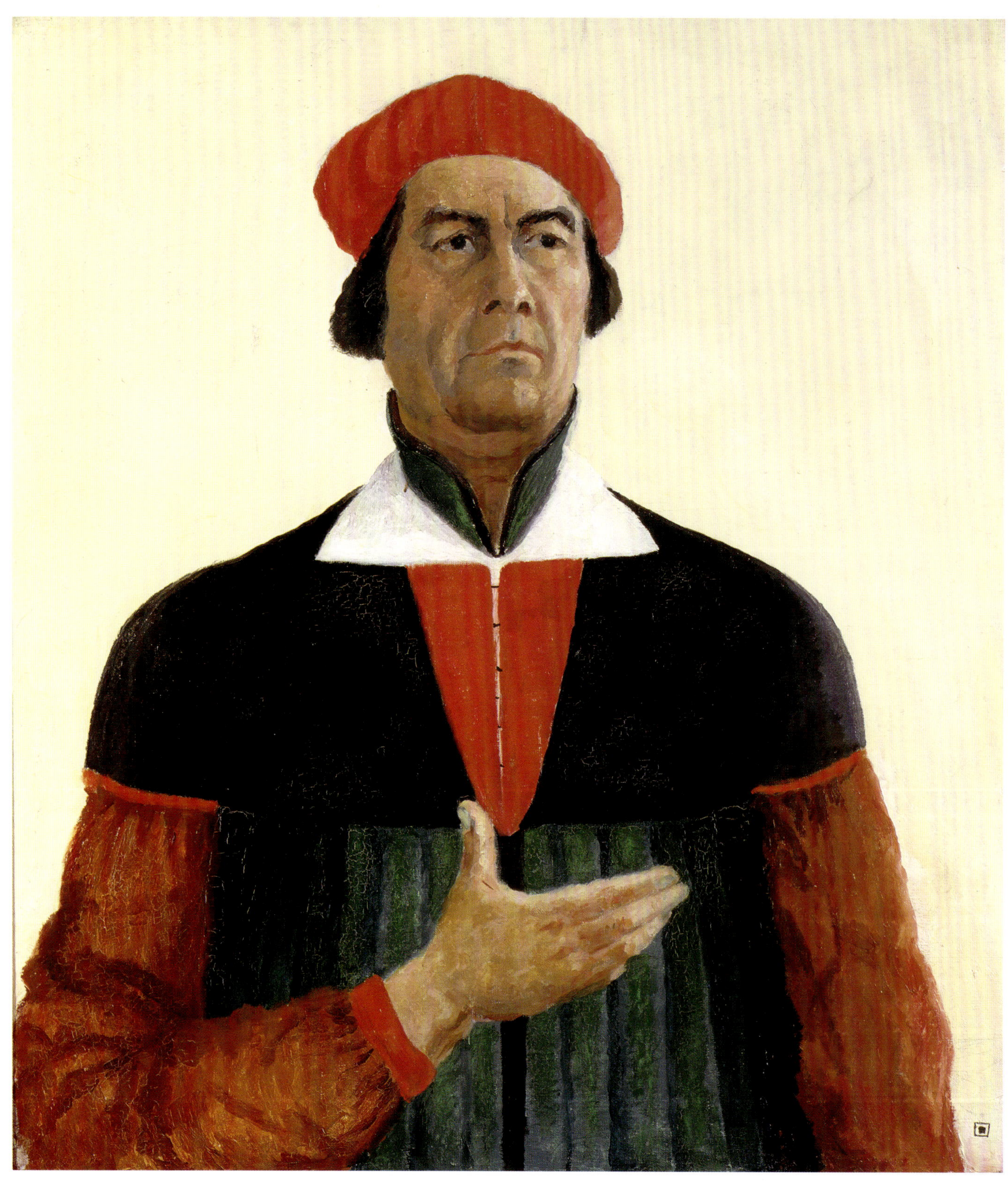

20 Kazimir Malevich, *Self-portrait*, 1933. State Russian Museum, St. Petersburg.

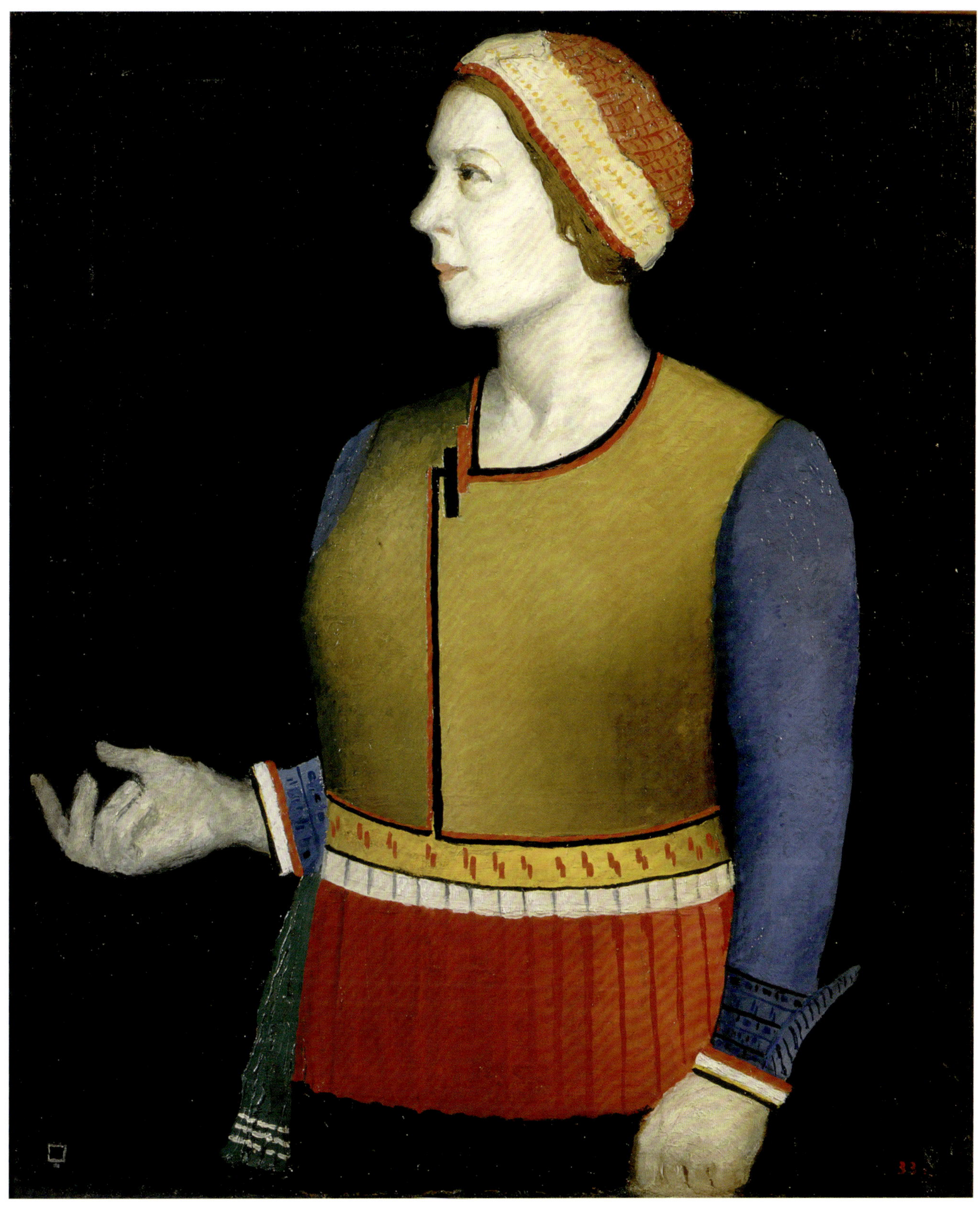

21 Kazimir Malevich, *Portrait of the Artist's Wife*, 1933. State Russian Museum, St. Petersburg.

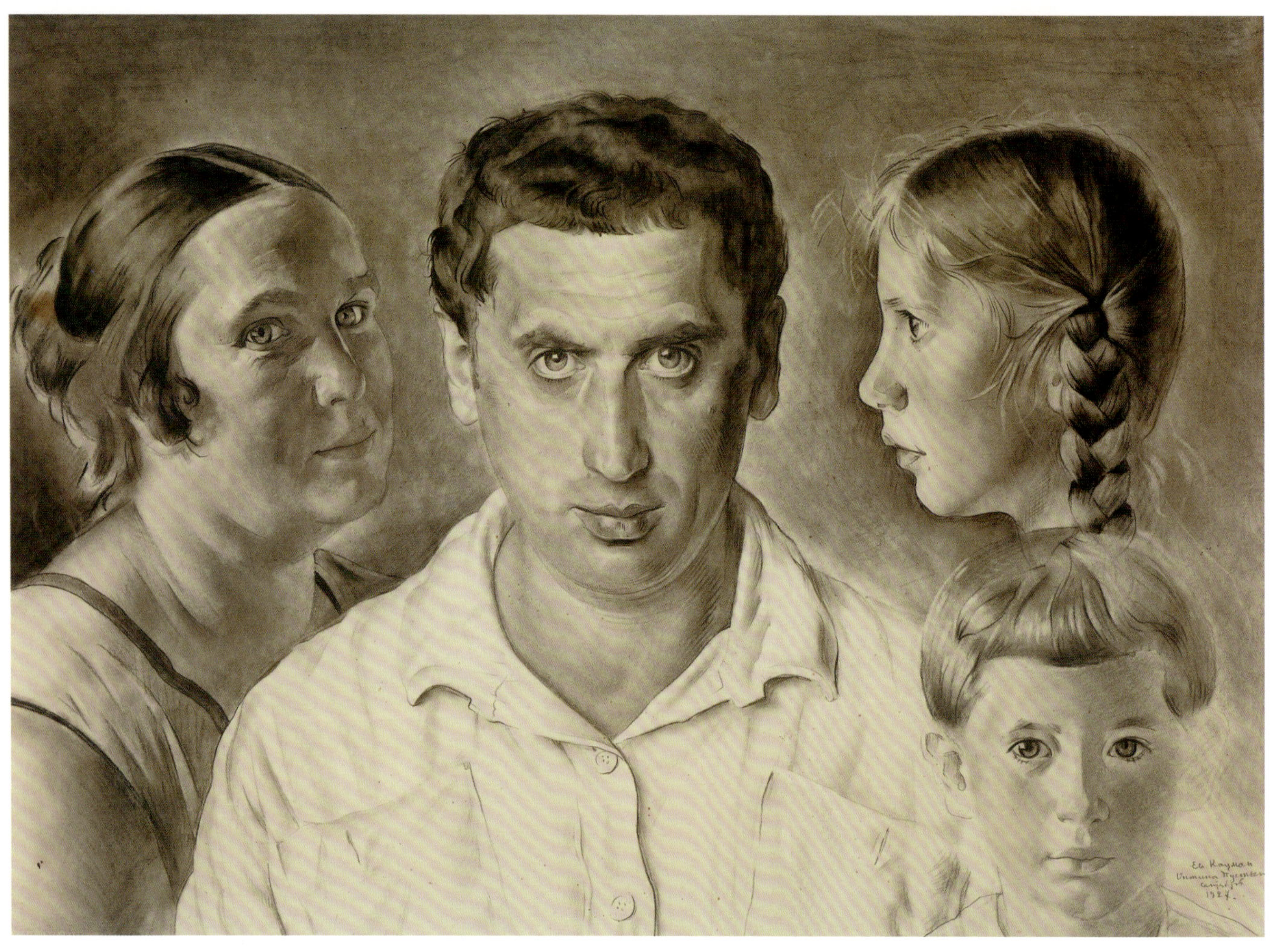

22   Evgeny Katsman, preliminary study for *Family Portrait*, 1927. State Tretiakov Gallery, Moscow.

then a stalwart dedication to industrial design and utilitarian aesthetics. A u-turn in their careers and attitudes took place early in the 1930s when they began to question production art, and painting, which they had categorically rejected at the beginning of 1920s, reemerged. Why? Kulagina answers this question when she claims that in painting "things…will remain as they are made."[40] Just as her husband Klutsis had convinced her in the early 1920s to switch from painting to graphic arts, now she was committed to reversing it and to "persuad[ing] Gustav to take up painting," characterizing his work in mass media as "wasting his enormous talent."[41] Kulagina was successful, for, starting in 1932, Klutsis' montage technique of cutting and pasting began to depend on preliminary drawings, and thus on more traditional means of execution (fig. 24). By pushing "drawn posters" to the foreground of IZOGIZ production, Kulagina, who preferred and practiced this technique all along, unintentionally endorsed the agenda of Klutsis' antagonists who, according to Kulagina, "attacked [photomontage] on every front" (fig. 25).[42] Under this pressure, the IZOGIZ editors, who had supported constructivist designs, began to favor easelism in the poster designs supplied to them by Nikolai Dolgorukov and Viktor Koretsky, and even turned to the work of the AKhRR painters Fedor Bogorodsky and Georgy Riazhsky.[43] By the spring of 1934, nonconstructivist poster artists were competing with Klutsis for the same projects, submitting "shoddy drawings to Pravda,"

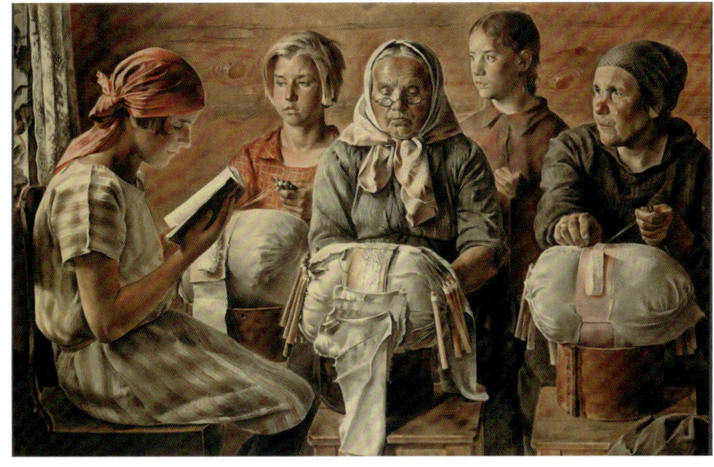

23   Evgeny Katsman, *Lacemakers from Kaliazin*, 1928. State Tretiakov Gallery, Moscow.

24   Gustav Klutsis, design for various posters, ca. 1932. Private collection.

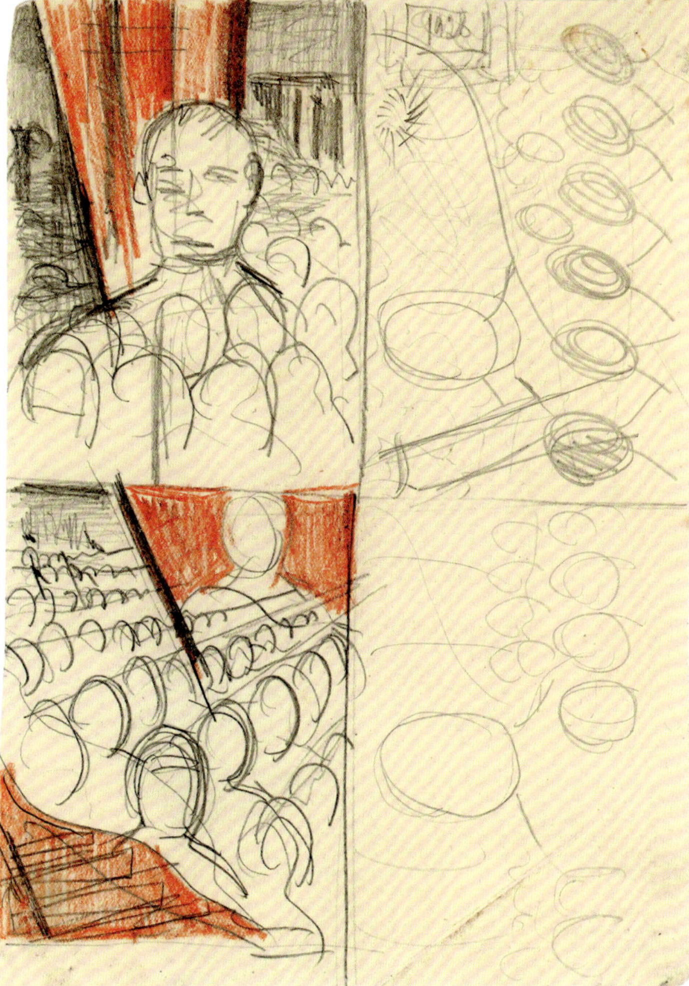

according to Kulagina.[44] By 1935, the virus of easelism had contaminated poster production, prompting Kulagina to characterize Klutsis' last series of poster designs as "painting-like" (fig. 26). As she wrote in her diary:

> This is a new type of poster; life has changed a lot, people no longer walk around in dirty shirts; girls now style their hair and the poster has become more substantive, more decorative, richer, merrier. Gustav's posters at least. As for [Viktor] Deni, Dolgorukov – in my opinion they are simply taking advantage of what Gustav has achieved, and doing it in a crude and untalented way, but it gets the go-ahead because of the illiteracy of editors and the lack of understanding of the art of the poster at the MK [Moscow Committee of the Communist Party].[45]

This entry signals the closing of the chapter in which posters had depicted coalminers, foundry workers, and oilmen – in schematic, anonymous, and utopian modes. After 1932 the reformed socialist bureaucracy, along with individuals held up as exemplars, had established its position and with this, Zhdanovian romanticism crept into mass-media representation. Yet Kulagina insisted on protecting mass-media production in terms of quality and talent.[46] She thus refused to submit mass-media works to the control of bureaucratic editors who would turn them into "hack jobs." AKhRR's eradication of experimentation in painting was now being applied to mass media, in which many avant-garde artists had worked since the 1920s.

Klutsis, who was promised a personal exhibition by Vsekokhudozhnik (All-Russian Union of Cooperative Comradeships of Workers of Visual Art), decided that in order "to join the ranks of major artists,"[47] he had to return to painting. However, without funding from the government, he could only paint family portraits and the landscapes outside his window. As Kulagina

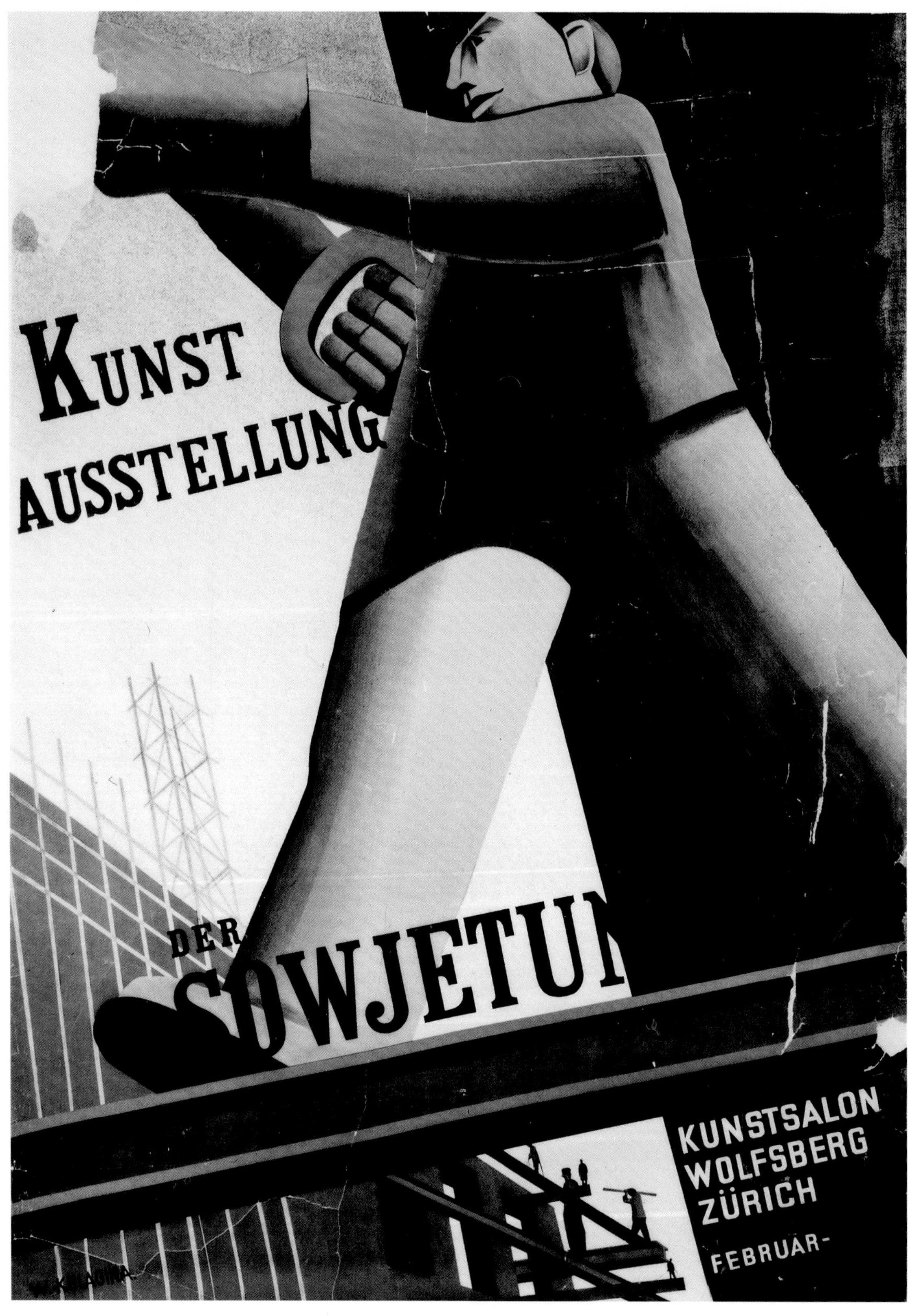

25   Valentina Kulagina, poster for *Kunst Ausstellung der Sovjetunion*, 1931. Wolfsberg, Zurich.

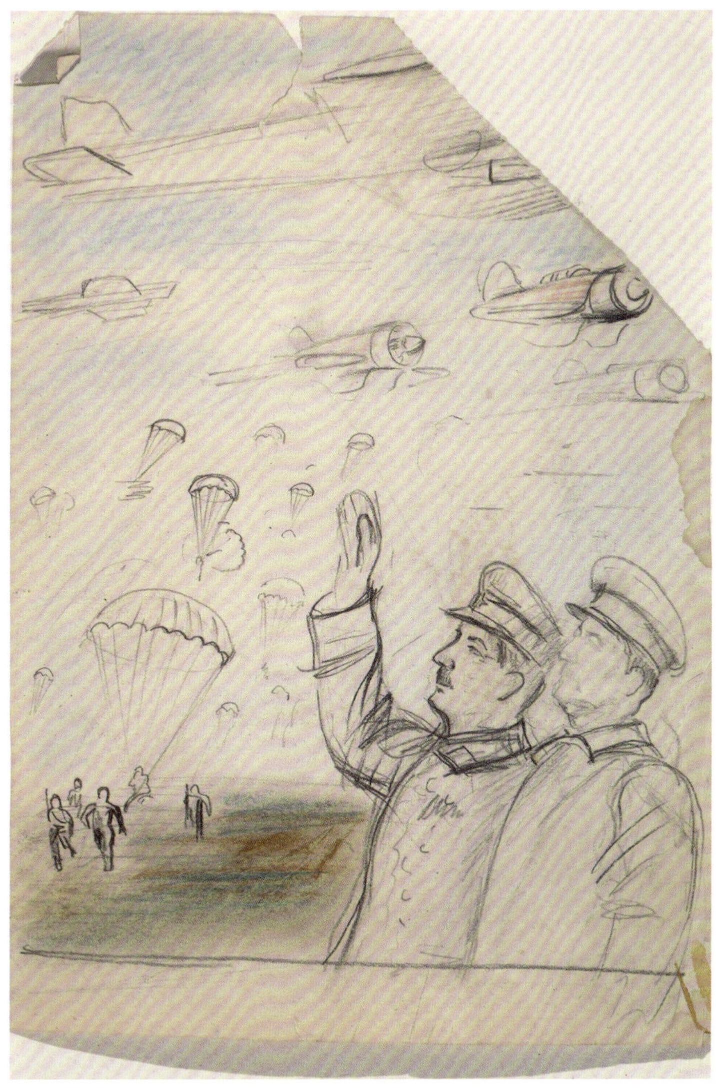

later admitted, neither MOSSKh nor Vsekokhudozhnik provided Klutsis with funds to travel to the sites of production, prompting him in 1936 to turn to a Latvian enlightenment society, Prometheus, which "gave him the opportunity to paint" (fig. 27).[48] Klutsis traveled all over the Soviet Union and recorded the labor achievements of various Latvian communities. His link to Prometheus, labeled in 1938 as "the Latvian fascist-nationalist organization,"[49] became, half a century later, the official explanation for his arrest and execution on February 11, 1938.[50] With this tragic end, painting had played a grim joke on Klutsis: first, he, along with other constructivists, had put this medium to death, then it had seduced him again, only to contribute to his own death.

Was Klutsis, then, a victim of his decision to conform to the prescriptions of cultural conservatives? Or did the new socio-political context lay bare the avant-garde generation's miscalculations in sacrificing the title of creator for operator, and thus autonomous art for social commissions? Kulagina believed in the second theory, and she met an acquaintance who proved that she was right. Still unaware of Klutsis' execution (the government had told her he was in a camp), she wrote in her diary:

> Today [March 10, 1940] I ran into a friend of Gustav from the Korovin studio. He told me a lot about Gustav's reputation as the best of Korovin's students [fig. 28], and how well he painted. How his obsessions with various "isms," and then with poster design, made many regret his unfulfilled talent in painting. This is true. When I look at his works made in the summer of 1937, my heart contracts and my fists clench – this is who should have painted and who by now would have joined the ranks of major artists.[51]

The government's building of prestigious housing for MOSSKh members in 1936 on Maslovka Street, where Klutsis and Kulagina moved that year,[52] was

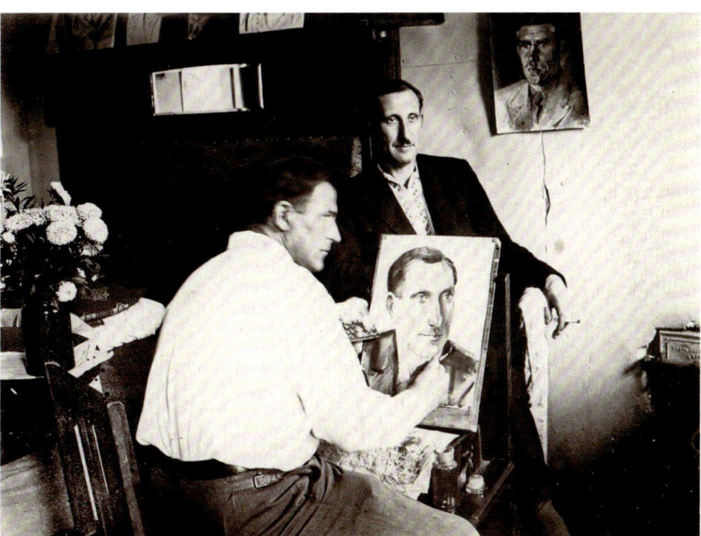

26   Gustav Klutsis, design for a poster, ca. 1935. Private collection.

27   Gustav Klutsis painting a portrait of "a distinguished Latvian person," 1936. Private collection.

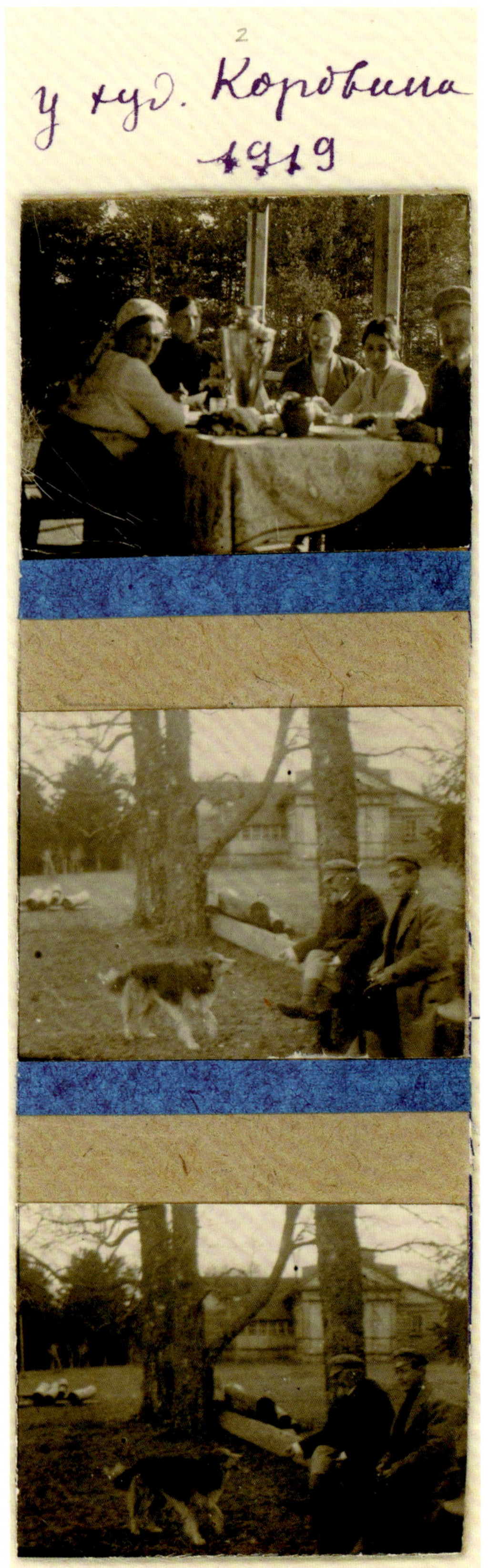

intended to downgrade the importance of left artists' homes on Miasnitskaia Street near VKhUTEMAS (fig. 29). Rodchenko was able to stay in his spacious apartment (occupied only by his family) on Miasnitskaia Street in spite of Katsman's and Voroshilov's mission to evict its avant-garde tenants.[53] Although Rodchenko had been a major nonobjective artist of the post-revolutionary period, by 1932 he was barely remembered as such, and not considered worth inclusion in *Artists of the RSFSR*. His exclusion from the milieu of Soviet painters was the result of his own rejection of painting in 1921, which by the end of the 1930s he regarded as one of his mistakes.[54] His expulsion from the October Group in 1932, where he was head of the photography section, was an altogether different story, catapulting him from constructivist and productivist periods into "a phase of seclusion."[55] His employment by the magazine *USSR in Construction* gave some financial support, but it also prolonged his isolation and hardship, as he traveled to the cold, remote region of Karelia to photograph the construction of the White Sea Canal, one of the most gigantic and ruthless industrial projects of the Stalin era (fig. 30). By 1934, Rodchenko experienced weakening of his assertive constructivist identity, and alienation from the cultural environment that had shaped it. For the first time, he questioned the Leica camera's ability to grasp reality; he thought that writing a diary could do this better.[56] Even as he packed for an assignment in Kramatorsk in March 1934, he pledged, "to keep a diary of the trip."[57] The commitment to *pisat*, to write, was soon followed by his urge to *pisat*, to paint. Rodchenko used this second meaning after visiting Vasily Surikov's exhibition in January 1937: "I feel like writing a response, though not with pen but paint."[58]

"Today," Rodchenko wrote in February 1934, "I began to paint the circus for myself, and thought: What if I painted the first painting, the circus, in black and pink, huge and complicated, 200 × 120 cm, and then the Dinamo stadium: gray and green." This entry's conclusion, "I'm reading about Courbet, he worked like an ox,"[59] indicates the scale of Rodchenko's

28   Gustav Klutsis visiting the artist Konstantin Korovin, 1919. Private archive.

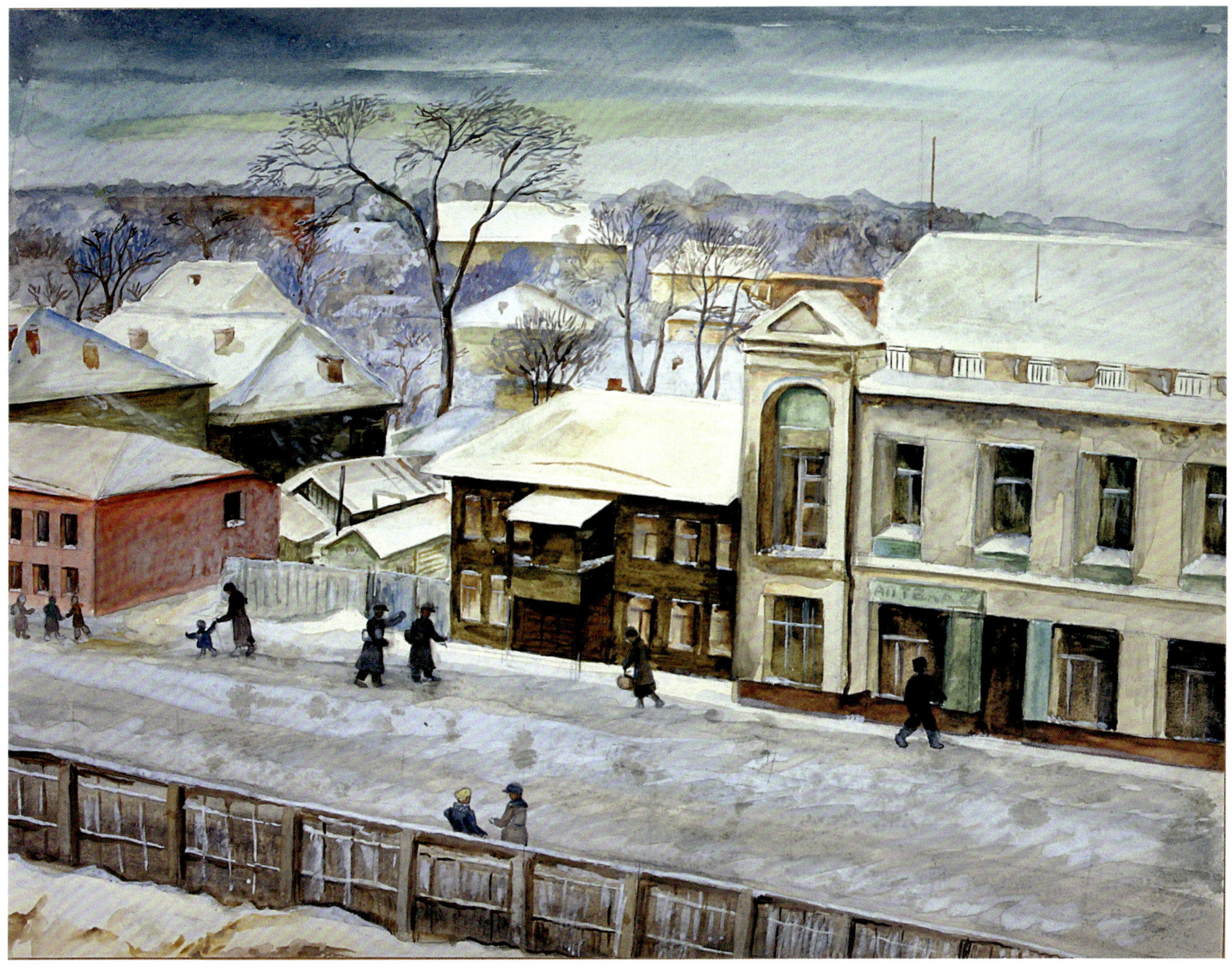

29 Valentina Kulagina, *Untitled* (Maslovka Street, Moscow), late 1930s. Collection of Edvard Kulagin, Moscow.

painting ambitions. It also overlaps with Malevich's concurrent aesthetic paradigm, of a retreat to the origins of French modernism. This is reiterated by Rodchenko three days later: "I am looking for myself…I look at magazines, read about painting… I want to start everything from the beginning."[60] Identifying with Courbet also meant adopting the nonconformity expressed in his remark: "I must free myself even from governments."[61] And again, like Courbet, Rodchenko continued to insist "on contemporaneity as the necessary condition of the concrete that separates the academic artist from the innovator."[62] Increasingly, Rodchenko had seen his studio as

the epicenter of his "personal iconography relevant to contemporary life and its major areas of experience."[63] Moreover, Rodchenko's studio, like Courbet's in *The Painter's Studio*, would function on the principle of dichotomy: friends and admirers (on the left in Courbet's painting) would be part of it, whereas all opposing and challenging forces (represented on the right by Courbet) would be expelled from it.

Rodchenko's diary comes to a halt in the spring of 1934, and only resumes in the summer of 1936. He explains that his silence was due to a "monstrous apathy," which "seems to be passing."[64] He also reveals that he had been thinking about painting and

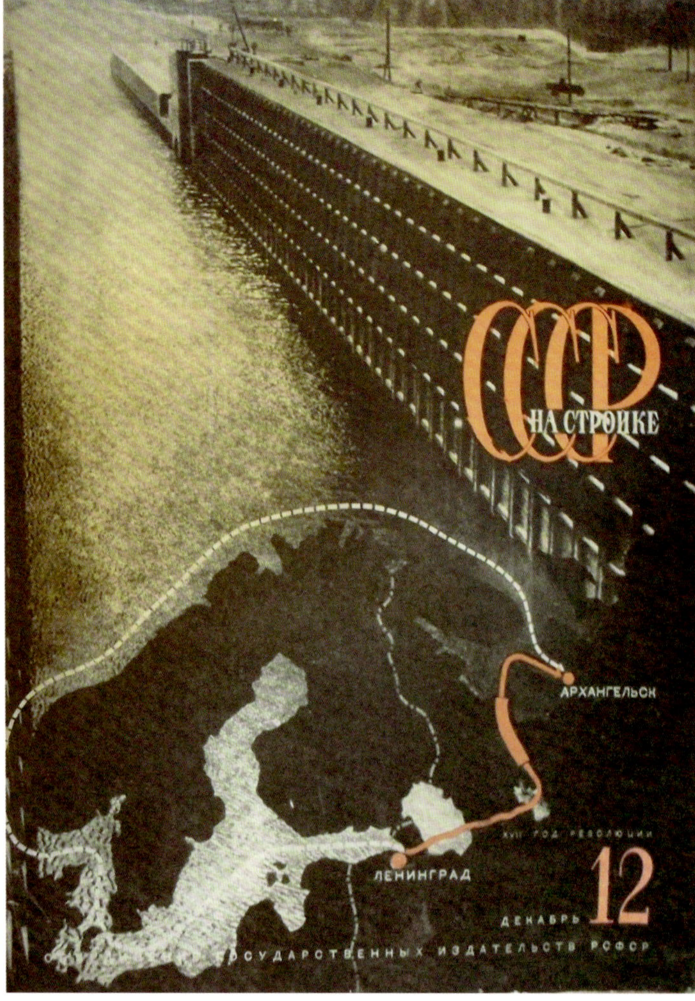

30 Aleksandr Rodchenko, cover of the magazine *USSR in Construction* no. 12, 1933. A. Rodchenko and V. Stepanova Archive, Moscow.

photography as well as color photography, refusing, like Klutsis, to give up on experimentation. He writes: "our art here is horribly behind the times…Art workers have nothing to fight for, and they don't want to fight for ideas, they want a quiet life."[65] Rodchenko again suspended his diary until the New Year of 1937, when he concludes that he "must write," and reports on spending much time in his "photo laboratory…where I think and write."[66] The word "laboratory" is key here, for in constructivist vocabulary it signifies a longing to experiment; for process rather than product. Rodchenko's emphasis on thinking as his daily task testifies to his determination to resist the

main instrument of totalitarianism, namely to eradicate a free process of thinking; to assign someone else to think on one's behalf. Yet, Rodchenko admits to the crippling impact of pressure from above, and how "the persecution of formalism leads to depression, and then it's hard to bounce back."[67] Since he had long considered that art should reflect the contemporary world, Rodchenko defined historicism (as in the case of Surikov) as, "boring," illustrative, and oriented toward a psychotic rewriting of "times long past."[68] Rodchenko also opposed the imitation of Nature and "masters," as well as painting by copying newspaper clippings and black and white photographs. "I cannot even paint from my own photographs,"[69] he concluded. Instead of making paintings that look like "painted photography," of which Rodchenko accused Deineka,[70] he considered making color prints large enough to look "like paintings."[71] This would also replace the time-consuming act of painting, and transportation and preservation of works, by the faster and cheaper production of color prints. "It's enough to have five big pieces for an exhibition," he concluded in 1938.[72] By proposing a photographic model of Soviet realism, he repeated his earlier break with the medium of painting. Then he had replaced nonobjective painting with photography; now he wanted to replace painterly mimesis with color photography, once again rejecting the notion of art as commodity in socialist society.

By May 1938, Rodchenko's analysis of the most effective method of Soviet realism was constantly being derailed by the grim social environment: "It's a strange time, everyone's whispering, everyone's afraid…This shouldn't have to concern an honest man."[73] His naïveté, however, dissolved in the fall of the same year: "Rumors are going around that innocent people are suffering from denunciations…They tell some incredible stories…So I am not guaranteed against someone writing a false denunciation and everything collapsing…My family will be sent into exile, and that'll be the end."[74] Rodchenko's anxiety regarding political repression manifested itself that spring 1938 in the desire to visualize the horrors of fascism, eerily a year before the Soviets signed the German–Soviet Nonaggression Pact. He conceptualizes "a big painting, 200 × 300 cm, in the spirit of

Peter Breughel, called *Fascism*." In addition to being identical in size to Picasso's *Guernica*, Rodchenko's disjointed verbal portrayal of his imagery reverberates with items from Picasso's fragmented canvas: "Huge ears, Eyes, Tentacles, Money, Debauch [*sic*], Murder of children, women, old people, Destruction: Cities, Gardens, Museums, Burning of books, Flight: Einstein, Heinrich Mann, [Arnold] Zweig, and others, Armaments: Piracy at sea."[75] Paradoxically in that year, at the height of the purges, a more moderate MOSSKh board was formed, prompting Rodchenko to define the nature of his dissent. "I almost know what not to do, like [Aleksandr] Gerasimov and Brodsky," he wrote that summer,[76] blaming individual artists rather than a political diktat for the domination of Socialist Realism.

Brodsky and Aleksandr Gerasimov were Katsman's cronies and accompanied him to Stalin's dacha, a visit I described at the outset of this chapter. The former artist, who died in 1939 at the age of fifty-five, lived in Leningrad, and, like Gerasimov and Katsman, was fixated on the academization of Soviet art. Through the academy these artists planned to gain more respect and material reward. A predisposition toward idealization and canonical realism was to their liking and advantage, but not the pursuit of academic mastery: the intention was not to preserve the fine arts, but to please the Kremlin. Brodsky understood the appeal of academic references earlier than any other AKhRR artist. The writer Kornei Chukovsky, who visited him in 1926, remembered that Brodsky lived "magnificently," and was primarily involved in having "hack-work painters" copying his portraits of Lenin and other images for which he became famous. "He has a commission for 60 of the same 'shootings' [Brodsky painted *Shooting of Communists in Baku* in 1925] for clubs, village Soviets, etc., and he paints these canvases with others' hands, puts his name on them, and lives in clover."[77] In this sarcastic account of Brodsky's lifestyle and working practices, Chukovsky creates one of the earliest images of the Soviet bourgeois, marking the beginning of the Soviet culture industry. Brodsky should be remembered for his 1917 portrait of Aleksandr Kerensky, the leader of the February Revolution and a rare subject in Russian art (fig. 31). The canvas synthesized the spontaneity that

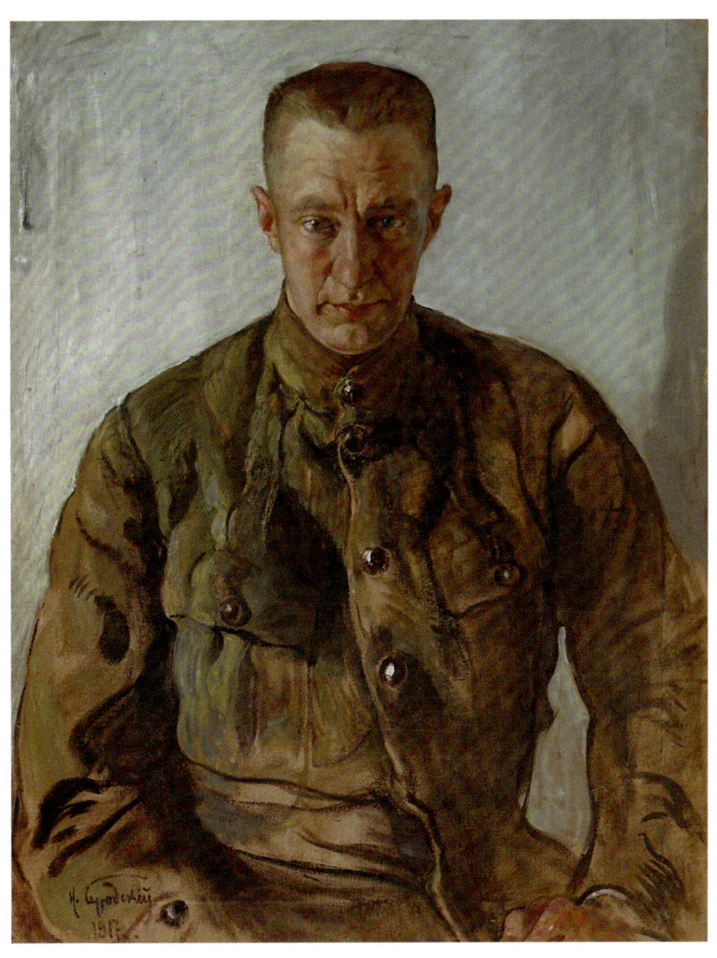

31   Isaak Brodsky, *Aleksandr Kerensky*, 1917. State Central Museum of Contemporary History of Russia, Moscow.

later disappeared from Brodsky's art, and documented his readiness to conform to any regime.

A student of Ilia Repin, Brodsky had traveled widely around Europe between 1909 and 1911 under the auspices of the Russian Academy. Familiarity with academic painting as well as Impressionism divided his oeuvre into two polarized groups: his single portraits of leaders are executed with almost paranoid attention to detail, whereas his genre paintings are clumsy in form and messy in color application. Perhaps to compensate for his lack of creativity, Brodsky was fascinated by the work of other artists, which he was able to acquire even during the hungry years of the Civil War. This is reflected in a portrait of Brodsky by Boris Kustodiev. Painted in 1920, during the Civil War, it depicts him as a dandy of Gulliver size strolling on

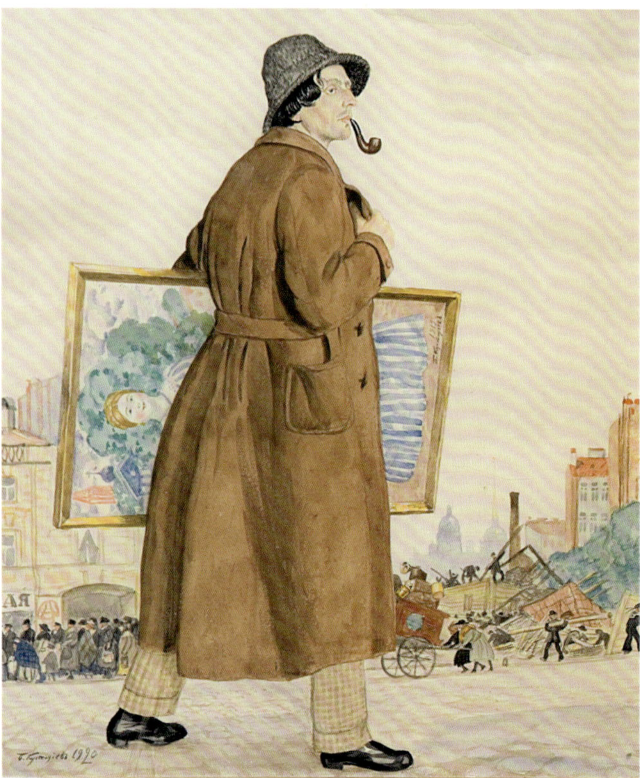

32 Boris Kustodiev, *Isaak Brodsky*, 1920. Academy of Arts, St. Petersburg.

the street with Kustodiev's painting under his arm. His head is turned away from the activities of the proletarian "Lilliputians" (fig. 32).[78] Not sharing Katsman's and Gerasimov's hostility toward modernism, Brodsky was impartial as regards individual left artists. For example, in the official press, he called Pavel Filonov, "a master-painter…the greatest not only in our country but in Europe and America,"[79] and befriended Malevich around 1930, when the latter headed to GINKhUK.

Malevich's student Konstantin Rozhdestvensky gives description of his teacher's Leningrad studio and his portrait methods, which is strikingly different from Brodsky's:

A huge room. Half of it is dark, without windows. Here K.S. worked with electric light. In this studio he was, to be specific, painting my portrait. Malevich worked calmly, concentrating. But almost every time, every session he repainted the portrait: changed

the background – included sportswomen, took them away; changed palette – from blue to orange-red…The portrait remained unfinished.[80]

Malevich's agony over the form and content of his canvas comes across as low-tech next to Brodsky's cynical management of his assembly-line production of works, which involved assistants copying the same painting again and again. The two artists' odd relationship in the early 1930s was probably stimulated by Malevich's financial difficulties, which were eased by Brodsky's acquisition of several of his paintings.[81] By 1933, particularly after Bukharin's attack on *Black Square*, Malevich became a bitter opponent of Brodsky's Leicism, picking up on the denunciation of Brodsky's photographic realism by AKhRR youth, as I noted earlier. What angered Malevich most was Bukharin's claim that *Black Square* was an expression of "bourgeois life devoid of meaning and content,"[82] a description diametrically opposed to Malevich's intention "to completely destroy the face of bourgeois art."[83] As a retort to Bukharin's association of nonobjective art with bourgeois values, Malevich claimed that it was Leicism that was in compliance with bourgeois mentality. "In reality, [formalists]," Malevich asserted, "do not fit in precisely because they are not bourgeois, for if we were bourgeois-representational, distinctly object-oriented artists [*predmetniki*], then probably we would fit in."[84] Although at the time, Malevich was also preoccupied with "putting a man back together,"[85] he refused to let imitation of the object rule the artist and viewed it as the enemy of creativity. Attacking mimetic painting as if it were a person, Malevich erupted in mockery: "[an object] does not tolerate an exceptional painterly approach to itself…no, it demands representation based on an object. Being strong and rich with bread and water, it threatens every painter with death from hunger, should the latter refuse to depict it."[86] This vision of the object as "the silent and spectral Adversary" was one that Malevich held in common with de Chirico, and in his late figurative series Malevich was prepared to turn "the most ordinary objects into something quite 'other,' something strange [and] fearful."[87]

Unlike Brodsky, Aleksandr Gerasimov (the second artist Rodchenko refused to resemble artistically) traveled to Europe for the first time in 1934. Visiting such important museums as the Louvre and Uffizi, Gerasimov produced numerous city sketches in which his realism was "enriched by the Impressionist techniques of Arkhipov and others as far as skillful expression of light and air goes."[88] From Korovin, his other teacher, Gerasimov adopted "a bold brushstroke, a love of juicy and full-blooded colors."[89] Seeing works by French nineteenth-century artists undoubtedly reinforced his desire to become a painter of David's caliber at Stalin's court, and in general to associate with greater "masters" than the Wanderers.[90] From Paris he wrote to Katsman and Grigory Perelman:

> the nineteenth century belongs to David, Delacroix, Courbet…I was amazed by David, I did not expect him to have been such a force; in reproductions he is dry, but, imagine, in reality he is a wonderful painter…But I liked Courbet the most. What a master in drawing and painting….then come great C. Monet and E. Manet.[91]

Such excitement with the protomodernists and modernists found an immediate reflection in Gerasimov's frequent inserting in otherwise pseudo-academic painting isolated patches of uncontrolled brushwork that attempted or, rather, simulated Wölfflin's concept of *malerisch* (the painterly). Thus, setting aside Brodsky who faithfully copied photographs or Katsman who, being primarily a draftsman, was unable to deal with large-scale canvases, there was no one to compete with Gerasimov in creating an image of a free Soviet artist working in a spontaneous manner and without previously censored photographs.[92] An illustration of this can be found in the 1943 film footage of Gerasimov, from the series *Masters of Soviet Painting*, which commenced with Gerasimov caught in a moment of spectacularization, or what Malevich called "painterly temperament," as he executes a still life of a bouquet of lilacs. This scene of painting intimate subject matter is theatrically interrupted by the arrival of four artists from an older generation. They have come to model for Gerasimov's government-commissioned canvas, *The Four Oldest Artists*, which he finished in 1944. As the maestro, wearing a bow tie and a white shirt (rather than worker coveralls), he greets the visitors outside of the studio, the viewer catches a glimpse of his set-up – copies of an antique vase and a bust as well as two cropped paintings in carved gilded frames (which undermine the practice of framing nonobjective paintings with cheap wooden planks) against which the freely conversing artist-models are placed. Gerasimov painting the elders in front of the camera is on par with his spirited execution of the still life. It suggests that there was no gap between private unrestrained creativity and public, supposedly spontaneous, official portraiture. In the footage, both practices are shown as equal beneficiaries of Gerasimov's creative persona.

That same pastiche of rhetorical grandeur and freer rendition of the backgrounds is present in two major court paintings by Gerasimov: *Stalin at the 16th Party Congress* (1933) and *Stalin and Voroshilov in the Kremlin* (1938). Gerasimov's theatricality reflects his work in the 1920s as a theater designer, for which he was also indebted to Korovin, who was an acclaimed designer for major theaters. The *Masters of Soviet Painting* footage validates Golomstock's conclusion that "whatever an artist drew – a portrait of the Leader or a cucumber – he must be guided by this general worldview or 'Weltanschauung,' accepting that what he depicted could only be viewed in an ideological setting. The concept of so-called 'art for art's sake' was regarded with profound hostility by every totalitarian ideology."[93] In other words, painting non-ideological subject matter such as landscapes or still lifes could only be allowed if it followed dialectical principles, that is, in the presence of an overtly ideological subject. Another example of this conformist alliance between the so-called "lyrical" and ideological Socialist Realist easelisms is a photograph of Katsman's studio with three female portraits: a woman with medals in the foreground, then a modest working woman, and a nude in the background.[94] Such mixed production aimed to relieve the overwhelming load of historico-heroic canvases and create a mechanism of control over not only the public's minds but also their feelings. There has been a tendency to pull the Socialist Realists' nonideological works (traditional nudes, landscapes, and still lifes) out of their ideological context and consider them as free of censorship. For example, Susan Buck-Morss believes that even in "the propaganda content, the utopian effect of these artworks was sensual: the paintings are full of light, warmth, and an atmosphere of bodily pleasure." And Christina Kiaer has acclaimed this "newfound concern with 'feeling' as one of the positive or productive contributions of Socialist Realism to the project of revolutionary art, to be distinguished from its negative aim of eliminating the avant-garde from that project."[95] However, documents show that often it was not the subject matter that was purged but who was executing that subject matter, how it was executed, and who sanctioned it. In this sense the difference between Robert Falk's cubist *Nude* (1916; State Tretiakov Gallery, Moscow) and Aleksandr Deineka's representations of a new Soviet female physique that conformed to cultural bureaucrats' prescriptions (as did his 1933 rejection of photomontage) is the same as that between Picasso's and fascist artists' nudes of the 1930s. This virus of positivizing and romanticizing Socialist Realism initiated by a small group of European critics and scholars and some Russian émigrés during perestroika not only increasingly blurs the fundamental gap between the official dogma of Socialist Realism and the theoretical and stylistic objectives of the avant-garde, but also obscures the power of the "modernist retort" or revolt staged in the 1930s by Malevich (with his unemotional, unlyrical, and unsensual paintings), Rodchenko, Kulagina, Suetin, and others. In fact, it would have been grist to AKhRR's mill, given that their initial aim was to dissipate the revolutionary status of the avant-garde, and it perfectly fits the current agenda of those Russians who have started down the dangerous path of heroization and even humanization of the Stalin epoch. Aleksandr Gerasimov's voting in MOSSKh against a Korovin exhibition in early 1941, the year the former received the first of his four Stalin Prizes,[96] is the best evidence that his display of devotion to the impressionist method was not sincere and did not extend to support of modernists. Instead, his painterly spontaneity was a mere propaganda performance, aimed at creating the image of a Soviet genius.[97]

Like Rodchenko, who wrote that the Leftist artists' gradual demise was due to attacks from "the vappo-mappo-akhrov,"[98] Kulagina was direct and merciless in her evaluations of "the akhrov" and Socialist Realists. She concluded in 1933, based on her interactions with Katsman in IZOGIZ, that he gave "the unpleasant impression of an unintelligent and insolent man…a typical AKhRR man,"[99] and later called Aleksandr Gerasimov and his cronies "artists-diehards… occupying everything with their grabbing hands."[100] Kulagina credited Sergei Gerasimov, who replaced Aleksandr as the chairman of MOSSKh in 1939, with overruling his namesake's decision to cancel Korovin's exhibition, a brave action given that from 1922 until his death in 1939, Korovin lived in Paris.[101] Rushing to see the oeuvre of her husband's teacher, Kulagina wrote that Korovin was "a wonderful painter…made wonderful things, had such a free, sparkling, playful color, such brevity, wonderful."[102] Kulagina's diary entry positioned Impressionism as a beacon of modernist consciousness, which was paradoxically gaining presence in the first half of the new decade. This personal feeling was accompanied by lessening public censorship of members of MOSSKh, which Kulagina observed at the outset of 1940, after she had attended several MOSSKh meetings: "Many people had spoken…the questions raised were sharp and open; two years ago [Boris] Deikin would probably not say publicly that artists take and fulfill commissions that they think are suicidal for an artist."[103] Less than a week later she summarized her impression of another MOSSKh gathering: "People are unhappy about art politics, criticize the system of commissions, in particular."[104]

At the turn of the twentieth century, Korovin's contemporary Mikhail Vrubel, a central figure in the emergence of Russian modernism, decided to paint lilacs in order to demonstrate his bold pictorial innovations but also to relieve emotional distress.[105] With this fusion of the formal and the psychological (and thus in contrast to Gerasimov's approach to this subject), the theme of lilacs reappeared during the Stalin era in the works of marginalized painters such as Kulagina and Tatlin who refused to compromise by painting political imagery. In lilac's lavish blossom and large color fields, they could withdraw into painterly reverie, and it is not surprising that after the Second World War "attacks grew in strength on [artists], who painted pointless apples and lilacs, thus distructing [*sic*] the masses from pressing tasks."[106] In this modest

still-life genre (in comparison to the formal achievements of the avant-garde) rests the realization of
Malevich's 1934 instruction to Kliun quoted earlier, to
fight naturalism with Impressionism, and to follow
Renoir as an example of "representational and genre
painting."[107]

Kulagina last saw and photographed Malevich
talking to Klutsis in their apartment in 1933 (fig. 33),
in a staged-looking pose strangely reminiscent of
Malevich's contemporary portraits of friends and
family.[108] Five years later, she adopted his final instruction while agonizing over her husband's recent arrest:
"Tomorrow I will begin a still life [*nature-morte, sic* in
French]. I wonder if he feels that I think about him
uninterruptedly," she writes in her diary in March
1938 (not knowing that Klutsis had been executed on
February 11).[109] She describes the complex composition of her planned *nature-morte* and promises to work
"on form."[110] Kulagina's choice of writing the word
"still life" in French, thus breaking it into two parts,
allowed her to expose the term's etymology while
simultaneously revealing her fear that Klutsis was dead.
It also enabled her to describe the numbing state of
Soviet aesthetics. Kulagina, like the young woman in
Vrubel's *Lilacs*, envisions this robust flowering shrub
as a shield from the grim realities of her life, and
commits herself to a decade of painting the same
flower, in the same way that Van Gogh painted sun-
flowers, both deriving visual power and meaning from
obsessive repetition (figs. 34, 35). By the spring of
1940, Kulagina was able "to intensify [her] painterly
temperament," making "brushes walk and bend like
trees from The Tempest."[111] She noted: "Today I
worked surprisingly bravely. I must go on like this,
even more boldly, without fear of color, and hues. I
painted with a large brush, and large brushstrokes."[112]
Yet, a few days later she added: "I must paint more
bravely whatever I want rather than think – I will not
be able to do it, it will not work out."[113]

This kind of exhilaration over easelism reversed the
early 1920s rejection of painting in favor of utilitarian
practices. Kulagina, who in 1921, under Klutsis' influence at VKhUTEMAS, had converted to this new
ideology (though not without reservations),[114] was
more and more occupied with painterly tasks. Only
occasionally was she interrupted by Tatlin, who while

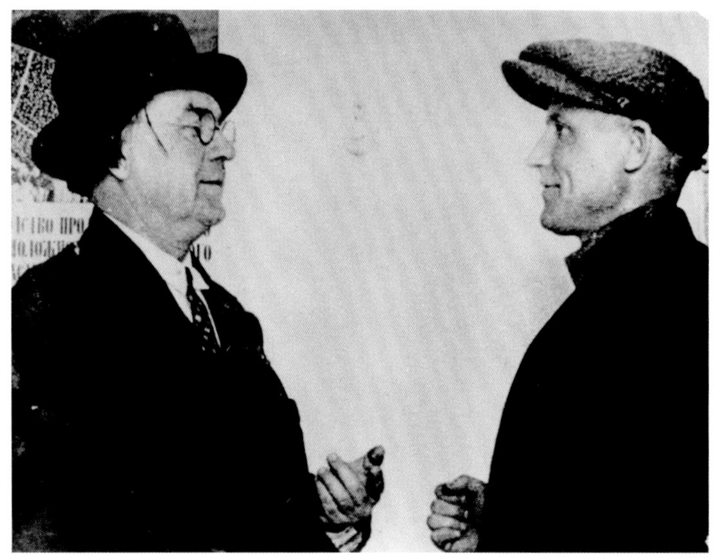

33   Valentina Kulagina, photograph of Kazimir Malevich and
Gustav Klutsis in Klutsis and Kulagina's apartment in Moscow,
May 20, 1933. Private archive.

visiting Kulagina in the 1940s, often geared conversations about art toward ideas rather than emotions.
Both Kulagina and Tatlin, who was the motor behind
the ideology of production art, by the end of the
1930s were working on the "Animal Husbandry"
pavilion of the All-union Agricultural Exhibition
(VSKhV).[115] Tatlin became the pavilion's chief designer
and Kulagina was commissioned to execute large
montage panels (figs. 36, 37). Initially, the preliminary
sketches from both artists were approved. However,
two weeks later, the decision was revoked, prompting
Kulagina to conclude that the new well-funded
opportunities for production art had been hijacked by
"people who unabashedly want to make a lot of
money."[116] From this point on, the radical concept of
"the artist as producer" was converted to one of finan-
cially driven labor by those artists excluded from
MOSSKh's "material support for creativity."[117]

With this transformation the famous Constructivist
slogan of "enter production" was substituted by "enter
creativity" (read "enter painting") in the minds of
avant-garde artists. It had become a new internal quest
that mesmerized even the most stalwart and successful
production artists, Klutsis, Rodchenko, and Tatlin. The
last two, in contrast to Malevich's call to follow Renoir

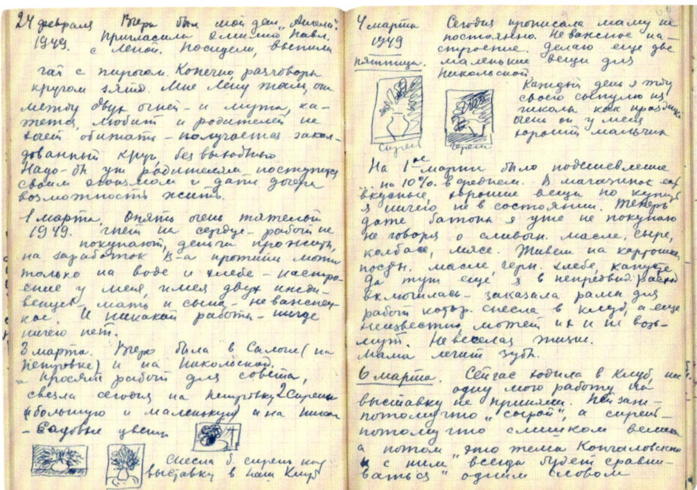

ABOVE 34   Double page from Valentina Kulagina's diary, February 24–March 6, 1949. Private collection.

RIGHT 35   Valentina Kulagina, *Lilacs*, 1948, with dedication to Aleksei Kruchenykh. Russian State Archive of Literature and Art, Moscow.

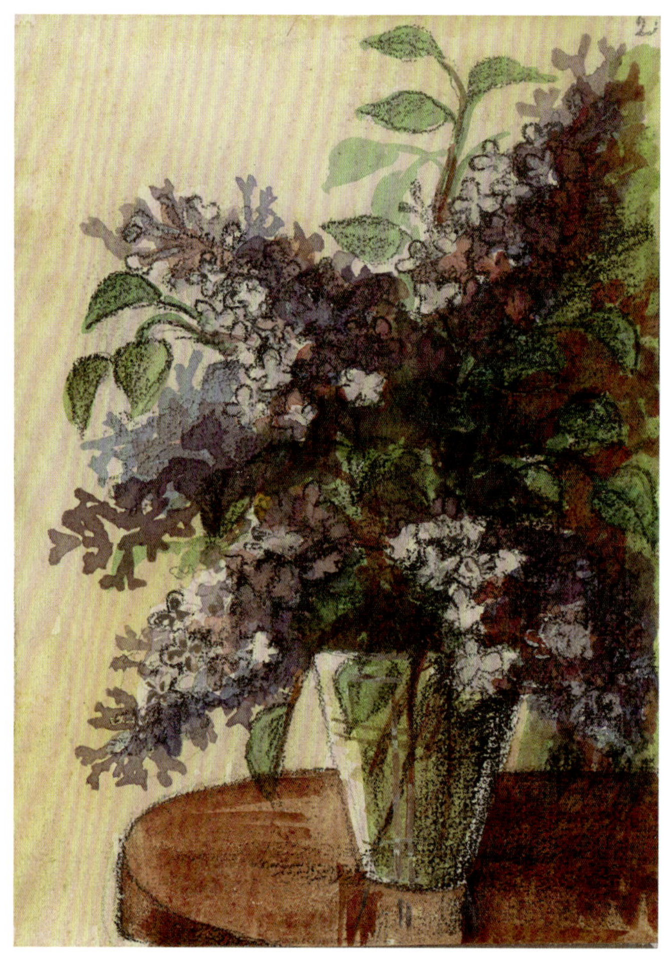

(taken on by many MOSSKh members), chose to identify with Van Gogh as a social outcast and willful individualist. Tatlin's vigorous bouquets, painted in 1936–8, adopt Van Gogh's passionate painting methods and robust coloring, and Rodchenko emphasized his kinship with Van Gogh's style, which he expressed with equal force both visually and verbally:

> What a marvelous person van Gogh was; I'm reading his letters. Makes you want to burn, write,[118] and love the same way. And how boring is the art of Blanter, Lebedev-Kumach, [Aleksandr] Gerasimov, Litvishko, Kravchenko, et al.…You lie there and interesting thoughts pop into your head, and as soon as you sit down in front of this blank piece of paper it's cold and empty, like the heart, which is tired and worn out with hopeless dreams, broken hopes, discredited ideas, obliterated work…It's hard to switch from painting to writing. Painting demands all one's time. Painting demands your entire life, entire head, eyes, and hands. Then something will come out of it.[119]

Sartre's expression, *l'ecriture blanche*, introduced in his review of Camus's *The Stranger*, fits Rodchenko's oscil-lation between empty page and empty canvas. In fact, the plot of *The Stranger* uncannily matches the events of Rodchenko's life after he was expelled from the October Group in 1932. The following year, he received a telegram about his mother's death while he was photographing the construction of the White Sea Canal. He chose not to go to the funeral. Many of Rodchenko's troubles and emotional distress occurred as a result of his relationship with the photographer Evgenia Lemberg, who died in a train accident in 1934, and whose memory haunted him as late as 1943.[120] Intensifying control over street photography forced him to retreat from Soviet daily life, thus depriving him of his long-standing commitment to serving contemporary reality, and creating a sense of imprisonment.

Reading Proust in the late spring of 1939 further agitated Rodchenko, who by this time was living off

LEFT 36 Page from Valentina Kulagina's diary, February 20, 1941. Private collection.

BELOW 37 Valentina Kulagina, design for the "Animal Husbandry" pavilion at the All-union Agricultural Exhibition, 1938. Private collection.

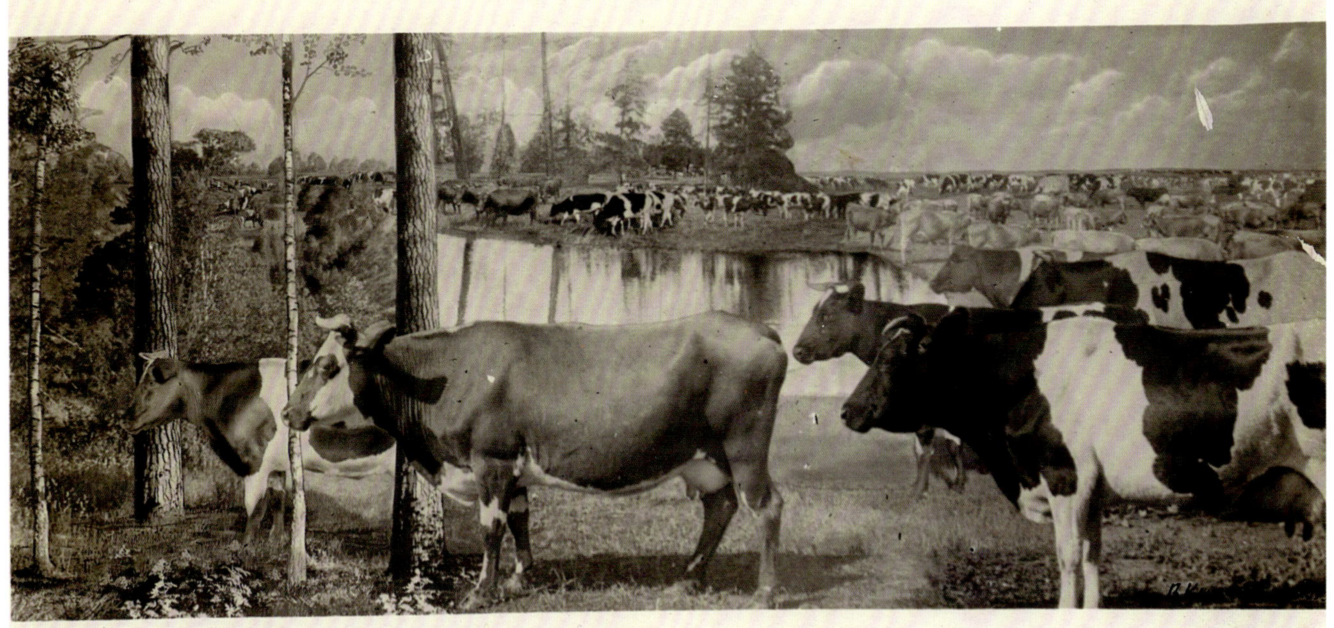

the memories of his avant-garde past. Brik's suggestion that he write about his work with Mayakovsky plunged Rodchenko into "remembrance of the *left* things past." As Rodchenko recorded in his diary in May 1939, Brik's recalling that, "we [LEF] ran ahead, the rest of them are walking and we arrived on a train,"[121] reinspired him: he would carry on with vanguard art and reject Zhdanov's 1934 cancellation of utopianism and nonobjective art. But could a collective-minded Rodchenko perform this mission alone? In fact, before he converted to constructivist thinking and making, Rodchenko's idea of nonobjective art had fed on individual and anarchic "creation." His text, "Rodchenko's System" (published in the catalogue of the *Tenth State Exhibition: Nonobjective Creation and Suprematism*, 1919), includes epigraphs from Max Stirner, Walt Whitman, and Aleksei Kruchenykh, and his own assertion of individuality. Here, with the fervor of "ego-futurist" rhetoric,[122] and conviction in individual inventiveness, Rodchenko rejects Malevich's collectivism: "The collapse of all 'isms' in painting was the beginning of my ascent....Painting – is the body, creativity – the spirit. My work – is to create the new out of painting, so look at my work in action."[123] Once again, and 21 years after this statement, Rodchenko left the Socialist Realist "house of dead truths," for in his eyes, "personal freedom...is the most valuable thing," as he wrote in his diary in January 1940.[124] His affirmation at the outset of this new decade, "I definitely still exist,"[125] testifies to the endurance of his "I" during the height of propaganda for collectivization and readiness for "new discoveries."

The outbreak of war with Germany on June 22, 1941 distracted Socialist Realist hawks in the administration from tightening their control. Kulagina described the situation in Moscow that October: "Horror, horror! There is panic in Moscow, everyone is fleeing, newspapers announced that the front has been defeated."[126] The next day, Kulagina named former AKhRR artists who were infamous for their affiliation with the Red Army: "There is a mass flight...Shame, shame! All the newly baked party members including medalists and laureates are gone! [Boris] Ioganson, [Georgy] Riazhsky, [Fedor] Bogorodsky, and many others. I am shocked."[127] Like these

Socialist Realists, Rodchenko too left Moscow, while Kulagina "decided not to go,"[128] matching boldness in painting with courage in life. Rodchenko returned to Moscow in September 1942 to face the capital's everyday hardships, alleviated only by modest card rations received from MOSSKh and other organizations, which gave him occasional work. One such place was the Grekov Studio, visits to which upset Rodchenko as he watched artists copying reproductions of famous paintings, thus throwing themselves into a deadening cycle of imitation. Rodchenko, like Malevich before him, concluded that Leicism had become "the favorite realism."[129] But even then Rodchenko refused to settle on homogeneity, fantasizing of plurality in exhibitions: "Let there be non-objective things...and real things, it would be interesting."[130] He reminisced about his international reputation as "an artist of the left front."[131] "I want to be the same as I was. I will never be a [Aleksandr] Gerasimov!" he pledged by July 1943.[132]

Rodchenko was not alone in surfing this growing wave of self-confidence and nostalgia over the identity of the left. That same summer, Kulagina wrote in her diary that she was no longer painting "coyly" but "confidently and freely.[133] Later she added that she was "an artist after all."[134] She also noted with regret, after Kruchenykh visited her in June, that he was "one of the last of the left Mohicans."[135] But, unlike Kulagina and Malevich, Rodchenko refused painterly Impressionism in an attempt to free himself from the pressure of Socialist Realist canons. Doing this would mean blindly engaging in work devoid of formal invention. In 1940, Rodchenko had decided to reclaim the curved line, which he had earlier renounced in favor of the straight line. He was convinced, to use Popova's expression, that the latter was "the revolutionary condition of form," a signifier of utopia. Now his goals were different: he was putting abstraction at the service of "collapsing bodily forms and fluid dispersal."[136] For him, the human figure had become associated with the literary heritage of Russian art that stretched from the Wanderers to AKhRR, and even included Suprematism. Since the mid-1930s, Rodchenko had tried to accommodate the human figure in his painting, working out a form of critical realism. In 1937, Deineka's sports paintings had made

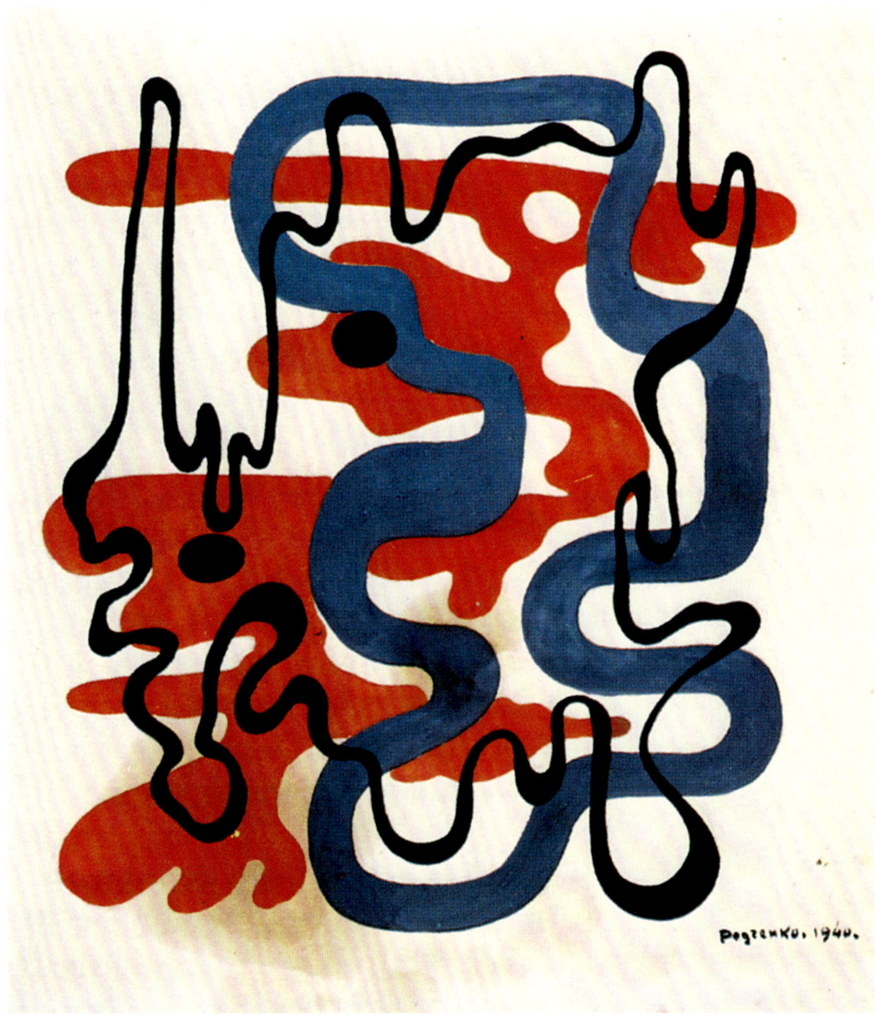

38   Aleksandr Rodchenko, *Untitled* (from the series *Streamlined Ornament*), 1940. State Museum of Contemporary Art, Costakis Collection, Thessaloniki.

him again "feel like writing a response…not with pen, but with paint."[137] Rodchenko's *Football* of that year followed Deineka's method of rendering the human body in action. But, being a photographer and a graphic designer, Rodchenko understood that Deineka was simply adapting graphic design techniques to the medium of painting. In 1940, he criticized Deineka for being "an illustrator and a poster designer,"[138] and, in rejecting that course, made his first abstract drawings in which he converted his footballers and circus performers into a swirl of colored lines, imprisoning their collective shadow within the curvilinear grid.

This was the beginning of Rodchenko's duel with what he called "the empire of pseudo-realism."[139] It differed from the duel orchestrated in 1933 by Malevich with Dmitry Toporkov, fought on the grounds of figuration, and positioning Malevich as "a right-wing formalist."[140] Instead, Rodchenko decided to radicalize the conflict of styles by creating a binary opposition to works he observed in official exhibitions, and thus to reclaim his left identity. To put this project of resistance into practice, Rodchenko could only return to non-representational art, unequivocally denounced by the ruling Socialist Realists. A series of small, surviving abstractions from the 1940s document

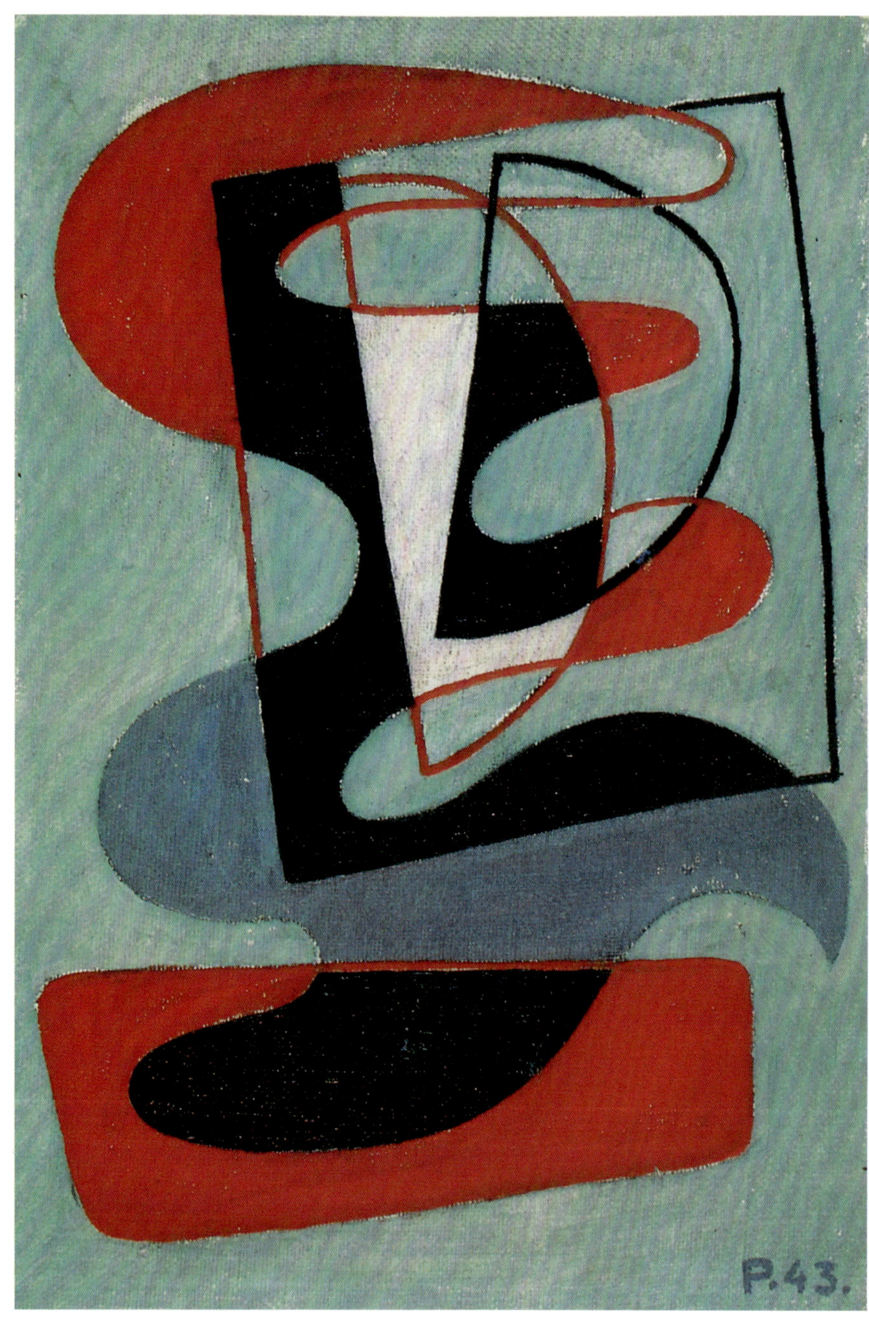

39 Aleksandr Rodchenko, *Untitled* (from the series *Streamlined Ornament*), 1943. Collection A. Rodchenko and V. Stepanova Archive, Moscow.

this effort, and include both sophisticated and awkward compositions. Together they create the impression that Rodchenko was reinventing abstract art. Under the title, *Streamlined Ornaments*, the series appears to fulfill Rodchenko's wish to make art "separate from politics" and propaganda (figs. 38, 39).[141] But this is an illusion, for the true subject of this abstract art is its opposition to Socialist Realism: hence its function is political. It has buried its ideological structure under a formal one.

Even the most spontaneous compositions from this series come across as calculated desk or easel exercises, as 1940s photographs testify (fig. 40). Lacking gestural freedom, they kept disappointing Rodchenko until, after days of despair, he had written in euphoria: "The painting has taken off! But horrors!!! It's leftist painting. And Lord Almighty, what a joy it is to be leftist…To be myself after all these torments, and against common sense. Not to break myself, to paint with pleasure!! What will be, will be!! But I'll die leftist and leave behind good works."[142]

A gouache on paper is Rodchenko's only known composition whose stylistic originality and gestural vigor correspond with his excitement (fig. 41). Emphatically horizontal (almost two meters in width), the work could only have been made on the floor. Here, Rodchenko's diary entries – non-narrative and against the status quo – proved fertile ground. Thin black scribbles that form the allover composition move from left to right in an uninterrupted flow. Rodchenko had finally found a formula to contest Socialist Realists "not with pen, but with paint."[143] A true internationalist, increasingly worried about his "European reputation,"[144] Rodchenko undermined Socialist Realism's "optical restructuring"[145] that requested "seeing through the eyes, or on behalf, of the 'collective Other.'"[146] And thus, in one of the rare Soviet abstract works of the 1940s, Rodchenko restated the uncollectivized model of vision, linking it to what would become the goals of the postwar abstractionists. In asking himself, "Why wasn't I born in America?", and painting a semi-abstract city of skyscrapers that he called *New America* (fig. 42), Rodchenko foresaw the new center of the international avant-garde.[147]

Rodchenko could not have become a cosmopolitan at a worse time. In the same year he painted *New America*, Zhdanov asked at a Central Committee meeting for an immediate shift from proletarian internationalism to explicit nationalism. The cold war had begun in 1947, which alienated the Soviet Union from the West. Also in August 1947, the Academy of Arts of the USSR was established in Moscow, and then set up its headquarters in the converted building of the State Museum of New Western Art, that had been closed in March 1948. The latter had displayed

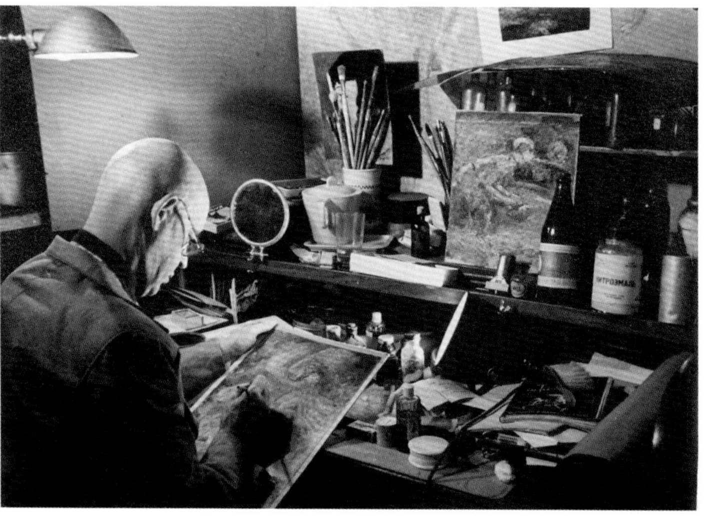

40 Aleksandr Rodchenko in his studio in Moscow, ca. 1948, photographed by Vadim Kovrigin.

a wide spectrum of French modernist art, drawn from the expropriated collections of Sergei Shchukin and Ivan Morozov. The relocation of some of these paintings to the Pushkin State Museum of Fine Arts did not lead, however, to their display, for it too shut its doors in 1949, giving way to the Museum of Presents to Stalin. Such orchestrated moves effectively exorcized all traces of Western modern art from the Soviet capital. The old plan of AKhRR's cronies was now backed by Zhdanov's anti-Western rhetoric, allowing them to allege that even Impressionism, still practiced by some of AKhRR's veterans, was "alien and hostile to the art of Socialist Realism."[148]

As with the Congress of Soviet Writers in 1934, and for secretaries of MOSSKh, there were several candidates for the post of president of the Academy. AKhRR's dream to obtain academic status, and stop sharing with modernists the state privileges available through MOSSKh membership, made this position especially political. In his memoirs, Katsman claims that Voroshilov asked him whether he would prefer Grabar or Aleksandr Gerasimov as the Academy's president. He is quoted as replying, "to choose Grabar would be to choose the intelligentsia, to choose Gerasimov – the proletariat."[149] With this answer, the well-to-do Katsman played the proletarian card, but gave preference to his even richer friend, at a time

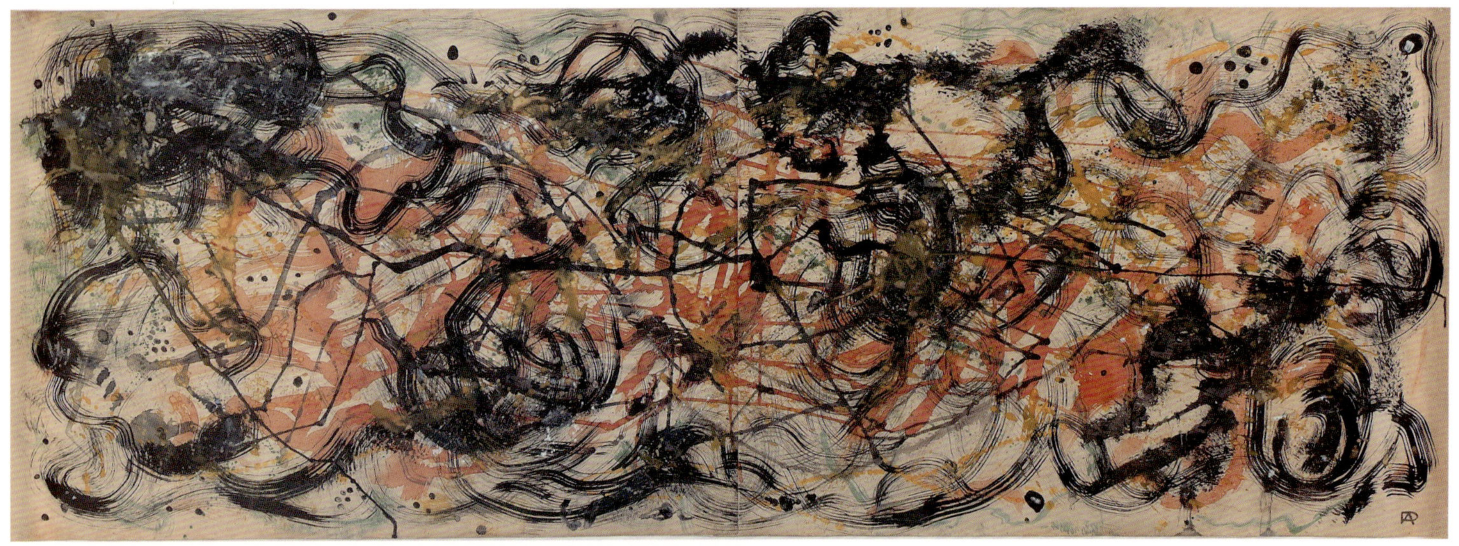

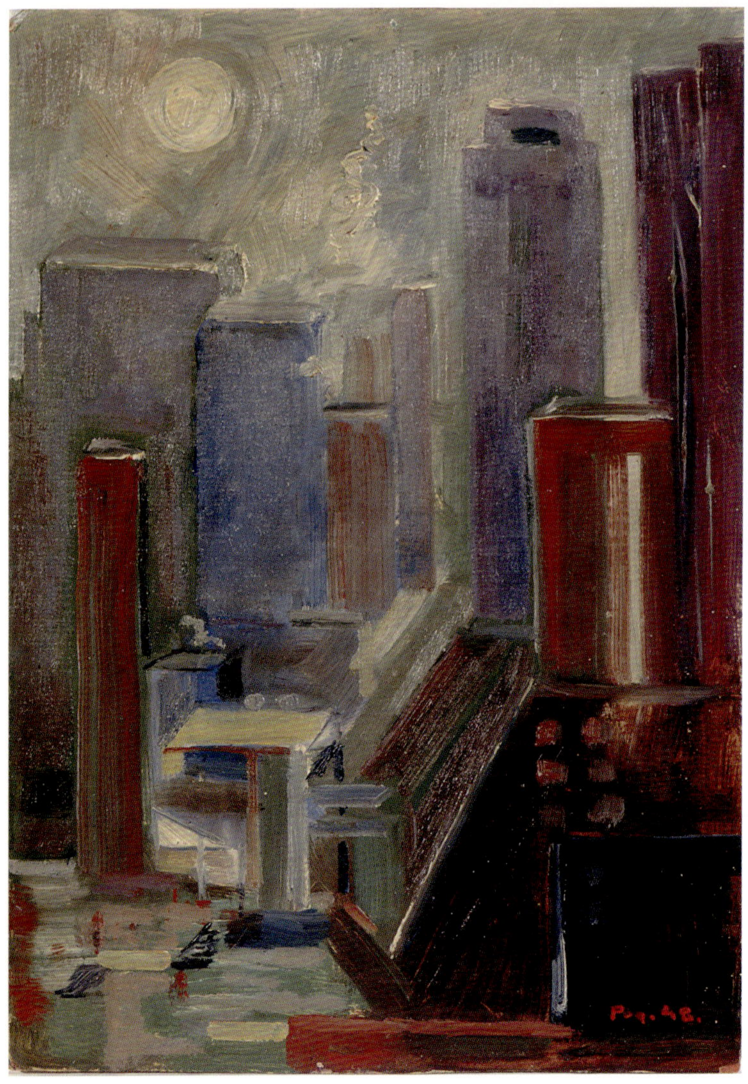

ABOVE 41   Aleksandr Rodchenko, *Expressive Rhythm*, ca. 1943–4. State Museum of Contemporary Art, Costakis Collection, Thessaloniki.

LEFT 42   Aleksandr Rodchenko, *New America*, 1948. A. Rodchenko and V. Stepanova Archive, Moscow.

OPPOSITE PAGE 43   Vladimir Tatlin, *The Tempest*, ca. 1949. State Museum of Contemporary Art, Costakis Collection, Thessaloniki.

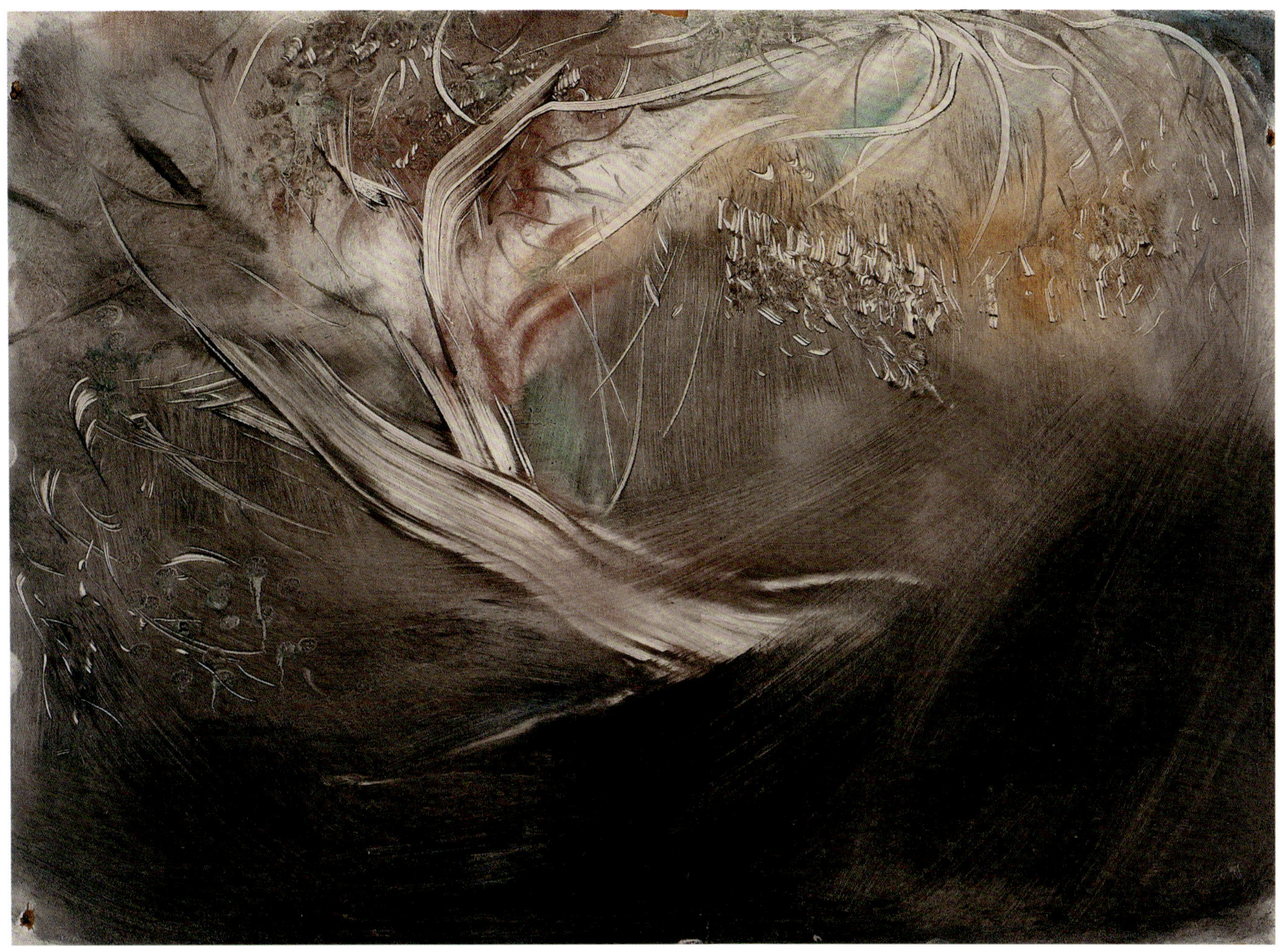

when, as Kulagina put it, "a permanent companion of all Soviet people was expensive life…constant fear…uncertainty in earnings, in a piece of bread."[150] With Gerasimov at the wheel of the Academy, academic classicism finally became the official style of Socialist Realism. Powerful committees condemned any stylistic diversity among the works submitted to the official exhibition committees, public commissions, and for sale. Eager to idealize Soviet life, newly fledged academics threw Russian art back a century, intensifying the level of "falsification and bad art." The English critic G.H. Lewes, to whom this statement and the term "falsism" belong, used them in 1858 in relation to nineteenth-century academic paintings, and his judgment is equally relevant to late 1940s Soviet academicism: "Either give us true peasants, or leave them untouched…either keep your

people silent, or make them speak the idiom of their class."[151]

Reacting to the Academy's opening, Rodchenko wrote: "The Academy: N. Pavlov, Bialynitsky-Birulia, A. Gerasimov, Kukryniksy. I'm gloomy as the night. Again they squeeze and pressure us. And art descends lower and lower."[152] Tatlin, whom at the well-attended MOSSKh meetings fearlessly stated that he would not "burn [his] old pieces,"[153] by the end of the 1940s exhibited the same feeling of dispair, expressed powerfully in two works. One depicted a semi-abstract, murky forest with a swirling tree (ca. 1949, fig. 43) that closely followed Malevich's instruction to wage war against Leicism by, to repeat Malevich's phrase, "rais[ing] one's painterly temperament so that brushes walk and bend like trees from The Tempest."[154] The other, painted in 1947, represented a still life with a

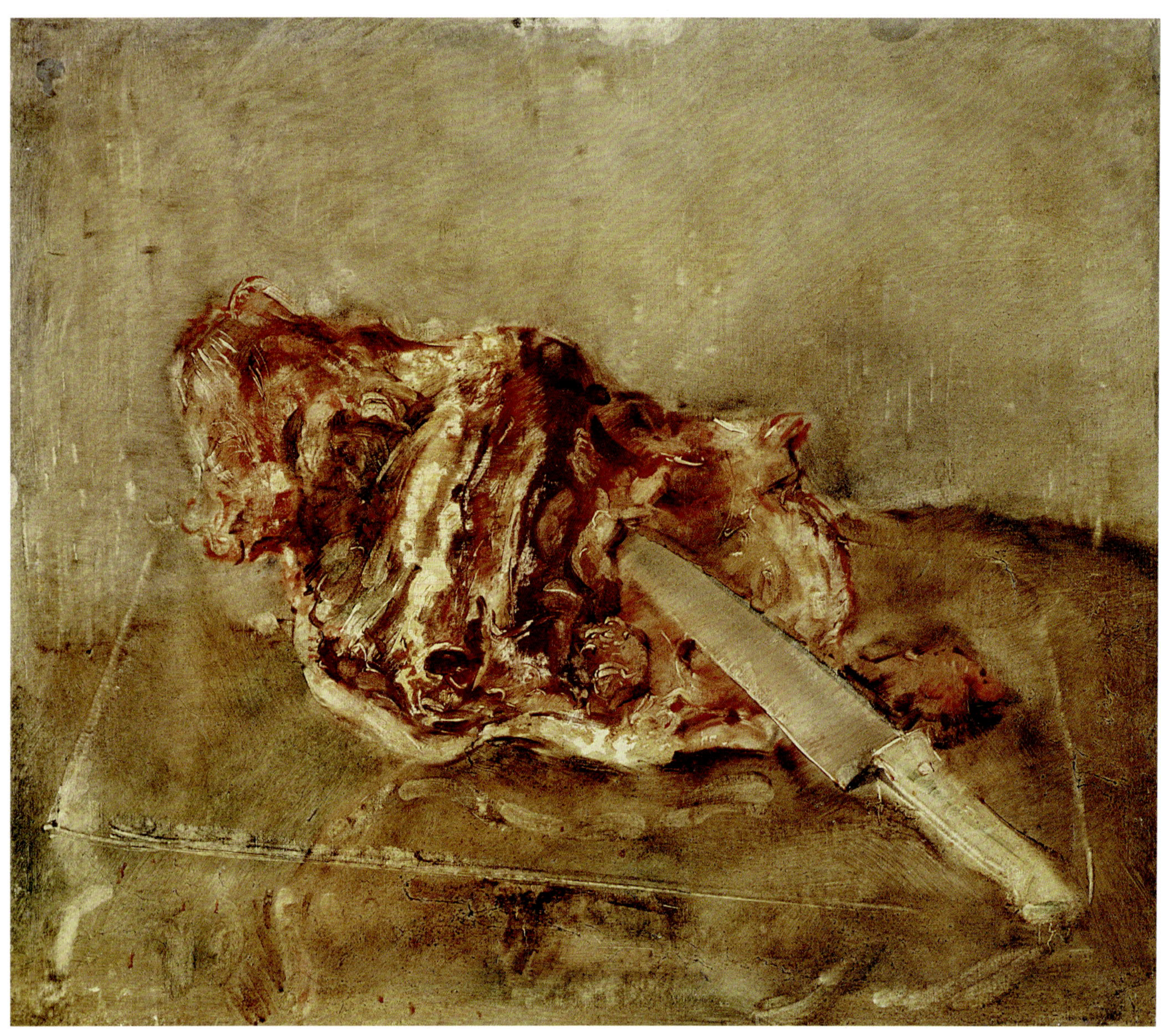

44 Vladimir Tatlin, *Meat*, 1947. State Tretiakov Gallery, Moscow.

piece of bloody meat pierced by a kitchen knife, that may be read as an allegory of the avant-garde's violent demise (fig. 44). For her part, Kulagina reported cases of multiple sackings from art institutions and schools of moderate Socialist Realists, including Grabar, Deineka, and Sergei Gerasimov.[155]

As the president of the Academy, Aleksandr Gerasimov regularly traveled abroad, where he lobbied against abstract art. This, as well as his hostility toward intellectuals, had made his participation in inter-national events, such as the World Congress of Intellectuals for Peace in Poland in 1948, objectionable for Western proponents of political and cultural freedom, such as the American sociologist and civil rights activist W.E.B. Du Bois. The latter's address to the Scientific and Cultural Conference for World Peace, held the following year in New York, comes across as a message in support of dissidents like Rodchenko. Du Bois believed that one of the barriers that "hem[med] us in [was] the world-old habit of refusing to think for ourselves, or to listen to those who do think. Against this ignorance and intolerance we protest forever."[156] Those Soviet cultural functionaries who had access to their Western colleagues did their best to create the impression that the Soviet art world was functioning under no strict censorship and had no voices of dissent. To sustain such myths, persecution of certain activities would occur simultaneously with permission for others, depending on the person concerned. For example, while Punin was arrested in 1949 for giving "anti-Soviet" art lectures, a privileged woman who had traveled to Europe freely shared her impressions of the Paris art scene in one of Moscow's workers' clubs: according to Kulagina, this woman discussed Picasso and Léger, claiming that, "at that moment in Paris they were the only artists worthy of attention."[157] As an example of how the brutal nature of Soviet cultural affairs was hidden from the international cultural community, Kulagina recorded that this lecturer added: "artists in Europe were amazed by how the Soviet State supported its artists with commissions whereas [Western artists] had nothing of this sort and thus lived badly."[158]

The heroic Socialist Realist period, though, was soon to end and, perhaps in a premonition of political change, in 1951 Gerasimov decided to commemorate the beginning of Socialist Realists' rule with the episode narrated at the outset of this chapter. An unusually medium-sized painting, *The Artists I. Brodsky, A Gerasimov, E. Katsman Visiting I.V. Stalin's Dacha*, depicts the group with Voroshilov, sitting at a table laden with food (fig. 45). The three artists are dressed like bourgeois, whereas Stalin and Voroshilov wear military uniforms. A samovar, a symbol of true *narodnost*,[159] stuck in the left-hand corner, dilutes Stalin's Georgian ethnicity. Only two years later Gerasimov painted his last portrait of Stalin lying in state (fig. 46). Executed swiftly in blazing red, the canvas conveys the high-voltage ideology that was about to be thwarted by the Khrushchev thaw.[160]

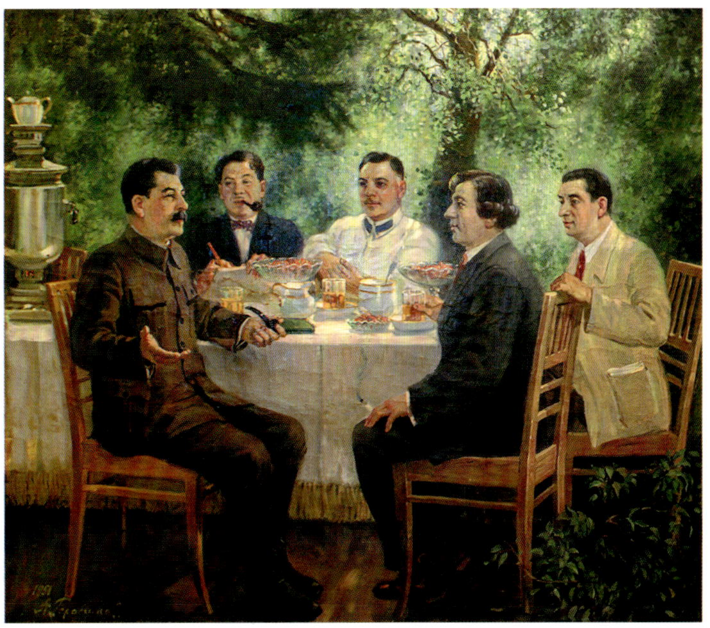

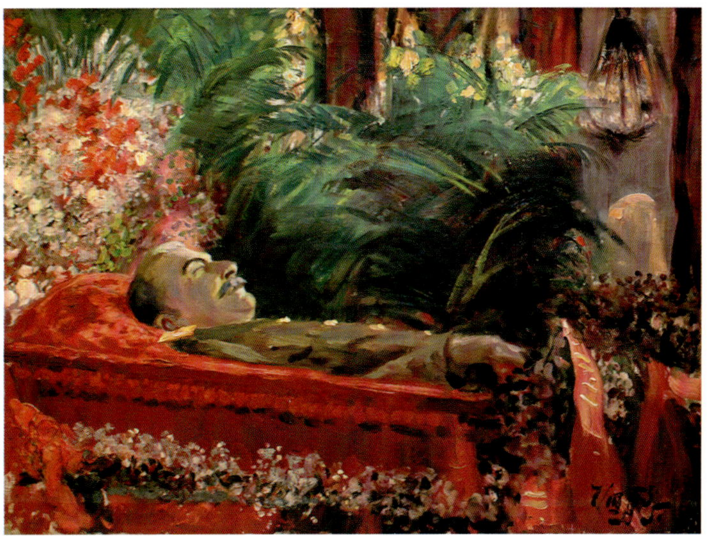

45   Aleksandr Gerasimov, *The Artists I. Brodsky, A Gerasimov, E. Katsman Visiting I.V. Stalin's Dacha*, 1951. Private collection, Moscow.

46   Aleksandr Gerasimov, *Stalin Lying in State*, 1953. Private collection, Moscow.

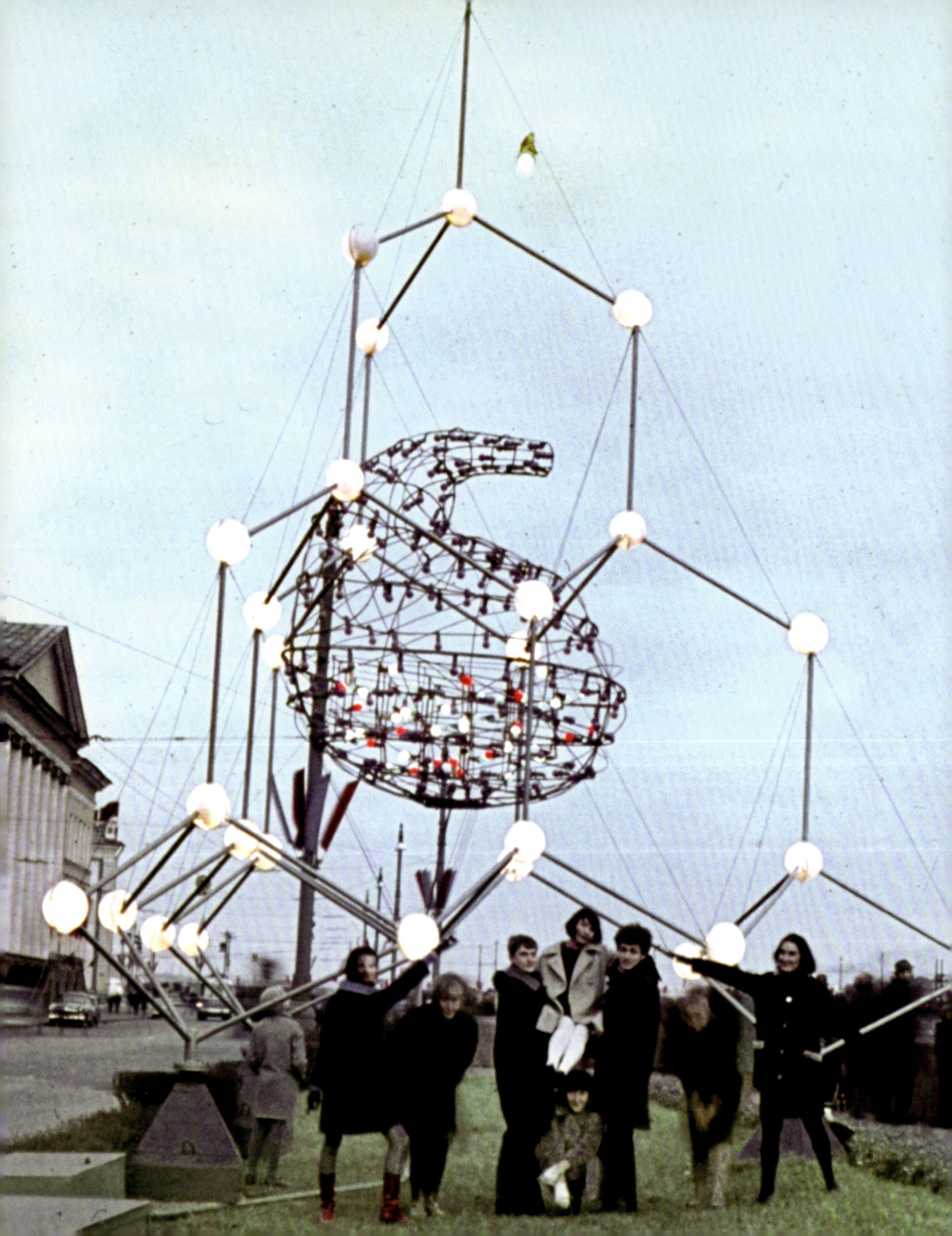

3

REINVENTING ABSTRACTION

Ilya Ehrenburg at the World Congress of Intellectuals for Peace in 1948 embraced and spoke to Picasso in French in front of Aleksandr Gerasimov, to taunt the latter for his nationalism and loathing of modernism, knowing that he would not understand.[1] Like the specter of a new epoch, Ehrenburg, though he received the Stalin Prize in 1952, after Stalin's death in 1953 lost no time in completing his prophetic novel *The Thaw*, which was published in 1954. When the Soviet leader Nikita Khrushchev caused a sensation by denouncing Stalin's cult of personality at the Twentieth Congress of the Communist Party, convened at the beginning of 1956, the word "thaw" was thenceforward linked to his name. Buoyed up by the popularity of his novel, Ehrenburg succeeded in overturning AKhRR's excoriation of modernism. This he achieved with the exhibition *Pablo Picasso in the USSR*, which, had it been installed as planned in the Academy, would have more explicitly undermined the Soviet academic artists. Instead, the show commenced in the reopened Pushkin Museum on October 26, 1956. This allowed Rodchenko, who died on December 3 of that year, to witness the resurrection of free art in his country and the deposition of those artists whom he had detested since the late 1930s.

Yet the surviving Moscow modernists were not invited to the celebration of Picasso's 75th birthday on the eve of the exhibition at the House of Architects. Rather, it was academicians who presided at this major event, some of whom had instigated or supported the closing of the Pushkin Museum and who considered modernism as their aesthetic foe.[2] Picasso chose to turn a blind eye to the fact that this celebration of his art and life was attended by his artist-opposites, and in a message sent from France he pledged his fidelity to communism, and his love to Soviet artists whose letters had always "deeply moved him." He still hoped to visit the Soviet Union, but "for now," Picasso concluded, "I delegate this [journey] to my paintings" (he lent nearly 40 recent paintings).[3]

The exhibition surveyed Picasso's oeuvre starting with the Pushkin Museum's own paintings from his Blue and Rose Periods. Well attended and intensely discussed, it reinstated a sense of creativity in young artists suffocating from official schooling that was based, in the words of Ilya Kabakov, on making work "'for them' rather than for yourself."[4] Picasso's stylistic diversity served to open up – with actual works rather than reproductions – the genealogy of prewar European modernism. The result was described by the artist Iury Sobolev in his recollection of 1956: "We would set up a still life or invite a model, drawing and acting as Cubists, Dadaists, and Surrealists. The whole year was spent on studying Picasso, who 'turned' to us one time with a classical face, and another with a Cubist one."[5]

Such schizophrenic self-healing from the trauma inflicted by the "painfully deadening rules" of teachers, as well as by the "terrifying and incomprehensible work of the last of Stalin's 'art hawks,'"[6] was quickly converted into a desire to find a countercultural mode of producing art. As Rodchenko's case had shown in the 1940s, non-representational art continued to be the ultimate "other" of official painting, particularly in the form of automatic painting. Vladimir Slepian adopted just that kind of practice when in 1957 at the age of 27 he attended an international exhibition with many abstract works on view, organized in conjunction with the Moscow Festival of Youth and Students (figs. 47, 48). He later remarked that "the psychological climate…[was] extremely favorable to abstract art…we were able to look at current Western art magazines for the first time in two public libraries in Moscow, reviews like *Art d'aujourd'hui, Artnews, L'Oeil*…and I realized that art has no ending."[7] Slepian occupies a unique position in the history of the Moscow vanguard: several of his early abstract paintings reached the West through a French art dealer, Daniel Cordier, who while visiting the Festival was introduced to Slepian's works. In October of that year they were exhibited anonymously at Cordier's gallery in Paris.[8] If this was not brave enough

for an artist in the USSR only four years after Stalin's death, Slepian miraculously reached Paris via Poland in 1958. In an interview with the Matisse scholar Pierre Schneider, published in *Artnews* in 1959, Slepian, speaking under the pseudonym "Woks," describes seeing works by Malevich, Kandinsky, and Chagall in 1957, "in the cellars of the Leningrad Museum [State Russian Museum] by special privilege," and "doing surrealist drawings of machines" while watching "the military parades."[9] He also outlined the course that he thought the Moscow vanguard should pursue:

> I believe that we are living in a critical moment in the history of painting. Since Cézanne, it has become evident that, for the painter, what counts is no longer the painting but the process of creation. Tachism, or whatever you call it, has drawn the lesson. Whether you regard painting as a means of penetrating the self or the world, it is a creation. When Pollock painted, his situation, his inner behavior as an artist, were certainly more complex than the painting, for he was living the process. Why should this creation be pinned down, shut up in a rectangle, hung on the wall? I believe when an "automatist" paints, there are actually two painters in him: the one who wants to act, the other who wants to create an object… the essential aim of painting must be the process of creation; the viewer must no longer be made to look at the painting alone, but at the very process of making it."[10]

In his emphasis on abstraction produced in action and the treatment of the canvas as an arena in which to express an artist's individuality, Slepian was reiterating Harold Rosenberg's famous 1952 essay, "The American Action Painters," also published in *Artnews*. According to Rosenberg, for some American abstract artists the canvas had become "an arena in which to act rather than as a means of representation. What was to go on the canvas was not a picture but an event."[11] Rosenberg's expression, "revolutionary gesturing," positioned abstract art once again in the realm of radical aesthetics. That is similar to the experience of Kandinsky during the Bolshevik Revolution. His paintings and drawings of that time are intensely gestural and automatic, reflecting the shaping of his own revolutionary identity.

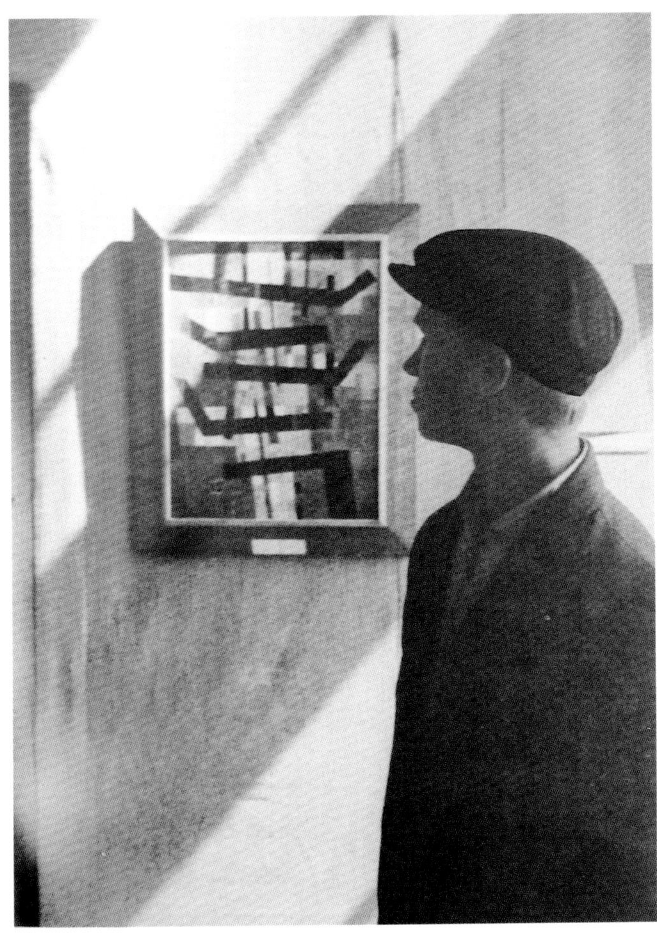

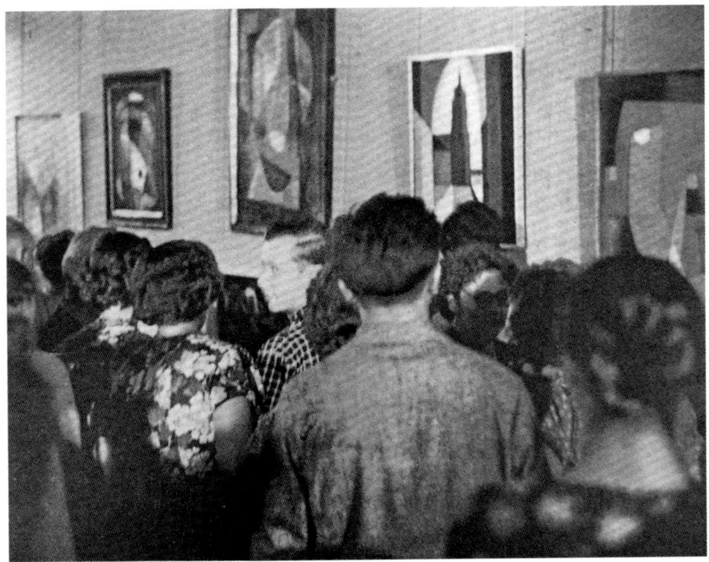

47 Newspaper clipping of a worker in front of an abstract painting at the Moscow Festival of Youth and Students, 1957.

48 Newspaper clipping showing viewers looking at abstract paintings at the Moscow Festival of Youth and Students, 1957.

It is possible that American expressionists, many of whom were left-leaning, expressed their true identity through "action painting." However, in the commercially driven Western art world, the final product was always the most important. In contrast, in the Soviet Union, which had no commercial galleries, "action painting" came across as the most relevant and feasible vanguard direction that, in the history of Soviet easelism, constituted the beginning of the next chapter. It reversed the anti-easelism of the 1920s as a path to street production and repositioned the artist's studio as a safe haven for acting out "the act of painting."[12] Thus, Slepian welcomed other underground artists to his rented Moscow studio, in what became an essential practice for such artists. His own experiments bluntly deconstructed what some other Russian modernists had held sacred, namely, painting on a canvas with a brush and a palette knife. During one such painterly happening in 1957, an anonymous photographer

caught Slepian (as Hans Namuth had photographed Pollock in 1950) attempting to paint with a gas torch (fig. 49). Iury Zlotnikov, with whom Slepian sometimes collaborated, defined the latter's "artistic consciousness" as that of "a barbarous intellectual aiming to understand the structure of painting through a scientific association with mathematical formulae, and [to feel] physical structures through a new relation to a flat surface."[13] Slepian's collective form of action painting went against the practice of most underground artists, who religiously defended individualism as a retort to Soviet collectivization. To him a collective practice was the only possibility within a society that lacked commodity exchange. He described in detail the creation of what may be defined as "dialogical painting":

In the center of a hall filled with a few persons, a screen is set up. The spectators place themselves on either side. The hall is plunged into darkness, but the screen remains lit on both sides by projectors. Two painters are at work, each on one side of the translucent screen. Each sees what the other is

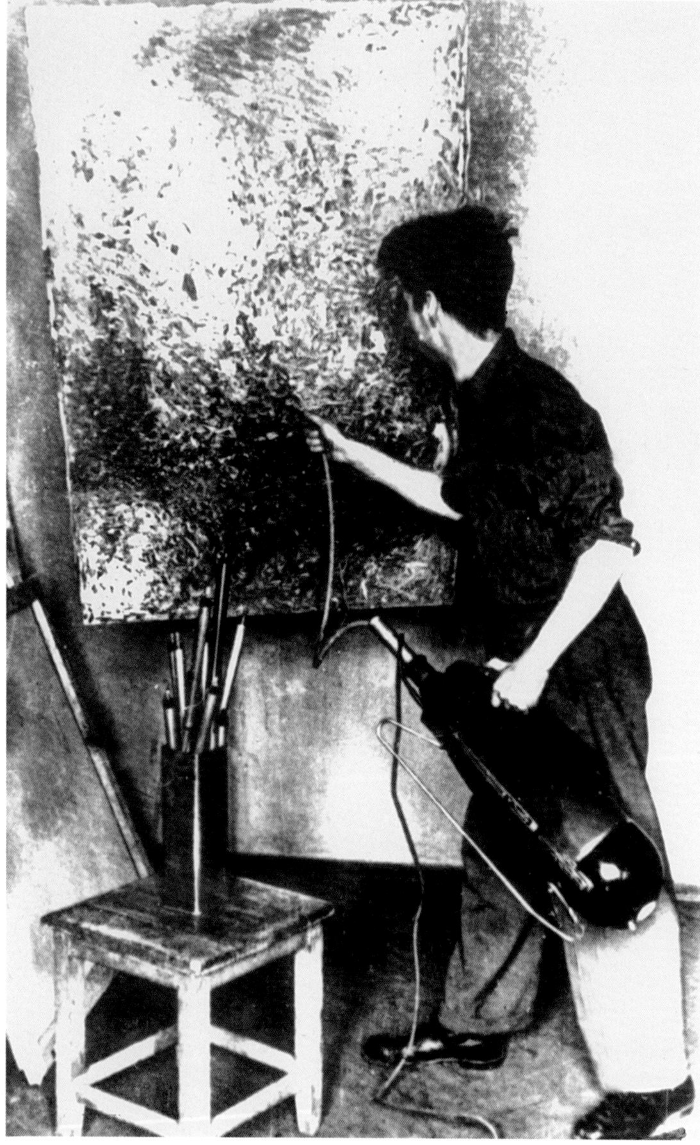

49 Vladimir Slepian painting in his studio, 1957. Moscow.

painting, and each imagines that everything is going on on his side of the screen. This type of screen is best suited for black and white painting. For many colors, a screen such as the one used by Clouzot in his film, *The Picasso Mystery*, is preferable. A dialogue, or a clash, of two personalities is obtained.[14]

It is not known whether Slepian actually saw Henri-Georges Clouzot's film *Le mystère Picasso*, released in 1955, a year before Picasso's exhibition in Moscow

(which Slepian visited) and thus possibly screened there, but he brilliantly expanded this film record of Picasso's genius into an open-ended experiment with collective creativity. However, in 1957 he was able to smuggle out to France a dozen modestly sized paintings, including *Rock and Roll Mathematics*, *Birth and Death of the World*, *Ten Thousand Meters*, and *Similitude*, all mentioned in the *Herald Tribune* review of Cordier's show. To protect Slepian's identity, his name was not mentioned in this or other reviews, whose descriptions established clichés for writing about Soviet nonconformist artists. These included obligatory anti-communist rhetoric (for example, that Slepian's father was "a Communist functionary" and thus he had gone against him by becoming a modernist), emphasis on the secretive atmosphere in the Soviet Union, the danger of smuggling out and exhibiting such art in the West, and downplaying underground artists' sophistication. And yet, overall, this and other reviews were positive, saying for example, that Slepian's works were "brilliant in color, and gaudy in a poster sense. And all show a strange, astral, 'babymoon' kind of design, including one that appeared to have been peppered with caviar"[15] (fig. 50). Cordier, quoted in another review, described Slepian's works as "too 'naïve' and violently experimental to suggest that he had seen any Western examples at close hand. Here is a young man reaching for expression in a field largely unknown and presumably forbidden to him. The paintings indicated little more than a novice's groping attempts at abstract art but they showed a high degree of artistic consciousness."[16] Slepian's "novice" style was in fact intentional and derived from his fascination with children's art that he had admired since 1943, and the exhibitions of which in the West made "the strongest impression" on him.[17] Cordier's expression "violently experimental" is noteworthy for it points to the loss of interest in experimentation in the postwar Paris art world, and its engagement in classical abstraction. It was clear that, as with Rodchenko's longing for America, Slepian's place was in New York.

Meanwhile, back in Moscow, Vladimir Nemukhin, another future major underground abstractionist who attended the 1957 Festival, later stated that he and his friends could finally see "what the art of the second part of the twentieth century was. It was a real shock but a therapeutic one that definitively enlightened us...everything that seemed to be have been forgotten, deleted from memory with 'Zhdanov's iron,' returned to life."[18] The *American National Exhibition*, which opened in Sakolniki Park, Moscow in 1959, brought another huge educational and emotional shake-up (fig. 51). In a private conversation with me, Nemukhin recalled that while returning home with his partner, the artist Lydia Masterkova, they were both silent, as if the abstract expressionists had helped save them from the prison of optics contaminated by narrativity, thereby letting visual sensations finally take charge of creative impulses. Nemukhin commemorated his visit to the American exhibition in an all-black, semi-abstract drawing of Sakolniki Park (fig. 52). What impressed these artists most was the gestural freedom exemplified by Willem de Kooning's 1948 *Asheville* and Jackson Pollock's 1947 *Cathedral*,[19] as well as the large scale of most of the abstract canvases.[20] Nemukhin eloquently describes the artistic and political impact of the style: "Abstract expressionism, which dominated the world of art then, was organically grafted into the new Russian soil...It woke up our unconscious, allowed us to liberate ourselves, gave the push to the formalist experiment...by becoming an abstract artist, one opposed oneself to society, to its bureaucratic ideology, and went into conflict with the authorities."[21]

Unlike Slepian, who admitted that "At the age of twenty [in 1950], I had never heard the names of Cézanne and Van Gogh,"[22] Nemukhin and Masterkova, several years Slepian's seniors, in the 1940s connected with a handful of older modernists both privately and in an art school on Chudov Lane opened in 1943 that coincided with the time when Rodchenko returned to abstraction.[23] The school took a risk in passing on the tradition of modernist painting to the next generation. Empowered by teachers and by rare editions of art books available in second-hand book stores during the war, by 1946 Nemukhin and Masterkova were committed to painting in a Cezannesque style. Looking back, Masterkova noted: "Painting must not be such that one could grab objects, but more in trembling, and every line should tremble and live, integrated in color and harmony. Subject matter does not have any significance."[24]

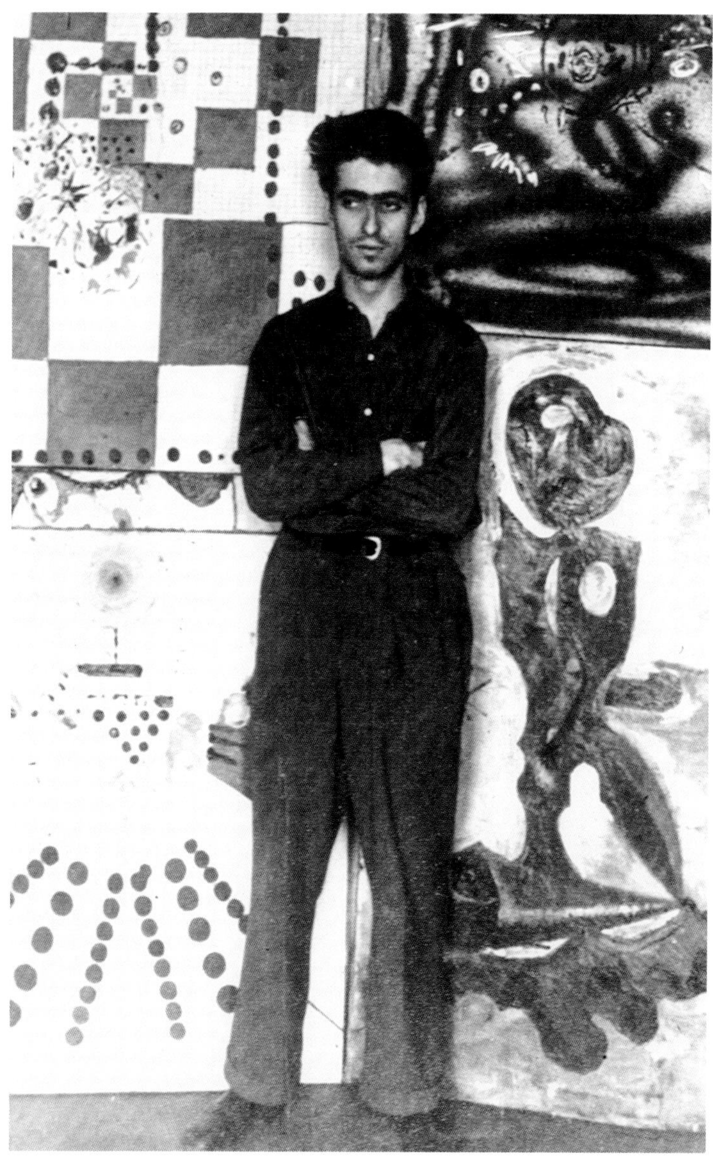

50   Vladimir Slepian in his studio, 1957. Moscow.

Although they could see various modernist versions of figuration in the Pushkin Museum's Picasso show, and in the canvases of Surrealists such as Yves Tanguy and Peter Blume (displayed in the *American National Exhibition*), for Masterkova and Nemukhin "contemporary forms" – given their experience with figuration – translated exclusively into abstraction.[25] This commitment allowed these artists to continue "the story of modernism," which, as Rosalind Krauss has pointed out, "has generally been one of a struggle to

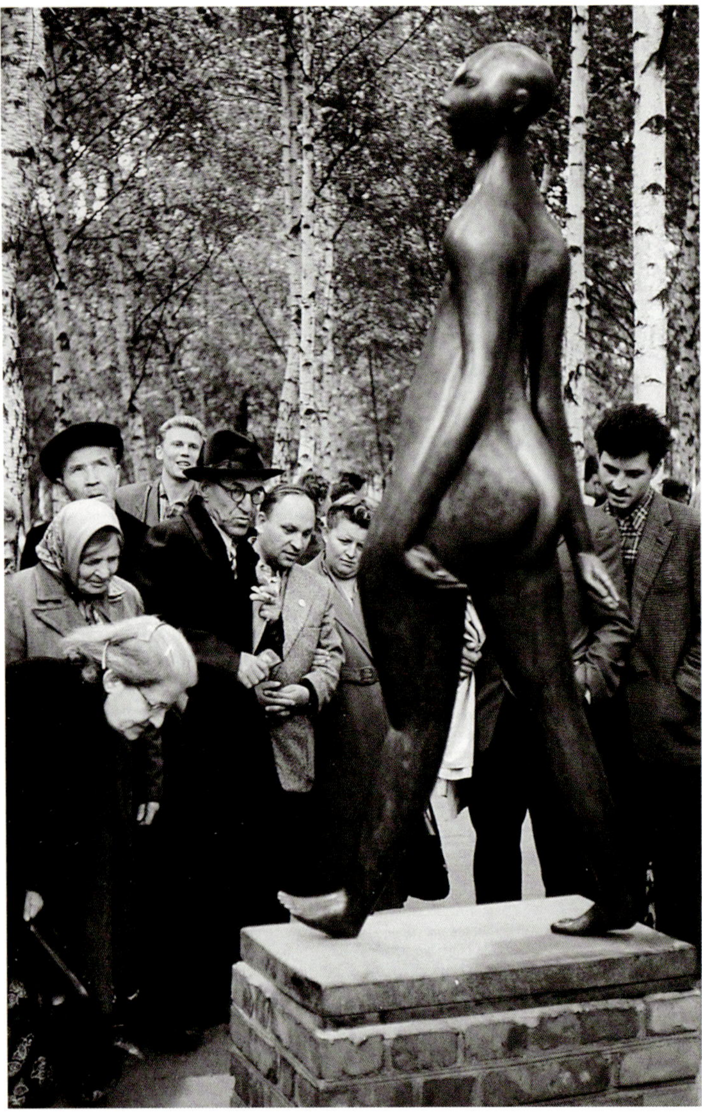

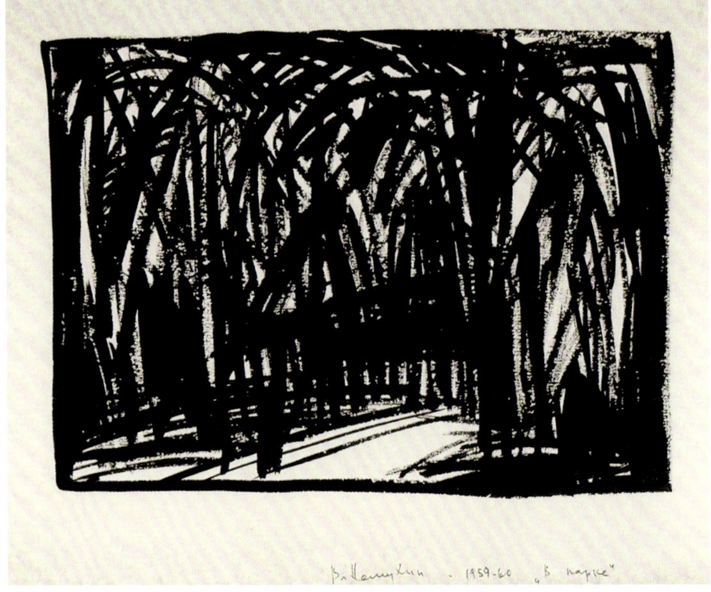

51 Gaston Lachaise's *Female Nude* in Sakolniki Park during *The American National Exhibition*, Moscow, 1959. Photograph by Valery Gente-Rote © Heirs of Valery Gende-Rote.

52 Vladimir Nemukhin, *In the Park*, 1959–60. Collection of Russian and Eastern European Art, Kolodzei Art Foundation, New Jersey.

throw off traditional forms of figuration in order to achieve the unmediated clarity of non-representational art."[26]

Unfortunately, there was no photographer at hand when Nemukhin, inspired by what he saw at the *American National Exhibition*, painted several abstract canvases that were remarkably mature in their employment of allover structure and in their gestural and coloristic freedom. Like Slepian, Nemukhin realized that the importance of Abstract Expressionism resided in automatism, in its ability to obliterate the figurative image and attain the condition of "beyond literary". Nemukhin called Socialist Realism "an imposter," insisting that in art there was a place for "indignation which can be expressed most dramatically in abstract art."[27]

If Nemukhin's *Blue Day* (1959) is still saturated with Impressionist light and color, as well as references to nature, in a series of compositions that followed it, his expressiveness, equally dependent on vivacious color and gestural force, reaches a peak (figs. 53, 54). These canvases match the sophistication of abstractions produced by Nemukhin's compatriot Kandinsky, as well as by his Western contemporaries exhibiting in Moscow, particularly De Kooning.[28] Moreover, Nemukhin's abstract works were two meters high, although they were executed in extremely small spaces. In one case, Nemukhin pinned a blank canvas to the wall and stood on a couch in order to paint it; he executed another composition in his rented room, scaring his landlord with his "painterly happening." The landlord concluded that Nemukhin was insane and started sleeping with an axe for protection.

Masterkova dated her "sudden switch to Abstract Expressionism"[29] shortly after she attended the 1957

Festival. To formulate her own direction, she relied on her understanding of modernist painting as well as on her fascination with music that ranged from Bach to "the sound of black singers."[30] This synthesis of color and sound rhythms resulted in an abstract style of interlocking organic shapes (fig. 55). She described her abstractions as "sound-visions," carefully orchestrating color fields as if they were a voice or a musical instrument and envisioning sounds along with colors as the materials of art. This led her to resurrecting the concept of *faktura* (facture) in a combination ranging from Mikhail Larionov's in the early 1910s as "the condition of [a] colored surface, its timbre," to Liubov Popova's understanding of it as "the content of pictorial surfaces."[31] In other words, the content can be both abstract and figurative but subject matter can only be mimetic, as in Socialist Realism. Pursuing this conviction Masterkova actively used the color red, thus reclaiming its aesthetic status from its primarily ideological function (fig. 56). Like the work of Georgia O'Keeffe, which was also included in the *American National Exhibition* and who was similarly fascinated with translating music into form and color, Masterkova's mode of abstraction stood apart from Nemukhin's significantly less controlled renditions, illustrating a gender split (also evident in the West) in perceptions and interpretations of abstraction in the postwar period. This differs from the 1920s practice of geometric abstraction that, in following the theories of Suprematism and Constructivism, both genders equally used nonobjective forms.[32]

As noted already, it was Rodchenko who moved non-representational art in the 1940s into the realm of political art simply because it was the antithesis of Socialist Realism. Rodchenko's desire to identify with American culture, expressed in his lamenting over not being born in America, was resumed by the next generation of artists, including Masterkova and Nemukhin. That artist couple regularly read the magazine *Amerika* (America), and displayed John F. Kennedy's photograph in their dacha; this attitude positioned them as outsiders in their own country, particularly after relations between the U.S.A. and the U.S.S.R. deteriorated shortly after Khrushchev's visit to America in 1959. America had become the topos of their aesthetic identity and social aspirations, and Abstract Ex-

pressionism had turned into the Zeitgeist or, in the words of another Moscow abstract painter, Lev Kropivnitsky, the "portrait of the time."[33] The reaction to Slepian's works exhibited in Paris in 1957 attested to an emerging aesthetic unity in the postwar art world. As Cordier noted, Slepian's works "gave proof that no matter how tightly sealed off Russian painters may be, there is, as one Parisian art goer put it, 'only one cosmos in art.'"[34]

This sense of abstract art being the international style was augmented with the opening in Moscow of the *French National Exhibition* in the summer of 1961, on the same site as the American show. It presented abstract works by artists affiliated with the School of Paris (Roger Bissière, Jean Bazaine, Charles Lapicque, and Jean Le Moal). By then, abstraction had been popularized by Eli Beliutin who at the end of the 1950s established a free studio that was attended by many artists who learned "the fundamentals of modern art – something entirely absent from the curriculum of the country's official art schools."[35] They painted together in Moscow and during country outings, creating an experimental collective comparable to Malevich's UNOVIS (fig. 57). Many of Beliutin's students were professional designers eager to insert an abstract language into official design production: that destabilized the artistic and financial status quo guarded by academics and the orthodox faction of MOSSKh. The last bastion in resisting such competitors, these conservative forces organized the exhibition *XXX Years of MOSSKh* in 1962 at the Manezh exhibition hall to celebrate that anniversary of Moscow art under the Union's control. The very fact of honoring this oppressive organization attested to the art establishment's refusal to abolish, or at least reform, MOSSKh and the Academy.

And yet the 'Manezh Exhibition,' as it became known, was diverse (some claim in order to have the evidence for an attack on modernists), and presented works by prewar modernists (hung in the exhibition's historical section), including Robert Falk and David Shterenberg, as well as such current rebellious union members as Beliutin (with his students) and the sculptor Ernst Neizvestny. Their paintings and sculptures were relegated to the Manezh's second floor and exhibited together with works by three non-Union

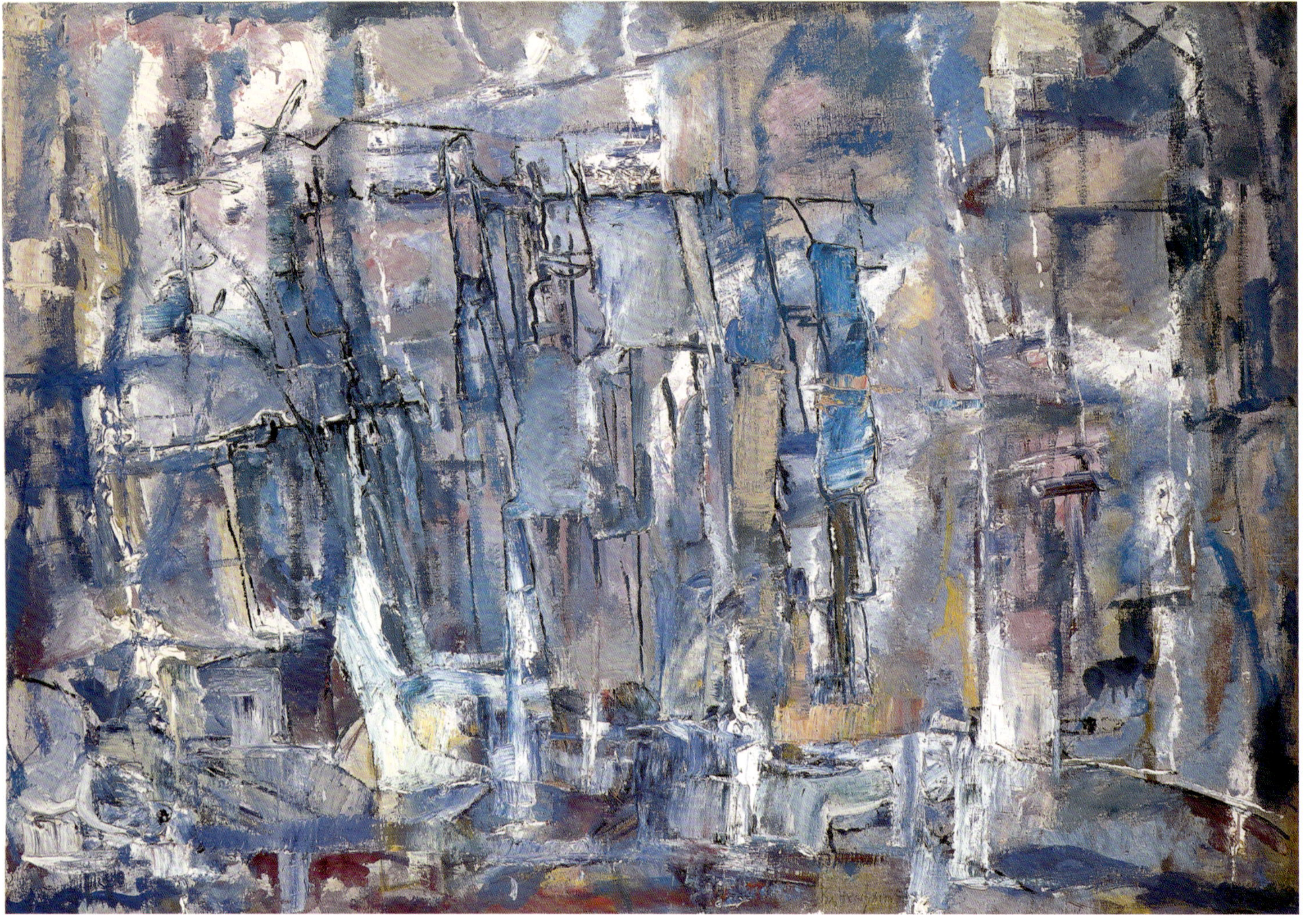

ABOVE 53 Vladimir Nemukhin, *Blue Day*, 1959. Collection Evgeny Nutovich, Moscow.

OPPOSITE PAGE 54 Vladimir Nemukhin, *Composition*, 1960. Norton and Nancy Dodge Collection of Nonconformist Art from the Soviet Union, Jane Voorhees Zimmerli Art Museum, Rutgers, State University of New Jersey.

participants – Ulö Sooster, Sobolev, and Vladimir Yankilevsky. They had participated not long before in an unsanctioned exhibition on Bolshaia Kommunisticheskaia Street. In the Manezh show these three significantly reinforced the second floor's challenge of the limits of liberalization, by injecting vanguard art into the Soviet mainstream. Yankilevsky's bird's-eye diagram of the second-floor spaces recreates Khrushchev's path as he toured the exhibition with a hostile group of political and cultural bureaucrats (figs. 58, 59). According to Yankilevsky, Khrushchev was particularly outraged by the first room,

probably because it was packed with abstract works by artists of the Beliutin Studio, and because his negative theatricality was then at its peak.[36] In general, Khrushchev's eccentric public behavior was consistent with a penchant for individuality and spontaneity; he was known for not sticking to written speeches, often plunging into more effective free improvisation. Nonetheless, Khrushchev's repetitive use of the word "daubing,"[37] with which he described most of the works on the second floor, was highly derogatory and authorized a view of abstract art as undeserving of civilized debate.

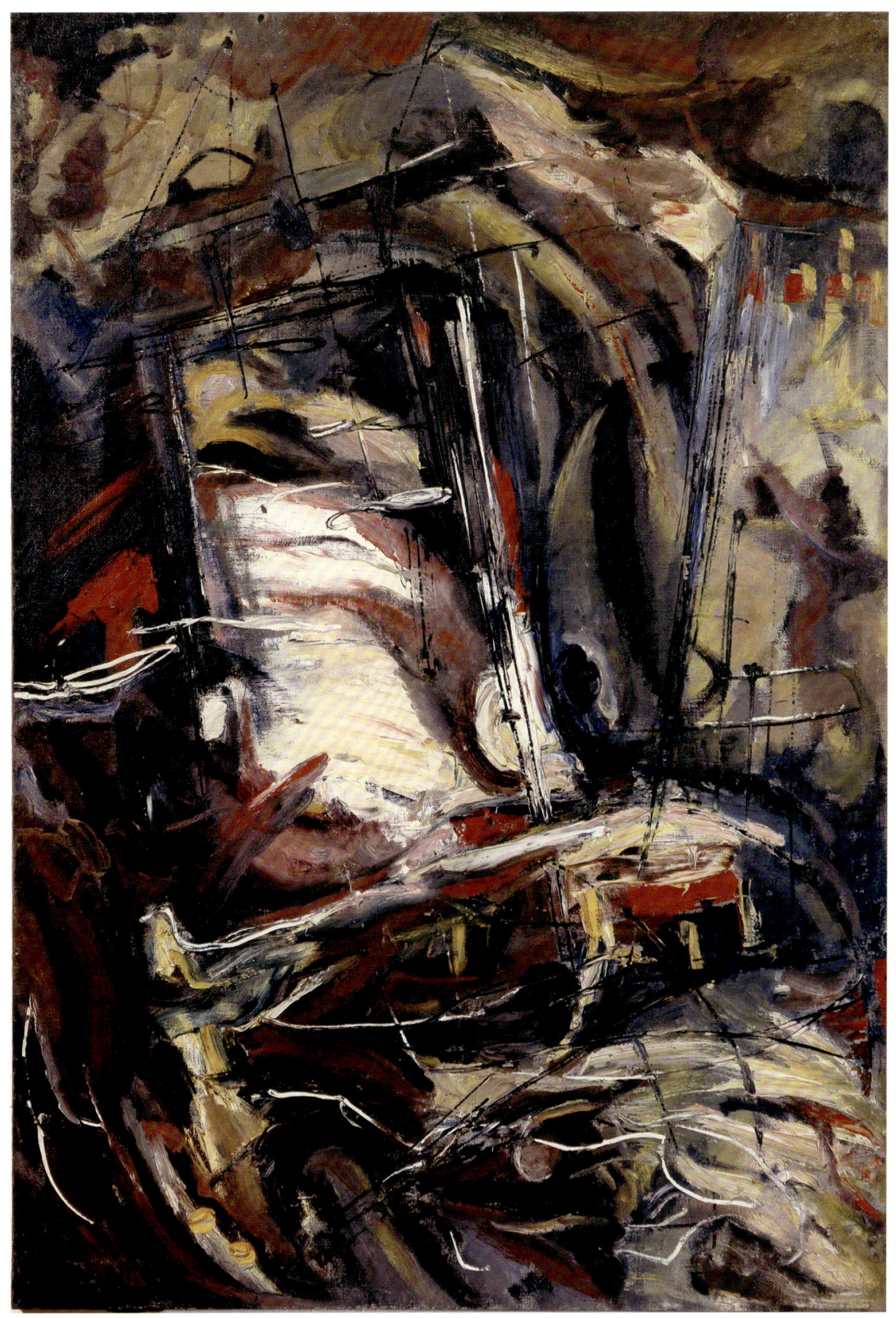

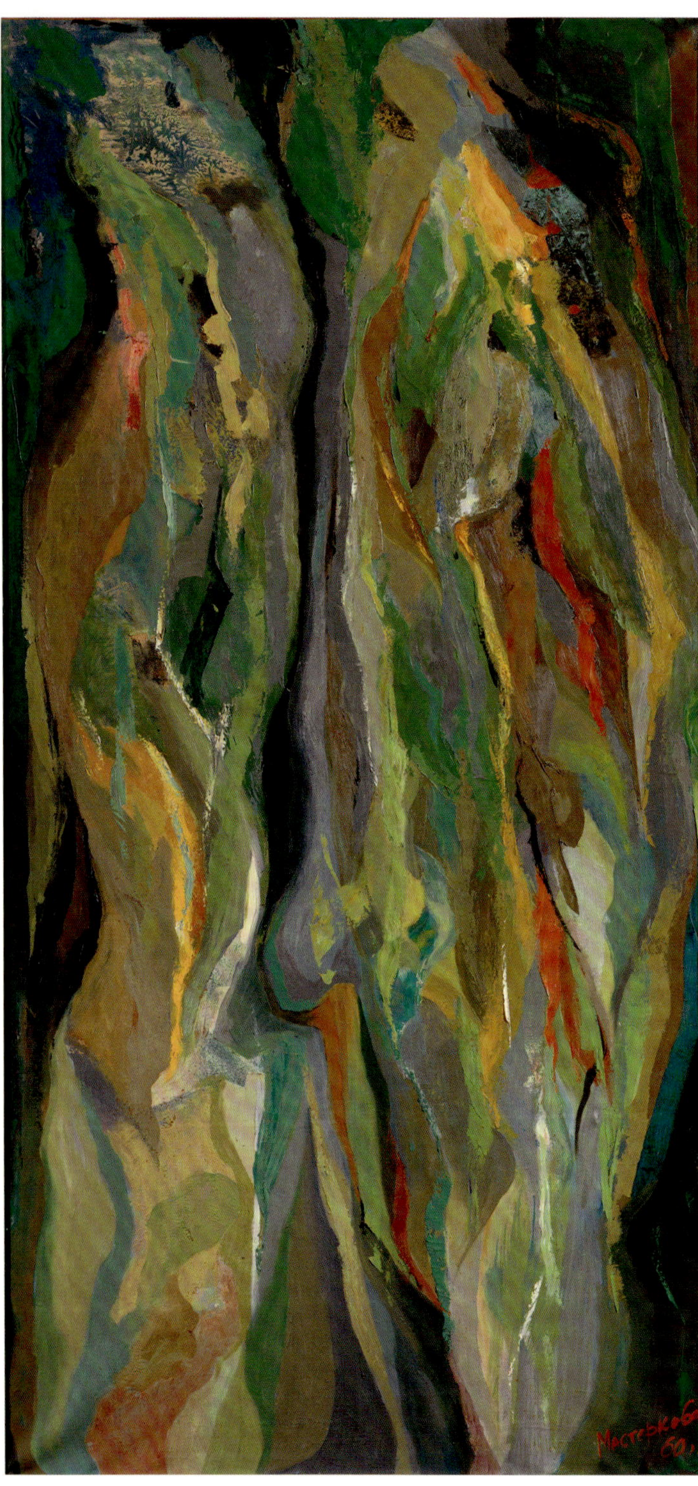

ABOVE 55   Lydia Masterkova, *Composition*, 1960. Collection Tsukanov Family, London.

OPPOSITE PAGE 56   Lydia Masterkova, *Composition*, 1960. Collection Tsukanov Family, London.

Moving up to the second space, Khrushchev encountered the works of Sooster, Sobolev, and Yankilevsky, whose art provided a window onto countercultural trends. Khrushchev's inquiry about the meaning of Sooster's surrealist abstractions was disrupted as the General Secretary was taken off guard by the artist's foreign accent and by "someone whisper[ing] in [Khrushchev's] ear. 'He's Estonian, spent time in a camp, he was freed in '56.'"[38] Across from Sooster's wall hung Yankilevsky's *Penaptych No. 1: Atomic Station*, which immediately impressed viewers with its scale (six meters in length), in bold competition with official academic painting (fig. 60). In *Atomic Station* and *Triptych No. 2: Two Principles*, Yankilevsky, just 24 at the time, showed that lack of space, materials, and transportation did not have to lead to small-scale works. His multi-section pieces also defied the automatic techniques of other Moscow abstractionists as they dealt with specific "themes" (abstract and anthropomorphic), and aimed at a coexistence of order and fantasy. Each section of *Atomic Station* is painted with intense color gradations and consists of elaborate details, ranging from the abstract to what the artist calls "being." As a whole, the painting comes across as a filmstrip in which each still is separately titled in a strange combination (then popular in Moscow) of the old concept of technological progress and a new existential mood. The filmic quality of *Atomic Station* was recognized and admired by the film director Mikhail Romm. His own documentary, *Nine Days in One Year*, released the same year, told the story of young nuclear physicists using factual means,[39] whereas Yankilevsky treated the same subject using abstraction, thus detached from official language. Today, *Atomic Station*'s iconography of disintegration (into particles or fluid essences), along with its title and the last section's subtitle "Presentiment," creates an uncanny reference to the Chernobyl nuclear disaster in 1986 that started off the Soviet Union's demise. The fact that in *Two Principles* Yankilevsky, like Malevich in his painting *Composition with Mona Lisa* (1914), introduces into a nonfigurative work a Renaissance portrait could only anger those who guarded figurative art from the intrusion of abstract "daubing."

Neizvestny, a veteran of the Second World War, was not easily intimidated. He had already announced

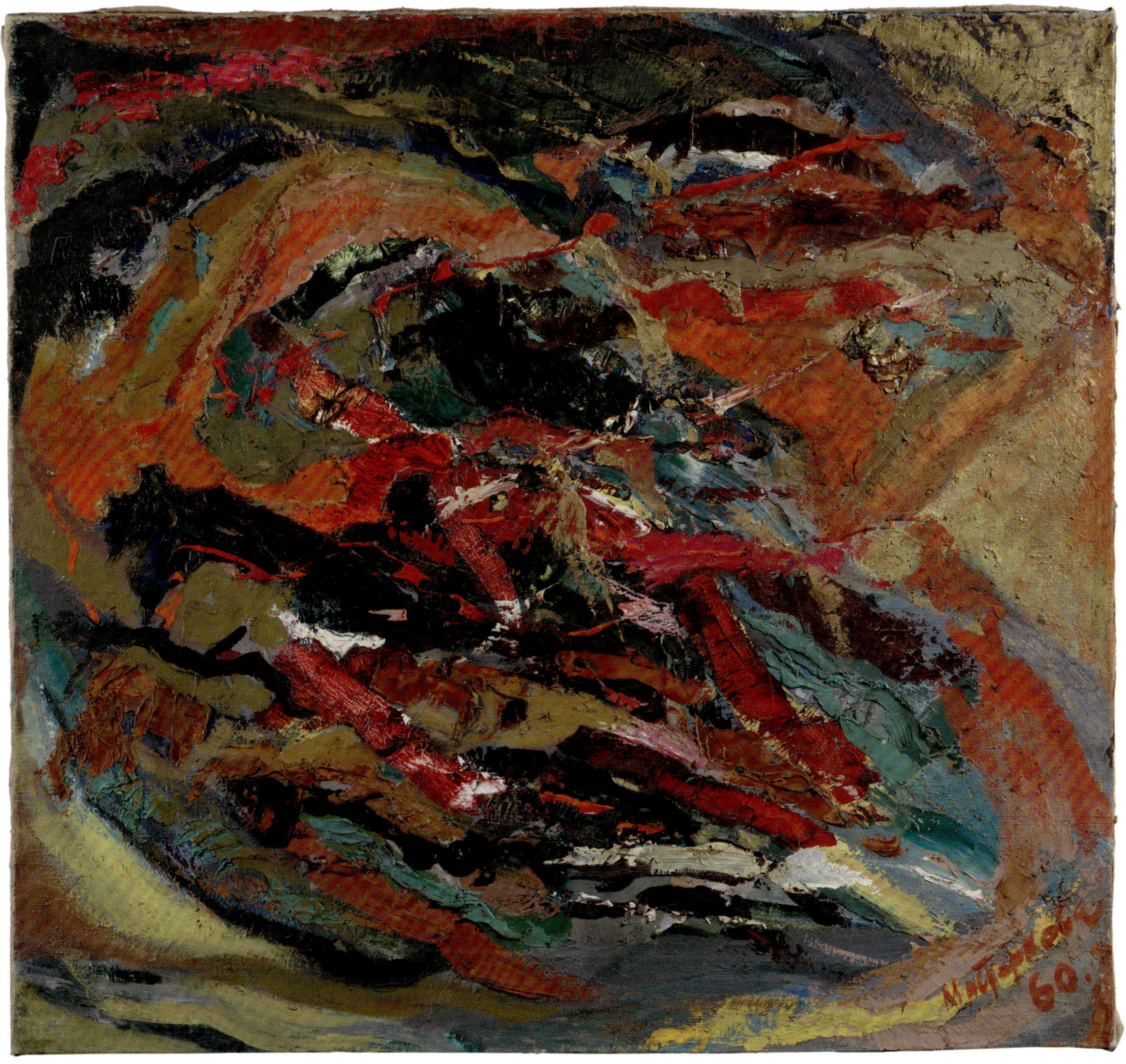

himself in official circles as a modernist sculptor and independent thinker about contemporary art. Writing for the conservative magazine *Iskusstvo* (Art) a few months before the opening of the Manezh Exhibition, he avoided the ingrained clichés of anti-modernist rhetoric and got away with free thinking. His article, "To Invent the New!," was illustrated by his 1962 sculpture of a cosmonaut rendered in futurist broken planes (fig. 61). The text discussed sculptural forms that defied Socialist Realism's preoccupation with mimesis. This, Neizvestny believed, must be replaced by experimentation in the modernist tradition, associated with progress and the search for the "unknown," as in science. Neizvestny also wrote about active

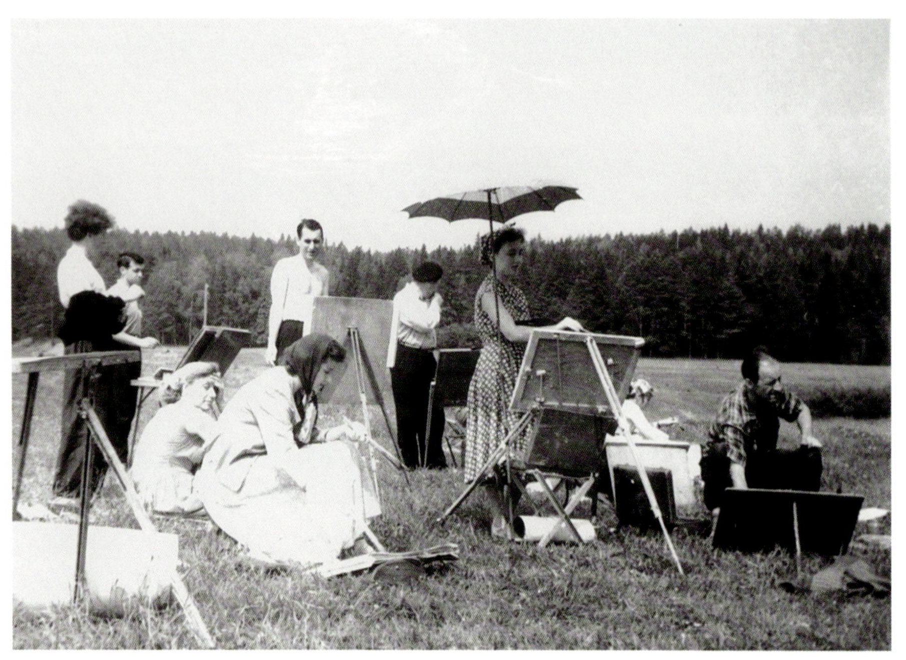

LEFT 57 Artists of the Eli Beliutin Studio painting *en plein air*, Moscow region, June 1957.

BELOW 58 Vladimir Yankilevsky, diagram of the second floor of the Manezh exhibition, 1962.

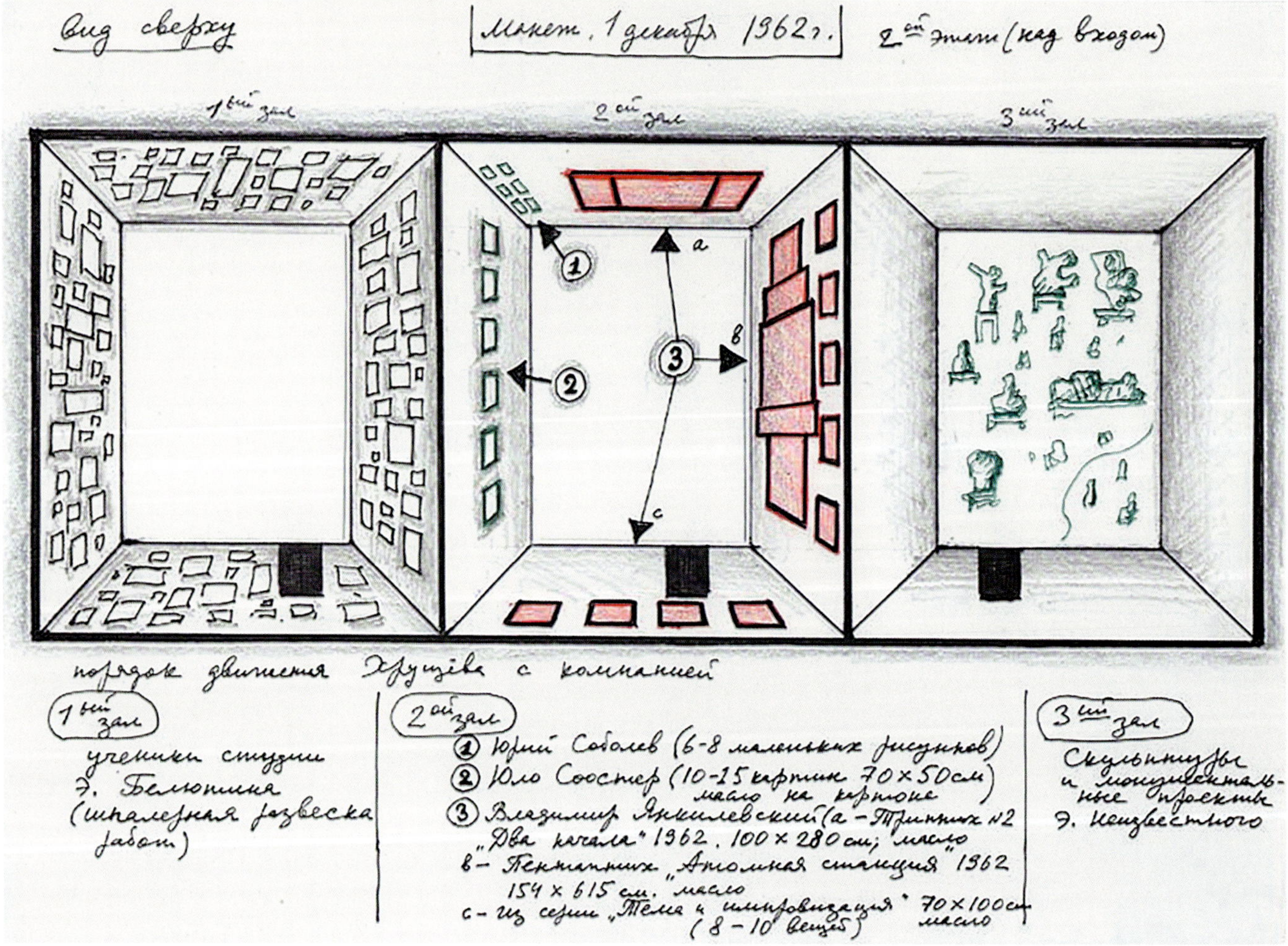

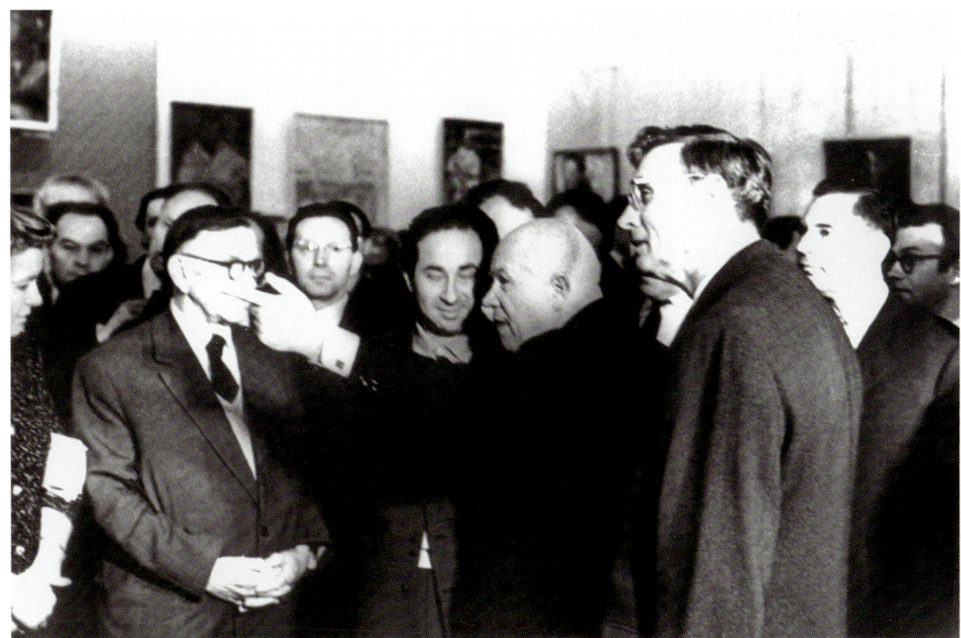

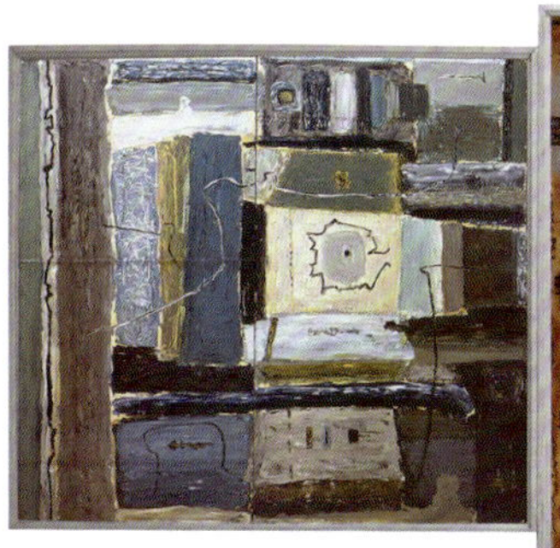
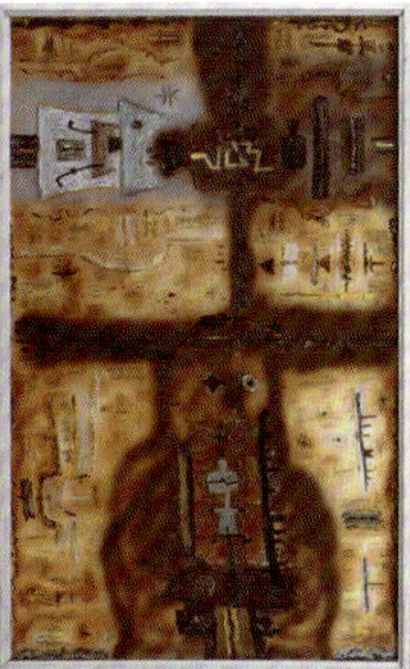
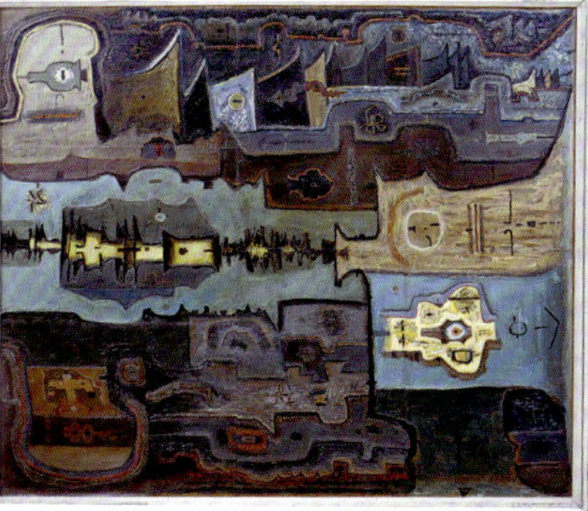
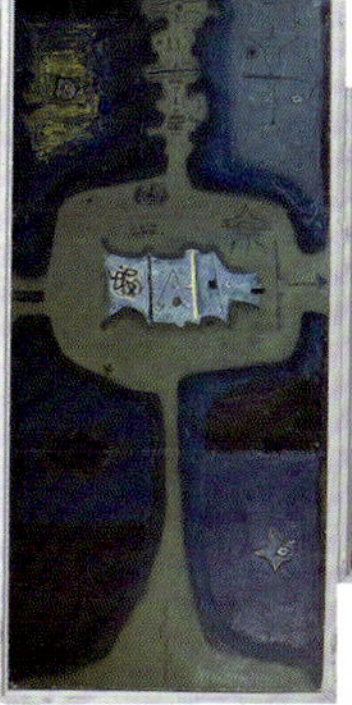
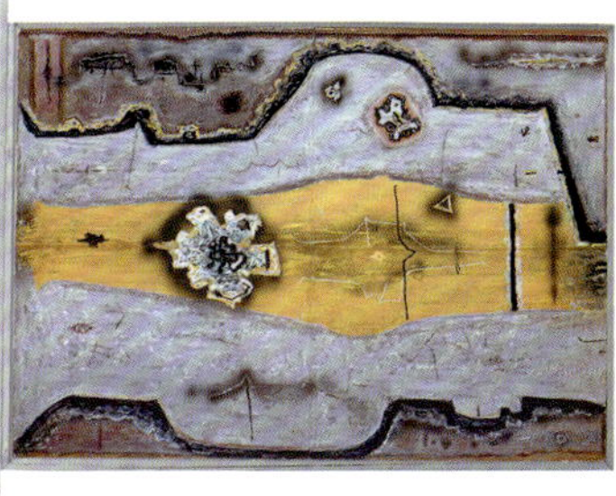

collaboration with architects and a redefinition of monumental art.[40]

By the time Khrushchev reached Neizvestny's space at the Manezh exhibition, which was the last room on the second floor, Neizvestny, unlike his colleagues, had had time to develop a counterattack on the leader. The result was the now infamous dialogue, which Neizvestny shaped by detailing his war heroism and blue-collar jobs such as stonemasonry, and challenging Khrushchev on aesthetic matters.[41] His sculptures also seduced Khrushchev with their overall expression of inhumanity. This is evident in one of Neizvestny's earliest bronzes, *Soldier Being Bayonetted* (fig. 62), an amalgamation of formal distortion and grotesque subject. With this sculpture, executed in the year of the Geneva Summit, which marked an era of optimism and more communication between the Soviet Union and the West, Neizvestny had defied the "smooth rendition of Socialist Realism."[42] It is possible that this bronze was inspired by Jacques Lipchitz's *Mother and Child* (1941–5), even though Lipchitz's sculpture was not exhibited in the Soviet Union until 1959, in the *American National Exhibition*. Neizvestny's work executed in 1959 adheres to a trend in modernist sculpture in which semi-abstract forms are politicized in their expression of human suffering inflicted by repression and the War (fig. 63). After Khrushchev's heated exchange with the sculptor, he was anxious to descend to the first floor. He asked the Communist Party chief propagandist, Leonid Ilichev (accused by

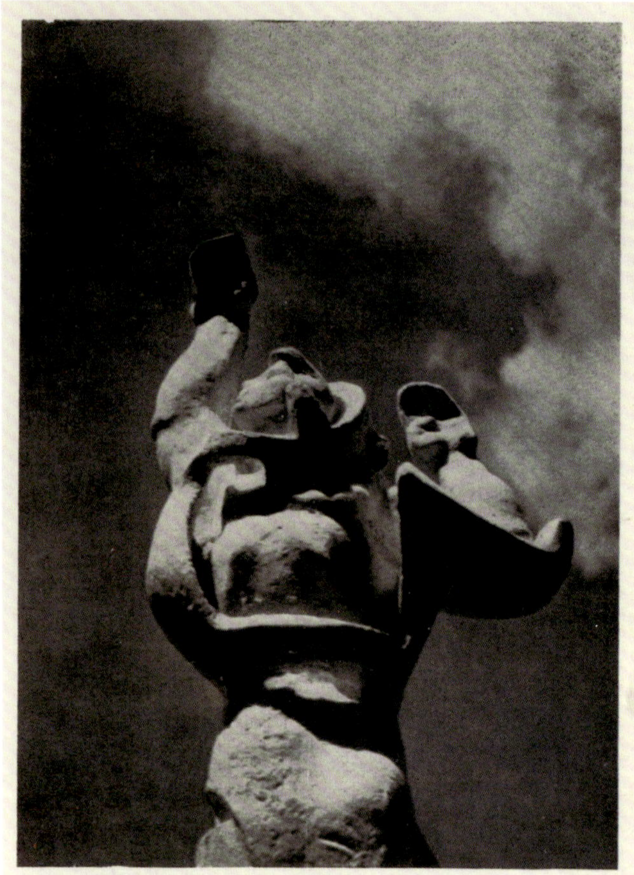

61 Ernst Neizvestny's *Cosmonaut*, illustrating his article in *Iskusstvo* no. 10, 1962.

some of being the main instigator of the spectacle), "Why did you bring me here? Why couldn't you deal with this issue yourself?" "The issue has received international coverage, they [Soviet dissident modernists] are written about in the West, we don't know what to do with them," Ilichev replied.[43]

During Khrushchev's tour of the Manezh show, his escort often yelled out: "Arrest them," pointing to the nonconformist artists, thus applying the same criminal methods of suppression as before. In fact, they acted much as had AKhRR's bosses in the 1930s during their campaign against the avant-garde, relying heavily on the Party and on individual leaders, including Voroshilov and Stalin himself. Khrushchev's visit to the Manezh exhibition was a repeat of the similarly

anomalous involvement of Stalin 30 years earlier, when he looked at the modernist publications that Katsman, Gerasimov, and Brodsky delivered to his dacha. Thus, the ideological divide between realists and modernists that had commenced in 1922 with the foundation of AKhRR was alive and well. Press comment on Falk's *Nude* (1916; State Tretiakov Gallery), also exhibited in the Manezh show, exemplifies this divide. Inspired by Picasso's brazen and distorted nudes, but painted in a postimpressionist style, this work, the press claimed, "annoyed…the majority of exhibition visitors…with its cynical display of ugliness."[44] But why, as the reviewer asks, "would one need to exhibit this painting given that it was painted in 1922, long before the foundation of MOSSKh?"

Probably for some defenders of formalism in painting and in other arts, it was important to underline, by including this painting, that the critique of formalism in painting conducted by the Soviet people in the 1920s and afterward should be seen in our time as irrelevant. All this can only be read as an attempt to "rehabilitate" formalism. And the fact that the organizers of the exhibition submitted to pressure from the adherents of this tendency is a display of liberalism [for the reviewer a negative term], and of the absence of principles.[45]

This passage reveals the determined backwardness of the visual art establishment in post-Stalinist Russia. In such conservative circles, the politics of "liberalism" remained alien, and modernists continued to be called "enemies of the people"; they were denied the rehabilitation that even political prisoners had been granted. And yet, repression and arrest, which had been essential for AKhRR to achieve hegemony in MOSSKh and in the Academy, became the exception in the 1960s, since the Soviet Union had become more open to Western visitors and was regularly covered in the foreign press. What the conservative faction of MOSSKh did manage to achieve after the incident in the Manezh was to keep the cultural infrastructure centralized, and to deny modernists, by publicly denigrating them, access to the many privileges previously available to official artists. Moreover, by exploiting populist sentiment, always

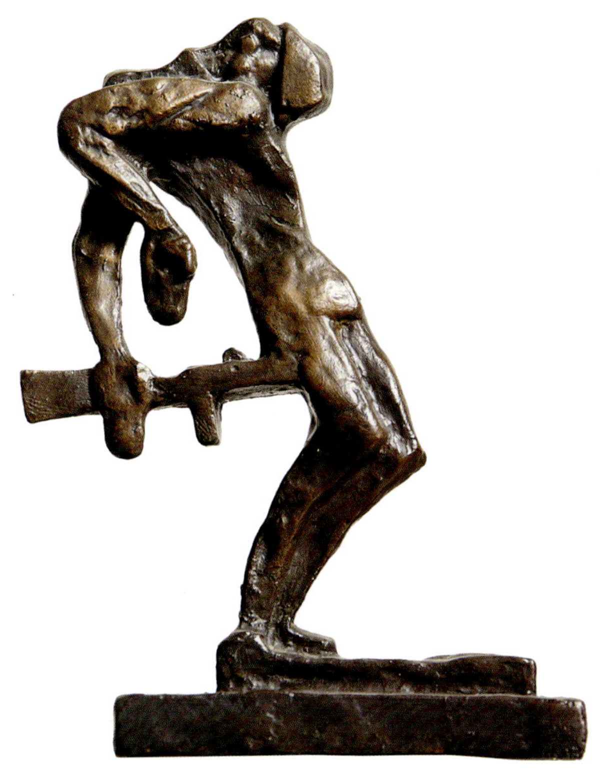

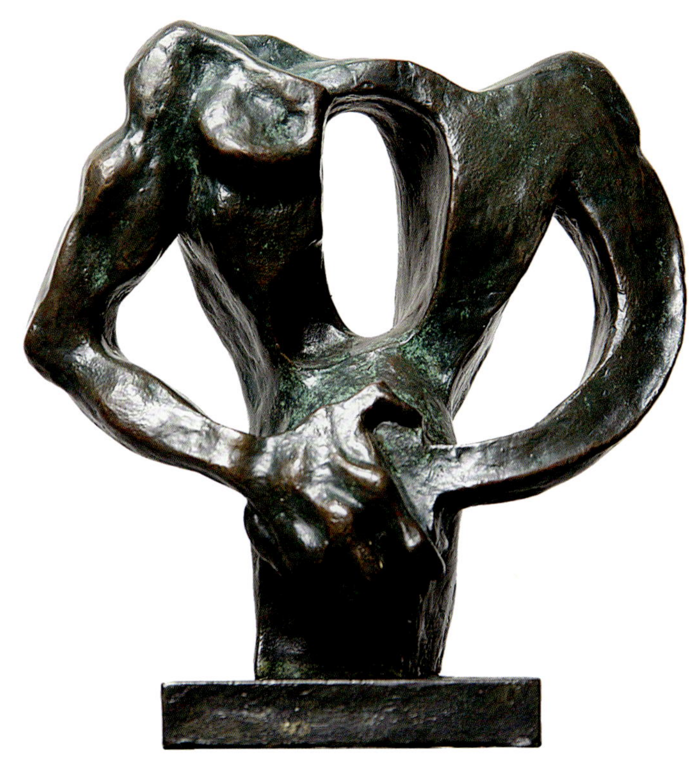

62   Ernst Neizvestny, *Soldier Being Bayonetted*, 1955. Collection of the artist's estate.

63   Ernst Neizvestny, *Untitled*, 1959. Collection of the artist's estate.

close to Khrushchev's heart, the reviews of the Manezh exhibition continued to control the style of official art production. All the official press coverage of the Manezh show was harsh in its criticism and condemnation of abstract artists, while still proclaiming the status of "great art" for Socialist Realism.[46] If those whose taste had been transformed by their exposure to international exhibitions dared publicly to support "practitioners of formalism," finding a "'justification' for abstract art,"[47] they were personally attacked in the press. As Yankilevsky points out, the officials' victory was "'ornamental'" for "it failed to correspond to the dynamics of the liberalization of society."[48] Similarly, "a barrage of abuse in newspapers and magazines" ironically served as an acknowledgment of the modernists' "existence."[49]

Publications against abstractionism of course had to include examples of their targets, thereby providing detailed and valuable information about such art, albeit extremely biased and negative. This was the case with the third edition of A.K. Lebedev's book *Against Abstractionism in Art* (first published in 1959; fig. 64), which came out after the Manezh show with a new introduction supporting the attack on the "so-called abstractionists."[50] What followed, though, was a range of information about Western abstract art, including descriptions of works, prices, discussion of various exhibitions including the Venice Biennales, and even a mention of collectors such as Solomon R. Guggenheim. Illustrated with works by Mark Rothko, Jackson Pollock, Mark Tobey, and Eduardo Chillida, such a thorough survey of international contemporary abstraction was indispensable for those who were able to read between the lines of its anti-modernist rhetoric. The existence of Lebedev's and similar books and articles in major official journals such as *Iskusstvo*[51] dispels the lingering opinion that postwar modernists worked in a total vacuum of information about their Western colleagues. Moreover, in several publications, such as S.E. Mozhniagun's *Abstractionism is the Destruction*

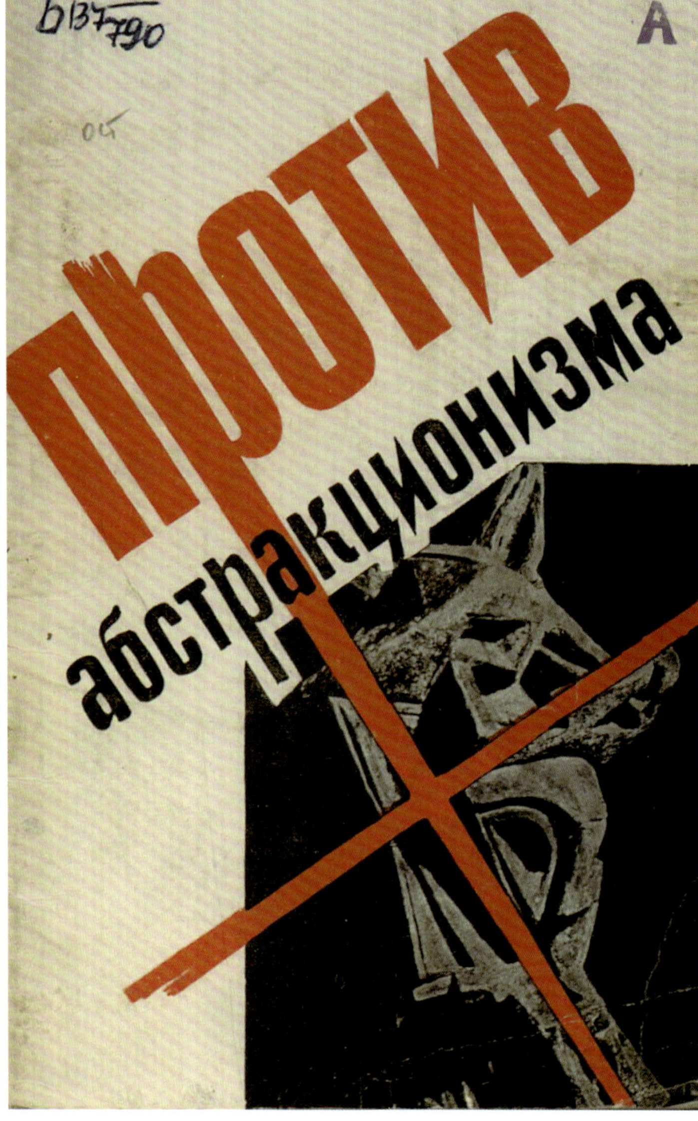

64   Cover of A.K. Lebedev's book, *Against Abstractionism in Art*, 1959.

of Aesthetics (1961),[52] the analysis of abstraction gave a comprehensive history with illustrations of seminal works by artists including Kandinsky, Malevich,[53] Tatlin, and Mondrian, as well as a survey of De Stijl, the Bauhaus, and the postwar movements, Tachism and Abstract Expressionism. Further on, the book outlined the "philosophical foundation of abstractionism," scrutinizing abstractionists' methodology and visual semantics in the context of twentieth-century philosophical notions of subjectivity.

While abstract art was tackled in the press, the State Mayakovsky Museum opened modest exhibitions of works by El Lissitzky in 1960 and Malevich and Tatlin in 1965. These were symbolic events, for they restated a genealogy of local canons of non-representational art. Paradoxically, the official press linked the avant-garde generation and the postwar vanguardists by positioning abstract art and formalism as the main enemies of official doctrine, and by referring in derogatory terms to the nonconformist milieu as "left" artists even though they were steadfastly against any association with Marxism. Moreover, by abusing the term "left," the Soviet establishment was continuing AKhRR's repudiation of the original communist goals.

By the early 1960s, there was already a new generation of geometric abstractionists in Moscow including Lev Nusberg, Francisco Infante, Vladimir Akulinin, and Rimma Zanevskaia. Together they formed the Movement collective in around 1963, detached themselves from what Malevich in the 1930s called "nonobjective painterly values," and pursued a universal language of geometry and flat surfaces associated with Suprematism and Mondrian. From the outset of his career early in the 1960s, Nusberg acknowledged the schism between the practitioners of expressionist and geometric abstraction, as seen in an early graphic work entitled *Collision* (1961). On the picture plane, he separated curvilinear and straight lines, demonstrating his understanding that the two types of lines lead to different forms and, ultimately, to different content. The rest of his 1961 works confirm Nusberg's ardent commitment to visually austere grids and lines, as well as to conceptualizing abstract painting, evident from such titles as *Beginning of Counting*, *A System of Two Structures*, *Penetrating Like an Idea*, and *A Moment of Structure*. These are rendered with commercial paint on nonflexible Masonite supports, which deprives them of traditional aesthetic properties and turns them into what Gustav Klutsis in 1919 had called "picture-object." The mathematical precision of their minimal compositions, most effectively demonstrated in *Beginning of Counting*, with its gridded and ruled picture surface and overall flatness, achieves his program of controlled creativity (fig. 65). With this series, Nusberg endorsed the conceptual operation of painting rather than the narrative practices of Socialist

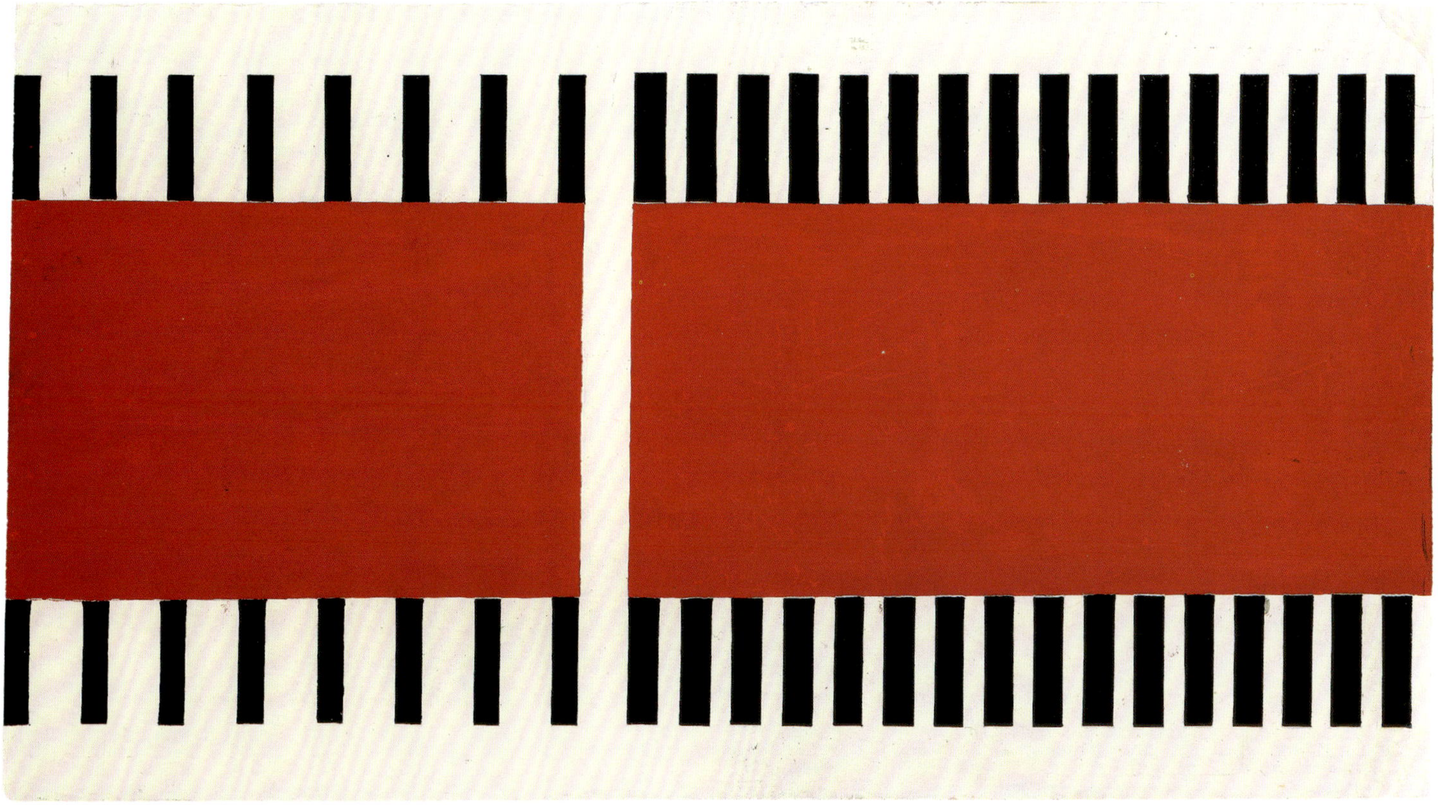

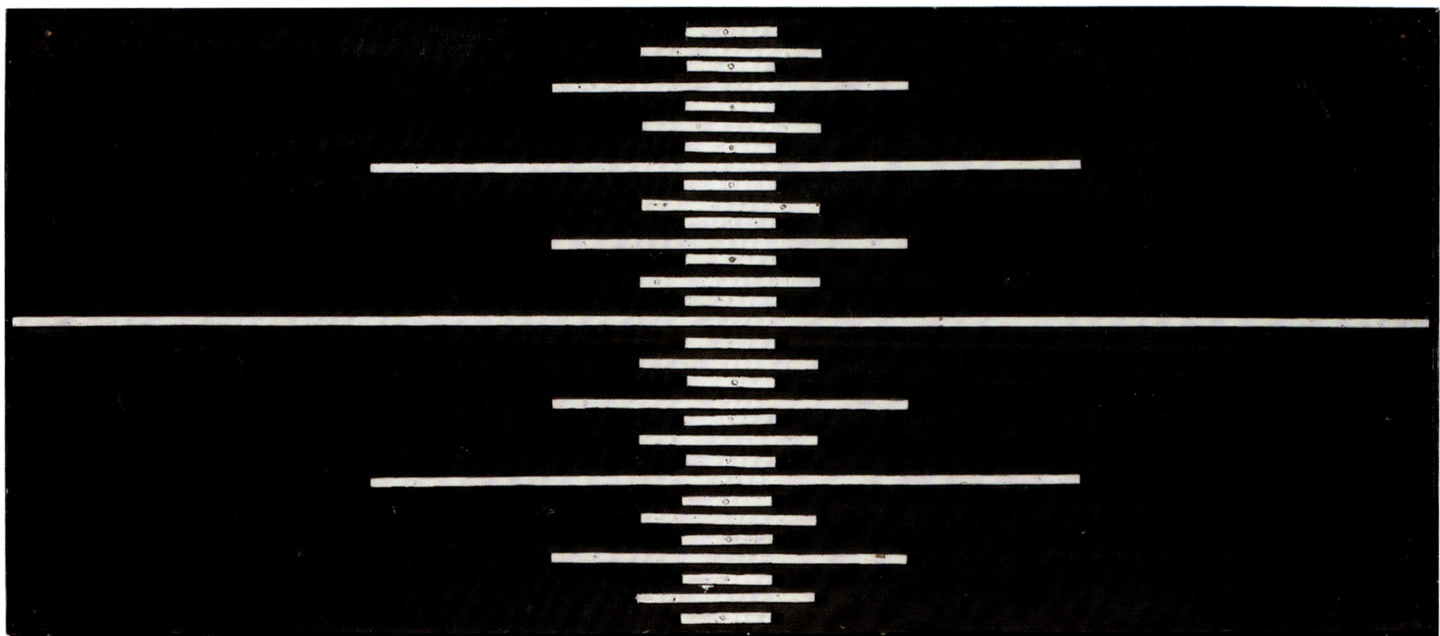

65   Lev Nusberg, *Beginning of Counting*, 1961. State Tretiakov Gallery, Moscow.

66   Francisco Infante, *Birth of a Vertical*, 1962. State Tretiakov Gallery, Moscow.

Realism or the unrestrained subjectivity of Abstract Expressionism.

Nusberg's pictorial reductionism and rejection of expressive color is equally observable in Infante's *Birth of a Vertical* (1962), rendered in black and white – Kandinsky's "silent colors"[54] – to match a schema of "silent" horizontal lines (fig. 66). These are made out of wooden slats cut into different sizes, painted in white, and assembled along a vertical axis on a horizontal Masonite support covered in black. Here Infante makes the leap from composition to construction based on a "system of lines," defined in 1921 by a Constructivist architect, Nikolai Ladovsky, as "a combination of material elements organized according to a specific plan for the attainment of force effects… without superfluous materials and elements."[55] Like any construction, *Birth of a Vertical* was conceptualized through a process of multiple drawings, notes, and mathematical calculations, finally settling on the shape of a cross. Again, Constructivists had identified the cross as "the fundamentally irreducible articulation of the minimum requirement for the existence of any structure."[56] The cross also presents an opportunity, as in the case of Frank Stella and Carl Andre, to explore the correlation between flat surface and actual space, for, as Krauss pointed out, "the Cross itself relates to the most primitive sign of an object in space."[57]

Put in Kandinsky's terms, Infante's "painterly relief" epitomized "a desire, at one moment, to abandon PP [the picture plane]; at another to assert it."[58] Later, Infante abandoned the picture plane to produce *Space–Movement–Infinity* (1963–5), a mobile double-cube structure, webbed with nylon threads and fitted with a light (fig. 67). Viacheslav Koleichuk, who became a member of Movement in 1966, has described Infante's spatial construction in movement: "it created the impression of an object that overcomes gravity and freely moves in space. The impossibility of catching all of the detailed transformations, taking place in each part of the total composition, turned it into a new, single object woven by movement and form."[59] It is exactly this ability to convey the power and effects of movement that positioned *Space–Movement–Infinity* as the exemplar of the group's manifesto, written in 1965 by Nusberg: "What we are doing can roughly be called Kinetic art, but it is necessary to add that it is also

synthetic. The most important thing for us is Movement! Movement I understand as change – the move – interpenetration – development – struggle – state of mind, etc."[60] Here the idea of movement functions both as a formal property and as a metaphor against isolation and art for art's sake practices. It also stands for socially engaged art.

Nusberg's text, written at the beginning of the Brezhnev era (Leonid Brezhnev became General Secretary in 1964), called for artists to resist stagnation. Shortly after Khrushchev's removal in 1964, the group demonstrated its commitment to development and struggle by organizing an exhibition, *Towards the Synthesis of the Arts*, in Moscow. For this event the Movement's artists joined with architects to make the shift from visual art to industrial design and technological innovation, thus lessening the show's threat to official artists. The result was a display of interdisciplinary production as nurtured by Naum Gabo, László Moholy-Nagy, and Malevich, and based on a commitment to examining modernist painting and sculpture and other related theories in order to revolutionize three-dimensional art. As happened with the avant-garde groups, although many of the Movement's architectural and environmental projects remained on paper, they are valuable testaments to the artists' unrestrained utopian visions.

Like the avant-garde artists in the 1920s, the Movement was eager to erect monumental abstract works in Moscow. Of course, public projects were under state control, and guarded by MOSSKh's administrators, for monumental art generated the highest and easiest income, since it consisted primarily of the repetitive production of statues of Lenin and other propagandistic sculptures. Movement's opportunity to enter this competitive field came from their exhibition in 1965 at the prestigious Moscow House of Architects, which included an ambitious project of urban transformation dubbed by the official press, "Square of the Nine Muses" (fig. 68).[61] In Koleichuk's estimation, this was:

the first attempt to give concrete urban meaning to the group's experiments. Standing and floating constructivist compositions, illuminated or radiating light on their own, were positioned on a huge

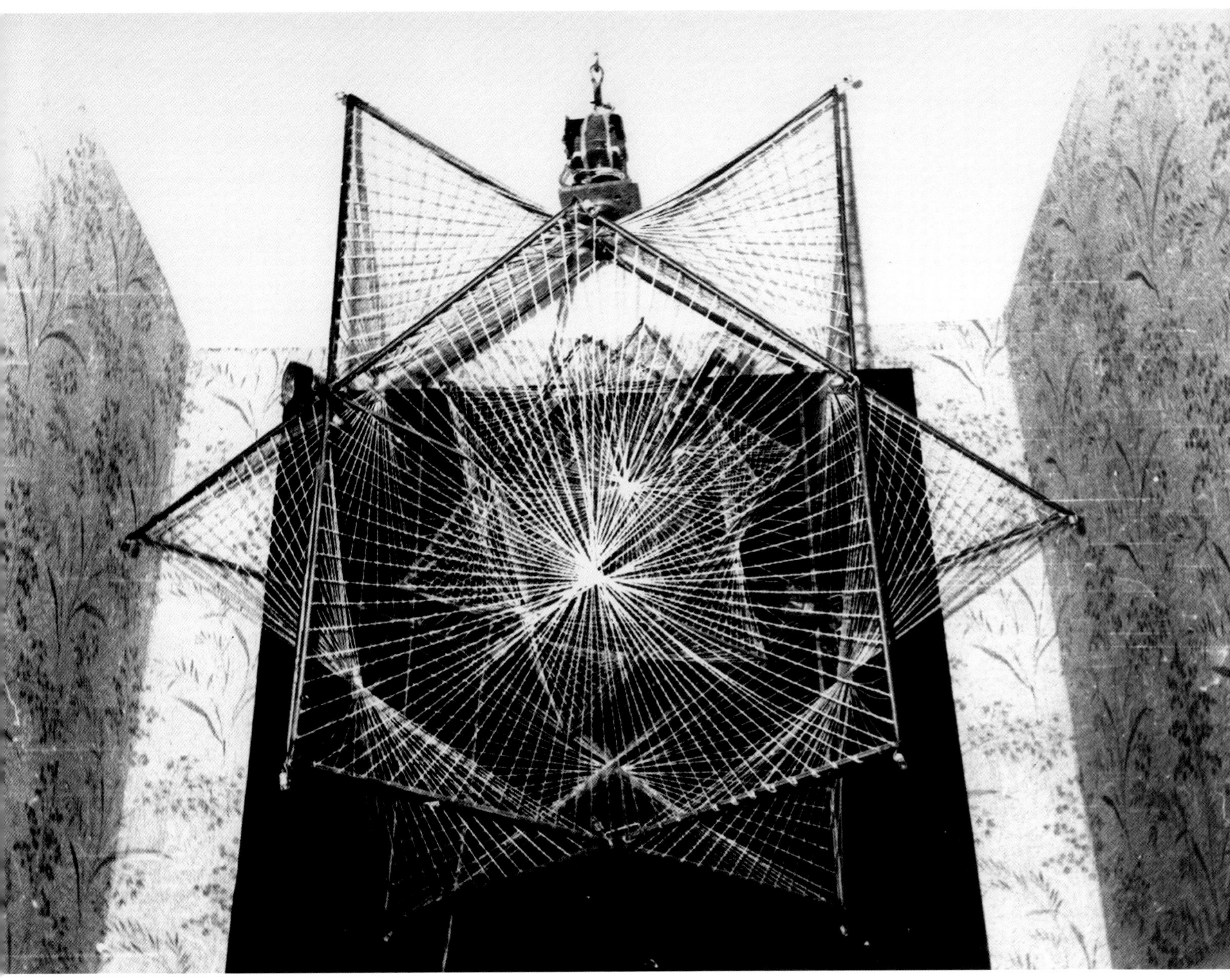

67   Francisco Infante, *Space–Movement–Infinity*, 1963–5. Centre Georges Pompidou, Paris.

square segmented into pedestrian paths. The absence of people and the grand size of some compositions, as well as of the square, subtly alluded to the projects of the Soviet architect I[van] Leonidov, and also responded to the concepts of our 1960s urban development, with its practice of creating vast city districts, esplanades, and city centers with large-scale separate edifices infrequently "floating" in them.[62]

The exhibition was followed by Movement's manifesto, which was signed by all of the members. Nusberg's text promoted collective and interdisciplinary creativity, supported the union of art and technology, and took into consideration the psycho-physiology of human perception. Like Ladovsky in the early 1920s, Nusberg sought to keep his colleagues and students in a state of creative tension in order to test

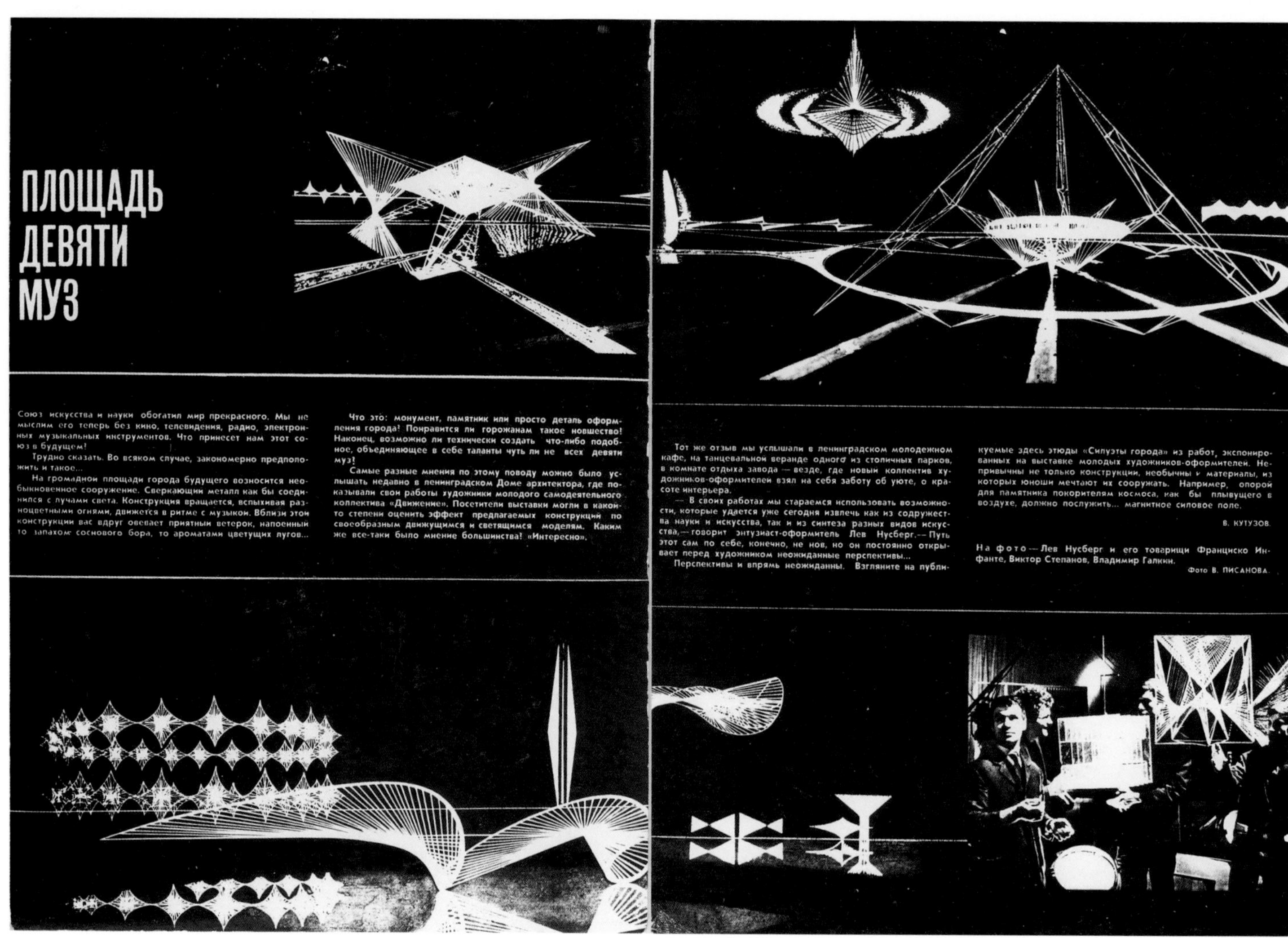

68   Double page from *Soviet Union* no. 12, 1965, with works by the Movement group.

the limits of abstraction. Apparently, the official head artist of Leningrad was so impressed by Movement's theory and practice that in 1967 he entrusted it with the ideological task of decorating the city for the commemoration of the fiftieth anniversary of the October Revolution. This gave Movement an unprecedented and unique opportunity (for vanguard artists) to realize some of their projects in public spaces, and after many decades to bring abstract "art into life." Working in various parts of Leningrad, the collective created site-specific installations that included light and cinematographic projections, along with large-scale mobiles and stabiles. One of these stabiles had an affinity to Buckminster Fuller's geodesic dome, which

Nusberg had no doubt seen at the *American National Exhibition* in 1957 (figs. 69, 70).

In 1967, Movement also participated in an exhibition, *Creativity of Scientific and Technological Youth*, that took place on the premises of the Permanent Exhibition of the Achievements of the People's Economy (VDNKh, formerly VSKhV) in Moscow. This was a site inaugurated in 1939 in celebration of Soviet economic achievements of the two Five-Year Plans and, ultimately, Stalin's empire of ideological signs. Close to one of the VDNKh's neoclassical pavilions, Infante installed his large-scale lattice construction equipped with lights, titled *Galaxy* in a scientific spirit (fig. 71). Although its lifespan was brief, many visitors were

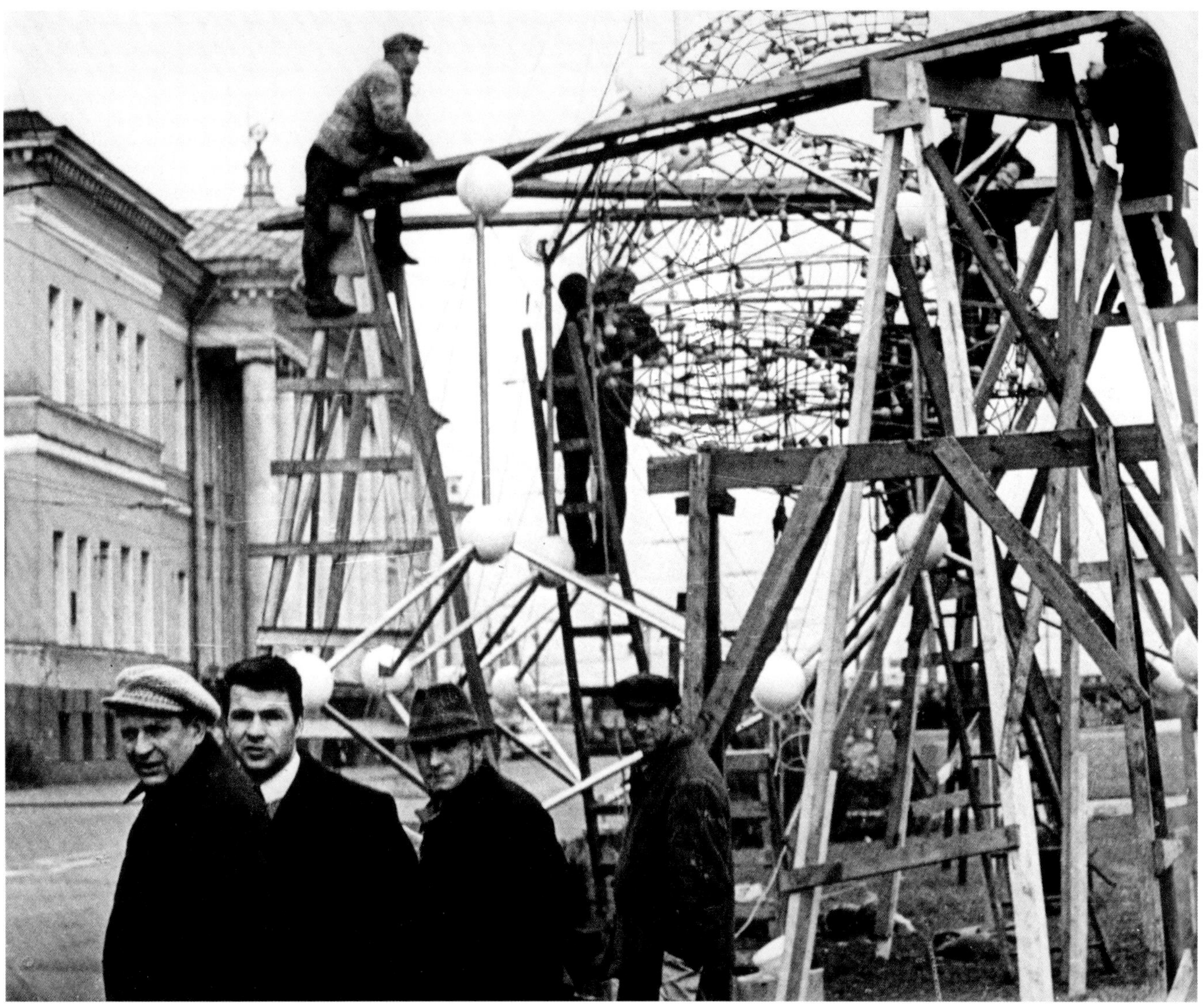

69   Members of the Movement group installing a sculpture dedicated to the fiftieth anniversary of the October Revolution, Leningrad, 1967.

given the chance to enter it, to become participatory viewers observing the arrested development of the Soviet cityscape through the grid-like and transitory *Galaxy*.

Although Movement's public activities were more favorably received than those of their colleagues in the Manezh exhibition, they did not result in permanent support for this vanguard movement by state institutions or in the creation of "a normal art world."[63] In fact, as I suggested earlier, opportunities to organize and construct various exhibitions and monumental projects came about primarily because the collective acted under the umbrella of technological progress, including space exploration, so revered in the 1960s. This association guaranteed a lack of interest from the conservative forces of MOSSKh and the Academy, who were not aware that the gap between art and technology had long been collapsed. What made them finally realize that Movement was just as threatening to their monolithic power as the artists who had exhibited on the second floor of the Manezh show, was the growing success of the collective in the West.

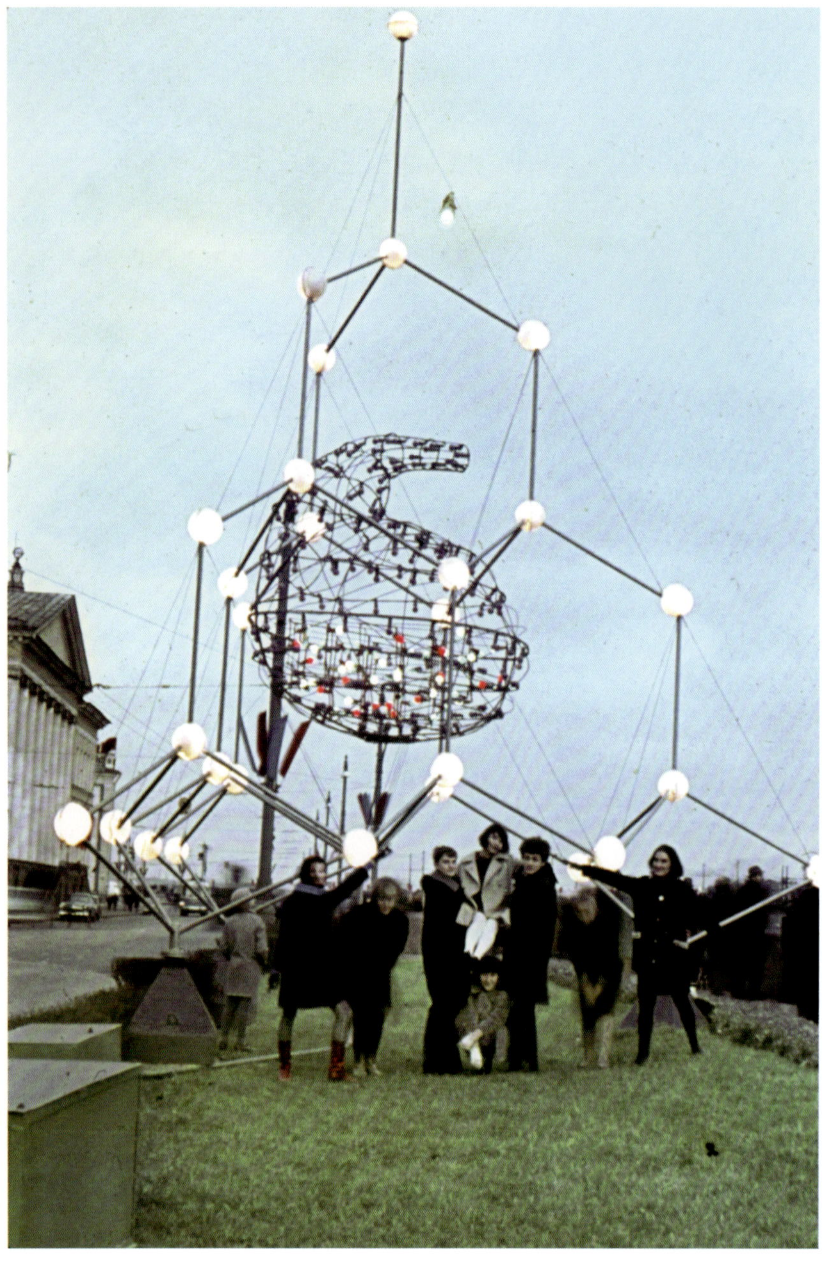

70   Members of the Movement group standing before their sculpture dedicated
to the fiftieth anniversary of the October Revolution, Leningrad, 1967.

Movement participated in the international one-day exhibition *Luminism*, on May 25, 1967 at the Artists Club in New York by Willoughby Sharp, the artist-editor of the avant-garde magazine *Avalanche*. With this and similar exhibitions, he helped to position Kinetic art as the new international model of abstraction.

If Movement aimed at reinstating abstract art in public places, Mikhail Chernyshov, Mikhail Roginsky, and Kabakov signaled the conceptual potential of common objects that embodied the failure of Constructivism's utilitarian utopia. Viewed as an accomplice to official ideology, this was forbidden material for an artist with transcendental values. But for these

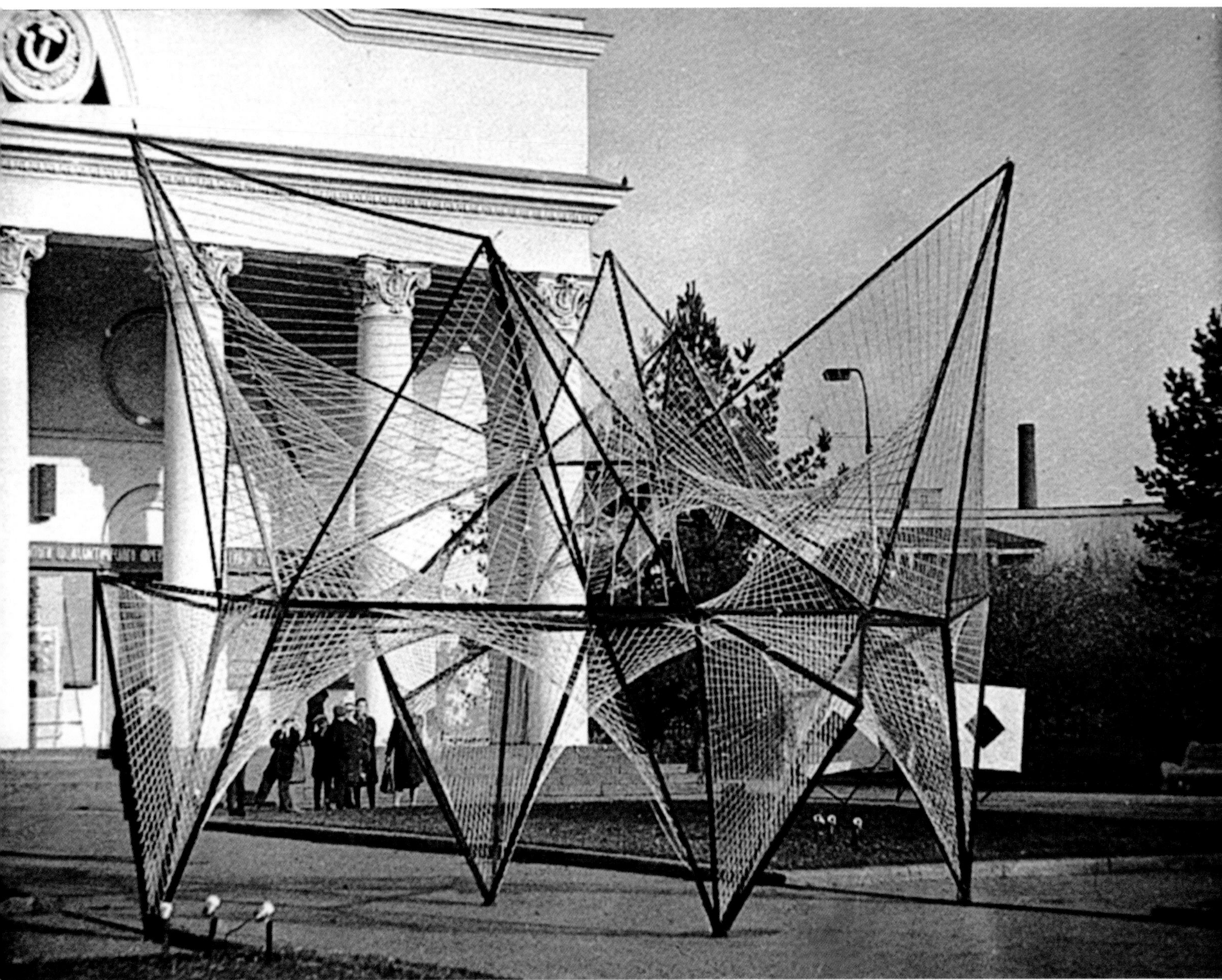

71   Francisco Infante, *Galaxy*, 1967, installation view in VDNKh, Moscow, 1967.

three artists such damaged objects laid the ground for abstraction built upon their simulation and appropriation. These artists thus left behind the idea of abstraction as a universal language without subject matter, and replaced what Lee Krasner called "the unframed space"[64] of an abstract expressionist work with the framed space composed out of an object's physical destruction or fragmentation.

Like Slepian, Chernyshov dispelled the reputation of Moscow underground artists as provincial and uninformed. Referring to Chernyshov only as "the young pop artist" (imparting the same clandestine sense of anonymity as Cordier had with Slepian), this is how Paul Sjeklocha and Igor Mead (Americans who went to Moscow in 1963 in conjunction with an exhibition, *American Graphic Art*, and later co-wrote a book on postwar nonconformist art) described him:

> As we began to discuss art, we were amazed at the scope of the young man's knowledge. The last person we expected to encounter in Moscow was an eighteen-year-old who knew more about the New York artistic scene of the moment than either of us…Our young friend was not only well aware of the numerous subtleties of abstract expressionism, but knew fully as much about pop and op art. He spoke of Anuszkiewicz, Oldenburg, Lichtenstein, Johns, Indiana, Rauschenberg, and many others, as if he knew them personally.[65]

Chernyshov was fourteen years old when he went to Sakolniki Park to see the *American National Exhibition* and, like many people of his age, he was as fascinated by American cars, electronics, clothing, and hairstyles as he was by Pollock and De Kooning. By then he had seen reproductions of Kandinsky's work during regular visits to the State Library for Foreign Literature in Moscow (a source of information for other artists as well) and he hung one such reproduction next to his desk at home, alongside a portrait of Pollock and Krasner. In these surroundings, Chernyshov, only a few months after he had seen contemporary American painting, acted like an abstract expressionist:

> In November I thought about Abstract Expressionism again. Once, when my parents left for a whole day, I put down several plastic sheets on the floor for protection, dissolved some watercolors, and opened a couple of bottles of ink. I was familiar with Pollock's method of working from the photos I saw at the exhibition. I used school paper, gluing two or three sheets together. Then, I glued some cut-outs from an American magazine for the background…and I dipped a house painter's brush into the plate with the watercolors, which covered the paper very well and avoided the glossy letters…I began then to pour ink, got carried away, and ruined almost everything, for I was constrained by the fear that I would damage the walls in the room. My parents would never forgive me for this. So, I dried one piece and hung it over my bed. The rest had to be thrown away.[66]

Abstract Expressionism, rather than the street, provided Chernyshov with a field for teenage mischief. Not having a perspicacious father like Picasso's, he received no encouragement from his parents to enter an art institution and remained self-taught. Remarkably, by 1962, Chernyshov had created enough original work to have a show in the apartment of Roginsky's brother. The inspiration came from Malevich and Tatlin in whose works Chernyshov saw an alternative to what he called the "'carpet' compositions"[67] of the artists of the School of Paris, who became popular in Moscow after their exhibition in the summer of 1961. But, in addition to turning to "experimenting with pure geometric forms,"[68] as was the Movement group, Malevich taught Chernyshov how his art could become brutal, awkward, not attractive. The way to achieve this was to look outward, around, rather than inside, finding and using material that would correspond to "anti-form" and the concept of the *enfant terrible*, not as regards the official art establishment but to the canonical vanguard. Accordingly, Chernyshov called his apartment show *Red Truck*, provoking an enraged reaction from abstract expressionists, who were trying to avoid subjects from everyday life at all costs. He exhibited a series of symmetrical collages using simple, artificial colors. "These works were not supposed to make a positive effect," he explained. Instead, "they provoked the viewer with their pretension to easelism."[69] The symmetry and monotony was demonstrated not only in hand-made collages but also in readymades such as framed pieces of Soviet wallpaper with geometric designs (figs. 72, 73); these took any question of mastery out of his work and made a piece of patterned wallpaper the subject matter of this type of abstraction.

Twelve years senior to Chernyshov, Roginsky belonged to the first generation of postwar vanguard artists fortunate enough to avoid a Socialist Realist art education, and after the war, studied with surviving modernists in the Moscow Art Institute, along with Masterkova. Unlike her fascination with abstract art, Roginsky, while visiting the *American National Exhibition*, admired such realists as Edward Hopper, Raphael Soyer, and Ben Shahn. Roginsky felt he had been given permission (essential after figuration had been contaminated by Socialist Realists) by the American artists to express his discontent in ways other

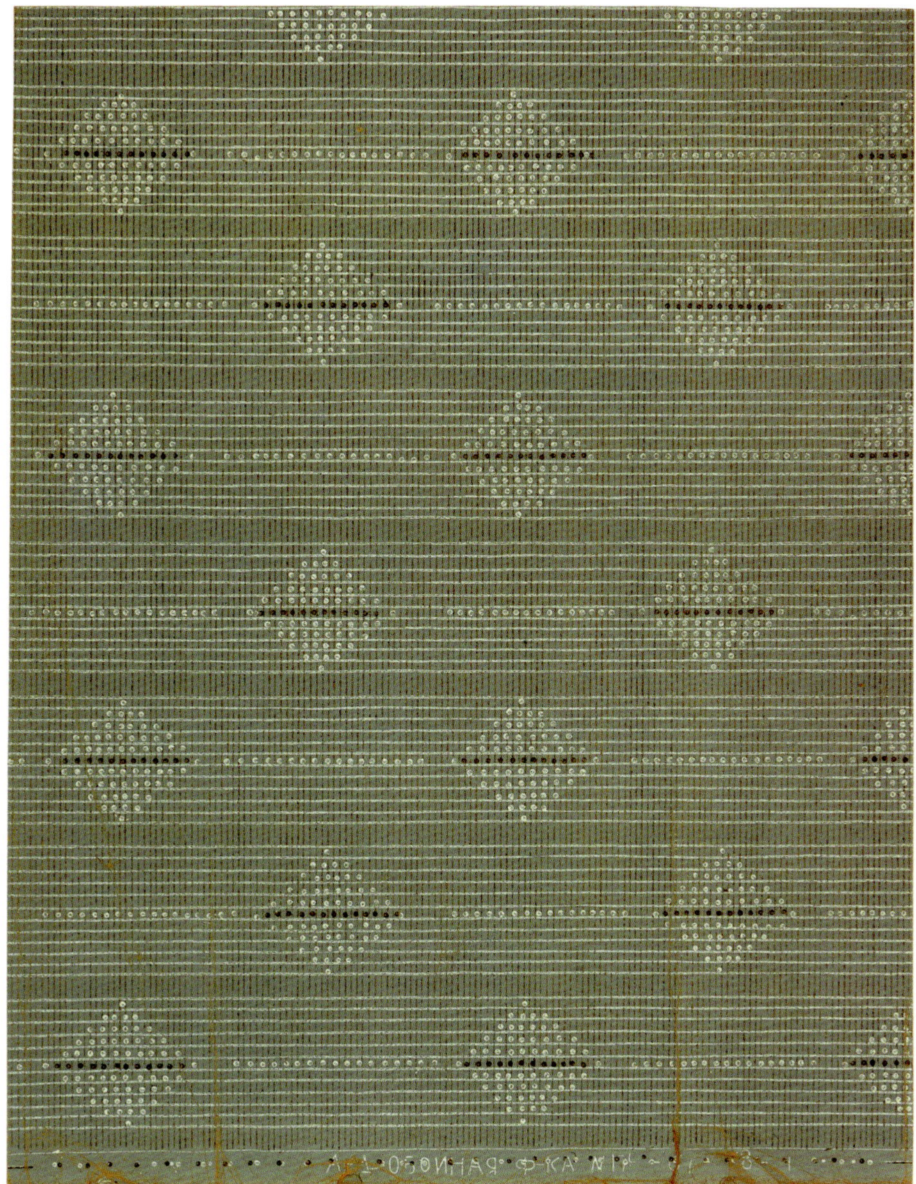

72   Mikhail Chernyshov, *Untitled*, 1960–1. Norton and Nancy Dodge Collection of Nonconformist Art from the Soviet Union, Jane Voorhees Zimmerli Art Museum Rutgers, State University of New Jersey.

than modernist abstract styles. As an alternative he began to generate geometric forms from external phenomena, as with Constructivism, by appropriating or imitating readymades that had a predisposition to abstractness. These were flat surfaces such as painted doors and walls, and objects arranged in grids, such as tiles (fig. 74). Additionally, he assembled common objects such as an electric socket on a monochrome surface, upgrading utilitarian things to the status of ideal forms (fig. 75). In 1965, Roginsky and Chernyshov's interest in reducing the layers of ideology packed into Soviet objects was manifested in a joint exhibition held in the Club of Youth. Although the show lasted less than two days, it was attended by at least 300 people, which in the 1960s was an impressive audience for vanguard art anywhere.

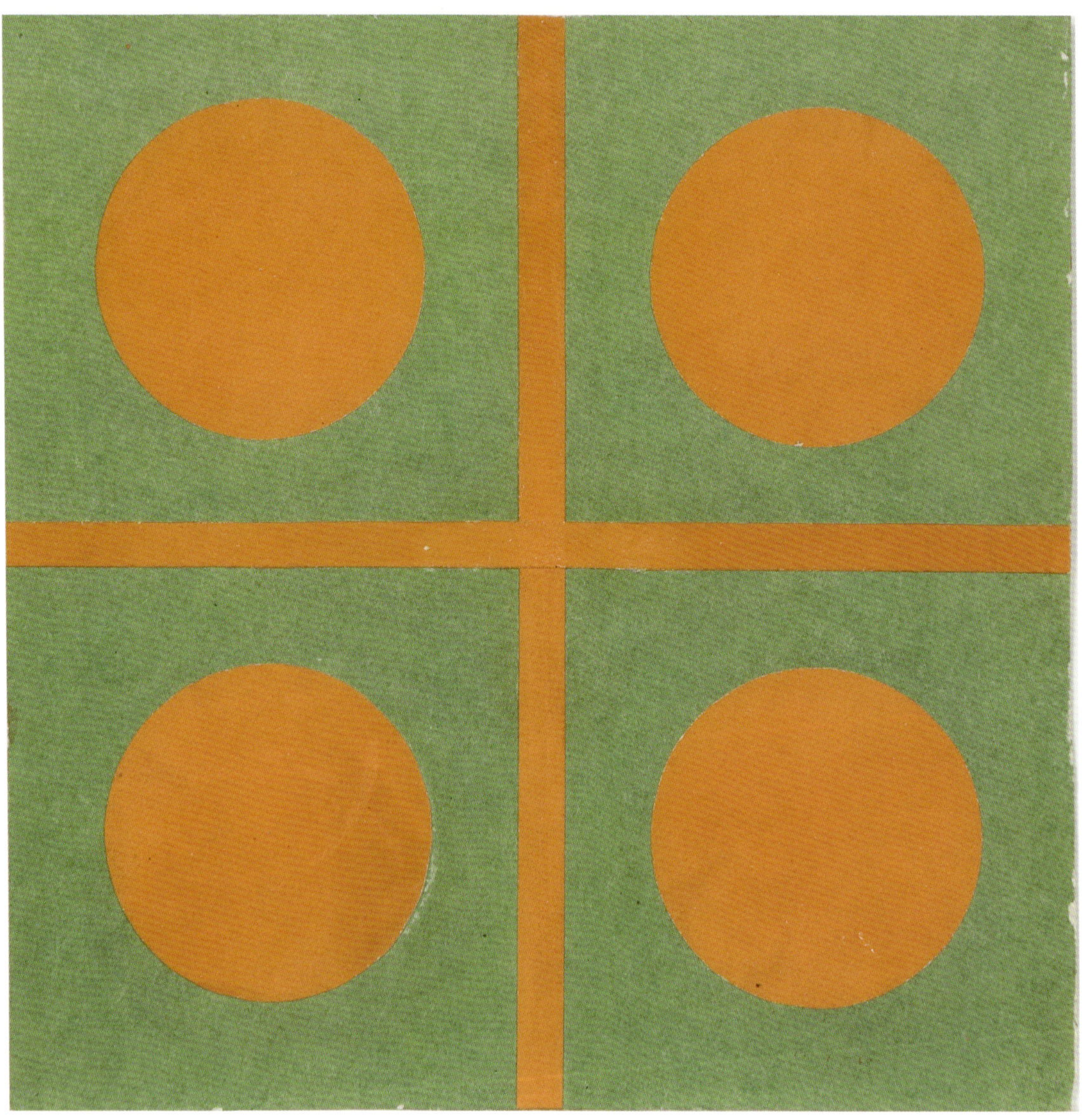

73   Mikhail Chernyshov, *Untitled*, 1962. Norton and Nancy Dodge Collection of Nonconformist Art from the Soviet Union, Jane Voorhees Zimmerli Art Museum Rutgers, State University of New Jersey.

In "Before 1961," the first chapter of Kabakov's memoirs, the artist notes that during that period "the profession of 'artist' was 'for them [officialdom],' and for their approval I produced 'an artistic work.'" The first thing that he "'encountered' inside himself" involved automatic drawing, "an unconscious impulse to move, wave a pencil and pen on a small page of paper when, thanks to unintended and unconnected gestures, there appeared internally, from the psyche, some impulses, which somehow connected with these scribbles."[70] Kabakov continues:

After the execution of 5–6 drawings like this, there was some release of powerful energy coming from deep inside me. To predict the result of these movements of a pen, of these "wavings," was impossible, it appeared on its own, but in its own configuration, and a composition, "a memory," and experience of this energy coming from deep inside me, was preserved…for me…I did these after I came home from the institute, and as a style it was called abstract expressionism…there were 600–700 drawings like this…These "executions" were "organic," "unpred-

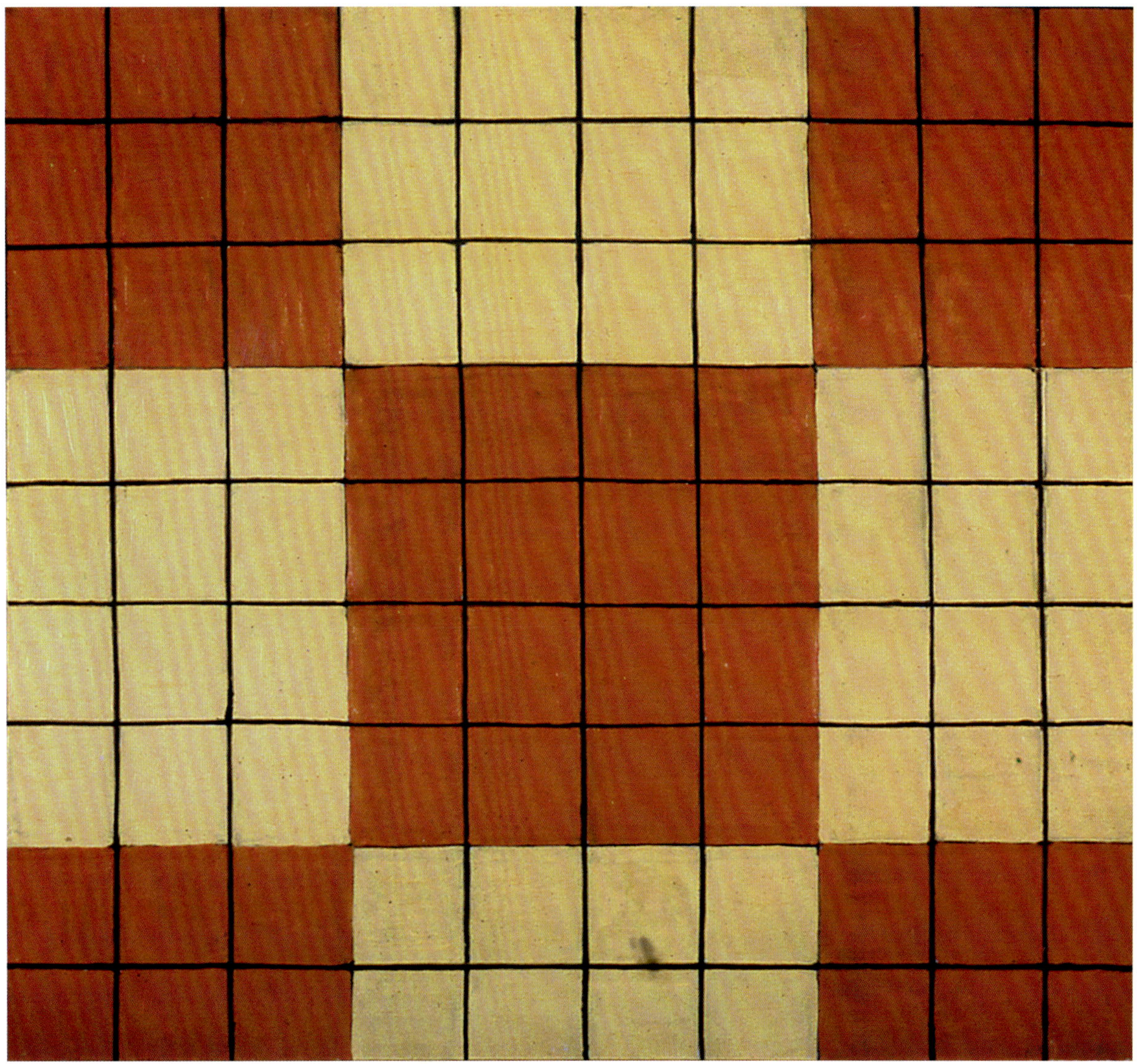

74   Mikhail Roginsky, *Floor Tiles*, 1965. State Tretiakov Gallery, Moscow.

ictable," "uncontrolled," and "mine," but there was no "reflection" in them, with which I have always been abundantly endowed, then and now."[71]

That last sentence explains why Kabakov found a common language with Sooster, whom he met the year of the Manezh show and with whom he soon after began to share a studio. Sooster's predilection for philosophizing glued the two together until Sooster's death in 1970. When they moved into the first of their three shared studios, Sooster "had thousands of draw-ings…and stacks of paintings which he displayed on regular and travel easels, and placed along walls…and I had nothing," remembers Kabakov.[72] The weight of easelism, as well as Sooster's reputation for his "extraordinarily high level of technical ability,"[73] did not leave Kabakov unaffected. Once again, his sense of alienation and disjunction, experienced earlier with respect to Socialist Realism, resurfaced as he witnessed Sooster's eclectic modernism. This set Kabakov off on a rebellious path, working on tables rather than easels, and conceptualizing forms of serial art in order to

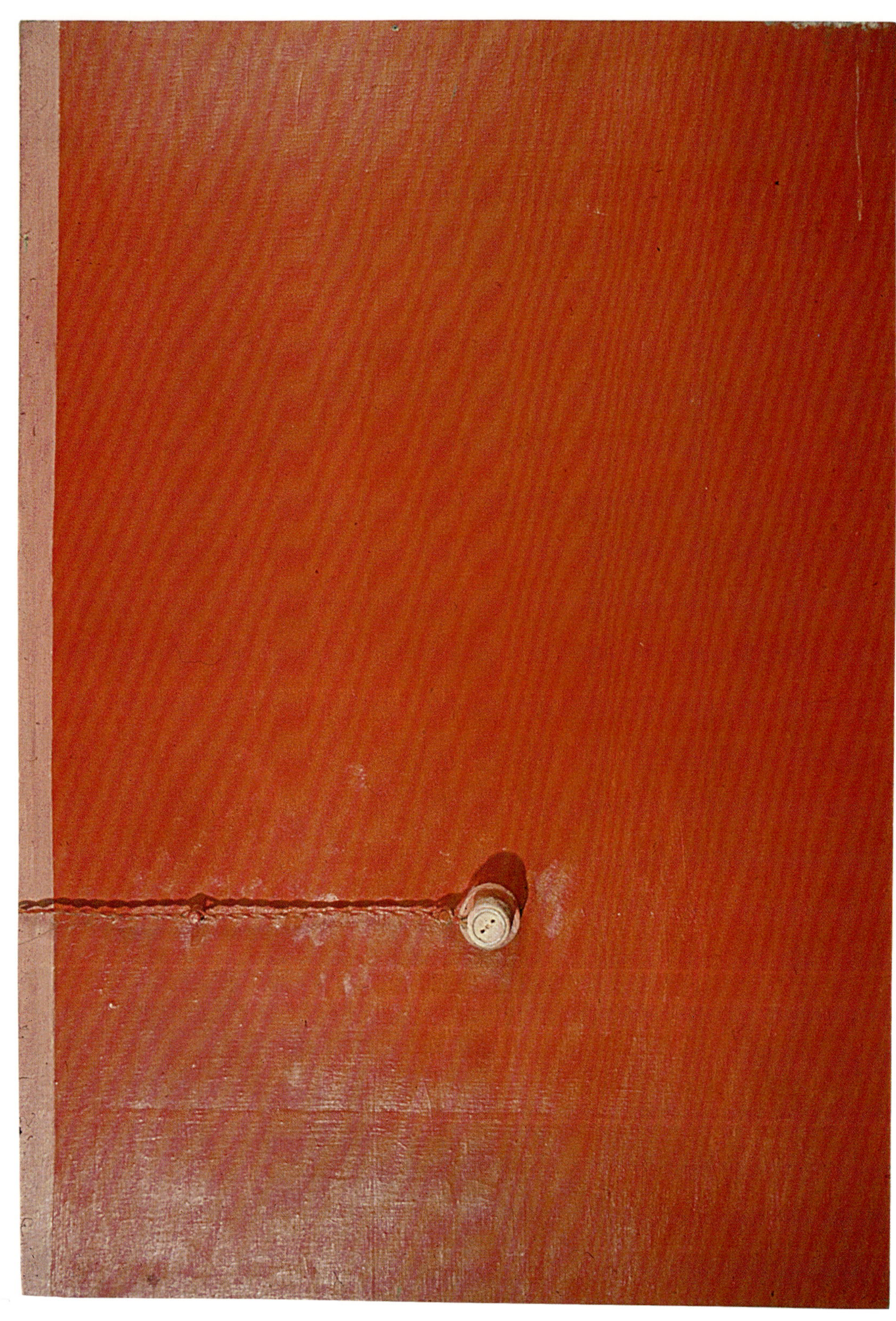

75   Mikhail Roginsky, *Wall with an Electric Outlet*, 1965.

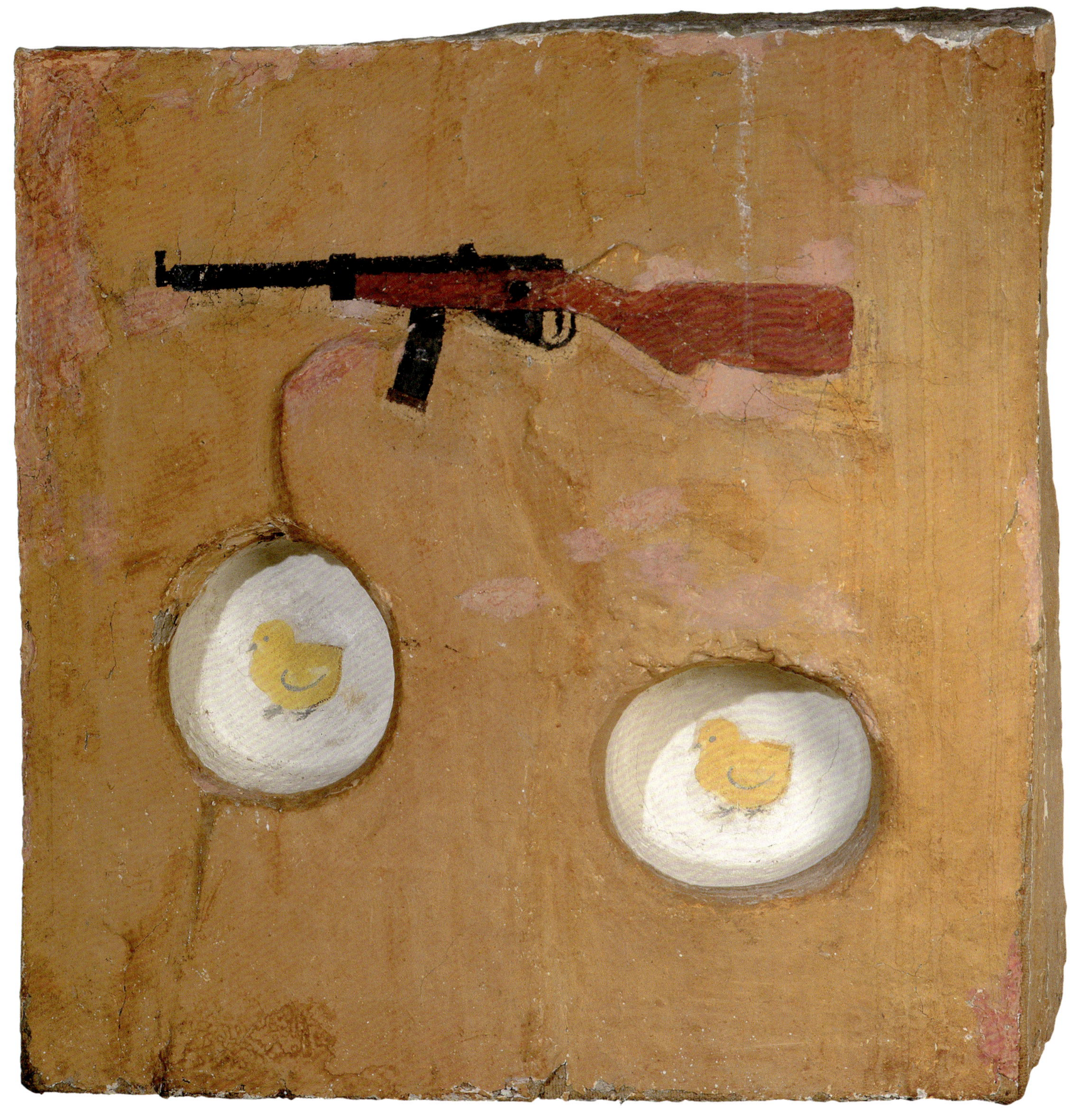

76   Ilya Kabakov, *Machine Gun and Chickens*, 1966. State Tretiakov Gallery, Moscow.

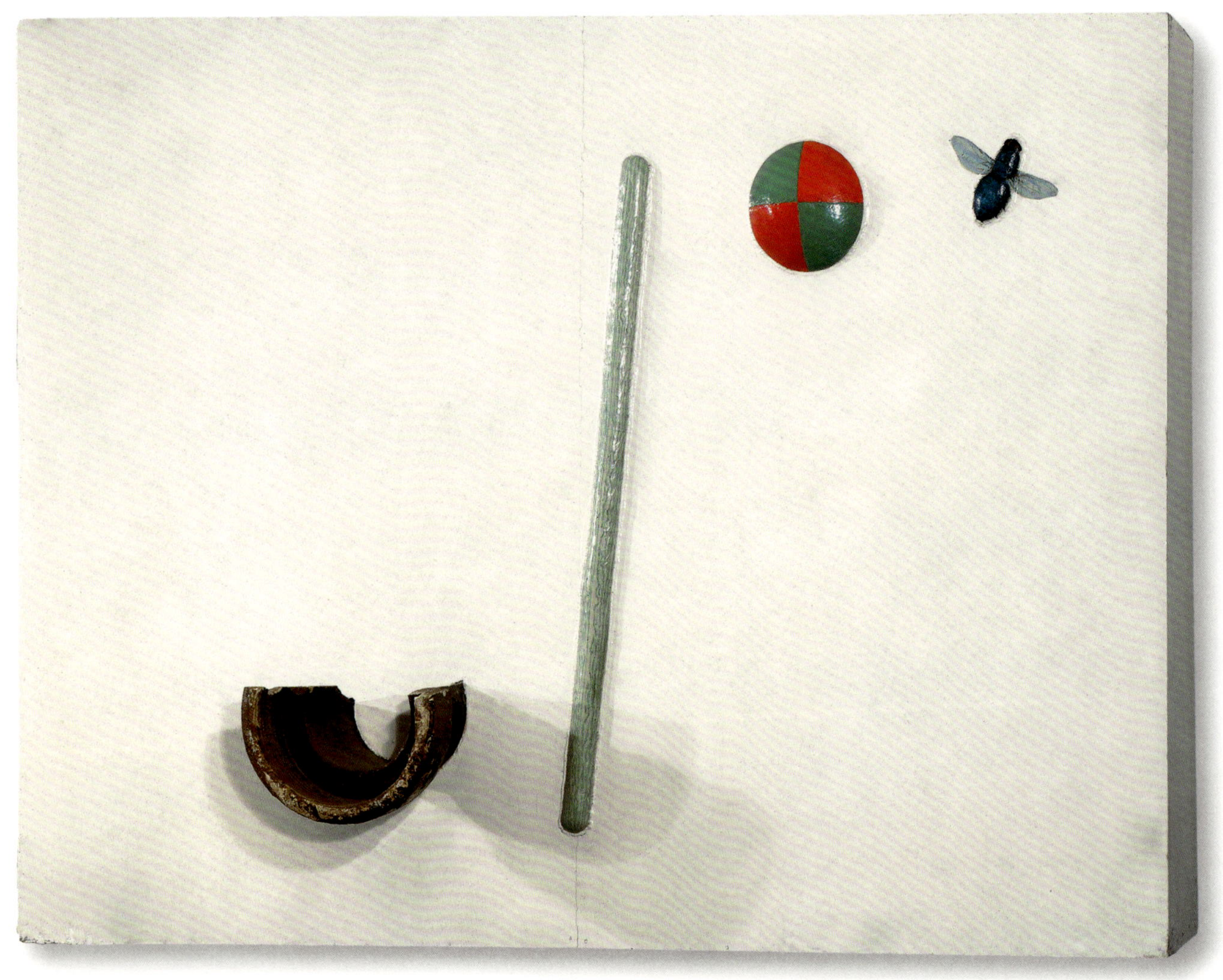

77 Ilya Kabakov, *Pipe, Stick, Ball, and Fly*, 1966. Collection Ludwig Forum für Internationale Kunst, Aachen.

escape from the pressure to be original. But most importantly, working next to Sooster impelled Kabakov toward a deconstructive approach to easel painting, or what he referred to as "picture-objects" and "'strange' objects" executed in discarded materials and commercial paint.

Kabakov's "strange" object was a materialization of his theory that in the Soviet Union an aesthetic object had no function outside of its ideological exploitation. The historical and contemporary art that was displayed in Soviet museums could be viewed as "utilitarian," for its primary role was to propagandize. Art works that could not be used to advance official

ideology either stayed in storage or were sold to Western collectors. Kabakov applied his concept of dislocated aesthetics in his first series of "strange" objects, also called "white large objects" because of their large scale and monochrome color. Kabakov made them in order to claim that while, as Marcel Duchamp had shown, bringing a readymade into an art space confirmed the authority of aesthetics in the Western world, in Kabakov's homeland there was no cultural context that could achieve Duchamp's conversion of an ordinary object into an art object.

In 1965, Sooster and Kabakov moved to a new studio near the State Mayakovsky Museum, which the

78 Ilya Kabakov, *Couch-painting*, 1967. Collection Claudia Jolles, Zürich.

latter described as "a refuge for all rejected talented bohemians; there 'progressive' exhibitions were organized…our studio, being located opposite it, became more visited with such a neighbor, especially after exhibitions and evening events organized by the museum."[74] In this studio, Kabakov's space was a dark basement room, which he filled with light from hundreds of drawings on white paper. This work created a sensation of either floating in its light (three-dimensional objects) or blocking it (flat elements). While conceiving the first three "white large objects," among which are *Machine Gun and Chickens* (although it is not entirely white) and *Pipe, Stick, Ball, and Fly* (figs. 76, 77), Kabakov attempted to achieve this meeting of abstract light (abstract white) and groups of unrelated objects that he rendered on or attached to white surfaces, as if making graffiti on abstract works. This was done under the influence of "alogism," a Russian term for the shift from rationality to illogicality, practiced by artists and poets including Malevich and Aleksei Kruchenykh. One of the main characteristics of alogism (particularly in montage) was the combination of abstraction and figuration in order to reduce the former's illegibility and the latter's narrativity. In this practice, Kabakov's "'strange' objects" were in dialogue with the work of Bruce Nauman,

Louise Bourgeois, and Eva Hesse, in their turn influenced by Surrealism and united by the critic Lucy Lippard in her 1966 exhibition, *Eccentric Abstraction*, at the Fischbach Gallery in New York. Twenty-five years later, a curator at the Museum of Modern Art (MoMA) in New York, Robert Storr, recognized the common conceptual ground between Kabakov and the "eccentric abstractionists" and featured his work with Nauman's and Bourgeois's in MoMA's 1991 *Dislocations* exhibition.

Kabakov's *Couch-painting* (fig. 78) is a laborious imitation of the back of a sofa, made of papier-mâché and painted a "hundred times with English enamel,"[75] in a conflicted attempt to achieve the literalness of a minimalist object on the one hand, and to refine it until it looked like the surface of a painting on the other. The result would have become a dialectical abstract object if Kabakov had not added to its surface a medallion-like male portrait, asymmetrically close to the left border and thus not at "'a point of importance,' not in optical focus."[76] Kabakov denied *Couch-painting* aesthetic status by destroying its internal logic with external illogicality.

In spite of Kabakov's conviction that the Soviet Union was a "no-aesthetics zone," he was "dying to exhibit"[77] his heavy picture-objects even in one-day

79   Erik Bulatov, *Diagonal II*, 1966. Musée Maillol, Fondation Dina Vierny, Paris.

80   Erik Bulatov, *Horizontal I*, 1966. Musée Maillol, Fondation Dina Vierny, Paris.

shows. For Kabakov, such a brief showing underlined the difference between pompous official "exhibitions" and informal displays of unsanctioned art,[78] and spoke of the hermetic state of the Soviet exhibition industry for outsiders like himself. Oddly, he chose to display *Machine Gun and Chickens* (see fig. 76), a block painted in a "disgusting rufous color"[79] with a rough surface. Inside its two cavities, against a white background (to imitate eggs) he painted chickens and a machine gun on top of them. Yet Kabakov's decision to exhibit this particular work, which looked eccentric to both official and nonconformist artists, was not accidental: it was a full-blooded allegory of the relationship between these artists and the authorities; of the difference between controlling, militant officialdom and a pacifist underground milieu.

In 1966, Kabakov's art school classmate Erik Bulatov made a radical shift in his own abstract style. He replaced his compositions of toxic-colored celestial bodies dashing into blackness with black and white diptychs, *Diagonal I* and *Diagonal II*, and *Horizontal I* and *Horizontal II* (figs. 79, 80). In reducing these canvases to a single color, Bulatov, much like other producers of monochrome works, appears to be demonstrating his frustration with Abstract Expressionism. However, unlike Rodchenko's, Bulatov's reductivism did not bring him to abandon the canvas support, nor did it demonstrate a concession to the canvas's flatness. Contrary to Rodchenko's dynamic lines that glide over the surface to indicate real space, Bulatov's static lines are what he called "incisions" that assert the internal properties of a canvas: "while [it is] flat, it simultaneously encompasses space, and thus lives a double, pulsating life."[80] The crystallization of this dual nature of the canvas prompted his reinvention of realism based on the modernist structure of the grid. Being what Krauss called "antinatural, antimimetic, antireal,"[81] it served as a cover for Bulatov's noncompliance with Socialist Realism.

Bulatov's *Entrance* (fig. 81) elucidates this pro-cess: the canvas is webbed with a red grid, signifying the politicized position of abstraction in Soviet Russia. The blue arrows painted on the four sides of the canvas chart "an infinitely penetrable depth behind the [canvas's] surface" (Krauss again).[82] But there is one more thing that Bulatov does in *Entrance* that is at odds with the grid's defiance of speech practices. He enforces the indexical power of the arrows by doubling the word "entrance." This announces that his figurative painting, for which he was about to abandon abstraction, and which I will discuss in the next chapter, would be discursive rather than mimetic. That is, it establishes painting's textual modality and thus breaks away from the pervasive literary heritage of Socialist Realism. Further, Bulatov painted his canvas smoothly and thinly, and thus, in opposition to Moscow abstract expressionists, took faktura out of the painterly surface.

If Bulatov turned to the grid to shift figuration from the affirmative to the negative, Vitaly Komar and Aleksandr Melamid adopted this structure to silence the dominance of the verbal over the visual. In *Quotation* (fig. 82), they replaced a fragment of a propaganda speech with fourteen rows of white quadrilaterals and a shorter row in place of a signature, all painted against a red background. The painting's title and the quotation imply an ideological phrase, and thus again demonstrate the grid's ability to silence a text. *Quotation* also asserts that a critique of ideological rhetoric can be performed by abstract art, without including the corroded speech of officialdom.

This "purification" of ideology, or ideologization of abstraction, further evolves in *Color Writing: Ideological Abstraction No. 1* (fig. 83), a strongly vertical canvas. In the accompanying text, Komar and Melamid explained that they assigned each tube of paint a letter from the alphabet and applied this code to create "the grid image" of an article of the state constitution that guaranteed Soviet citizens freedoms but that had been gridlocked for decades.[83] Their multicolored palette (an actual palette is included in the work) far exceeds the official fixation on the color red and is assigned decoding, rather than optical, functions.

Komar and Melamid's political discourse is realized through their "abstracting" of propaganda and their following of the avant-garde conviction that geometric forms were instrumental in the creation of an ideal reality. For *Documents: Ideal Document* (figs. 84, 85), Komar and Melamid used Soviet documents of control (passports, trade union cards, diplomas, and so on) to make transparent Plexiglas panels, one of which is painted red and called "ideal document," in

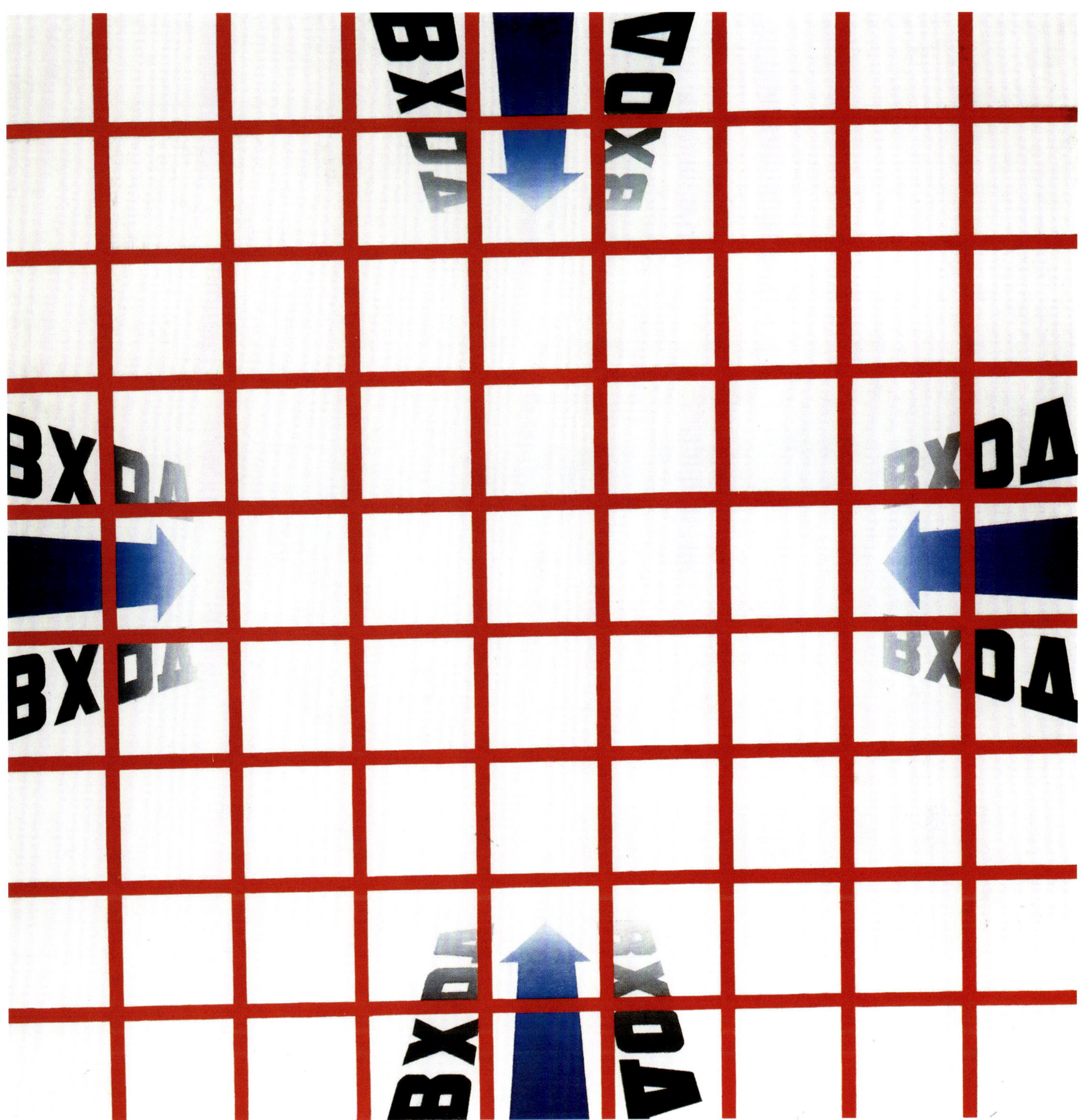

81 Erik Bulatov, *Entrance*, 1971. Musée Maillol, Fondation Dina Vierny, Paris.

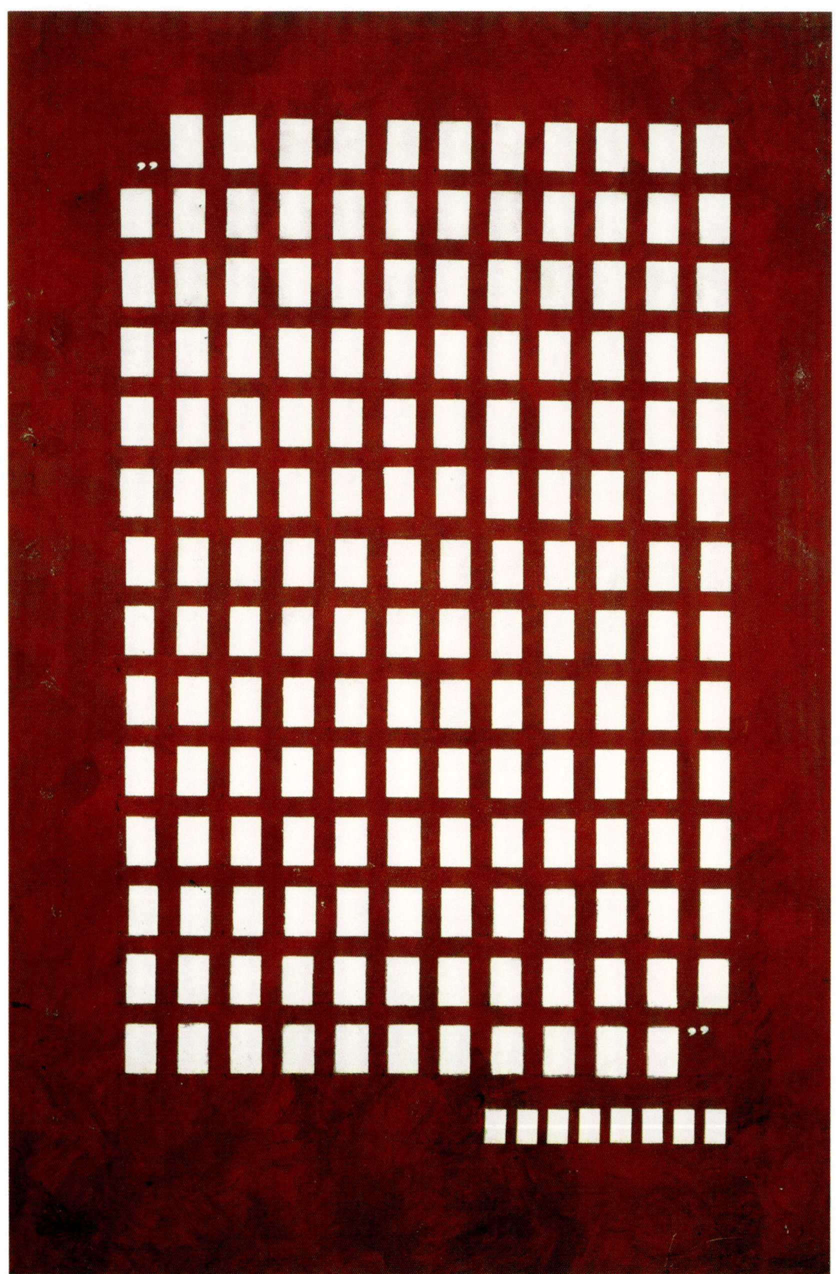

82 Vitaly Komar and Aleksandr Melamid, *Quotation*, 1972. Collection Frayda and Ronald Feldman, New York.

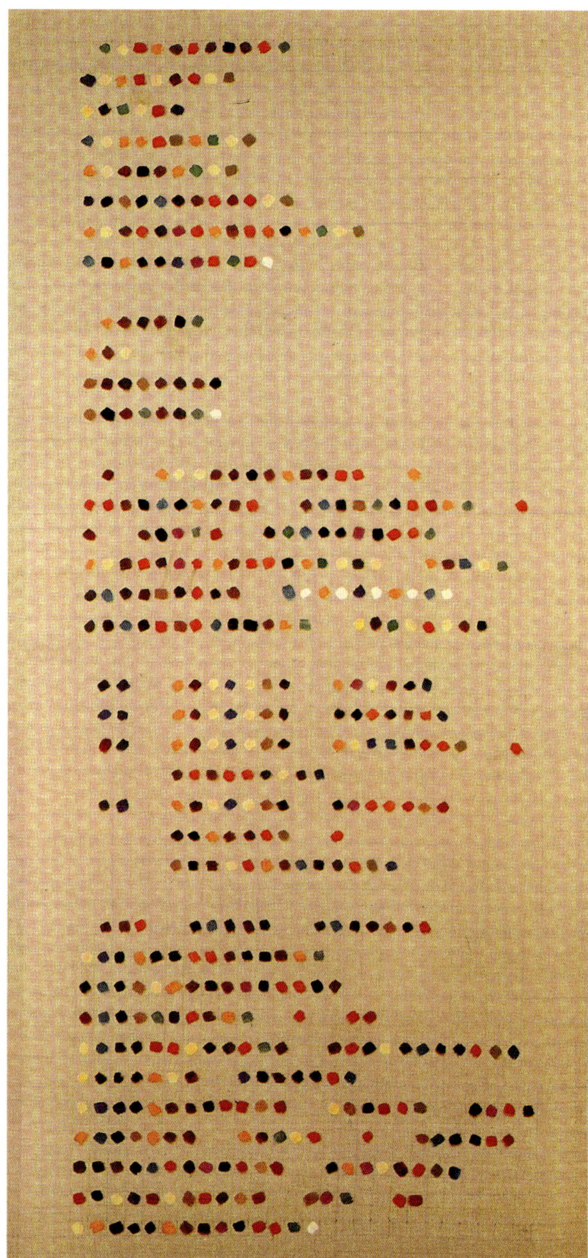

83 Vitaly Komar and Aleksandr Melamid, *Color Writing: Ideological Abstraction No. 1*, 1974. Collection Frayda and Ronald Feldman, New York.

OPPOSITE PAGE TOP 84 Vitaly Komar and Aleksandr Melamid, from the series *Documents: Ideal Document*, 1975. Tate, London.

OPPOSITE PAGE BOTTOM 85 Vitaly Komar and Aleksandr Melamid, *Documents: Ideal Document*, 1975. Tate, London

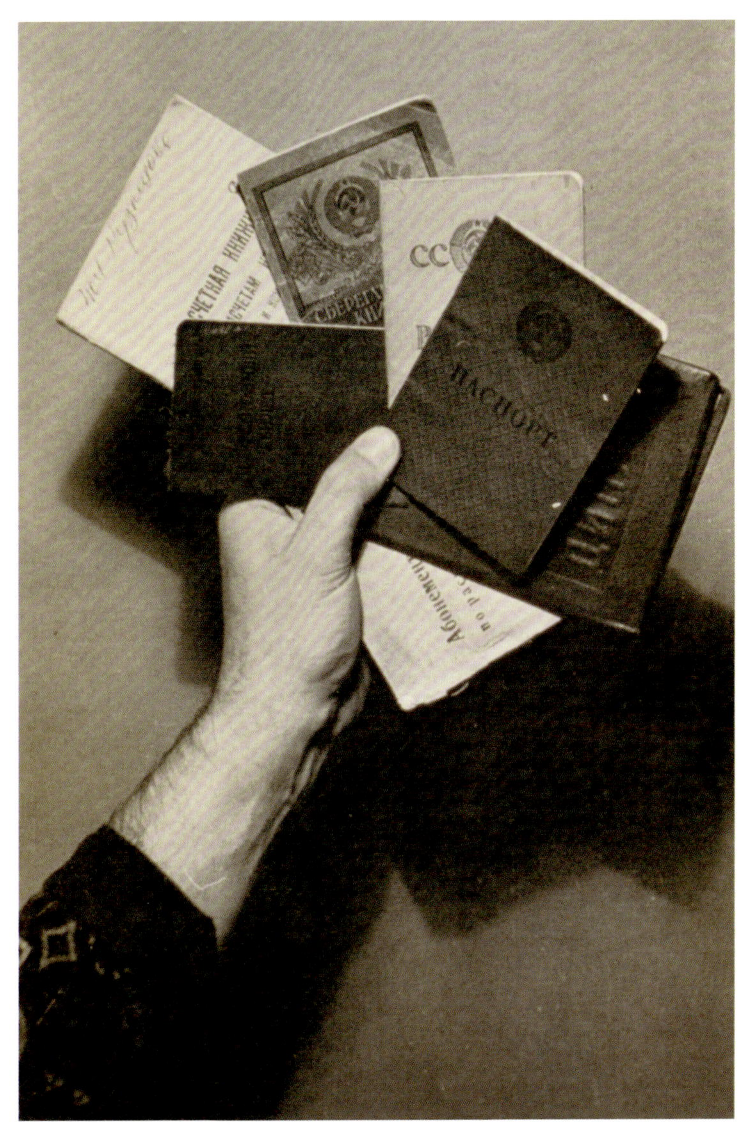

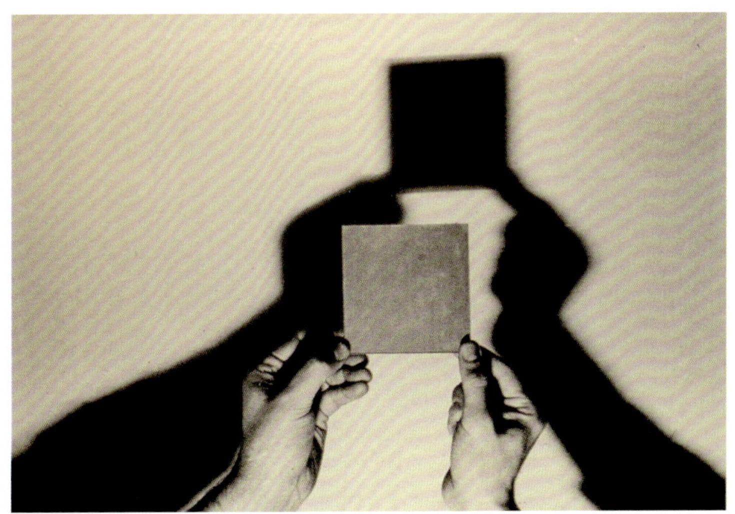

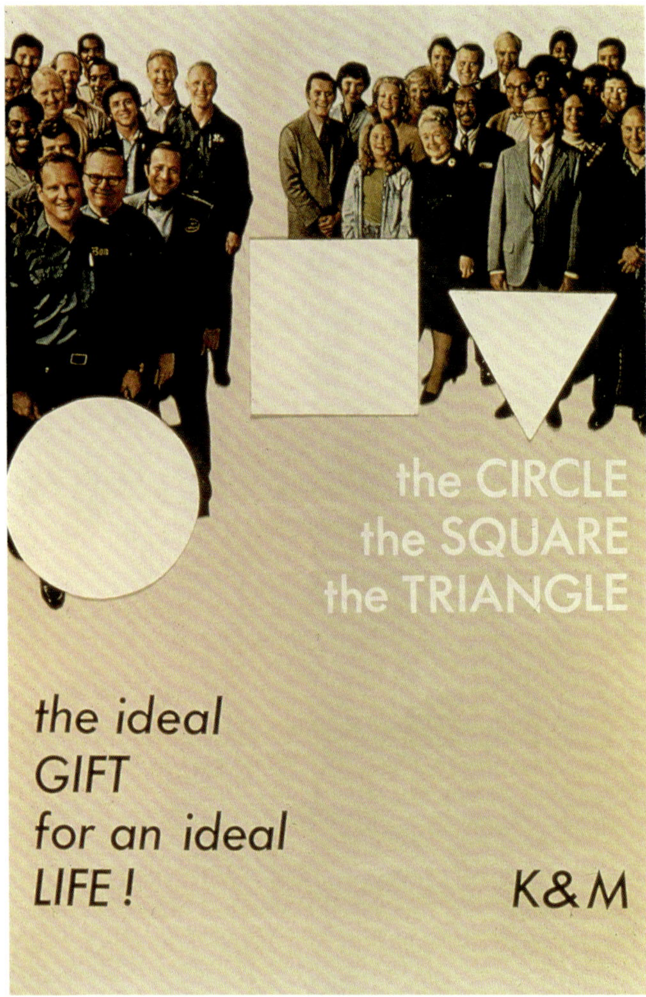

86 Vitaly Komar and Aleksandr Melamid, poster advertising *Circle, Square, Triangle*, 1974–5.

an allusion to Malevich's *Red Square* and specifically to its full title (*Pictorial Realism of a Peasant Woman in Two Dimensions, Called Red Square*), which identifies a conversion of figuarative into abstract. A dialogue with Malevich continues in *Circle, Square, Triangle* (figs. 86, 87), engaging with Malevich's ambition to "geometricize" Soviet everyday life. Komar and Melamid were here mocking the aim of transforming the world that had been held by production artists teaching in VKhUTEMAS (in whose contemporary form, the Moscow Institute of Arts and Industry, or Stroganovka, they themselves had been students) and by Suprematists in GINKhUK, by

advertising themselves as having therapeutic powers. Komar and Mela-mid made a connection:

> Like some other of our works of the early 1970s, *Circle, Square, Triangle* is a sort of "missing link" in the evolution of the Russian avant-garde's production of objects…We have done what Suprematists and Constructivists did not have time to do when their advantures were driven out by totalitarian and commercial art…along this path…of the production of objects, there should have appeared the production of ideal geometric figures with the goal of replacing their representation in a painting.[84]

Once in New York, where they moved in 1978, they continued this project by holding a production session with a group of female art students from the Pratt Institute whom, in a reference to the purity of white, they dubbed "virginal maidens" in a textual part of the work. Laboring with a saw in white kerchiefs, the young women evoke a faded photograph of Malevich's students, who also used saws when constructing *architektons* in GINKhUK.

I suggest that Komar and Melamid, in extending *Circle, Square, Triangle* to the New York art world, from the start conceived their work in response to minimalists' reaction to Malevich's works after his 1973–4 exhibition at the Guggenheim Museum. At precisely that time, Komar and Melamid first saw the magazine *Artforum*, which initiated several series dedicated to the deconstructive reading of American art movements, such as Pop art, and a critique of museums including MoMA and the Guggenheim. After Male-vich's exhibition, there was a discussion about his relation to geometric abstraction. Donald Judd concluded that Malevich had "no doctrine about geometry itself" and, in a conversation with the critic John Coplans, Mel Bochner claimed that Malevich did not have the same "'belief' in geometry"[85] as American postwar abstract painters. In the same conversation, Coplans asked whether Malevich could be considered a "Conceptual artist" because "it's almost as if…he never really had to paint the works." Bochner respon-ded: "the 'ideal Conceptual work' would be that it have an exact linguistic correlative, that is, it could be described and experienced in its description, and that it be infinitely repeatable. It must have absolutely no 'aura,' no

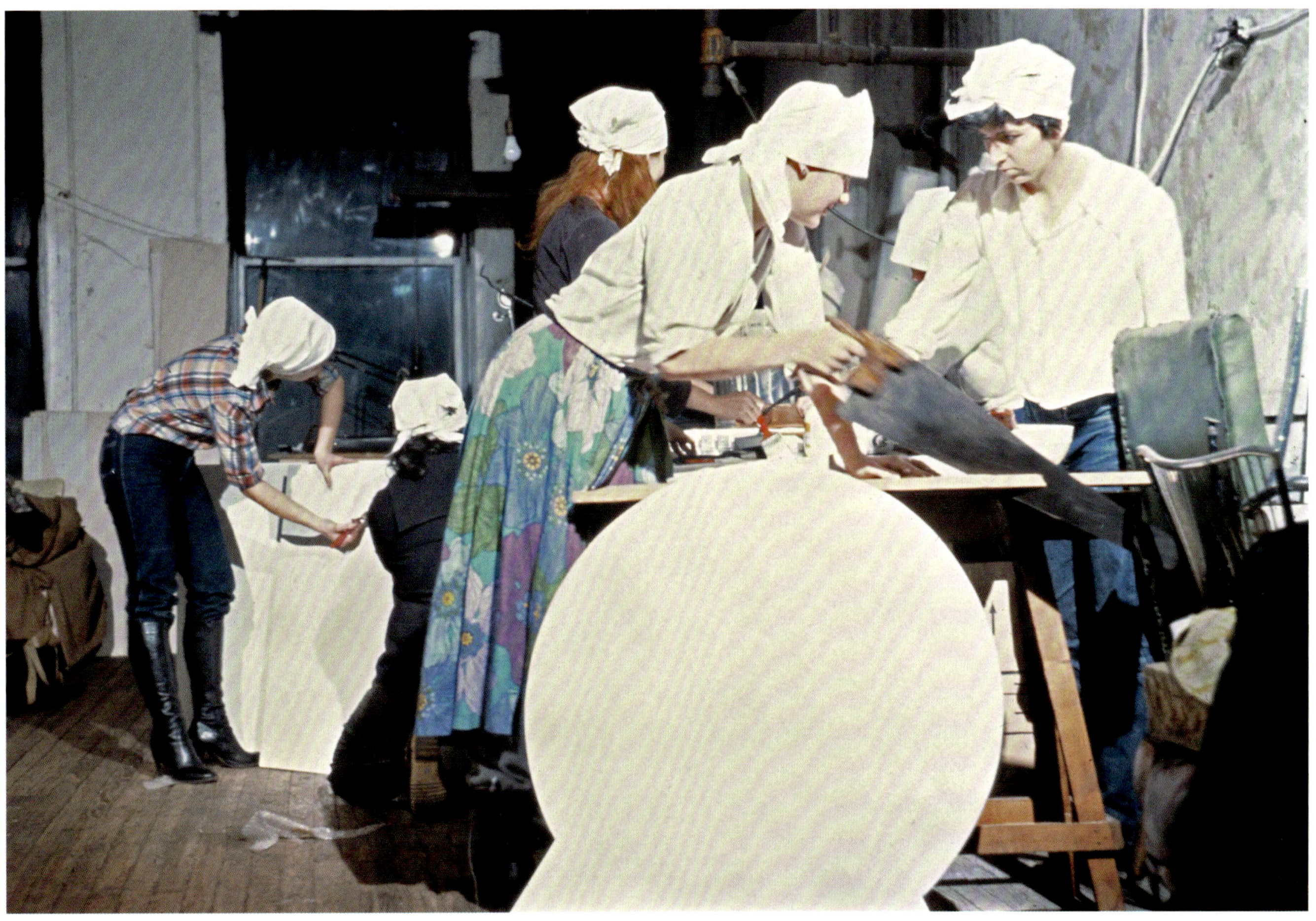

87   Vitaly Komar and Aleksandr Melamid, *Circle, Square, Triangle*, 1978.

uniqueness to it whatsoever. Obviously neither of those two imperatives fit Malevich."[86] While considering Malevich's relation to geometry, the discussion was solely based on his painting and excluded (as had the Guggenheim show) Malevich's design and architectural practices. It was in this domain of production art that Malevich believed in geometry as a universal language for communication (at UNOVIS) and for everyday consumption in the form of domestic objects (at GINKhUK). While developing these two programs, Malevich stripped Suprematist forms of their aura by submitting them to mechanical reproduction and to a free and infinite repetition. The UNOVIS street projects almost always included a "linguistic correlative" to an image, and GINKhUK's dedication to "volumetric Suprematism" opened up an infinite space for the dissemination of Suprematist forms in the public sphere. Komar and Melamid's *Circle, Square, Triangle* is built around this doctrine of Malevich's geometry, and it prompted them to create their first "ideal Conceptual work," and conclude the genealogy of non-representational art as the locomotive of the Moscow vanguard.

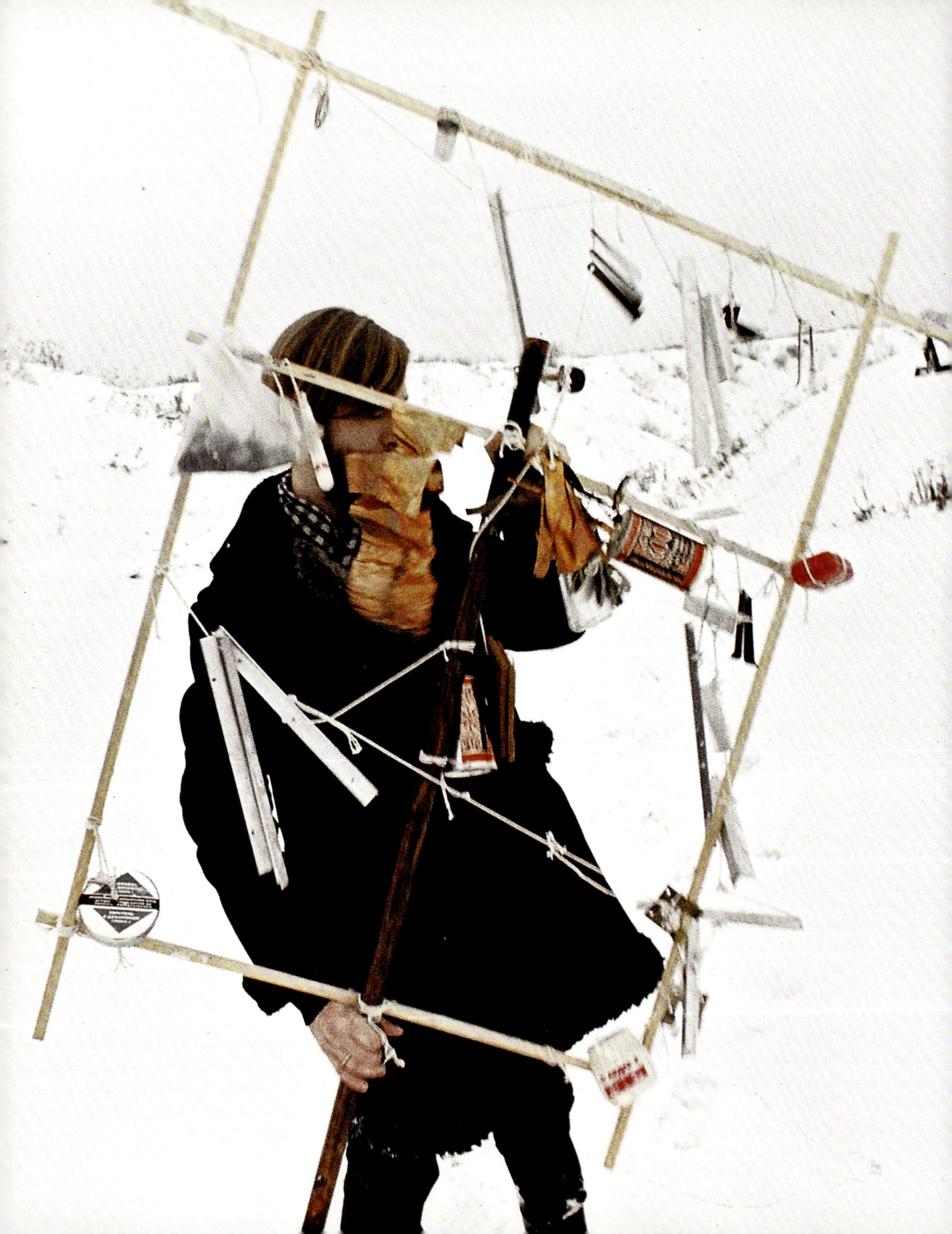

4

DANGEROUS LUNCHEON ON THE GRASS

I cannot get rid of the feeling that in our de-urbanization there was something "urban" in the highest sense.

Nikita Alekseev, 1982.

In the mid-1960s, in conjunction with ideological celebrations, the Movement group succeeded in implementing its vision of an urban utopia by installing abstract sculpture at Moscow's and Leningrad's iconic sites. Movement's ambitious projects of urban planning and interior design were discussed publicly and featured in the mainstream press. Although this participation in the organization of public space was unprecedented for vanguard artists, Movement's members were also the first to realize its finite nature, and indeed it evaporated as soon as Brezhnev's reign began.

Losing the opportunity to function within "the social mainstream as a professional like any other,"[1] Movement reclaimed the status of the vanguard artist as that of belonging to an aesthetic and moral world apart. Yet, after experimenting with laboratory and utilitarian Constructivism for almost a decade, a retreat to the studio and to easel painting would have been regressive. Given the vanguard's engagement with abstraction in the 1960s, Movement's Francisco Infante marked his exit from studio production with an action installation, *Suprematist Games* (1968), in which he released the Suprematist grid into no man's land, insisting on its transitory nature and objectlessness (fig. 88). Infante emphasized that in an environment so hostile to abstraction, works made in this style were doomed to stagnate in studios and therefore should to be created as impermanent marks. He charted an uncontaminated rural setting as the ideal site for experimental art, initiating a dialogical paradigm of Moscow conceptualism – studio and rural – that was developed throughout the 1970s and early 1980s. Infante replaced Movement's support of technological progress and use of industrial materials by adapting elements from the natural world, and preferring primitive execution. The nature of this transition replayed the historical schism between Italian Futurism's urban

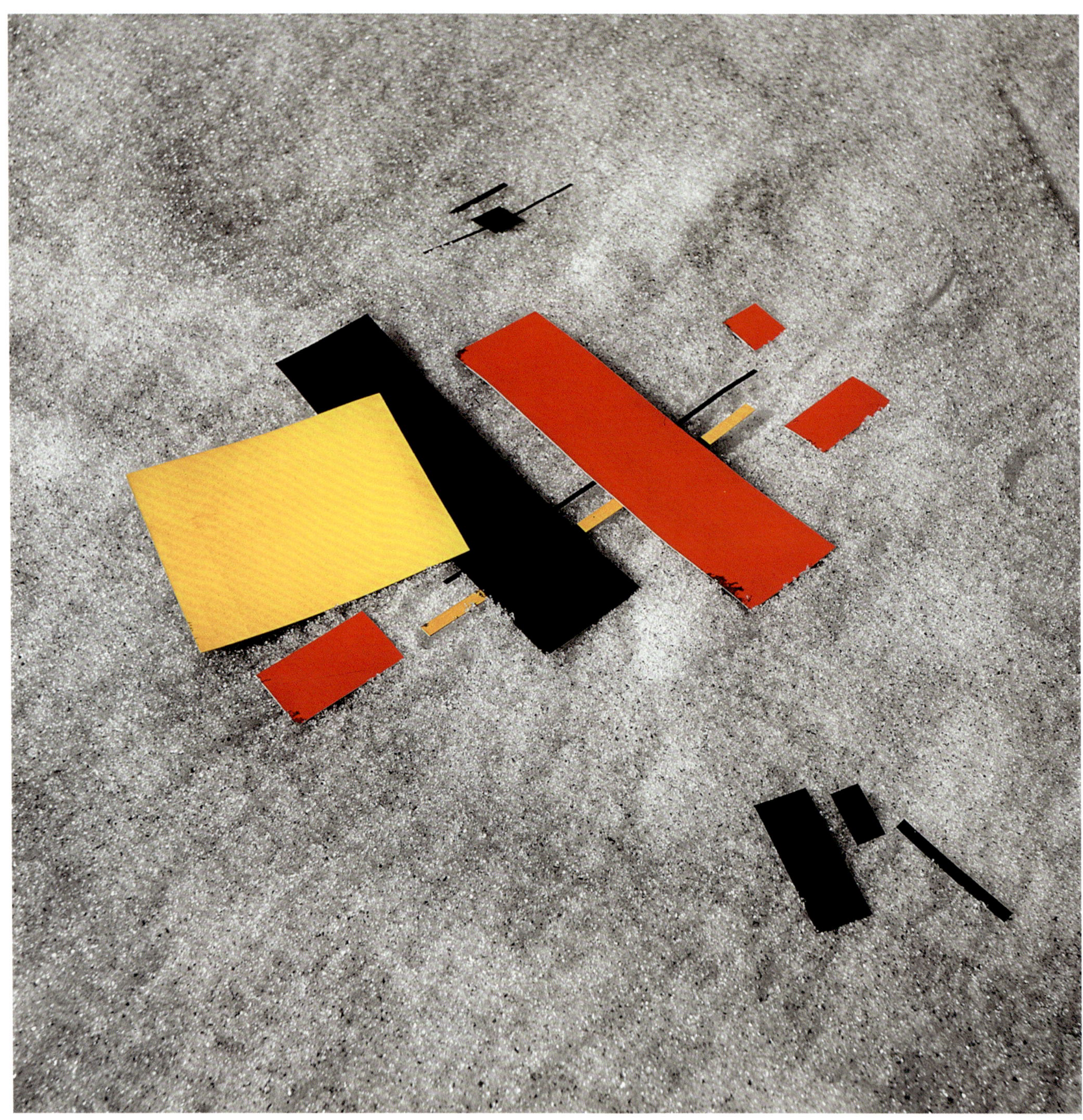

88   Francisco Infante, *Suprematist Games*, 1968.

and machine culture, and Russian Futurism's rural orientation and cult of the primitive.

In *Snow Ritual* (1968), Infante, together with his wife and collaborator, Nonna Goriunova, animated the landscape by literally and symbolically playing with fire (figs. 89, 90). The two artists erected a snow wall with candles inside that when lit melted the snow and created gaps to expose Goriunova standing naked behind the wall. Undressing in the winter was a doubly dangerous venture: it threatenend Goriunova's

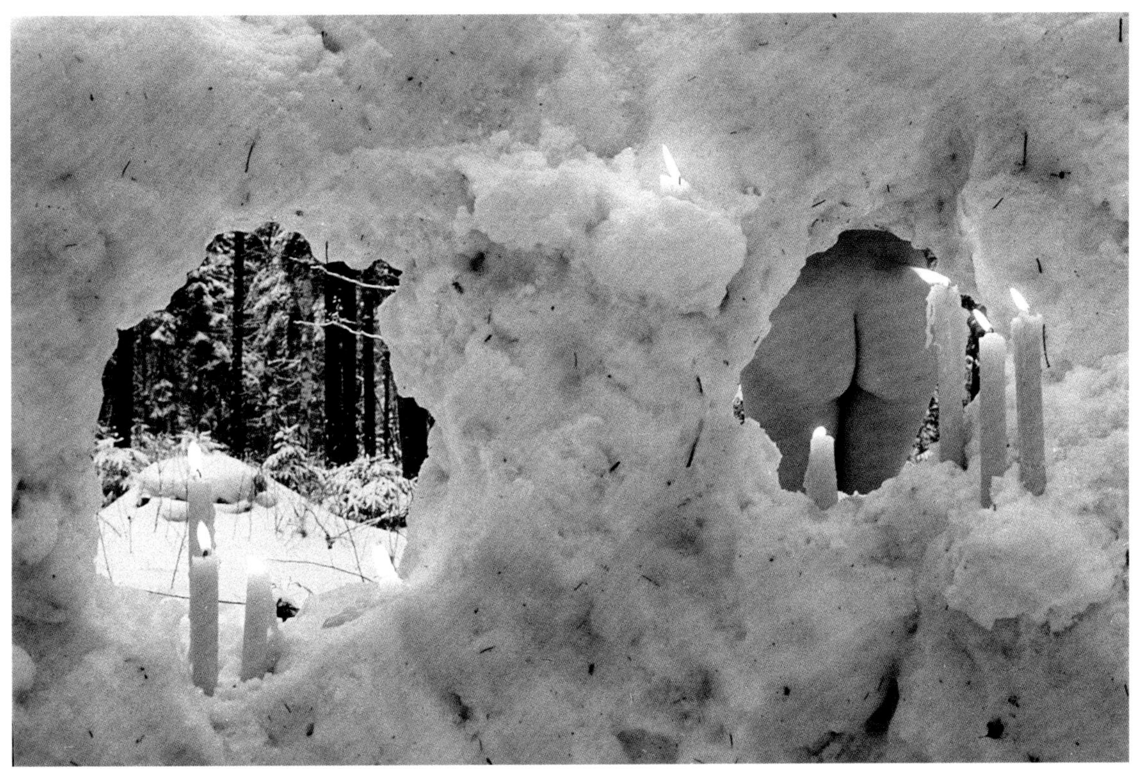

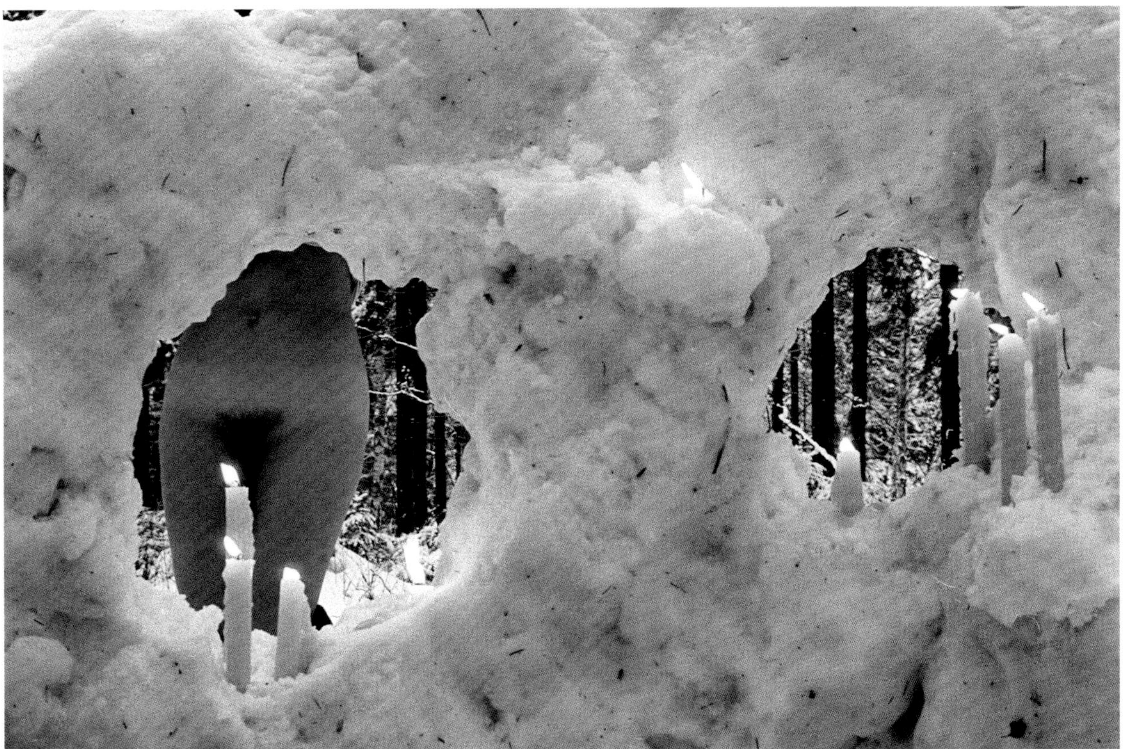

89 & 90   Francisco Infante and Nonna Goriunova, *Snow Ritual*, 1968.

health and subjected her to possible arrest for appearing naked in public, or, more precisely, in nature. However, public nudity was not only a provocative gesture for the authorities, but also radical for the nonconformist artists, who at least outwardly were not sexually emancipated, and who considered that excessive concentration on the physical would block the desired experience of the transcendental.

Other dissident modernists failed to resolve their sense of alienation in such forms of alternative practices, and in response to the lack of official opportunities held a collective open-air show in a field on the outskirts of Moscow on September 15, 1974. The event, described in the invitation as "the first Autumn view of paintings in the open air," has come down in history as *The Bulldozer Exhibition*. Classified by the authorities as a dissident act, an exaggerated reaction was certain. To disband both the show and the viewers, the authorities brought in the militia, KGB agents, and heavy machinery, including bulldozers and water hoses. The event culminated in arrests and damaged paintings (figs. 91–3).

Erik Bulatov did not participate in *The Bulldozer Exhibition*, but had finished a series of landscapes, all painted with painstaking realism. Like Edouard Manet's

Déjeuner sur l'herbe (Luncheon on the Grass), Bulatov's *Danger* (fig. 94) is built around the theme of a picnic place as a "suburban pleasure-ground."[2] However, unlike Manet's stylish and provocative trio of protagonists, Bulatov's unglamorous and overweight couple are enjoying their leisure on the bank of a shallow river. Also in contrast to Manet, Bulatov has removed his couple from the foreground, depriving the viewer of eye contact, and marks the depth of field not by a classical nymph but by two banal cows at pasture. Finally, if in Manet's *Déjeuner* the combination of clothed men and a naked woman looking straight into the eye of the beholder sends "a jolt through the picture,"[3] in Bulatov's canvas a similar shockwave is generated by the word "danger" stenciled in red on

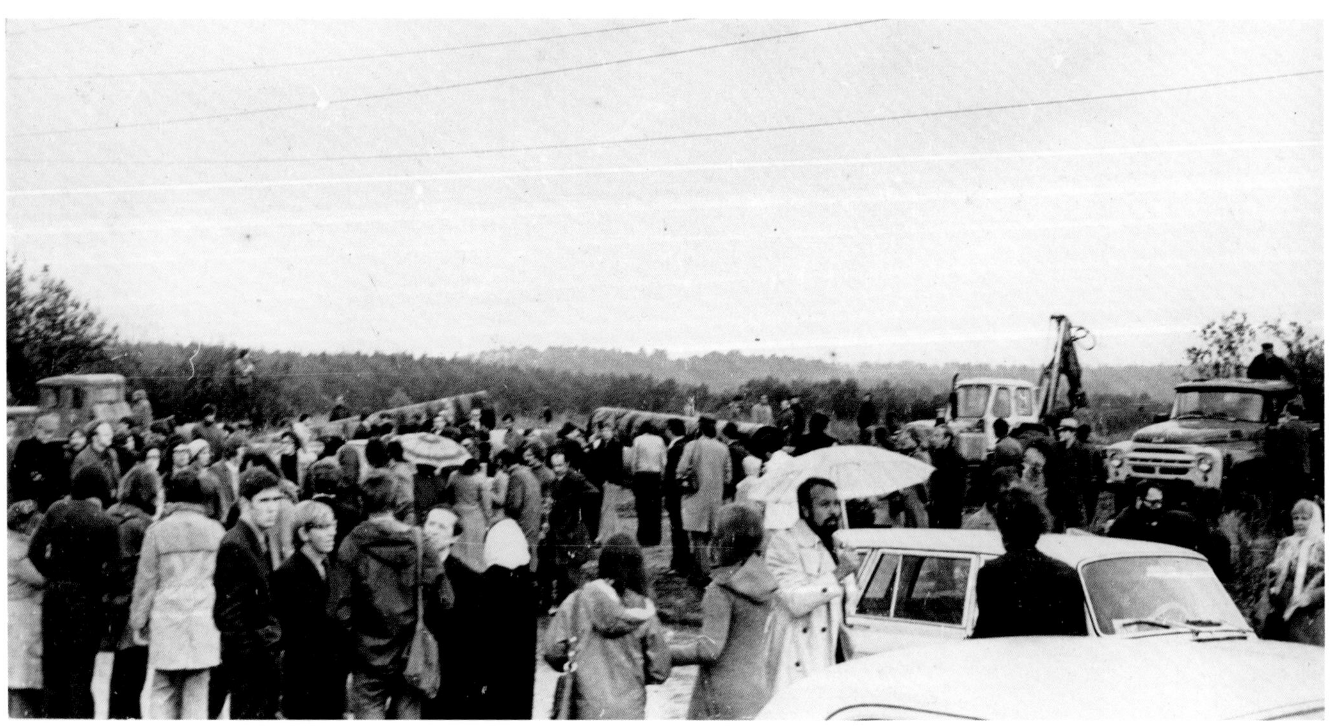

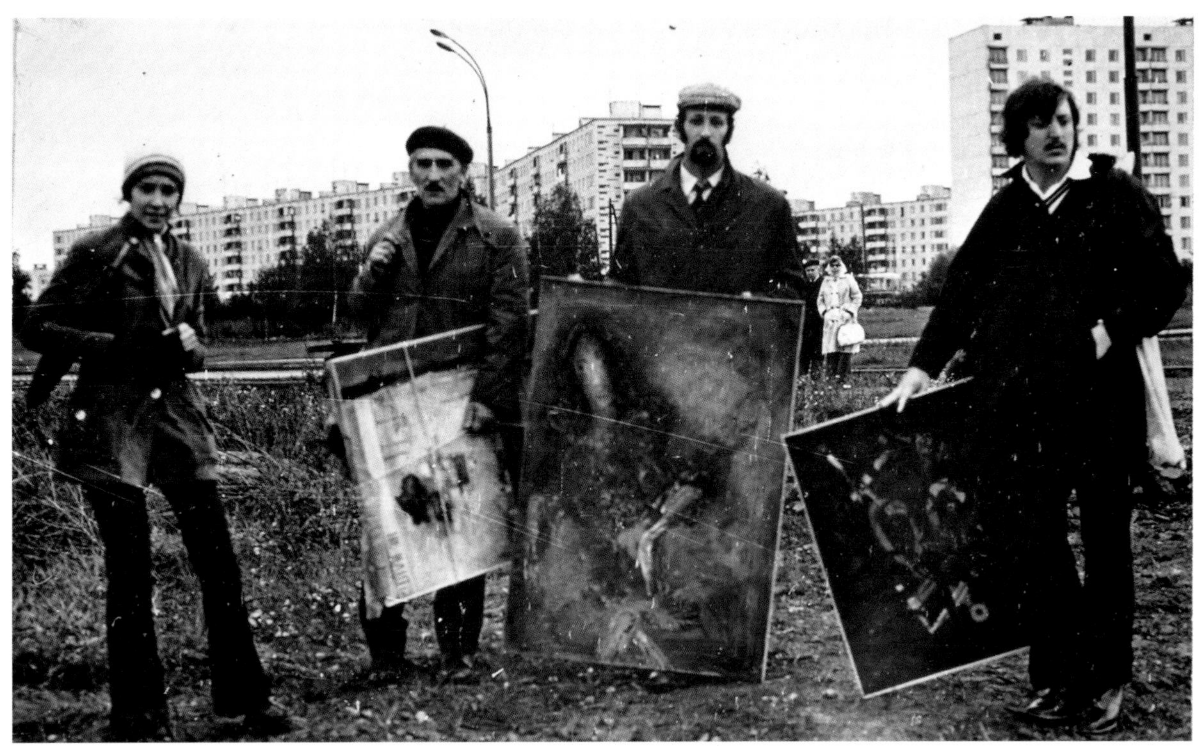

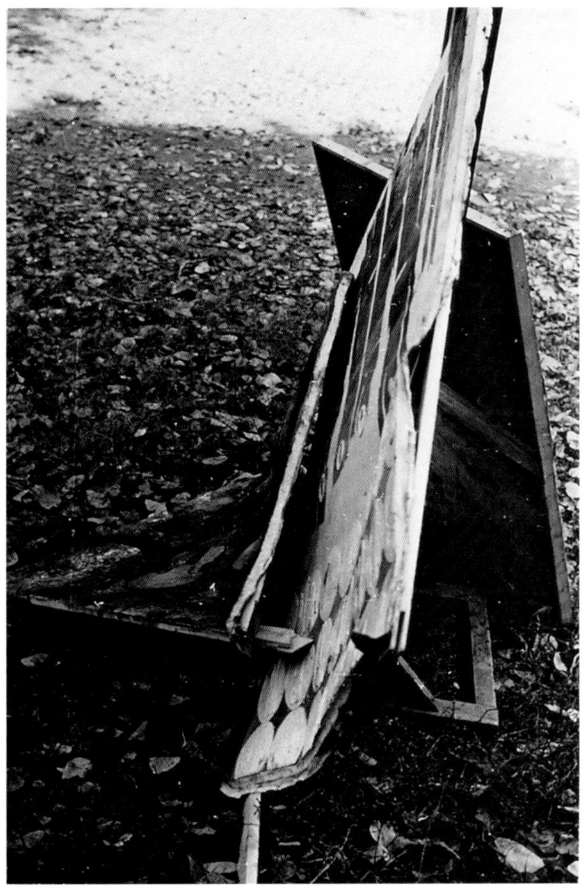

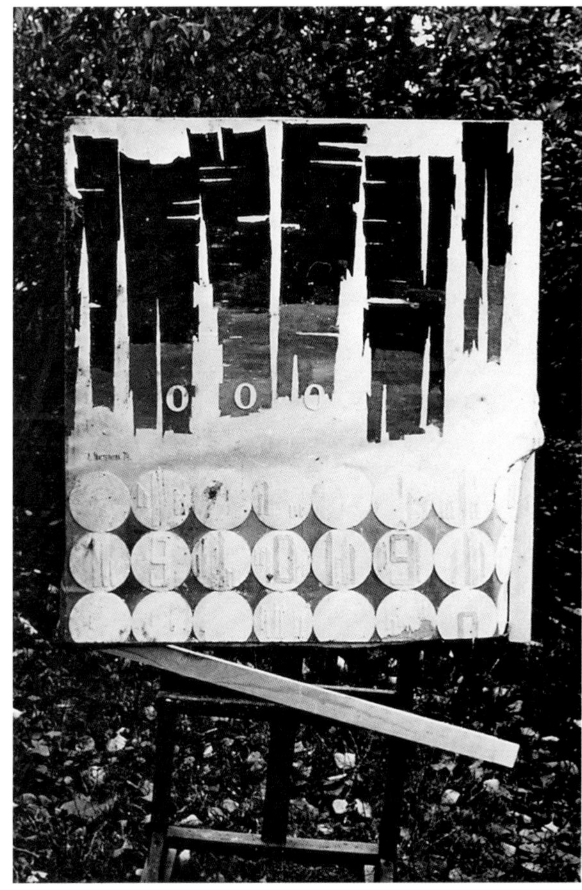

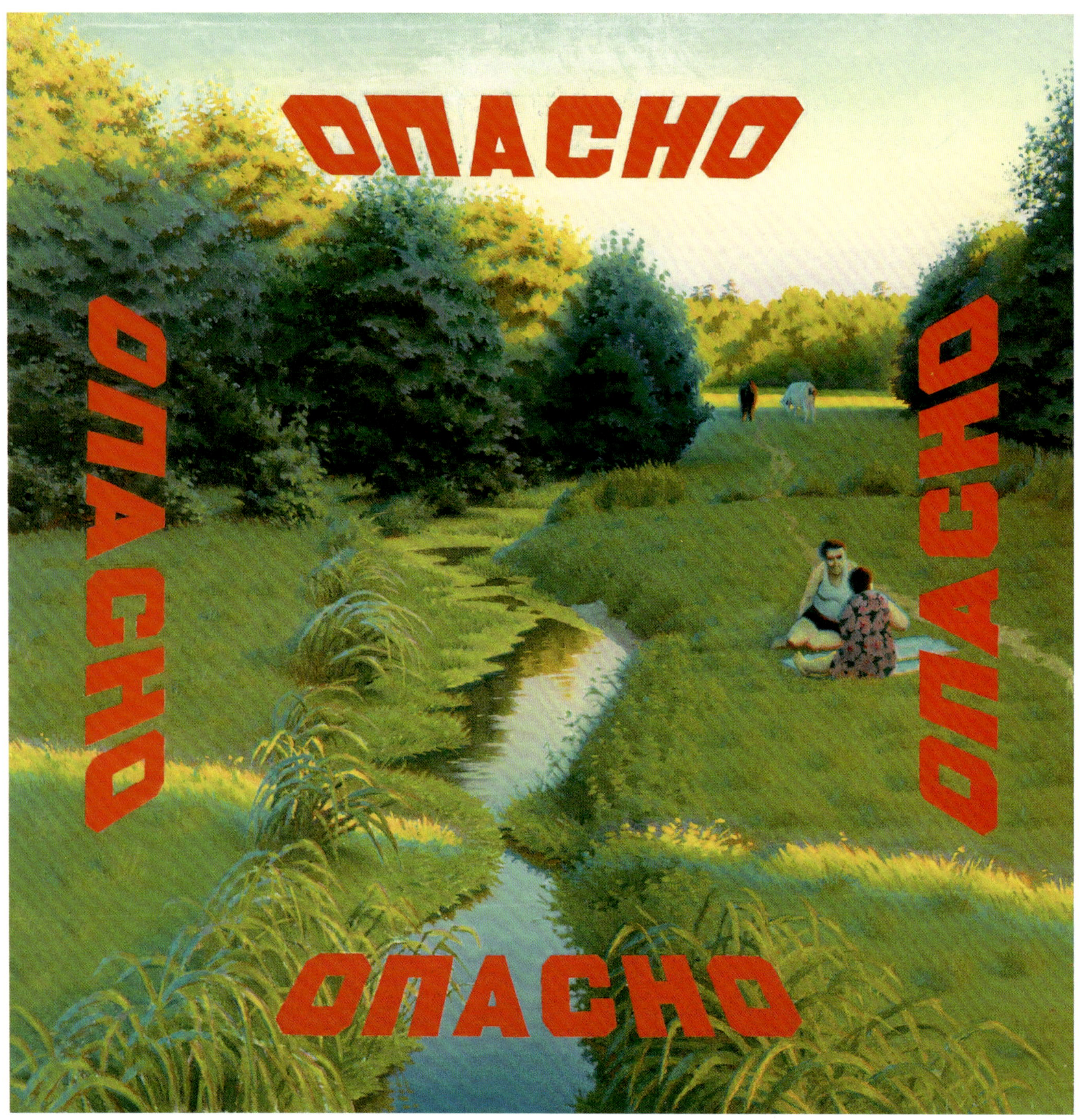

94   Erik Bulatov, *Danger*, 1972. Norton and Nancy Dodge Collection of Nonconformist Art from the Soviet Union, Jane Voorhees Zimmerli Art Museum Rutgers, State University of New Jersey.

each side of the square canvas. Next, in Bulatov's *Beware* (fig. 95), the canvas's surface is split by a punctuated line – a device registering its flatness; in Kandinsky's terms, the "nought" or "geometrical point" of a painting that "belongs to speech and indicates silence."[4] The silence is broken by the reading of the cautionary word "beware" that, painted in perspective twice, draws the viewer's gaze into the painting's depth.

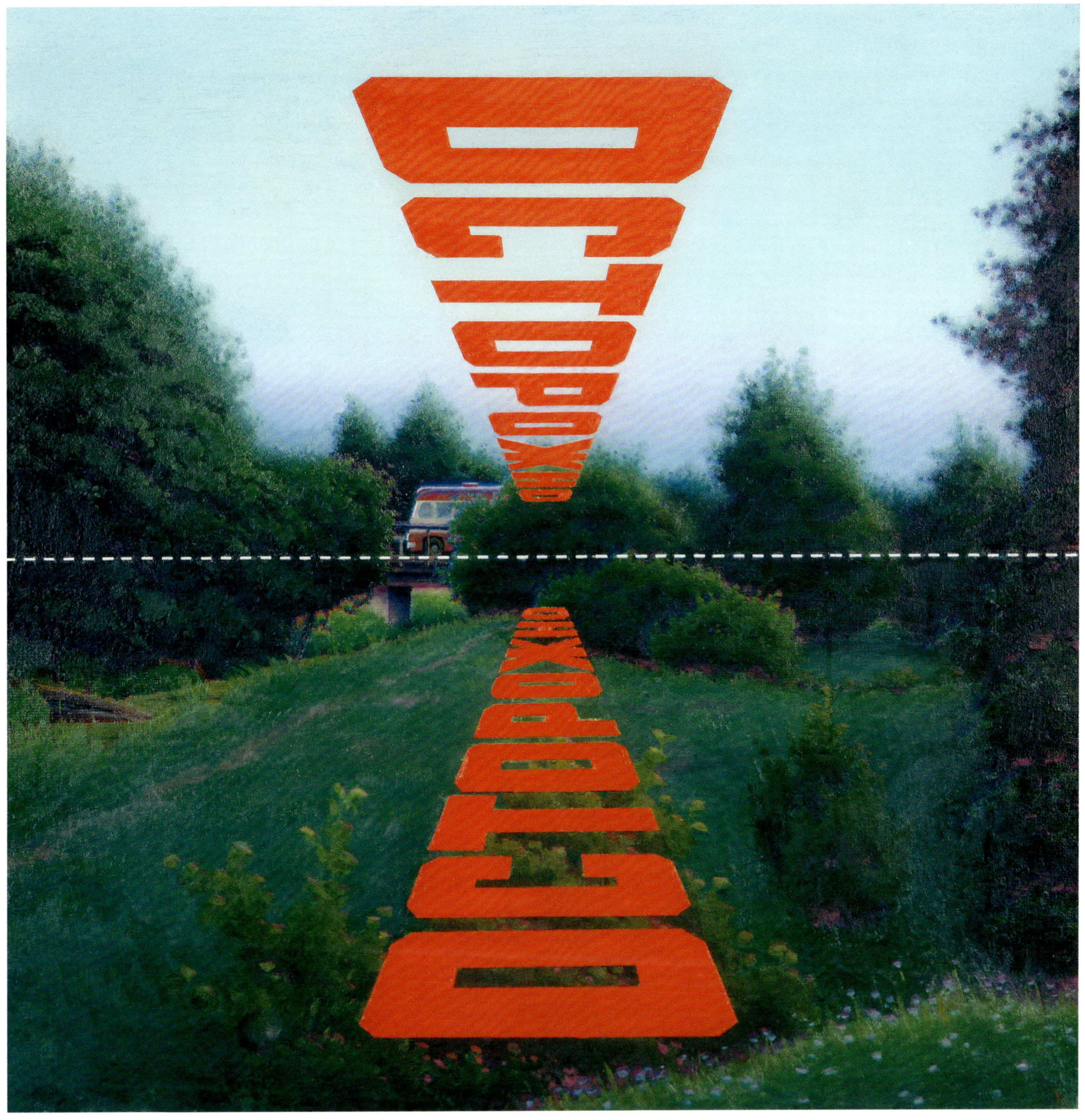

95   Erik Bulatov, *Beware*, 1973. Musée Maillol, Fondation Dina Vierny, Paris.

One is tempted to compare the "visual narrativity" of Socialist Realism with this red carpet of words that defines the spatial parameters of ideological manipulation. Thus *Danger* and *Beware* are discursive landscapes that together declare the Soviet countryside as a danger zone. In them the color red is not an aesthetic appendage, but a signifier of dystopia; an intruder – in the forms of words – that converts spaces of desire into what one may term "minus desire;" a desirable luncheon into a dangerous one. Bulatov's virtual spaces of danger warned that the *plein-air* space had not been freed of ideology.

Worldwide media condemnation of the authorities' brutal treatment of dissident modernists and of their art works at *The Bulldozer Exhibition* led to official permission for another open-air exhibition, in Izmailovsky Park (hence its name the Izmailovo exhibition two weeks later (figs. 96–8). This peaceful outcome of *The Bulldozer Exhibition* benefited both parties. On one hand, the authorities elevated their international reputation from savages to supporters of modern art, which, to judge by the high attendance at the Izmailovo exhibition, was of genuine public interest. On the other hand, underground artists were unprecedentedly uncensored in their selection of works, and were allowed to interact with the public. These new conditions marked the end of the systemic hegemony of MOSSKh, whose bureaucrats and artists, for the first time since the postwar period, did not play a definitive role in the nonconformists' relationships with the government and public. For the participants of *The Bulldozer Exhibition* this resulted in an official invitation to join the Moscow Committee of Graphic Artists (Gorkom Grafikov). Created for book designers and professional photographers, Gorkom Grafikov became willing to admit painters. A modest exhibition space in the basement of an apartment building, at Malaia Gruzinskaia Street 28, was assigned for regular exhibitions of hitherto unofficial art. This unintentionally preserved an atmosphere of underground culture. Gorkom Grafikov membership also made it possible to exhibit in other official venues, including

96   Crowds of viewers approaching the site of the Izmailovo exhibition, September 29, 1974.

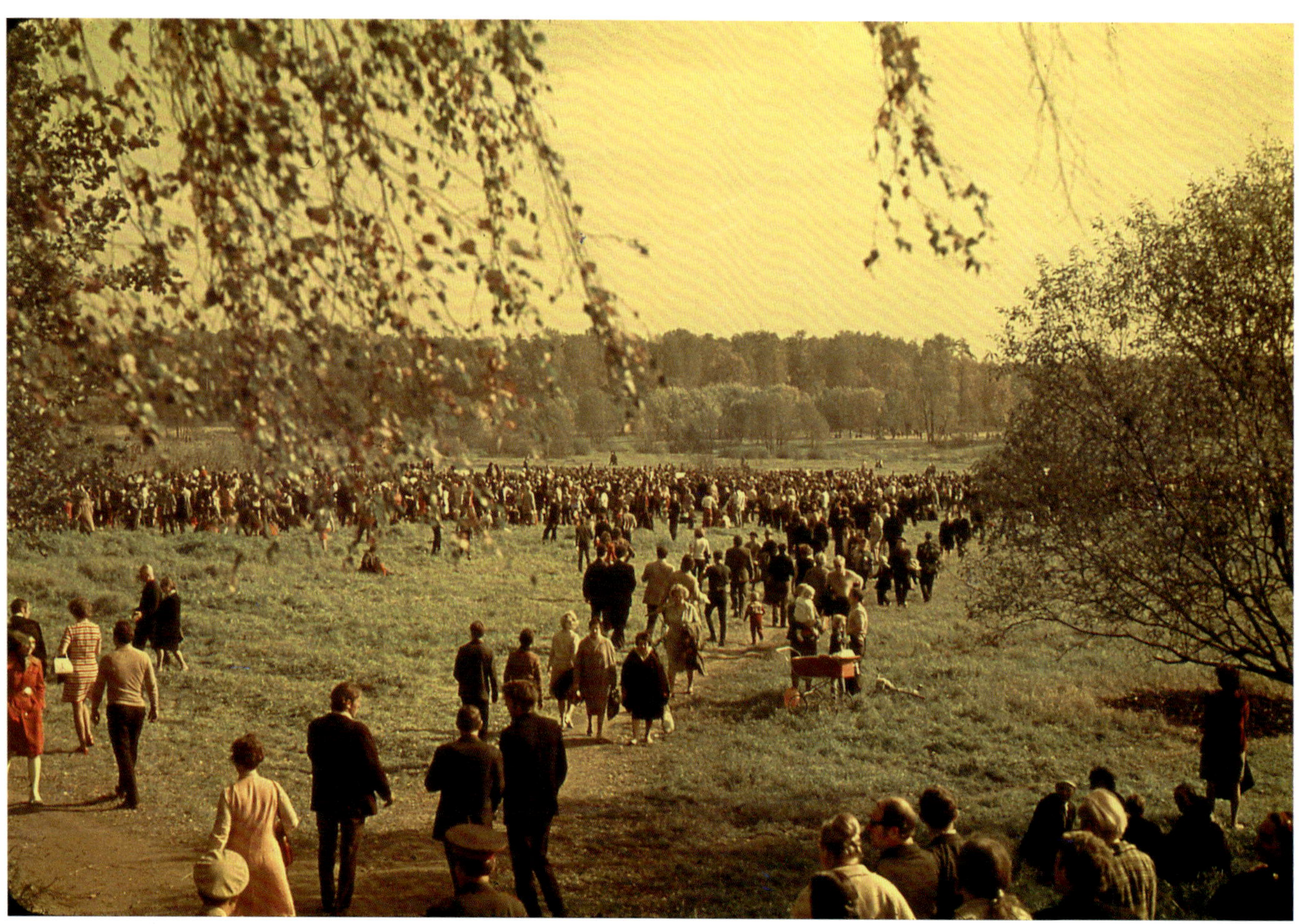

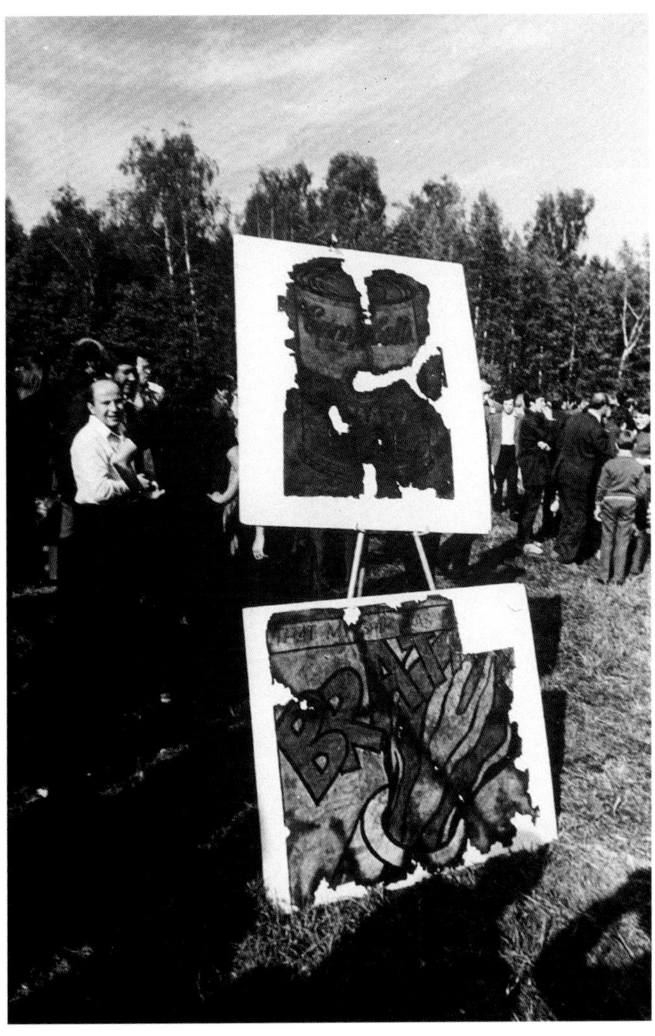

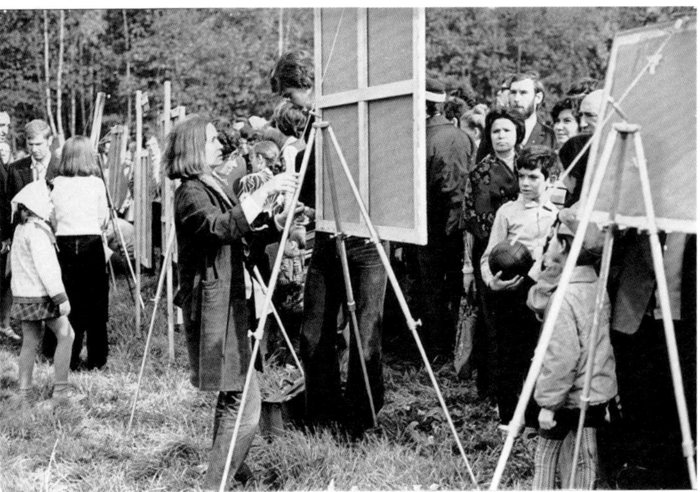

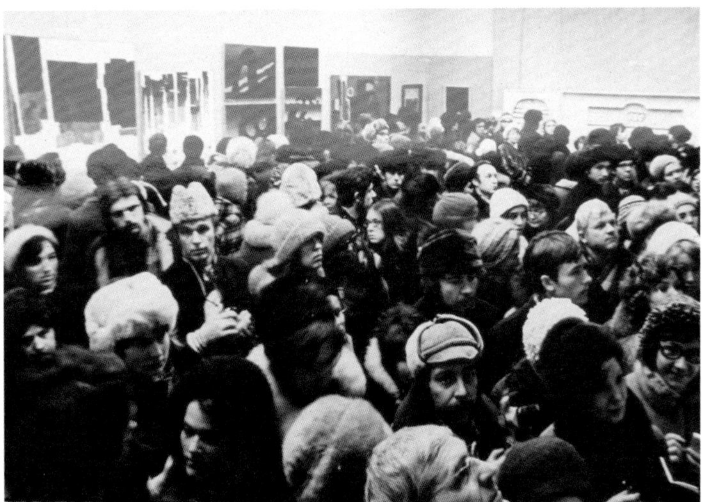

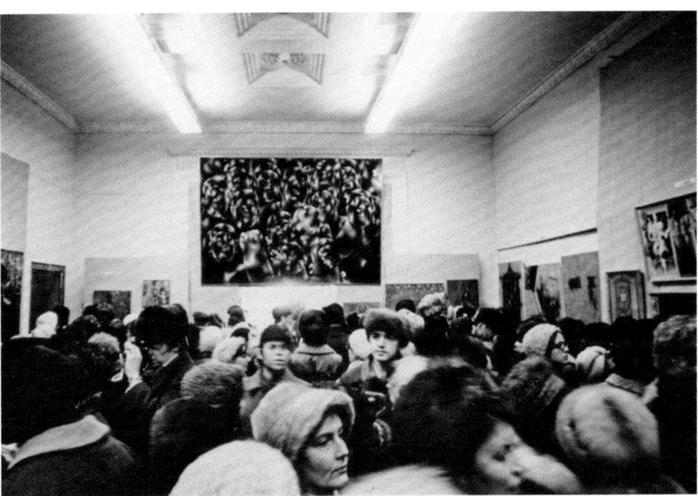

ABOVE 97   Vitaly Komar and Aleksandr Melamid's *Post Art* series in the Izmailovo exhibition, September 29, 1974.

TOP RIGHT 98   Lydia Masterkova standing near her painting in the Izmailovo exhibition, September 29, 1974.

MIDDLE & BOTTOM RIGHT 99   Exhibition in VDNKh's Beekeeping Pavilion, February 1975.

a one-week exhibition (February 19–26, 1975) in the Beekeeping Pavilion of VDNKh (fig. 99). Unlike the reaction to the Manezh exhibition in 1962, this display of modernist art at a site not associated with prestigious exhibitions could not evoke competitive feelings from MOSSKh artists and bureaucrats. Such rapid developments in exhibition policies for the dissident modernists eased their anxiety, but it did little for

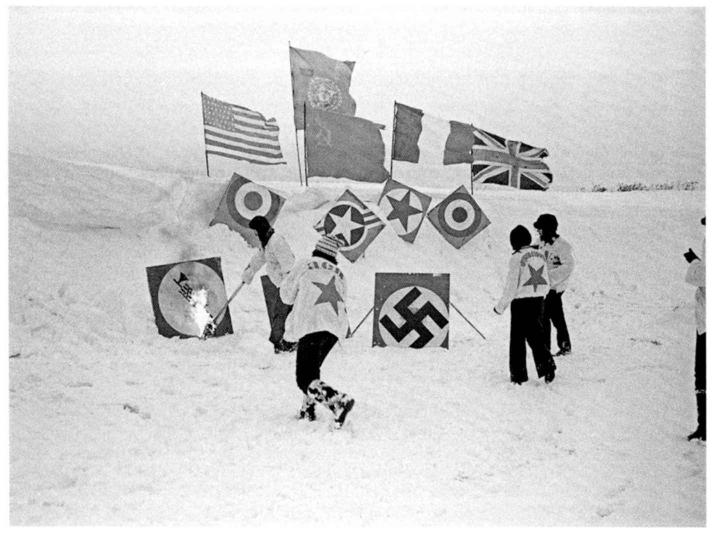

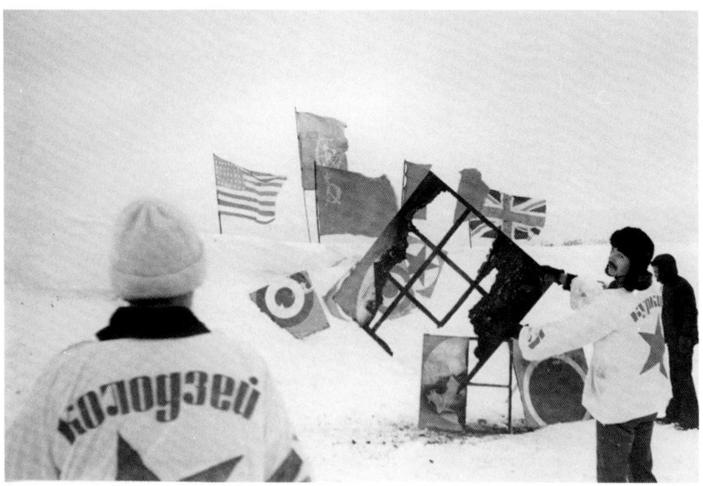

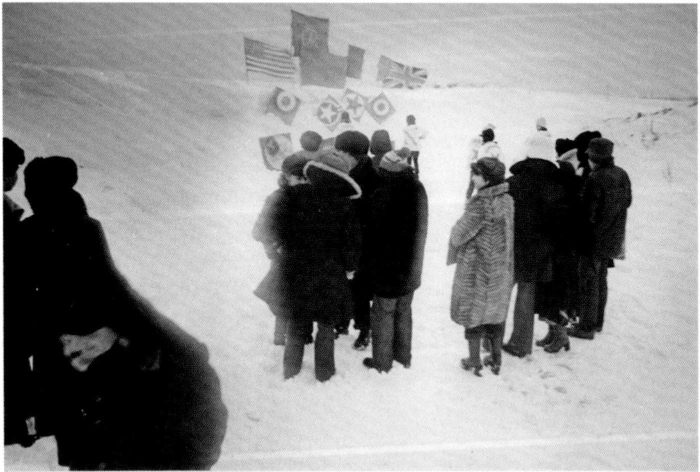

100–102   Red Star group, performance dedicated to the thirtieth anniversary of the United Nations, December 1975.

those artists who embarked on producing more radical content and forms. These artists formed their own milieu that bifurcated into rural and urban (or studio) production. The trajectory of formal and theoretical reaction and resistance between these two poles I analyze in this and the next chapter.

Mikhail Chernyshov's 1960s use of readymade materials and military imagery in two-dimensional art made it easy for him to exchange the studio for open space. In December 1975, together with Boris Bich, Chernyshov assembled the Red Star group to stage a performance in commemoration of the thirtieth anniversary of the founding of the United Nations (figs. 100–2). Joined by two more artists, they set up in a snowy field a mixture of homemade flags (American, Soviet, British, and United Nations) and signs (a star, a circle, and a swastika). To blend into the white natural space, and distinguish themselves from the audience, the performers wore white jackets decorated with stars and their names. Together with the audience, the group manipulated these foreign signs and symbols, which were dangerous for a Soviet citizen to associate with, by installing them randomly in the snow and setting some on fire. Taking power into their own hands, everyone present was able to rethink the established political clichés.

The political references and high energy of Red Star's performance can be seen as an extension of Chernyshov's earlier practice of action painting, which, given the official press's fierce attack on abstract art after the *American National Exhibition* and the Manezh show, had constituted a radical act, albeit one without implicit political iconography. In contrast, Red Star's event was saturated with political symbolism and thus the approach can be reversed and its reading conducted in visual terms. Political icons became geometric shapes, colors played against the whiteness of the snow, performers dressed in white contrasted with the audience dressed in black, and a still field covered in snow was animated with fire, as in Infante's *Snow Ritual*. A documentary photograph records the four group members posing after the event as they look through the grid structure, a trace of political imagery obliterated by fire. The image emblematizes Chernyshov's concept of the reversibility of political and apolitical readings of the same art work. For

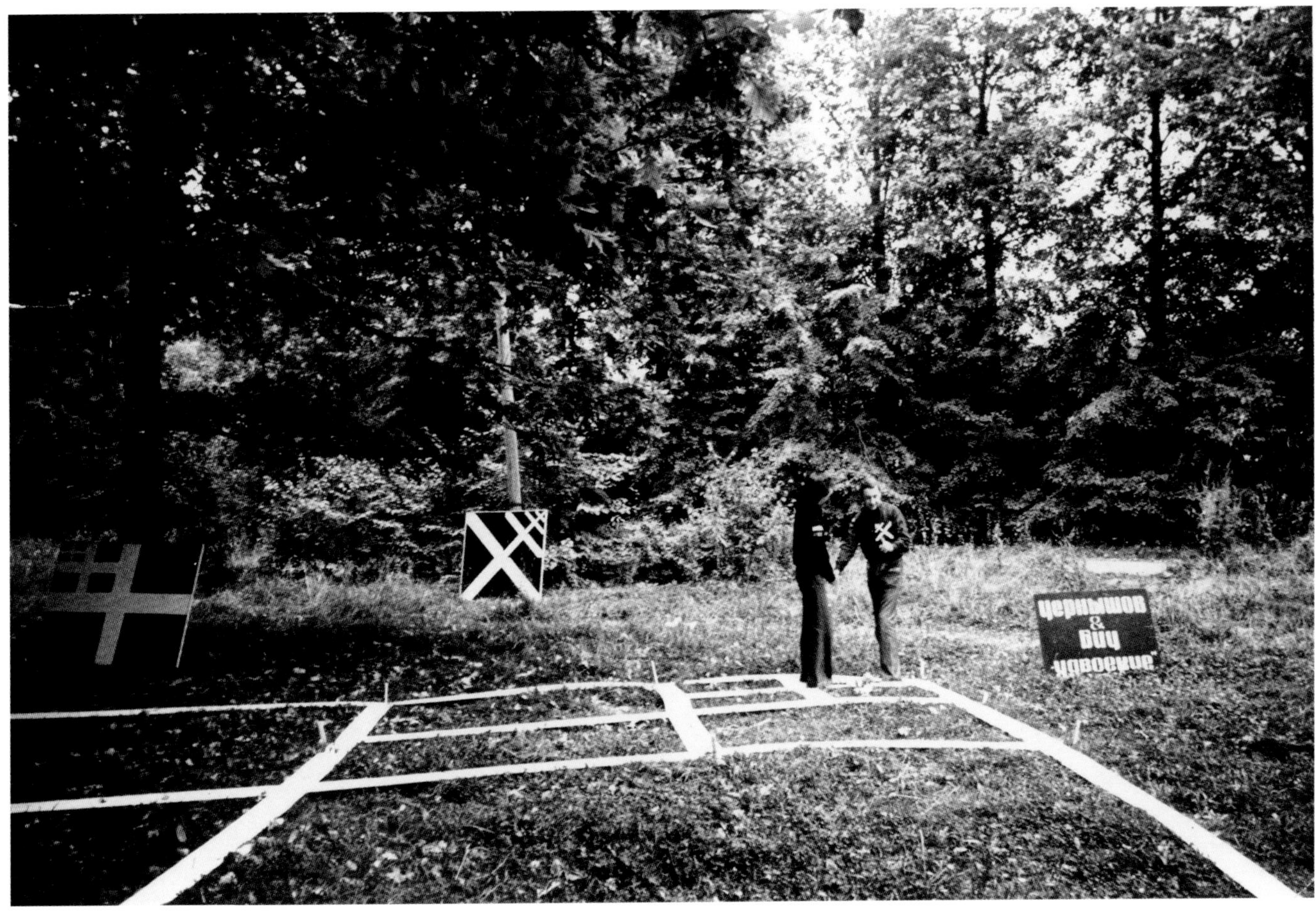

103   Mikhail Chernyshov and Boris Bich, *Doubling I*, September 1976.

Moscow vanguardists, this had been embedded from the beginning, simply because they worked in a totally politicized environment. This automatically radicalized their production, but it also exempted these artists from consciously conceiving political art. Further, this fixed union between aesthetics and politics could only work in the context of a single ideology, and it caused all sorts of problems for artists and Russian art when, after the collapse of the Soviet Union, the country's ideologies multiplied.

The Izmailovo exhibition inspired Chernyshov and Bich to create a performance, *Doubling I* (fig. 103), in which Chernyshov returned to his earlier critique of abstract art's self-referentiality. He was now discontented with how dissident modernists mechanically relocated their paintings from studios to Izmailovsky Park, showed them on easels, and engaged in a traditional author–viewer dialogue with the audience. In effect, the participants at the Izmailovo show were denying that they were showing their works in an unconventional space. *Doubling I* contested this artificial set-up by placing paintings on the ground and leaning them against trees. The paintings' compositions were configured according to Chernyshov's concept of doubling from the early 1960s. The idea was to shift symmetry from the center to the edge of the surface by doubling a central image on the scale of 1:2. As Chernyshov rendered this game of multiplication, painting's spatial limitations became obvious, necessitating a sequence of doubling spilling beyond the painting's edge and spreading onto the ground. This was what Malevich had discovered in Vitebsk, which led to his release of Suprematism's formal vocabulary onto the streets. In *Doubling I*, Cherny-

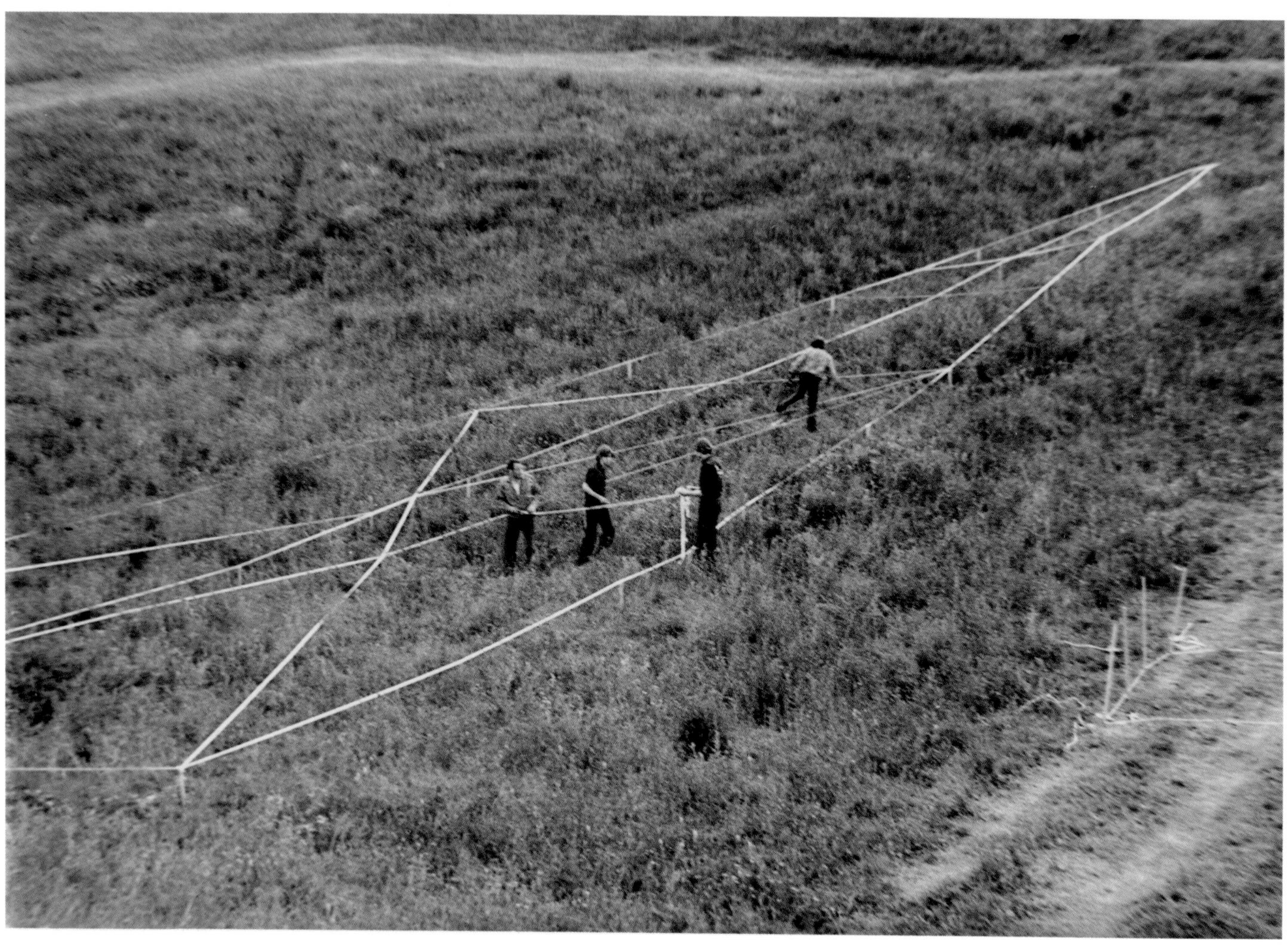

104   Mikhail Chernyshov and Boris Bich, *Doubling II*, September 1978.

shov did not use geometric forms for political ends – although, as I noted earlier, every unsanctioned aesthetic act was *a priori* politicized in Soviet Russia. By imitating a painterly concept on the ground, Chernyshov proposed an unusual form of mimesis: not of a landscape in a painting, but of painting in a landscape. In *Doubling II* (1978), Chernyshov's method of formal expansion attained a condition of sheer striving toward the infinity of time–space, but which in a geometric painting can only be connoted (fig. 104). This was achieved by a collective realization of doubling, during which the participants and the artists wove geometry across a field. Significantly, the resulting geometric configuration repeated a trajectory of participants' movements during the Red Star perfor-

mance. This similarity permits one to observe how political experience was rendered in the semantics of geometry, as in Russia's post-revolutionary geometric abstraction.

Both the place and the participants' arrival with their paintings at the second open-air exhibition (fig. 105) provide the context for a discussion about *The Appearance,* the first performance by the Collective Actions Group (CAG), which was staged at Izmailovsky Park on March 13, 1976 (figs. 106–8). The action's script concisely states: "Invitations were sent out for the action *The Appearance.* When everyone invited arrived (30 people) and gathered on one side of a field, five minutes later, two participants of the action appeared from the forest on another side. Carrying

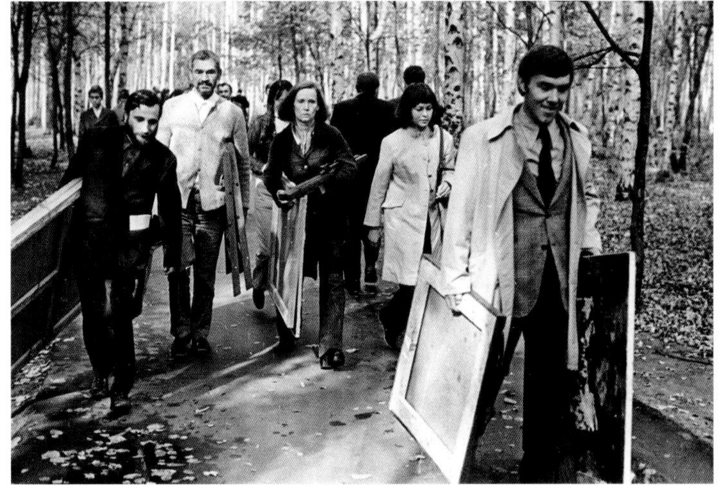

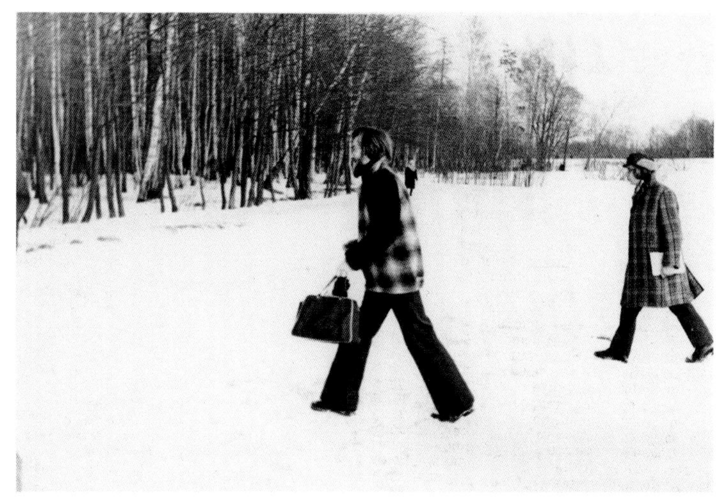

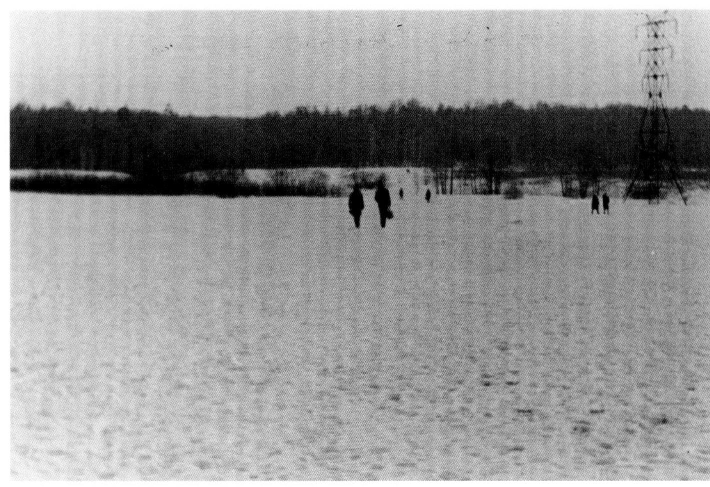

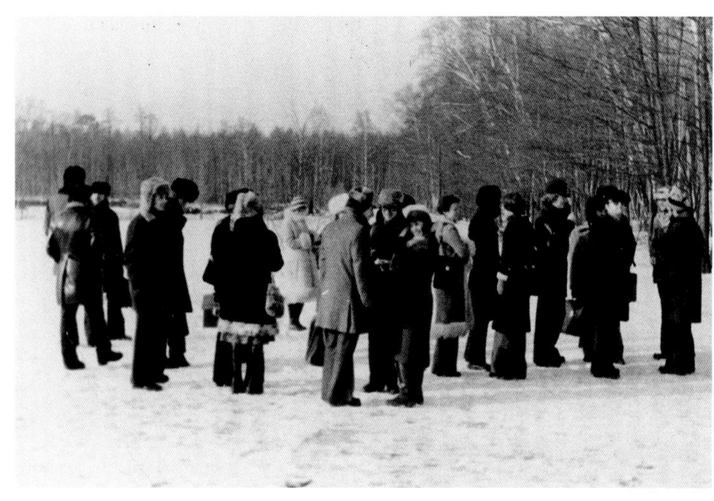

105   Artists approaching the site of the Izmailovo exhibition, September 29, 1974.

106   Collective Actions Group, *The Appearance*, Izmailovsky Park, March 13, 1976. Archive of Collective Actions Group.

107   Collective Actions Group, *The Appearance*, Izmailovsky Park, March 13, 1976. Archive of Collective Actions Group.

108   Collective Actions Group, *The Appearance*, Izmailovsky Park, March 13, 1976. Archive of Collective Actions Group.

only a bag and documents, they crossed the field, approached the audience, and handed out a certificate ('Documentary confirmation') of presence at *The Appearance*."[5] Under the text, the collective's original members are listed: Andrei Monastyrsky, Lev Rubinshtein, Nikita Alekseev, and Georgy Kizevalter.[6] Since the first two were poets, they directed the initial discourse away from art objects toward the exploration of transgressive forms of poetry. As Monastyrsky wrote on the back of a photograph of *The Appearance* that he sent to Victor Tupitsyn in New York: "These are the viewers-listeners-readers," broadening the viewers' experience from being solely visual.[7] This more complex interactive aesthetics was transposed to the *plein air* from Monastyrsky's series, *Elementary Poetry*. Conceived a year earlier in his Moscow apartment, it deconstructed the revered Russian practice of reciting poetry to compensate for the absence of formal publication. An active practitioner and master of this form, Monastyrsky decided to expand the performative aspects of poetry: he proceeded with an action, *Pile* (see fig. 141), that started on December 12, 1975, and

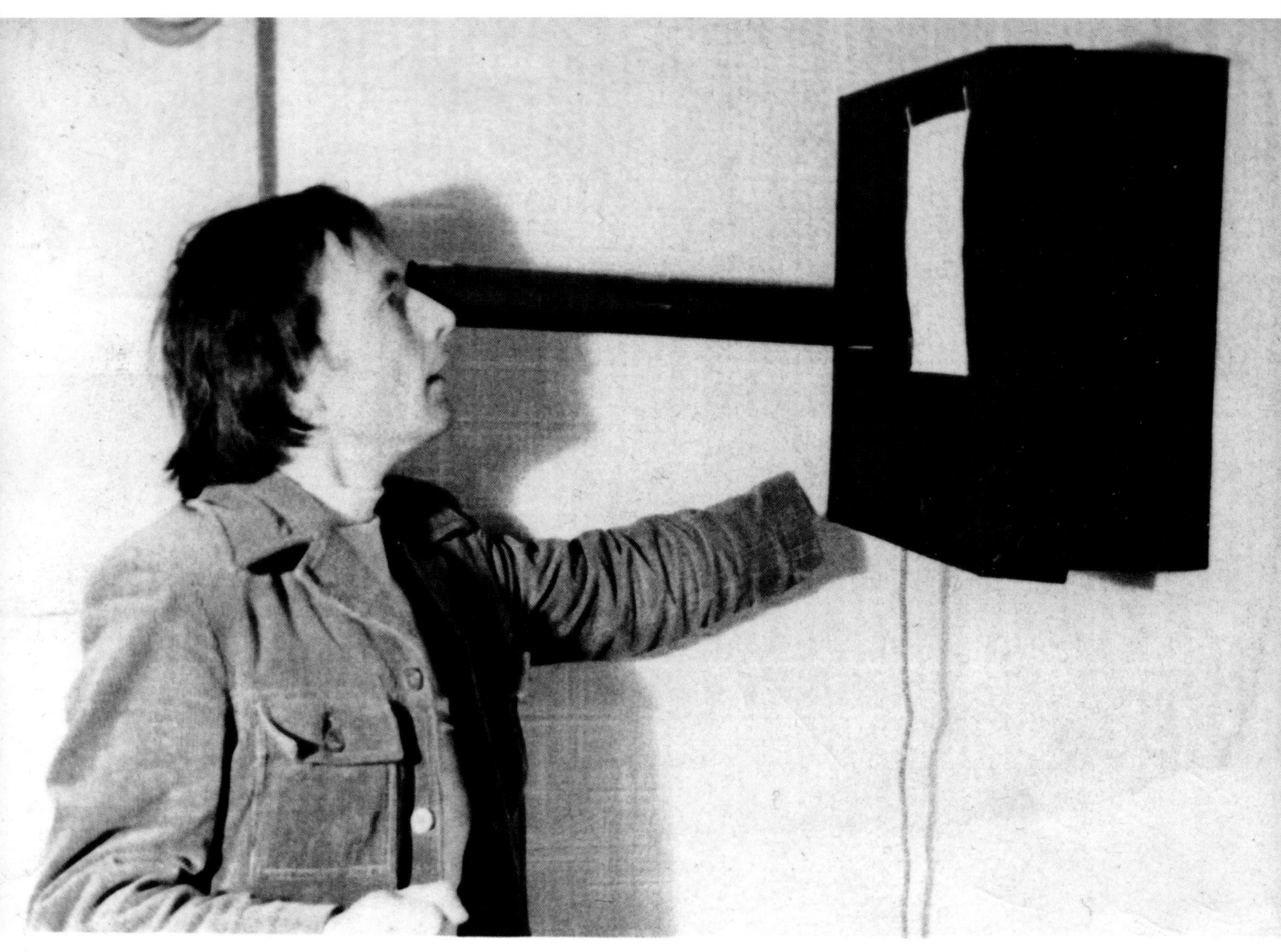

109 Andrei Monastyrsky, *Cannon*, 1975, with Rolf Fieguth.

was still functioning at the time of *The Appearance*'s staging. During this time, 44 participants left 87 objects on the podium and recorded their participation in a notebook. *Cannon* (1975), Monastyrsky's second experiment with transtextual poetry, consisted of a black box with a long tube and a switch attached to it (fig. 109).[8] While looking into the tube and turning on the switch, instead of an optical experience, the participant would hear a buzzer. In the second CAG action, called *Lieblich* and also performed in Izmailovsky Park on April 2, 1976, Monastyrsky tested *Cannon*'s aim to shift perceptions rather than shifting its status as an art object in an "expanded field." For this, a buzzer buried in a snow-covered field rang prior to the arrival of 25 "witnesses" and it kept ringing after they had left, uncertain about the meaning of their experience. CAG's interest in sound comes from a fascination with concrete music in general and with John Cage's *4'33"* in particular. On April 10, 1977, CAG received Cage's response to their earlier letter to him, in which he specifically says: "Your work with bells outdoors and the idea of bells under the seats in a concert hall are

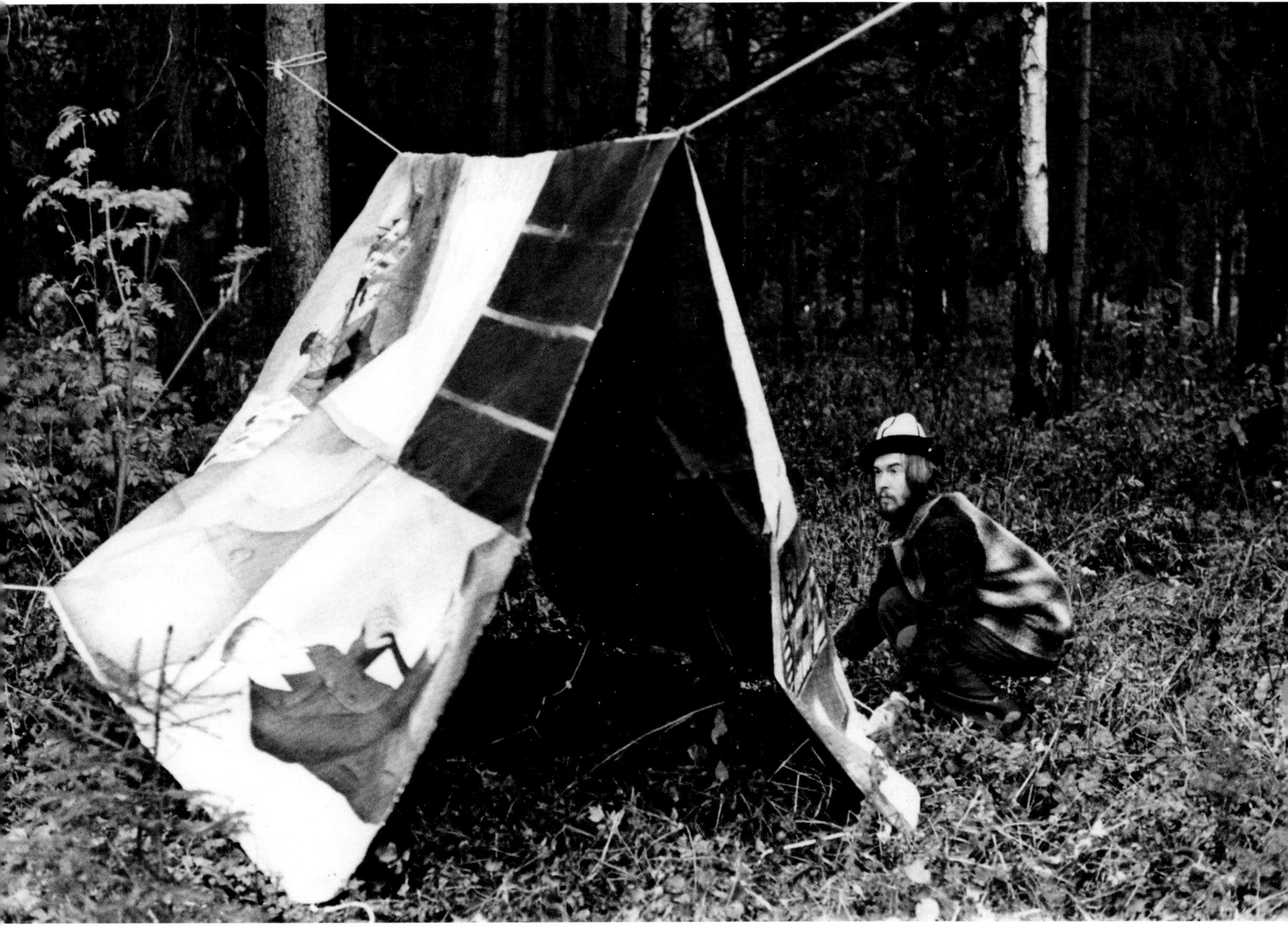

110   Collective Actions Group, *Tent*, October 2, 1976, with Nikita Alekseev.

excellent." He expresses an interest in collaboration and inspires Alekseev to think about the difference between underground practices in New York and Moscow. Alekseev believed that Cage's idea – that independence from mainstream culture would necessarily create "an embryo of a happy future" – was utopian and that, in general, the idea of a happy future in this world is absurd. This statement is noteworthy because it amply demonstrates the divide between the West and the East in terms of utopian thinking, formed due to Stalin's destruction of the embryo of

the Revolution, and later by Krushchev's false promise of a communist future. And yet, I believe there was a utopian aspect (distinct from romanticism, a concept ruined by Andrei Zhdanov) to CAG's performances, and I will address it later.

The CAG's third action, *Tent*, performed on October 2, 1976, was conceived by Alekseev, a visual artist eager to address the socio-cultural displacement of modernist painting in Russia. Alekseev roughly painted twelve canvases and used them to build a tent that the group installed in a forest and left there. They returned a year

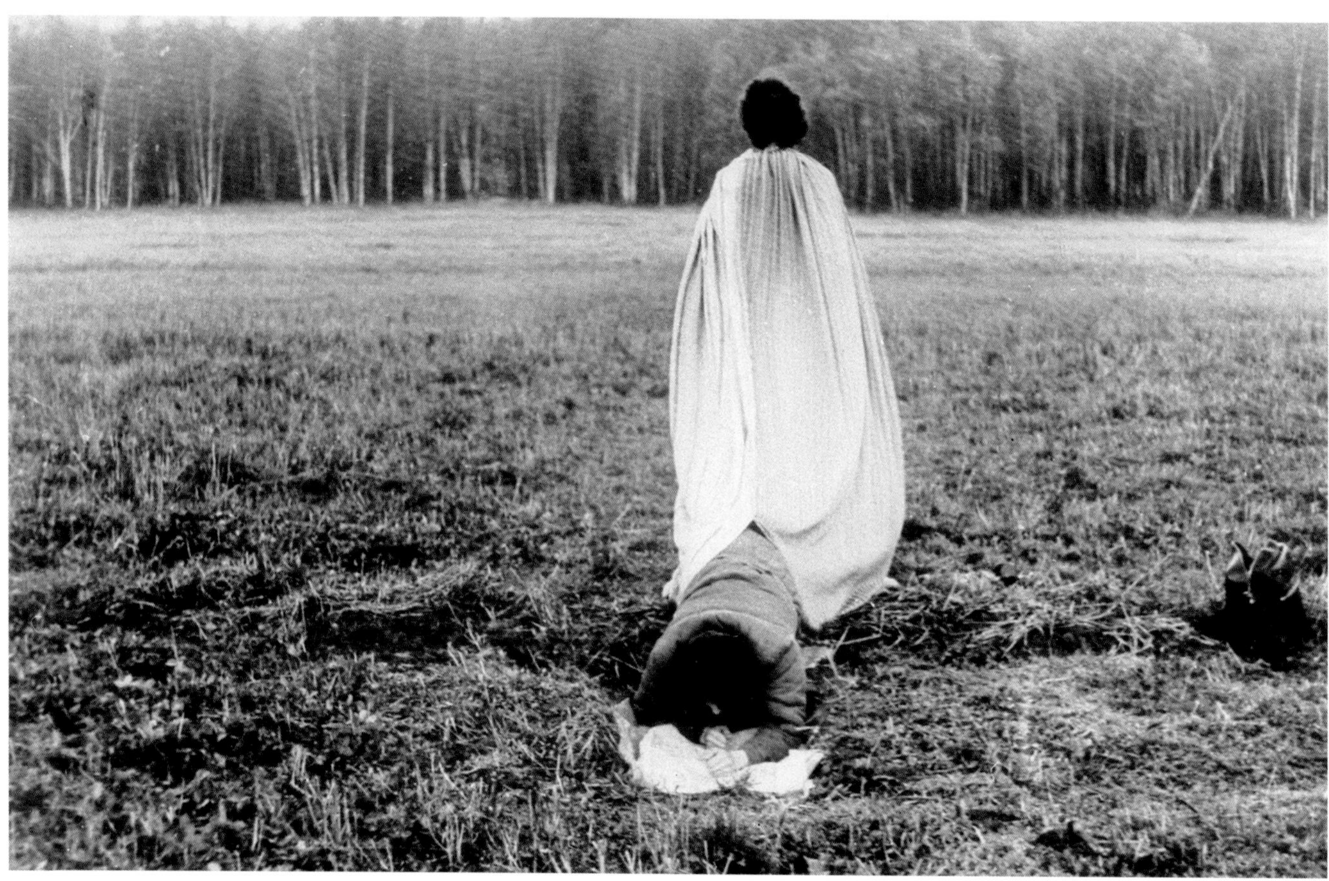

later to witness the damage made to the art works by the elements (fig. 110). This act of misusing – dumping paintings in the countryside and leaving them to turn into rubbish – called on the spectator not to forget the destruction of paintings by the authorities (during *The Bulldozer Exhibition*), even though artists were later included in exhibitions by way of compensation. Furthermore, Alekseev's staging of an encounter between an accidental viewer and a common, familiar object such as a tent executed in an unfamiliar fashion was an attempt to shake up Soviet citizens' alienation from modernist art.

Monastyrsky believes that the next action, *Comedy* (October 2, 1977), shifted the "not very compulsory" performances of the group into "a more narrowed, specialized field, a genre…It was then that definitive principles in the actions' structure began to be formed, and the language of a small collective had taken shape

as a result," he explained to Victor Tupitsyn (fig. III).[9] At that point, the CAG stopped seeing its activities in relation to the overall Moscow cultural situation, which Monastyrsky believes catapulted the group into open space. Instead, they chose to develop a theoretical kinship with a group of older artists who had departed from classical modernism. Among such were Oleg Vasiliev, Ilya Kabakov, Bulatov, Ivan Chuikov, Viktor Pivovarov, and Eduard Gorokhovsky. Together they could challenge Brezhnev's stagnation by stimulating the alternative spaces outside of the mundane and controlled everydayness of urban life. As poets, the CAG's founding members, Monastyrsky and Rubinshtein, were perhaps unconsciously responding to the assertion by Roman Jakobson in relation to Mayakovsky that stagnation "is the poet's primordial enemy."[10]

In order to reach the site of *Comedy*, Kabakov and Gorokhovsky undertook a long journey out of town

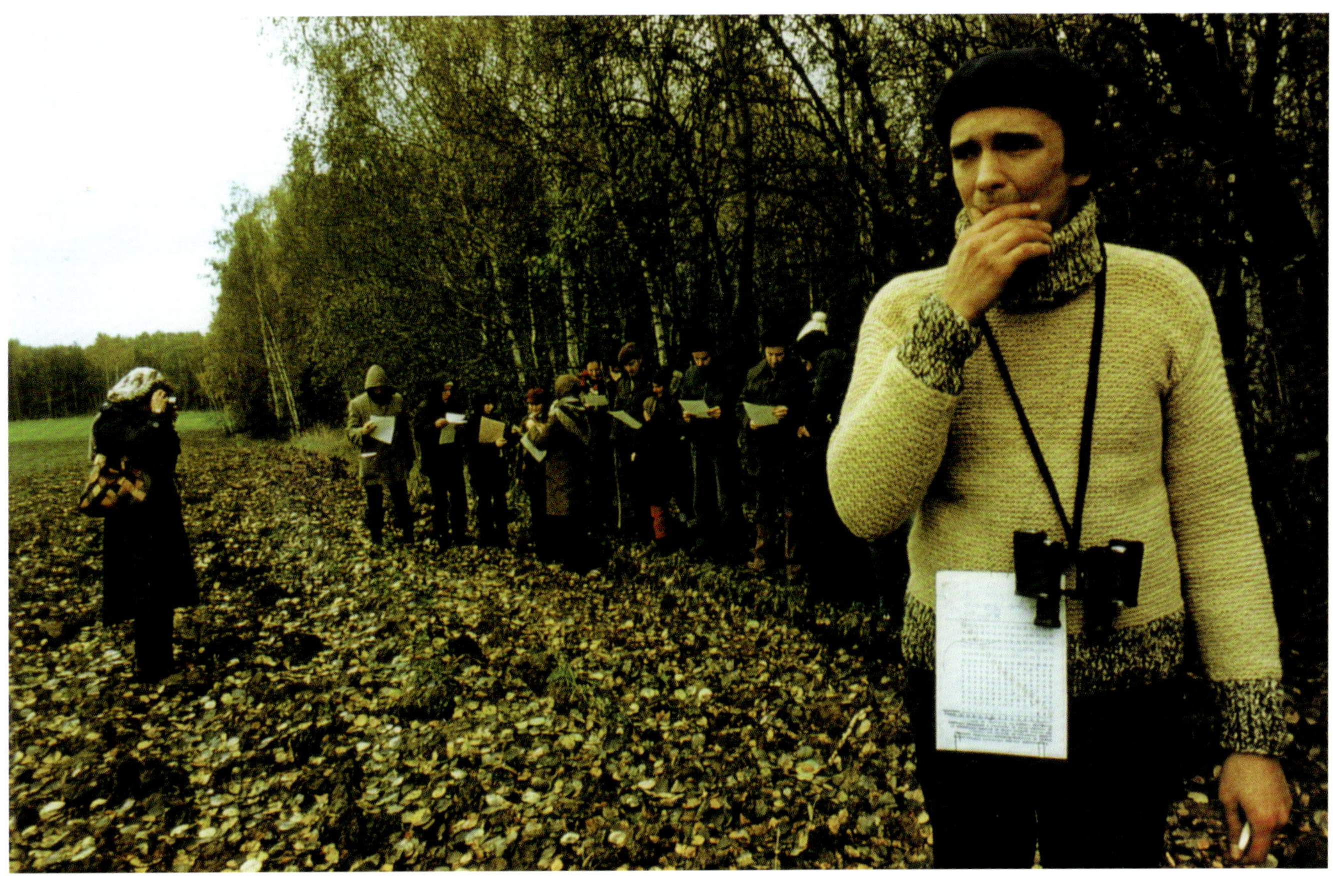

112   Collective Actions Group, *Place of Action*, October 7, 1979. Archive of Collective Actions Group.

by train, bus, and a walk through the forest. All this effort was made in order to witness a brief event enacted by Monastyrsky and the artist Nikolai Panitkov (a member of CAG since *Tent*), who wore an over-sized cloak. Eighty meters from viewers, Monastyrsky faked crawling inside the cloak, giving the impression that the two performers were together moving toward the viewers. From a distance of 25 meters, Panitkov lifted his cloak to show that Monastyrsky had gone, and then he himself disappeared into the forest. Although *Comedy*'s action fitted in with the theater of the absurd, it initiated the group's "laws of demonstration" that, according to Monastyrsky, included "a movement of figures and objects…along a straight line and in two directions: either toward or away from the audience. In this context this movement should be understood as a movement along 'a line of perception.'"[11] The rest of the activities took place on the

"'margins' of an action's 'demonstration field.'"[12] In other words, CAG members began to script their events according to fairly precise structural rules that were similar to those of two-dimensional works made at the time in Moscow's studios. There were two reasons to do this: first to expand the discursive space of conceptual works such as Kabakov's, and second to provide a paradigm of a vanguard practice that would dematerialize an art object, make it fully independent of the local socio-cultural environment, which supported an entirely "different 'culture.'"[13] Monastyrsky believed that in the Soviet Union "only those artists who do not make 'things,' but rather look at art as a form of existence can survive…that is, do not make art consciously. Here everything is rotting because no one consumes these art goods in time. We function independently from society because we make nothing that could rot."[14] Thus CAG's aesthetic choices were based on the "objectlessness of our desires,"[15] and the group arrived at the same paradigm of de-reification as had early 1920s nonobjective artists after they abandoned painting and before they turned to production.

Writing shortly after the event, Monastyrsky called *Place of Action* (fig. 112) "a monumental 'canvas,'" and stressed the participation of Bulatov, Kabakov, Chuikov, and Vasiliev. "I think we were finally able to over-saturate the salon to such a degree that no one understood anything, thus fulfilling our task," Monastyrsky concluded.[16] For this piece, the group wanted to take aesthetic energy from the studios (or, in Monastyrsky's terminology, "the salon") to a country field, or at least to create a correlation between them. With this objective, CAG shifted from their earlier minimizing of visual material to generating a detailed photographic archive.[17] This move was crucial in that CAG could formally reinstate photography as an experimental medium – the position it had played in the avant-garde but had lost as soon as it had been adopted by the state as its main propaganda instrument. CAG's photographers such as Kizevalter, Igor Makarevich, and Andrei Abramov not only performed the utilitarian function of documenting the actions, but also took a formal and conceptual approach to the medium. During a session of *Place of Action* called "Shooting," fifteen participants posed for the camera as they moved singly in a straight line across a field according to strict instructions, toward the forest. A participant was photographed only after the previous one had disappeared into the forest. These shots were compiled into a slideshow presented and discussed in Makarevich and Elena Elagina's studio, both conceptual artists and CAG members since *Place of Action*. The result is a model in which performance artists test the principles of two-dimensional work in an open space – the photographs in the form of a slideshow in their turn allowed the action to enter the studio space for interpretation and a visual experience.

There is a specific Kabakov work that I believe impacted CAG's late 1970s performances. In 1975,

when Monastyrsky, then 26 years old, started regularly visiting Kabakov's studio, Kabakov's triptych *Along the Edge* (1974) no doubt overwhelmed the space (fig. 113). Its monumental size (each panel three meters high), coarse and monochrome surface of Masonite covered in white enamel paint, and imagery of peasants pushed out to all four edges, constituted a challenge in representation and technique to the small easel painting practiced by most modernists. There is no record of how Kabakov described his triptych to Monastyrsky, but in the early 1990s, while living in the West, Kabakov emphasized that in *Along the Edge* he had rejected perspective: "Here the foundation of the painting is the center…thus all the painting's edges are identical and equal in relation to the center."[18] He also related this structure to the Russian avant-garde's collapsing of the difference between "top, bottom, right, and left" of an art work, as demonstrated in such nonobjective works as Gustav Klutsis' *Dynamic City* (see fig. 5) and Lissitzky's *Abstract Cabinet*. As in those works, Kabakov's figures ignore the laws of gravity and the viewer's vertical position. Furthermore, this kind of composition allows the work to be placed flat on the ground to be observed from above. Such possibilities convinced Monastyrsky that painting could be translated into action. He first tried this by showing objects on the ground, in *Pictures* (fig. 114),[19] and then, as some shots of *Place of Action* demonstrate, positioning that action's participants at the edge of an empty field.

Kabakov's recollection of *Place of Action* stresses the physical sensations that show his awareness of Monastrysky's conceptual move: "Finally [other participants] turned into rather small groups entirely indistinguishable…I was now alone moving across the field. I have to say, it was rather large for crossing fast, and I spent a large chunk of time in the middle of this dirty plowed field between the two edges of the forest, surrounded by the incredible emptiness."[20] It is this memory of optical effects and psychosomatic experience that reverberated in Kabakov's definition of his own *Along the Edge* as "geometrically narrated psychedelia."[21]

OPPOSITE PAGE 113   Ilya Kabakov, *Along the Edge*, 1974, one of three panels. Collection Erna and Paul Jolles, Bern.

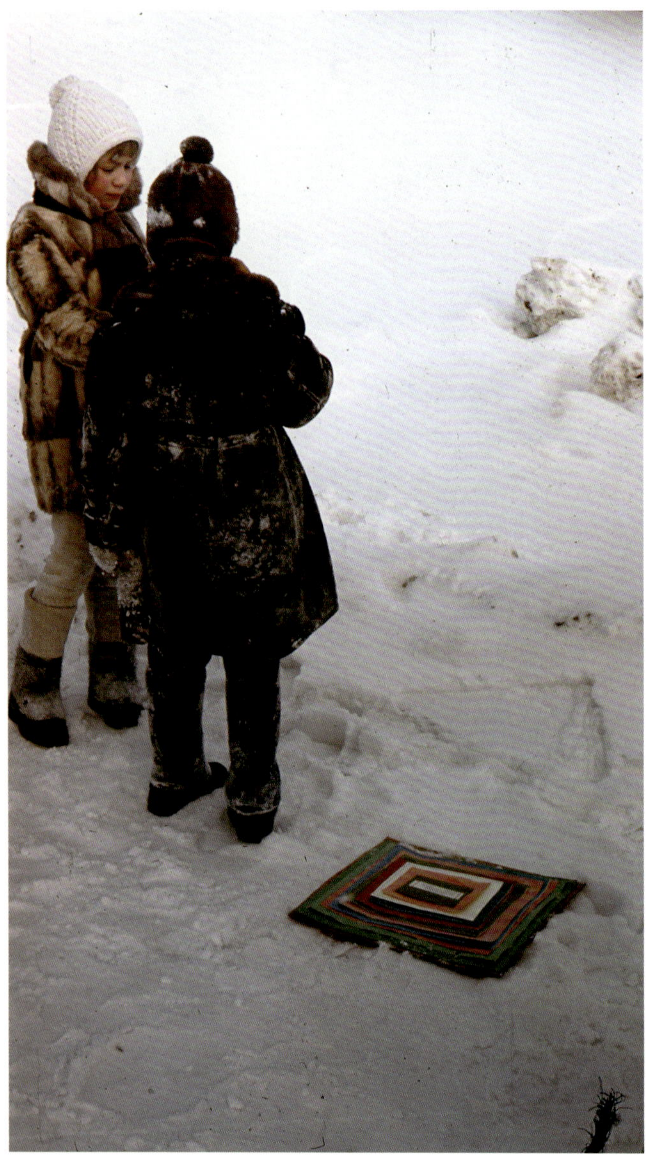

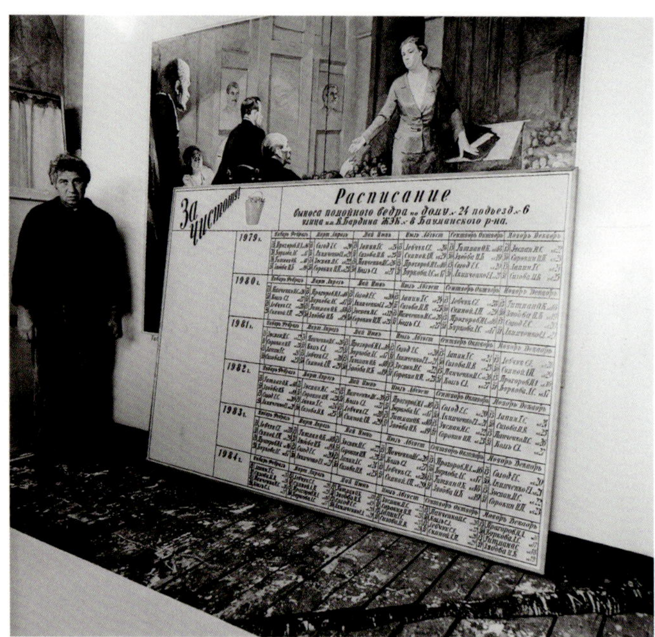

LEFT 114   Collective Actions Group, *Pictures*, February 11, 1979. Archive of Collective Actions Group

ABOVE 115   Ilya Kabakov standing near *Schedule for Taking Out the Garbage Bucket*, 1980, in his studio. Schaulager Basel, Sammlung der Emanuel Hoffmann-Stiftung.

There is one more aspect of CAG's *Place of Action* that also demonstrates a correlation and reciprocity between performance art and conceptual art executed in studios. In Kabakov's 1983 essay, "Can One Write Words on 'White?'" he described his concept of that color, which he had been developing from the 1960s. The text was written after he had participated in several major CAG actions, and its painting terminology and metaphors reflect the spatial and metaphysical sensations he had experienced during the actions. The main significance of white (including *Along the Edge*[22]) arises when "the 'white' surface and the center of a painting remain undisturbed and untouchable. In this case":

> "White"…is understood, seen, and perceived as an uninterrupted and even stream of emanation, the emanation of bright, almost blinding light that functions not as a flash but as a constant current of even energy…the "white" painting itself ceases to exist. It becomes a place where this action occurs, a screen from which comes this emanation. In this case the definitive meaning and content are carried by the edges of such a "pseudo-painting." These edges become the contact points, the intersections between this "non-painting" and common objects of our reality…The latter blur the edges of such "[non-]painting," creating a sort of "green halo" around the light discussed above.[23]

Another series of white paintings came about, I believe, as a result of Kabakov's participation in *Place of Action*, and was characterized by Monastyrsky as:

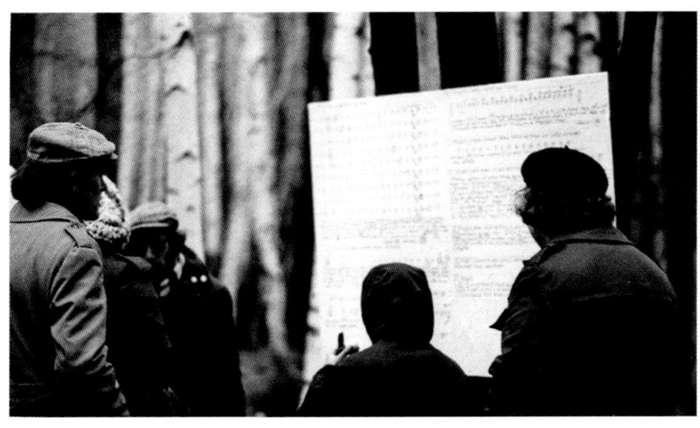

116   Collective Actions Group, *Place of Action*, with Ilya Kabakov (right), October 7, 1979. Archive of Collective Actions Group.

117   Collective Actions Group, diagram for *Ten Appearances*, February 1, 1981. Archive of Collective Actions Group.

some kind of flattening, blending, fading; in place of the ontological depths of emptiness came the depth of banality, details, neurotic reactions, and personal sensation. On white panels, Kabakov is inscribing a schedule for taking out the trash by the tenants of some communal apartment…every day and for many hours [I] draw nonsensical scribbles and crosses, unsuccessfully trying to conceive a plan for the next trip to an empty field.[24]

Monastyrsky was referring to Kabakov's *Schedule for Taking Out the Garbage Bucket* (fig. 115) in which he inscribed in black on a white background a tenants' schedule covering six years for performing this most mundane chore. The result is a textual (anti-modernist) grid where characters are named instead of depicted, and a drawing of a bucket is the only image. This way of building up an art work by systematizing ordinary events was *Place of Action*'s achievement. A white panel displayed on a tree at the end of the action documented this process. Kabakov's study of it, captured by the camera (fig. 116), propelled him toward his next model of a "pseudo-painting," such as *Schedule* where the "background is always white, and a representation…consists of texts, numbers, drawings, etc., executed in black enamel."[25]

CAG's *Ten Appearances* (February 1, 1981) was a successful resolution of Monastyrsky's frustration, just described, over how to continue their activities in the new decade (figs. 117, 118). The action's script

assigned ten people, among whom were eight artists (including a woman), a poet, and a collector (probably in homage to Kabakov's seminal drawings and text albums, the "Ten Characters" conceived in the early 1970s and discussed in the next chapter), to walk in deep snow, from the center of the field to the forest, each participant pulling a thread from ten spools installed at the center of the field. At the end of each thread was a piece of paper that certified the participation. The decision about what to do afterward was left up to each participant, resulting in two people leaving and eight returning for a group photograph.

Kabakov and Monastyrsky recorded a conversation about *Ten Appearances* a week after its staging: "I must say that I have never experienced anything like this as far as being in a congenial and joyful state of mind…a completely irrational state of mind," Kabakov recalled.[26] When he finally reached the end of his thread, instead of receiving what he calls "a present," he found a routine acknowledgment of his participation. But, since he had already experienced the pleasure of anticipation, the concreteness of this document was not so important since the very experience described earlier had already taken place.

…Here was realized one of the most pleasant and basically unfamiliar forms of social interaction…which is not hostile to you…but is certain and benevolent in the highest degree. This is such

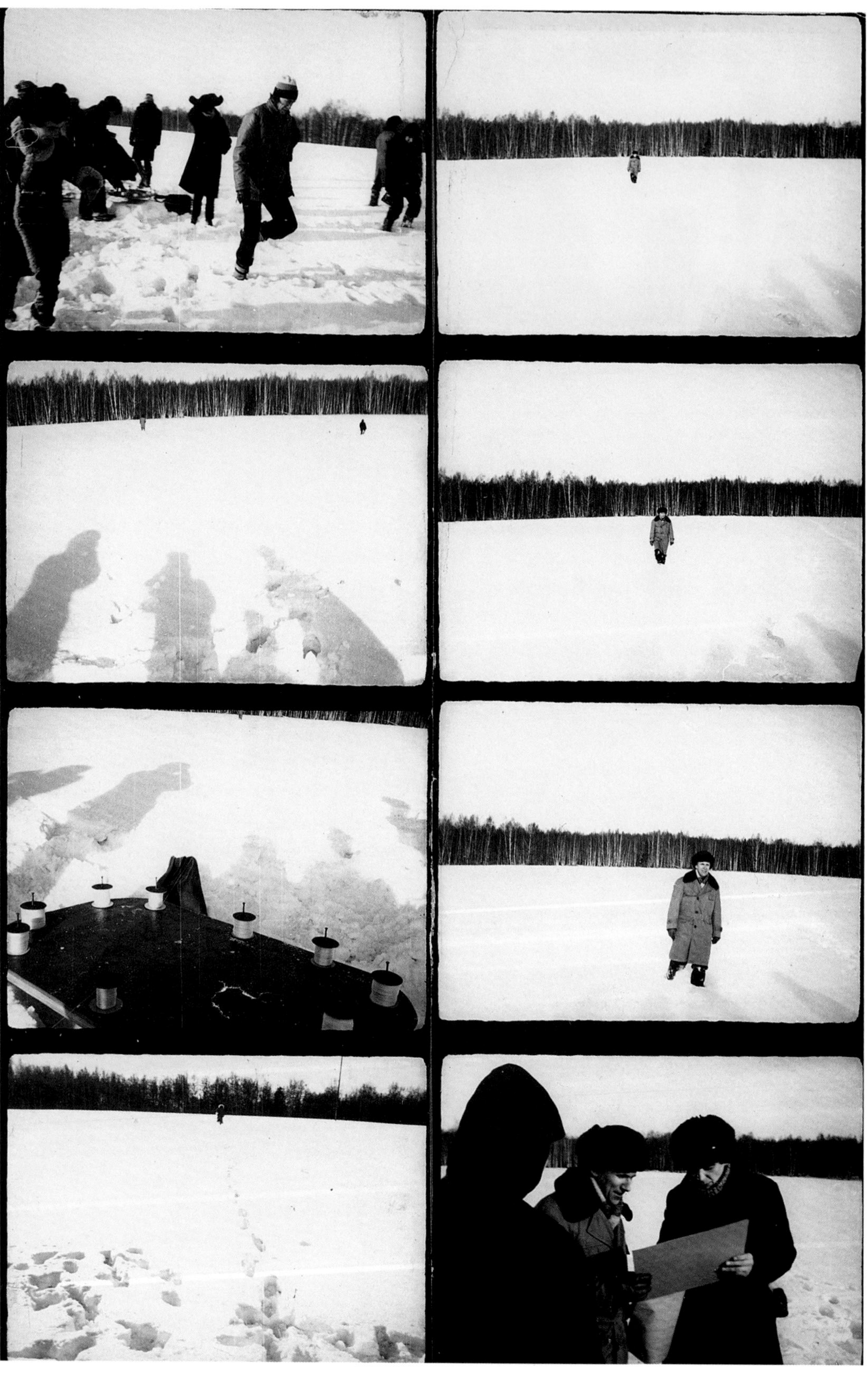

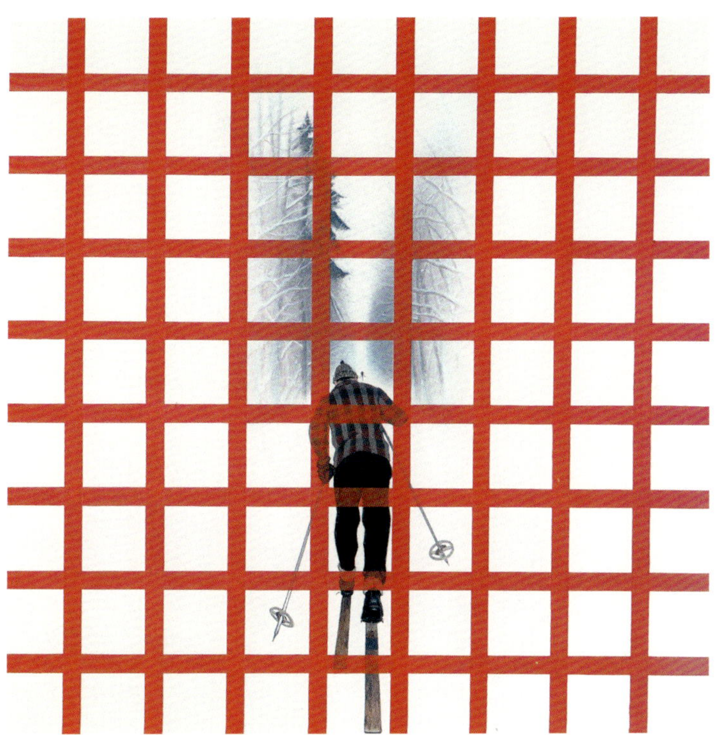

119   Erik Bulatov, *Skier*, 1971–4. Collection Erna and Paul Jolles, Bern.

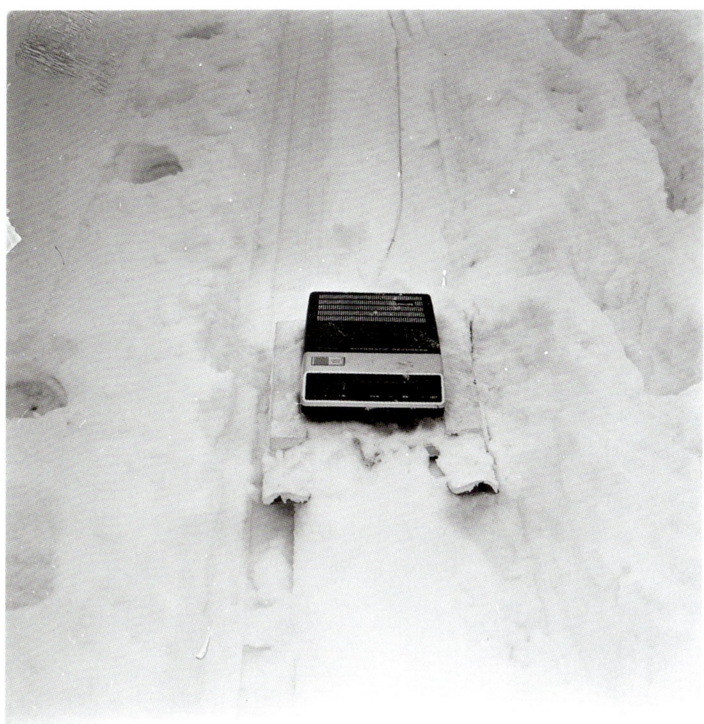

120   Collective Actions Group, *Sound Perspectives of a Country Trip*, February 14, 1983. Archive of Collective Actions Group.

a rare, unfamiliar sensation that it not only invigorates, it serves as a gift against the background of everything we have.[27]

Kabakov's description of his sensations is close to "the house of utopia" proposed by Kandinsky.[28] "Let this structure be characterized by its mobility, its flexibility, so as to accommodate not only what is alive today, even if only in dreams, but also what will first be dreamed of tomorrow," Kandinsky wrote in "The Great Utopia."[29] In other words, by adhering to the notion of utopia as "no place," rather than concretizing its aspirations as constructivists had done,[30] Kandinsky kept "the house of utopia" forever open. In order to test the limits of such metaphysical abstraction, one had to stay in permanent creative tension and indeed intensify the psychophysiological mechanisms of human perception. This explains CAG's cultivation of empty spaces and of "empty action," as well as their rejection of objects from their practice. Similarly, Kabakov called the last painting from his "white series" *Empty Painting* (1983), a monochrome surrounded at the edges by a thin black line that guards such utopian space against reification.

Monastyrsky's acting out on a field the structural properties of painting lead him to study Bulatov's landscapes. By the late 1970s, Monastyrsky was emphasizing the fact that Bulatov had distanced himself from sanctioned exhibitions such as Gorkom Grafikov's *Color, Form, and Space*.[31] "Everyone has surfaced except E. Bulatov, who preserves his esotericism and thus comes out a big winner," wrote Monastyrsky, justifying his own escapist behavior.[32] In *Sound Perspectives of a Country Trip* (February 14, 1983) he decided to probe Bulatov's iconographic and spatial templates just as Bulatov had for *Skier* (fig. 119), when he had himself

OPPOSITE PAGE 118   Collective Actions Group, *Ten Appearances*, February 1, 1981. Archive of Collective Actions Group.

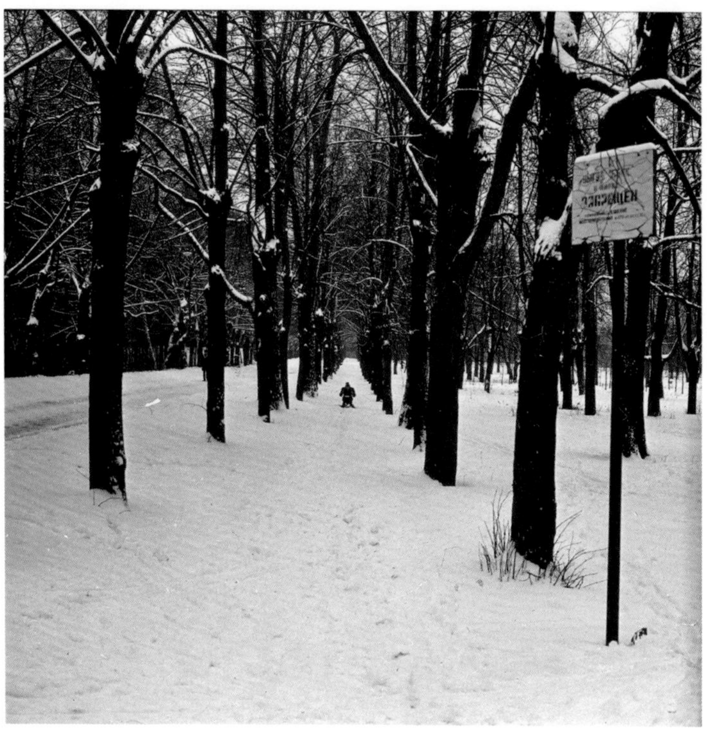

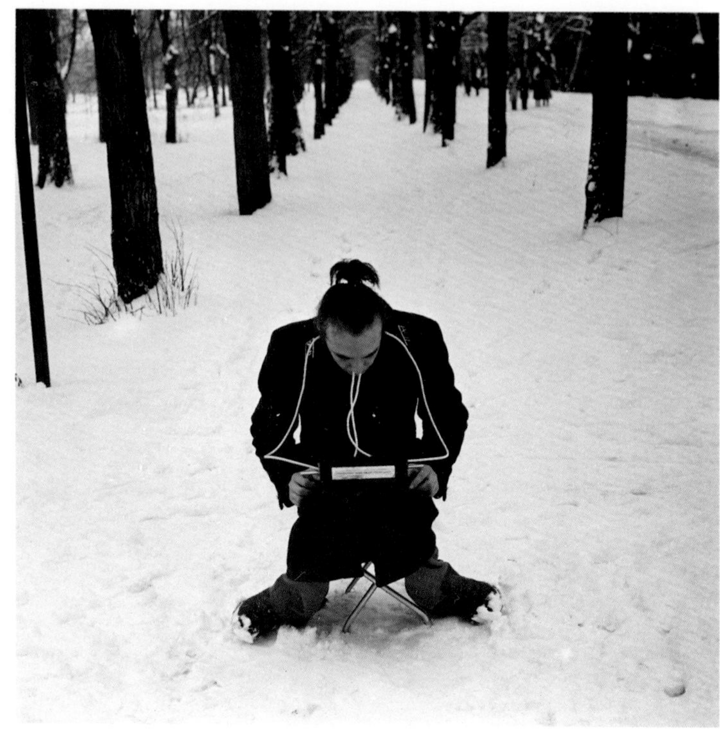

121   Collective Actions Group, *Sound Perspectives of a Country Trip*, February 14, 1983. Archive of Collective Actions Group.

122   Collective Actions Group, *Sound Perspectives of a Country Trip*, February 14, 1983, with Andrei Monastyrsky. Archive of Collective Actions Group

photographed skiing. This was in line with Bulatov's later dictum that, "a painting interests me as some spatial system, not hermetic (closed in itself), but open into the space of my everyday existence. By opening into that space (which is social, by and large), a painting sort of highlights that space, makes it and myself in it visible and comprehensible."[33] In *Skier* Bulatov used a red grid to demarcate the internal and external borders of the canvas. The task of the skier, separated from the viewer by the grid, is to surmount, or even eradicate, the canvas's flatness by moving toward a distant forest, drawing with him – as the words and arrows did in his *Entrance* (see fig. 81) – the viewer's gaze. To accentuate the depth of space, Bulatov renders a second skier in the background in the form of a barely visible dot.

CAG staged *Sound Perspectives of a Country Trip* in Moscow's Sakolniki Park, bringing it closer to the urban environment than their previous actions. Together with the group's members, fifteen participants pulled a rope connected to a sledge made from

skis and carrying a tape recorder to record the sound of gliding on the snow (fig. 120). This sound was later combined with those of breathing and of a moving train, creating a blend of sound "perspectives" from Bulatov's *Skier* as well as his *Danger* and *Beware* (see figs. 94, 95). The last two had been inspired by railroad posters warning about approaching trains. Separately, CAG staged a photographic session, during which Monastyrsky, sitting on a folding chair, was slowly moved down an avenue of trees from far away toward the fixed position of the photographer, who was standing near a notice forbidding various activities in the park (figs. 121, 122). By wearing the black coat of a railroad worker and yet with his hair tied into a ponytail, Monastyrsky looked both ordinary and enigmatic. A black box sitting on his lap was bureaucratically labeled with names of train stations, while a set of plastic tubes connecting the box to Monastyrsky's ears and nostrils intensified the oddness and signified "I breathe, I hear," a response to Bulatov's recent cityscape *I Live, I See* (1982). Called after a line in a poem

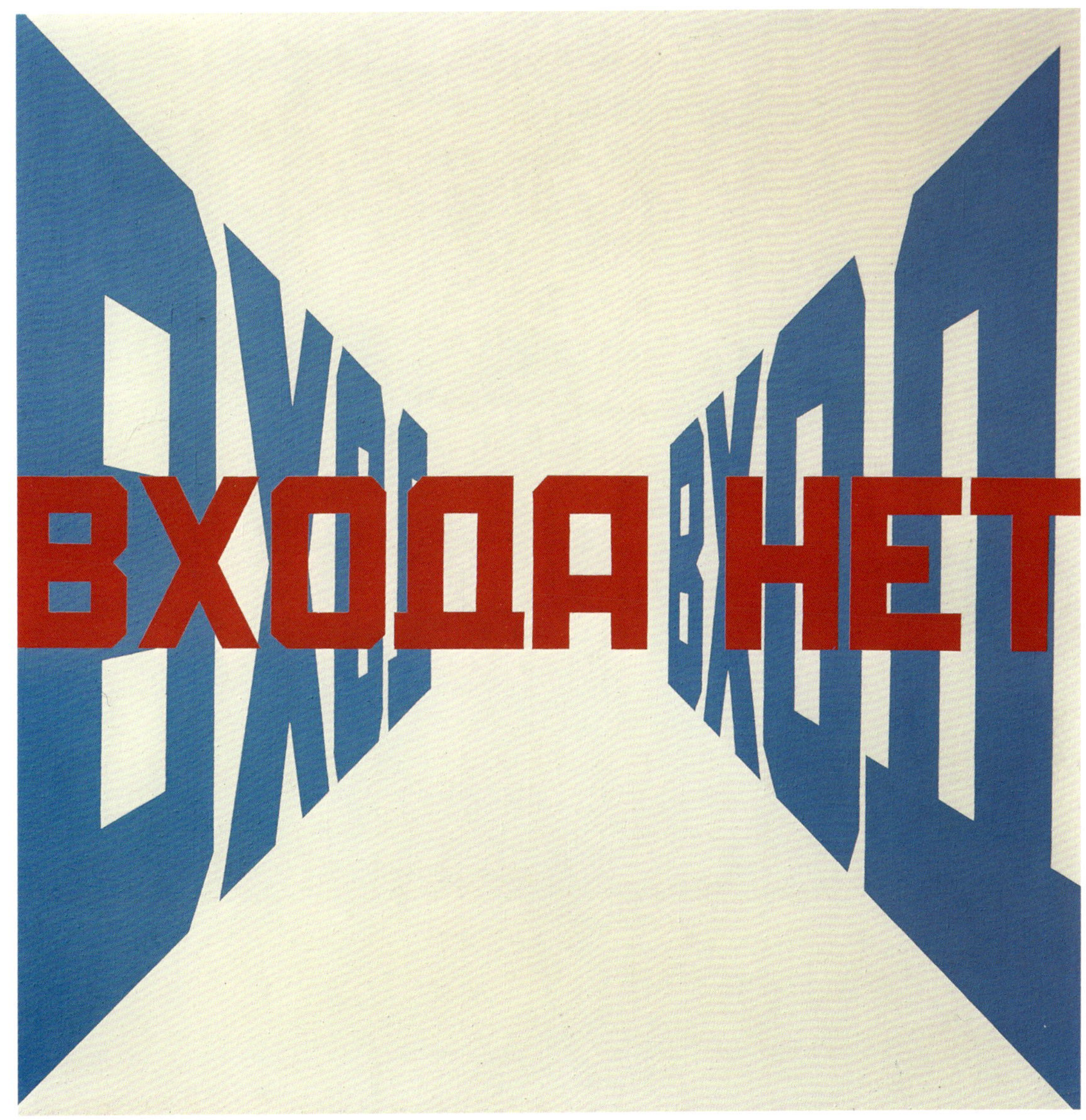

123   Erik Bulatov, *Entrance–No Entrance*, 1974–5. Centre Georges Pompidou, Paris.

by the nonconformist Vsevolod Nekrasov (finished a year earlier and dedicated to Bulatov), it equally stimulated the poet Monastyrsky. The assertions, "I live" (Bulatov) and "I breathe" (Monastyrsky) relate to physical being, whereas "I see" and "I hear" state Bulatov's "im/pulse to see" and Monastyrsky's "im/pulse to hear," respectively.[34] In reality, there is no clash between them, for in *I Live, I See* Bulatov prompted viewers "to see words instead of objects" (as Kabakov put it).[35] This was in line with Monastyrsky's dictum that "in order to understand sound, one must see it."[36]

These perceptual systems are locally specific and depend on their cultural context being infected with propaganda.

Nothing attested better the truth of Monastyrsky's phrase cited earlier, "everything is rotting because no one consumes these art goods in time,"[37] than Bulatov's paintings. After all, more than any other art form, they depended on being exhibited. Yet each of his 1970s canvases, after being worked on for more than one year, was certain to stagnate in the studio and be viewed by only a handful of colleagues and friends.

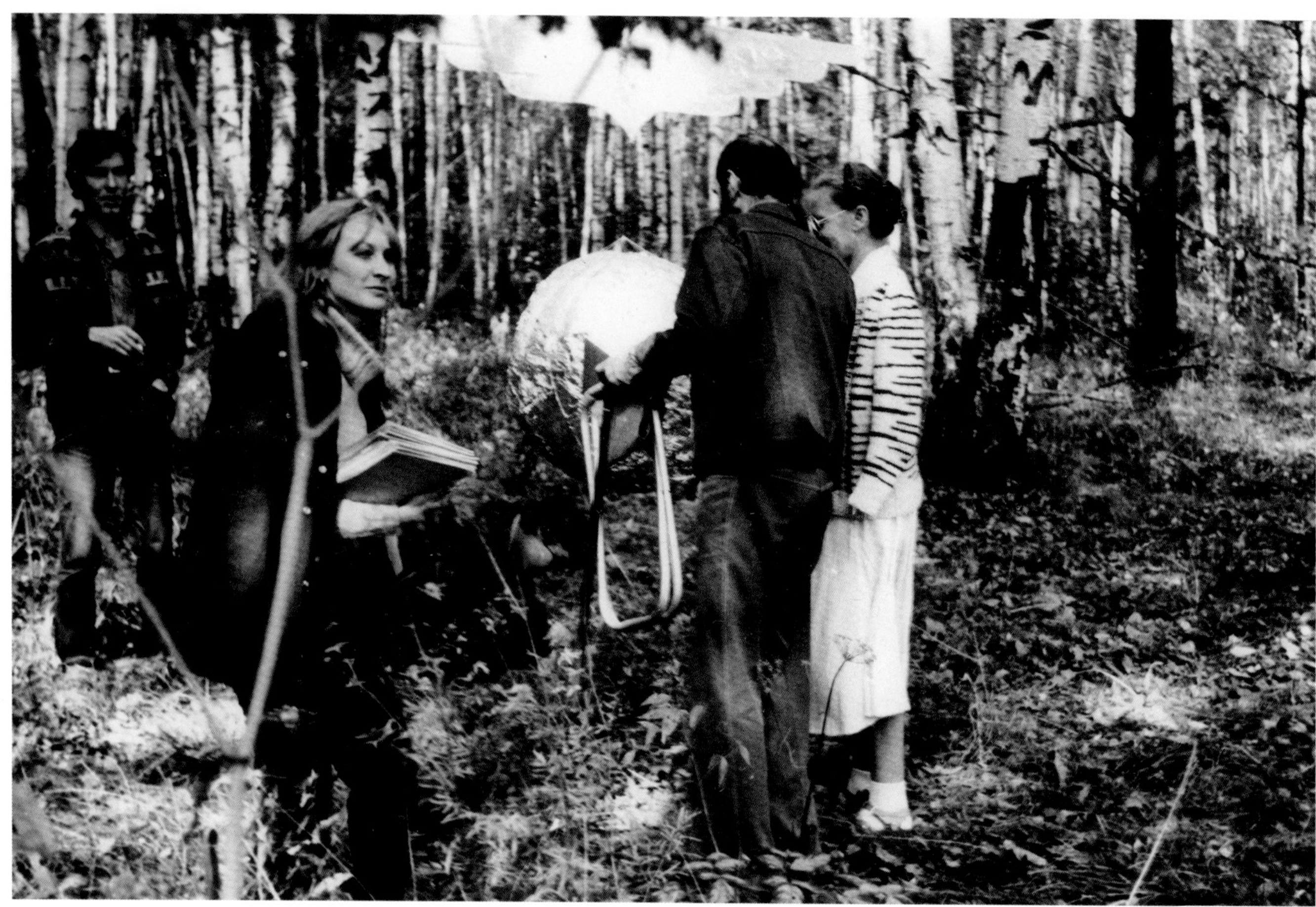

124   Collective Actions Group, *M*, October 18, 1983, with Erik Bulatov (right).

In the early 1970s, Bulatov reflected this dilemma in a series of paintings that created a dialectic of entrance–no entrance – the only possible movement in this closed off reality. In a textual painting called exactly that, *Entrance–No Entrance* (1974–5; fig. 123), the word "Entrance" appears twice in blue and in perspective, like the panes of an open window, implying the possibility of exit into a social space. However, "No Entrance," painted in red and in the foreground, restricts this expansion, ordering an immediate withdrawal into the studio.

CAG's *Exit* (March 20, 1983), dedicated to Bulatov, responded to his iconography of constraints, and overcame their own fear of the city by performing in the center of Moscow, in the era when the ex-chief of the KGB, Iury Andropov, held power as the General Secretary. Two group members and participants rode one stop on a trolley bus to meet other CAG members and receive an envelope with the inscription, "'Exit' has taken place on March 20, 1983 at 12:24." With this trivial act, CAG postulated that the practice of painting itself was at fault because of its existential limitations. Later that year, Monastyrsky visited Bulatov and Vasiliev's shared studio and recorded his fascination with their "light-bearing paintings,"[38] emphasising *en plein air* quality. He then invited Bulatov to participate in CAG's action *M* (October 18, 1983; fig. 124), following instructions (to whistle, look into binoculars, obtain drawings, and so on) acted out by 30 people in the forest over two hours. This was all accomplished to the accompaniment of live music (played by a jazz musician, Sergei Letov, on saxophone and other instruments) and multiple audio recordings including such loud and alien sounds as announcements on the

Moscow metro system (hence the name *M*) in that rural setting. Bulatov arrived at the site of *M* with a cane and stool, having sustained leg injuries when he had been hit by a truck. His disability and warning announcements such as "beware of the closing doors" prompted a sense of urban dangers as effectively as the words "danger" and "beware" had of the rural dangers in his canvases. This time, though, Bulatov took pleasure in *entering* a rural environment and when he *exited* the site of *M*, his perception of rurality had been detoxified of ideological threats. The difference is akin to that between the disquietude of Manet's *Déjeuner sur l'herbe* and the tranquillity of Claude Monet's canvas of the same title, which, as Nochlin pointed out, was "radically affected by light, air, immediacy of pose, and spontaneity of attitude."[39] Bulatov's recollection of *M* is informed by the same impressionist flow, though not in concrete form: "I have seen for the first time that a day itself can become an art work. For me this was unexpected and amazing. I would never have believed it if I myself had not become a participant and a witness."[40] In fact, one could suggest that in Bulatov's subsequent landscapes the level of ideological threat has been visibly reduced.

At the time *M* took place, Monastyrsky wrote: "The conceptual center of our group has shifted toward the two 'Taoists,' myself and Panitkov. Alekseev has almost seceded, has become interested in other things, has rushed into the thick of *narodnost* (the national principle), into the passion for pure art, a timeless trip has drained him."[41] Indeed Alekseev had criticized CAG's ritualism and theatricality, insisting that, "it has become clear that art can't be a spiritual practice, and [that] trying to behave (in current conditions) like an icon painter…'while doing avant-garde [art]' is absurd." Alekseev elaborated: "After all, art is art and one must either…drop it, or not overestimate its potential and try to be an artist. We did not understand it right away and as a result the last actions make a burdensome impression. They are suspended between hermetic constructions and citations from our own works, quasipsychology and painful self-enjoyment."[42] Alekseev's feeling that CAG's actions had been diverging too much from the category of aesthetic project was reflected in his own works of the late 1970s. These include *Noise* (1978) and *Star* (1978), which are

"Sculpture[s] to be Lost in the Forest," to use Jean (Hans) Arp's title for a 1932 bronze (figs. 125, 126). As with the earlier *Tent* (see fig. 110), Alekseev tested an art object "made in an interior space but meant for and installed in the open air."[43] In the Soviet context, his intentional misplacement of an art work metaphorized the uselessness of any art that was not Socialist Realist.

Alekseev elaborated on this issue in a performance called *Speech* (1980), during which he stood in a forest bare-footed on melting snow and read out a text (fig. 127). His act equated the vanguard artist's voice with that of the prophet crying in the desert. Alekseev's "speech" was a critique of the Moscow vanguard's situation at the turn of the decade. In addition to stressing its extreme marginality at home, Alekseev argued that, regardless of that vanguard's "participation in international 'avant-garde' activities (irregular exhibitions, publications, and personal contacts)," such interaction is "illusory, for it works only in our direction."[44] In conclusion, Alekseev laid out the creative advantages that, in his opinion, Moscow vanguard artists paradoxically gained from having no support or demand for their work:

> One of the major factors contributing to the distinctive activities of local "avant-garde" artists is their complete social unconditionality, an absolute freedom, for the only limitation of their activities is that they are totally negated by the established structures. Needless to say, this limitation cannot be considered such: if, despite the complete lack of interest, something is going on in this country, it means that those who participate are completely free from social pressures. Other forms of pressure coming from the State can be ignored in this context. The effect of this situation is an immense personal responsibility for the participants in the local "avant-garde," given an incredibly broad range of choices. The unfeasibility of investing millions of dollars into an art action, using helicopters or laser technology – which is the reality for local artists – does not destroy their choices. This condition, from my point of view, is unique, very difficult and at the same time charged with high energy.[45]

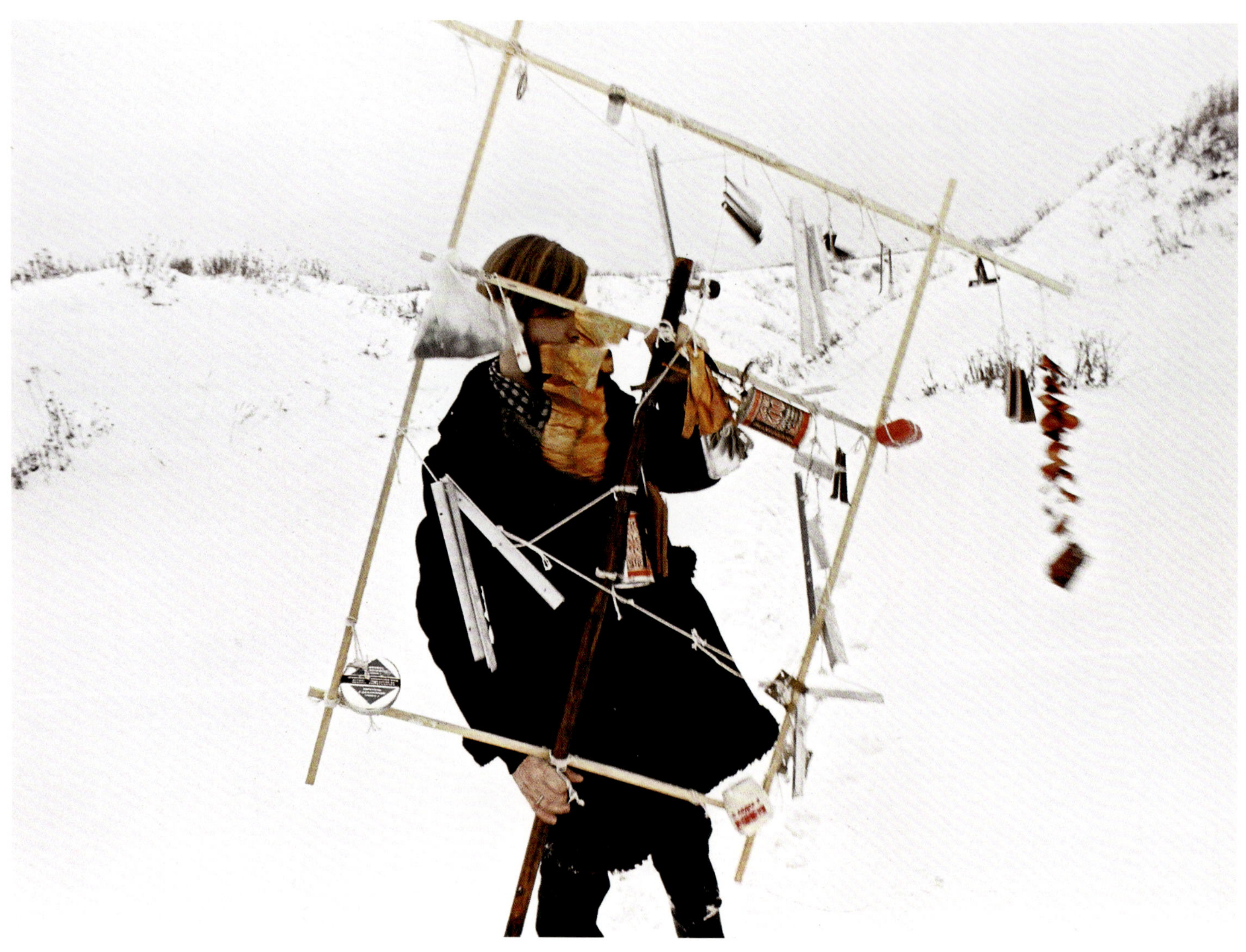

125 Nikita Alekseev, *Noise*, 1978, with the artist.

Alekseev put his convictions into practice when he gave up his privacy and set up his studio apartment as a site for the eruption of creative energy that had been gathering force among young artists since the late 1970s. From this a movement dubbed Apt Art emerged that aimed to recontextualize the showing of unsanctioned art in apartments and artists' studios. In order to rise above this enforced situation, Alekseev gave his apartment institutional status by calling it "the avant-garde gallery on 1/6th of the globe."[46] Together, Aptartists conceived a new form of collective installation that blurred individual authorship and achieved

a unified, whole spectacle. The Apt Art gallery commenced two weeks before Brezhnev's death in November 1982 and was disbanded by the end of Andropov's rule (in February 1984), which had reactivated KGB agents from their tamed stagnation during the Brezhnev era. I will discuss the Apt Art gallery activities in the following chapter, but here, in order to maintain the theme of rural practices, I will focus on their refuge *en plein air* after the troubles that Aptartists experienced in the city.

Preparation for *Apt Art En Plein Air* (May 29, 1983) occurred under "almost partisan conditions" that,

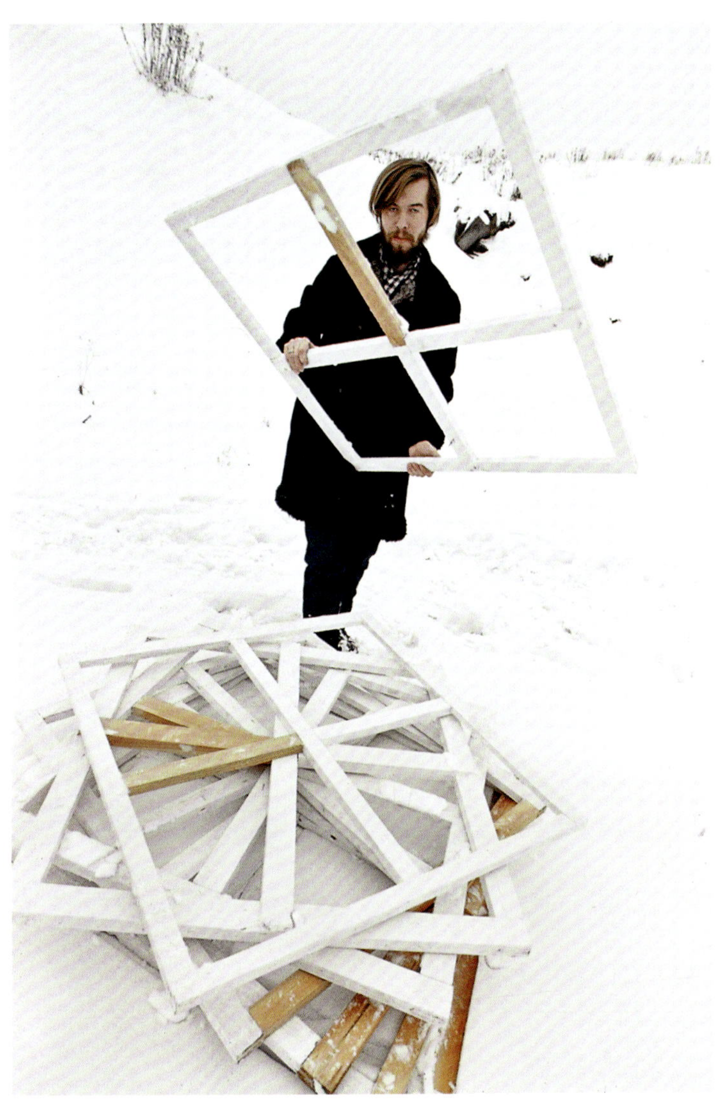
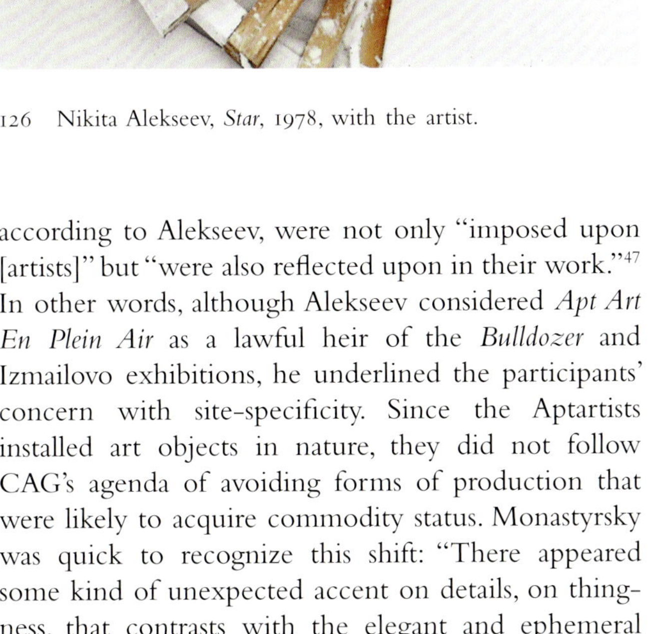

126   Nikita Alekseev, *Star*, 1978, with the artist.

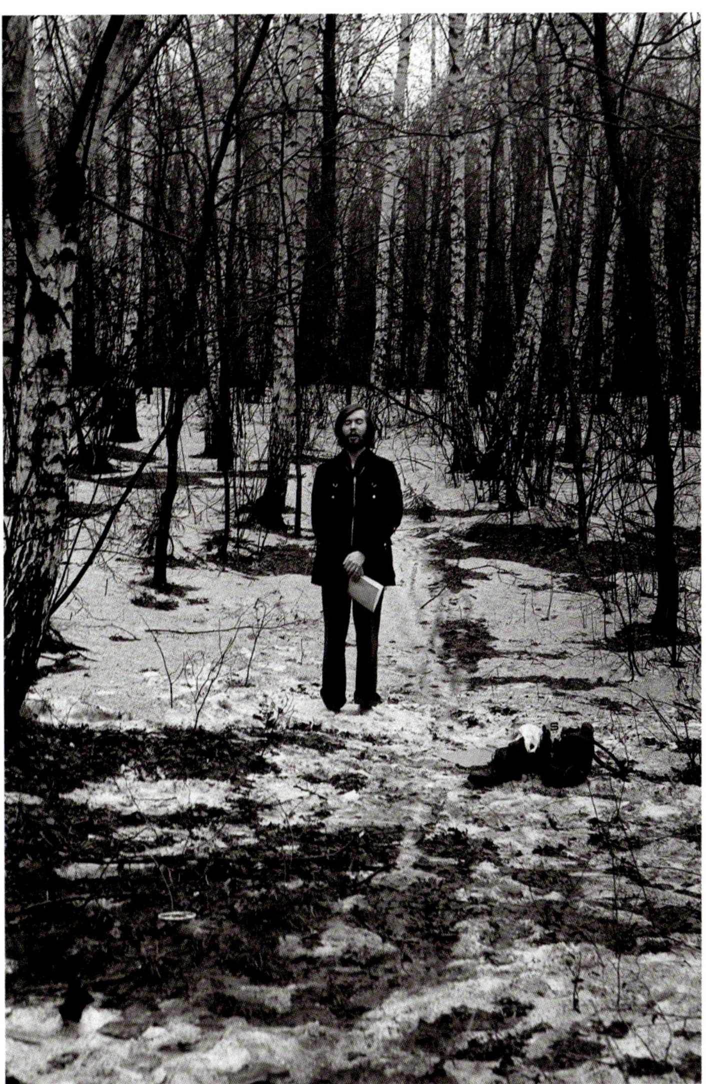

127   Nikita Alekseev, *Speech*, 1980.

according to Alekseev, were not only "imposed upon [artists]" but "were also reflected upon in their work."[47] In other words, although Alekseev considered *Apt Art En Plein Air* as a lawful heir of the *Bulldozer* and Izmailovo exhibitions, he underlined the participants' concern with site-specificity. Since the Aptartists installed art objects in nature, they did not follow CAG's agenda of avoiding forms of production that were likely to acquire commodity status. Monastyrsky was quick to recognize this shift: "There appeared some kind of unexpected accent on details, on thingness, that contrasts with the elegant and ephemeral *faktura* of the emptiness of our ideal fields, with lonely, appearing/disappearing figures somewhere on the periphery of one's internal vision."[48] Here Monastyrsky uses the Russian term *faktura* not of surfaces and materials, but in the expanded, nontangible sense that Vladimir Markov, in his 1914 essay, *Principles of Creation in the Visual Arts: Faktura*, had described as "nonmaterial *faktura*" that is linked "to all principles of creativity."[49] Similarly, Monastyrsky's making a distinction between the two aesthetic practices reverberates with the debates that took place in the late 1920s on whether collectively to cultivate ideal forms as

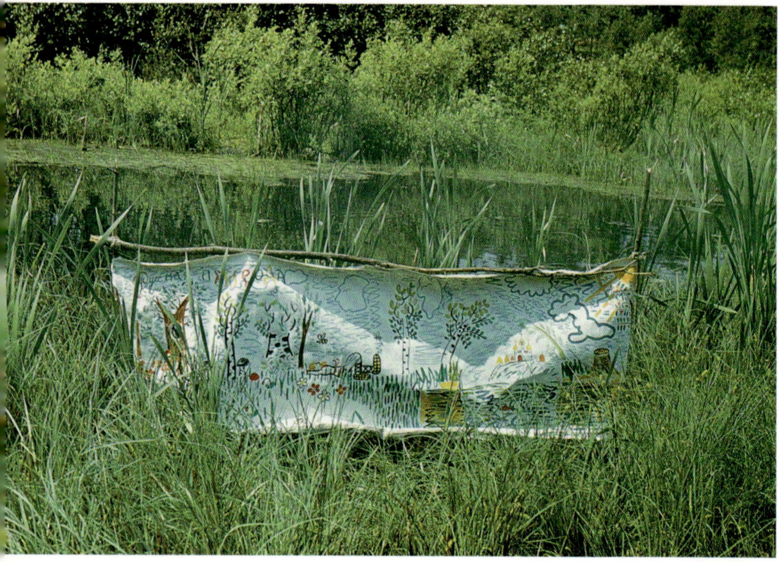

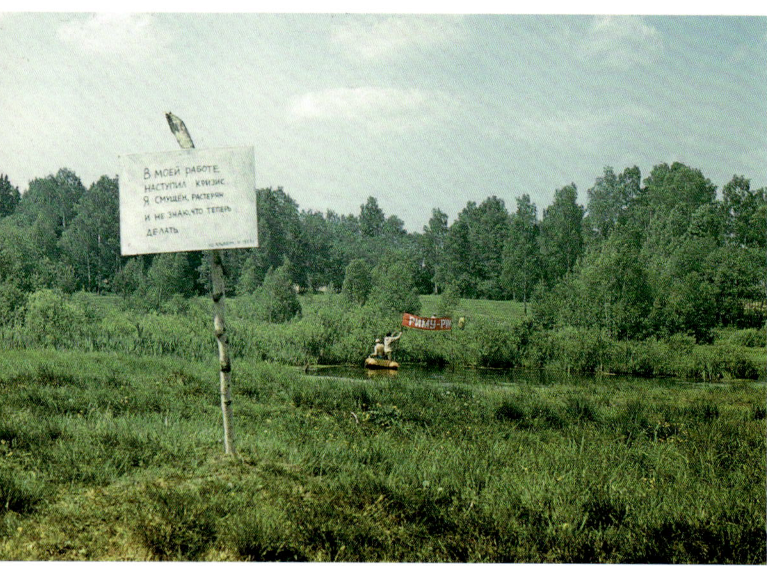

128   *Apt Art En Plein Air*, Kalistovo, May 29, 1983, installation view: Konstantin Zvezdochetov, *Russian Nature*, 1983.

129   *Apt Art En Plein Air*, Kalistovo, May 29, 1983, installation view: Iury Albert, "There is crisis in my work," 1983 (foreground), and Andrei Filippov, *Rome to Rome*, 1983 (background).

signifiers of utopian conditions, or invest in the production of objects as signifiers of contemporaneity.

In total, *Apt Art En Plein Air* included 30 installations by 16 artists, many working in collectives,[50] and 4 actions,[51] all realized on "a sward of incredible beauty bordered by a forest on one side and with a peaty half-lake half-swamp on the other" (fig. 128).[52] Made in Moscow with found materials of no particular quality, art works were hung on rope lines, tree benches, and trunks, or installed on the lake with the help of a boat; other structures were assembled on site with no intention of preserving them after the event. All these methods negated the pompous exhibitions of easel art in local museums as well as dissident modernists' quest for a right to be shown in official spaces. The meaning of the works was absurdist and ironic, easily discernible from their laconic titles and the works' texts. Sven Gundlakh, a member of the Mukhomor group, was instrumental in distinguishing Apt Art as the neo-Dadaist alternative to CAG's production, which was comparatively oblique and laden with instructions and interpretations. Gundlakh went as far as calling one of his installations *Hell with Tao*, a direct attack on Monastyrsky's philosophical influences. Iury Albert's discourse *en plein air* conveyed a collective sense of frustration, expressed in phrases such as: "there is a crisis in my work. I am lost and hesitant, and don't know what to do," which were inscribed on white boards attached to twigs set in the ground (fig. 129).

Gundlakh also considered the *Bulldozer* and Izmailovo exhibitions as the "two older sisters" of *Apt Art En Plein Air*, but at the same time underlined their differences: "The participants of these shows had created their works for galleries and museums, and thus these kind of necessary and ludicrous shows signified a heroic position, a challenge to conservative authorities, and, of course, a typical Russian mode of 'special suffering'. This is exactly what we tried to avoid," as he wrote shortly afterward.[53] He summarized what Apt Art pursued and achieved in *Apt Art en Plein Air*:

Art must organically correlate with the exhibition environment; this is why works were conceived as such so that everyone understood that their place

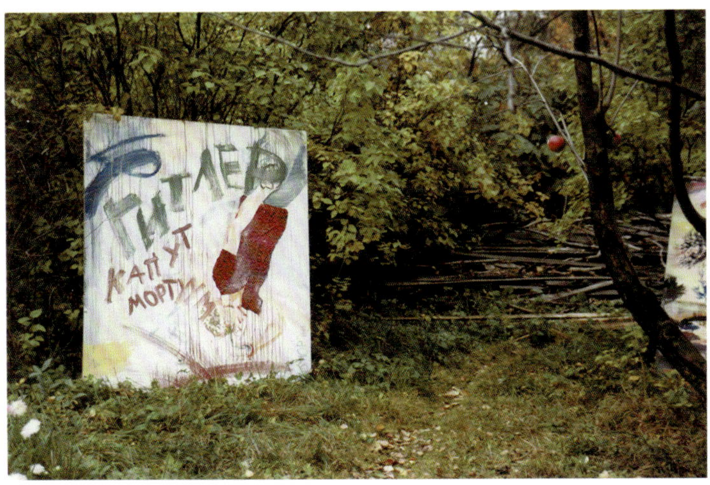

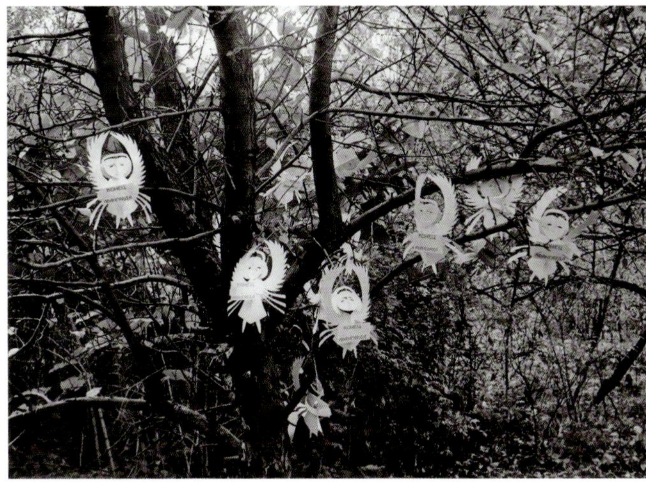

130   *Apt Art Behind the Fence*, outskirts of Moscow, 1983, installation view: Sergei Mironenko, *Hitler-Kaput-Mortem*, 1983.

131   *Apt Art Behind the Fence*, outskirts of Moscow, 1983, installation view: Larisa Rezun, *The End of the Avant-garde*, 1983.

was here on the grass. On purpose, we spread out works over a large area so that they would not attract attention, would not destroy a particular local beauty. The result was a symbiosis of the natural and the artificial. Such…presentation required significant attention at the time of viewing. One could pass by some of the works without noticing them for, with all their explicit foreignness, they were logically inserted into the landscape.[54]

The next show, *Apt Art Behind the Fence* (September 25, 1983), was a one-day event that took place on the smaller ground of a dacha of Sergei and Vladimir Mironenko, two other members of the Mukhomor group. This catapulted Apt Art from a public space (the Kalistovo field) back to a private space. A protective fence gave the artists a sense of safety, which they needed after *Apt Art En Plein Air* without borders. It also drew together the participants and considerably fewer visitors, creating a picnic atmosphere. A handful of color photographs document another distinction from *Apt Art En Plein Air*: there the wild greenery of the landscape often overpowered or even buried timid

art works or created a sharp contrast to them. Here multicolored Fall foliage harmoniously mixed into the works, creating an overall "expressionist" *faktura* that, in a completely new conceptual framework, resonated with the first nonconformist generation's conviction that Abstract Expressionism was the polar opposite of Socialist Realism. This smaller area was shared with several artists from Odessa (Sergei Anufriev, Iury Leiderman, Leonid Voitsekhov, Sergei Iakhimov, and Larisa Rezun). As a result, works were squeezed together rather than dispersed among the trees and fruit bushes. There was a visible shift from the site-specificity of *Apt Art En Plein Air* to delicate paintings and works on paper, whose place was in galleries and museums. The canvases by Sergei Mironenko u-turned to the modernists' earlier showings of paintings in *plein air* (fig. 130). All of these perhaps unintentional references to the Moscow vanguard's earlier tenets and practices were reflected in Rezun's installation, *The End of the Avant-garde* (fig. 131). Paper cutouts of angels suspended from a tree conveyed this misfit atmosphere, and heralded the end of the Moscow rural vanguard.

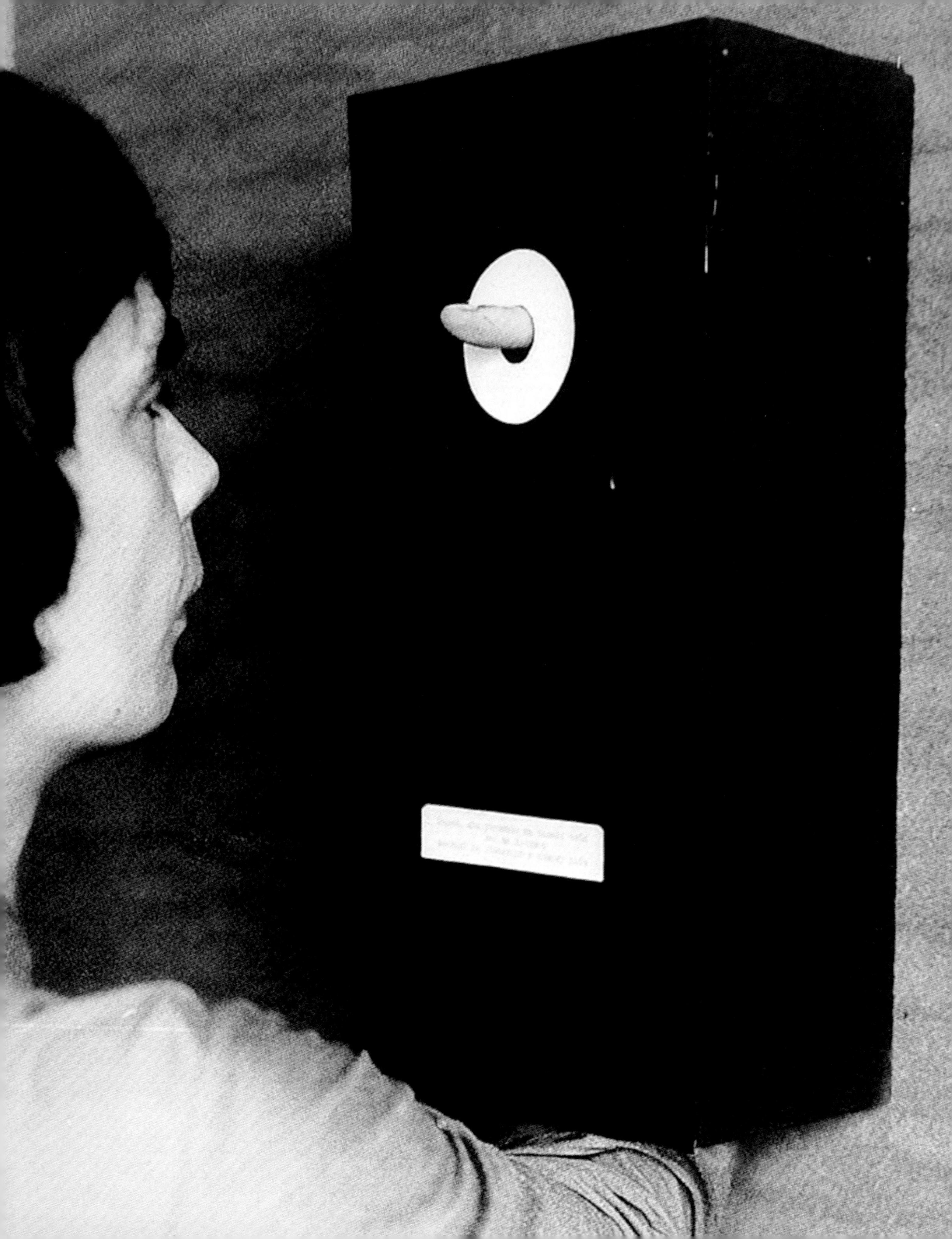

5

THE RAISON D'ETRE OF INSTALLATION ART

In the 1960s and 1970s, rare photographs of noncon-formist artists in their studios would typically show the artist displaying paintings to a guest who was rarely included in the picture (fig. 132; see fig. 115). Sometimes, paintings are stacked against a wall, while others are placed on an easel. The abundance of art works, while betraying a lack of demand, led to the invention of a type of display that would compensate for the chronic inaccessibility of authorized exhibi-tions. In these personal shows, artists acted as curators and interpreters, giving rise to a greater sense of control over their production, which was otherwise threatened by censorship. By the mid-1970s, the first generation of postwar modernists had lost hope of accessing public exhibition spaces and felt burdened by domestic showings. A comparison of two photo-graphs of Lydia Masterkova in her studio shows how her earlier eagerness to share her painting with the

viewer, in 1968, had turned to resentment by 1974, as she posed with her paintings facing away from the viewer, including those she was holding (fig. 133). This disengagement demonstrated her longing for an alternative mode of display, which would allow artists to step back from their production. It was under the increasing pressure of such anxiety that the dissident modernists exhibited their work in *The Bulldozer Exhibition*.

The artists who decided not to participate in that pivotal event were those who had accepted the lack of institutional support, and began to see this situation as a stimulus to rethink their forms of production and display. Bulatov, for example, expressed his frustration over the inability to test his ideas in a public space through a greater emphasis on the structures and ico-nography of entrance and exit. Grids, arrows, words, horizons, and deep perspectives became his forms for expressing frustration with his studio imprisonment. Bulatov also intensified this sense of stagnation by spending a notoriously long time executing each canvas, often working on several paintings at the same

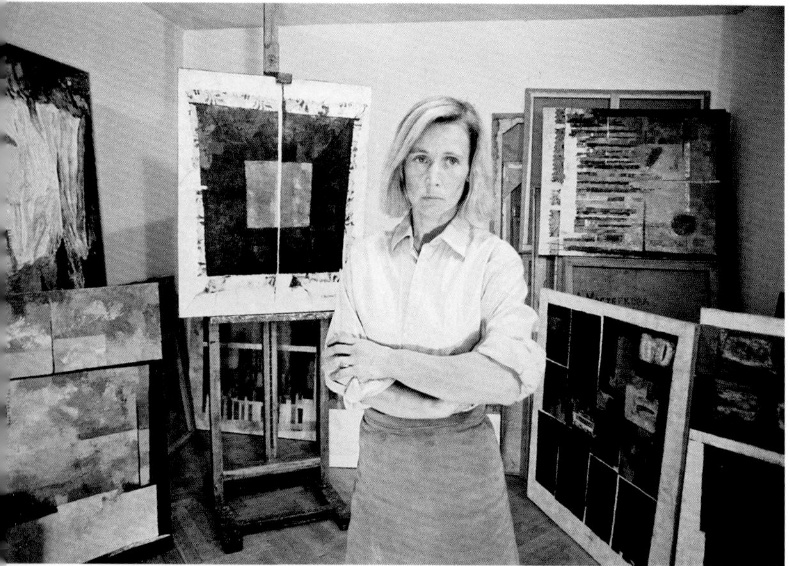

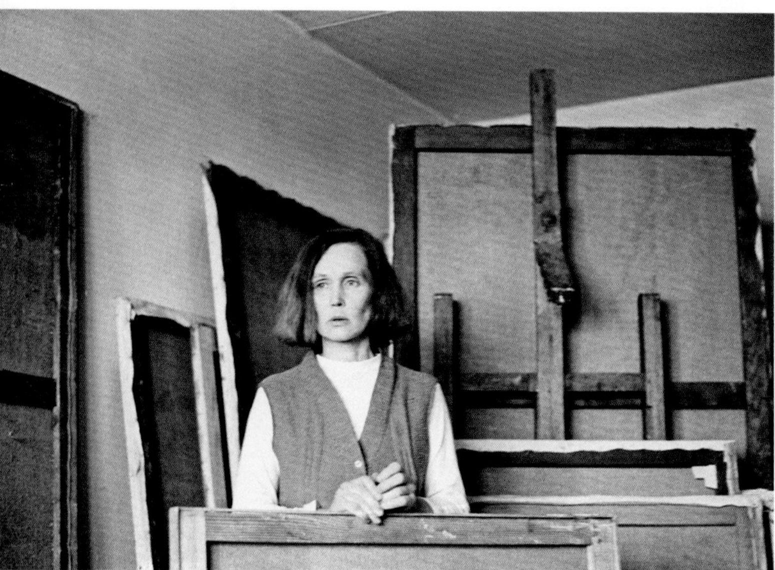

132   Lydia Masterkova in her studio, Moscow, 1968.

133   Lydia Masterkova in her studio, Moscow, Spring 1974.

time, as if to suppress their significance as singular works. Bulatov's painting *No Entrance* (fig. 135) presents metaphors of incarceration with a half-length self-portrait that partially obstructs the phrase "no entrance" painted twice in red in the middle of the canvas. *No Entrance* evokes the feeling of *bezvykhodnost* (literally, "without exit"), yet Bulatov's resolute face (though his eyes are oddly covered with a black cloud

speckled with dots of light) and muscular hands speak of his determination to keep fighting against imposed methods of creation.

In Yankilevsky's *Door* (fig. 134), the same feeling of spatial and psychological suffocation is expressed in the form of installation art, one of the first in Moscow. His prolonged involvement with large works, which was rare for underground artists before the 1970s, made Yankilevsky's studio particularly crowded. *Door* is a structure built out of two sets of doors, the first of which is faced by the figure of a dowdy male inhabitant of a communal apartment returning home after shopping. Yankilevsky explains in the accompanying text that his character is imprisoned by the "existential box," and the scene, in all its mundane attributes, communicates the inertness of being. Within the second set of the doors, one sees only the character's white outline, his specter, with a blue horizon drawn on the back, thus allegorizing the yearning for personal liberation. As did the *Bulldozer* artists who moved into open space, Yankilevsky here locates the idea of escape within a landscape, but his attachment to producing large objects ultimately prevented him from exiting the studio.

In *Couch-painting* (1967; see fig. 78), discussed in Chapter Three, Kabakov questioned the underground artist's preoccupation with two-dimensional art in a state that constantly sabotaged its public display. It was clear that such production depended on a conventional exhibition framework and mechanisms of viewing. Under these conditions, Kabakov paid attention to something that most underground artists tried to ignore, namely the decommodified common objects that bluntly spoke of the failure to realize a "concrete utopia." In *Couch-painting* and in *Along the Edge* (1974; see fig. 113), Kabakov pushed imagery to the edges, and ultimately to a space outside of a painting frame. In these works or "pseudo-paintings," edges meet with the common objects such as "walls, doors, other things." To Kabakov, this part of a painting "was always unpredictable,"[1] that is, optically uncontrollable owing to its bordering on real space, which resulted in the illusion of his imagery spilling over edge of the frame. In such white and decentralized compositions Kabakov not only took a step toward installation practices, but also realized the dialectical relation between peripheral

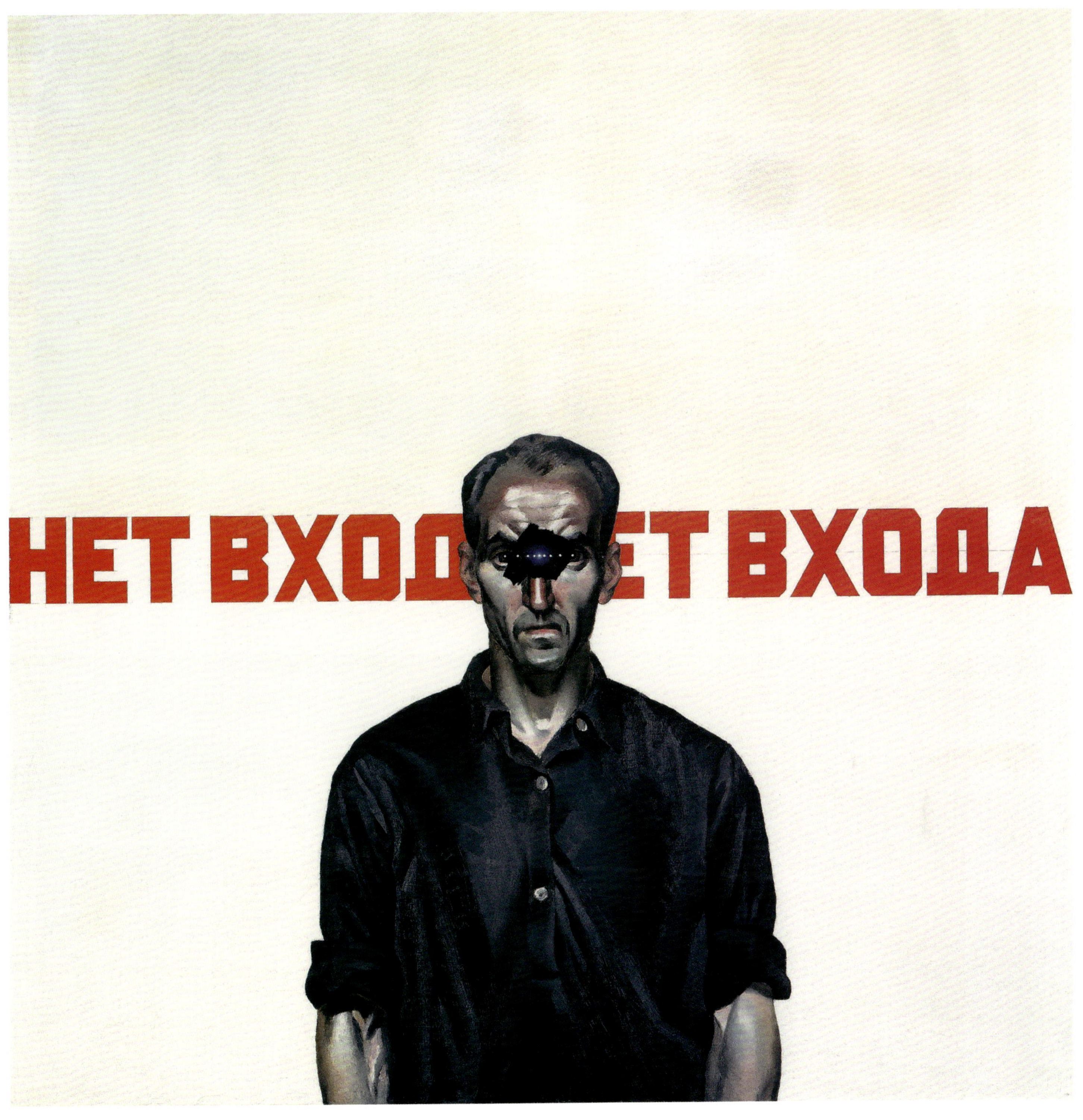

135 Erik Bulatov, *No Entrance* (self-portrait), 1971–3. Musée Maillol, Fondation Dina Vierny, Paris.

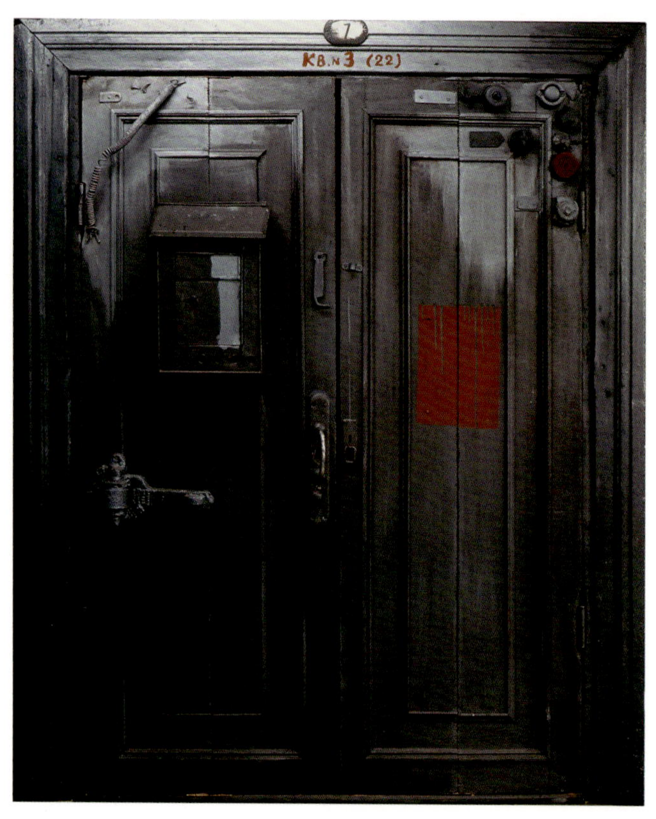
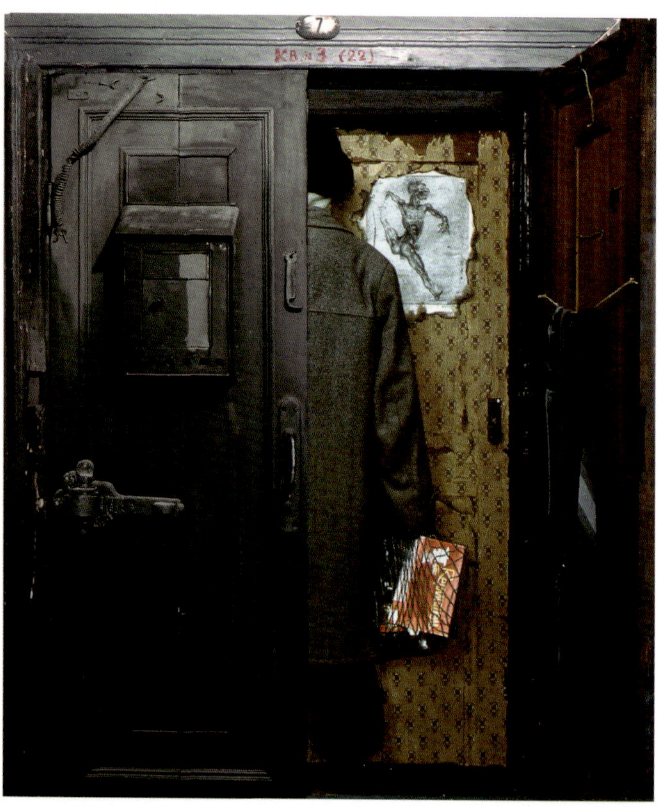
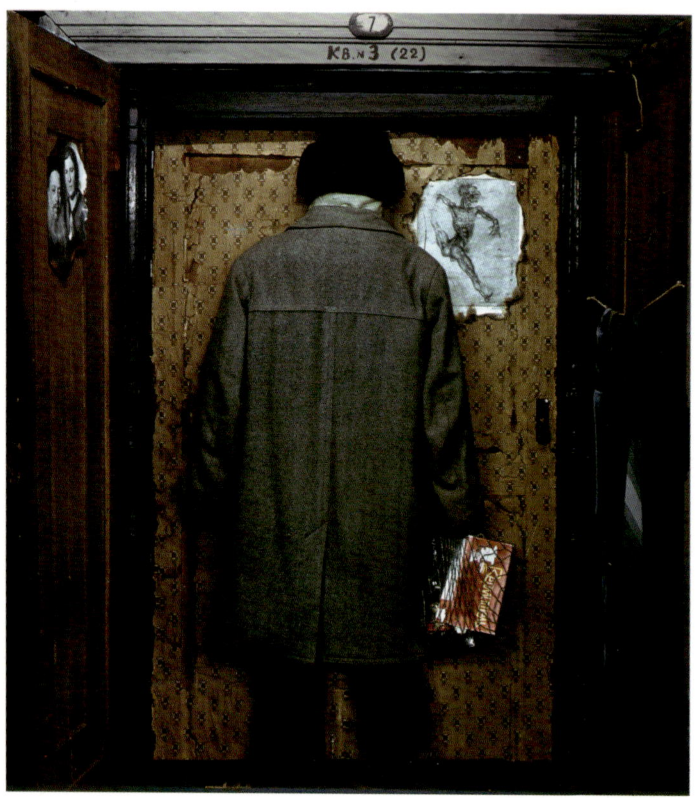
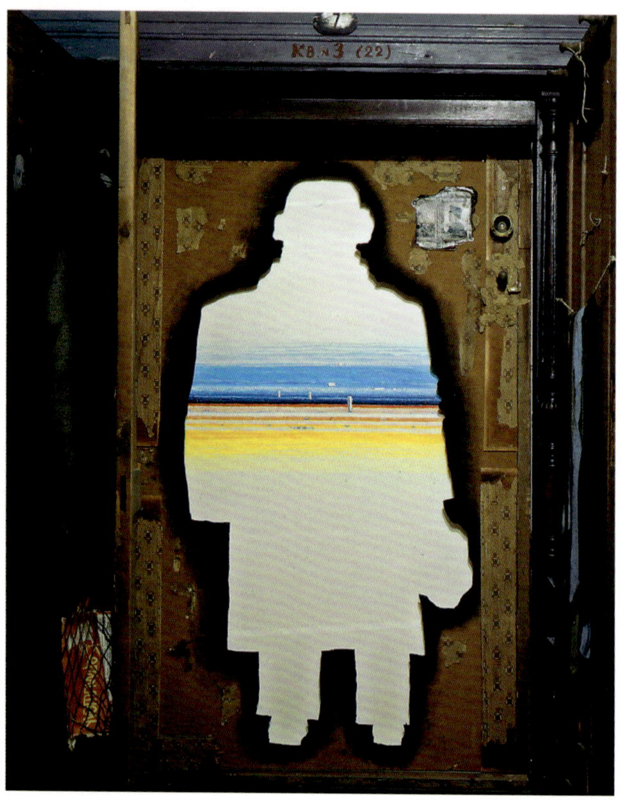

vanguard art dense with creativity and experiment, and central official art empty of innovation. Monastyrsky commented that Kabakov's works with empty centers were "wonderful signs that characterized the moulded situation [of society by the authorities in the 1970s]…[they] are a sort of 'state' report about the condition of our Empire…emptiness had completely eaten up the center, performing a 'genocide' and what is left is only along the edges."[2]

While making his "pseudo-paintings," Kabakov came up with a new art form that he called an "album," which was a set of drawings and texts dedicated to a single fictional character – a communal apartment-dweller – and executed on loose sheets of paper, packed according to a specific order in a home-made box covered in fabric. Unlike Kabakov's sizable and heavy Masonite panels that he had to lean against a wall, or hold up for private viewings, his albums were compact and portable, expanding the field of display within the studio space. For invited guests, he would "perform" the album's content, reading out the texts and showing the pages with images, thus encroaching upon the necessarily domestic presentations of paintings attached to walls in imitation of a display in a museum (fig. 136). In this freer performance-like presentation, the chances for interaction with studio visitors increased.

This represented an important shift in Moscow vanguard circles, where independent artists had aimed to counter collectively oriented Socialist Realism with individualism; to invent an original (read modernist) language that would effectively contradict and dissoiate itself from official canons of representation. Kabakov stepped over this by adopting the language of the communal dweller (alien for modernists) and thus tackling the peripheral, reverse side of Soviet reality that was veiled by the myths of a Soviet communal paradise. There were no heroes or antiheroes among Kabakov's characters. Instead, their *faktura* was rendered through image and language.

In contrast to most vanguardists' detachment from Soviet reality, Komar and Melamid, too, around the same time broke a code of silence about all the clichéd images and slogans used in propaganda. Being a decade younger than Kabakov, they came of age in the Khrushchev thaw, thus developing in a significantly

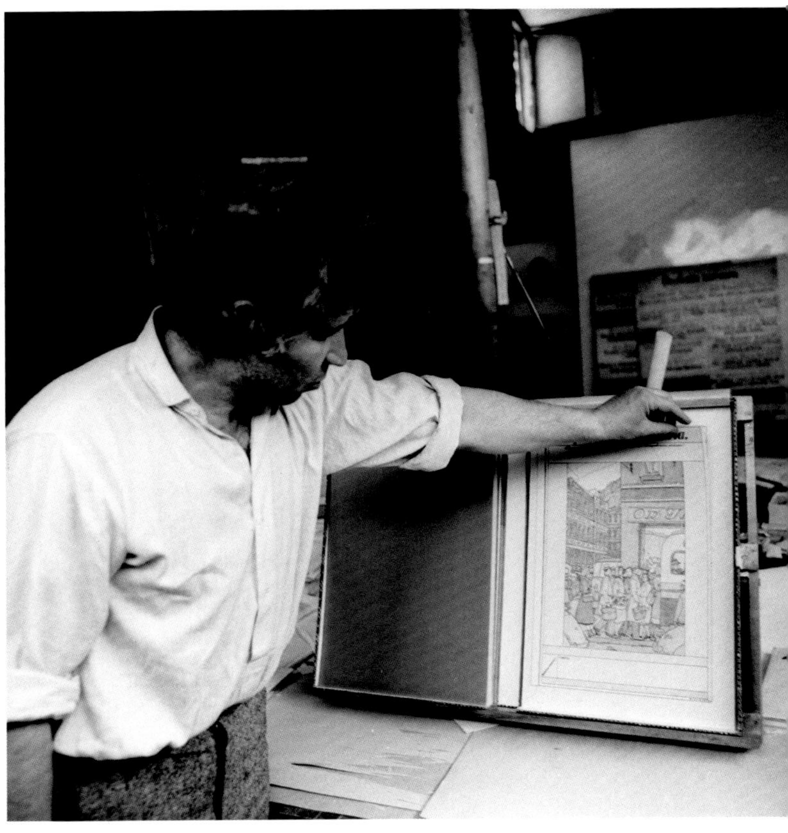

OPPOSITE PAGE 134 Vladimir Yankilevsky, *Door (dedicated to the parents of my parents…)*, 1972. Musée Maillol, Fondation Dina Vierny, Paris.

ABOVE 136 Ilya Kabakov shows his albums in his studio, Moscow, 1979.

more liberal environment, with less fear of official institutional forces. As a result, they refused to be incarcerated in a studio, and, eager to integrate into the vanguard community, chose to disseminate their provocative oeuvre by means of slideshows, disrupting the traditional studio viewing of original art works.

Whereas Kabakov's stories of communal dwellers might have evoked empathy among his studio viewers simply because most of them had experienced the distress of communal life, Komar and Melamid's appropriation of Soviet propaganda, unyieldingly refused and even repressed by the modernists, automatically gave them *enfants terribles* status. This, no doubt, energized the pair to work out a radical arsenal of subversive devices. Referencing AKhRR's

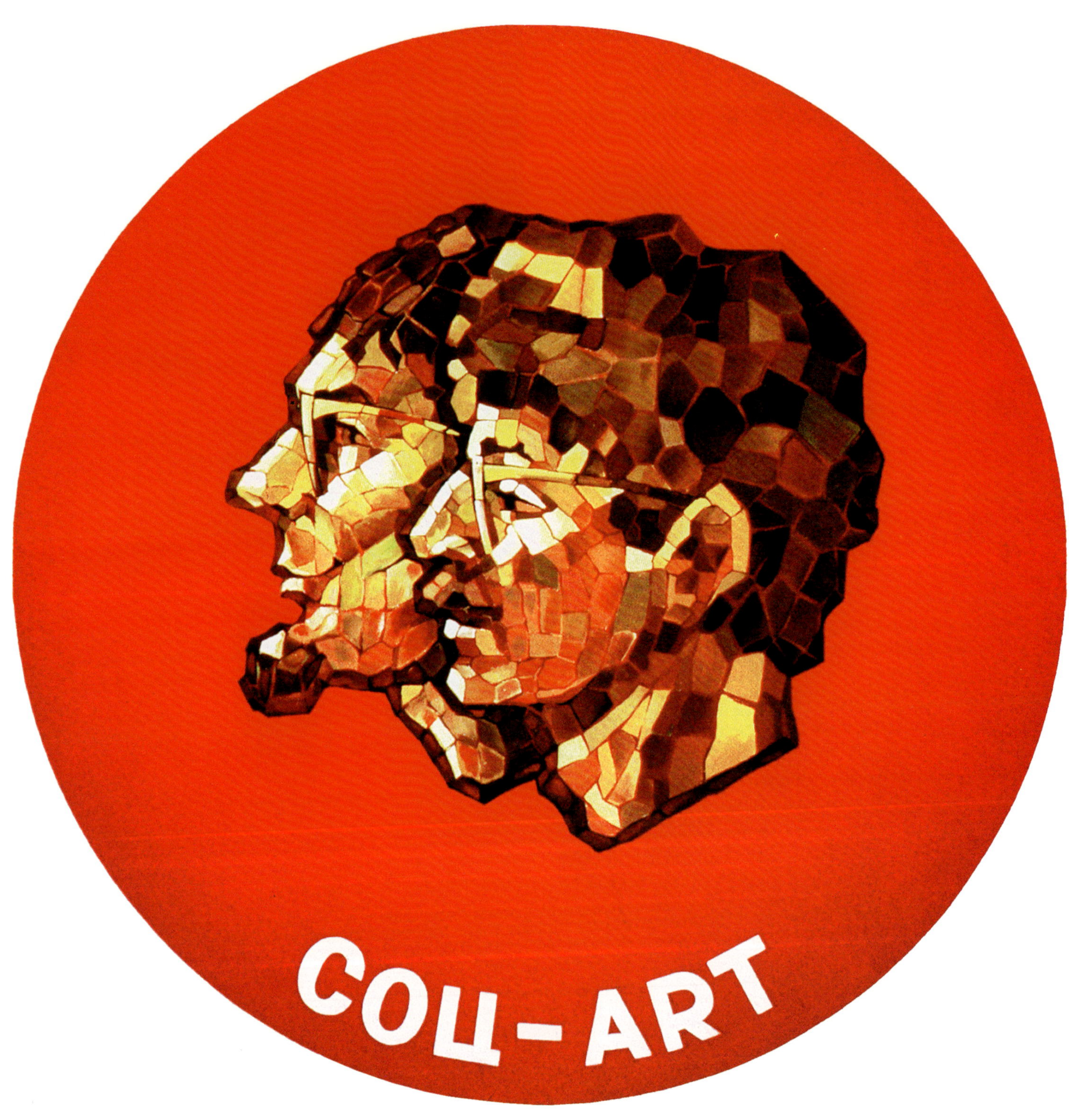

137 Vitaly Komar and Aleksandr Melamid, *Double Self-portrait* (1972), replica 1984. Private collection.

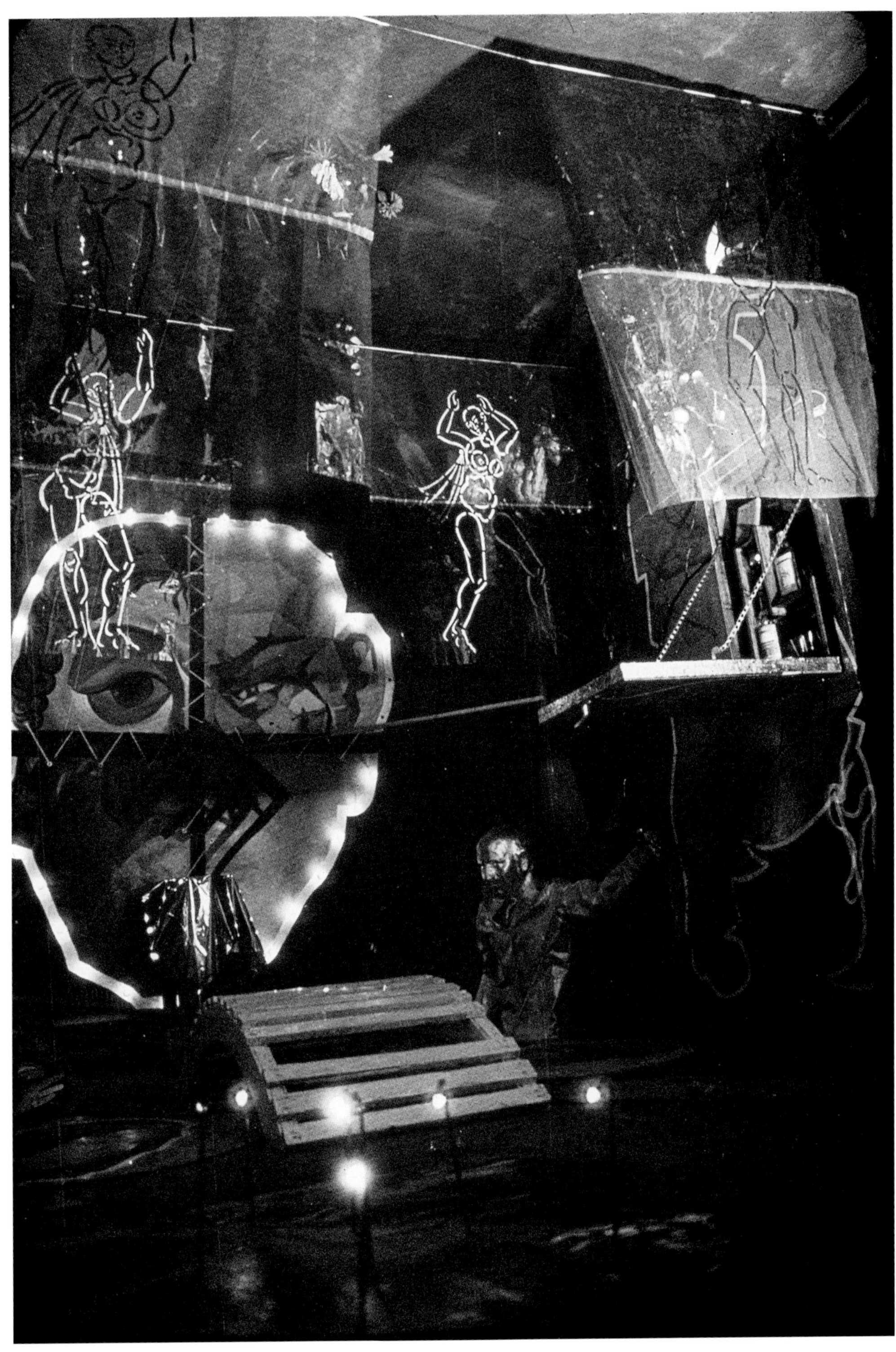

138 Vitaly Komar and Aleksandr Melamid, *Paradise*, installation view, private apartment, Moscow, 1972.

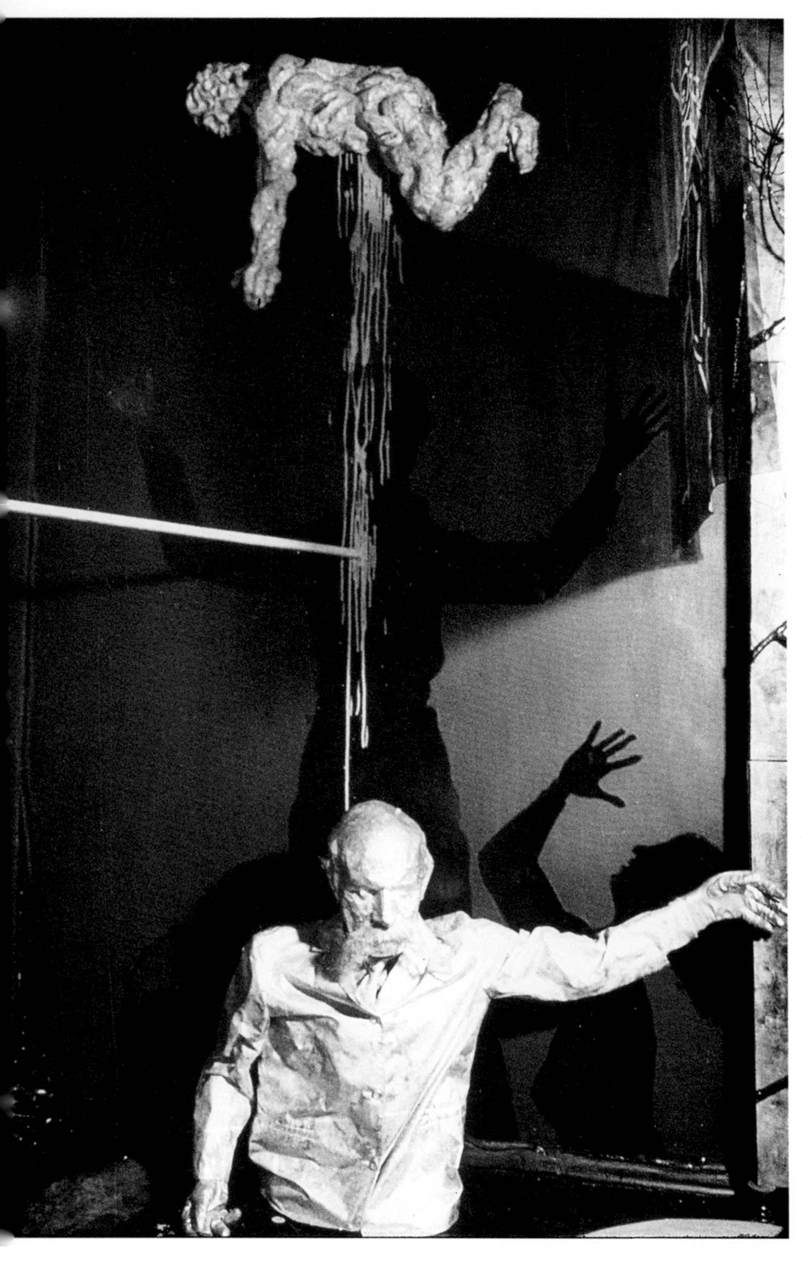

139 Vitaly Komar and Aleksandr Melamid, *Paradise*, installation view, private apartment, Moscow, 1972.

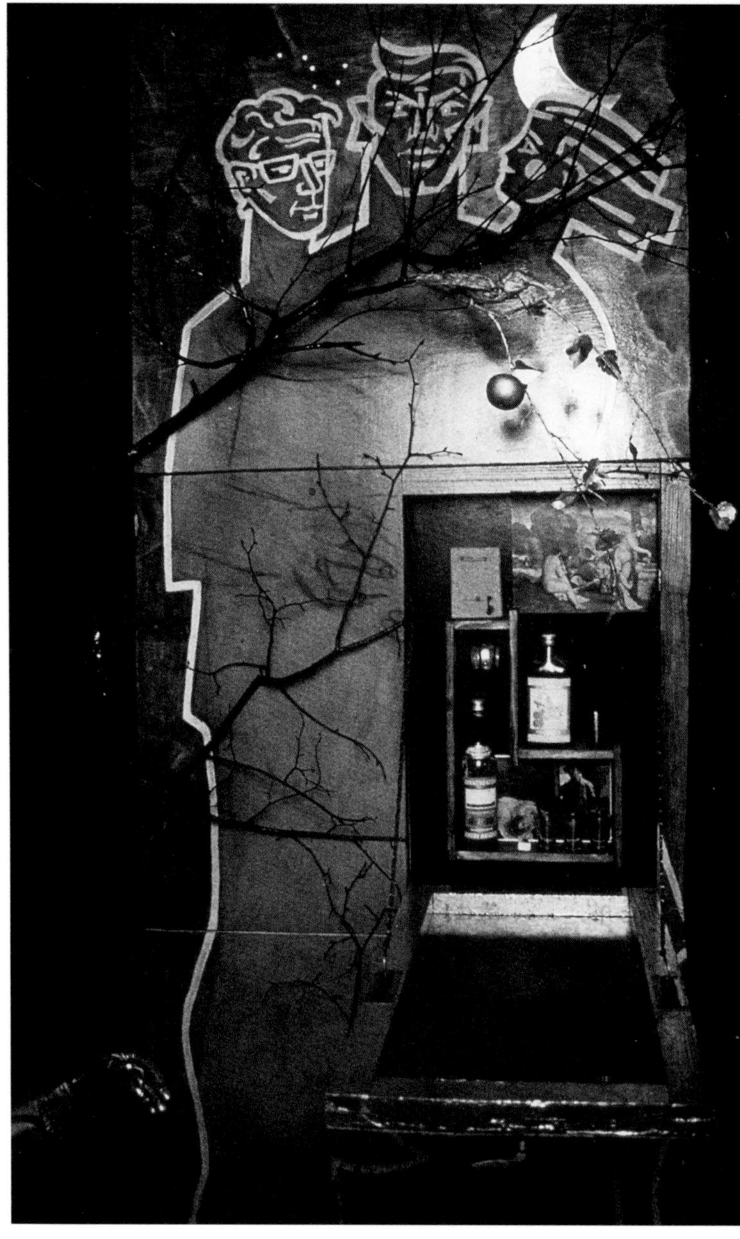

140 Vitaly Komar and Aleksandr Melamid, *Paradise*, installation view, private apartment, Moscow, 1972.

recognition that leaders' portraits were the easiest genre for mass consumption, Komar and Melamid started off by publicizing themselves in vanguard circles with a *Double Self-portrait* (fig. 137).[3] On a round piece of Masonite, it depicted them in profile, just as in the ubiquitous representations of Lenin and Stalin, except that their heads were painted in imitation of mosaics, a favorite technique of Soviet public spaces such as the metro. At the bottom of the portrait's red background, Komar and Melamid stenciled, "Sots Art," the name of the art movement they had launched. The term ("Sots" short for Socialist) asserted its dialectical relationship with the dominant culture's signifiers and master narratives. After the double portrait was destroyed in *The Bulldozer Exhibition*, Komar and Melamid made another one with a new inscription – "Famous artists of the early 1970s of the XX century. Moscow" – which depicted the two artists without spectacles and looking in a different direction. The changes reflected their assumption that the publicity that they had received in the Western press after *The Bulldozer Exhibition* guaranteed them international fame.

Komar and Melamid's objective of destabilizing, redefining, and, through appropriation, personalizing the Soviet propaganda apparatus appeared in a total environment, *Paradise* (figs. 138–40). The artists began to install it at the end of 1972 in a relative's private apartment on the outskirts of Moscow. It stayed intact until the beginning of 1975, when the authorities, right after *The Bulldozer Exhibition*, told the occupier of the apartment to dismantle it. Through a door mock-bureaucratically labeled "Paradise," one visitor at a time entered a barely lit eight-square-meter "black box" or "sweet coffin for the viewer," to use Komar and Melamid's words.[4] Their other metaphor of *Paradise* as "'the square' [that]…locks in when the viewer completes his/her journey only to start it again"[5] links up with Malevich's *Black Square* and his famous Suprematist coffin designed by Suetin.

Perceiving no clear boundaries for top and bottom, and guided only by small lanterns, visitors to *Paradise* found their customary sense of a three-dimensional space undermined. This corresponds to Komar and Melamid's intention to create the illusion of entering a painting where "the smell of paint is mixed with that of cheap cologne." The artists initially planned to title their environment *Paradise/Pantheon*, claiming that it was "the first conceptual eclectic mix of various art styles and images (religious, legendary, mythological and historical)," including its imagery of gods and heroes. As in a theater, their materials were ephemeral and cheap, and comprised papier-mâché, Masonite, plywood, commercial paint, and colored mica. Several of Komar and Melamid's earlier paintings, made before the two became a team late in the 1960s, swayed like curtains from the ventilators installed behind them, which, sprayed with cheap cologne, diffused an intense odor. The radio was constantly on, with a flow of authorized music and news delivered by the em-phatic voices of Soviet anchormen and women. These and other primitive effects animated two- and three-dimensional images of Prometheus, the goddess Flora, nymphs, and the Buddha, whose coarsely made figure dangled in space. A papier-mâché Prometheus in the style of an expressionist sculpture[6] displayed front-page headlines of Soviet newspapers that effectively desta-bilized their ordered propaganda. The viewer was led over a bridge to the "face of humanity" placed on the "altar wall" of *Paradise*, this face roughly sewn with white thread on four separate pieces of fabric. A frag-ment of a Mongol face was rendered in the upper left corner in the style of Florentine mosaics, a Jew exe-cuted in the manner of a Russian (or Greek) icon painting in the upper right corner; the bottom left section of the face was painted in white in impres-sionist style, and the bottom right section in that of Cubism. The entire head (with an obvious resem-blance to Christ) was crowned by a nimbus of small flashing bulbs, as in decorations of Soviet leaders' por-traits circulated during Soviet holidays. Banners made from transparent multicolored mica with stenciled figures of nymphs partially obstructed the "face of humanity" and made the color of *Paradise* oscillate from blue to yellow to red. Such overwhelming het-erogeneity sprouted from the "eclectic consciousness of atheists" and signified a desire for emancipation from all possible doctrines.

This assembly of classical iconography was overlaid with stereotypical Soviet constructs of a paradisiacal world. One example was an open bar with good-quality vodka, often found in the offices of high-ranking bureaucrats, but available only from a store for foreign-ers called *Berezka* (little birch tree). Komar and Melamid underscored the corrupting nature of such bourgeois privilege in a socialist society by inserting an artificial fly into a sugar cube in their dream bar. Another image of a Soviet utopia featured a trinity consisting of a female collective farmer, a male worker, and a portrait of a "working" intellectual. The last had been missing from the emblematic first two proletarians sculpted by Vera Mukhina for the Paris Fair in 1937.

Melamid fell off a stool during the last phase of the installation and broke his arm, which generated an unintended extension of *Paradise*'s concept. The signif-icance of the accident was heightened by the fact that

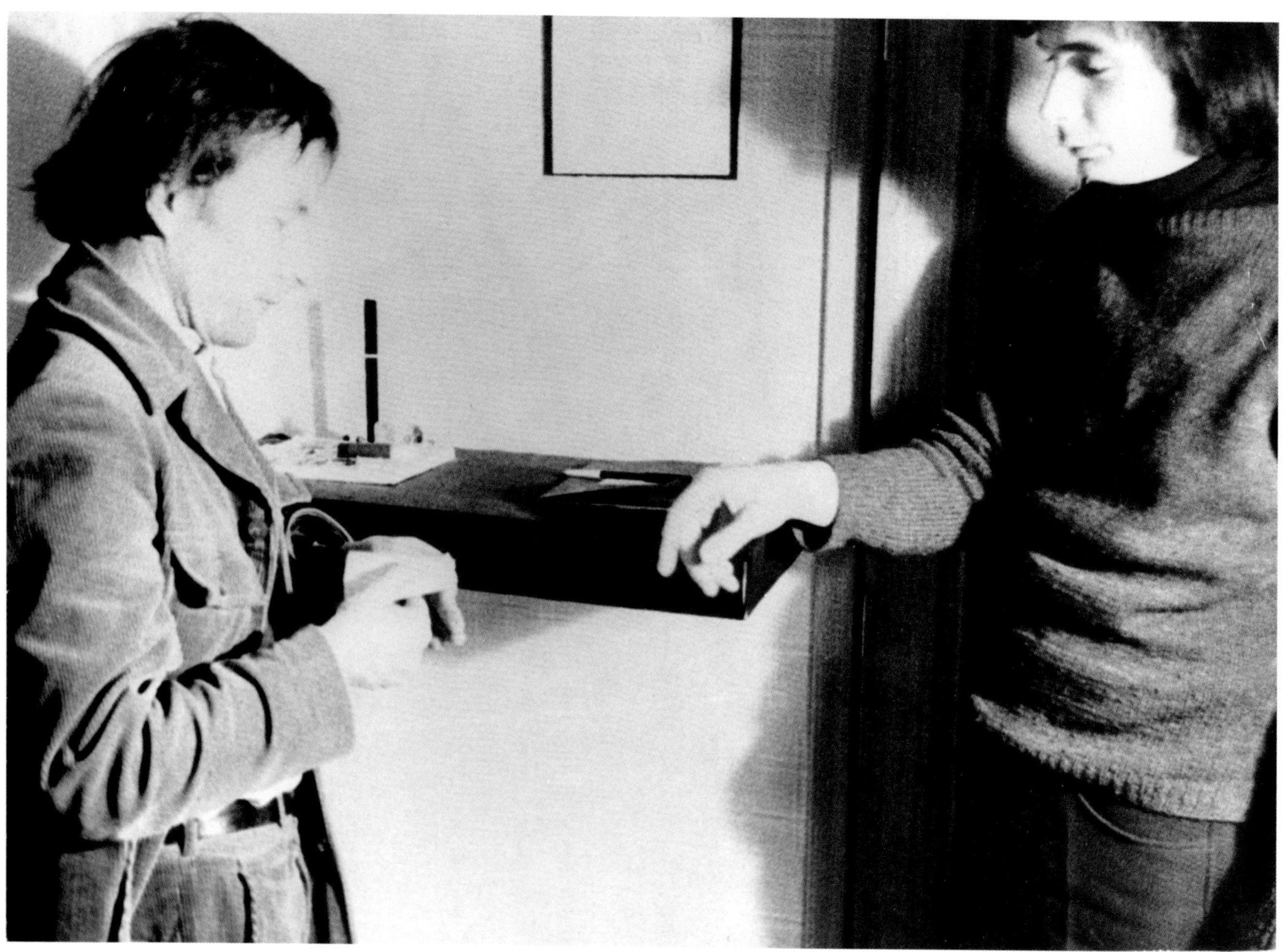

141 Andrei Monastyrsky, *Pile*, Moscow, 1975, with Rolf Fieguth (left) and Andrei Monastyrsky (right).

a few days earlier, Komar had dreamt that he had fallen and fractured his hand. His prophetic dream called for a commemorative performance which they staged in front of the "face of humanity," but with the color eliminated. Their left hands are bandaged, their mouths are covered with medical masks, and a stool – the cause of the injury – hangs in front of their faces.

According to Komar and Melamid, *Paradise*'s structuring principal depended "like Tolstoy's *War and Peace*, on the conjunction 'and,'" the principal that allows "extension to the next war or the next peace in both past and future directions." This is the general "principal of ironic consciousness fractured by nihilism," the two artists conclude. Their subversive *vsechestvo* (every-

thingness) was an important example for the Moscow counterculture of liberation from the pervasive binary thinking in which everything domestic was perceived negatively and everything foreign positively. *Paradise* also assaulted the government's protection of social and ideological homogeneity, which formed a grotesque contrast with the fact that "[t]he space in which…our time and our history occurs…is a heterogeneous space," as Michel Foucault wrote in his 1967 text, "Of Other Spaces: Utopias and Heterotopias."[7] By exposing this problem of the totalitarian regime, Komar and Melamid anticipated the more diverse cultural situation that emerged after *The Bulldozer Exhibition*. The critic Joseph Bakshtein, who visited *Paradise*, later described the sense of a historic rupture taking place, and the

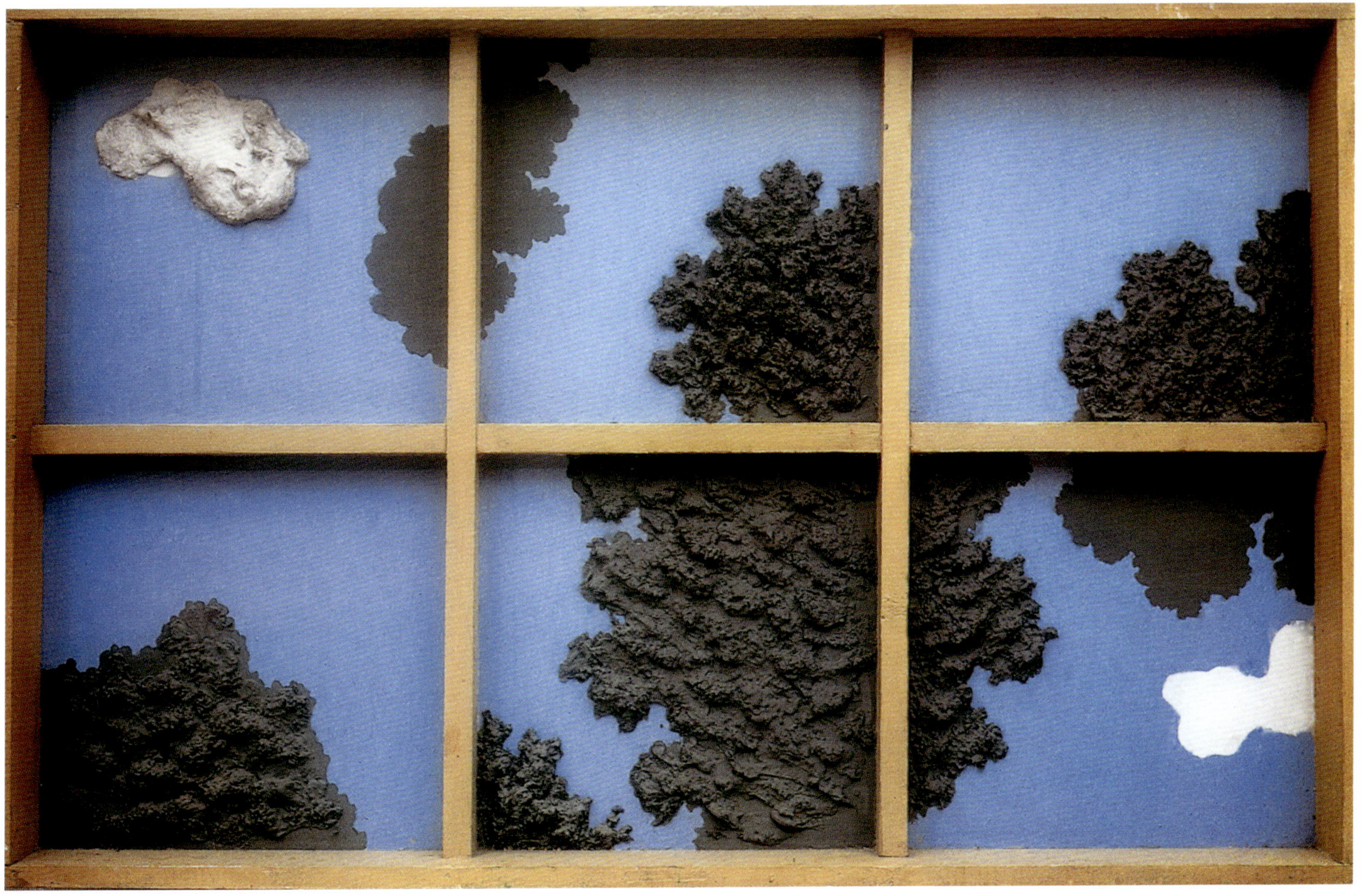

142   Ivan Chuikov, *Window IV*, 1974. State Tretiakov Gallery, Moscow.

elimination of the "single space of interpretation" that was endemic in both official and vanguard circles. Bakshtein continued: "Conditions were created such that each viewer, due to the fantastic diversity of objects offered, had to create his own, completely contingent, accidental, not verified and yet undeniable, conceptual and spatial interpretation. One could feel it very clearly. In this sense some qualitatively new level of freedom was created."[8]

Kabakov and Komar and Melamid's call for new perceptual systems and more interactive vanguard practices were developed in Monastyrsky's *Pile* (fig. 141) for which, as described in Chapter Four, he installed a shelf, inviting guests to leave on it a small object that they happened to have on them. Guests had to register their items in a notebook under their name with a number, description, and date of participation. Monastyrsky's recording of the shaping of an art work in a non-institutional context and with viewers' collaboration commenced a cultural account of this particular participatory aspect in underground aesthetic practices.[9]

In a conversation with Victor Tupitsyn in 1988, Ivan Chuikov talked about what it meant to make art for a small circle of viewers (who would perform a finite role) and within the spatial limitations of an artist's studio:

For a long time we were accustomed to think...that it's some narrow group of people (with [bona fide] references), whom you respect and who, probably, respect you...An appeal to a broad and unknown…viewer was simply unreal in those years. Now I understand how different these two situations are. The first…circle consists of people from whom you know what to expect. This significantly simplifies the game.[10]

From this statement it is clear that being understood and supported by a small group of likeminded people helped artists to sustain their vanguard agenda, and yet the inability to disseminate their ideas to broader audiences ended in frustration. Like most 1970s conceptual artists, Chuikov did not participate in *The Bulldozer Exhibition* but shared with its organizers a similar sense of claustrophobia that he expressed in the series *Windows*. Using a readymade window or making one himself, Chuikov obscured this transparent object by painting on its opaque surfaces. *Window IV* (1974; fig. 142), made in the year of *The Bulldozer Exhibition*, insisted on landscape as a representation rather than as a stage for displaying art. Chuikov's fascination with James Joyce's "linguistic layering" influenced how his art appeared.[11] This varied from figurative to abstract,[12] and included many landscapes as well as images of windows, all of which spoke of the "clash of representation with harsh reality."[13] He wanted to endow these structures with the dialectical power of "destruction and erection of illusions, an attempt to break through the walls erected by me or someone else. If we are to speak about the unconscious aspect of my works, it has to do with all kinds of borders, walls, either stating their presence or attempting to break them, to overcome limitations."[14]

While immuring his private space in the first series of windows, Chuikov made a counter-series called *A Window into the Studio*, in which compositions were applied to the glass surfaces, reversing the previous series' impenetrability, and using a window's liquid properties that "point[s] in two directions…toward the flow of birth – the amniotic fluid, the 'source,'" and "toward the freezing into stasis or death – the unfecund immobility of the mirror."[15] Once again, for Chuikov a window served as a dialectical format, reflecting a schism in the life and work of a vanguard artist in an authoritarian state – between feeling within one's studio walls simultaneously liberated and imprisoned.

This was a different resolution of pressures from that of the other artists discussed in this chapter. Unlike them, Chuikov refused to operate through the metaphor of exit, whether as a way out of contemporary existence or as a compromise that transformed reality into representation. In *Virtual Sculptures* and in *Virtual Objects* (1977), he created an antidote to the tangible pressure of Soviet everyday life (figs. 143, 144). Chuikov delineated geometric shapes and drew landscapes on the ceiling and walls of his studio, proposing that sculpture should be freed from a static and permanent position. With this he entered into the struggle later outlined by Rosalind Krauss: "From Tatlin's corner reliefs and his insistence on productivism to the Earthworks of the 1970s, many twentieth-century sculptors have wanted to smash the glass bubble that encases sculpture in a world of illusion, representation, idealization. They wanted it to exist, to function, to act, in the field of the real."[16] Chuikov's "virtual objects," designed to be installed in the corners, expanded this discourse to his historical context in which Socialist Realists had subverted the principles of Constructivism and Productivism in order to misuse sculpture for the state's ideological ends. In view of this, Chuikov's "Virtual Sculptures" make an about-turn into the corners and zones of the workplace that Soviet constructivists had exchanged for the streets in the early 1920s. In these projects Chuikov insisted that the zones of installation mattered more than what was being installed.

Igor Makarevich's articulation of such tensions took an overtly subjective form, as he made self-portraiture central to his *Transformation* series (1978). He conceived it while producing a cast of his face for another project. Waiting for a warm mass of plaster to solidify, he remembered experiencing the "stone coldness that separated [him] for some time from the surrounding world, and served as the inspiration for…Transformation."[17] In other words, in order to be able to convey a certain distance from reality he had to experience a boundary of reality first. Executed in the medium of photographs, in both color and black and white, *Transformation* consisted of scenes of Makarevich's face being trapped within the cramped spaces of identical wooden boxes (fig. 145). For Makarevich, a box became a stage for

143   Ivan Chuikov, *Virtual Objects* (project for the four corners of a room), 1977.

144   Ivan Chuikov, *Virtual Object* in the corner of the artist's studio, Moscow, 1977.

145   Igor Makarevich posing for his *Transformation* series, Moscow, 1978.

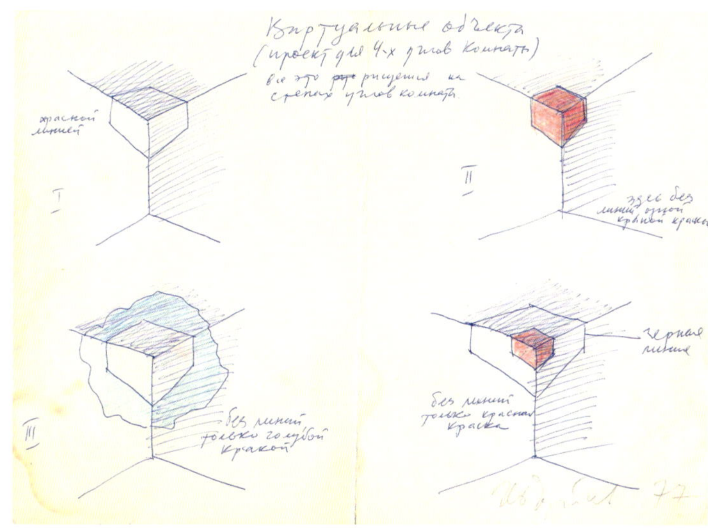

what might be termed a theatricalized ontology – he himself defined it as a hybrid of a real stage and "a border of reality."[18] In the color version of *Transformation*, Makarevich's face was buried in bandages and ropes, eventually reappearing as a death mask. Finally, that too disappeared, and so what might be called this "Box for Face," after Robert Morris, was deserted.[19]

In the black and white version of *Transformation* (fig. 146), Makarevich's representation of alienation and invisibility, or what he calls "temptation to despair," similarly fits into a discourse of political subjectivity, for Makarevich deals with ideas of power and resistance in an explicitly personal way. At first, he was going to call this work "Stratigraphic Structures," since "it is based on the process of immuring,"[20] thus in line with Chuikov's discourse. In this version, Makarevich stages a more brutal attack on the human subject by assaulting his face with a rough mass of plaster, and at one point confining it in a boarded-up box. This is followed by the shattering of "stratigraphic" traps – the cracking of the plaster covers, made to allegorize repression, and the face's disimmuring, the return of the subject that resisted repression. In 1979, the color version of *Transformation* was exhibited at the Pompidou Centre in Paris in the group photography exhibition that also included Andrei Abramov and Chuikov (fig. 147). For their exhibition poster image, the organizers chose a detail of Makarevich's face with his mouth bandaged, which underscored the relationship of *Transformation* with the then influential ideas of Foucault on the interconnection of language and power.

Monastyrsky's *Finger* (fig. 148), also a box-object, is an interactive construction aimed at providing the domestic viewer with an instrument to experience the physical and psychological effects of the

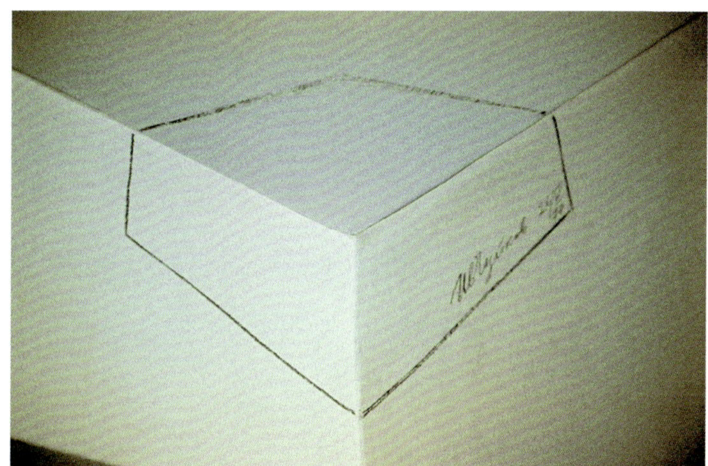

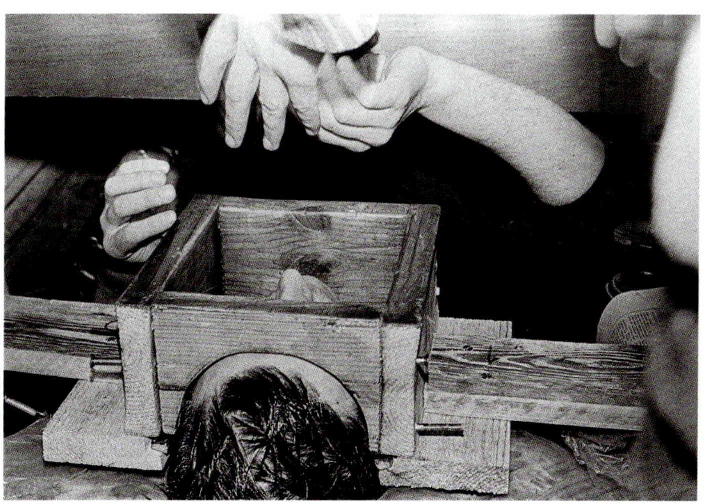

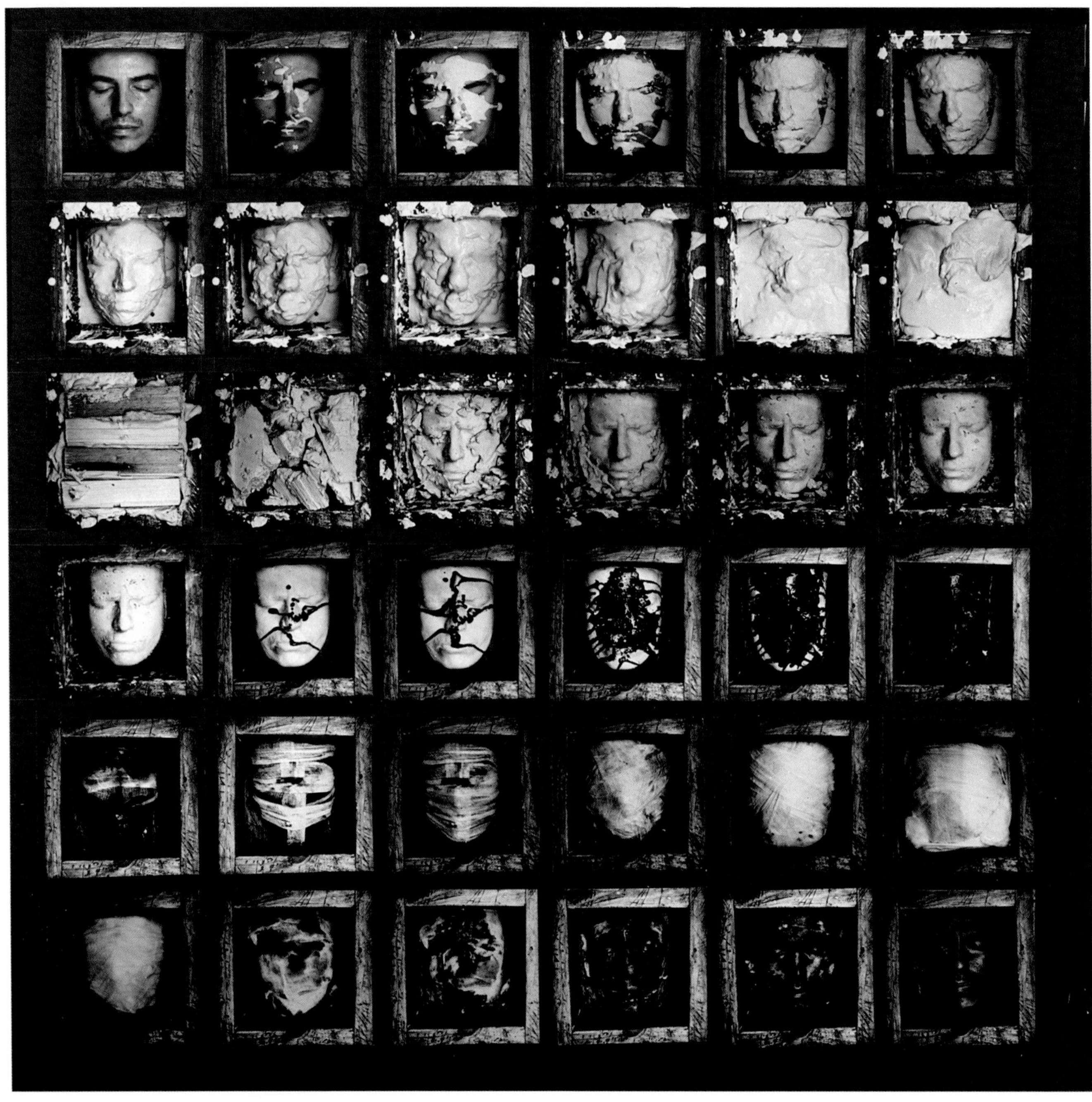

146　Igor Makarevich, *Transformation*, 1978.

conditions under which artists showed their works in studios. Covered in black fabric, *Finger* is bottomless and has a round opening. A label instructs the viewer on how to become the object's user: insert your arm inside and stick your index finger out of the hole, thereby pointing toward an action. Another label says: "Finger, or pointing at oneself as an object external in relation to oneself," on which Monastyrsky expanded two years later: "Finger," he wrote in a letter to Victor Tupitsyn, "is a sign of a personality split over the empirical 'I' ('an external object') and the spiritual 'I' ('toward oneself')."[21] While agreeing to Tupitsyn's

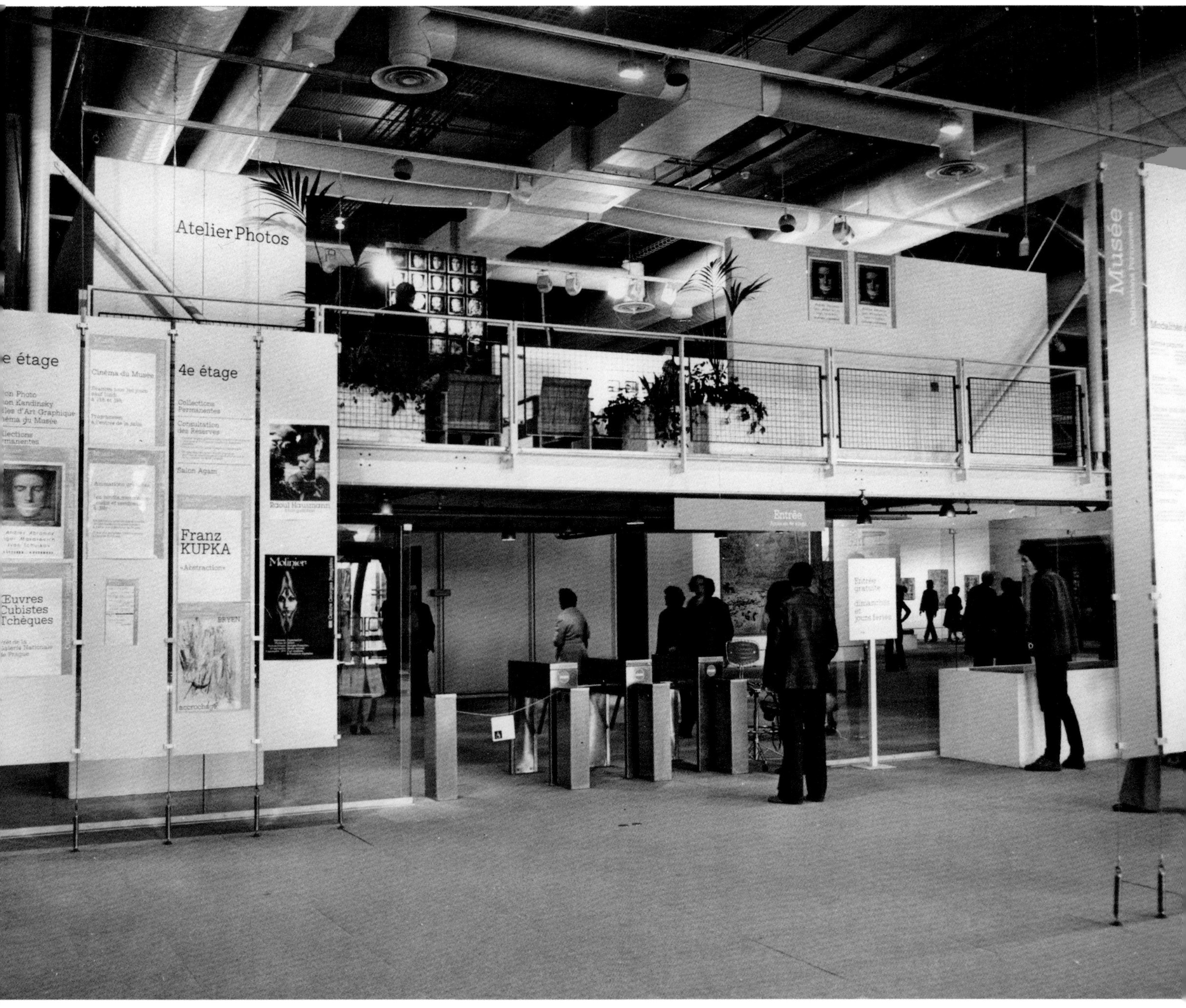

147   Igor Makarevich, *Transformation*, 1978, in the Centre Georges Pompidou, Paris, 1979.

proposal to recreate *Finger* in New York, Monastyrsky warned that this object was not for "public showing, but for domestic use because…[it is] purely existential…it is not a thing, but a principle."[22]

Unlike the easel painters, Kabakov worked on Masonite, a rigid, heavy material that made his works look more object-like, and when shown, more grounded. Kabakov's visible presence within the space of display resulted in a condition not unlike Monastyrsky's split between "the empirical 'I'" and "the spiritual 'I,'" in this case between Kabakov a handler of heavy objects, and Kabakov a subject integrated into

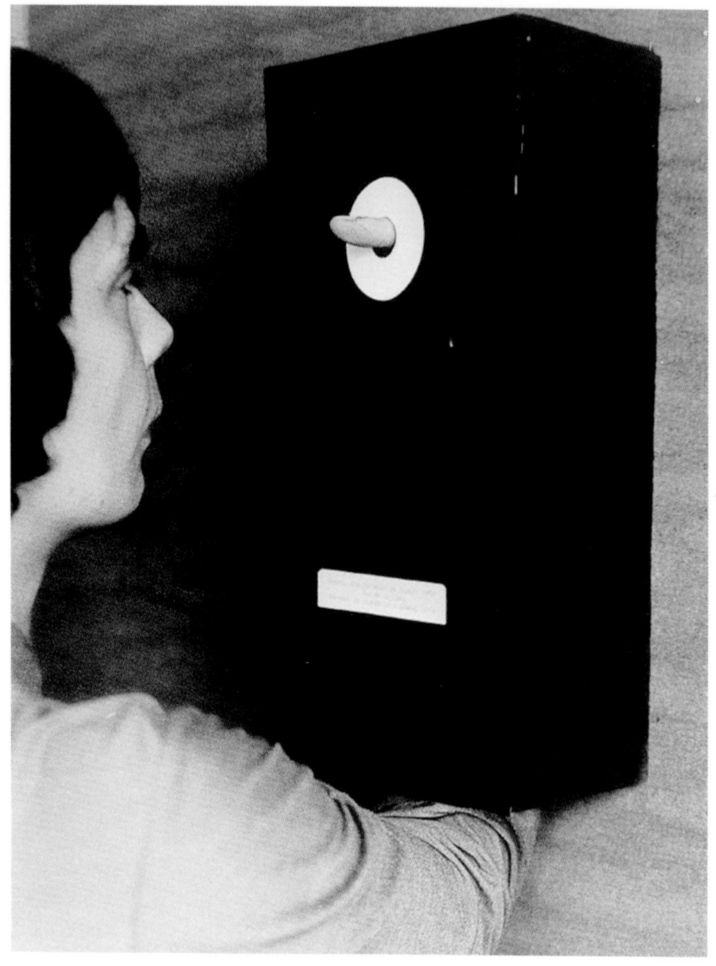

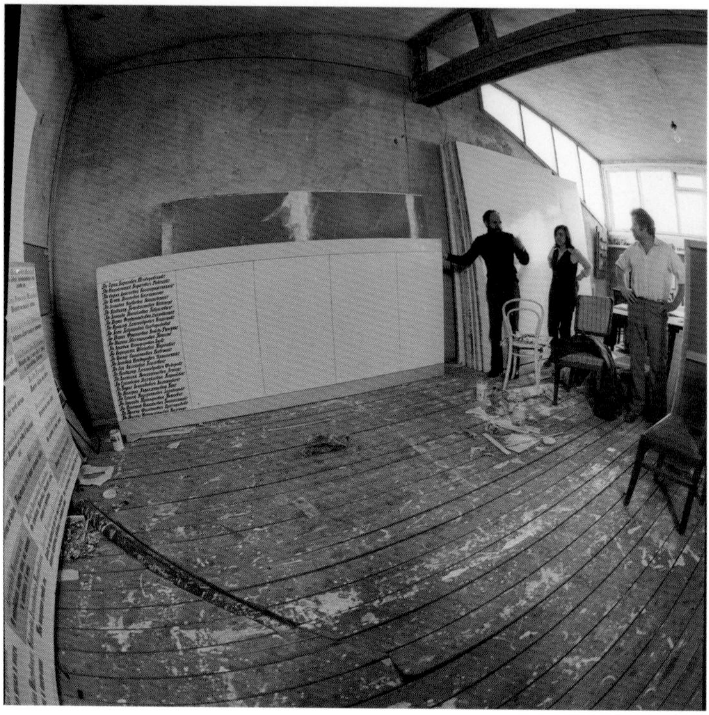

the space of his works. The viewer was discouraged from entering this space. Monastyrsky's *Finger* exposed the mechanism of this privatized display and charted a new collective one. A photograph taken by Makarevich in Kabakov's studio a year after Monastyrsky made *Finger* records a moment of this change (fig. 149). During a visit to Kabakov, a young conceptual artist, Valery Gerlovin, became involved in holding and showing Kabakov's work *Where Are They* (1971) and, judging by the gesture of his hand, Gerlovin was engaged in its interpretation. Standing at a distance enabled Kabakov to observe his work as an outsider and listen to the interpretive voice of the other. This is the moment when Kabakov experienced alienation from his production, something that was normal for Western artists exposed to critical evaluation and parting with their works, but at the time not typical for Moscow underground artists. A viewer's "physical

insertion into the painting,"[23] or what Bakshtein, in a reference to Monastyrsky's *Finger*, described as "the viewer's hand's 'penetration into a painting,'"[24] orchestrated an intersubjective space, instead of the one available only to the artist.

This marked a historical shift in relations among vanguard artists as well as between them and their studio viewers. In the 1960s, these artists empathized for the sake of independent creation, and in support of a counterculture, but in the process they ignored the issues they had as regards the nature of aesthetic objects. In the second half of the 1970s, consensus on the cultural terms of the vanguard started to be influenced by the collective activities of conceptual and performance artists of the next generation (discussed in Chapter Four). With Kabakov's active communication with them, new forms of display were conceived and different art-viewing experiences invented.

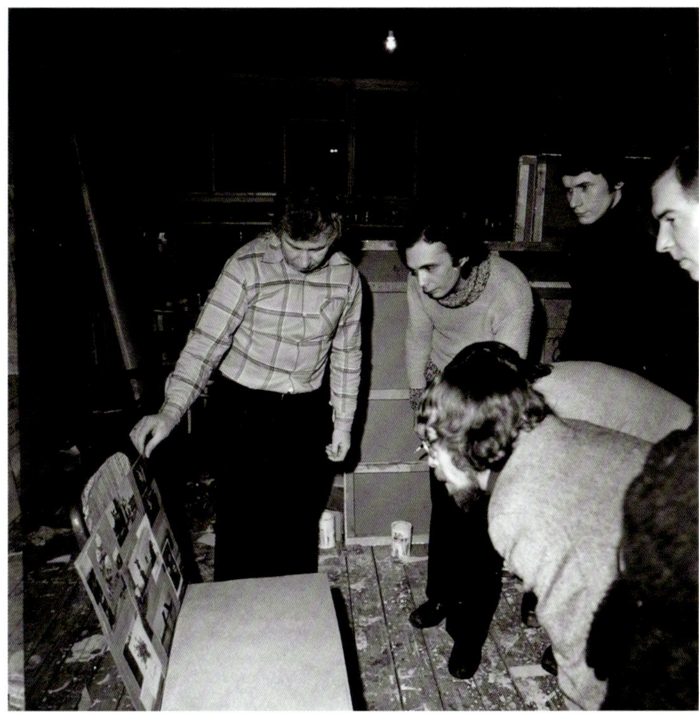

ABOVE 150   Ilya Kabakov's studio in Moscow, 1980, with (clockwise from left) Lev Rubinshtein, Nikita Alekseev, Victor Skersis, Andrei Monastyrsky, and Ilya Kabakov.

RIGHT 151   The Mukhomor group, *Drainage*, July 7, 1981. Moscow.

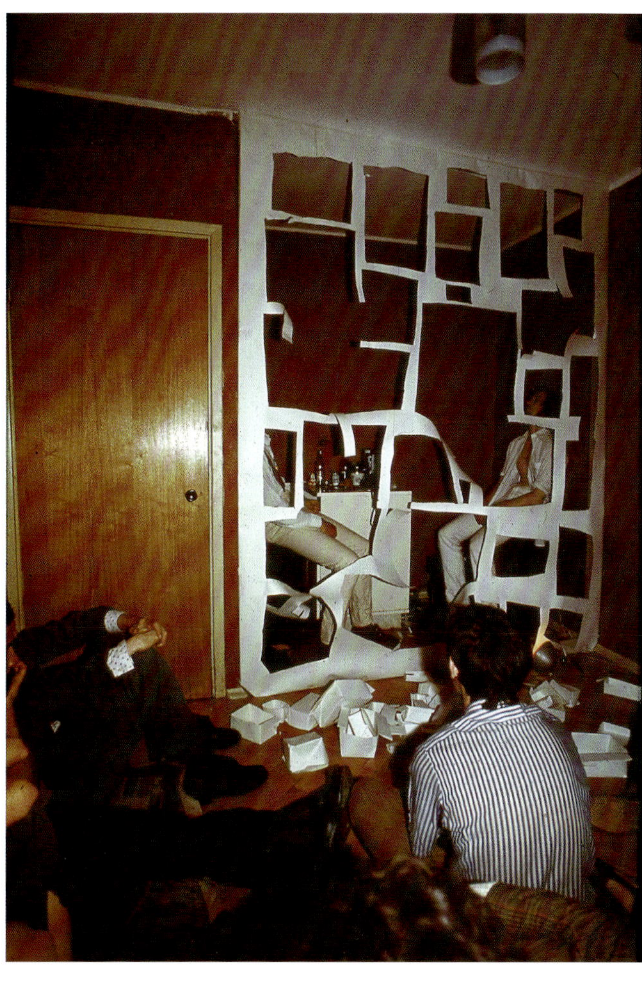

Another group photograph, taken in Kabakov's studio by Georgy Kizevalter in 1980, underscores the paramount importance of verbal exchange in the formation of an alternative sociocultural microcosm. Kabakov presides at his studio's dinner table with a group of young conceptualists, artists, and poets, namely Nikita Alekseev, Elena Elagina, Maria Konstantinova, Monastyrsky, Lev Rubinshtein, and Victor Skersis. Together they are engaged in generating what Mikhail Bakhtin called "utterances," which until then, Kabakov took from overheard ordinary speech. Bakhtin wrote: "The intention – the subjective aspect of the utterance – merges with the objective-semantic aspect and forms an indissoluble whole limiting the latter by linking it to the specific (unique) context of the verbal communication, with all its individual circumstances, with the people participating in it, and with their preceding speeches – utterances."[25]

Other Kizevalter photographs capture the same group looking at Kabakov's new collages (fig. 150). Composed from official magazine cutouts and postcards, these works delivered the counterfeit image that the counterculture had loathed. Besides ignoring such modernist values as originality and skill, this material disturbed the exclusive, liberating experience associated with viewing vanguard art. Now Kabakov more explicitly than in his albums was challenging this uncritical interaction with the viewer by showing art as a subversive and critical field. Writing shortly after seeing Kabakov's collages, Monastyrsky initially concluded that these "works are indigestible."[26] However, less than a year later, he wrote that Kabakov's appropriation of found material presented a convincing conclusion to his albums: "[Kabakov] created with this series a very clear and energetic sign that formulates an incredible…connection with the world through reproduction. This is how Kabakov's hitherto elusive 'conceptualism' becomes defined."[27] A series of Makarevich's photographs, titled *Kabakov's Space*, provides a key to understanding how Kabakov became fascinated by "Soviet litter," be it mass-media imagery or ordinary trash. As Kabakov climbed up a long set of stairs to his studio every day, he passed discarded toilets, stoves, refrigerators, cupboards, and garbage cans – a collection of unwanted objects whose constant presence made him into their regular spectator. Thus he learned how, psycho-optically and aesthetically, to perceive Soviet mundanity, and aspired to teach others to do so first in his collages and later in installations.

Kabakov's nihilistic attitude toward the unofficial art canons of the 1960s carried great weight with the young conceptualists who had already left modernism behind. By the end of the 1970s, among the boldest adherents of the anti-art stance were the Mukhomor group, formed in 1978 by the young artists Sven Gundlakh, Aleksis Kamensky, Sergei and Vladimir Mironenko, and Konstantin Zvezdochetov. Like Komar and Melamid, they started off with appearances in Moscow studios, bringing suitcases of ephemeral pieces, which consisted of original drawings and miscellaneous objects with no apparent function. Their sharing of this material with mock seriousness scoffed at modernists' solemn presentations of easel art. For the performance piece, *Metro* (October 28, 1979), Mukhomor infiltrated the revered public metro, riding trains the whole day according to a schedule distributed to members of the underground art community for participation. They even managed to have their photograph taken at one of the stations despite the official restrictions on photography in the metro. Yet, as Makarevich points out, Mukhomor's fearless behavior in highly populated and controlled public spaces at times gave way to "a persecution complex" and to "feelings of oppression and anxiety."[28] It is precisely these kinds of sensations that CAG's later *M* (see fig. 124), similarly based on the metro, was trying to free itself from by performing in rural spaces.

In *Drainage* (July 7, 1981), Mukhomor further interrogated 1960s modernist values, including those associated with Kabakov (fig. 151). In a private apartment, they separated themselves from viewers with a white paper wall, in this way constructing a stage for a skit based on the concept of a white surface as a source of energy and as an "emanating stream…of bright, almost blinding light."[29] Not aware of the performers sitting behind the wall, the viewers were caught off guard when the former started making holes and cutouts in the paper wall, through which streams of water were discharged. They also threw small objects into the room. As the openings became larger, the viewers could see the two performers sitting at the table-as-altar, on which tenets of modernism were being "sacrificed" among bottles of Pepsi-Cola and unemptied ashtrays. While this was happening, the shower was running in the bathroom, referring to Kabakov's best-known series of drawings, 'Shower' (1965–78), which were eventually assembled and called *Comedies of a Theater of One Actor*. Each drawing depicts the same man standing under a shower, but with differing amounts of water, which allegorizes his dreams and fantasies. *Drainage*'s viewers were invited to the bathroom to receive a jar of its water as a trace of liquidated modernist narratives. During the performance, a soundtrack of "mooing, quacking, and incoherent puffing of disconnected words"[30] mocked the impenetrable intellectual performances of CAG. Monastyrsky, who attended *Drainage*, described it as "'a goofy ocean,' presented so inconspicuously that it was a pleasure to be immersed in it."[31]

This novel experience of immersion in a vigorous artistic atmosphere was what the young conceptualists aspired to achieve by employing an allover display of multimedia material. A veteran of collective practices, Alekseev readily surrendered his studio apartment to the creation of such an environment, inaugurated under the name "Apt Art" on October 20, 1982. Coining this term, a direct reference to the postwar showing of unsanctioned art in apartments, Aptartists converted this narrow option into a radical form of collective installation art. They made a point of calling the first Apt Art display the "anti-show" and a "working exposition" (figs. 152–4), resisting any association with academic exhibitions and those of modernists currently organized in Gorkom Grafikov.

According to a checklist, Alekseev's apartment accommodated 106 works executed specifically for this event by Natalia Abalakova and Anatoly Zhigalov

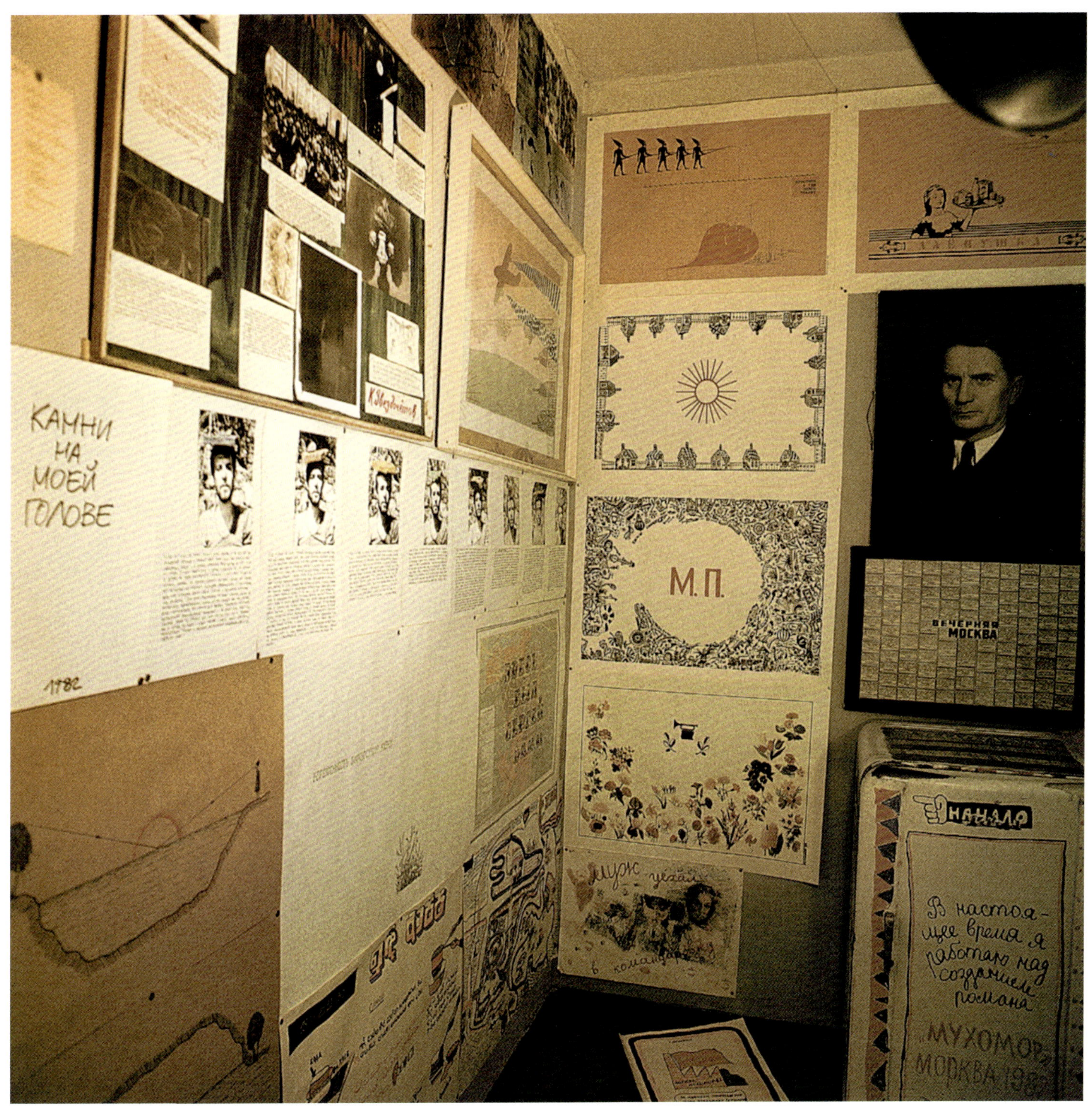

152   The first Apt Art exhibition, October 20–31, 1982.

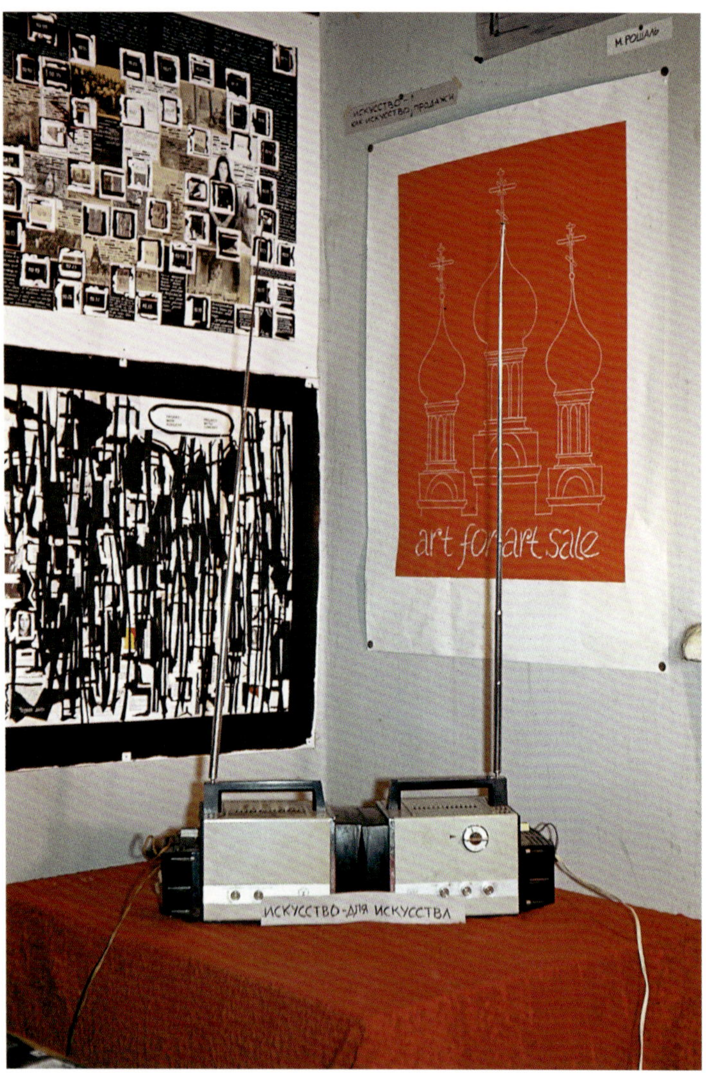
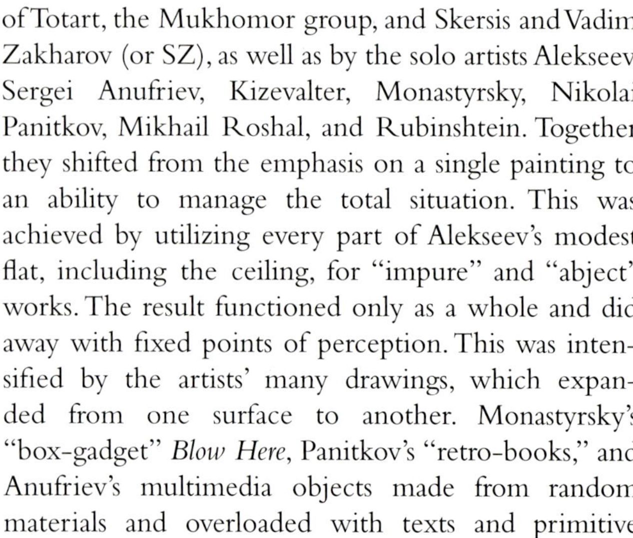

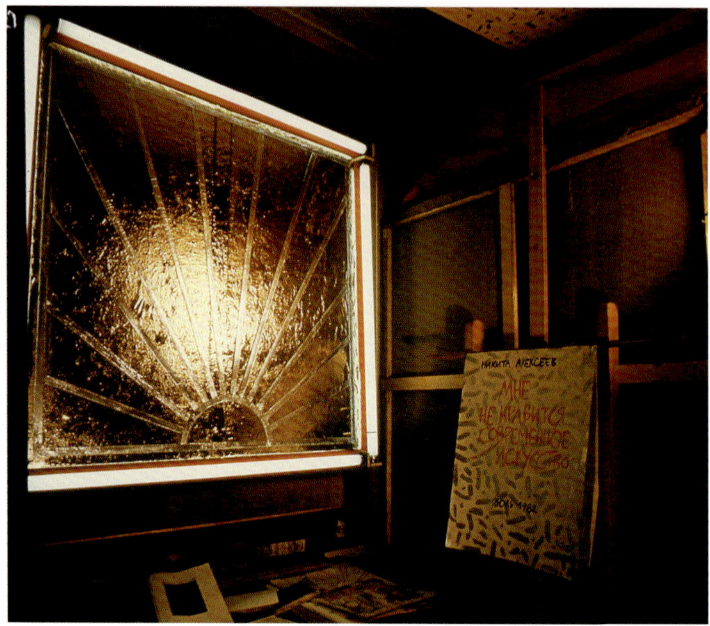

153 & 154   The first Apt Art exhibition, October 20–31, 1982.

of Totart, the Mukhomor group, and Skersis and Vadim Zakharov (or SZ), as well as by the solo artists Alekseev, Sergei Anufriev, Kizevalter, Monastyrsky, Nikolai Panitkov, Mikhail Roshal, and Rubinshtein. Together they shifted from the emphasis on a single painting to an ability to manage the total situation. This was achieved by utilizing every part of Alekseev's modest flat, including the ceiling, for "impure" and "abject" works. The result functioned only as a whole and did away with fixed points of perception. This was intensified by the artists' many drawings, which expanded from one surface to another. Monastyrsky's "box-gadget" *Blow Here*, Panitkov's "retro-books," and Anufriev's multimedia objects made from random materials and overloaded with texts and primitive

drawings, were displayed wherever possible. Mixing with domestic objects, they created micro installations in "which everything could be pulled at, leafed through, touched, etc."[32] Such a visual bombardment, along with what Zhigalov called the "avalanche of unreadable texts, labels, slogans, posters," overwhelmed the viewer and energized the entire visual field. Zhigalov used such terms as "works-actions," and "energetic production art."[33]

Aptartists also transformed scarce socialist commodities into bizarre structures. This included the Mukhomor group's object *Novel*,[34] a refrigerator that was decorated with an abundance of found elements. It attacked the novel, that revered literary form in Russia and the Soviet Union, with a schizophrenic visual assemblage. A stretched arm with the word "beginning" was drawn on the front of the refrigerator, pointing to where to open it, thus giving the kind of freedom to the viewer that the reader has with a book. Mukhomor's television screen, with a primitive drawing of a Kremlin tower and a sky with red stars, together with a self-rebutting inscription, "This is not what I wanted to say," unmasked the deceiving rhetoric of Soviet media. Roshal took up the same theme in his two working television sets, tied up monitor to monitor and labeled "art for art's sake." This modernist slogan was appropriated to insinuate the frozen regime of Soviet ideology less than a month before Brezhnev's death. Abalakova and Zhigalov's placing of a label on a chair, "the chair is not for you, it's for everyone," also deflated the cult of creative individuality. Their *Black Square*, a garbage bag filled with paper, responded to Malevich's seminal canvas, which had been exhibited the year before at the Pushkin State Museum of Fine Arts in *Moscow–Paris, 1900–1930* (June 3–October 4, 1981), which they considered a gesture that failed to compensate for the official trashing of the historical avant-garde.

Aptartists' disenchantment with the state of art, official and underground alike, was expressed in another group of works. Among them is Alekseev's album *I Don't Like Contemporary Art*, in which he wrote a mock art essay on large sheets of paper using color markers, at times disrupting the text with drawings and cut-outs (see fig. 154, right). Here, Alekseev says that he does not like the state of contemporary art because it lacks a critical discourse, and as a result constantly collides with visual and verbal (interpretive) regimes. Mukhomor's *The Most Important Painting* was a collage of sunrays in silver and gold leaf assembled on a canvas framed by neon tubes (see fig. 154, left). This is yet another example of the group's blunt debunking of Moscow modernists' fixation on the notion of masterpieces and on the creation of a self-determined rather than institutional hierarchy in the underground art world. The latter's regard for painterly techniques and claim of transcendental knowledge are demystified in the collage's imitation of precious metals and use of artificial neon-white light.

Without much advertising, the Apt Art installation attracted many visitors, including those from official circles: some high-ranking bureaucrats initially provided the necessary protection for the project. But this backing was cut off three months after Andropov, following Brezhnev's death, became General Secretary, as noted in Chapter Four. After several more shows and performances, Apt Art paused its activities in Alekseev's apartment.[35] Alekseev described, in English, how it happened:

I am informing you with deep regret that "APTART" ceased to exist on February 15, 1983. Early in the morning of that day, the employees of a "well known" organization [KGB] came with a search warrant and smashed the exhibition of Skersis and Zakharov, confiscated some of the works along with other materials which were in no way anti-Soviet…From the "employee's" remarks it was clear that they tend to interpret all works if not as anti-Soviet then pornographic or both…Most likely, this signals the beginning of a new campaign for complete extirpation of new art…All this is quite sad but at least we have already achieved something. And maybe the situation will get better.[36]

Kabakov admits to his fascination with the Aptartists' conceptualism in a text of 1985, "The Artist-character," which he begins by mentioning the Apt Art installation. Summing it up, Kabakov writes that the Apt Art works "were made not by the artists themselves, but by 'artist-characters.' The author-artist invents such a character, and then art works like 'things' are made by this invented character."[37] Kabakov adopted this split authorial construct because of his prolonged absence of distance from his production that, as I suggested earlier, had led to the necessisty of his estrangement from his own art works. Kabakov felt this more strongly than most artists of his generation because of his high productivity, stylistic diversity, and refusal to work on canvas, which reduced his chances of selling works to those foreign collectors who had been buying underground art since the 1960s. Well aware of these issues, the '80s generation underplayed the role of individual art works and single authorship. Thus, while Western artists, notably Marcel Duchamp, had assumed various characters in order to escape accepted definitions of artist and existing institutional structures, the Moscow vanguardists, not being able "to participate in a normal art cycle: artist–painting–exhibit–viewer," experienced a splitting of themselves.[38] Kabakov continues:

The appearance of the "artist-character" is rooted in this prolonged experience of interacting with this glowing "panorama" of art. I repeat, it continuously exists in the imagination of every artist working here. Being plunged inside the work itself, made by the artist himself, leads to fantastic, unknown patterns, junctions where, like in a psychedelic dream, one fragment connects with the other, flowing into the other."[39]

At this point, Kabakov figured out how to channel these shortcomings into a new genre: installation art. Its early stages are linked to Kabakov's *Empty Painting* (1983, the last in the series of white paintings), which he included as one of the illustrations in *The Artist-character*, a book he made himself. Its sizable Masonite panel is entirely covered in white enamel paint, with a thin black line stretching around the perimeter. Instead of wrapping the color white in esoteric meanings as he had done before, Kabakov added to it an explanation board painted in dirty brown that tells the story of an official painter who, owing to illness, failed to deliver a commissioned canvas and asked for more time to finish it. The trusting committee told him to exhibit an empty canvas instead – an "invisible painting" – together with an explanation board. Kabakov's diptych is dialectical: he was assaulting Socialist Realism's fixation on narrative and suspicion of the visual. He also concluded that the counterculture's estrangement from Soviet mainstream culture meant that its impressive painting inventory would remain "invisible" in the eyes of officialdom.

Acknowledging these realities resulted in Kabakov giving up two-dimensional art as a self-sufficient medium. Now he could release his rich cast of characters from flat surfaces into the panorama of his studio. *Little White Men* has been registered in his oeuvre as the earliest example of his installation practices.[40] Kabakov stretched a rope from a stack of paintings leaned against the wall to a spot on the floor of his studio and tied to the rope descending cutout figures (figs. 155, 156). Kabakov extended the march of this specter of cutout characters into the window that was his usual passage to the roof. Up there, he liked to sit leaning against a white chimney and facing the splashes of white paint, the kind of environment that could have shaped his white creatures and where he could imagine "fantastic, unknown patterns," and connect one fragment with the other, as well as flee as an invisible man (fig. 157).

The breaking free of *Little White Men*, which signified Kabakov's distress about a prolonged underground existence, was paralleled by that of a young painter, Irina Nakhova. She also expressed her discomfort with limited spaces by painting roofs so that they barred the view of repressive Soviet everyday life and turned Moscow into an ideal city. Nakhova conceived her installation idiom as an alternative to the cluttered spaces of underground studios. Her initial impression of those spaces goes back to the early 1970s when, still a teenager, she visited Yankilevsky's studio (fig. 158):

At the very beginning, it was Yankilevsky who made the strongest impression on me – especially the huge coffins in his studio near the Turgenevskaia Metro stop. I now understand that that studio was as much a work of art as what we later began to call installations, because there wasn't a single bit of space in it that wasn't filled with images.[41]

Throughout the 1970s, Nakhova painted canvases peopled by odd creatures, which were also politically provocative, as in the case of *The General's Funeral* (1973), with its unconventional representation of this pompous Soviet ritual. In 1974, she collaborated with Monastyrsky on an installation, *Adoration of a Word* (fig. 159), that sets up a competition between verbal and visual practices. With a globe in the place of his head, the poet Monastyrsky kneels over a carpet of books arranged on the floor. On his back sits Nakhova's still life depicting a chessboard that symbolizes both a competition and a search for a balance between image and language. At the edge of Monastyrsky's grid of books stands Nakhova's small canvas *Stoning: After Fra Angelico* (1974), which resists the conceptualists' privileging of language. Moreover, it can be suggested that Nakhova's allusion to Fra Angelico's *Martyrdom of St. Mark* serves as an allegory of government aggression, expulsions from institutions, and harassment of vanguard artists.

For her own first experiment with installation art, called *Room No. 1* (fig. 160), Nakhova entirely covered a room (39 × 4.2 × 2.6 m) in her small apartment with sheets of white paper, creating an "empty white space…that had no visual borders, and

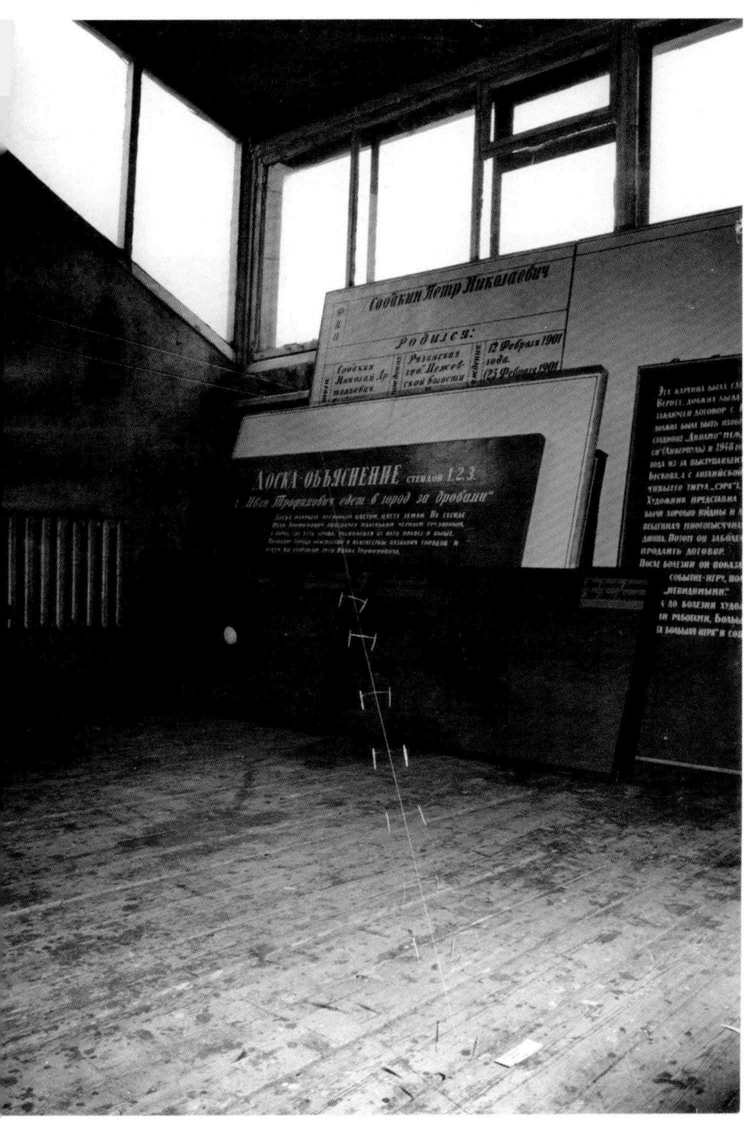

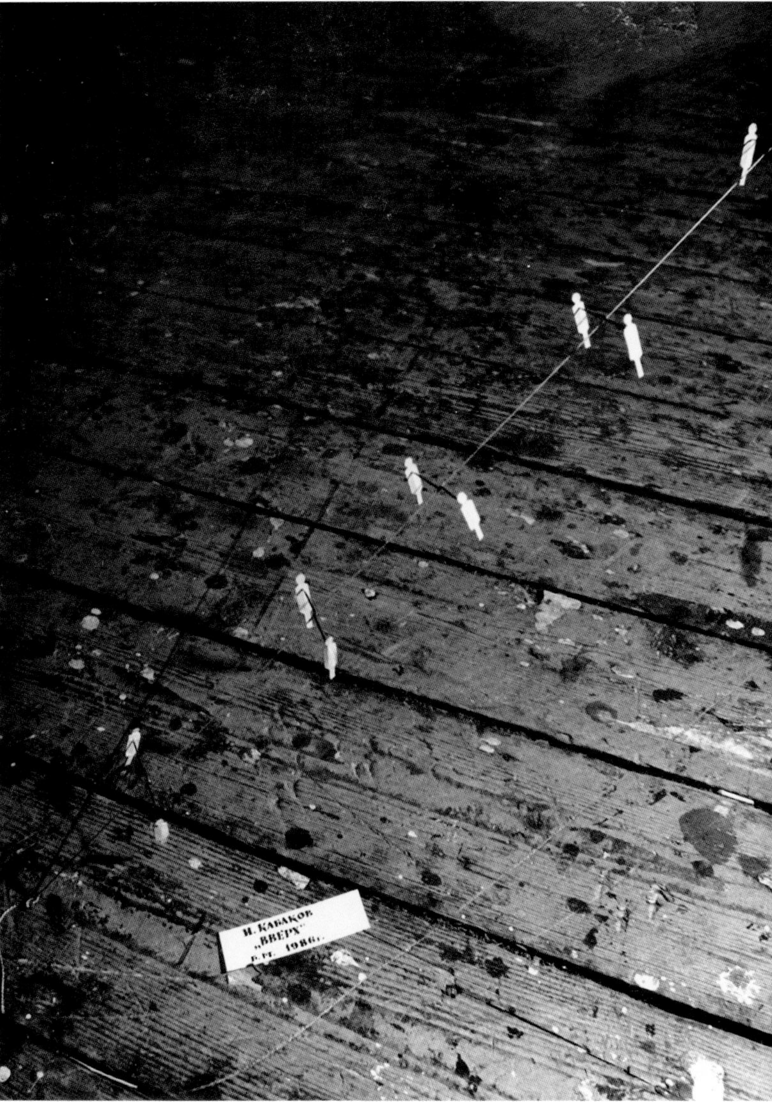

155   Ilya Kabakov, *Little White Men* in the artist's studio, Moscow, 1986.

156   Ilya Kabakov, *Little White Men* in the artist's studio, Moscow, 1986.

was built on the principle of a 'scattered and spinned bowl.'"[42] Over the white paper surfaces she pasted "pronouncedly bright, shiny, and colorful" clippings from Soviet fashion magazines.[43] In what was then an intuitively feminist interpretation of woman-as-construct, Nakhova dissected female fig-ures – those for the walls, lengthwise, and those for the floor, across. This turned *Room No. 1* into "figurative architectonics," an optical mirage, that stood in opposition to the invasive readability of official art.

The next two Moscow installations, Kabakov's *16 Ropes* (ca. 1984) and Nakhova's *Room No. 2* (1984) were formal and iconographic opposites (figs. 161, 162). In *Room No. 2*, Nakhova once again covered the walls with white paper, upon which she now glued large shapes of black and gray paper. With a powerful sense of tension, and feeding off the psychology of perception, *Room 2* evoked Kandinsky's concept of the "house of utopia" in conjuring a wholly abstract environment.[44] Her shift to the nonobjective and colorlessness

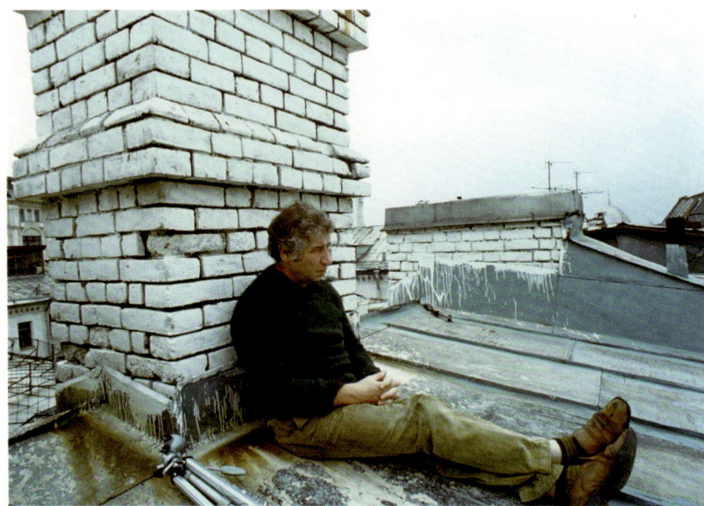

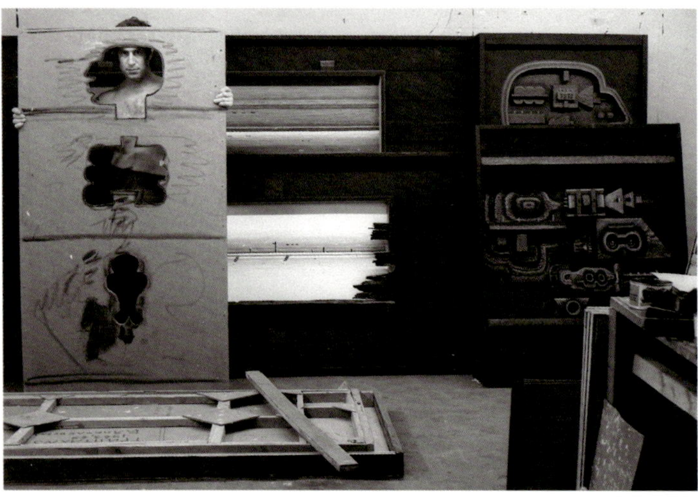

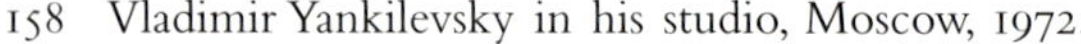

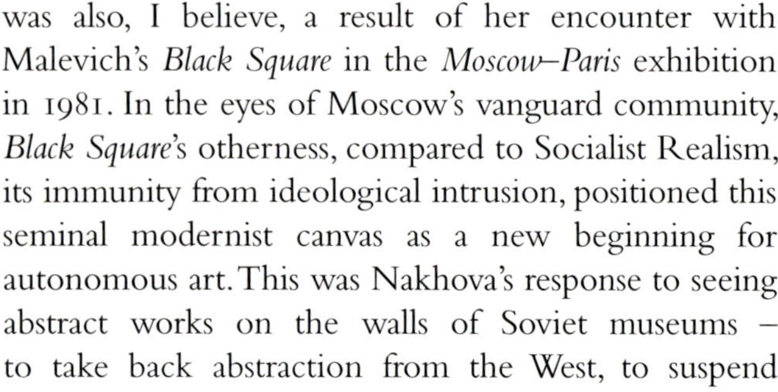

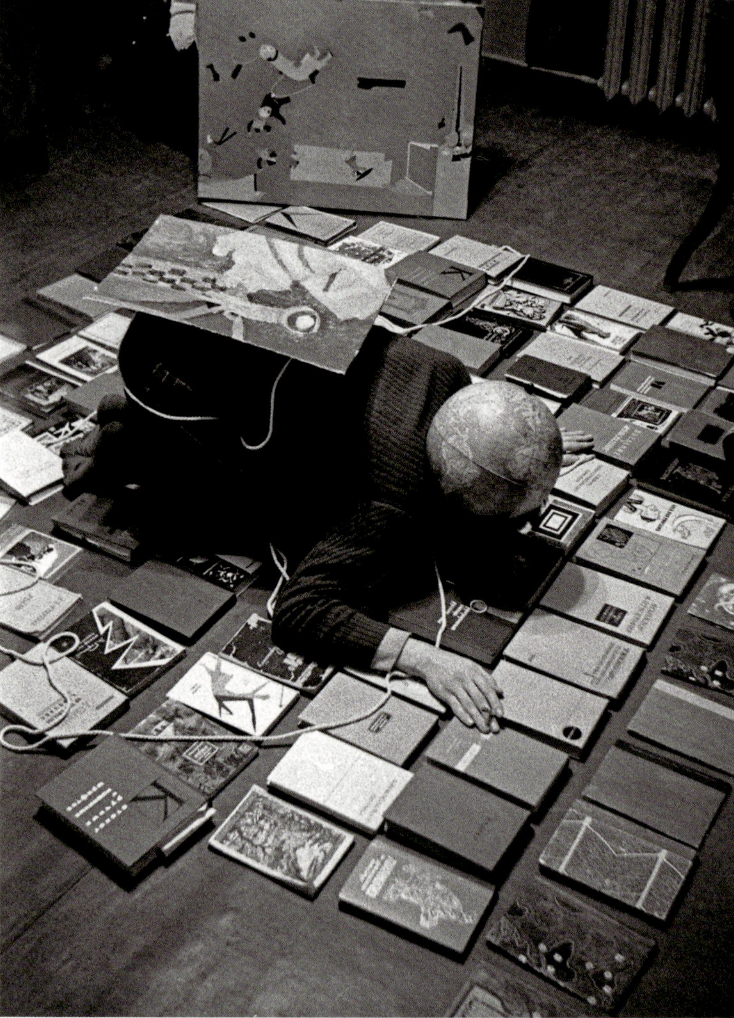

157   Ilya Kabakov on the roof of his studio, Moscow, 1983.

158   Vladimir Yankilevsky in his studio, Moscow, 1972.

159   Andrei Monastyrsky and Irina Nakhova, *Adoration of a Word* in the artists' studio, Moscow, 1974.

was also, I believe, a result of her encounter with Malevich's *Black Square* in the *Moscow–Paris* exhibition in 1981. In the eyes of Moscow's vanguard community, *Black Square*'s otherness, compared to Socialist Realism, its immunity from ideological intrusion, positioned this seminal modernist canvas as a new beginning for autonomous art. This was Nakhova's response to seeing abstract works on the walls of Soviet museums – to take back abstraction from the West, to suspend alienation from the avant-garde's utopian aspirations, amply expressed by Zhigalov after he saw *Moscow–Paris*: "I don't see Malevich as my grandfather. I learnt about Suprematism…only through the West. And when in Russia there is a tendency to present him as the closest relative, I do not agree with it."[45] He illustrated this attitude in an action for which he outlined a square on the wall of his country house then stood inside it in the pose of a crucifixion (fig. 163).

OPPOSITE PAGE 160   Irina Nakhova, *Room No. 1* in the artist's studio, Moscow, 1983.

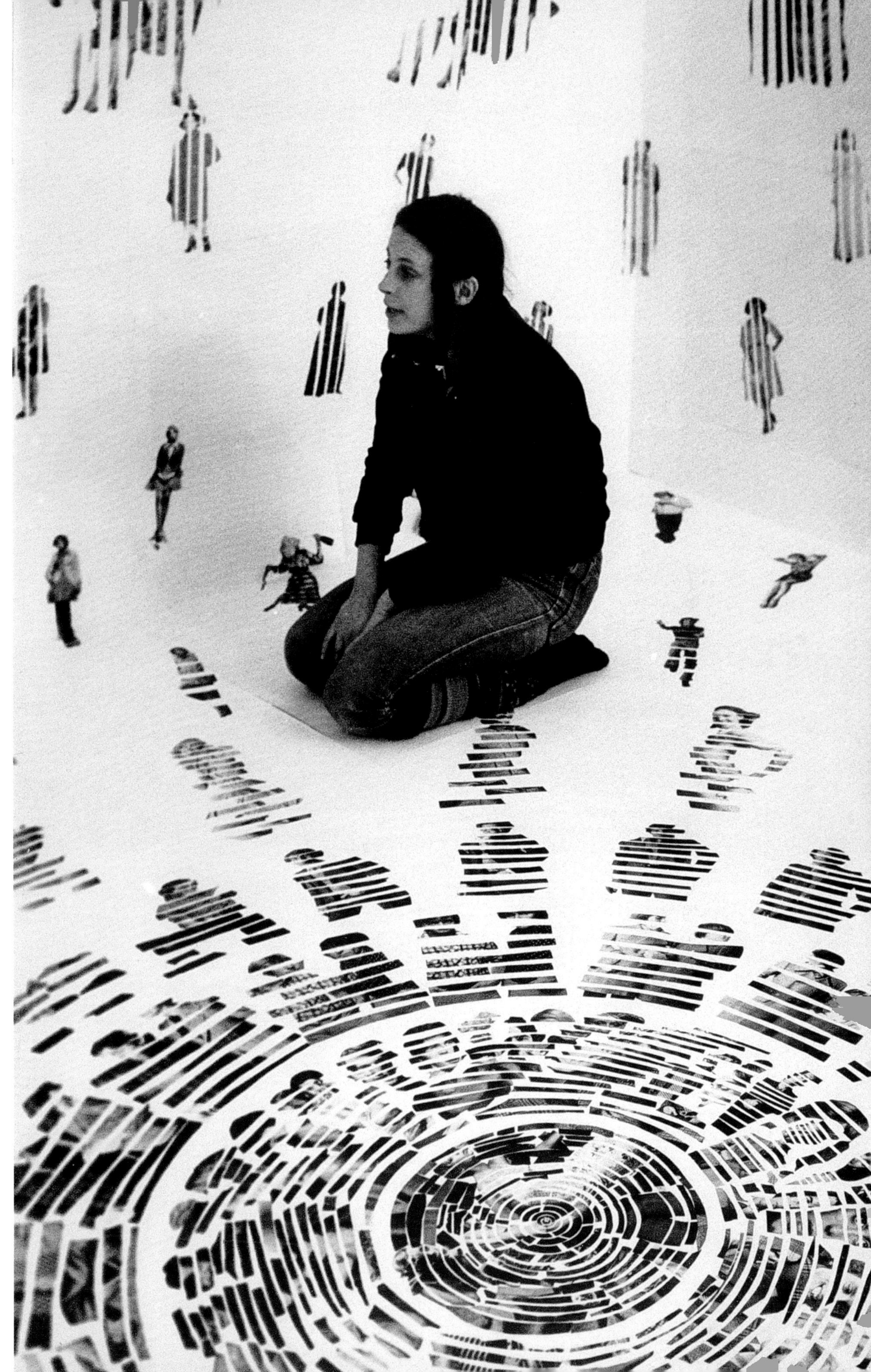

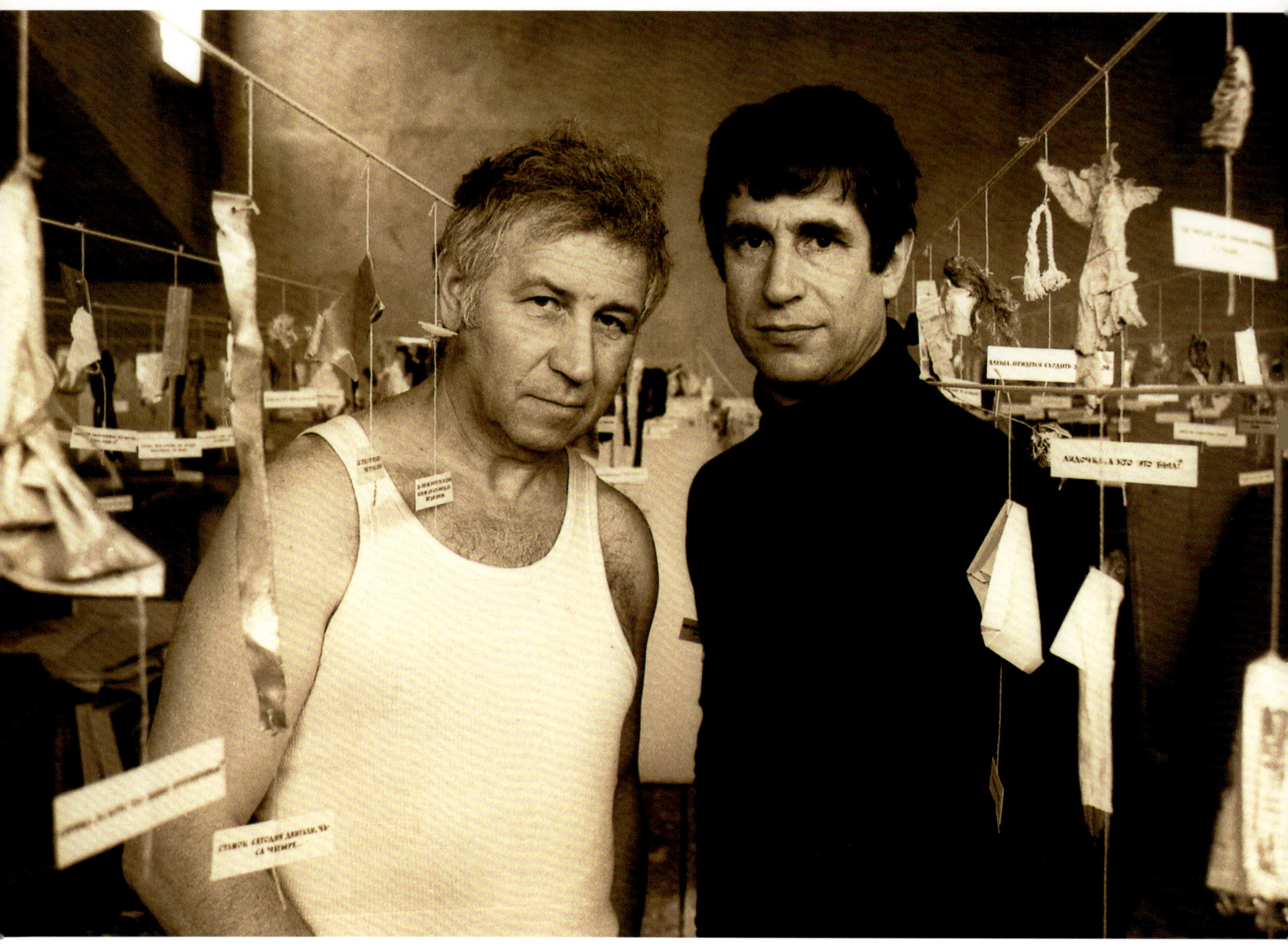

161   Ilya Kabakov, *16 Ropes,* in the artist's studio, Moscow, ca. 1984, with Kabakov (left) and Vladimir Yankilevsky (right).

In contrast, Kabakov reacted to *Black Square* in writing,[46] but made *16 Ropes*, which threw the viewer into a dystopian grid. He explains:

All of the hanging garbage forms…a unique sea in which the viewer can submerge [himself], if he makes the effort to go between these rows, taking in hand [handling] the labels and reading the texts written on them. But then he will wind up in yet another sea, this time a verbal one. All of the texts consist of phrases, and not even phrases but scraps

of them. This is everyday, ordinary noise, pieces of non-individualized speech which could belong to "each and every person."[47]

His goal was to cut through common speech with individual voices ("utterances"), creating a space of intersubjectivity in the "third dimension." "This is not the place," Kabakov continues, "for the function[ing] of an aesthetic object. [P]articipation itself is an aesthetic phenomenon. This is a succession of pulling out of the painting's space. Out of the painting, out of the

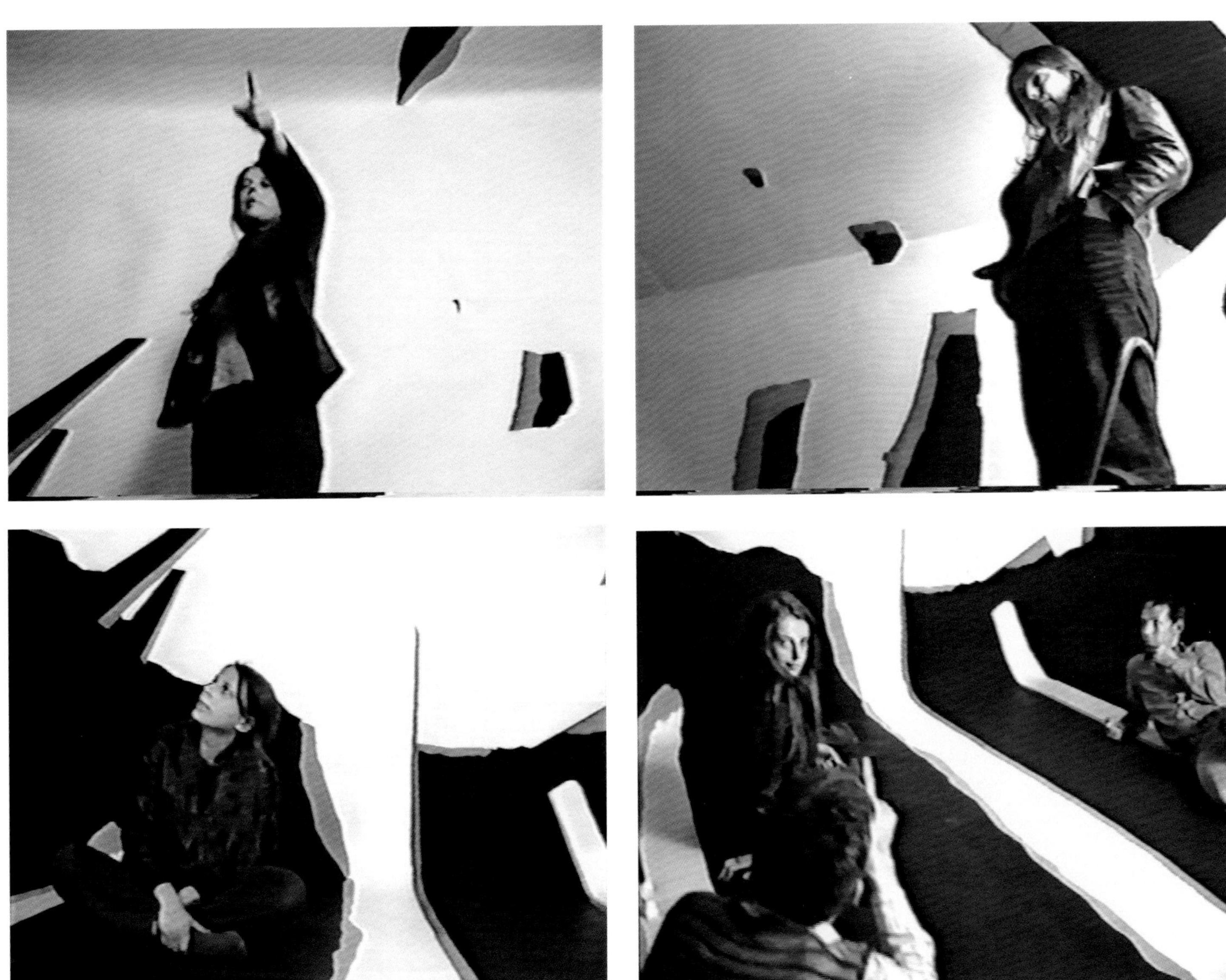

162   Irina Nakhova, *Room No. 2* in the artist's studio, Moscow, 1984. Stills from Sabine Hänsgan's video of *Room no. 2*, 1985.

'window' of the painting things fell out, then came the viewer and now he is part of the painting."[48] The viewer is simultaneously the subject and object of representation.

The silence of Nakhova's *Room No. 2* was broken when a group of male artists, including Bulatov, Kabakov, Makarevich, Oleg Vasiliev, and Eduard Gorokhovsky came to view it and were interviewed by Bakshtein, then Nakhova's husband, thus generating an important criticial response, which was lacking in underground circles.[49] The resulting avalanche of male "utterances" interrupted Nakhova's text-free environment. Just as the contents of *16 Ropes* fell out of Kabakov's panels, Nakhova's *Room* gave the impression that, as Gorokhovsky observed, one had "gotten inside the painting, and now...know[s] what it looks like on the inside." Vasiliev admitted to the therapeutic effects of *Room No. 2*, putting one "at peace," eliminating "fatigue," and he "recognize[d]" the *Rooms'* relation to Nakhova's paintings, to "her theme."[50] For

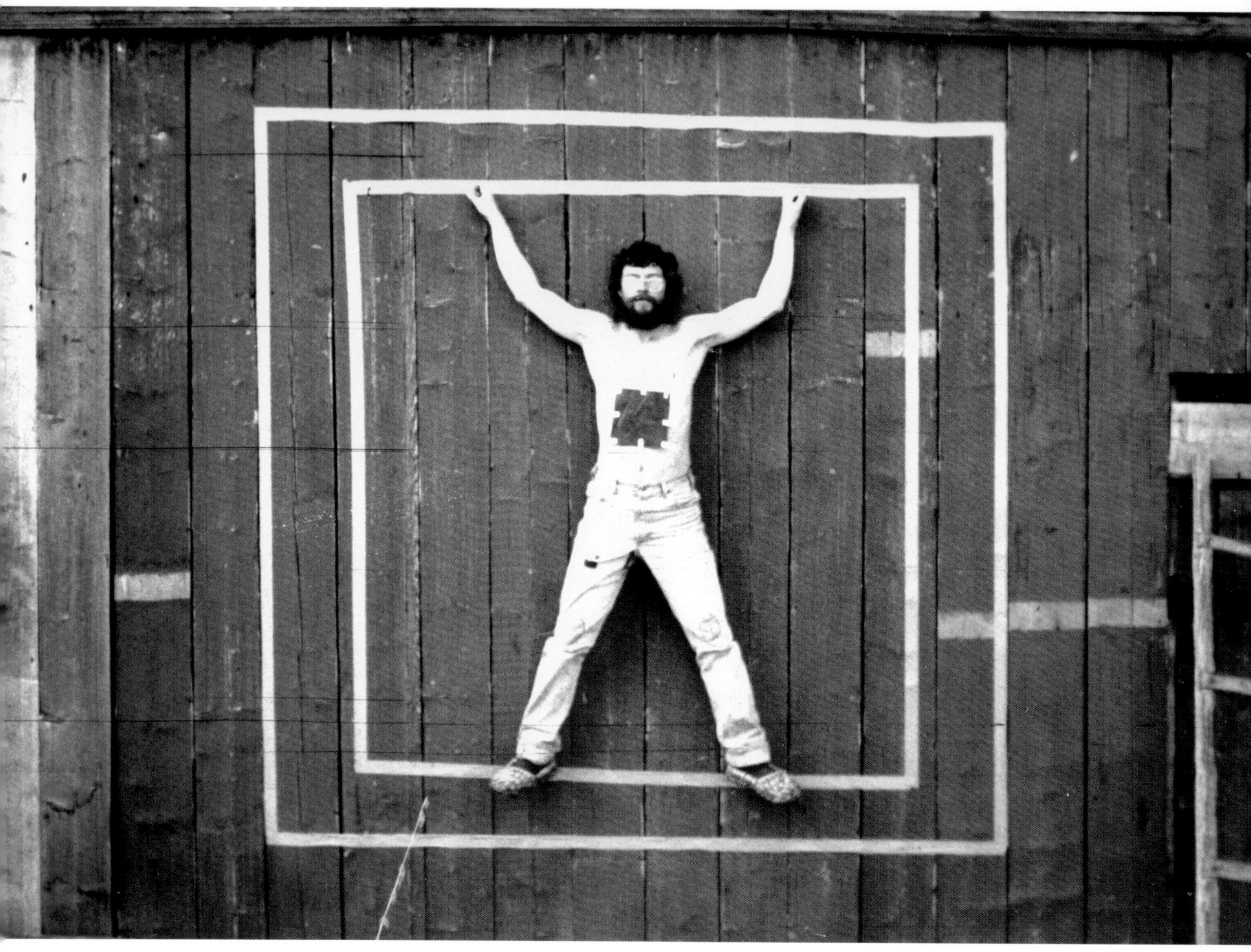

163 Anatoly Zhigalov, *Black Square*, from the series "Study of a Square," 1981.

Makarevich this was a space of "meditation" inherent in abstract art. "It was wrong to break this moment, the moment of silence,"[51] concluded Makarevich, referring to Bakshtein's interviews. Gorokhovsky politicized Nakhova's "abstraction" by alluding to the current political volatility (first Brezhnev's death and then Andropov's terminal illness) and the Russians' downing of a Korean plane on September 1, 1983:

I see in this an apocalyptic mood; to me, it's sort of a localized end of the world. I'll even say more specifically – a plane crash. The very moment of impact…everything bursts…and that's why everything is shapeless…As far as color, this gray is reminiscent of the gray aluminum paneling of an airplane, while the black – also symbolic – is the color of the explosion, the end, in contrast to the white…that's the path to freedom.[52]

Bulatov called Nakhova "a heroic woman," for her *Room* "will have to be dismantled, and can't be reconstituted."[53] The transience of her *Rooms* was a radical concept for the underground artists, whose very existence had been defined by the preservation of their art in the hope of a better political climate. Moreover, Nakhova's photographs of her laborious dismantling of *Room No. 2*, and the discarding of it in a garbage bin, amply demonstrated the disposability of the vanguard product (fig. 164). Significantly, Kabakov's embrace of "forms of garbage" for a new genre diverged from Nakhova's installation ending as garbage – the former the reverse of the latter.

Kabakov's reaction to Nakhova's *Room No. 2* was far from dispassionate: "Yes, yes, a very strong impression – wonderful – a genuine artistic image. Everything Ira [Irina] does in this respect is pure genius, is marvelous. An entirely blind, internal action, monstrous energy and power. I must say that I'm struck by the general concept – by its power and originality, and this concept is made real, it's here."[54] Kabakov's seminal installation, *The Man Who Flew into the Cosmos from His Room*, followed in 1985 (figs. 165–7). His use of the word "room" (*komnata*, which has been wrongly translated as "apartment"[55]) reveals its kinship with Nakhova's *Rooms*. Kabakov built a tall, freestanding shack out of plywood in the back of his studio. The entrance was boarded up with wooden planks (a reminder of Makarevich's image of incarceration) that left slits through which to peep inside, and evoked the structure of Duchamp's *Étant Donnés*, albeit with paradigmatically different contents. Kabakov gave up his initial idea of installation as a "materialize[d] grid," and, like Nakhova, here constructed a closed space that he later dubbed a "total installation." Yet, unlike Nakhova's rooms, Kabakov's could not be entered.

As viewers gazed into the interior of *The Man Who Flew*, they would observe in "the small room [1.4 × 3 × 2.5 m]…a spectacle of total devastation."[56] Walls were cluttered with propaganda posters, mag-azine covers, and reproductions of well-known nineteenth-century paintings. This printed matter was mixed with Kabakov's original work – designs for the room and a brightly lit model of a utopian city laid out on one of three battered chairs. Other furniture and belongings included a cot with a blanket and

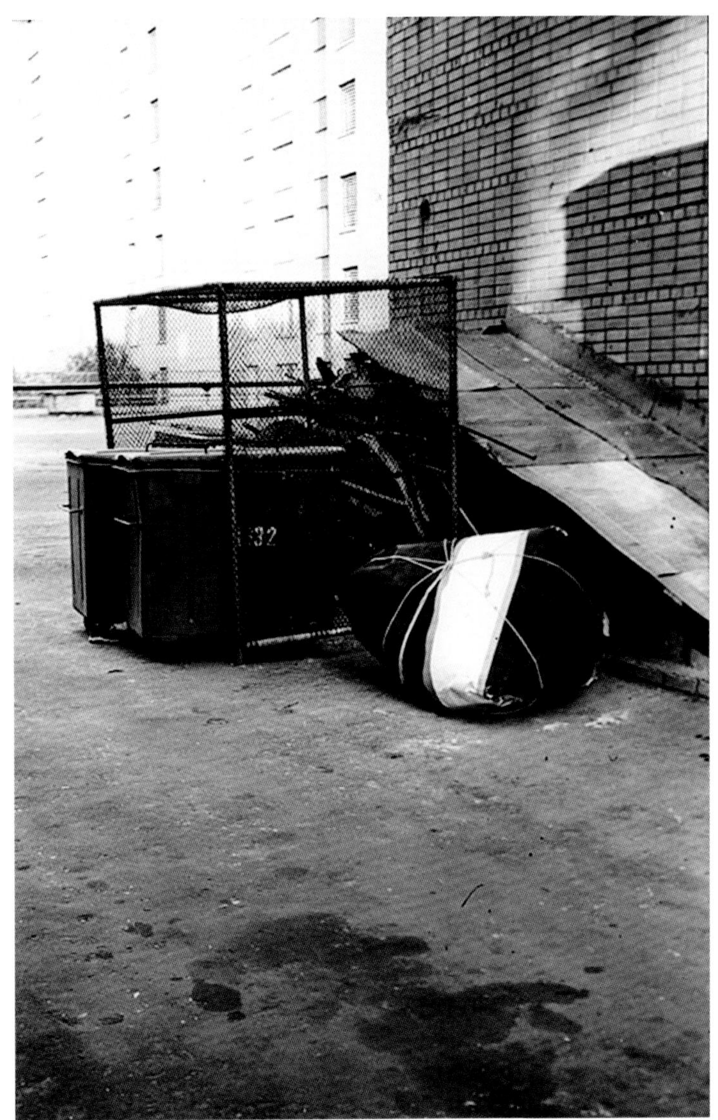

164   The dismantled material of Irina Nakhova's *Room No. 2* in a garbage bin, 1984.

pillow, and a pair of worn-out shoes. A catapult hanging above the cot, under the destroyed ceiling with a large opening, were pointers toward the character's escape. Thus, having "no entrance," Kabakov's "room" enacted a scene of exit, the opposite direction to that of the discourse of the 1970s that I have outlined in this chapter. Like Komar and Melamid and Bulatov, Kabakov decided to express his existential desperation through ideological stereotypes. In fact, in this aspect *The Man Who Flew* can be seen as a reaction to Bulatov's *Soviet Cosmos* (fig. 168). That

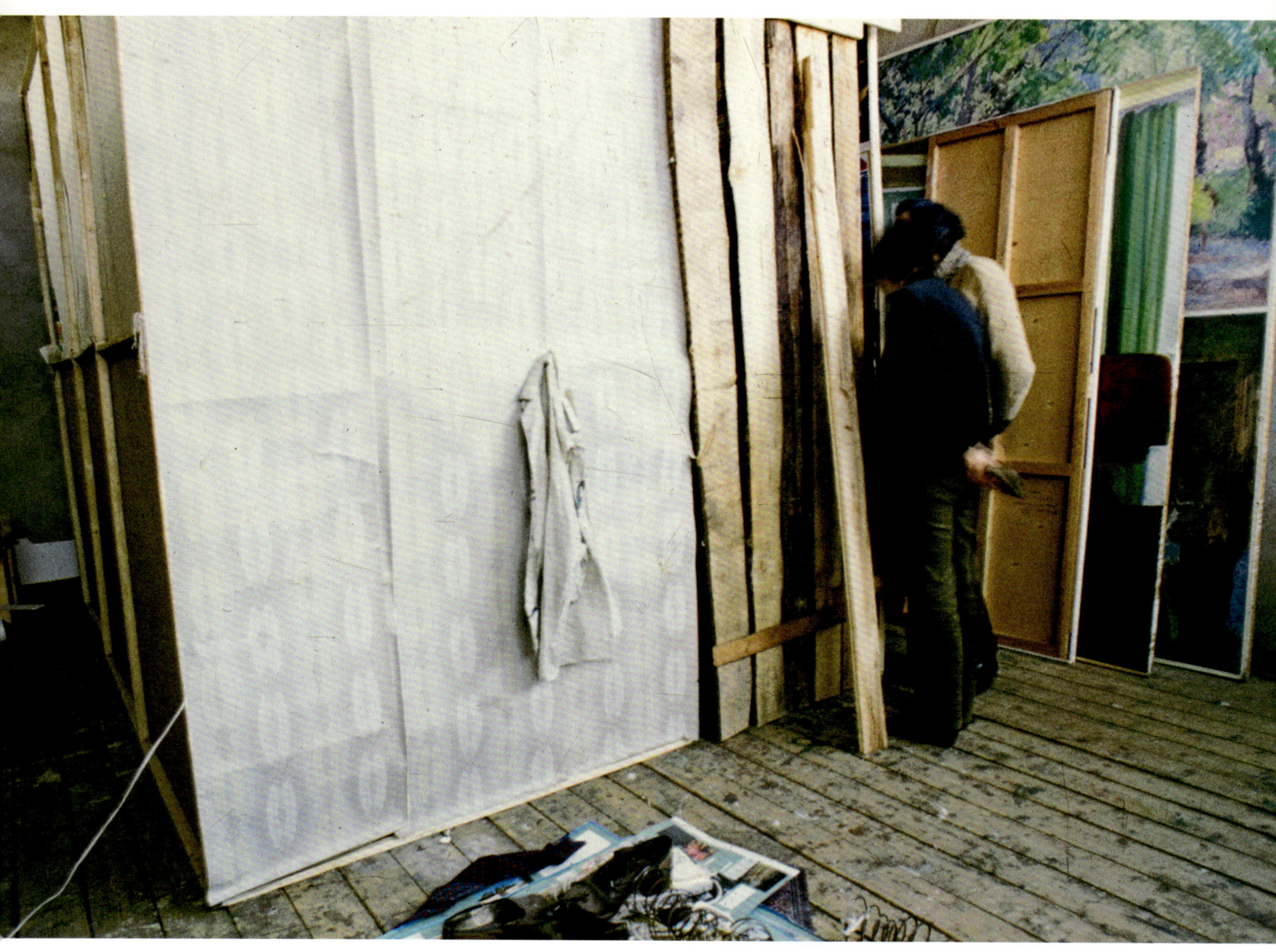

large-scale canvas had outraged the counter-culture because it aggrandizes the loathed Brezhnev, without Komar and Melamid's explicit irony. Brezhnev is shown as chief engineer and guardian of Soviet sociocultural stagnation, and is painted in the official style of public spectacle, here achieved by crowning him with the state emblem and flags of fifteen Soviet republics. The latter Bulatov meticulously copied from the cover of the picture magazine *Ogonyok* for the Revolution's sixtieth anniversary. The titles of *Soviet Cosmos* and *The Man Who Flew into the Cosmos from His Room* also connect the two works. However, when "Cosmos" was translated in the West as "Space," both the connection between the two works, and their allusion to the philosophy of Russian Cosmism, was obscured.

Kabakov stages in a three-dimensional format what Bulatov had insisted upon on the picture plane: as Bulatov wrote in "On My Attitude to Social Reality" in 1984, "social reality touches us too close" and, regardless of how much the counterculture had tried to exorcize it from their discourses, it would enter

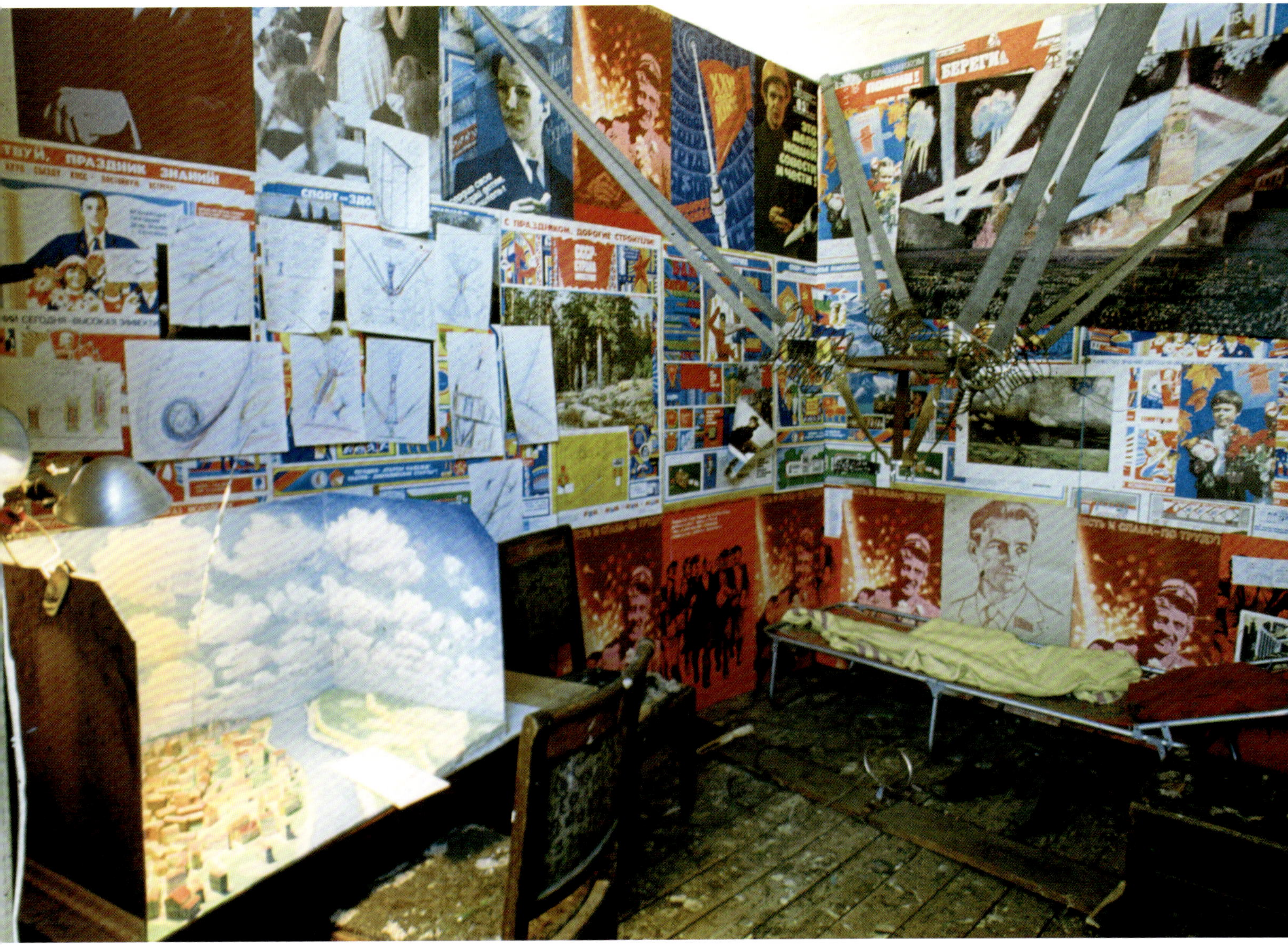

166   Ilya Kabakov, *The Man Who Flew into the Cosmos from His Room*, in the artist's studio, Moscow, 1985.

their aesthetic practices.[57] Bulatov's text outlined his strategy of recharging mechanically reproduced imagery with the aura of the transcendental, reversing Walter Benjamin's project. Bulatov's metaphor of the "space beyond the painting" from which "a stream of light is moving toward us through the painting," reverberates in Kabakov's description of his room: "There is an enormous hole in the ceiling through which a blinding light is falling into the room."[58]

With *The Man Who Flew*, Kabakov endorsed a theatrical type of installation art. By doing this he declared war against his own and his fellow artists' modernist oeuvre and their fear of theatricality as an element of official life and a polar opposite of modernist consciousness. This was the kind of conflict that Michael Fried had outlined in "Art and Objecthood": "theatre and theatricality are at war today, not simply with modernist painting…but with art as such – and to the extent that the different arts can be described as modernist, with modernist sensibility as such."[59]

Nakhova's *Room No. 3* (figs. 169–71) stood in contrast to Kabakov's abundance of details, intensity of

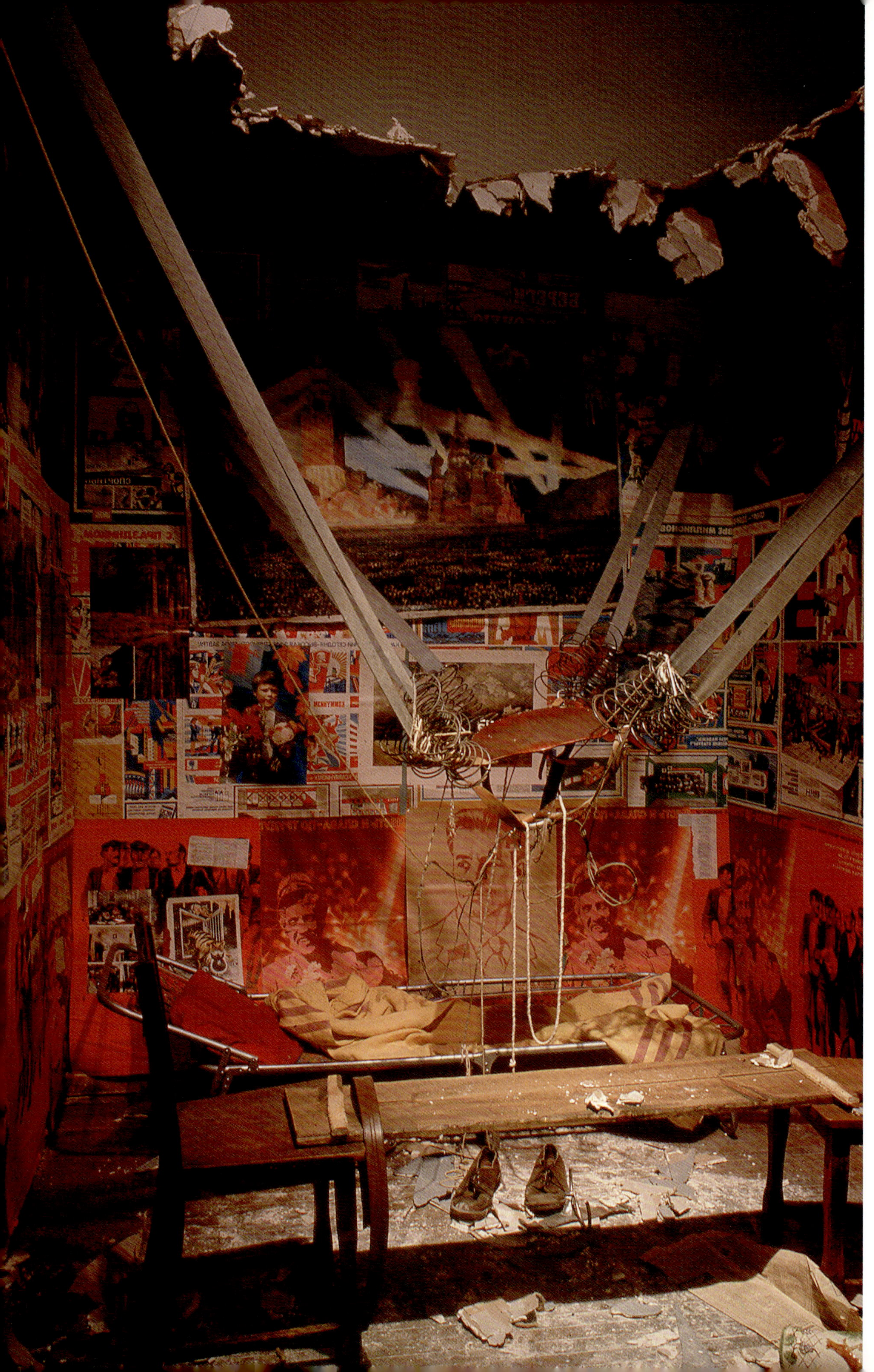

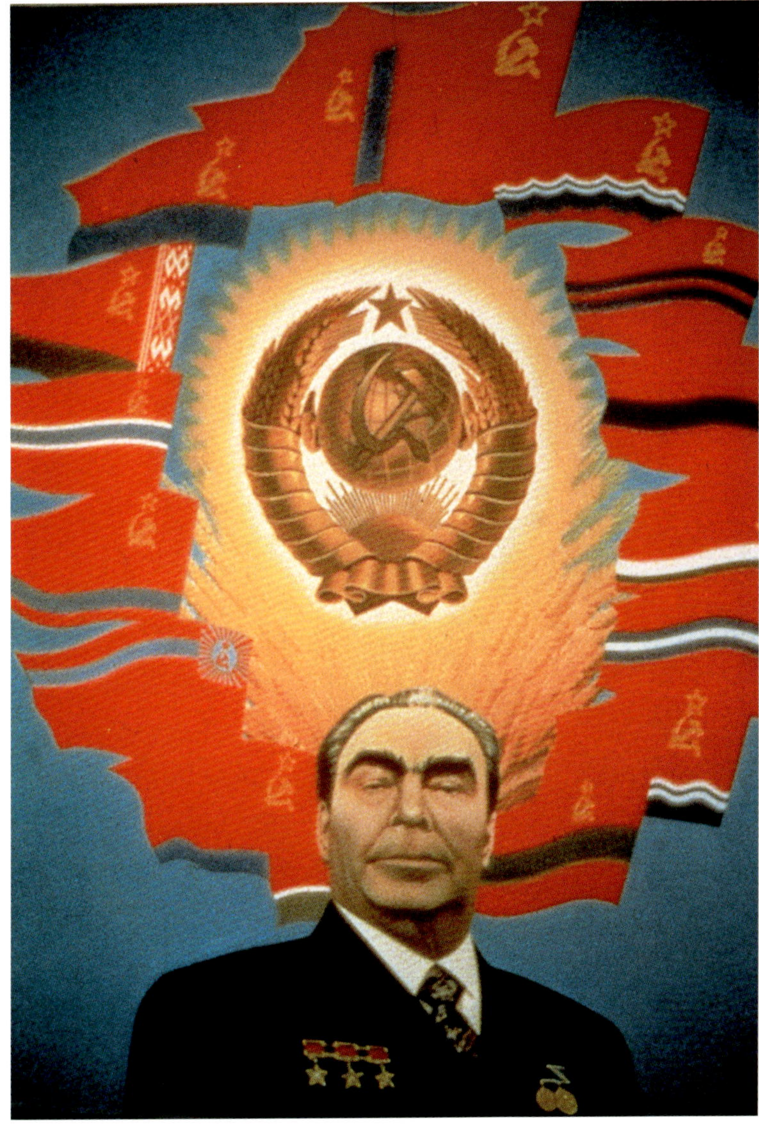

color, and a passage for escape. Hers was minimalist, monochromatic (black), and hermetic. This time Nakhova wrapped a painting on an easel and sprayed the entire room and the furniture black, creating the sensation of being inside of a black painting. This installation evokes Monastyrsky's concept of painting's third space, "a metaphysical, nonexistent space" that "had been always in the realm of ideas, ideologically charged. But it had not been elaborated in actuality."[60] He continues: "Let's look at *Finger.* It's hanging on the wall and is perceived as a conceptual object. But curiously (and it's not important whether it's an object or

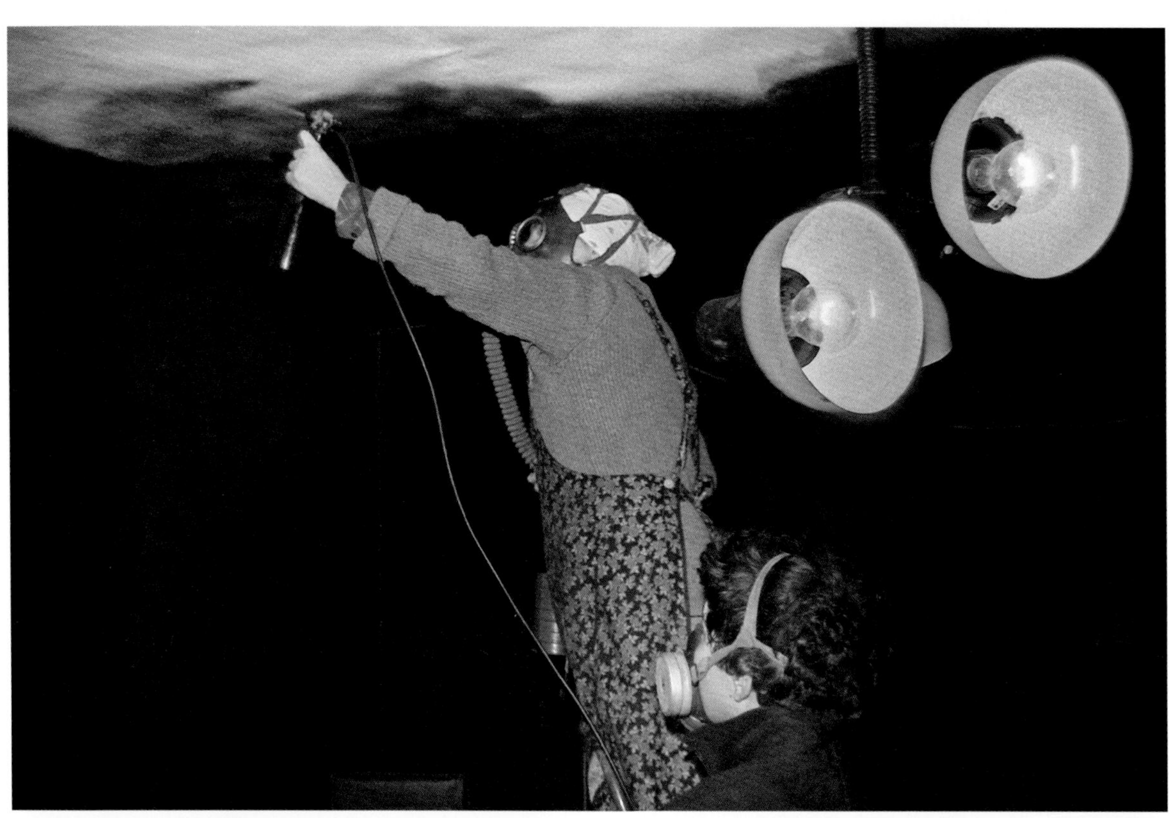

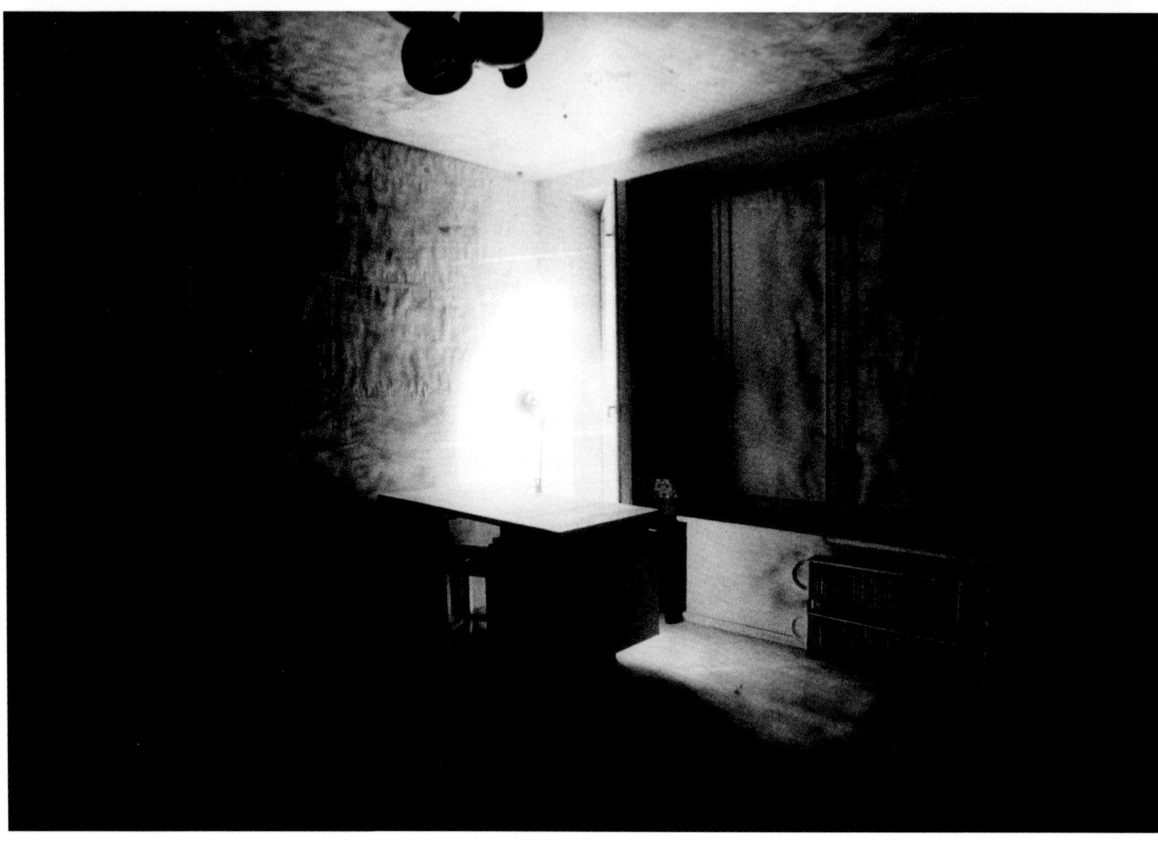

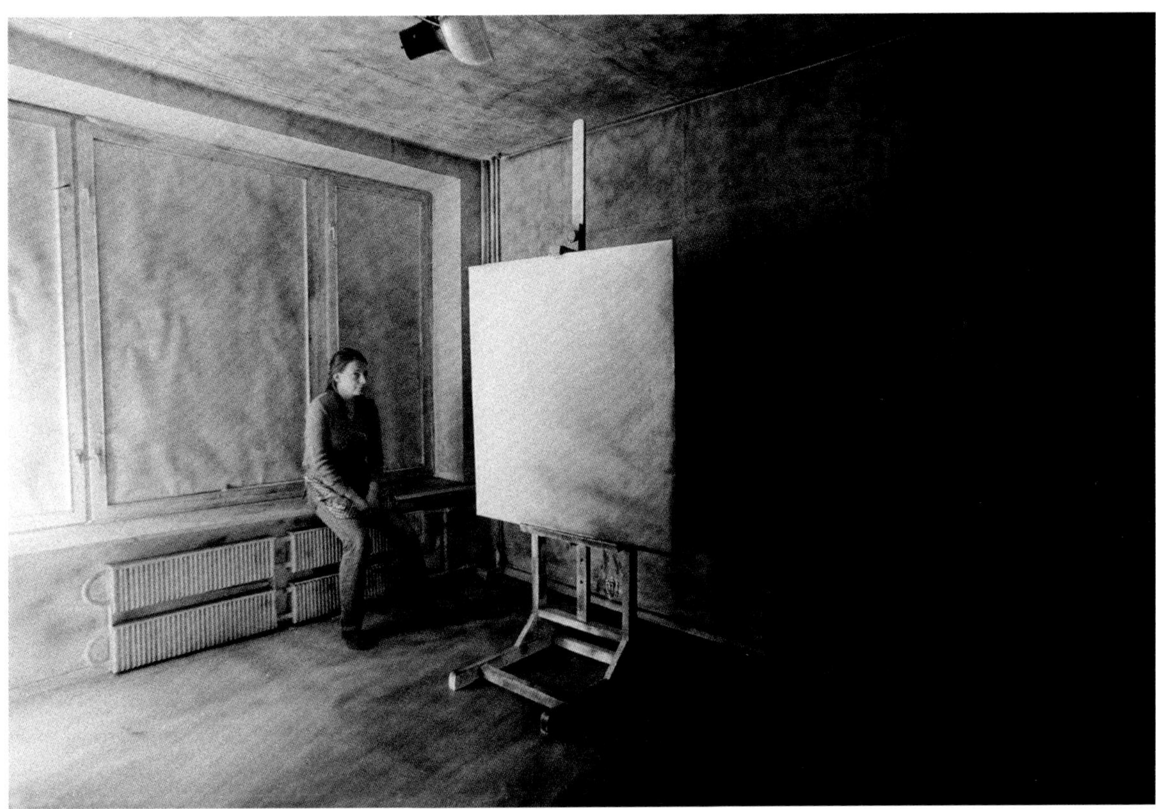

a painting), the viewer ends up inside this 'painting' physically…In this case, this 'interior' is actualized not ideologically…but purely physically."[61]

Nakhova's *Room No. 3* functioned within this theoretical paradigm of the bodily experience of modernism. Here Nakhova invited observers to experience the "inside" of a black square. I would suggest that she had in mind Malevich's *Black Square* that had been discussed in vanguard circles since its showing in Moscow. Kabakov, too, seems to have been thinking of Malevich in 1983 while conceiving *The Man Who Flew*:

The "old" land has ended. Ahead is the "new" land, the breath of the cosmos, a new class of being…A few will go with him [Malevich] into this new, precipitous world…There is a system of tests for this, which will determine your preparedness for spiritual flight. If, for those left, a square is simply a square…then, for those who have grasped the new spirit, have entered into it, these are signs of the new spiritual space, the gates beyond which lie the "new land," the koan whose solution is on a new, unprecedented plane.[62]

If Kabakov mapped a passage to that "unprecedented plane," Nakhova attempted to recreate it physically. By having light fall on the balcony door (not a door to the street), she cast doubt on the possibility of exit. The difference between the two installations thus is existential, as they reflect the two artists' response to the early and hitherto unimaginable steps of Gorbachev's reforms, later known as perestroika. Nakhova's *Room No. 3* spoke of her initial wariness of Gorbachev's ambitious project, and Kabakov's *The Man Who Flew into the Cosmos from His Room* asserted the approach of the counterculture's opportunity to escape the constraints of the Soviet prison-house.

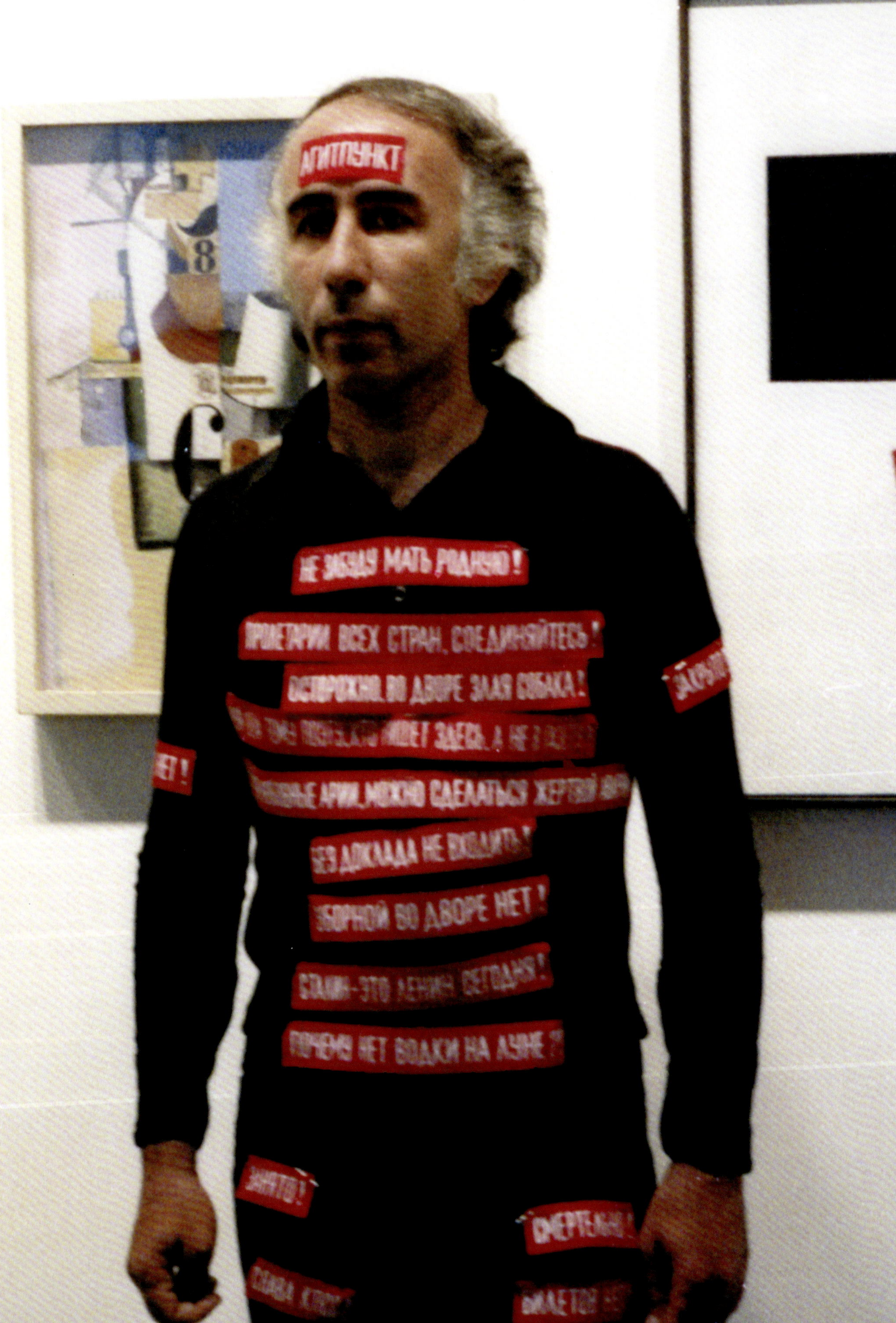

АГИТПУНКТ
НЕ ЗАБУДУ МАТЬ РОДНУЮ !
ПРОЛЕТАРИИ ВСЕХ СТРАН, СОЕДИНЯЙТЕСЬ !
ОСТОРОЖНО, ВО ДВОРЕ ЗЛАЯ СОБАКА !
БЕЗ ДОКЛАДА НЕ ВХОДИТЬ !
СТАЛИН - ЭТО ЛЕНИН СЕГОДНЯ !
ПОЧЕМУ НЕТ ВОДКИ НА ЛУНЕ ?!
ЗАНЯТО !
БИЛЕТОВ НЕТ

6

MOSCOW—NEW YORK

Vladimir Slepian: I had conceived a project: a new method of collective painting. Pierre Schneider: In other words, you left a country of collectivism for the West because you wanted to do collective painting?

Artnews, March 1959.

In our Soviet situation…it's inadequate to produce "things," objects that are handmade, rather than imaginary values. Indeed we only imagine that we exist, that we mean something. In reality…here there is another "culture" and what we are doing is evaluated in the West as having only ethnographic rather than aesthetic values.

Andrei Monastyrsky, letter to Victor Tupitsyn in New York, March 8, 1979.

In 1974, Vitaly Komar and Aleksandr Melamid collaborated on a performance, *Where Is the Line Between Us?*, with the American artist and critic Douglas Davis. The Russians and Davis were photographed in their respective countries standing divided by a thick black line, and holding two square boards on which the question, "Where is the line between us?" is written in English (Komar and Melamid's) and Russian (Davis's; fig. 172). Created in the year of the U.S.–Soviet linkup in space, this rare collaboration revealed that the two Moscow conceptualists believed in the translatability of their ideas and wanted to engage in an active dialogue with their Western colleagues.

To manifest this, Komar and Melamid attacked both local and international sociopolitical and cultural icons. For example, along with their paintings, *Quotation* and *Double Self-portrait* (see figs. 82, 137), which disturbed the semantics of Soviet propaganda, they produced in 1973 the futuristic series *Post Art*, in which they mapped out possible scenarios of the demise of American iconic art works and museums. To do so, they copied Andy Warhol's *Campbell's Soup Can* and Roy Lichtenstein's *"That my ship was below them"* on same-size canvases, scorched the reproductions with a blowtorch, and aged them using a dark varnish. By damaging these reproductions of pricey Western canvases, Komar and Melamid reminded Western artists of the unstable status of any masterpiece, which the turbulent history of the Russian

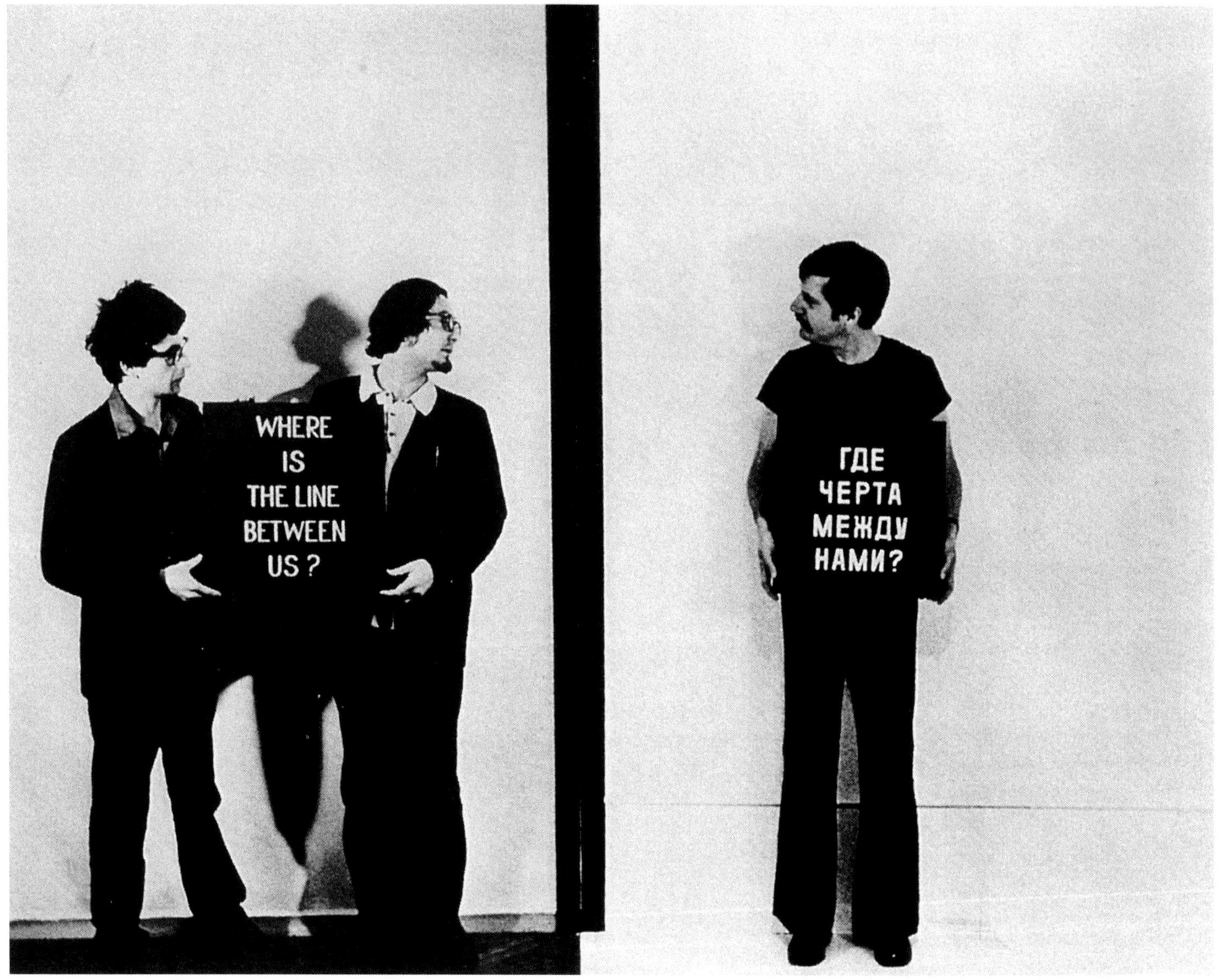

172 Vitaly Komar and Aleksandr Melamid (with Douglas Davis), *Where Is the Line Between Us?* (detail), 1974.

avant-garde had proved. Further to alert viewers to government destruction of art, including their own *Double Self-portrait* during *The Bulldozer Exhibition*, they showed *Post Art* at the Izmailovo exhibition, which was given official sanction (see fig. 97).

Komar and Melamid's conceptualism, which stressed collaboration and communication with the international art community, immediately attracted younger followers, three of whom formed the Nest group (Victor Skersis, Gennady Donskoy and Mikhail Roshal) that adopted Komar and Melamid's postmodernist agenda. Nest also copied their kind of collaboration, which, unlike CAG's flexible membership and preservation of individual authorship, was based on joint creativity. Skersis conveys this sense of artistic bonding:

1974…My closest friend and collaborator, Gennady Donskoi, and I are heading toward our third collaborator, Mikhail Roshal…We know that we've gotten beyond the boundaries of conventional art. We can do anything now. The problems of painting do not apply. Aesthetic criteria – cancelled. We don't do the art of images any more. We do imaginary art…We will make thermo graphic art, where the image is sensed directly by the hand as a function of temperature. Eyes are not needed, man![1]

Abandoning "retinal" art, further on Skersis demonstrated Nest's intention to fit into an international context:

We belong to this [Moscow vanguard] circle because we live, we think, we work the same way…Even such advanced artists as A[leksandr] Iulikov and M[ikhail] Chernyshev, who at the time impressed me immensely with their marvelous interpretations of geometric abstraction and Minimalism, still the problems they were dealing with were largely aesthetic…We know that the distance between our circle and official art is immense. But we also know that we have to go further to transcend the boundaries of visual art. We are also members of another circle, a virtual one, one that does not know the bounds of space and time. Joseph Kosuth, Andy Warhol, Yves Klein, and, of course, the majestic Marcel Duchamp, all of them make up our other company. We know them. We've heard their thoughts. We don't need an explanation as to what the artist wanted to say with his picture.[2]

Two examples of Nest's "imaginary art" are *Iron Curtain*, made from a square piece of iron and painted red, and *Communication Tube* (figs. 173, 174). *Iron Curtain* functions within the semiotic concept of the imaginary that is aligned with the "icon" – an image that is "understood" with no (or little) mediation.[3] By making *Iron Curtain* out of metal, Nest imbued this political weapon with symbolic and actual weight. *Communication Tube* is a device intended to break through communication blockages on an imaginary level.

As I pointed out earlier, the two open-air exhibitions, the *Bulldozer* and the Izmailovo, were a turning point in the careers of Moscow vanguardists. Those at the *Bulldozer* were officially invited to join Gorkom Grafikov and to have a major exhibition in the

Beekeeping Pavilion of VDNKh, in Febuary 1975 (see fig. 99). Komar and Melamid submitted *Documents: Ideal Document* to the selection committee, thus challenging its exclusive concentration on painting (see figs. 84, 85). For that work, Komar and Melamid measured various Soviet documents (passport, trade-union card, diploma) and used those measurements to make twelve rectangular Plexiglas panels, as noted in Chapter Three. A thirteenth panel, an "ideal square" (or ideal document) painted red, completed the work by referring to the political aspect of the avant-garde's geometric forms. On the surface, the committee's explanation for why they could not include *Documents* was purely practical: "How can we hang these transparent rectangles on the wall? This is not a painting."[4] But in reality, this response was a cover for the organizers' intention to minimize irritants, already in abundance in the form and content of the modernist paintings.

The next exhibition of underground art took place in VDNKh's House of Culture and ran from September 20 to 30, 1975. This time there were no restrictions on easel art, resulting in a more diverse and experimental exhibition, albeit not without censorship. Nikita Alekseev provides an eyewitness account:

By September 20 in VDNKh's House of Culture 145 artists brought 650 works, 522 of which were shown…before the opening of the exhibition some works were taken down…In a large nest woven from branches sat Mikhail Roshal, Victor Skersis, and Gennady Donskoy. They were hatching eggs and asked the viewers to do the same. This action caused an outcry from the KGB agents watching over the exhibition…. The over-heated authorities decided that some works could not be displayed. Roshal, Skersis, and Donskoy were chased away and the nest was removed as a "flammable" object.[5]

Nest's eponymous work was the first public installation in Moscow that grounded its meaning in encouraging viewers' participation (fig. 175). In this case, "the visitors joyfully sat, drank, or simply lived in it."[6] *Nest* is equally significant for its dialogue between its rural and urban manifestations. During the former, called *Hatching*, the trio created a Beckettian atmosphere of endless waiting, as they sat inside a hay nest, with their eyes closed and backs against each other. In the urban

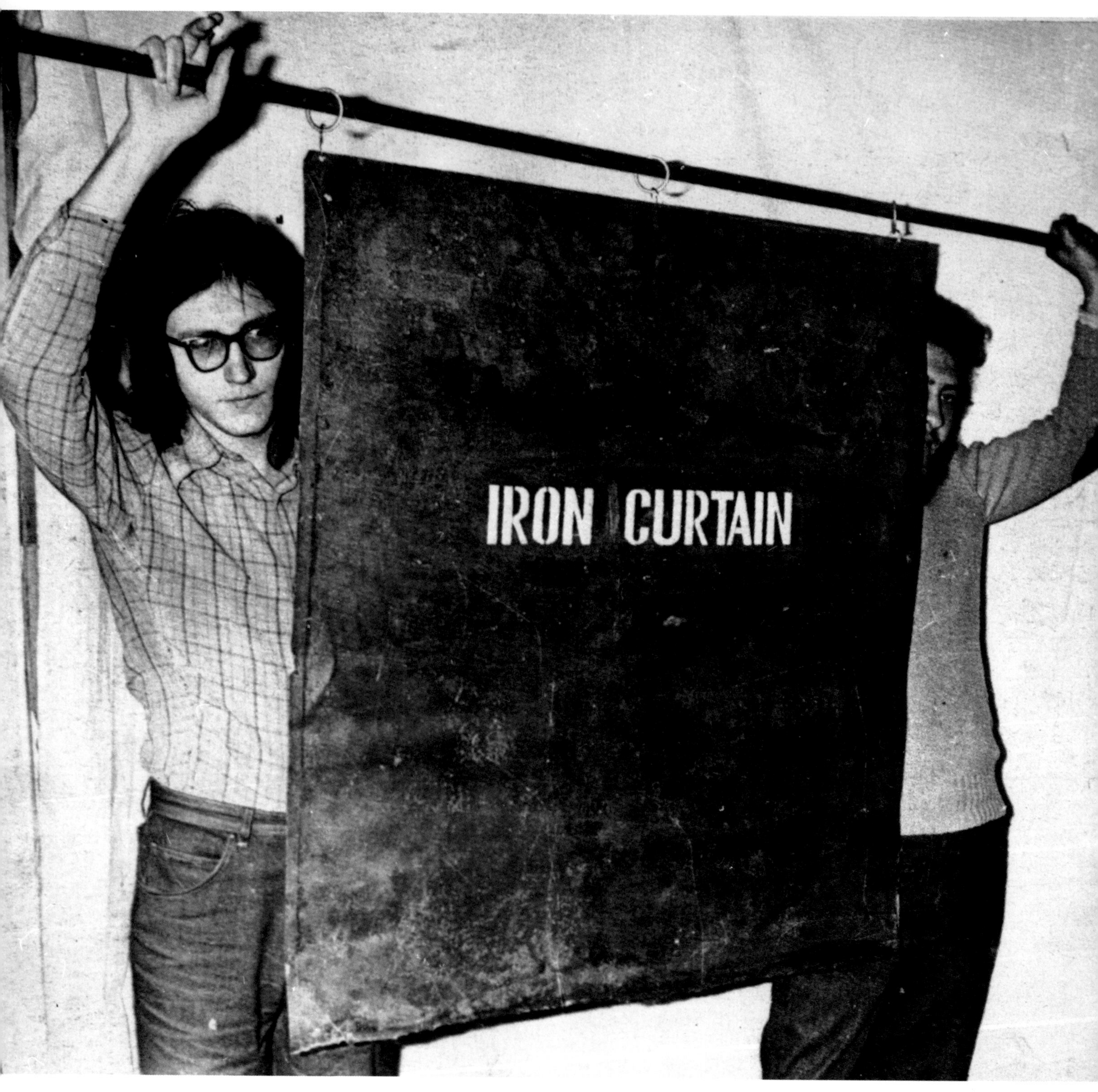

173   The Nest group, *Iron Curtain*, 1974, with Gennady Donskoi (left) and Mikhail Roshal.

THE COMMUNICATION TUBE

RECOMENDED BY DONSKOY-ROSHAL-SKERSIS
FOR OVERCOMING THE UNCOMMUNICATION AMONG PEOPLE

INSTRUCTION FOR THE USE OF THE COMMUNICATION TUBE
PLACE THE COMMUNICATION TUBE HORIZONTALLY
ON THE NEEDED LEVEL.
YOU COULD MAKE EITHER SOUND OR SIGHT CONTACT
THROUGH THE COMMUNICATION TUBE.
FOR SOUND CONTACT ONE OF THE CONTACTING PERSONS
HAS TO PUT HIS EAR TO ONE END OF THE COMMUNICATION TUBE,
WHEN AT THE SAME TIME THE OTHER PERSON
HAS TO PRONOUNCE ANY WORDS OR SOUNDS
INTO THE OTHER END OF THE COMMUNICATION TUBE/plate NI/
FOR SIGHT CONTACT TWO OF THE CONTACTING PERSONS
HAVE TO LOOK INTO THE COMMUNICATION TUBE
FROM THE OPPOSITE ENDS/plate N2/

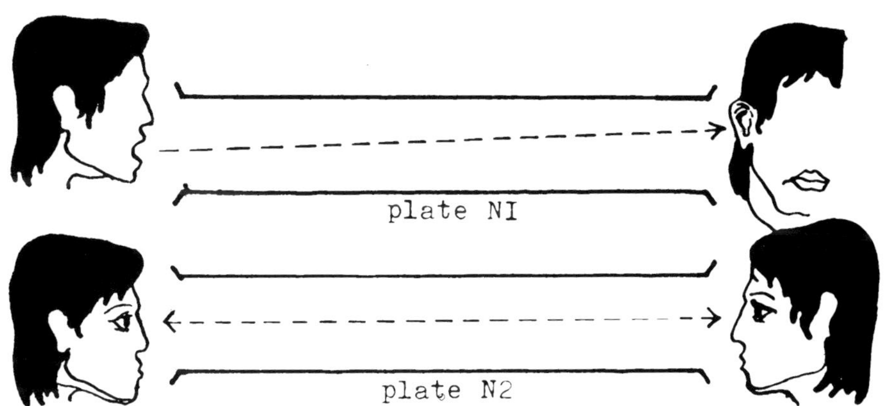

THE COMMUNICATION TUBE

174   The Nest group, diagram of *Communication Tube*, 1974.

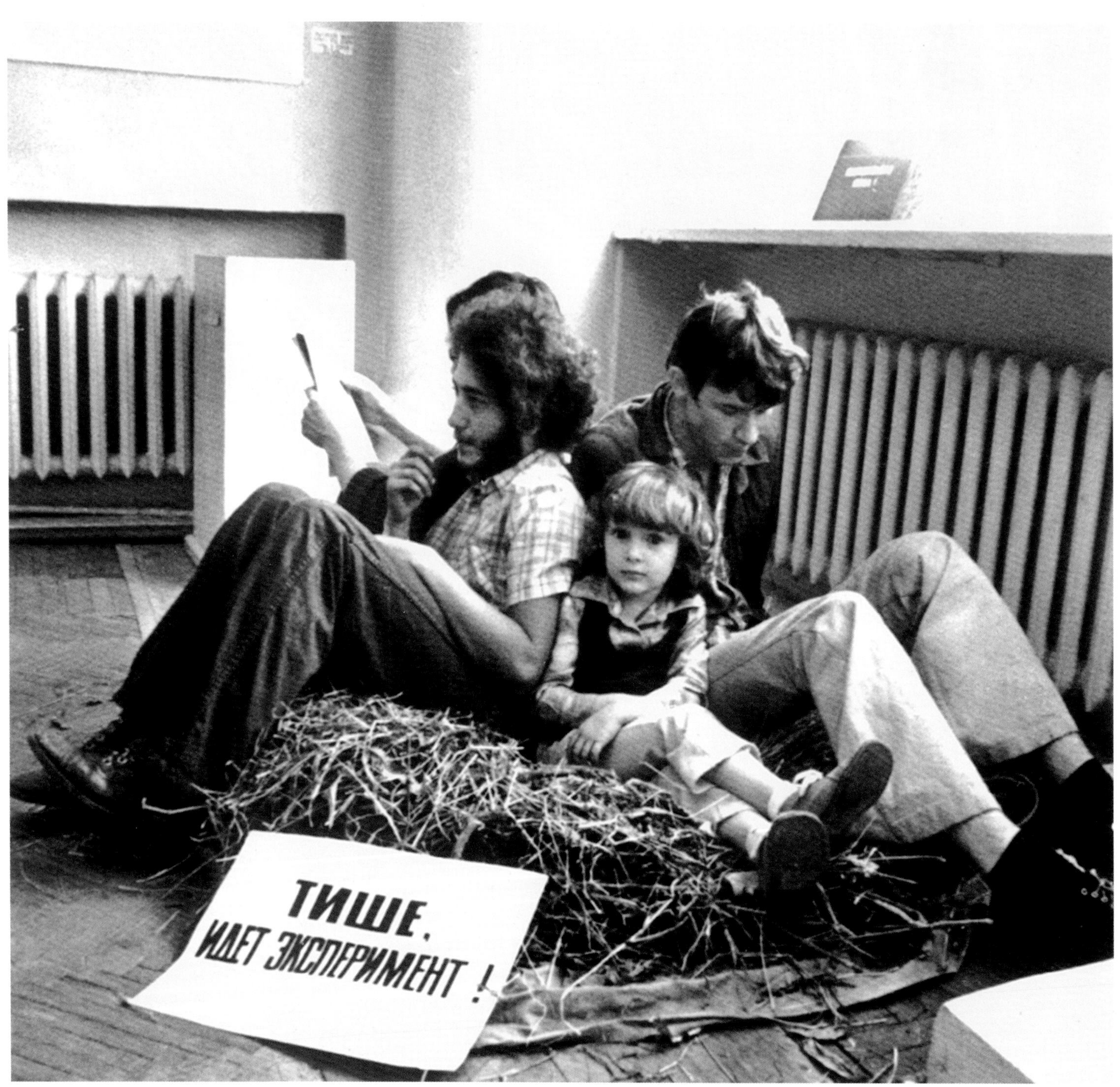

175   The Nest group, *Nest*, 1975.

setting in VDNKh, they sat in the same position, sometimes with a girl, as if her presence could protect them from the authorities' aggression. A sign, "Silence. The experiment is taking place!" near the nest, informed the public that they were witnessing not sanctioned, but experimental, art. Another sign, "hatching eggs!" ridiculed the officials' idea of exhibiting art in the venue of a permanent display heavily associated

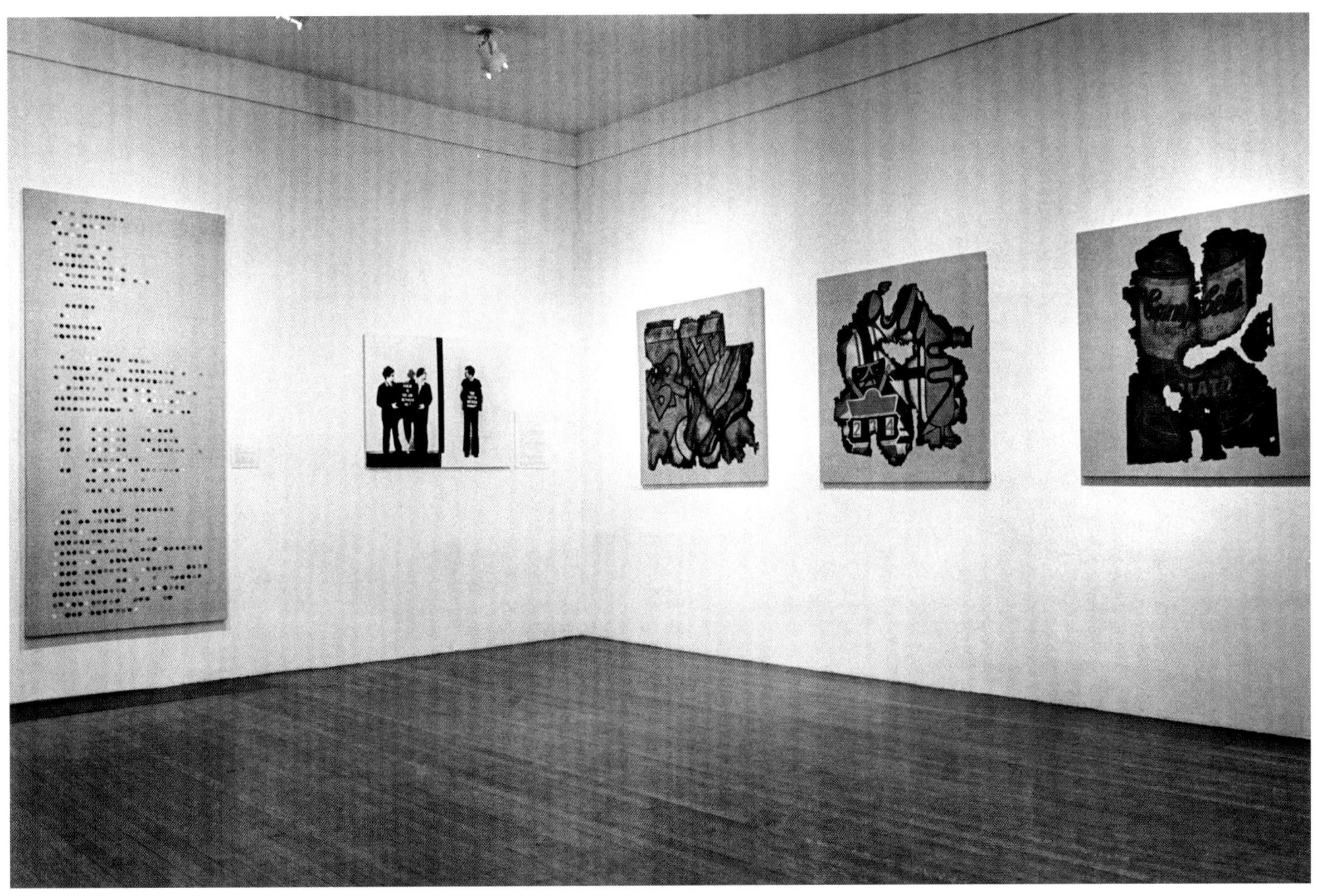

176   Installation view of Komar and Melamid's exhibition, *Color is a Mighty Power!*, with the series *Post Art* on the right, at Ronald Feldman Fine Arts, New York, 1976.

with achievements in agriculture. The group's staging of *Nest*, first in a rural, supposedly safe environment, and then on the potentially antagonistic site of the VDNKh, distinguished Nest's readiness for engagement with the controlled urban environment from such performances of escape as CAG launched six months later in March 1976 in *Appearance* (see figs. 106–8). By the time this official display of underground art at VDNKh ended, Komar and Melamid, once again not among the participants, had managed to smuggle a major portion of their works to New York. Those works formed a "one-men" show that opened on February 7, 1976 at Ronald Feldman Fine Arts, and was called (after one of Komar and Melamid's works), *Color is a Mighty Power!* (fig. 176). A grid of

"colored plaques," "manufactured" by Komar and Melamid, promised to cure a viewer's ailment if they "gaz[ed] intently for a certain time at one of the plaques."[7] This attitude toward color was in dialogue with the psycho-ideological rather than the utilitarian attitude of the productivist artists that had been repressed in postwar abstractionists' insistence on the autonomy of color.

Komar and Melamid's query addressed to the Western art world, "where is the line between us?," found its reflection in the way the Ronald Feldman gallery installed *Color is a Mighty Power!* to create a space of difference as well as of communication. At the opening, Charlotte Moorman, the Fluxus artist, performed Komar and Melamid's *Music "Passport"*

(1976) on the cello. The artists executed this piece in collaboration with a professional Russian musician who matched each note to a letter spelling out the Soviet passport's ten regulations. Komar and Melamid's substitution of words with musical notes returns us to the concept discussed earlier of the "im/pulse to hear" as a substitute for the "im/pulse to see." Moreover, by translating a repressive text into an abstract form of music, Komar and Melamid allowed visitors to experience this material on a new level accessible even to non-Russians.

The exhibition at Ronald Feldman Fine Arts received a positive critical response, unusually for Russian underground art. New York critics interpreted Sots Art as an original art movement and emphasized the importance of Komar and Melamid's creative teamwork. In the majority of reviews, the *Post-Art* series was illustrated and evaluated as an attempt to "give historical perspective to contemporary art such as Pop by making artifacts of it."[8] Such deconstruction of Pop art's icons, together with Komar and Melamid's provocative comparison of American and Soviet mass culture as material and immaterial consumerism, could not go unnoticed by Pop artists. It is likely that Andy Warhol saw Komar and Melamid's exhibition, for his dealer Leo Castelli's uptown gallery was located only a few blocks from the Ronald Feldman gallery. Further evidence pointing to Warhol's seeing *Color is a Mighty Power!* lies in his exhibiting the *Still Lifes* (*Hammer & Sickle*) series at the downtown Leo Castelli Gallery at the end of 1976. The canonical narrative behind this series is that Warhol produced it after a trip to Italy where he encountered the hammer and sickle as common graffiti. By appropriating them from a capitalist society rather than a cold war enemy, Warhol had mediated this hostile image. Exhibiting the hammer and sickle symbol as a still life at a commercial gallery further disarmed this communist icon, preparing the ground for its safe passage into the capitalist culture industry.

Although Warhol never acknowledged Komar and Melamid's influence on his *Hammer & Sickle* series, the fact that he agreed to meet the two Moscovites after they emigrated and settled in New York in 1978 may indicate that he was familiar with their first New York show. Astounded by the American predilection for

commodification, in 1979 Komar and Melamid established the fake corporation, "We Buy and Sell Souls," which obtained souls and conceived concepts for their promotion and sale. They contacted Warhol about buying his "Pop art soul," which they ended up receiving free of charge (fig. 177). Two "sales" staged during the same season in Moscow and New York once again searched for an answer to Komar and Melamid's inquiry "where is the line between us?," revealing a sizable gap between the value systems of the two art communities. Warhol's soul barely sold to the artist Elena Kirtsova in Moscow, while the soul of Norton Dodge, at the time the principal American collector of nonconformist art in the U.S., received the highest bidding from the Moscow collector Tatiana Kolodzei (fig. 178).

Given that Moscow vanguardists had practically no exhibition opportunities back home, it is not surprising that the artists who emigrated were particularly keen on getting public exposure. To discover that the New York art institutions were not eager to show their work was unanticipated and traumatic. The success of Komar and Melamid's first exhibition in New York did not stir interest in other Moscow conceptualists, however, which suggests that the pair quickly satisfied the low demand for non-American art, including Russian.

Vagrich Bakhchanian settled in New York in 1974, before the two exhibitions at VDNKh took place. Soon after, he realized that the New York galleries were just as inaccessible as the Soviet institutions back home. This pushed him toward executing a series of projects focused on a critique of institutions. Unable to enter the art world in a conventional way, Bakhchanian decided to use his body as a vessel to invade the New York art establishment. On November 18, 1977, he staged *Save Time! 30 Exhibitions in One Day* by visiting uptown and downtown galleries as well as the Whitney Museum with the plaque "Save Time" (fig. 179). In this action, Bakhchanian questioned artists' fixation on exhibitions by shifting the premise of public display from "quality" to "quantity."[9] As a way of overcoming his disappointment with the nondemocratic mechanisms of the Western art world, Bakhchanian ridiculed the entire exhibition process by equating it with any competition. Given that "In

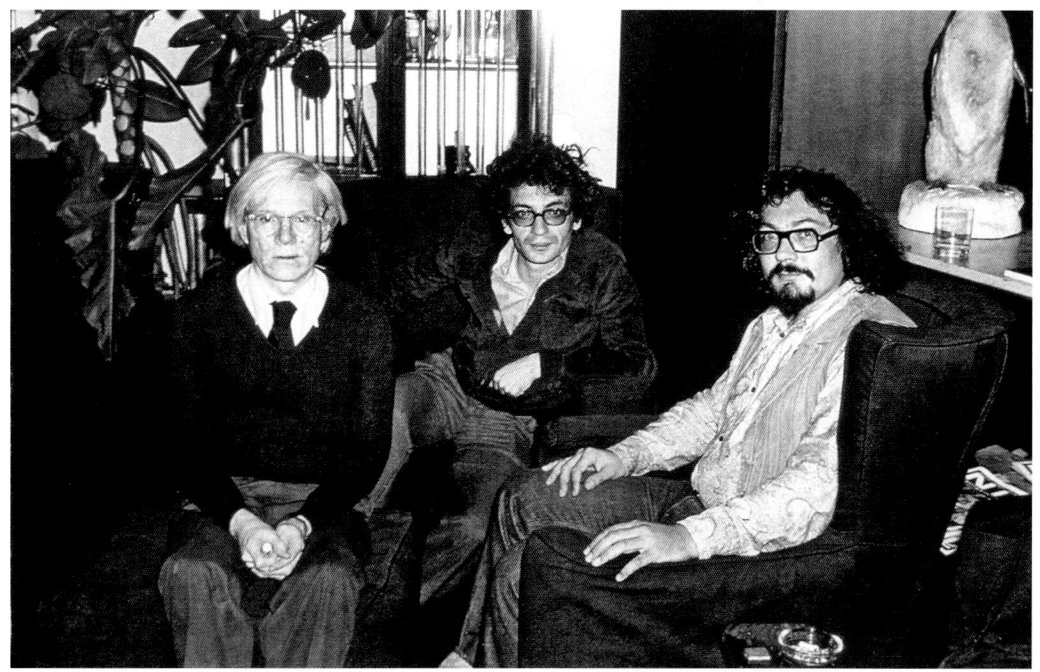

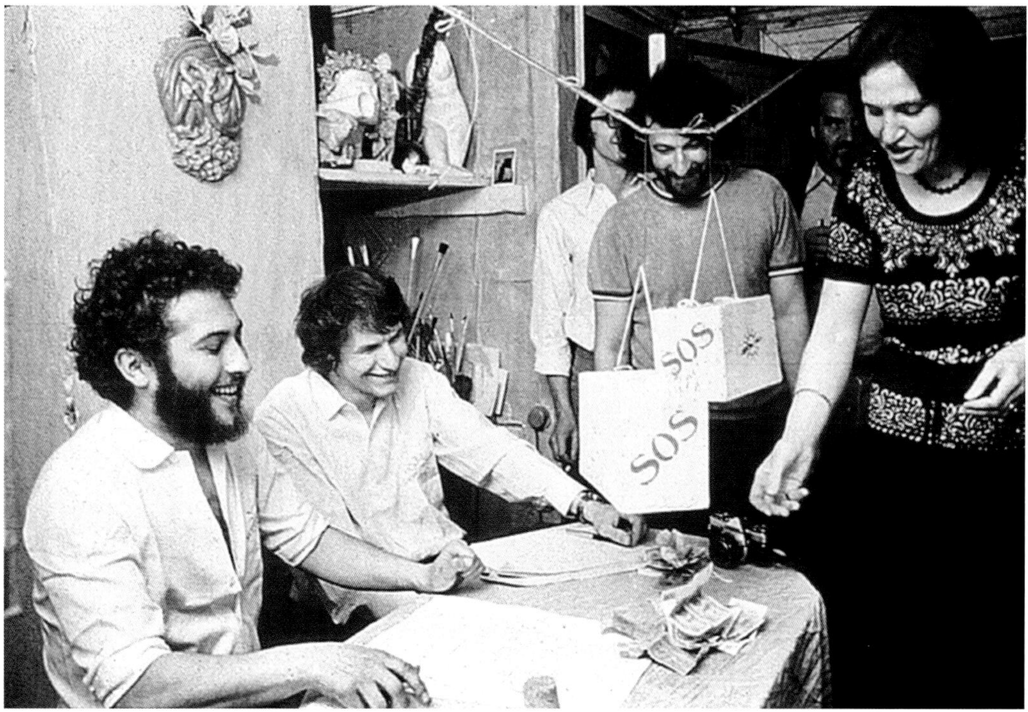

177   Andy Warhol with Aleksandr Melamid and Vitaly Komar (right) after they had bought Warhol's soul as part of their project *We Buy and Sell Souls*, February 6, 1979, New York.

178   Vitaly Komar and Aleksandr Melamid's collection of "souls" (clockwise from right): the collector Tatiana Kolodzei, Aleksandr Iulikov, Victor Skersis, and Mikhail Roshal, auctioned in Moscow, May 19, 1979, by the Nest group. Collection of Russian and Eastern European Art, Kolodzei Art Foundation, New Jersey.

Galleries and times of the exhibitions:
1 ALLAN STONE 12.10 p.m.
2 ELKON 12.22 p.m.
3 GIMPEL & WEIZENHOFFER 12.27 p.m.
4 FORUM 12.34 p.m.
5 BORGENICHT 12.39 p.m.
6 CASTELLI UPTOWN 12.50 p.m.
7 CORDIER & EKSTROM 1.03 p.m.
8 WHITNEY MUSEUM 1.12 p.m.
9 RONALD FELDMAN 1.23 p.m.
10 KNOEDLER 1.33 p.m.
11 ROSA ESMAN 2.14 p.m.
12 ARRAS 2.17 p.m.
13 ZABRISKIE 2.21 p.m.
14 FISCHBACH 2.24 p.m.
15 MARILYN PEARL 2.30 p.m.
16 MARLBOROUGH 2.36 p.m.
17 AARON BERMAN 2.44 p.m.
18 DINTENFASS 2.48 p.m.
19 LILIAN HEIDENBERG 2.57 p.m.
20 ALLAN FRUMKIN 3.08 p.m.
21 MEISEL 3.49 p.m.
22 WESTBROADWAY 3.52 p.m.
23 NANCY HOFFMAN 3.55 p.m.
24 SONNABEND 4 p.m.
25 WEBER 4.04 p.m.
26 JOHN GIBSON 4.15 p.m.
27 HOLLY SOLOMON 4.12 p.m.
28 HEINER FRIEDRICH 4.18 p.m.
29 O.K. HARRIS 4.23 p.m.
30 CALDWELL 4.26 p.m.

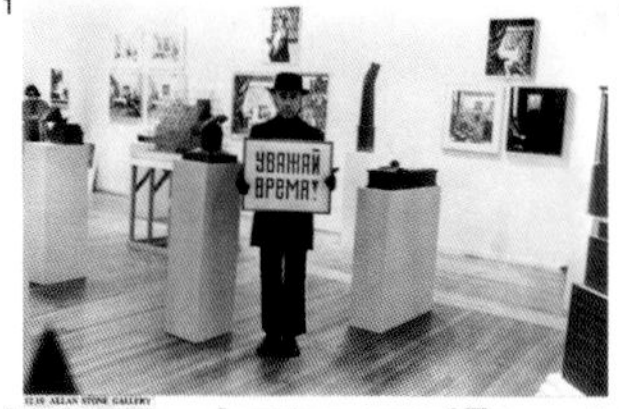
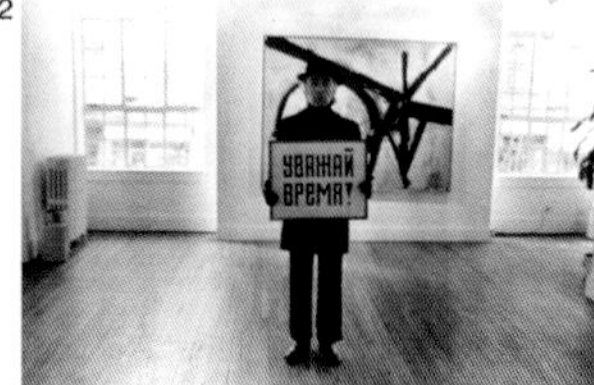
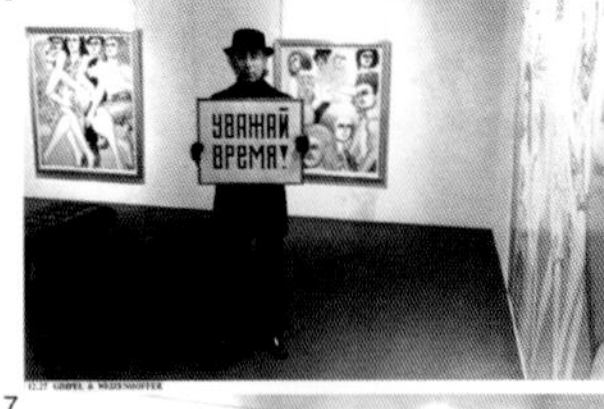
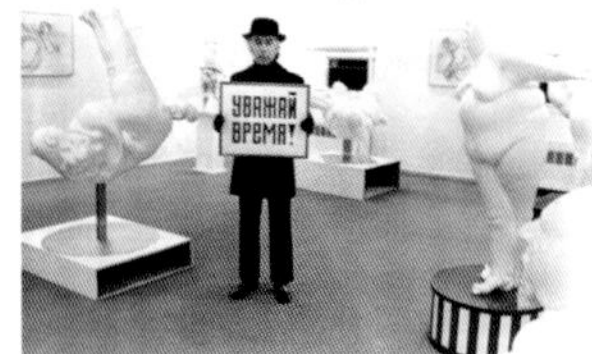
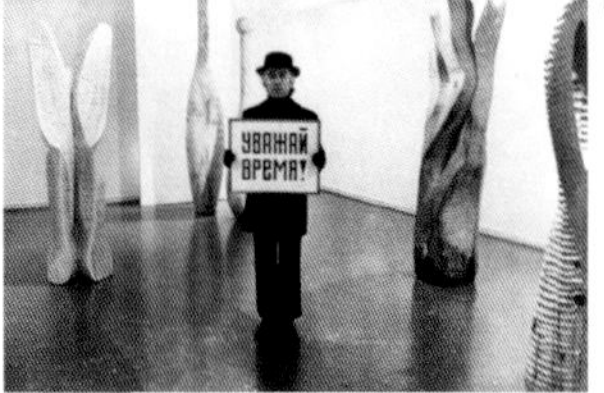
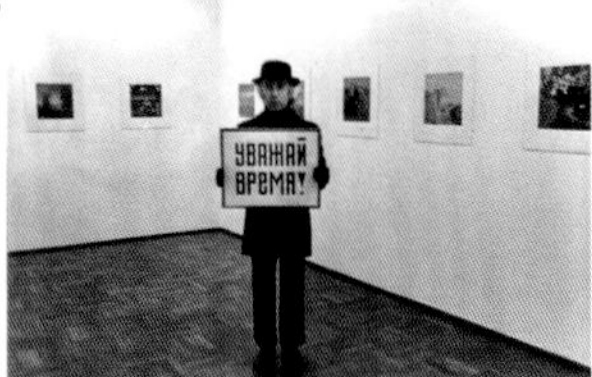
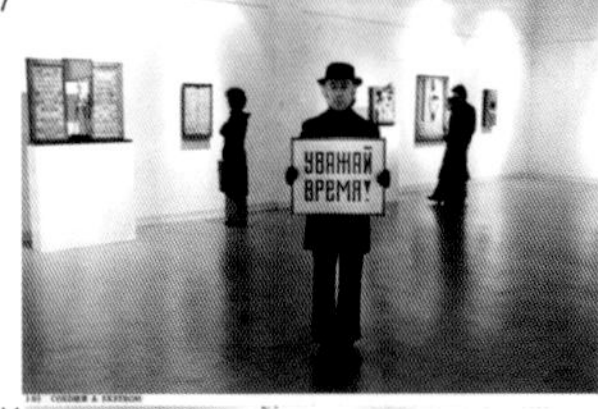
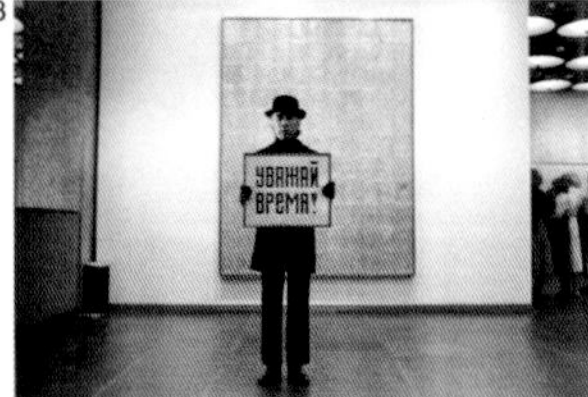
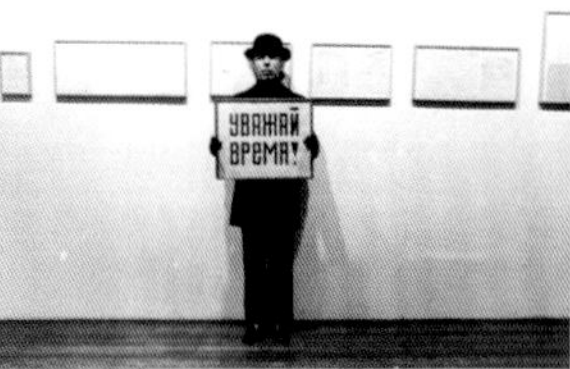
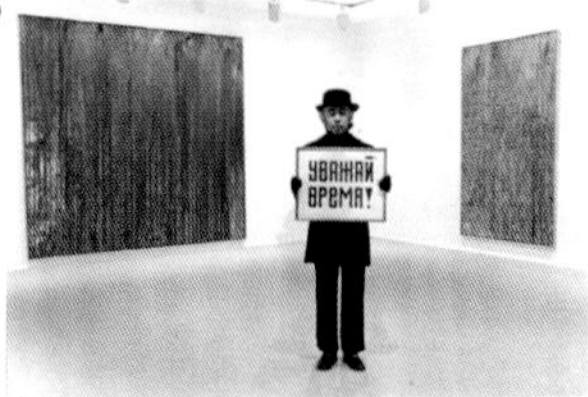
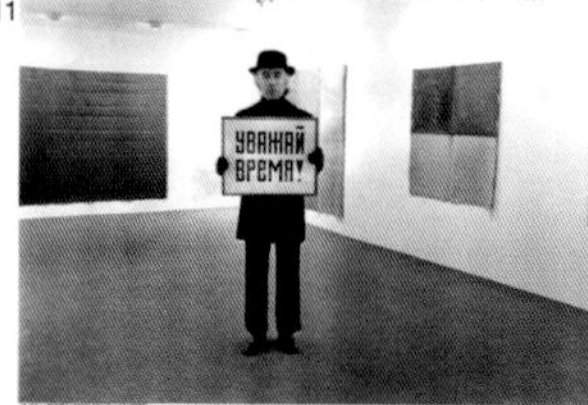
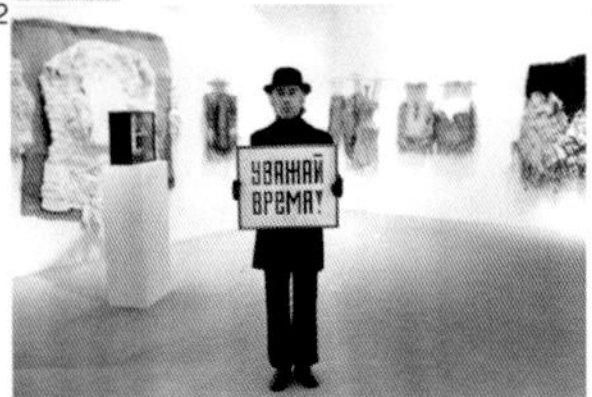
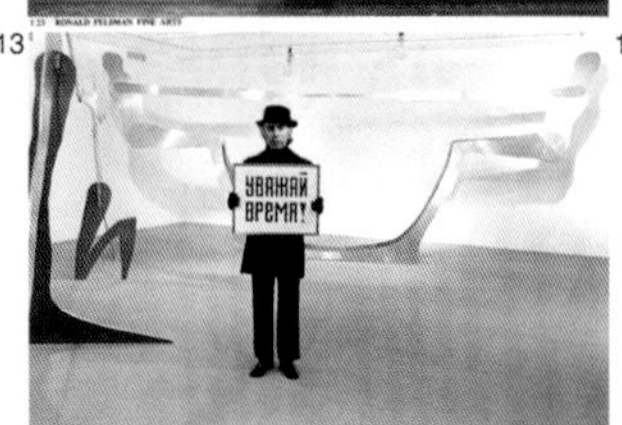
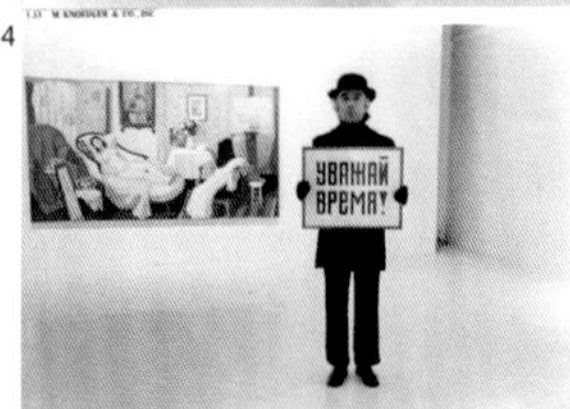
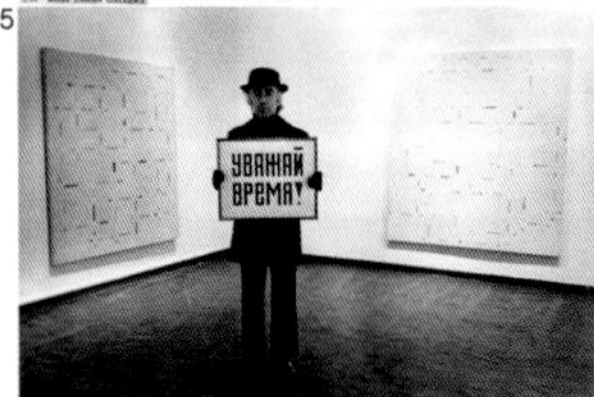
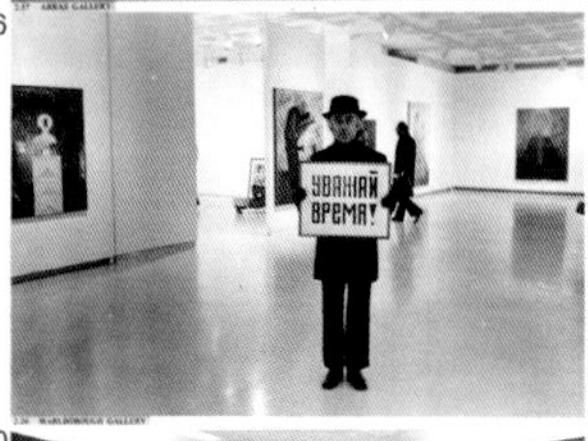
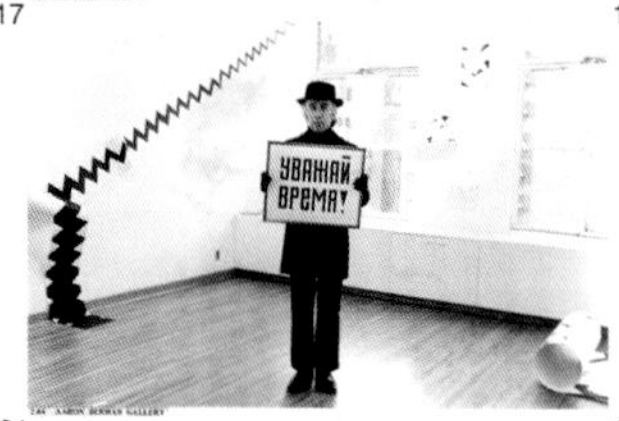
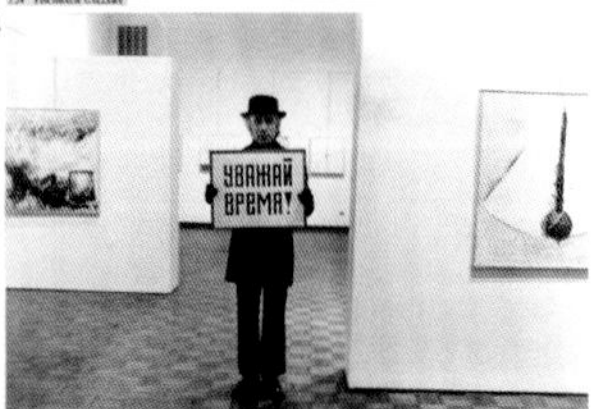
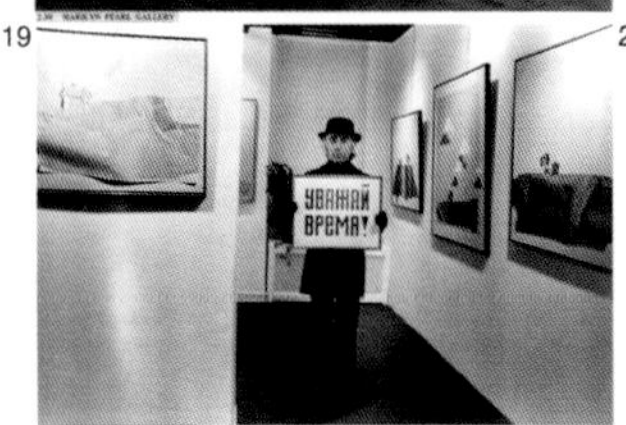
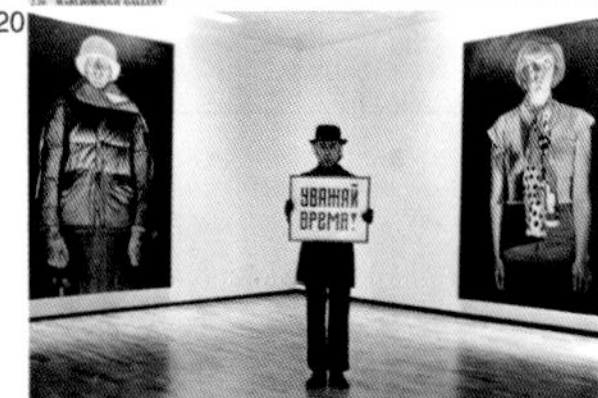
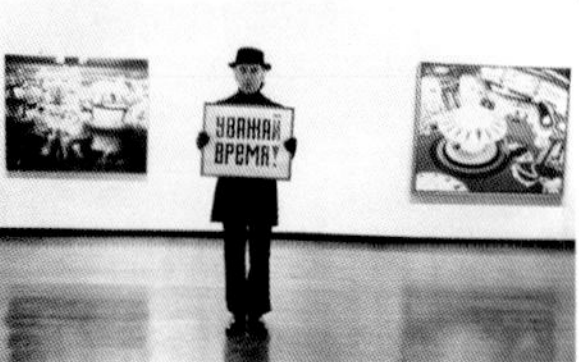
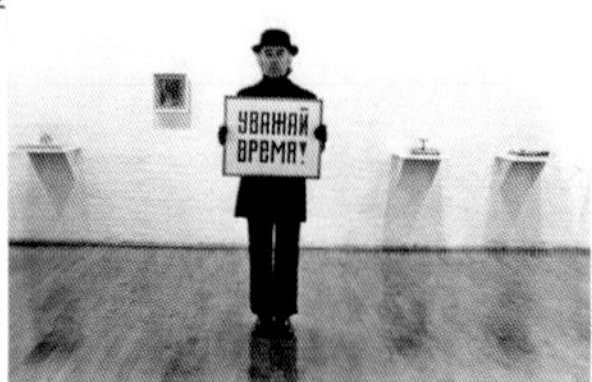
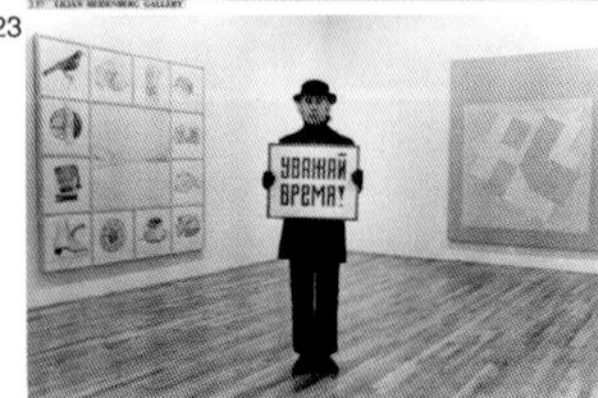
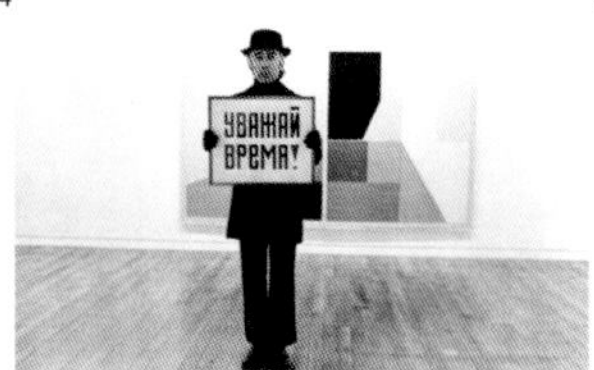
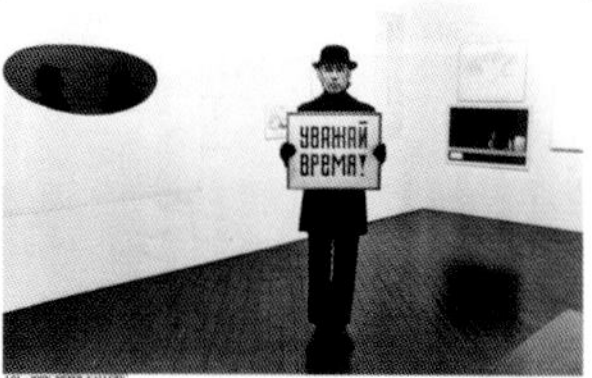
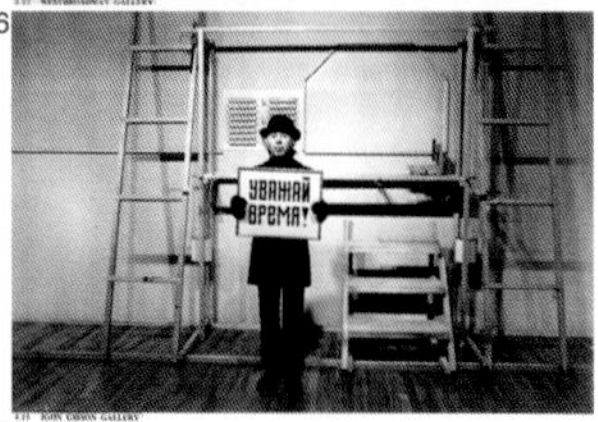
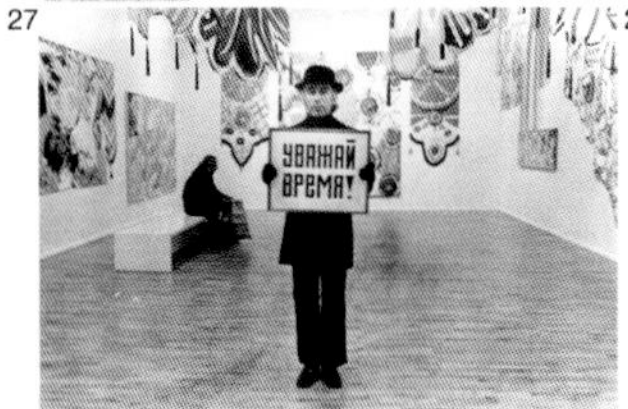
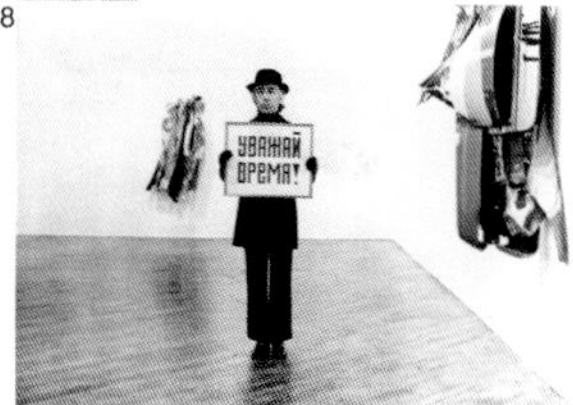
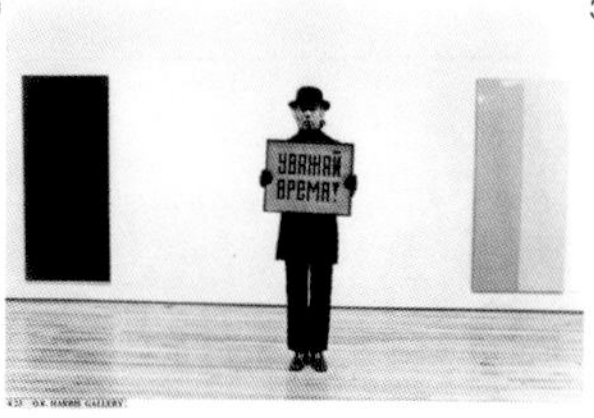
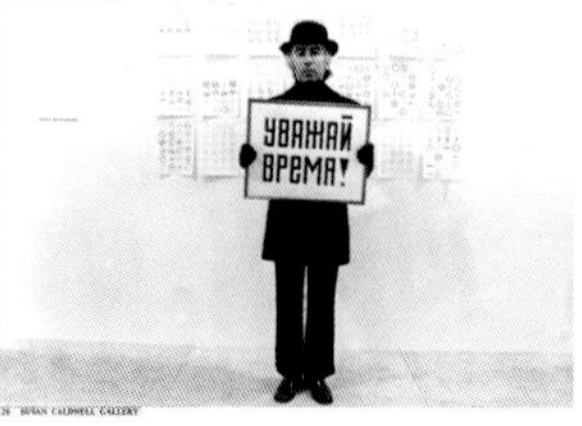

New York there are three hundred galleries," he disparagingly remarked, "one could be involved in such sport till one dies."[10]

An informal student of Vasily Ermilov (whose assemblage *Composition Number 3* [1923] is now in the collection of New York's Museum of Modern Art), Bakhchanian chose this showcase of modernism as the next site for his institutional critique, as well as an attempt to repossess the legacy of the Russian avant-garde that by then had been diverted to American Minimalism. On June 13, 1978, he appeared in the museum's gallery, which displayed Russian avant-garde paintings, to stage the *First Russian Propaganda Art Performance at the Museum of Modern Art, New York* (fig. 180). His body was covered in horizontal red stripes of fabric with slogans, stenciled in white paint, taken from standard propaganda as well as ordinary speech. To his forehead Bakhchanian attached the *Agitpunkt* (Russian for "agitation center") sign, becoming a walking agitator. Most avant-garde artists, including Malevich and Rodchenko, designed the *Agitpunkt* locations with nonobjective forms, thus assigning them sociopolitical meanings. Having photographed himself covered with these slogans next to Malevich's and Rodchenko's nonobjective canvases, Bakhchanian stood as a reminder of their original political context, which had been downplayed in the West. Nevertheless, by writing the slogans in Russian at an American venue, he also suggested that the power of abstract art lies in its ability to transcend particular sociopolitical referents, and to blend into multiple contexts.

Bakhchanian returned to MoMA in May and June of 1979 with the Moscow Sots artist Aleksandr Kosolapov, who had settled in New York in 1975, and the New York artist of Belarusian descent, Valentin Goroshko (fig. 181). Together they picketed the museum entrance with a banner with a red cross proclaiming "Art Salvation Inc," along with a cross saying the same attached to a pole, another kind of agitprop for the salvation of art. Bakhchanian stated that in this performance his:

> true intention was to try to shake up at least a little this and similar institutions that had grown stale to the core…nonstandard exhibitions – from Christo to video art…are rare occasions of animation against

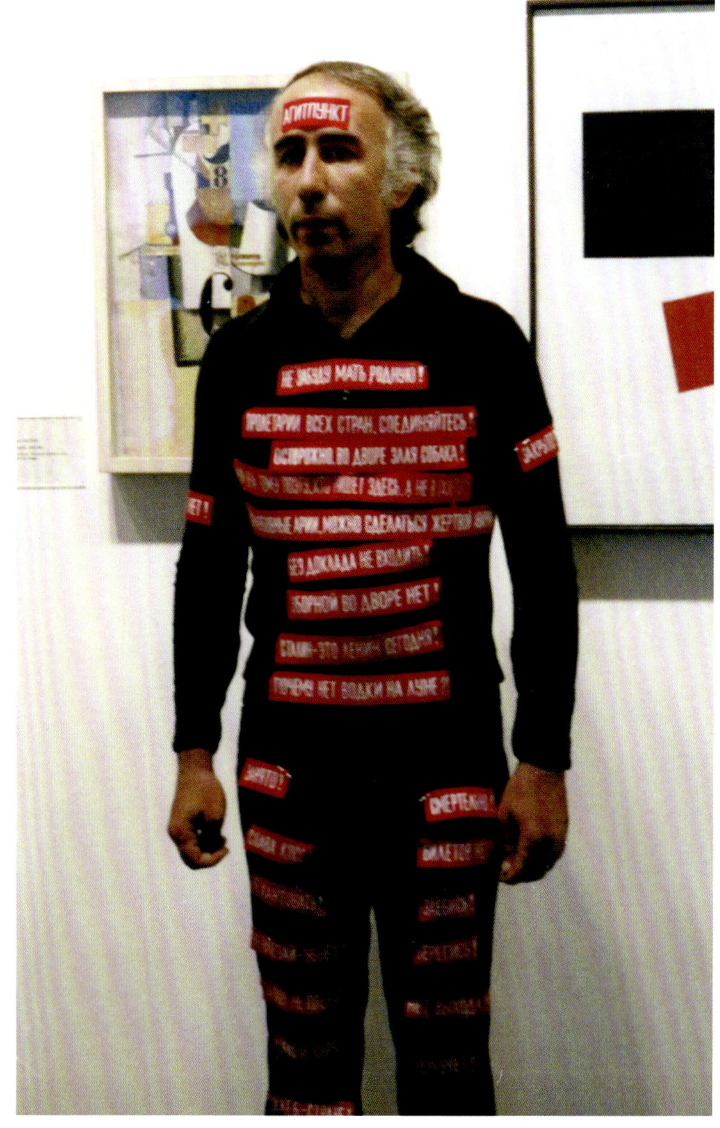

OPPOSITE PAGE 179 Vagrich Bakhchanian, *Save Time! 30 Exhibitions in One Day*, November 18, 1977, New York.

ABOVE 180 Vagrich Bakhchanian, *First Russian Propaganda Art Performance at the Museum of Modern Art, New York*, June 13, 1978, New York.

the general comatose background…Moreover, contemporary styles and forms cannot be represented and displayed by traditional means. One needs correspondingly new forms of display. Already during the period of the Russian avant-garde in the 1920s art left the museums to enter the street.[11]

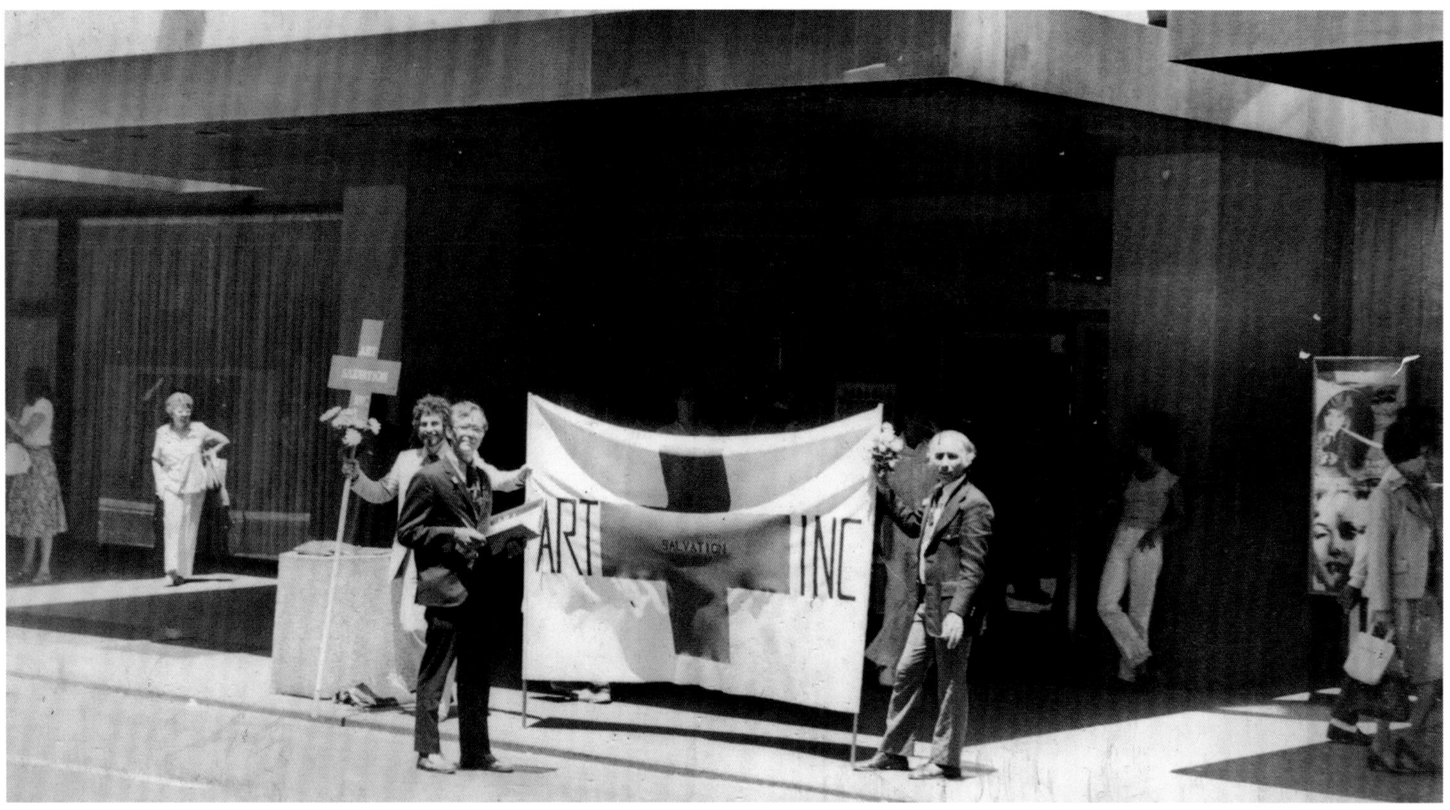

181 Vagrich Bakhchanian, Aleksandr Kosolapov, and Valentin Goroshko, *Art Salvation*, June 1979. New York.

This critique of institutions by Bakhchanian also manifested itself in his interview with Joseph Beuys, conducted with the Russian artist Anatoly Ur during Beuys's exhibition, *New Sculpture*, at Ronald Feldman's at the end of 1979. This interview, along with Komar and Melamid's collaborations with Davis and Warhol, constituted the first examples of "significant contact[s] between contemporary Russian and Western art, an important step on the path of exchanging information."[12] Bakhchanian and Ur suggested to Beuys that his exhibition at the Solomon R. Guggenheim Museum (now renamed simply, "Guggenhcim Muscum") in 1979 had not reflected the political ideas that he expressed elsewhere, and instead "presented relic-like remains of [his] former activity." "You could have put forward a new body of work," they continued, and further probed him on his claims of being a political activist, yet associating with the art world's financial system:

You made a statement that you fight against money power. You say, you are for changing the structure of society. You say, you want to create a new society – a free one…you organize your shows at traditionally established institutions, such as museums or galleries. You deal with money-minded people, such as museum curators or art dealers, collectors. Don't you feel that the system in which you are functioning might change you according to its own standards rather than you change it? They will use you as an extravagant example of a truly free artist just to exploit your aura and use it for their own profit.[13]

Beuys refused to accept this assessment of his situation, claiming that "this is impossible, because all such things stand in relationship to the free will of the person involved. It is my outspoken goal to struggle against state and money, and there is never a possibility to misuse this thing."[14] At best, this response sounded naïve in view of the cancellation of Hans Haacke's show at the same museum in 1971 because the artist had used one of his works to expose the questionable real-estate dealings of the museum's trustees.

Bakhchanian and Ur's interrogation of Beuys with respect to the authenticity of his practices predates the harsh analysis of him by critics such as Benjamin H. D. Buchloh.[15] Indirectly, this skewed the reputation of those Russian artists in the same circle of critics, portraying them as politically conservative. Instead, from the angle of their Soviet experience, with its lack of exhibition opportunities, Bakhchanian and Ur proposed a radical reassessment of the impact of exhibitions on vanguard art, and argued that exhibitions in established institutions could de-radicalize and corrupt artists. Georgy Kizevalter, as a conceptual artist and photographer who undoubtedly read this interview, commemorated Beuys's death at the beginning of 1986 with a portrait made out of a negative print (fig. 182), thus conveying the controversies surrounding Beuys's art and politics, especially after his 1979 Guggenheim exhibition. The phrase, "Just shoot and you'll see me again," painted on Beuys's hat, reads as a retort to the critics. On Beuys's chest, Kizevalter painted a hare, a reference to both Beuys's performance, *How to Explain Pictures to a Dead Hare* (1965), and CAG's *The Russian World* (March 17, 1985), in which a plywood cutout three meters high of a hare played a key part. The illusory function of interpretation and the degree of artist's control over viewers underlay both performances. Overall, Kizevalter seemed to suggest that Beuys's philosophy and aesthetics were much closer to the Russian than the Western world. As if to illustrate this point, in 1987, Beuys's portrait was stolen from one of the Moscow exhibitions, prompting Kizevalter to produce a replica.

At the outset of the 1980s, enough Moscow vanguardists had settled in New York to form the "American wing." In spite of Soviet government censorship, communication between Moscow and New York was established via a correspondence with Victor Tupitsyn and the Moscow conceptualists. Nest's *Let's Become One Meter Closer!* (fig. 183) summed up the

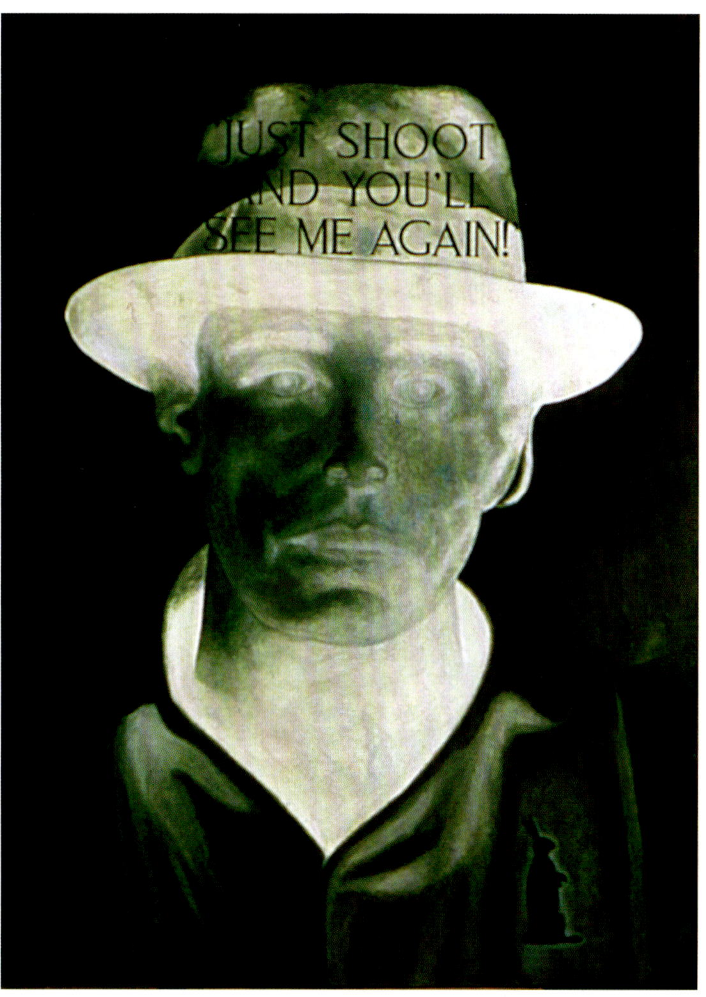

182   Georgy Kizevalter, "Just shoot and you'll see me again" (portrait of Joseph Beuys), 1986. Work now lost.

artists' desire for cultural exchange, and served as a Moscow addendum to Komar and Melamid's first New York show. Roshal, for whom *Let's Become* was "a reflection on so-called détente," has explained the group's concept: "By digging from the eastern part of the globe toward the western for fifty centimeters, and likewise from the West toward the East, we offered people the chance to become closer by one meter."[16] Yet, with the exception of Komar and Melamid's successful exhibition at the Ronald Feldman gallery, the hope of Moscow artists "becom[ing] closer" to the New York art world remained unfulfilled. Kosolapov remarked on this challenge:

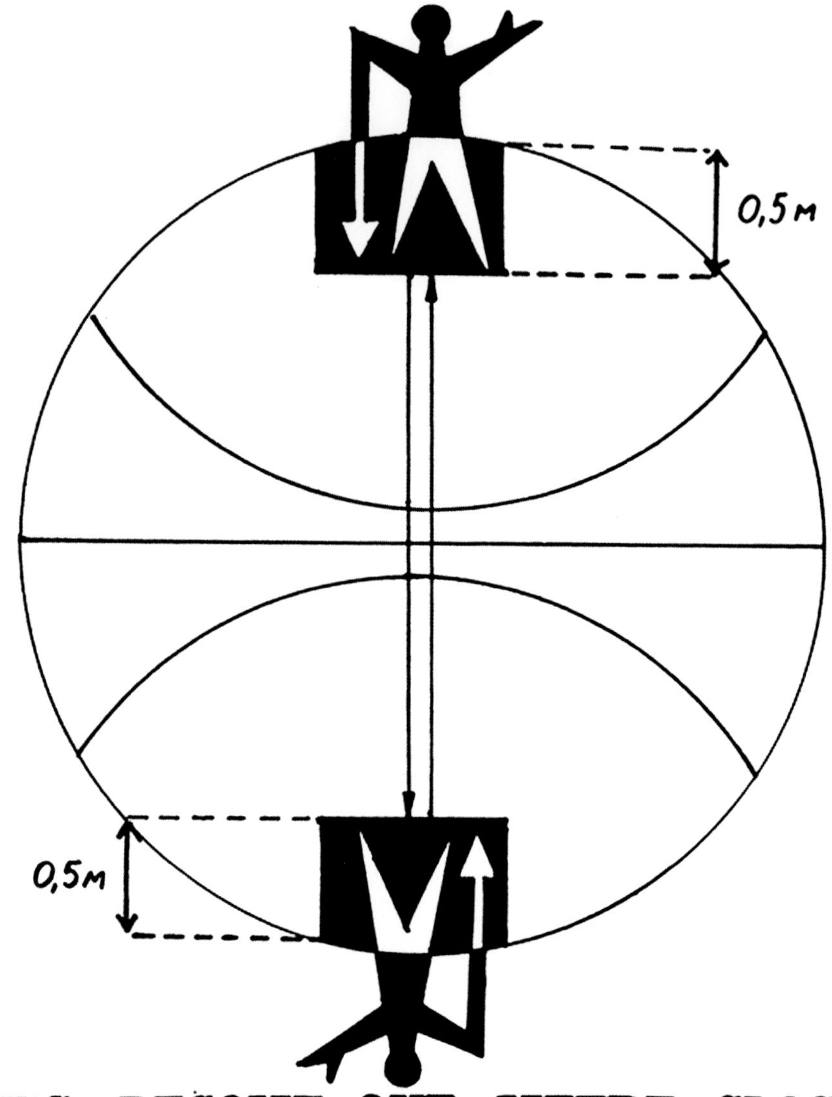

LET'S BECOME ONE METRE CLOSER!

FOR THE RELIEF OF THE PEOPLES RAPPROACHMENT

DONSKOY-ROSHAL-SKERSIS PROPOSE TO ALL INHABITANTS

OF WESTERN PART OF THE WORLD

DAILY AT I2.00 GREENWICH MEAN TIME

TO DIG A HOLE 0,5 metre DEEP.

AT THE SAME TIME DONSKOY-ROSHAL-SKERSIS WILL DIG A HOLE

OF THE SAME DEPTH FROM THE OPPOSITE SIDE OF THE GLOBE.

TAKE YOUR SHOVELS, FRIENDS,

LET'S BECOME ONE METRE CLOSER!

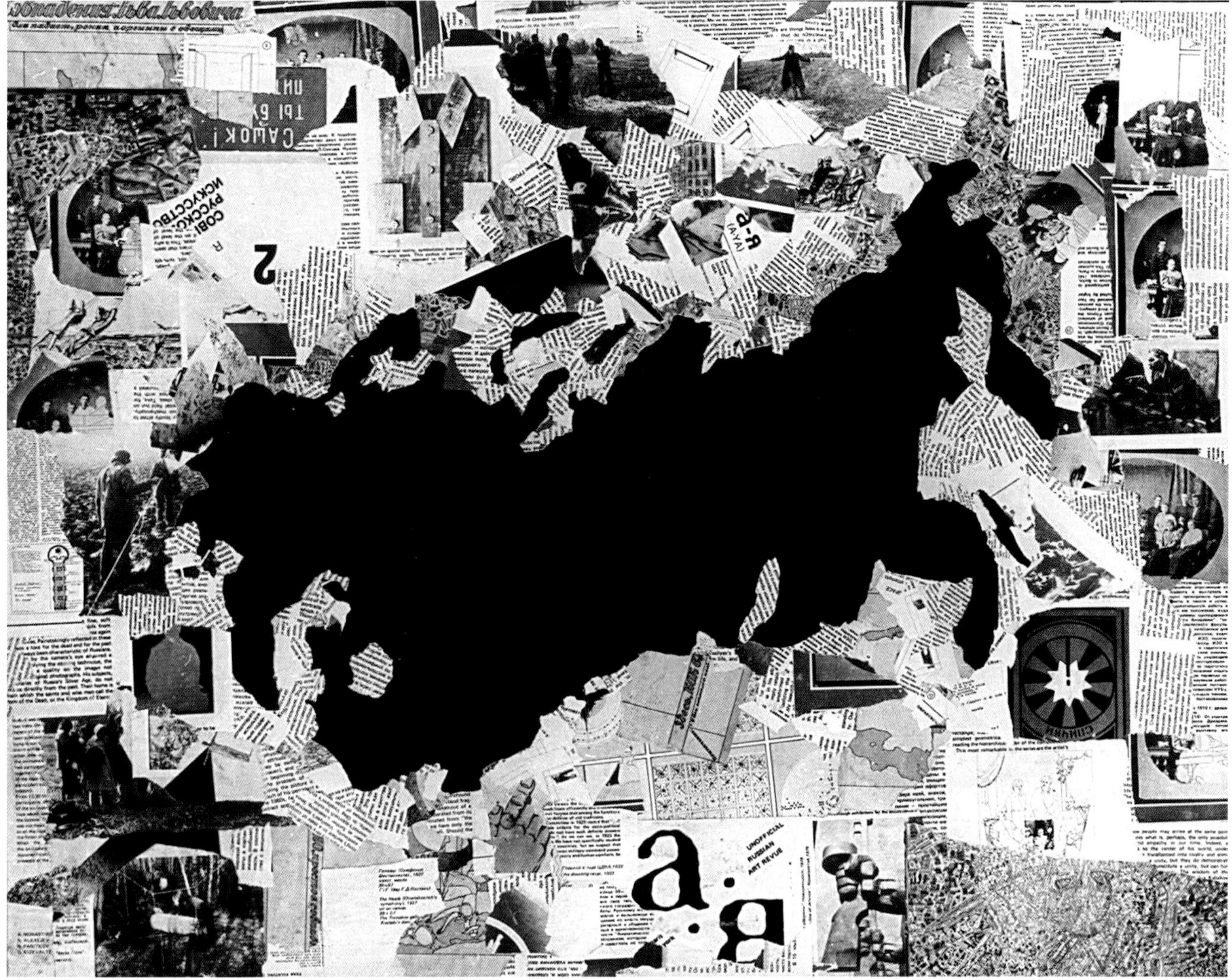

OPPOSITE PAGE 183   The Nest group, *Let's Become One Meter Closer!* 1976. Private collection.

ABOVE 184   Natalia Abalakova, *Black Hole*, 1981. Norton and Nancy Dodge Collection of Nonconformist Art from the Soviet Union. Jane Voorhees Zimmerli Art Museum, Rutgers, State University of New Jersey.

Russian artists have trouble showing their work not only in Moscow but also in New York. Everyone thinks that Russian culture lags, that we are yesterday's artists. But it's a different generation now, a younger generation that has advanced a lot. They are very well informed, they know what's going on in the West, and their work is not dissimilar from Western work. What they produce is not necessarily "dissident" art, though if it is, it's dissident culturally rather than politically.[17]

Kosolapov considered the launching of the periodical *A-Ya* in 1979 in Paris (a Russian version of the New York magazine *Avalanche*) as a substitute for exhibitions. "For us, the magazine is like a gallery," he concluded.[18] Vanguard artists who were still in Moscow shared Kosolapov's opinion: finally, they could not only see their most recent work on the pages of a bilingual periodical but also express their ideas in writing. Natalia Abalakova amply expressed the significance of *A-Ya* in a 1981 collage made out of cut-up issues of the magazine that conveyed the intellectual and artistic energy of the vanguard milieu (fig. 184). With this image of collective experimentation encroaching on a blackened map of the Soviet Union, Abalakova created a powerful clash between free creativity and the force geared to disbanding it.

The conceptual artists Rimma and Valery Gerlovin, who arrived in New York in 1980, also agreed that it was essential for the vanguard to have a platform in the form of a periodical, yet passionately argued for the need to exhibit.[19] This became possible after Norton Dodge, started the Contemporary Russian Art Center of America (CRACA) on the eleventh floor of a high-rise building located at 599 Broadway in SoHo. An exhibition, *Russian New Wave*, inaugurated the space on December 4, 1981, displaying collectives and individual artists from both the New York and Moscow wings of the vanguard.[20]

Included in the Russian *New Wave* was Kosolapov's Sots Art of the Moscow period. It is based on a montage of primitivist renditions of Soviet icons, ideological narratives with cosmonauts and ballerinas, and political symbols of the Revolution such as the battleship *Aurora* and Palace Square. He assembled all of these in one piece from the series *The Soviet Myth* (1974) in bold defiance of Soviet academicism. In another work, he depicted Lenin on an armored car, following the official history that, upon return from exile to Petrograd in April 1917, the Bolshevik leader spoke to the people in this fashion. By questioning whether it was myth or fact, Kosolapov pointed out the falsifications of Soviet historiography.

In the series, 'North' (1974), titled after a popular brand of cigarettes, Kosolapov surrounds a profile portrait of Lenin with packs of cigarettes and an inserted image of a couple making love (fig. 185). The composition speaks of ideological intrusion upon private life, which was intensified by such repressive slogans as, "Lenin is always with you." Yet, it also communicates the point that the propaganda machine, in making Lenin omnipresent, shifted his status from tyrant to prisoner of Soviet everyday life, as well as victim of boundless duplication. It is ironic that Lenin early on had recognized and criticized such heroization: "Everywhere I look, I see people writing about me. I find this completely unmarxist concentration on a single individual very harmful. It is wrong, undesirable and unnecessary. And as for these portraits! They are all over the place! What's the point of it all?"[21]

Sots artists' deconstruction of Soviet myths and their critique of stifling politics presents a puzzle for the Western viewer, something Kosolapov recognized upon settling in New York:

They are forms of a collective language, and "collective" is a limited concept, symbols lose their meaning beyond its [*sic*] borders. In a concrete sense these are barriers that seem to be national or cultural differences. This is why what can be easy on the level of ideas becomes insurmountable on the level of culture. In this I see one of the important difficulties concerning emigration.[22]

In an immediate reaction, Kosolapov retreated to formalism, making geometric constructions and employing them in performances. But then he decided to rethink his Sots Art iconography, applying it to more familiar emblems – cigarettes, Lenin (whose mask in the form of a red cube he made and wore in new performances), a mausoleum, a hammer and sickle. Kosolapov used the last particularly often, for by then it had been mediated by Warhol, whose elusive and innocuous rendering of this communist symbol Kosolapov countered with an aggressive readymade. These he combined with images of prehistoric people and their tools to assert the barbaric nature of Soviet communism (fig. 186).

Before Leonid Sokov settled in New York in 1980, he had made himself known in Moscow by organizing a group exhibition devoted to conceptualism and Sots Art in his studio in May 1976. Early on, Sokov positioned himself as an anti-Socialist Realist sculptor, challenging official sculpture's pseudoclassical coherence, monumental scale, and use of costly materials, such as bronze and marble. His sculptural objects were small, roughly executed from wood and gesso, and saturated with parody. Though he had the opportunity to become a well-paid and successful official sculptor, Sokov chose to refuse these privileges and join the underground milieu. In 1974 he marked this decision with an installation-happening of a sculpture of his last name in a heap of garbage (fig. 187). Many of

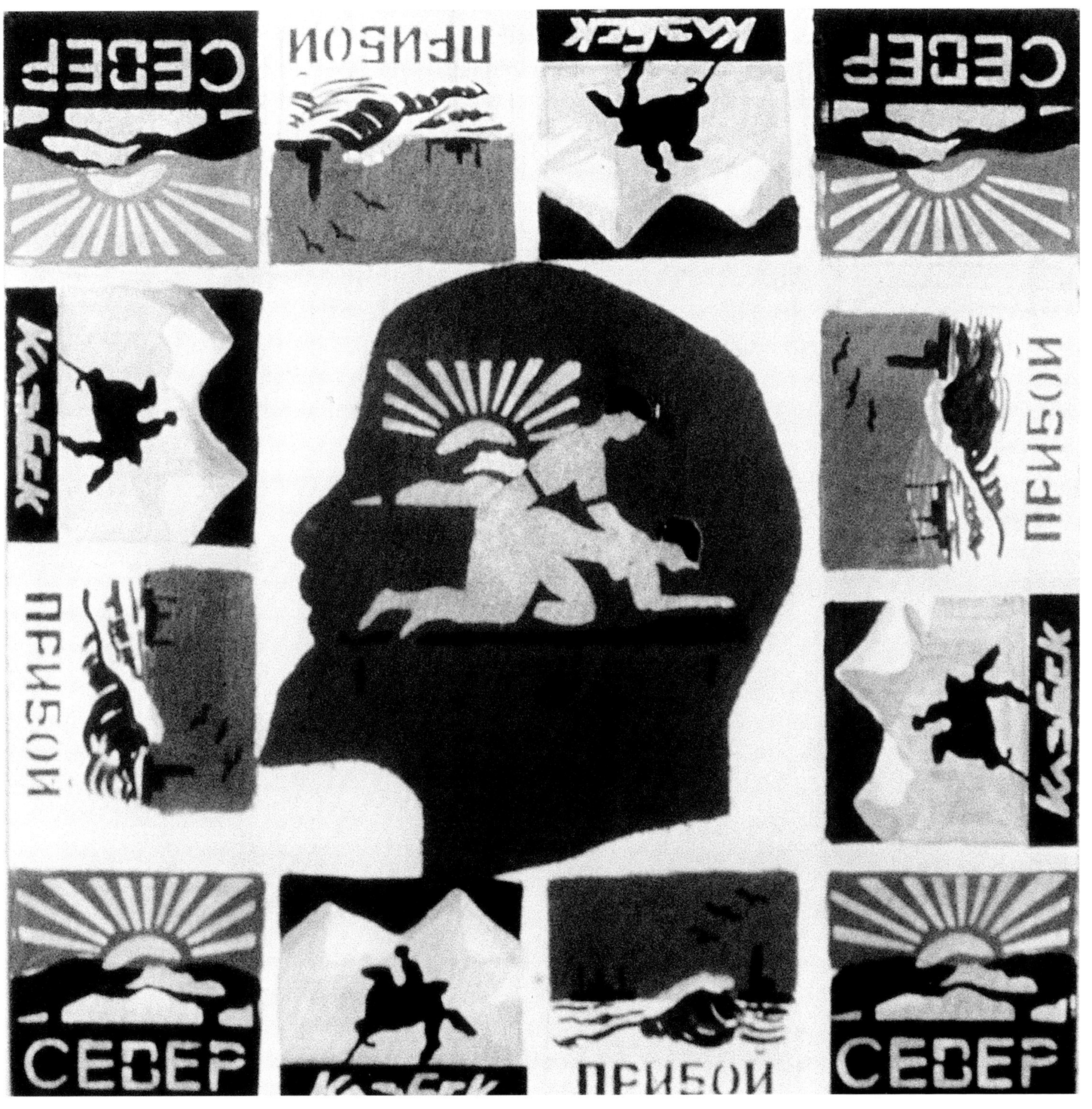

185   Aleksandr Kosolapov, from the series 'North', 1974. Norton and Nancy Dodge Collection of Nonconformist Art from the Soviet Union, Jane Voorhees Zimmerli Art Museum Rutgers, State University of New Jersey.

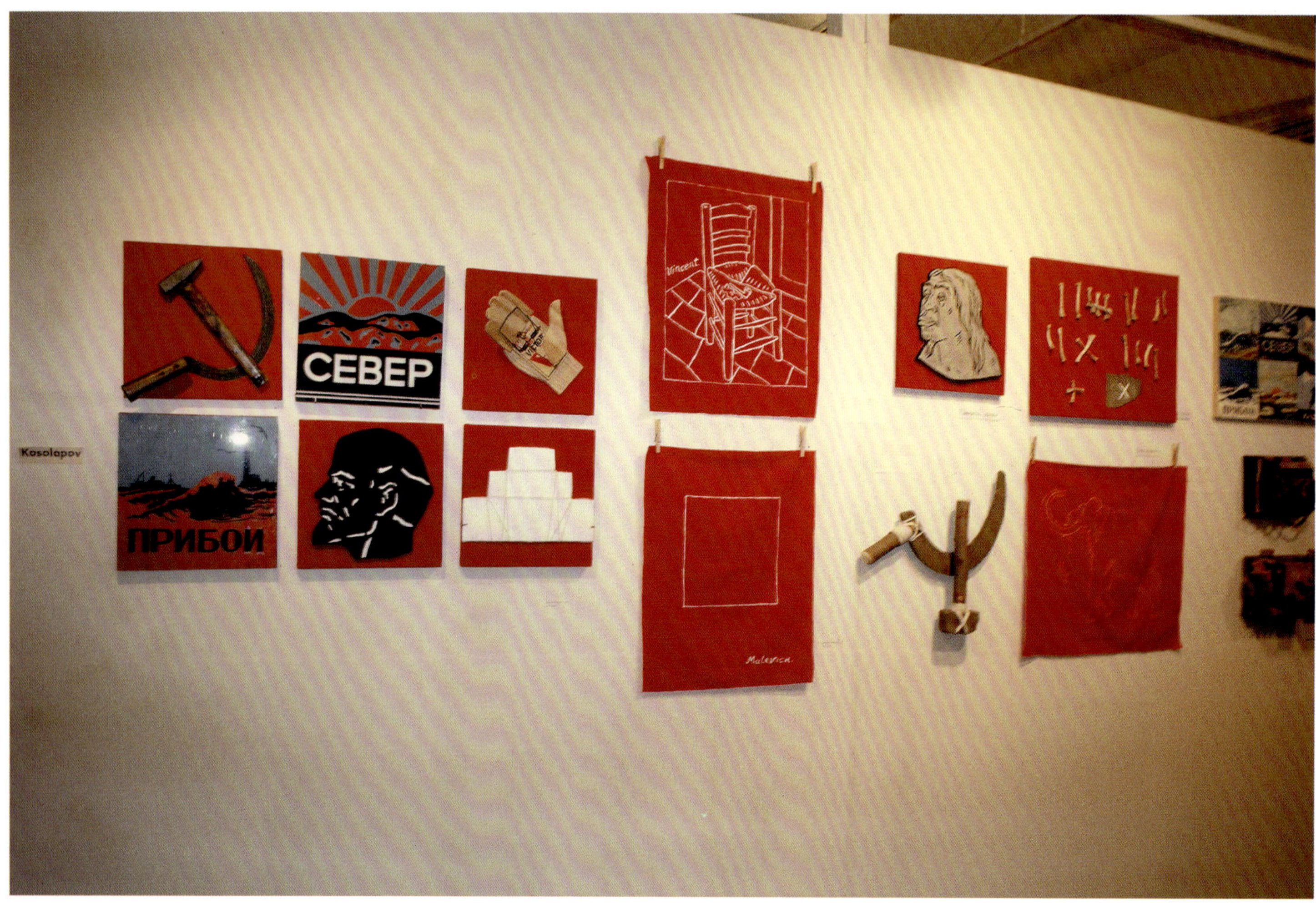

Sokov's works are mechanized toys rather than static monuments. His approach is rooted in the Russian folk tradition of producing puppets for mass entertainment, spanning buffooneries and masquerades from pre-revolutionary periods to post-revolutionary agit-prop activities. Sokov's "primitive" execution and lampooning of political events came out of this tradition, with which he elicited similarities between folkloristic and Soviet patterns of myth making. All of these devices are in play in his early unsanctioned sculptures: *Project to Construct Glasses for Every Soviet Person* (1976) uses red stars in place of glasses, commenting on the Soviet people's collective and stereotyped optics (fig. 188). *Alley of Heroes* (1975), another early Moscow installation, negates the official choices of heroes of the country: Sokov flanks a bust of Lenin not with authorized revolutionaries and party leaders, but with portraits of political dissidents. *Corvalan's Heart* (fig. 189) is also dedicated to a dissident, Vladimir Bukovsky, who was released from prison in 1976 in exchange for Luis Corvalan, the head of the Chilean Communist Party, imprisoned after General Pinochet's coup.

While in Moscow, the Gerlovins used performance art to test the limits of body politics, and to expose the illogicality of Soviet everyday life. Independently, Rimma made cardboard cubes draped in fabric that contained written statements and questions. The cubes functioned as single objects as well as elements of larger interactive structures – viewers could open or move the cubes (fig. 190). To some degree, Rimma performed a double release into the viewer's space of Kabakov's "cubes" since they were still attached to a surface (fig. 191), and also of his often-used question/

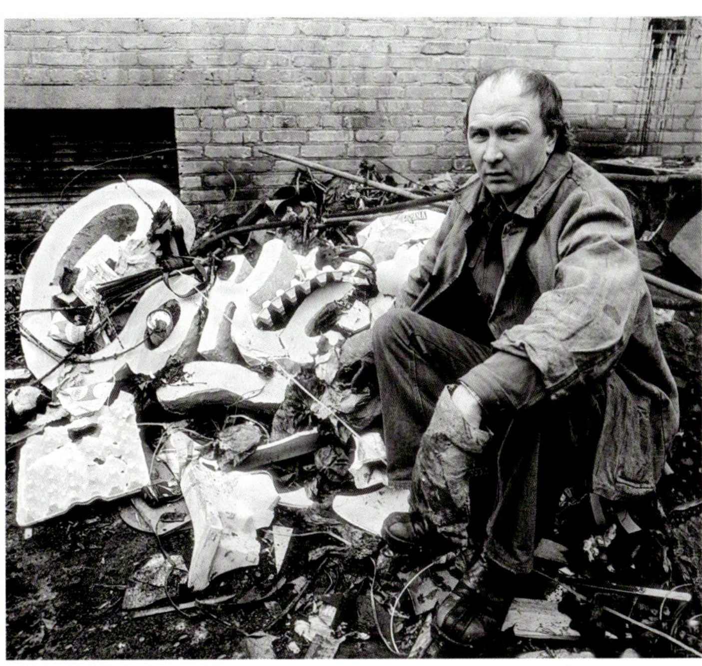

OPPOSITE PAGE 186   Aleksandr Kosolapov's installation in the exhibition *Russian New Wave*, Contemporary Russian Art Center of America (CRACA), New York, 1981.

RIGHT 187   Leonid Sokov with his sculpture of his name, Sokov, installed in a garbage heap, Moscow, 1974.

BELOW 188   Leonid Sokov's installation in the exhibition *Russian New Wave* (CRACA), New York, 1981.

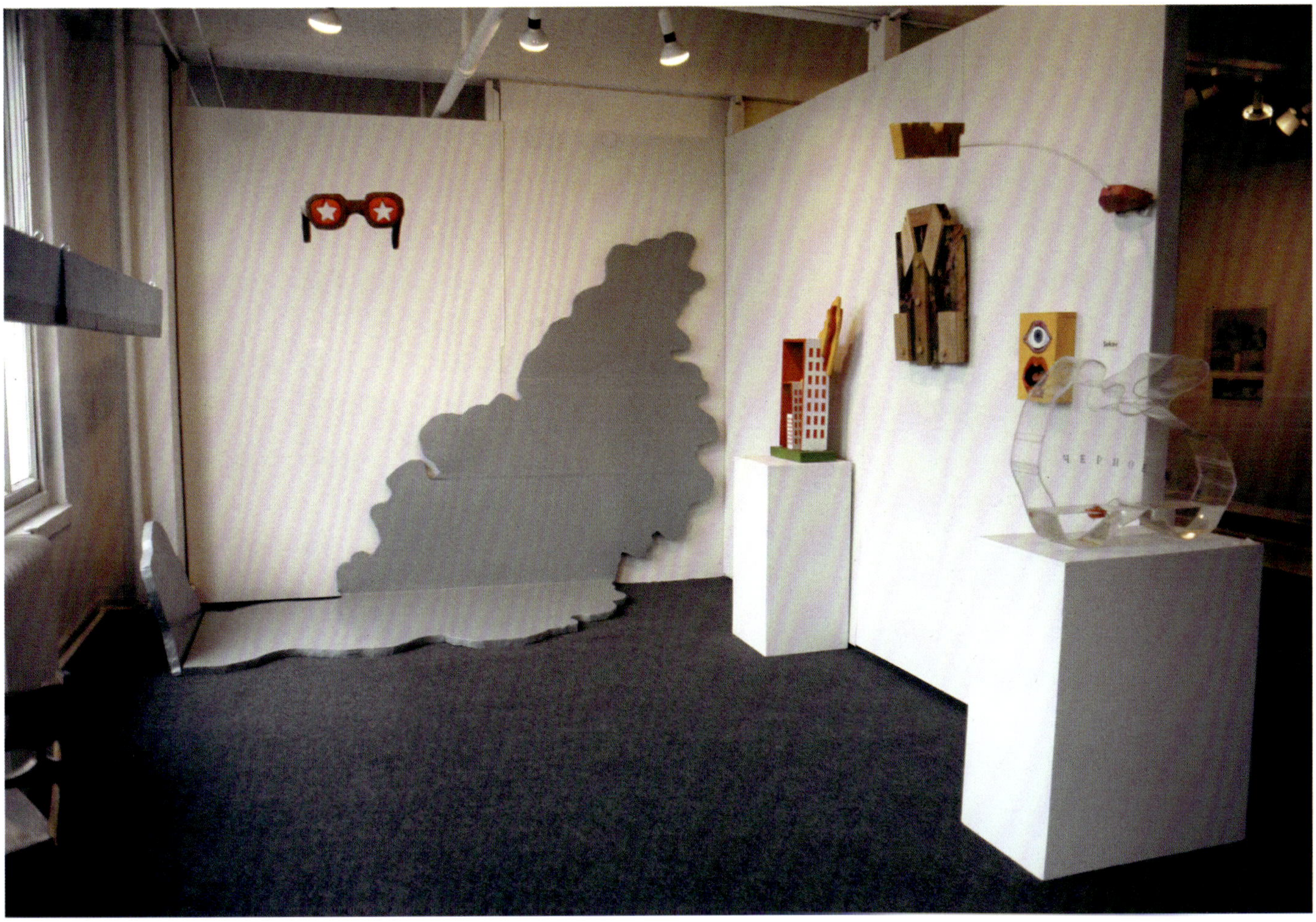

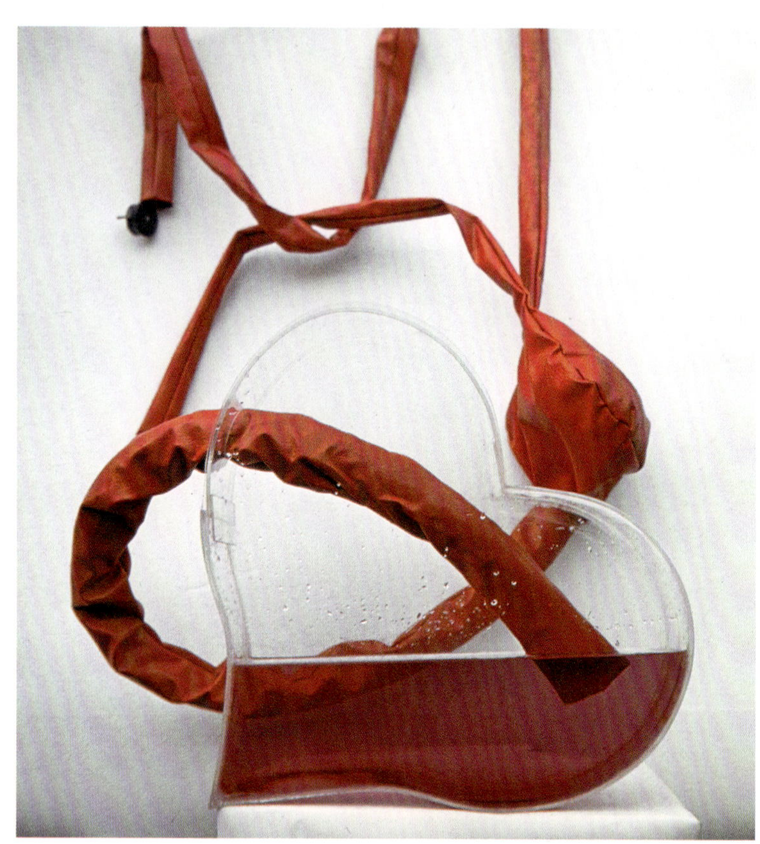

LEFT 189   Leonid Sokov, *Corvalan's Heart*, 1977.

BELOW 190   Rimma Gerlovin next to *Cubes*, ca. 1979. Moscow.

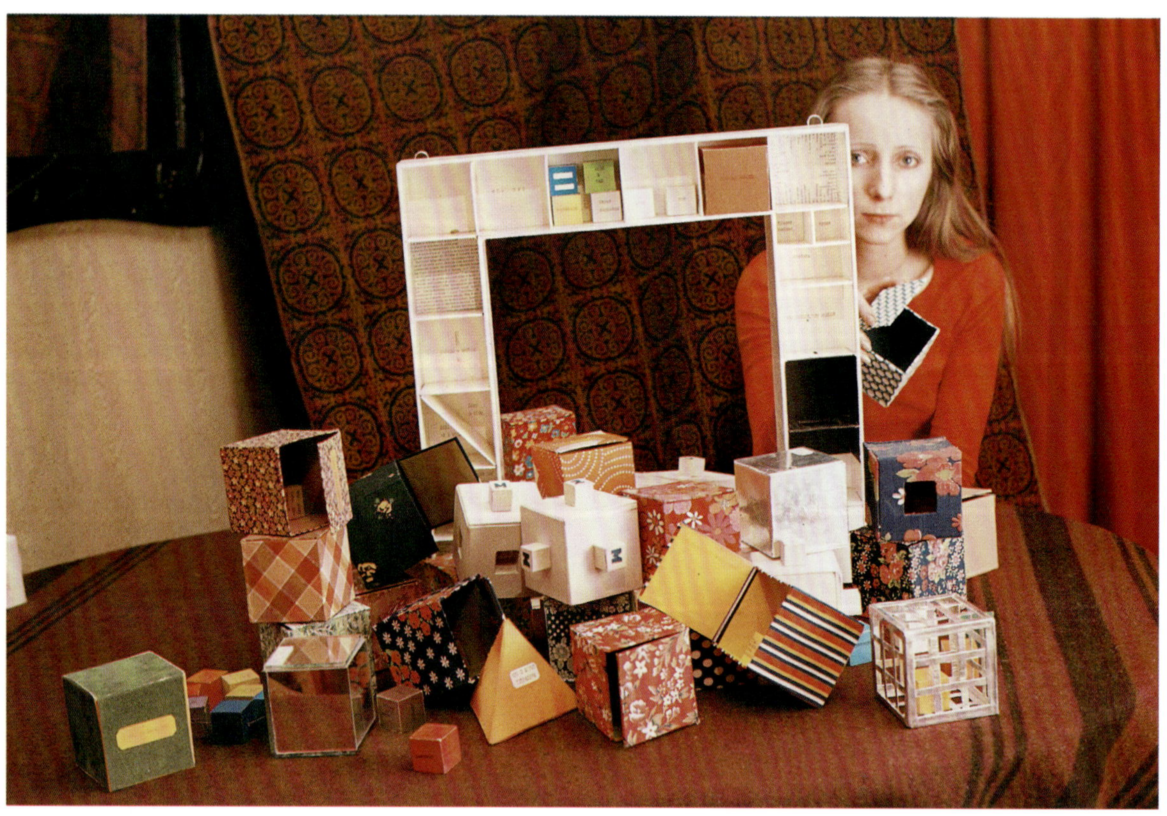

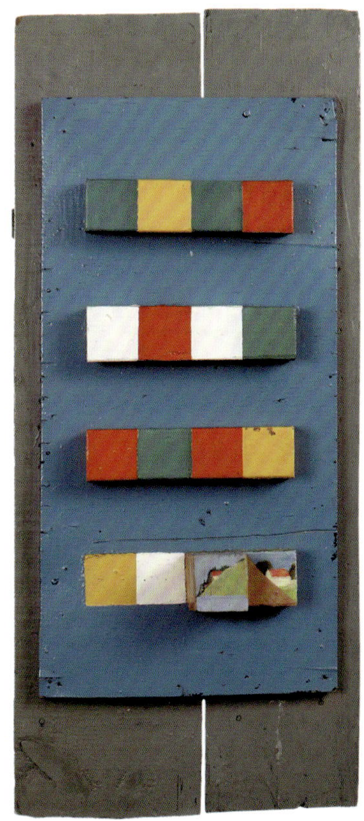

LEFT 191   Ilya Kabakov, *Cubes*, 1962. Norton and Nancy Dodge Collection of Nonconformist Art from the Soviet Union, Jane Voorhees Zimmerli Art Museum Rutgers, State University of New Jersey.

BELOW 192   Valery Gerlovin, *The Party Meeting*, 1975. Museum Haus am Checkpoint Charlie, Berlin.

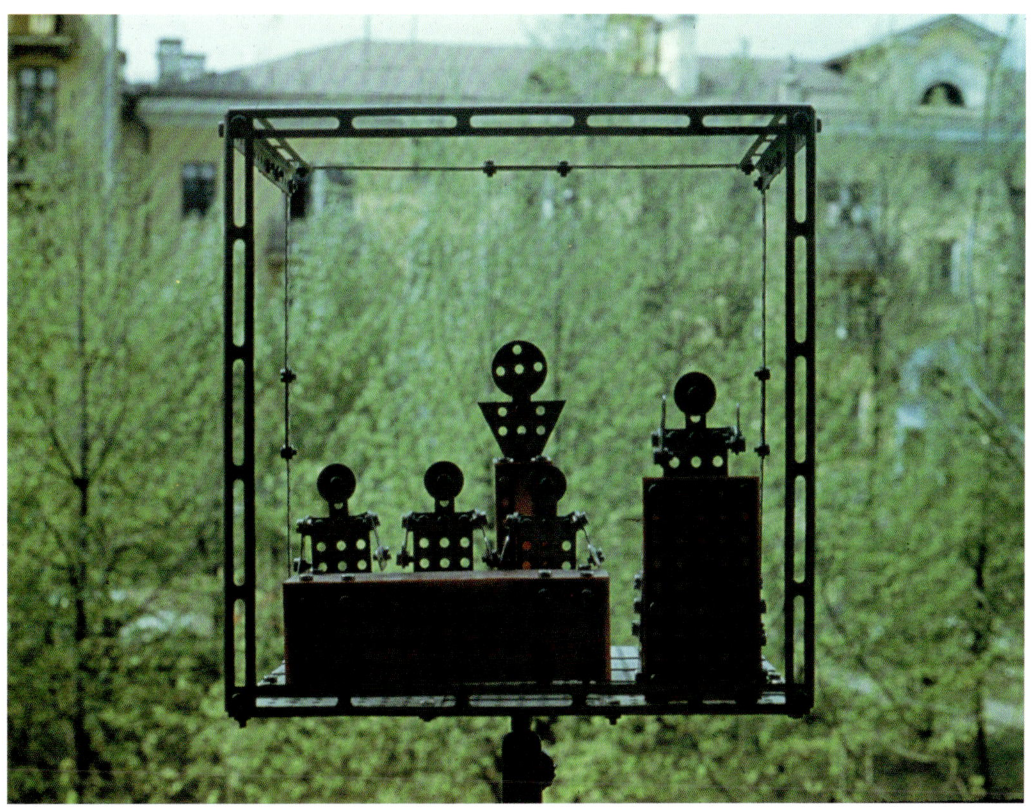

answer inscriptions, which were confined to their Masonite surfaces. Rimma's *Black Square on a White Background* (1975) is black on the outside and white on the inside, internalizing the white background of Malevich's canvas. In her words, "the cube opens like a Suprematist box in which the whiteness equals emptiness."[23] Again, this was a response to Kabakov's use of the color white as a signifier of emptiness, on which Kabakov and Monastyrsky based their conceptual discourse. *Black Square on a White Background* can also be read as a precursory model of Nakhova's *Room No. 3*, which, as I suggested earlier, created the sensation of being inside a black painting, more precisely, Malevich's *Black Square*.

To emphasize the utopian nature of Soviet Constructivism, Valery used children's metal construction sets to build common objects and activities of Soviet life and restage political events such as Communist Party meetings (fig. 192). A similar observation of Constructivism's obsession with formal innovation and transformation of human life can be found in Rimma's *Interchangeable Man* (fig. 193). Assembled from movable cubes with inscriptions like "rational," "queer," "normal," and "superman," the sculpture prompted viewers to restructure and rethink contemporary man.

Publicity and success for *Russian New Wave* was guaranteed by its month-long run at the same time as the exhibition *Art of the Avant-garde in Russia: Selections from the George Costakis Collection*, organized by the Solomon R. Guggenheim Museum. For postwar artists, Costakis's apartment and his collection (fig. 194) played a significant role comparable with that of Peggy Guggenheim for Western artists. It is this linkup with the avant-garde legacy that the participants of *Russian New Wave* wished to highlight by organizing a performance in front of the Guggenheim. The central object of the event was a replica of the Suprematist coffin designed by Malevich and executed by Nicolai Suetin, which the performers placed at the museum's Fifth Avenue entrance.[24] Near the coffin, they held banners saying, "Friends of New Russian Art," recited avant-garde poetry, and lit candles to

observe the "second death of the Russian avant-garde," from commercialization (fig. 195).

Afterwards, the coffin was brought to CRACA, where the performance artist Ann Magnuson invited artists to create a performance involving Malevich's coffin.[25] Aleksandr Driuchin, Kosolapov, Victor Tupitsyn, and Vladimir Urban responded by founding the group Kazimir Passion that staged its first performance on May 2, 1982, at PS1. They presented a mock-Communist Party Congress during which artists, dressed in an eclectic set of outfits (including an Uzbek robe, boxers, a formal suit, and a Trotsky-type military uniform), marched and gave speeches against the background of a propaganda slideshow (fig. 196). Lit in intense red, the stage acquired a transcendental air, intensified by Driuchin wearing a Brezhnev mask and dancing around Malevich's coffin with a hammer and sickle in his hands. Kazimir Passion argued that Soviet culture was a ritualistic rather than aesthetic construct that dominated Soviet society after the death of Malevich in 1935, which had allegorized (and historically coincided with) the eradication of avant-garde consciousness and experimental art. For Kazimir Passion, Malevich's coffin was a symbol of the shift from the ecstasy of the avant-garde to the ecstatic mask of Socialist Realism (fig. 197).

CRACA's *Russian New Wave*, along with these group performances, proved that Moscow vanguardists could succeed in New York only if they acted collectively, within a Russian postmodernist style. Despite its overall foreign subject matter, Sots Art was an obvious candidate for taking on this role, particularly because at the time in New York, other non-Russian artists began to probe Soviet symbols. For example, the Czech artist Milan Kunc in *Pravda Coca Cola* (fig. 198) orchestrated the earliest known collision between Soviet and Western objects of consumption. Francesc Torres's installation "What Is to Be Drunk?" (fig. 199) converted the fundamental, historic Russian question "What Is to Be Done?" (first posed in Nikolai Chernyshevsky's novel of 1863, and later in Lenin's key political text of 1901,

OPPOSITE PAGE 193   Rimma Gerlovin's *Interchangeable Man* in the exhibition *Russian New Wave* (CRACA), New York, 1981.

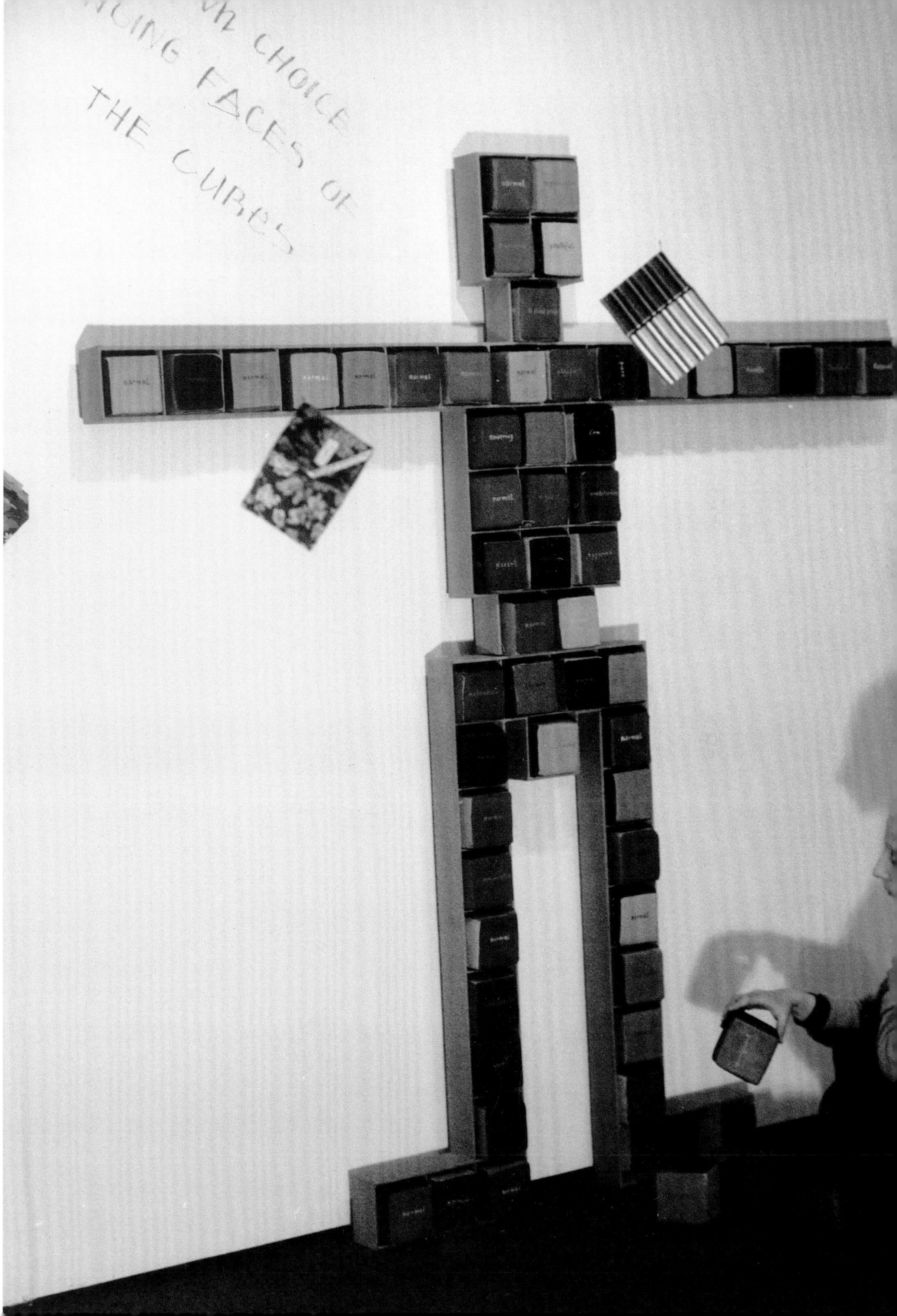

...vn CHOICE
...ING FACES OF
THE CUBES

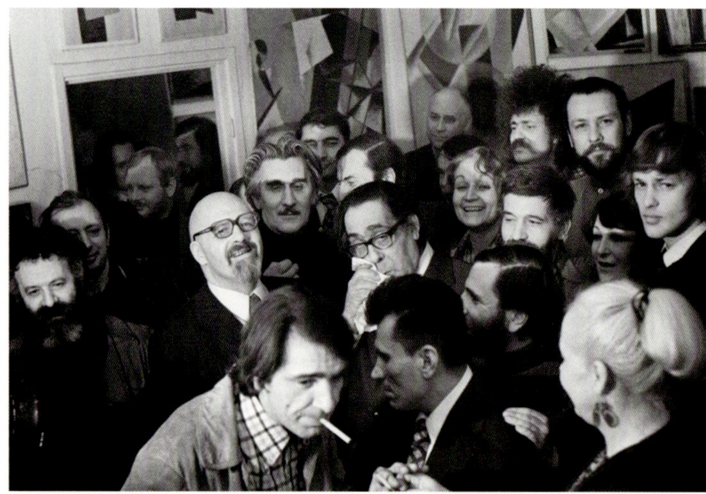

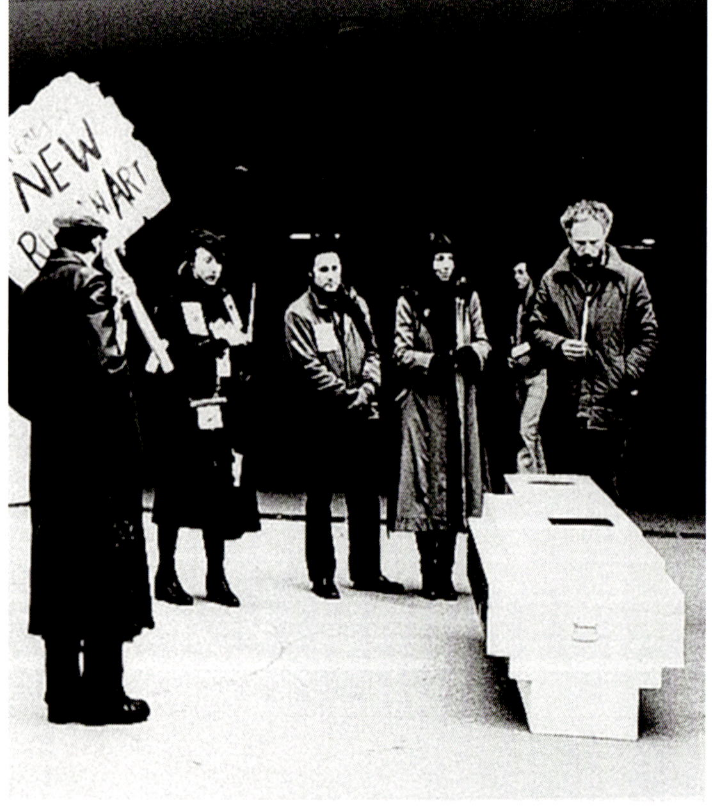

194   Nonconformist artists in the apartment of the collector George Costakis, Moscow, March 19, 1977.

195   Performance in front of the Solomon R. Guggenheim Museum during the exhibition *Art of the Avant-garde in Russia: Selections from George Costakis Collection*, December 1981, New York.

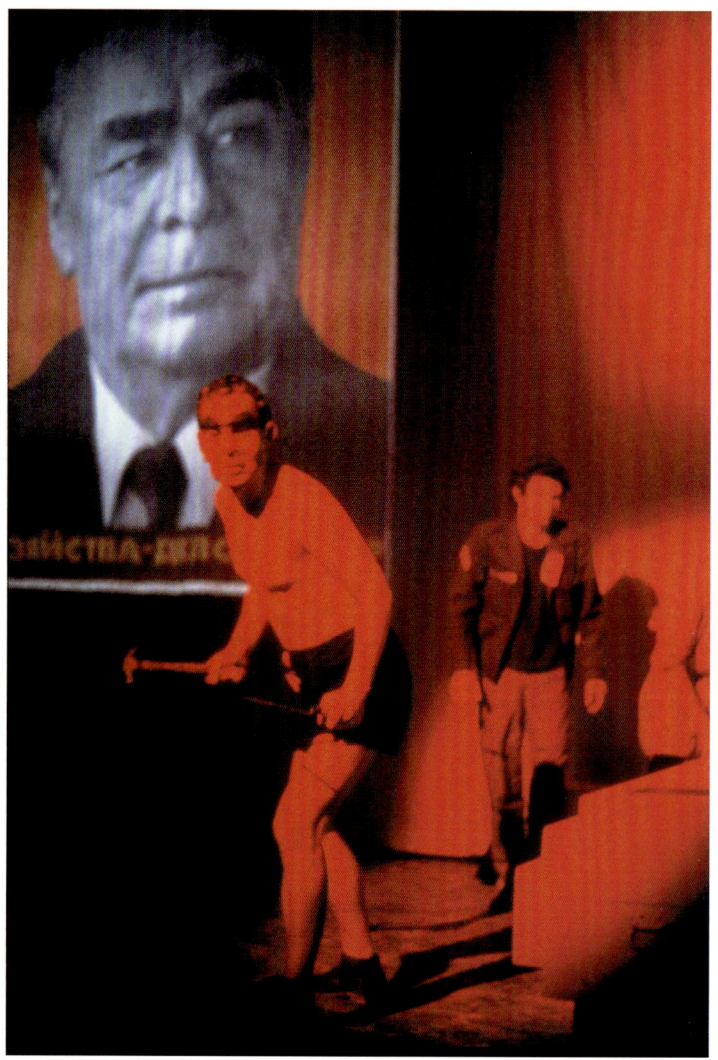

196   Kazimir Passion Group, *Communist Party Congress* at PS1, New York, May 2, 1982.

both of the same title) into a parody on Russia's heavy drinking culture.[26]

Unwilling to unite with other Sots artists into a movement,[27] Komar and Melamid responded to this dissemination of Sots Art practices with an exhibition, *Sots Art*, which opened on September 25, 1982 at the Ronald Feldman gallery (fig. 200). In the gallery, the lights were dimmed to set off the large, dramatically lit canvases executed in an academic style that imitated official Soviet and classical painting. Swags of drapery, columniated architecture, and Greek muses were combined with a veritable who's who of the Krem-

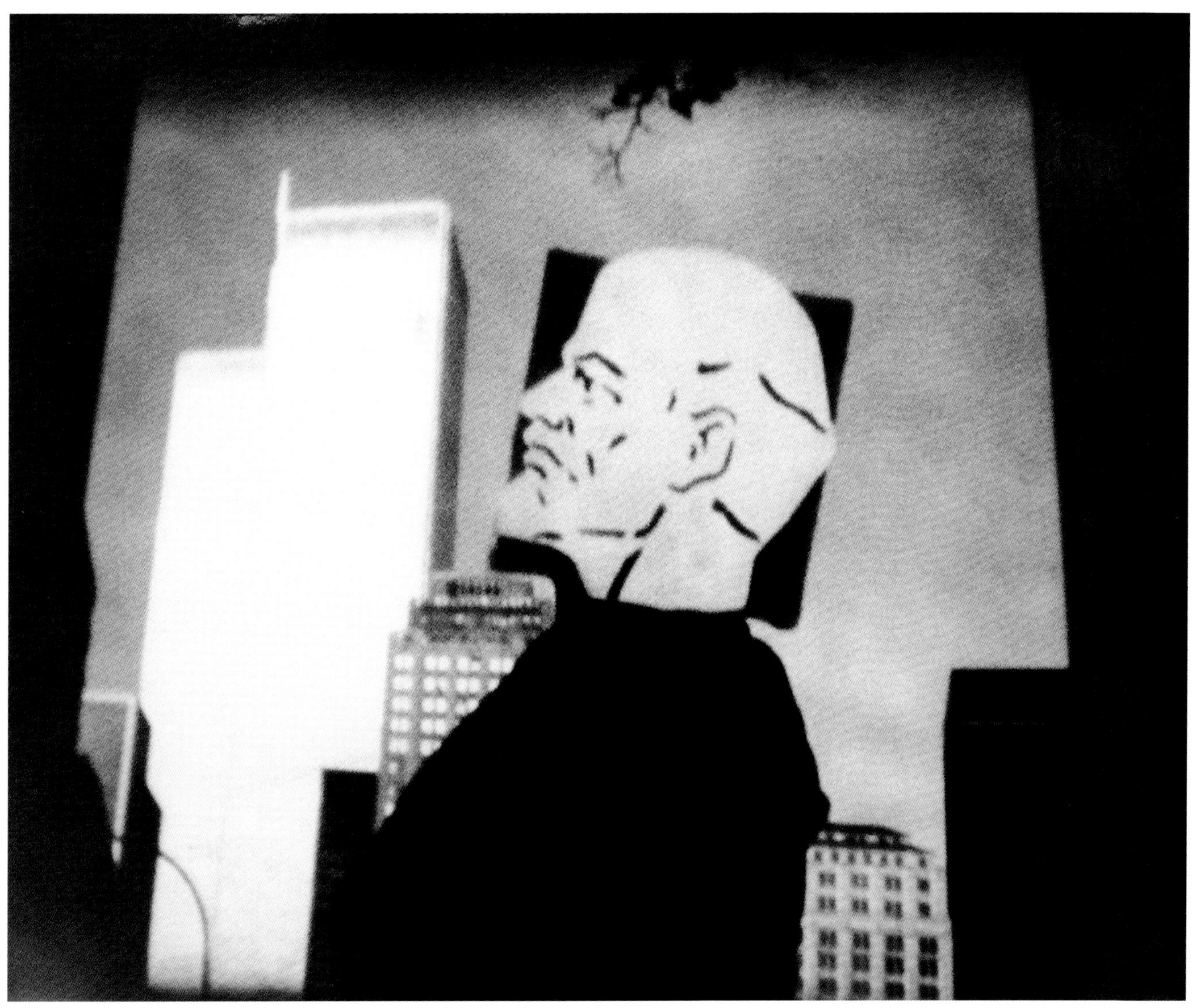

197   Kazimir Passion Group, still from the film *Lenin in New York*, 1982.

lin – Lenin, Stalin, and Khrushchev – resulting in jolting Brechtian alienation. Although a high degree of parody remained Komar and Melamid's principal device, the formal tools they had employed back in Moscow were abandoned. These are photography (here employed only to execute paintings), "utilitarian" painting (which ignored technical and aesthetic skill), the use of a readymade, and semantic analysis of the mechanisms of propaganda. Overall, their earlier broad range of formal, cultural, and political issues (extending beyond the Soviet context) was supplanted by an exclusive concentration on the Stalin empire. Being the only sculpture in the show, their bust of Stalin further emphasized this point.

The *Sots Art* exhibition included *Stalin and Muses* (1982), in which a jovial Stalin approves the unity between traditional and proletarian culture. The four muses welcome the new deity as well, validating his mythical status and endowing him with a high position in the representational hierarchy. In *Lenin Proclaims the Victory of the Revolution* (fig. 201), Komar and Melamid create their own version of Vladimir Serov's

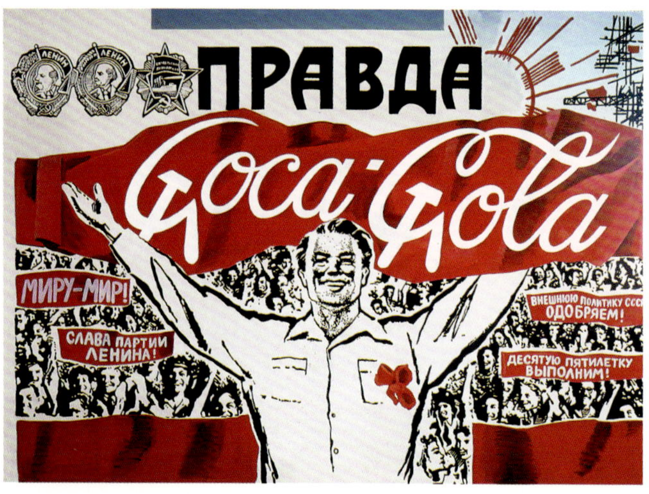

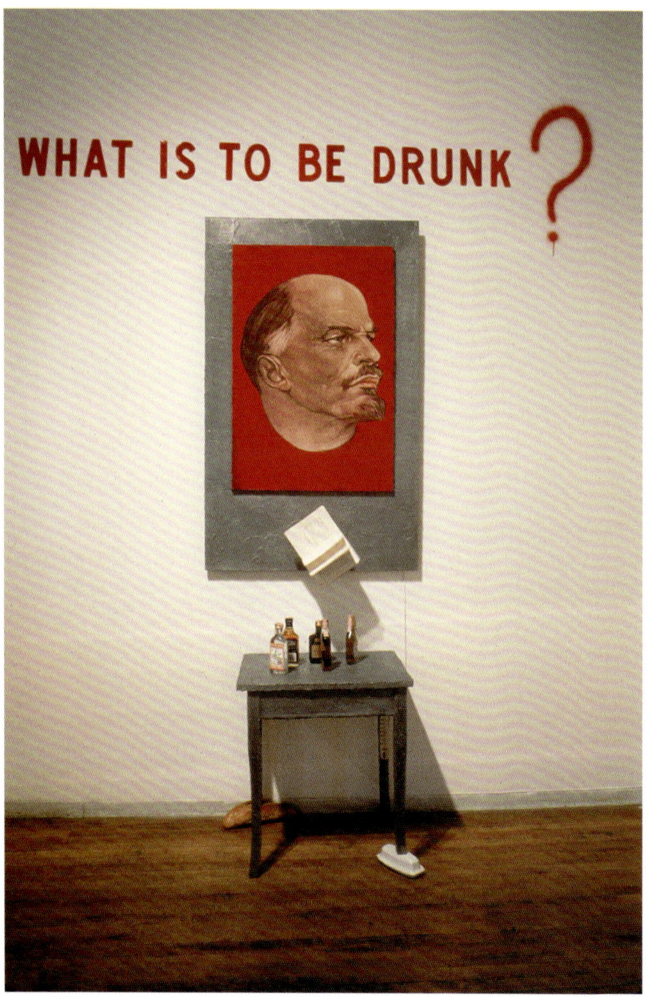

198   Milan Kunc, *Pravda Coca Cola*, 1978.

199   Francesc Torres, *What Is to Be Drunk?*, 1980.

painting of this subject (titled *Lenin Proclaims the Victory of Soviet Power*), which he executed twice to reflect different political climates and official adjustments of Soviet history. The first version, painted in 1947 at the height of Stalin's repressive rule and MOSSKh's unlimited power, includes Stalin standing behind Lenin during his speech. Serov repainted it in the late 1950s, removing Stalin in response to Khrushchev's denunciation of the cult of personality. In their canvas, Komar and Melamid reinserted Stalin by painting his figure in grisaille, alluding to photography's role in censoring official representations. Further, they demonstrated that, regardless of Soviet leaders' unlimited power at the time of their rule, their place in history is never secure. *Sots Art*'s subtitle, "Nostalgic Socialist Realism," positioned Komar and Melamid's new work as historical and biographical, rather than political. "To us, Stalin is a mythical figure," they insisted, in accordance with classical stories conceived to interpret the foundation of Socialist Realism. "We are not trying to do a political show. This is nostalgia."[28]

In their next exhibition at the Ronald Feldman gallery, *Business as Usual* (January 7–February 11, 1984), Komar and Melamid increased the nostalgia and created more intimate and sexually suggestive plots, which crossed the barrier of Andrei Zhdanov's "antisexual aesthetics." Here, in *Stalin in Front of the Mirror* (1982–3), even Stalin is caught in a moment of narcissistic admiration of his reflection. Komar and Melamid's *Origin of Socialist Realism* (fig. 202) pairs well with *Stalin and Muses* as it depicts Stalin in uniform next to a seminaked redheaded muse who is rendering his portrait as a shadow. That is the form that Stalin loathed so much that it is alleged that he damned Sergei Eisenstein's *Ivan the Terrible* for its excessive use of shadows.

Simultaneously with *Business as Usual*, the SoHo Semaphore gallery presented a group exhibition, *Sots Art: Russian Mock-heroic Style* (January 4–28), that cemented Sots Art as a movement in both Moscow and New York (fig. 203).[29] Among the exhibits were Kosolapov's *Perseus: The Assassination of Trotsky by Stalin* (1983), for which he joined his earlier strategy of presenting Soviet culture and history through myth and allegory with Komar and Melamid's academic

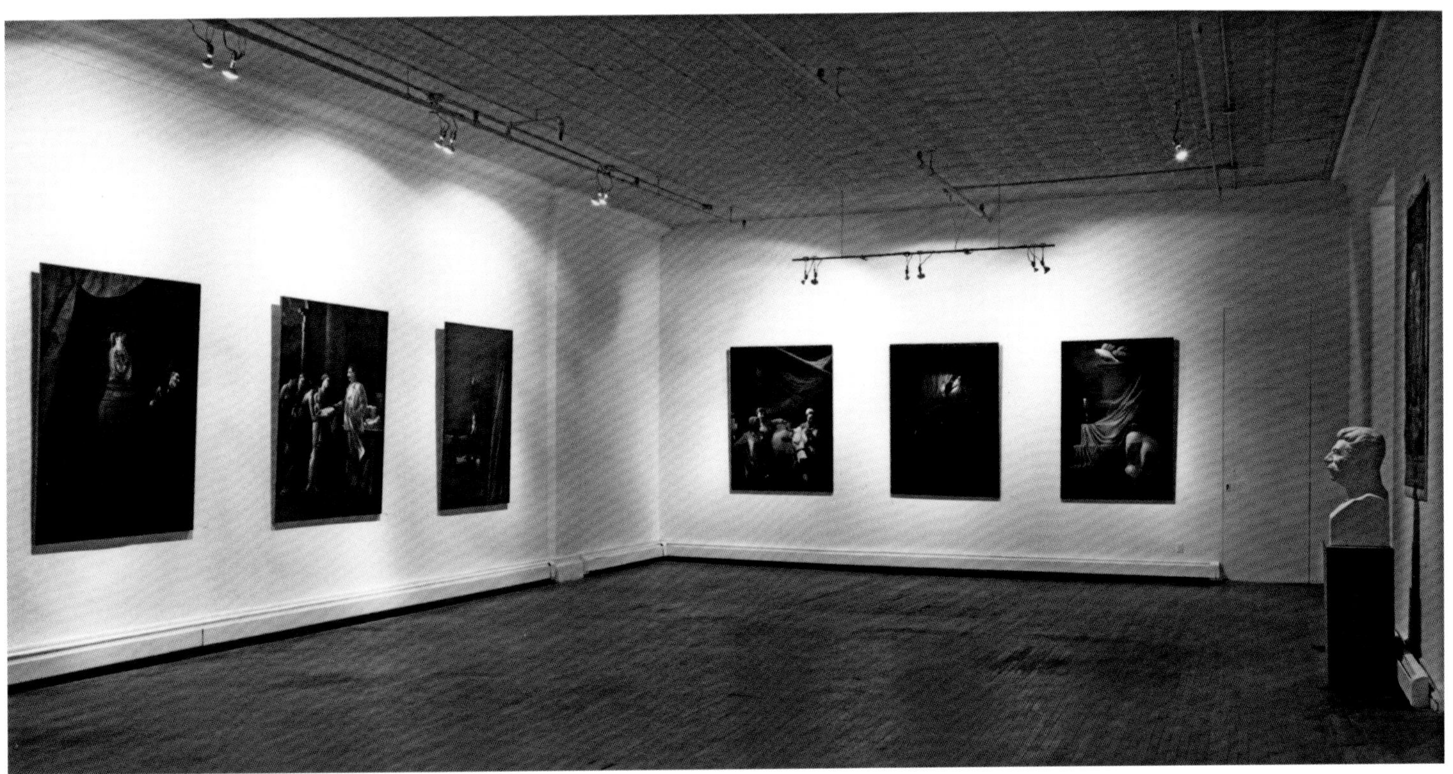

200   Installation view of Komar and Melamid's exhibition *Sots Art*, Ronald Feldman Fine Arts, New York, 1982.

painting style. In this work, Kosolapov replaced Stalin's plot to assassinate Trotsky in 1940 with the Greek myth of Perseus beheading Medusa. The parallel is decodable only through the title, and, as with René Magritte's paintings, the incongruity of word and image jolts the viewer.

In contrast to Komar and Melamid and Kosolapov's use of academicism as a deconstructive tool, Sokov remained true to his earlier rough and primitive techniques. His series, *History of the USSR: Leaders (1983–84)*, includes Andropov, Brezhnev, Khrushchev, Stalin, and Hitler – all movable pieces that confirm his revolt against pompous and monumental official representations – with which he establishes a carnivalesque atmosphere. For example, in the statue of Brezhnev, if one pushes down on Brezhnev's head, oversized genitals, concealed behind a speaking podium, become exposed (fig. 204).

Next to these heavy doses of parody and allegory, Bulatov's "enigmatic" canvas, *Danger* (see fig. 94), came across as a political statement reinforced by the word "Danger" inserted into a naturalistic landscape. In a review in *Artnews*, Bulatov's canvas was described as an example of "the disjunction between facts and words in Soviet culture." The same critic admitted that "what was surprising was that none of this work exhibited the bitterness that marks the also arguably political art of the new German expressionists."[30] Another reviewer similarly concluded that Semaphore's pairing of "wit" and serious content was "an impressive combination."[31] These two comments regarding Sots artists' reading of history are significant because it is precisely for their obsession with comic obscenity that they were criticized by Marxist art critics and art historians. This has resulted, for example, in no Sots artists being credited along with German artists for the renewal of history painting.[32] Yet, as Slavoj Žižek, also a Marxist scholar, has pointed out in relation to the Stalinist show trials, in them "there is a horror so deep that it can no longer be 'sublimated' into tragic

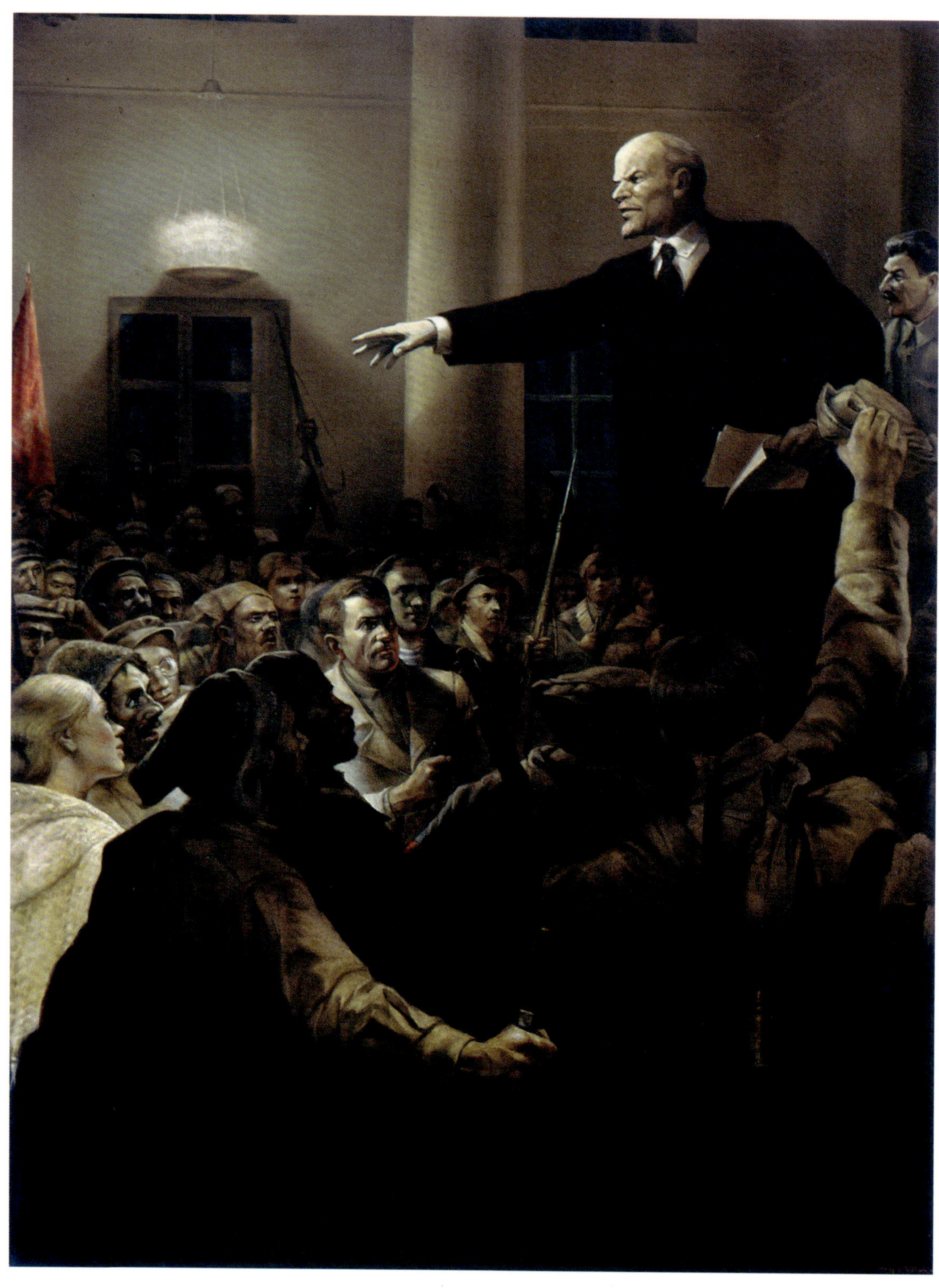

201   Vitaly Komar and Aleksandr Melamid, *Lenin Proclaims the Victory of the Revolution* (after first version by Vladimir Serov, 1947), 1981–2. Collection of Robert and Maryse Boxer, London.

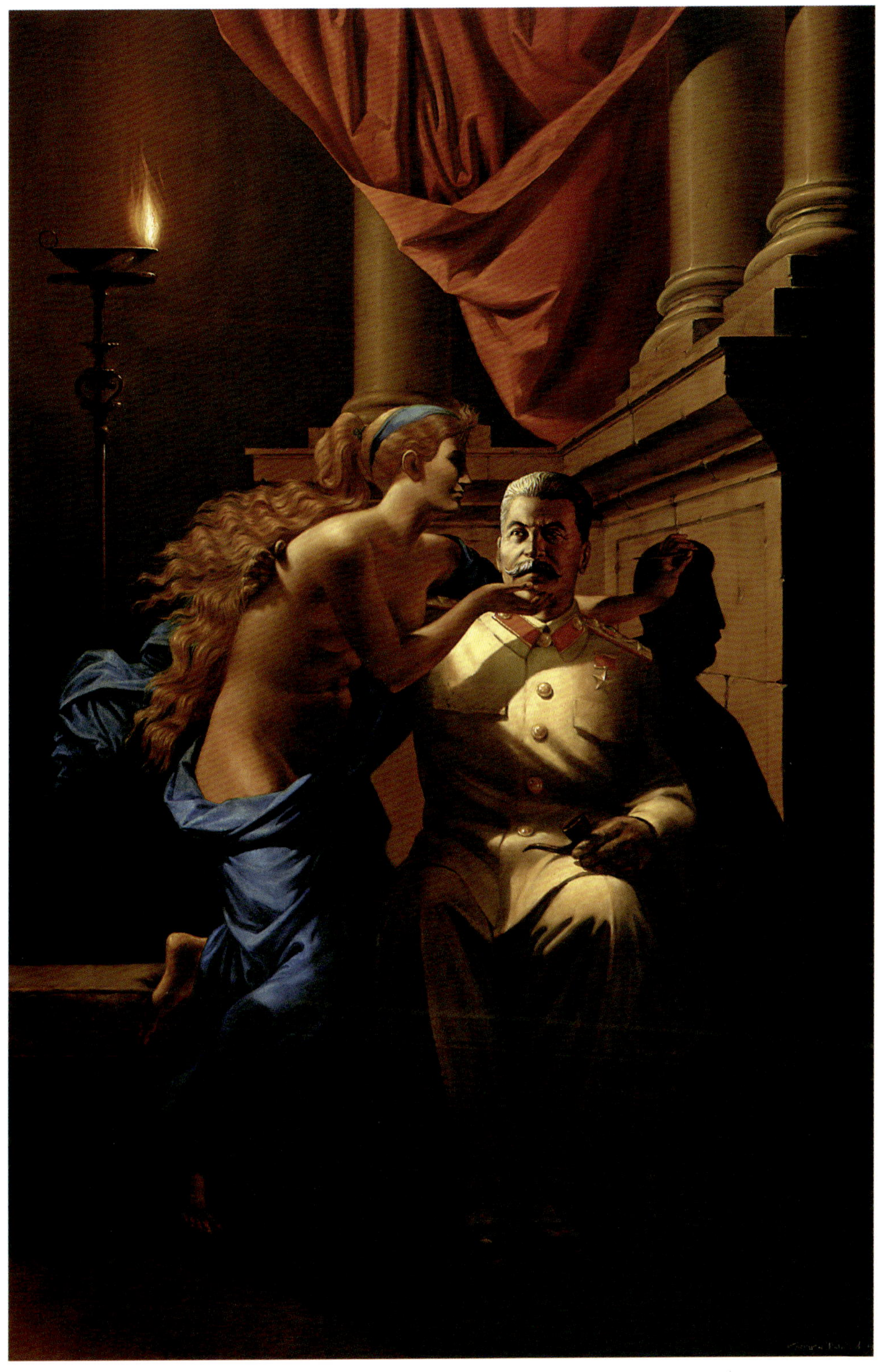

202 Vitaly Komar and Aleksandr Melamid, *The Origin of Socialist Realism*, 1982–3. Norton and Nancy Dodge Collection of Nonconformist Art from the Soviet Union, Jane Voorhees Zimmerli Art Museum Rutgers, State University of New Jersey.

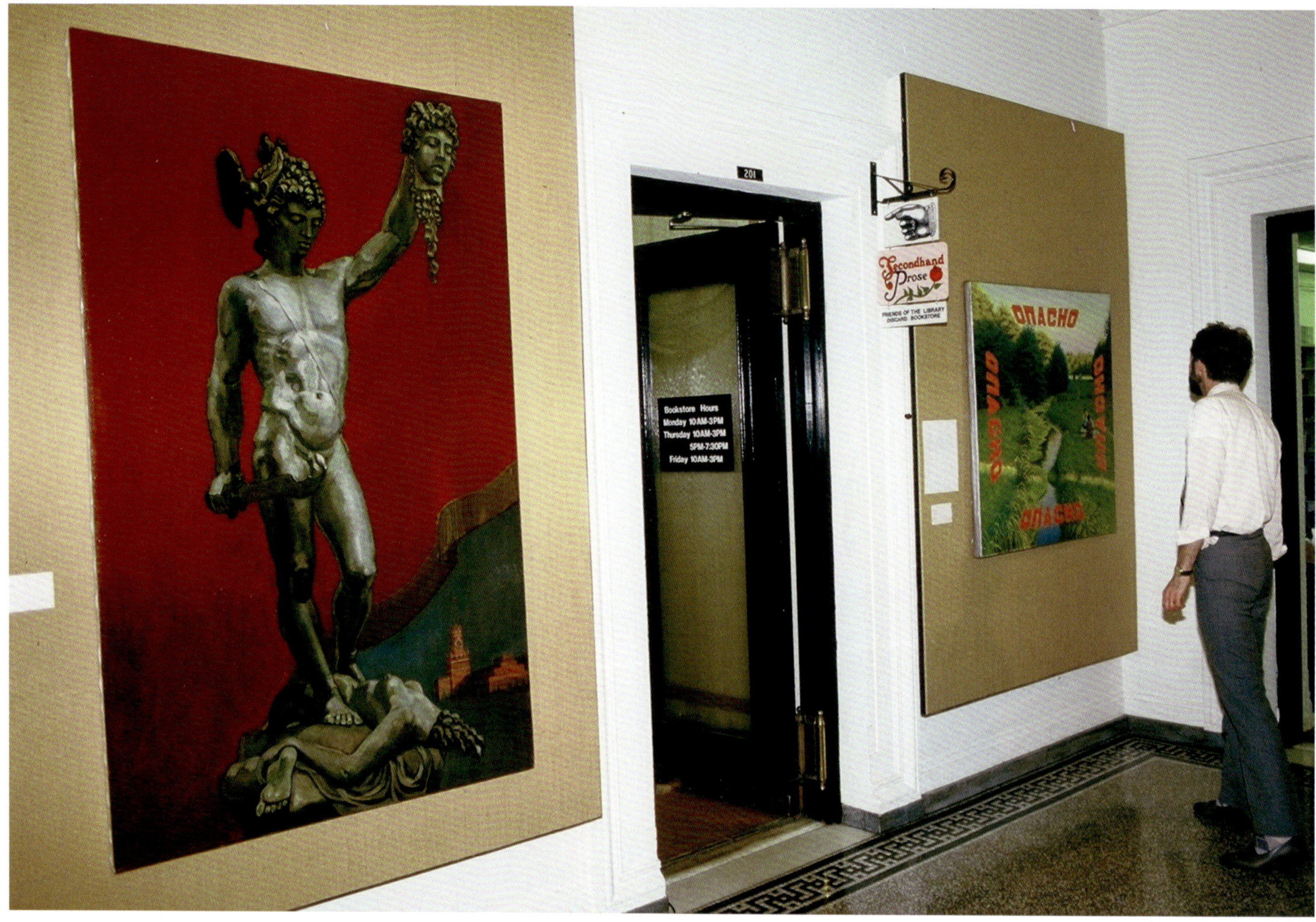

203   Installation view of *Sots Art: Russian Mock-heroic Style*, Semaphore Gallery, New York, 1984, with Aleksandr Kosolapov's *Perseus: The Assassination of Trotsky by Stalin*, 1983 (left) and Erik Bulatov's *Danger*, 1972.

dignity, and for that reason is approachable only through an eerie imitation/doubling of the parody itself."[33] That is exactly what Sots artists did in their history paintings.

Finally, after the Semaphore exhibition, Sots Art was being discussed in the Western press as a movement rather than an individual style associated exclusively with Komar and Melamid. This new critical consensus opened up the possibility of organizing the first museum exhibition of the Moscow vanguard in New York. *Sots Art* opened at the New Museum of Contemporary Art on April 12, 1986 (figs. 205, 206) with an expanded version of *Sots Art: Russian*

Mock-heroic Style. The Moscow Sots Art section benefited greatly from the arrival of Bulatov's major paintings, which included *Krasikov Street, Two Landscapes on the Background of a Red Banner*, and a rare entirely textual canvas, *Stop, Go* (1975). In many of the works at the New Museum, Socialist Realism remained the subject of nostalgic, historical, and allegorical constructs, resulting in a discourse that "borrows from a heritage the resources necessary for the deconstruction of that heritage itself."[34] More than any other Sots artist, Komar and Melamid continued to scrutinize Socialist Realism, measuring its strategies against those of Modernism. In this respect, their installation *Art*

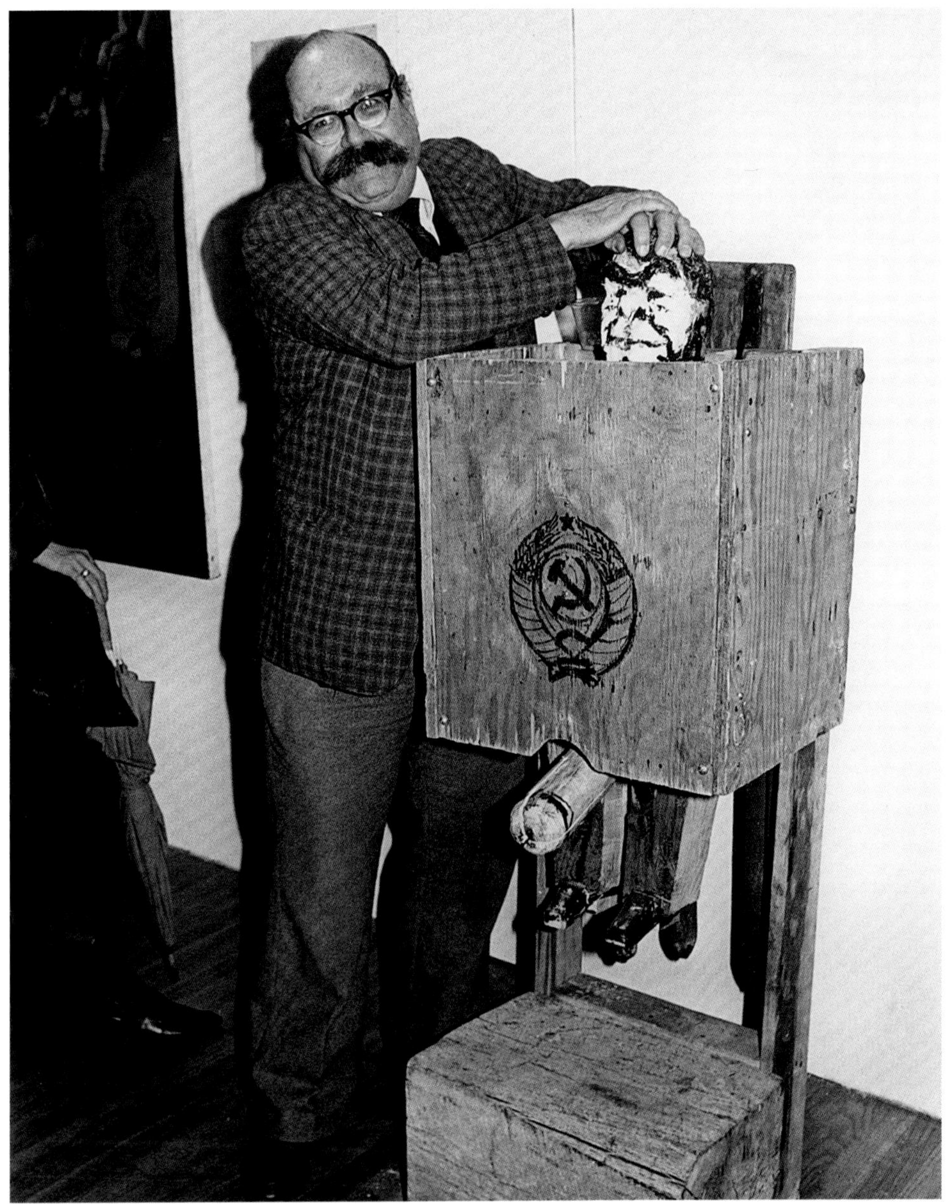

204   The collector Norton Dodge with Leonid Sokov's *Portrait of Brezhnev*, 1983 at the opening of *Sots Art: Russian Mock-heroic Style*, Semaphore Gallery, New York, 1984.

Belongs to the People (1984) commented on the binary opposition between Modernism and kitsch by referencing Clement Greenberg and earlier debates that took place in Western and Soviet critical circles in the 1920s and 1930s. The central piece of *Art Belongs to the People* was an oversized horizontal canvas executed by a group of friends during a performance staged by Komar and Melamid at The Kitchen on March 16,

1984 (fig. 207). The assignment was to depict John Hinckley's assassination attempt on President Reagan in Socialist Realist style. But because the amateur artists proceeded to paint in the style of Abstract Expressionism, the resulting canvas appeared to be saying that Socialist Realism and Modernism were equally guilty of distorting reality – the former by buckling under censorship and idealizing reality for

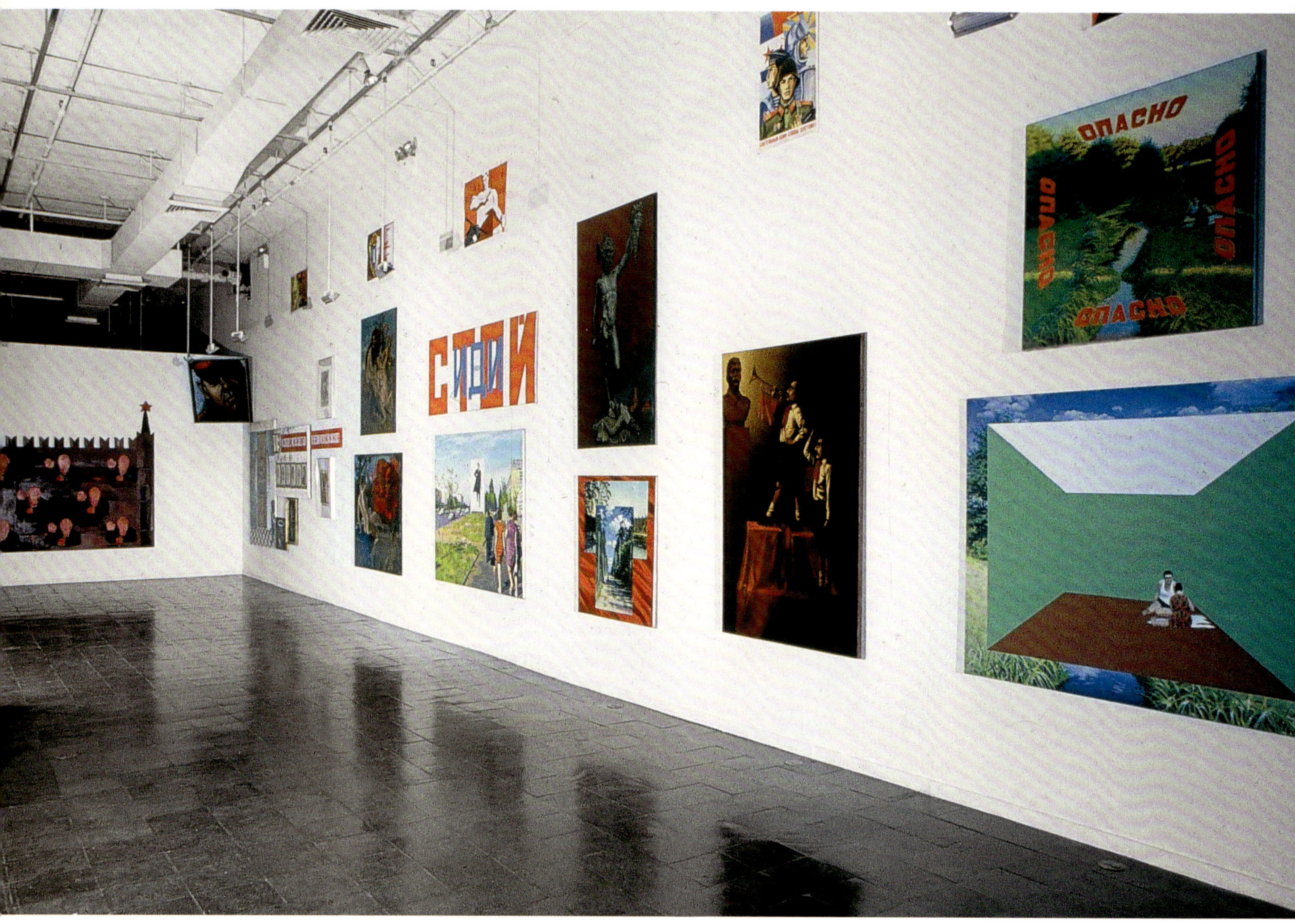

ABOVE 205 Installation view, *Sots Art,* New Museum of Contemporary Art, New York, 1986.

OPPOSITE PAGE TOP 206 Installation view, *Sots Art,* New Museum of Contemporary Art, New York, 1986.

OPPOSITE PAGE BOTTOM 207 Vitaly Komar and Aleksandr Melamid, *Art Belongs to the People* performance at The Kitchen, New York, March 16, 1984.

the benefit of the collective; the latter by heroizing individuality and the pursuit of creative freedom.

Kosolapov's installation, *Symbols of the Century,* propelled Sots Art into a critique of global corporations. In a poster, *Lenin-Coca-Cola* (1982), he assigned authorship of the American brand's famous slogan, "it's the real thing," to the architect of the Bolshevik Revolution. This is an example of double deconstruction, for it erased the differences between ideological and consumerist propaganda. Infuriated by the compromising juxtaposition, Coca-Cola threatened Kosolapov with legal action, but failed to stop him from exhibiting his image (fig. 208). The opening in the early days of perestroika of a McDonald's in the center of Moscow (January 31, 1990) made Kosolapov's *Symbols of the Century* a forecast of global corporations' infiltration

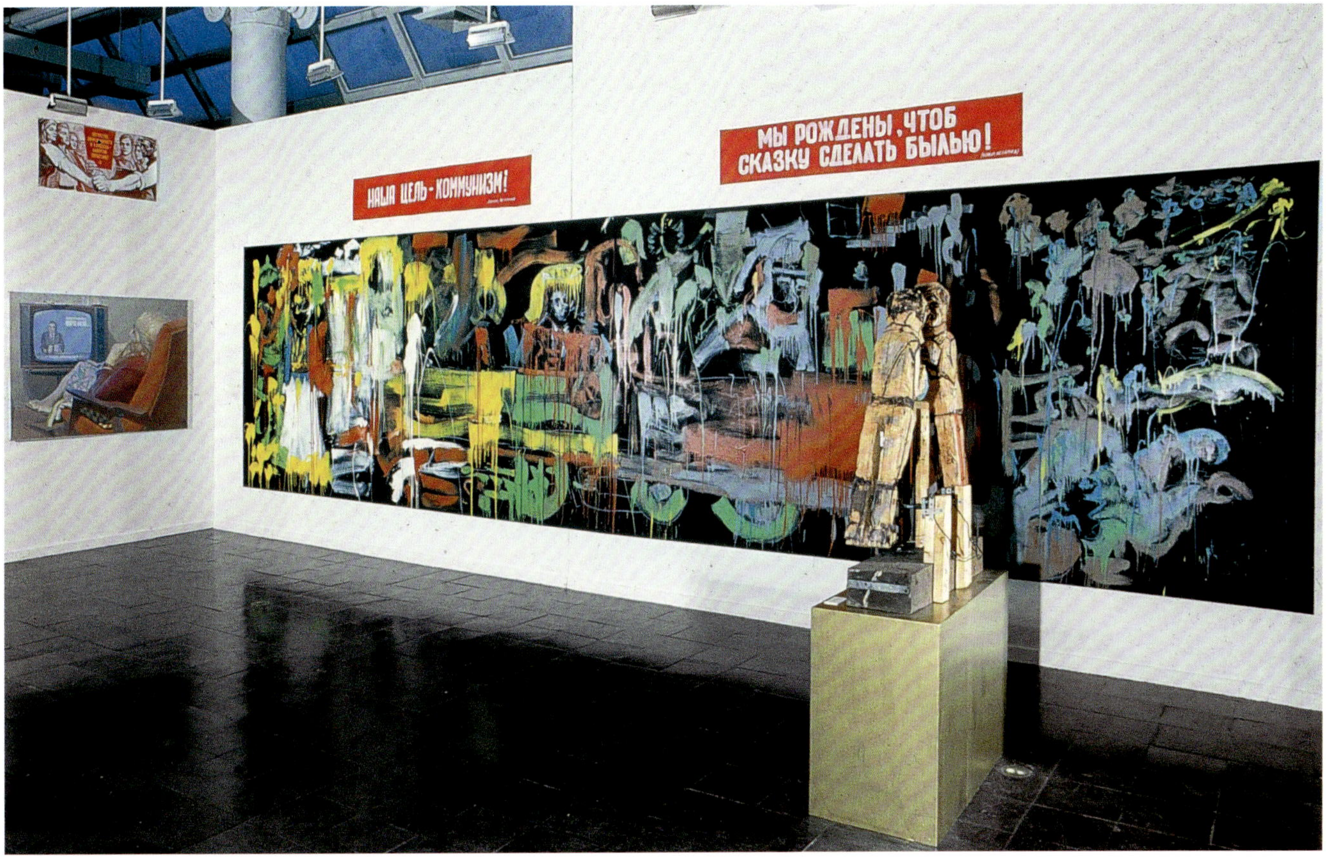

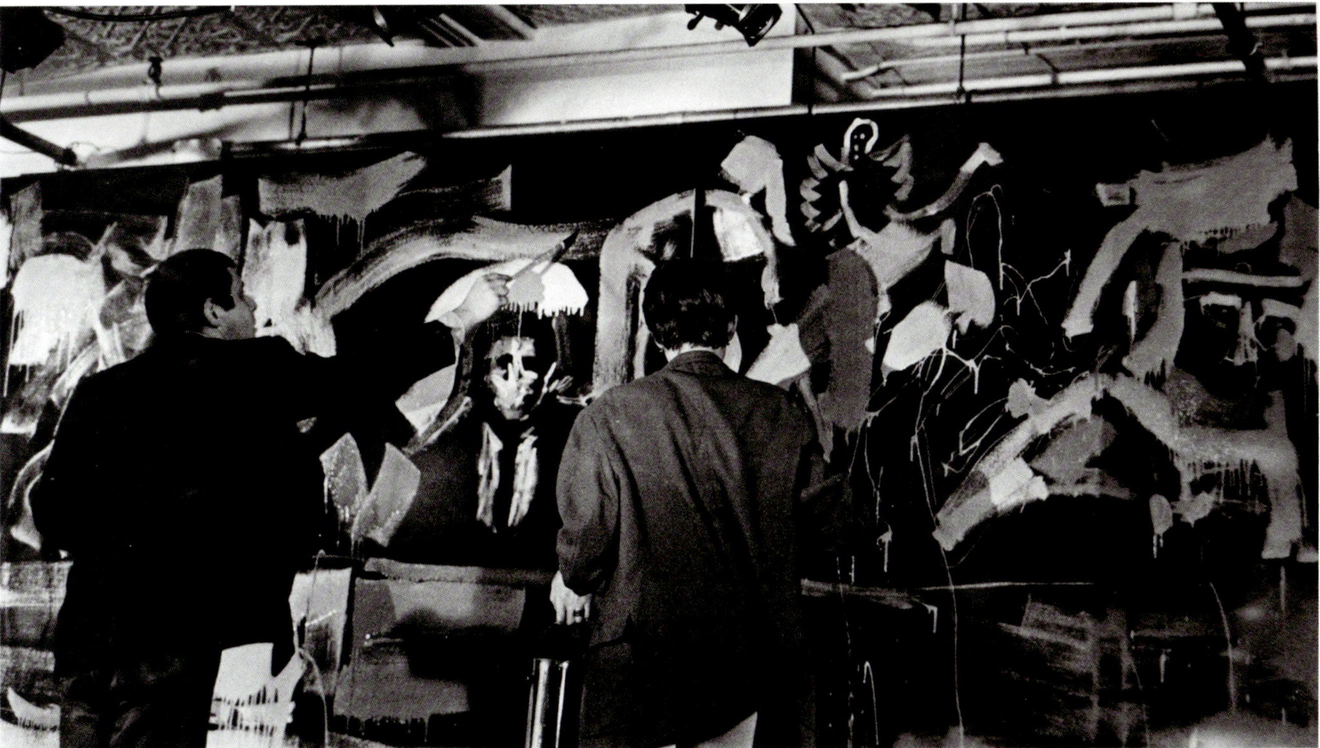

НАША ЦЕЛЬ - КОММУНИЗМ!
МЫ РОЖДЕНЫ, ЧТОБ СКАЗКУ СДЕЛАТЬ БЫЛЬЮ!

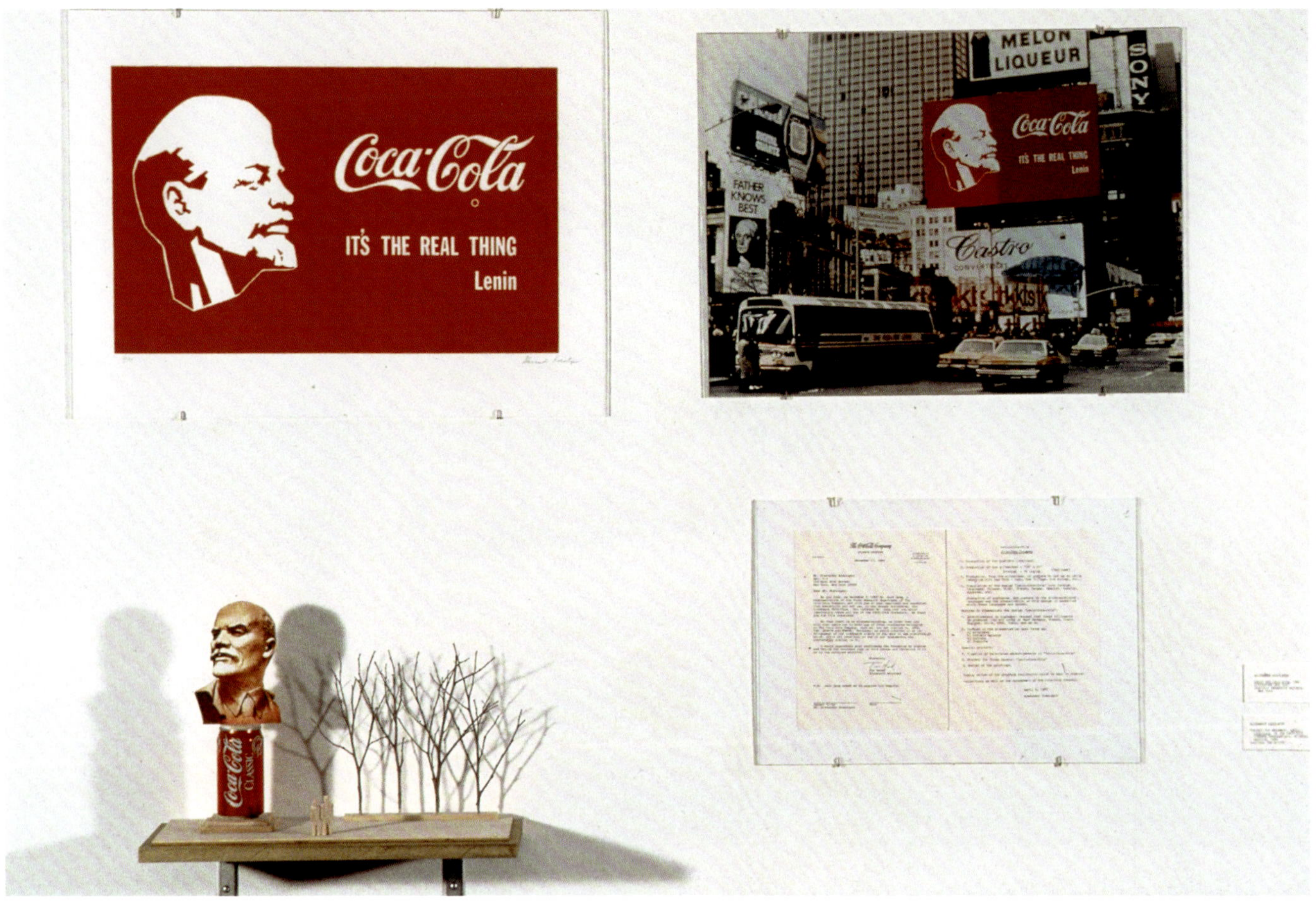

208   Installation by Aleksandr Kosolapov, *Sots Art*, New Museum of Contemporary Art, New York, 1986.

of the socialist economy prior to its official collapse. The accessibility of the fast food chain generated a queue comparable only to the lines formed to visit the Lenin Mausoleum, as Soviets, equipped with their under-the-mattress cash, awaited their first American junk-food experience. On the opening day, a massive population of around 30,000 waved red flags on which the McDonald's logo had seamlessly replaced Lenin's famous profile. Moreover, in view of current trade between capitalist countries and communist China, and Chinese artists' use of the Sots Art device of splicing capitalist and communist icons of mass persuasion, Kosolapov's montage *Lenin-Coca-Cola* only gains in historical significance.

At the time of the *Sots Art* exhibition, the New Museum was a magnet for all New York artists associated with political art. Thus there could not have been a more appropriate institution for the Moscow underground artists collectively to reach out to the international art community with their models of political and institutional resistance. However, a conversation with the Polish artist Krzysztof Wodiczko, conducted for *October* magazine shortly after the opening of *Sots Art*, revealed that left critics and artists were not prepared to embrace Soviet counterculture as a successor to the Russian avant-garde that they admired, and affiliated more with the practices of American neo-avant-garde such as Minimalism.[35] While briefly discussing the exhibition, the participants in the conversation paid no attention to Bulatov's contradistinctive paradigm of Sots Art and failed to address the affinities in the expositional strategies of the members of Apt Art and of the Group Material, though both collectives were exhibited at the same

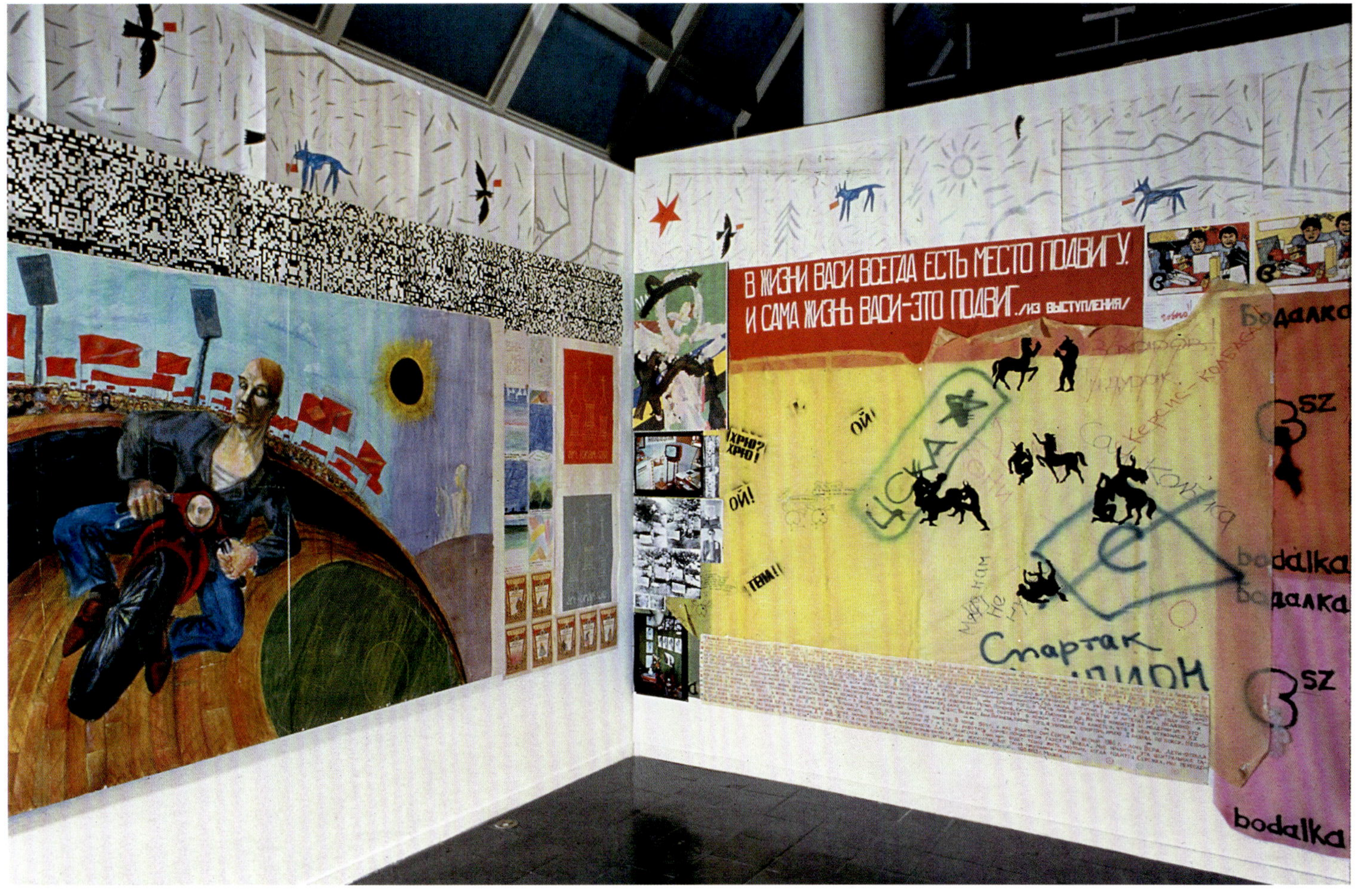

209   *Apt Art Exhibition*, New Museum of Contemporary Art, New York, 1986. Recreated by Victor Tupitsyn.

time as *Sots Art* (fig. 209). Instead, the discussion zoomed in on a critique of Komar and Melamid, diverting attention from Sots Art's broader significance. The participants in the conversation squabbled about the New Museum "relegat[ing] the critique of bourgeois culture…[to] the small, back space while giving much greater prominence to the art which purports to be a critique of Soviet society,"[36] and accused Komar and Melamid of cynicism, "political nihilism," and the failure to be "clearly critical of either system."[37] Wodiczko, whose political montages projected onto various public buildings were the main topic of conversation, expressed his objection to Komar and Melamid's "pop-art versions of Socialist Realism…I question the political clarity and social effectiveness of adopting pop-art strategies for the critique of Soviet culture," he remarked.[38] Was, then, Warhol's *Red Lenin*, made in 1987, a year after the *Sots Art* show in the New Museum, an endorsement of the very method Wodiczko had ruled out? Or was it Warhol's way of showing that, indeed, in the hands of a Pop artist, communist imagery becomes devoid of effective politics? After all, *Red Lenin* was made from a photograph that had been modified by censors before being sent to the West in 1948 by the Soviet press agency.[39] With these questions raised by the *Sots Art* exhibition, Komar and Melamid's decade-old query, *Where Is the Line Between Us?*, only gained in urgency, and Nest's appeal to the other side of the globe to "become one meter closer" had plenty of digging to do.

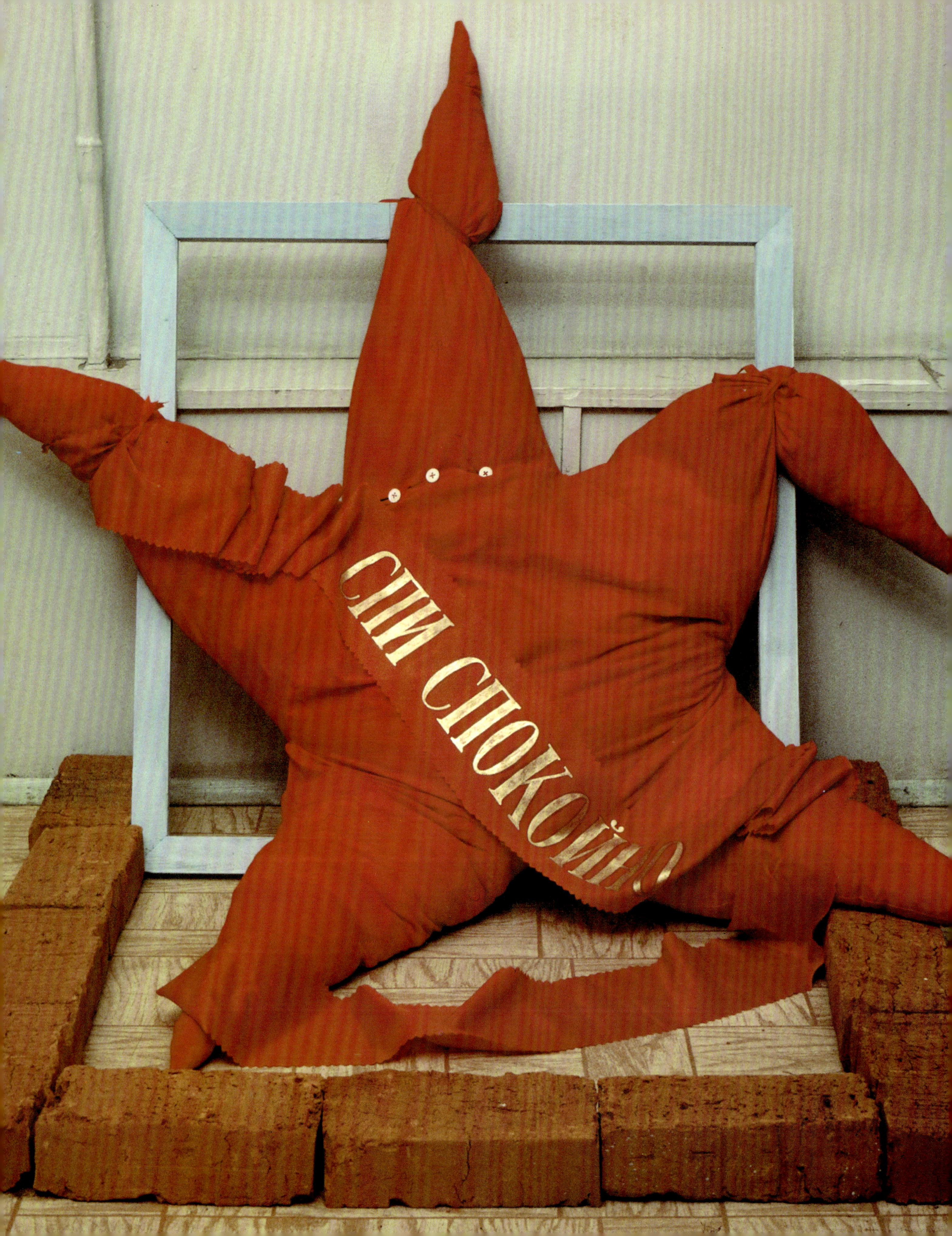
СПИ СПОКОЙНО

7

THE WORK OF ART IN THE AGE OF PERESTROIKA

At the height of Brezhnev's political and cultural stagnation, Oleg Vasiliev painted *Ogonek No. 25* (fig. 210), a reproduction of a Soviet magazine cover with the same name. Vasiliev added beams of light that obscure the original image of a Politburo meeting with a speaker at a podium. At the time only a radical fantasy about political change, *Ogonek No. 25* turned out to have prophesied Mikhail Gorbachev's historic disruption of predictable and confirmatory Politburo speeches, when he announced the new age of glasnost and perestroika at the Twenty-seventh Party Congress in 1986. This was thirty years after Khrushchev had denounced Stalin at the Twentieth Congress, and launched the "thaw" that was instrumental in the formation of postwar vanguard culture. Although Gorbachev's liberation campaign had no plans for dismantling the Communist Party – rather, a hybrid regime akin to today's China was planned – the freedom that transpired during his reign was irreversible. The irreparable loss of the epistemology of Communism is amply expressed in Andrei Fillipov's

installation *The Last Supper* (fig. 211), in which a red-clothed table is set with twelve white plates, along with hammers and sickles in place of forks and knives. Fillipov's *Last Supper* is also an icon for the new age of Moscow vanguard art, which was associated with the accessibility of the Western art world.

The harassment of vanguard artists was almost immediately brought to a halt and the rigidity of exhibition policies crumbled. Vladimir Mironenko's painting (later turned into an installation), *The Room of Protest* (fig. 212), which depicts a sealed black door labeled "the room of protest," epitomized underground art's committment to never again live or create under restriction. Nikita Alekseev, a veteran of artists' conflicts with authorities, conveyed the atmosphere of this swift democratization, in a letter of April 1987 that I quote at length for its first-hand witness:

What is going on now [in Moscow] is very interesting and has never been seen before, not even during the days of Khrushchev. As far as art is

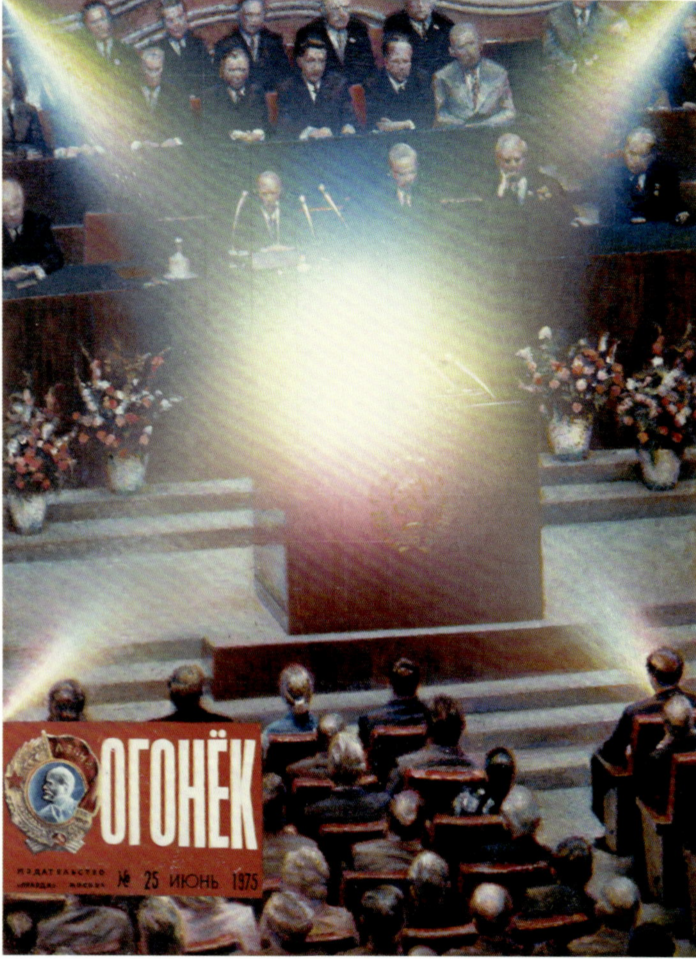

210   Oleg Vasiliev, *Ogonek No. 25*, 1980. Norton and Nancy Dodge Collection of Nonconformist Art from the Soviet Union, Jane Voorhees Zimmerli Art Museum Rutgers, State University of New Jersey.

concerned, there have been many changes. There is virtually no such thing now as unsanctioned art. Practically anybody can exhibit – with a few exceptions, of course. Prior to New Year's there was an exhibition of young artists on Kuznetsky Most, where everyone hung works[1]...The exhibition broke all attendance records. In February and March there was a large show in the regional exhibition hall on Kashirsky Highway where all of the "old guard" participated. In addition, there were constant poetry readings and other kinds of activities. [Dmitry] Prigov, who just a few years ago, was harassed by the KGB for his poetry, recited it before

a large audience (fig. 213). You have probably heard about the new act which gives Soviet citizens the right to organize "special interest clubs" for spending "leisure time" in a "healthy fashion," like growing cactuses, sewing, learning computer programming, jogging in the morning, etc. Well, [Leonid] Bazhanov organized the "Hermitage Society" and mustered all the best forces (I was a member of the council), and set himself the task of founding the Moscow Museum of Contemporary Art, for which he obtained a space of 5000 square meters and 150,000 rubles repairs.[2] Sven [Gundlakh] and [Sergei] Anufriev acted in simpler fashion. They found an exhibition hall somewhere in the Avtozavodskaia area, negotiated with the director, went to the city cultural section, and explained the following: "You've already given permission to everyone from special interest clubs, even heavy metalists with their studded jackets have one, but we avant-gardists, following the footsteps of Beuys and Warhol, what are we, worse or something? Accept us or else we'll kick up a fuss in your doorways again!" The officials scratched their heads and granted permission. The Club of Avant-gardists was formed...a fantastic set of rules was drawn up, having as its goal the dissemination of ideas [fig. 214].[3]

The rhetoric that Gundlakh and Anufriev employed to persuade local authorities to grant them permission for the use of exhibition spaces imitated the language of hooliganism with which they had often been charged by officials in the past. Members of the Club of Avant-gardists further tested perestroika's limits in January 1988, when they organized both an exhibition and a performance in the men-only part of the historic Sandunovsky Baths. Works of various media, by dozens of artists, were hung in the late nineteenth-century neoclassical interior with a columniated swimming pool (fig. 215).[4] During the opening, at which women were not allowed, some of the participants swam in the pool while others observed the scene from above. At the time, I was visiting Moscow for the first time since immigrating to the U.S.A. in the winter of 1975, and the event's organizer, Joseph Bakshtein, sneaked me in to see the works installed in the niches of a colonnade. In the visitor book, most

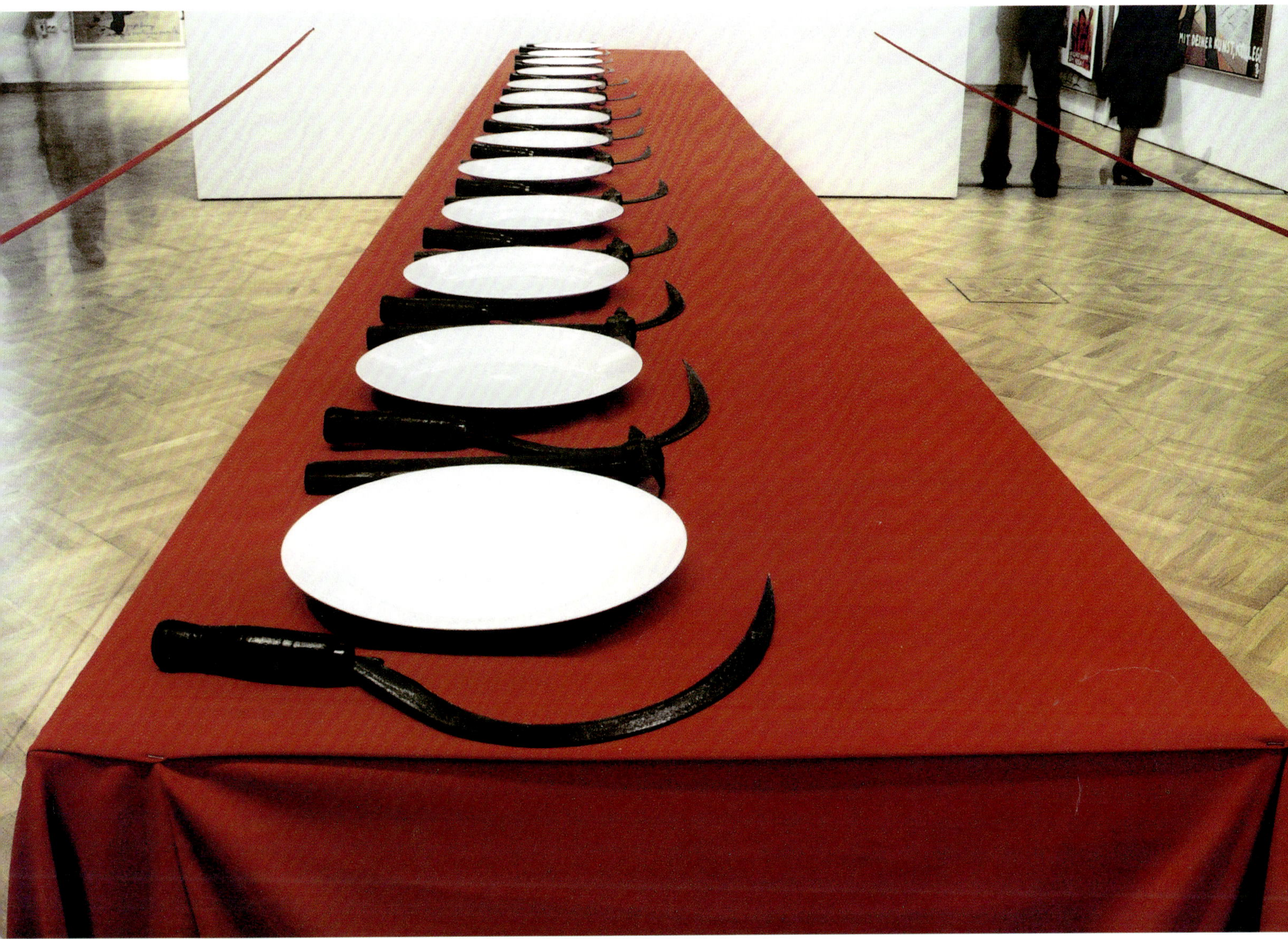

211 Andrei Fillipov, *The Last Supper*, 1989. Centre Georges Pompidou, Paris.

accounts hailed the event as "Great! This is glasnost, indeed." One negative review came from an American, who wrote, "I don't think that this art is good," thus clearly missing the event's neo-Dada anti-art and nonsensical origins, which targeted the positivist stance of official culture.[5] Moreover, the event's general lampooning atmosphere subverted this legendary bathhouse as a space of male bonding and power.[6]

This new tendency to confront male authority manifested itself at the highest political level. Gorbachev had no interest in erecting new monuments, so much so that he agreed instead to dismantle the Berlin Wall and engage in the disarmament campaign. For the first time since the Revolution, a Soviet leader gave up what might be called vertical mental images, and in general avoided the phallocentric syndrome of monument-making. This unusual mentality was registered in Anufriev and Sergei Bugaev's performances (Bugaev is also known as Africa), which involved climbing monuments in pursuit of their concept of artistic "inspection." For example, in *Birth of an Agent*, staged on July 31, 1990 (fig. 216), the two artists

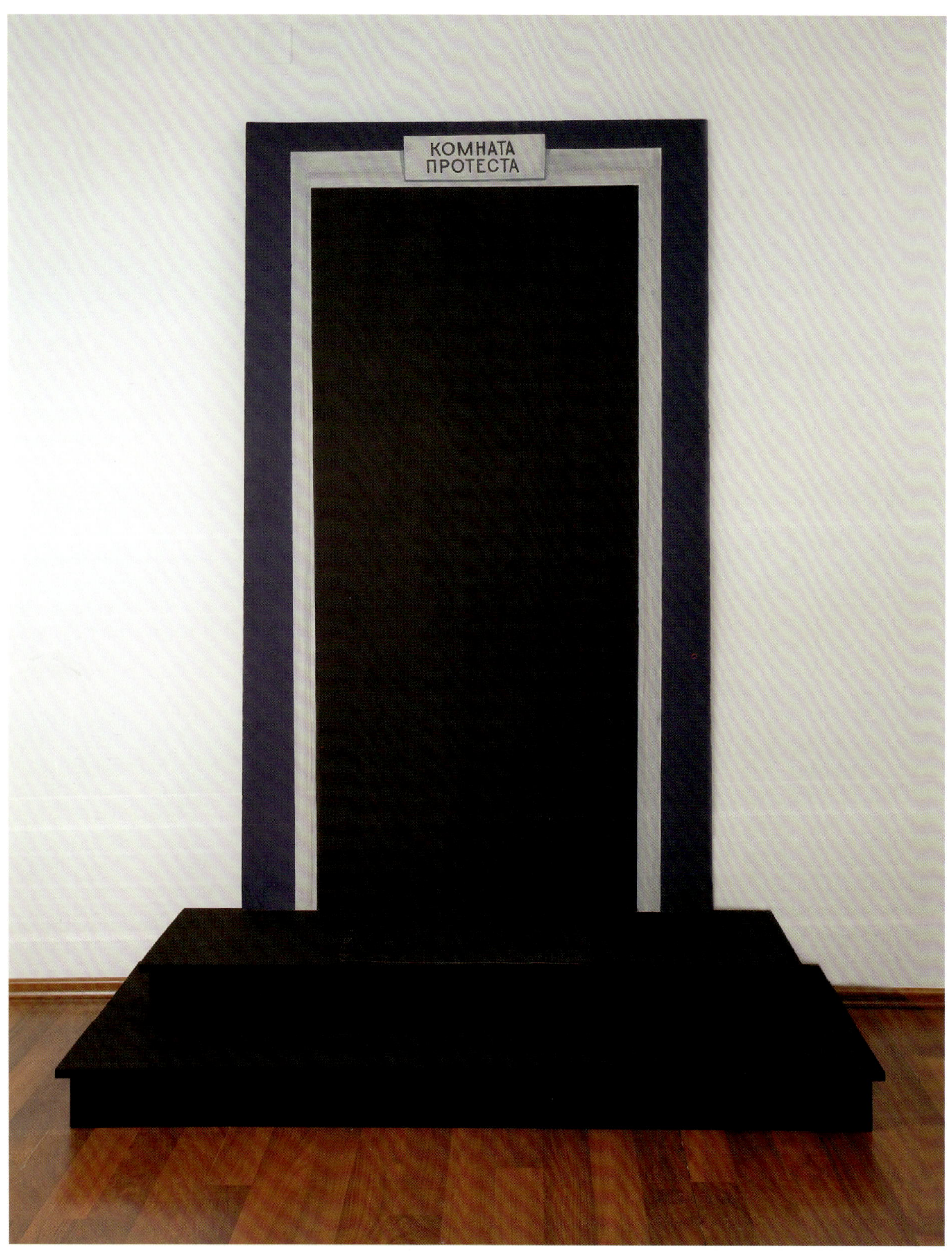

212 Vladimir Mironenko, *The Room of Protest*, 1987. Centre Georges Pompidou.

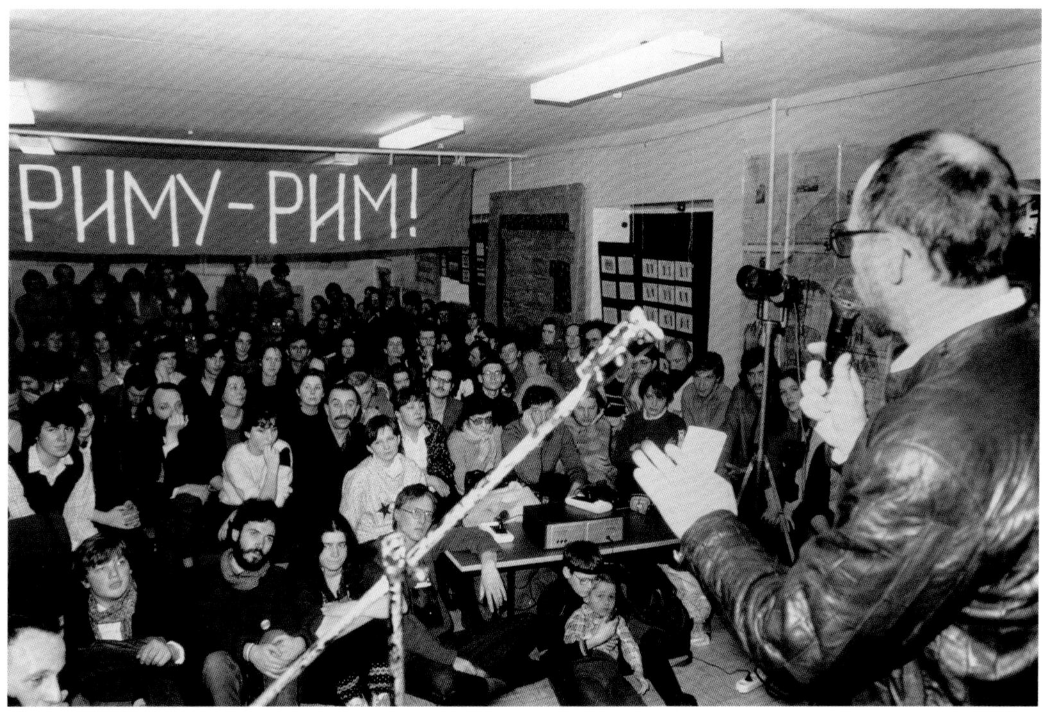

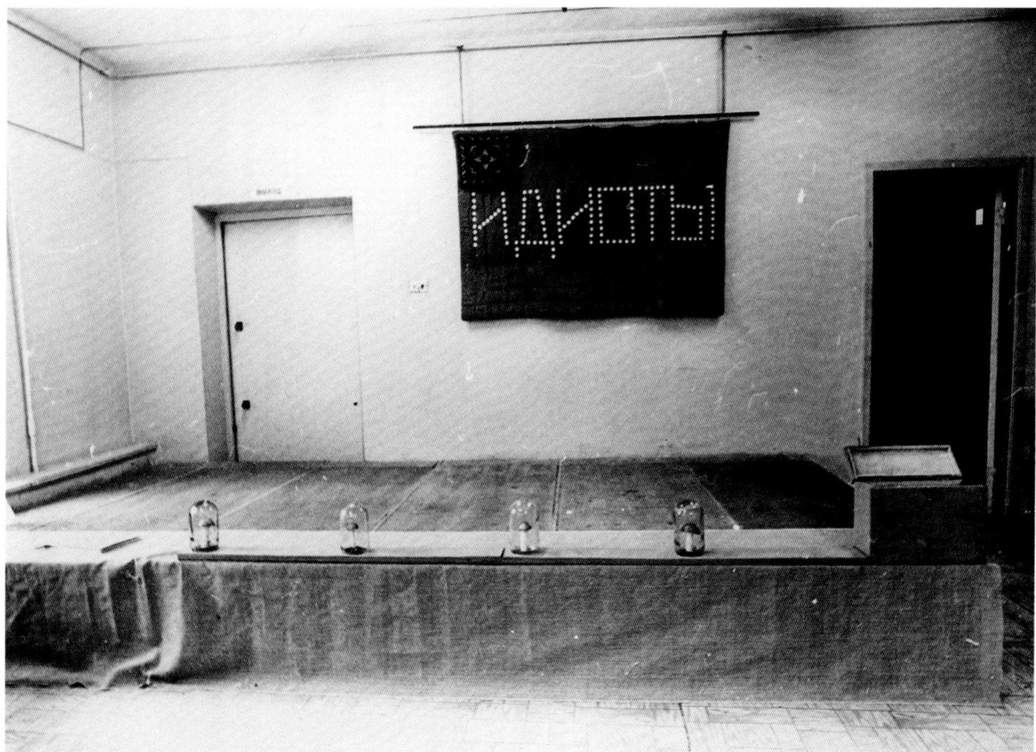

213   Dmitry Prigov recites poetry at the Club of Avant-gardists, Moscow, April 1987.

214   The first exhibition in the Club of Avant-gardists, Moscow, 1987: in the foreground Nikolai Panitkov's *The Mushroom Radiance*, 1987, and in the background Nikolai Kozlov's *Idiots*, 1987.

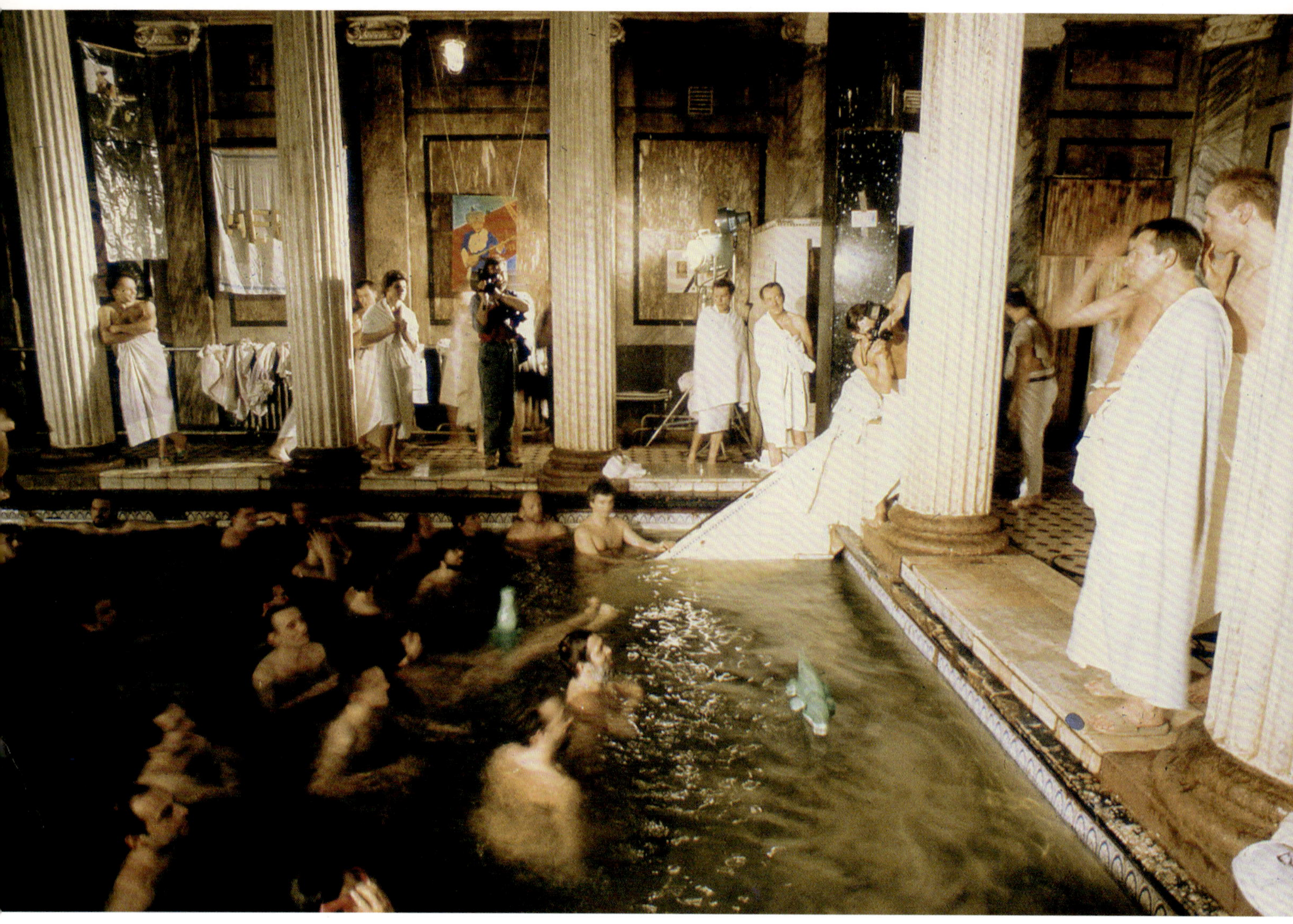

215   Exhibition-action of the Club of Avant-gardists in the Sandunovsky Baths, Moscow, 1988.

"heroically" detached a small detail from Vera Mukhina's colossal *Worker and Female Collective Farmer* (executed for the 1937 Paris Fair), a part that covered the opening between the farmer's legs. Such another neo-Dadaist treatment of ideological monuments denied the aggression of political revolutions. The idea was not to destroy the symbols of the previous regime, but to utilize them in the formation of critical discourses.

Gorbachev, furthermore, did not display any hostility toward his predecessors. The media, however, did set into motion a heated debate around Lenin, pressing for the closure of the mausoleum and giving his corpse a conventional burial. Such demands reversed the concerted Soviet effort to extirpate the notion of death using the myth of an eternally alive Lenin. This, in turn, had fortified the image of a communist paradise, for as Theodor Adorno said, "without the notion of an unfettered life, freed from death, the idea of Utopia, the idea of *the* Utopia, *cannot* even be thought at all."[7] Artists' reaction to perestroika's de-Leninization was immediate. The earliest example is Pavel Peppershtein's series, *V.I. Lenin on Vacation in Gorki* (figs. 217, 218), which features red-pencil doodles of Lenin sleeping, playing tennis and football, and meeting

Stalin. The series' title refers to the period following the assassination attempt on Lenin in 1918: after that, Lenin often stayed in his government dacha in Gorki, where he died in 1924. Peppershtein subjected Lenin's image to ridicule and mortality, much like Komar and Melamid had in their painting, *Lenin in Zurich* (1982–3). In the latter, the Bolshevik leader crawls through the forest in search of mushrooms. In the accompanying text to *V.I. Lenin on Vacation in Gorki*, Peppershtein explains that the drawings were "recently found," and attributes their authorship to one of Lenin's relatives, probably "the sister of comrade Lenin A.I. Ulianova-Elizarova," who, together with his wife, Nadezhda Krupskaia, looked after Lenin in his last year. In fact, Peppershtein's infantile drawings caricature the scribbles that Lenin made while paralyzed and unable to speak shortly before his death. Put on display in the Lenin Museum at the outset of perestroika, the disclosure of these documents of Lenin's degradation demonstrated how radical Gorbachev's reforms actually were, in allowing this kind of de-heroization of the iconic Soviet leader.

In *One Thousand Four Hundred Forty-eight Portraits of Lenin*, Eduard Gorokhovsky replaced the canonical double-profile portrait of Lenin and Stalin, appropriated by Komar and Melamid in their *Double Self-portrait* (see fig. 137), with a portrait *en face* (fig. 219). Contrary to the title, what one sees is a representation of Stalin composed from stencils of minuscule heads of Lenin. Following the principles of pointillism, the work offers a formally innovative portrait and connotes a chain of historical facts. Stalin's omnipresent image recalls Lenin's warning shortly before his death that Stalin would abuse his power. Lenin's tiny heads evoke the pockmarks on Stalin's face that were retouched in all official photographs, including the famous picture of Lenin and Stalin sitting on a bench in Gorki. The large number, 1,448, of heads of Lenin demonstrate Socialist Realists' obsessive duplication of his portrait. Finally, the effective fusion of the two politicians refers to the period during which they were laid together in the mausoleum, until Khrushchev ordered Stalin's removal in 1961.

In Erik Bulatov's *Revolution-Perestroika* (fig. 220), the standard sculpture of Lenin is painted in the background of the canvas as a symbol of the passing epoch.

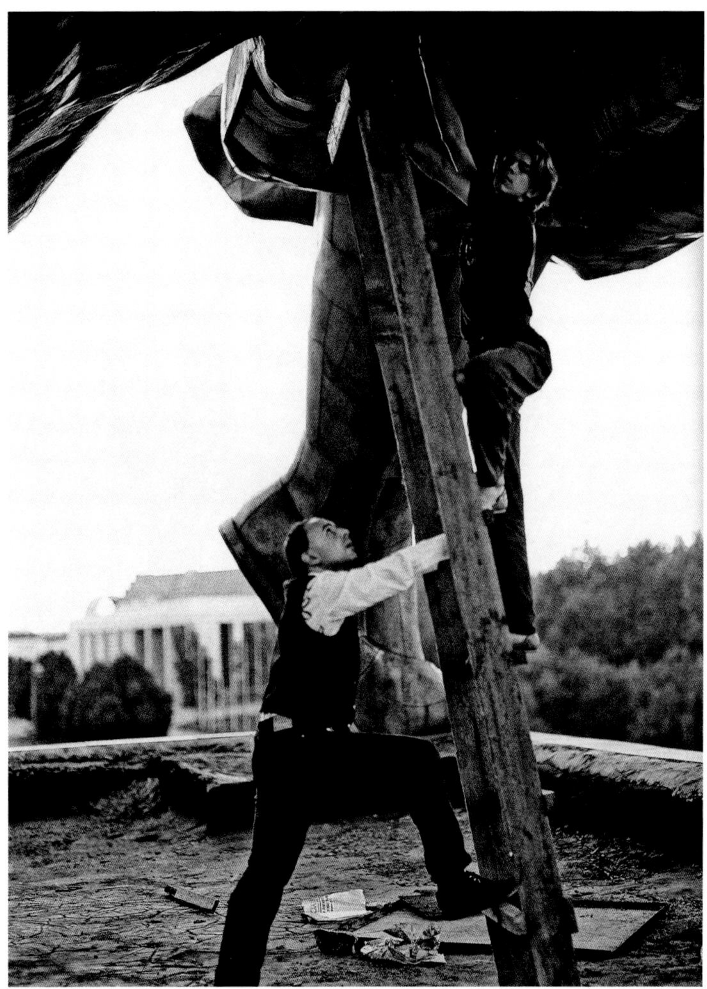

216   Sergei Anufriev and Sergei Bugaev ('Africa'), *Birth of an Agent*, July 31, 1990. Moscow.

By contrast, Gorbachev's portrait is executed with hyper-realism and depicts him as fervent. Positioned at the very edge of the painting, the figure seems ready to cross that edge. Bulatov's humanization of the Communist Party's general secretary, hitherto thought of solely as an instrument of power, implies that, with Gorbachev, the political process itself may take a less predictable course. Sergei Mironenko's *Bastards. What Have You Turned This Country Into!* (fig. 221), reflects upon this very possibility. With Mukhomor's taste for shocking viewers, Mironenko announced himself as the first free candidate to become the President of the USSR. He advertised his campaign message with a billboard, which consisted of several genial self-portrait

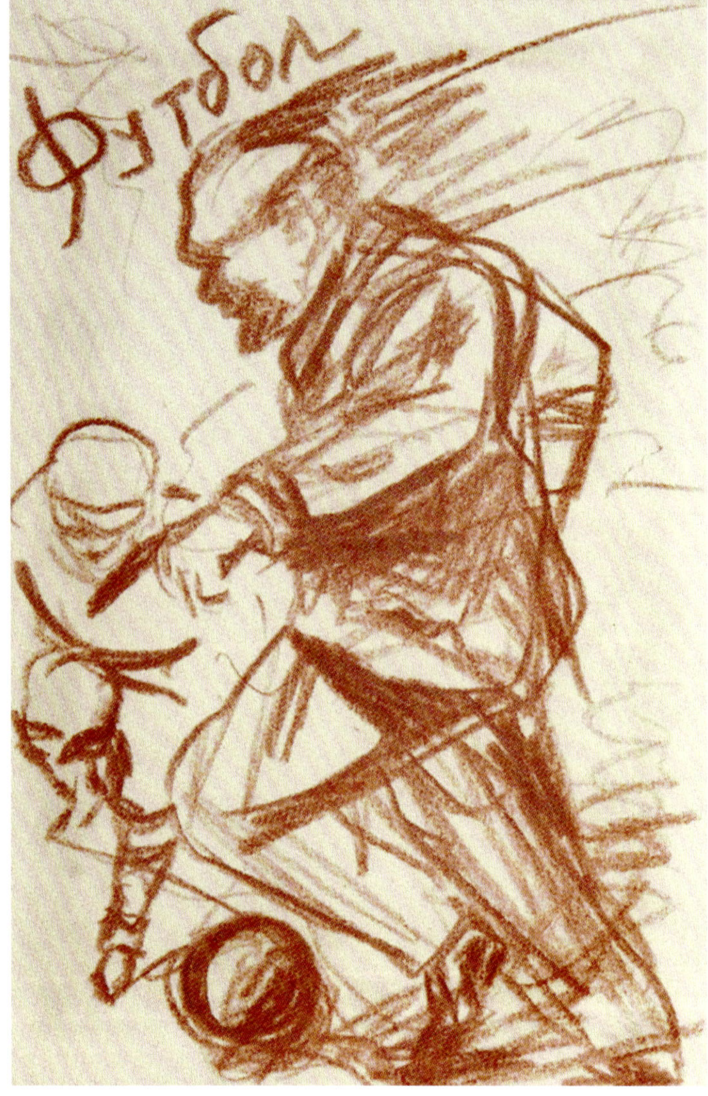
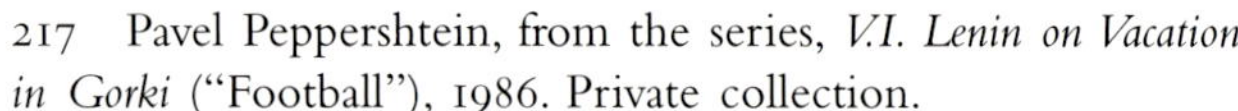

217 Pavel Peppershtein, from the series, *V.I. Lenin on Vacation in Gorki* ("Football"), 1986. Private collection.

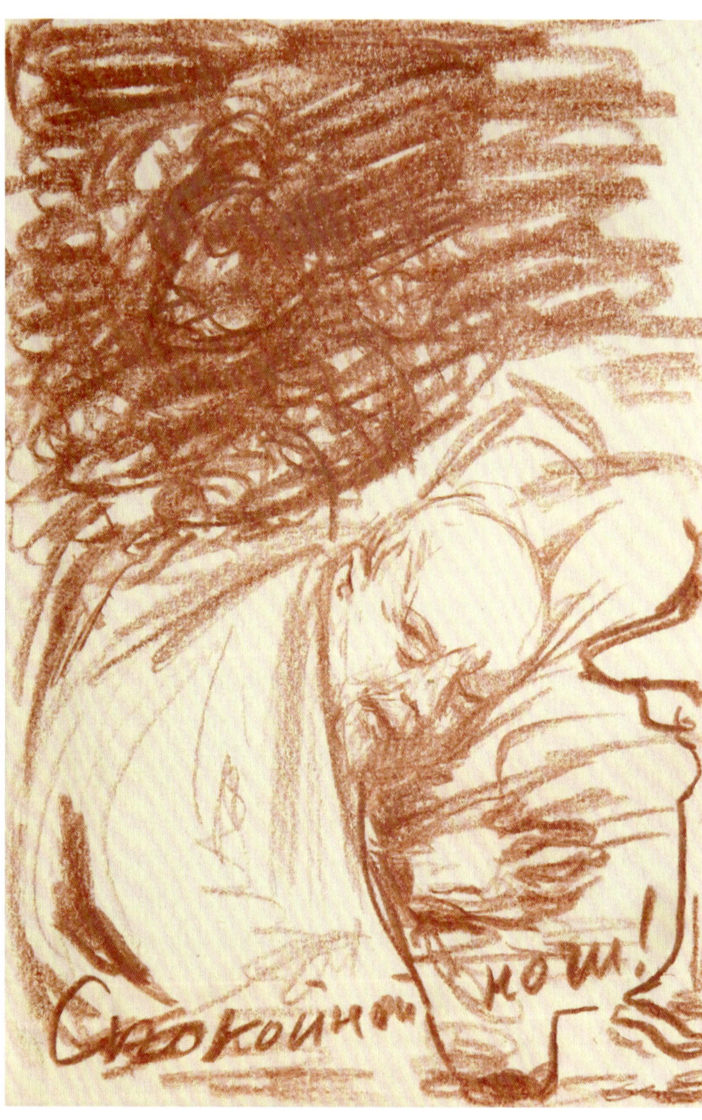

218 Pavel Peppershtein, from the series, *V.I. Lenin on Vacation in Gorki* ("Good Night"), 1986. Private collection.

photographs, along with an antagonistic slogan that accused Soviet leaders of bringing the country to its end.

Komar and Melamid's *Lenin with the Skeleton of Marx* (fig. 222), was executed between the fall of the Soviet Union and the Parliament's attempt to reinstate it with a coup. That led to another iconoclastic wave that swept out more Soviet imagery, and even abolished the sacred ritual of the changing of the guard by the mausoleum. Once again, the public demanded Lenin's burial. *Lenin with the Skeleton of Marx's* loaded

symbolism was a response to the Bolsheviks' unrelenting incarceration of Lenin's dead body. The piece is crowned with a model of the mausoleum, seized by "a fantastic creature: a hybrid of 'a symbol of evil – a serpent,' and 'a symbol of soul – a bird.'"[8] The serpent's heavy tail prevents the bird (the soul) from ascending over Soviet mundanity, symbolized by a teapot. Lenin carrying the skeleton of Marx on his back allegorizes the collapse of the Marxist utopia and asserts that the guilt of its dissemination in the Russian empire is laid on Lenin.

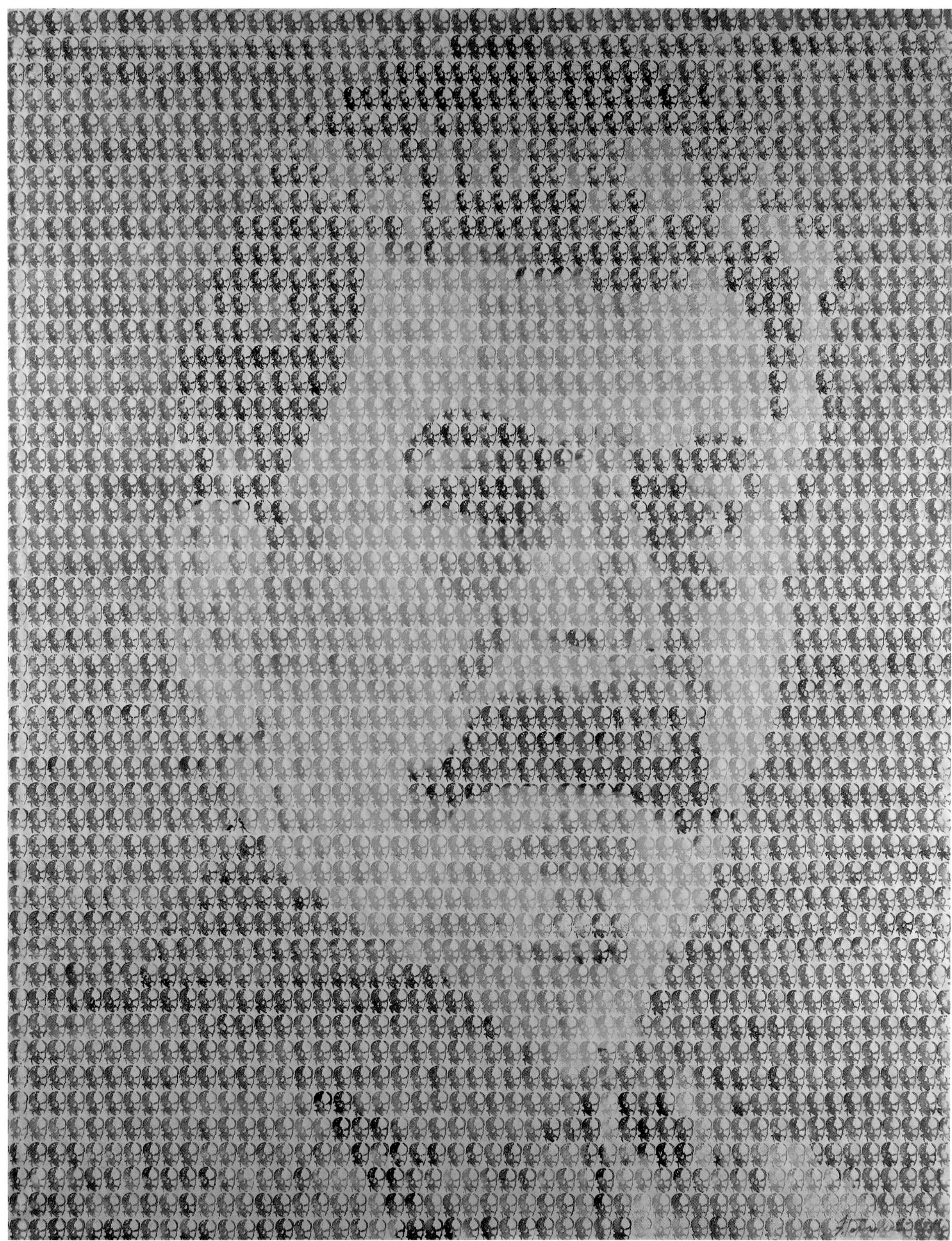

219   Eduard Gorokhovsky, *One Thousand Four Hundred Forty-eight Portraits of Lenin*, 1988. Private collection.

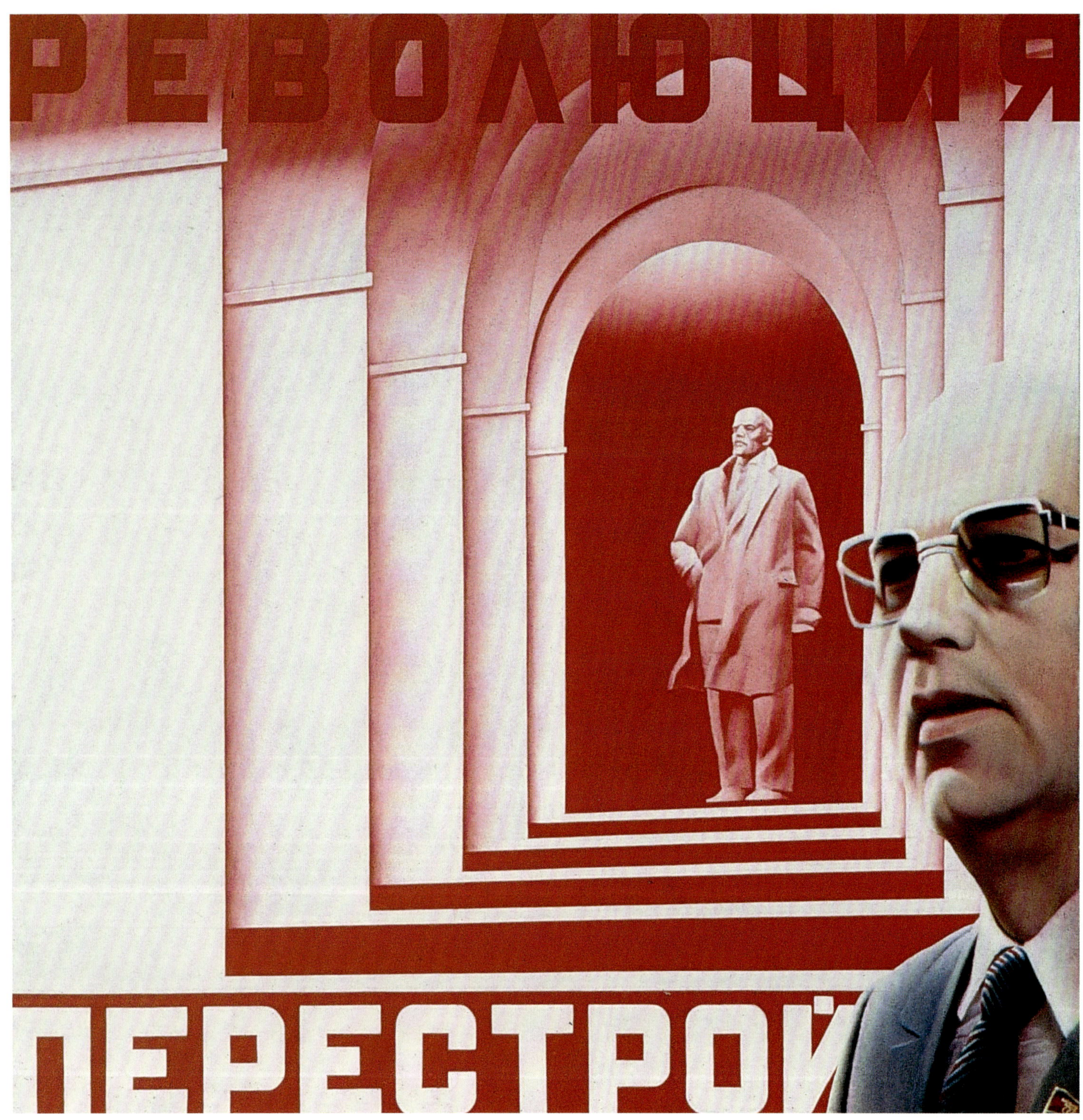

220   Erik Bulatov, *Revolution-Perestroika*, 1988.

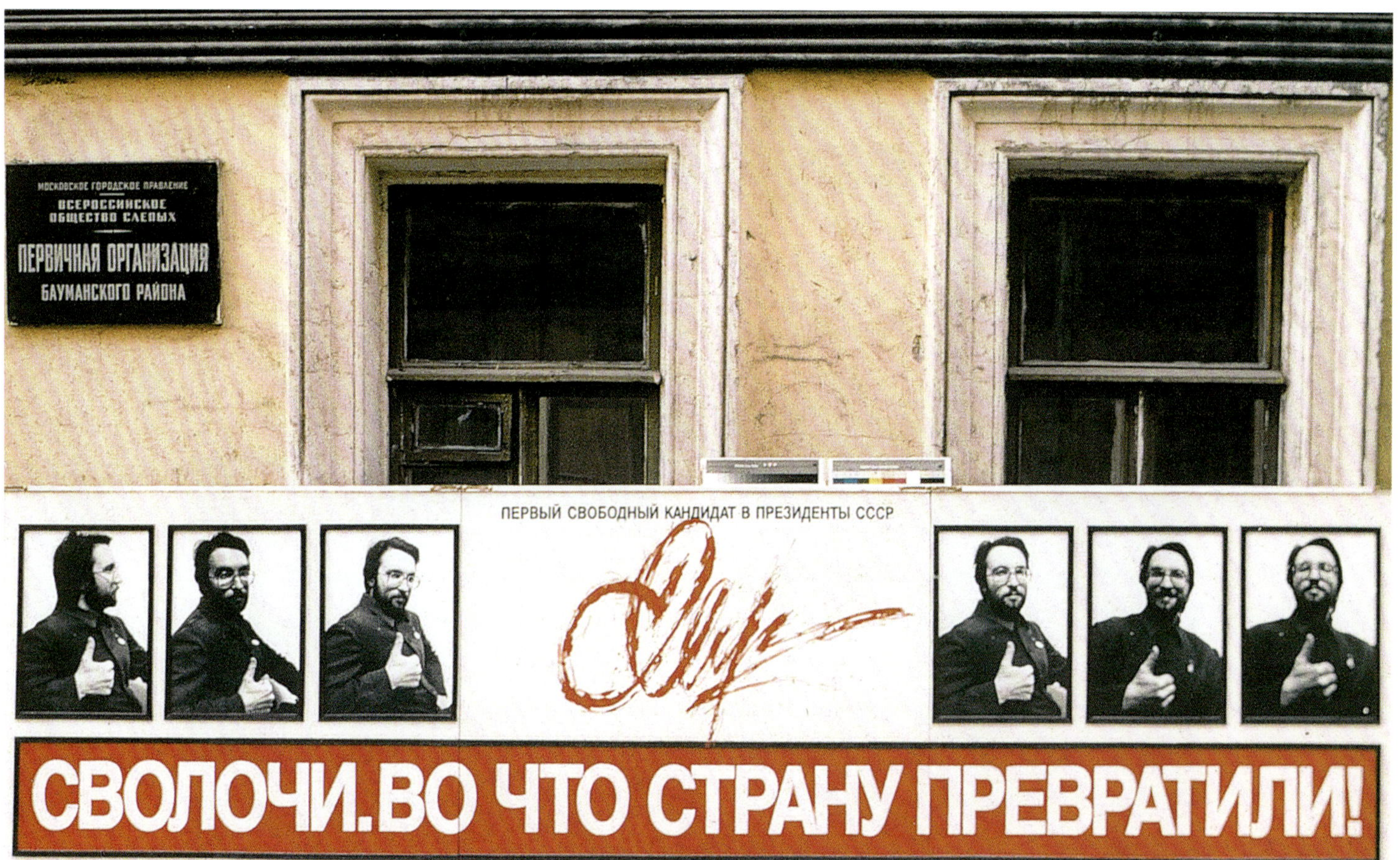

221 Sergei Mironenko, *Bastards. What Have You Turned This Country Into!*, 1988. Centre Georges Pompidou, Paris.

This avalanche of crushed myths resulted in the removal of propaganda paraphernalia from public spaces, taking with them the strictly maintained atmosphere of no conflict. Without it, images of squalor and decay moved to the forefront, capturing the subversive attention of artists. Some of them realised that, just as the color red was the pigment of the epoch before Gorbachev, the color green could have been nominated as the color of his rule.[9] Its essence could be expressed through the fresh grass growing on the graves of political ex-heroes, with the country's desperate quest for dollars (which, in the Soviet Union, were called "greens"), and with such major achievements as the Soviet–American disarmament pact. The latter inspired Nikolai Kozlov, in performances and objects (fig. 223), to address the rapid disintegration of the Soviet military-industrial complex.

For Anufriev, the color green became a marker of the post-red emptiness of Soviet reality – a reality that lay bare after the lifting of its ideological veneer. Vladimir Mironenko's painting, *The Room of Protest* (1987, see fig. 212), which he later turned into an installation by adding a step to it, depicts a sealed black door, labeled "the room of protest" and it epitomises the underground milieu's committment to never again live or create under restrcition. In 1987, Anufriev produced coarsely painted canvases in dull hues of green, with words written and cuts made in their surfaces, all of which imitated the textures of crumbling urban structures and objects (figs. 224, 225). Deliberately anti-aesthetic and anti-commercial, Anufriev's pieces take off from Ilya Kabakov's *Kitchen Series* (fig. 226). On the ten "board-installations" smoothly painted in dirty green, Kabakov attached to the

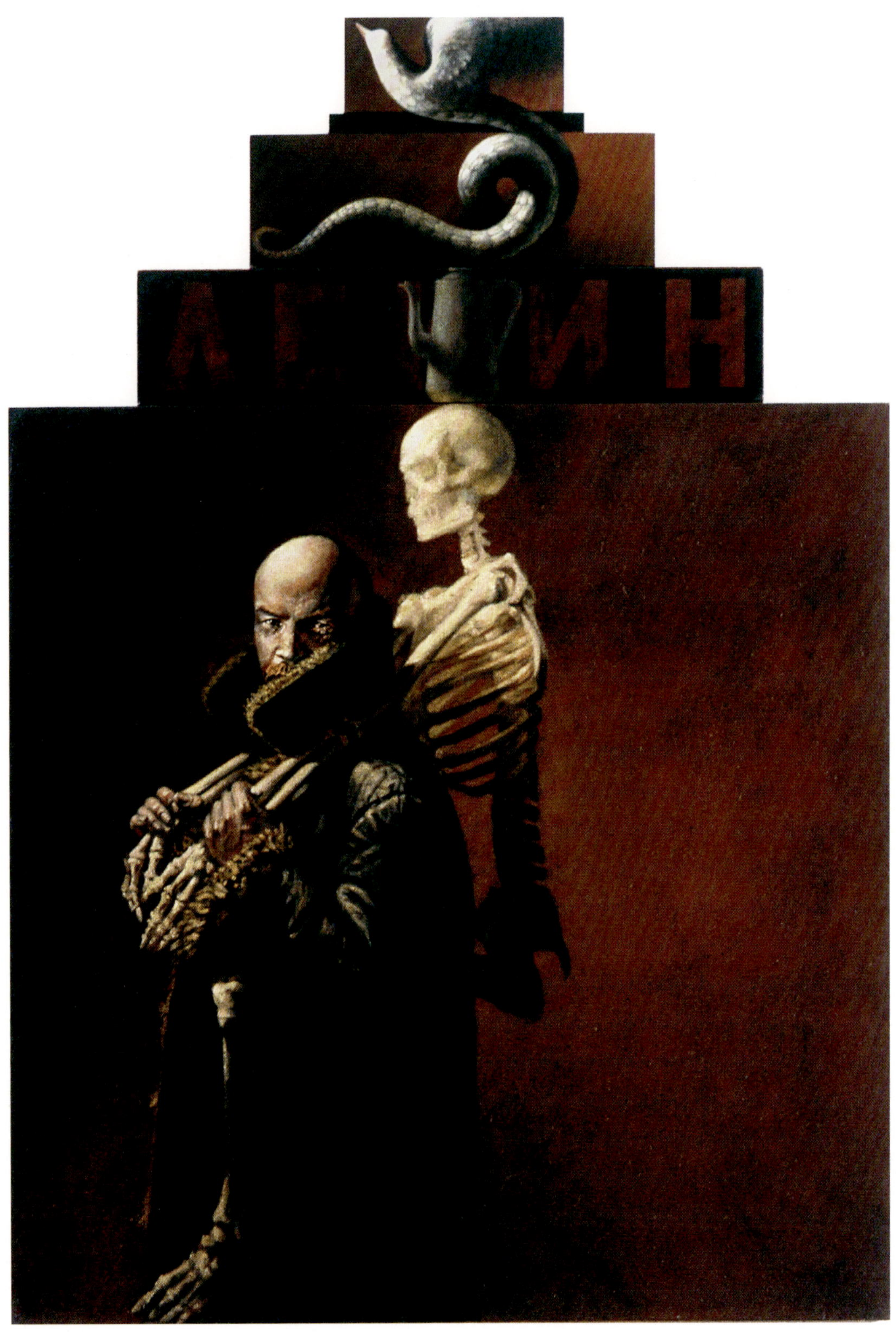

222 Vitaly Komar and Aleksandr Melamid, *Lenin with the Skeleton of Marx*, 1991–3. Ludwig Museum, Cologne.

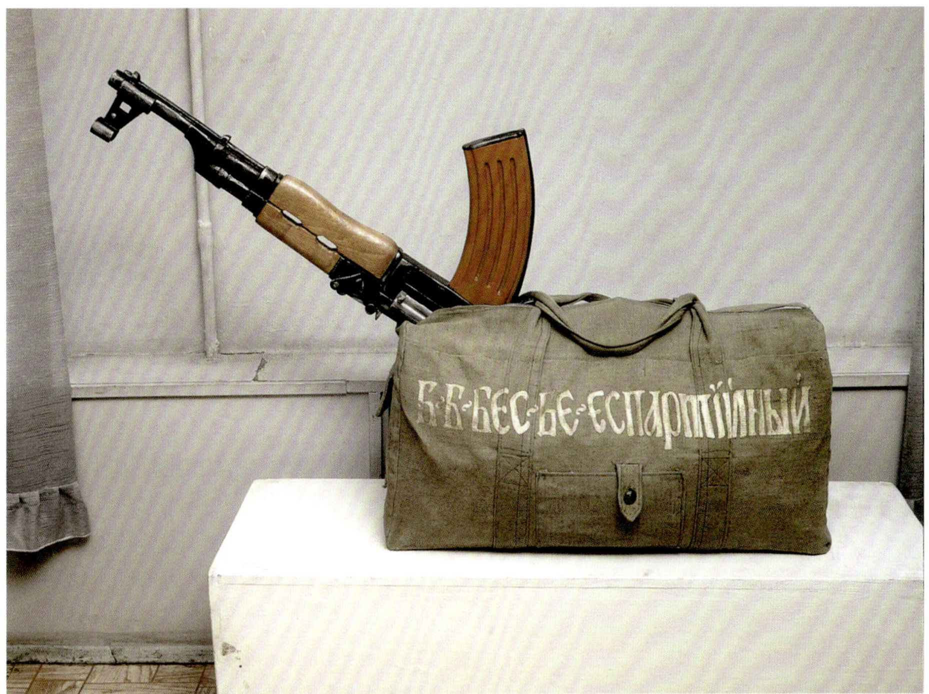

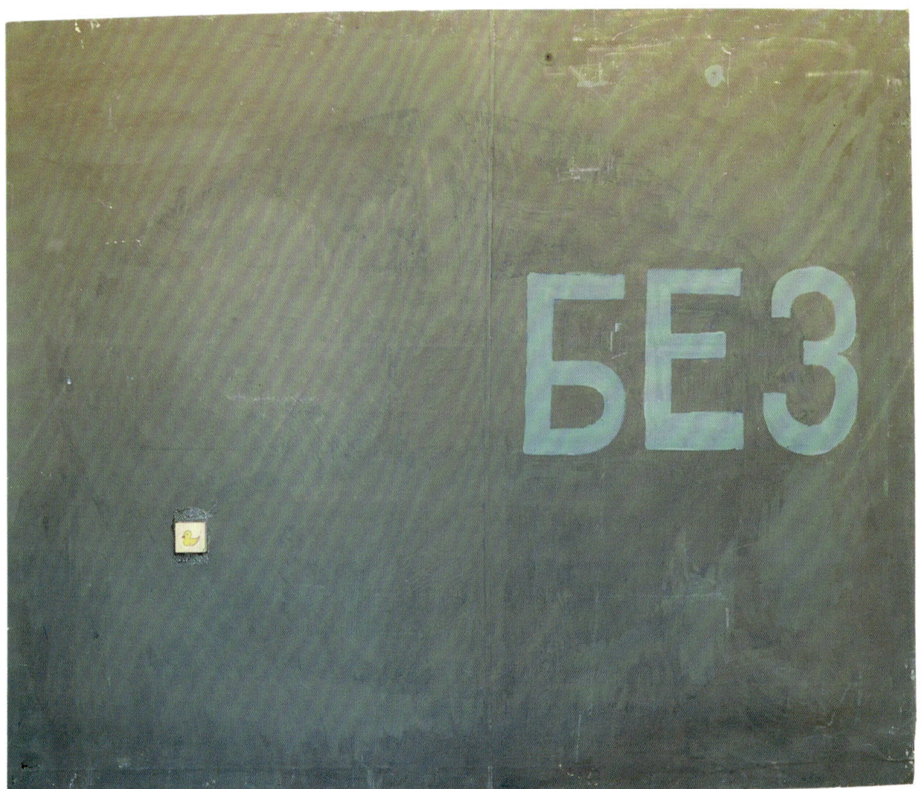

223 Nikolai Kozlov, *Untitled (Partyless)*, 1988. Private collection.

224 Sergei Anufriev, *Untitled (Without)*, 1987. Museum MANI, Moscow.

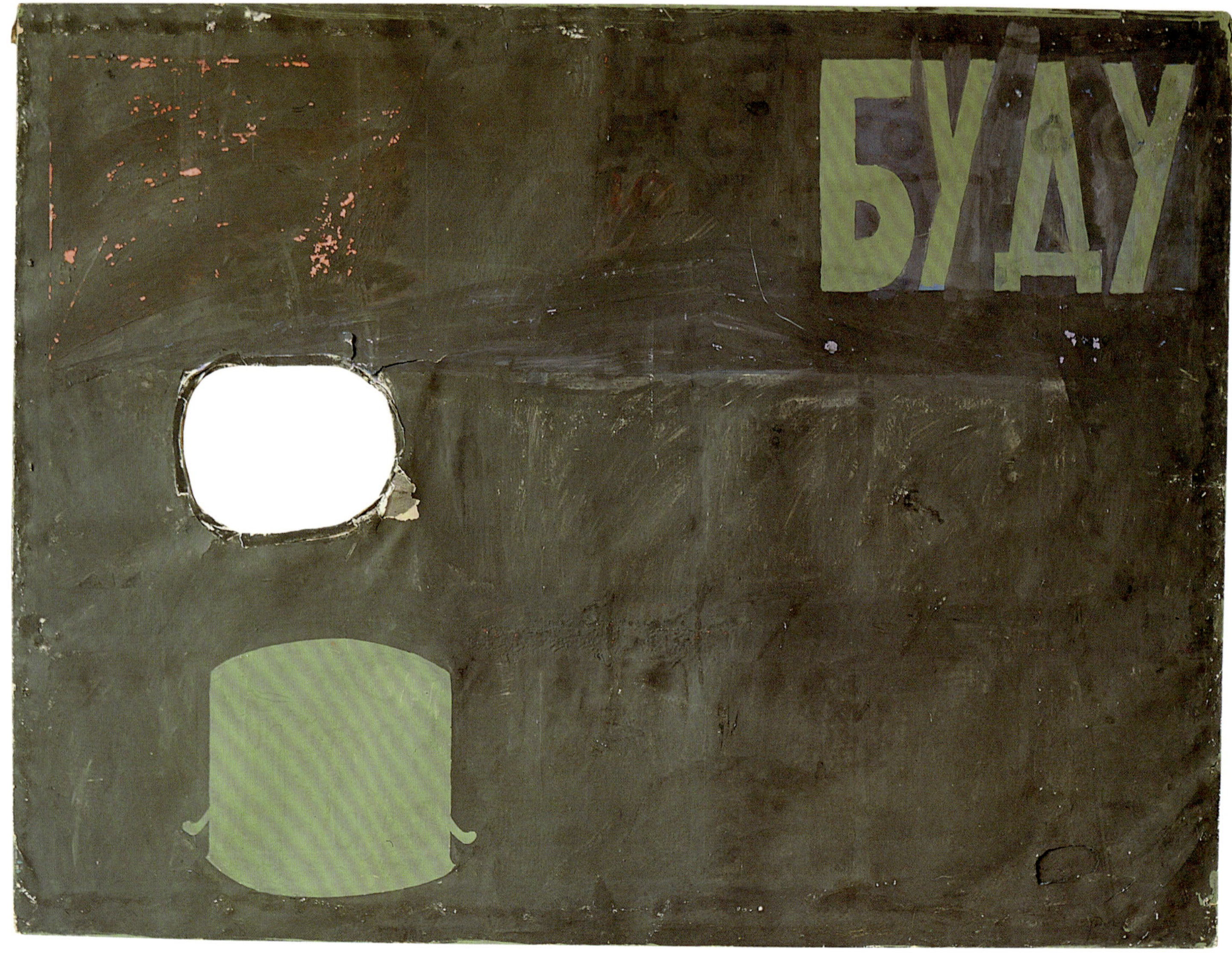

225   Sergei Anufriev, *Untitled (I Will Be)*, 1987. Museum MANI, Moscow.

surfaces so–called "zero objects"[10] of Soviet life: a grater, a tin cup, a coffee pot, a rolling pin. In the upper corners of the boards, he wrote the Chekhovian dialogues of communal dwellers regarding these "relics." The green area that surrounds the kitchen objects allegorizes Kabakov's concept of emptiness that "presents itself as an extraordinarily active volume – as a reservoir of emptiness, as a particular void–like state of being, staggeringly catalyzed, but opposed to genuine existence, genuine life, serving as the absolute opposite of any living existence…This very emptiness…is a special (however bombastic the word) hole in space."[11]

If, for Kabakov, emptiness was primarily a psychological issue, for perestroika artists it was experienced visually as a result of the sudden disappearance of a controlled picture of public space. Further, while Kabakov wrote an essay called "On Emptiness," Anufriev insisted, "there is nothing we can say about 'emptiness'"; instead one must come up with the tangible embodiment of this social phenomenon.[12] The rough surfaces of Anufriev's paintings created a

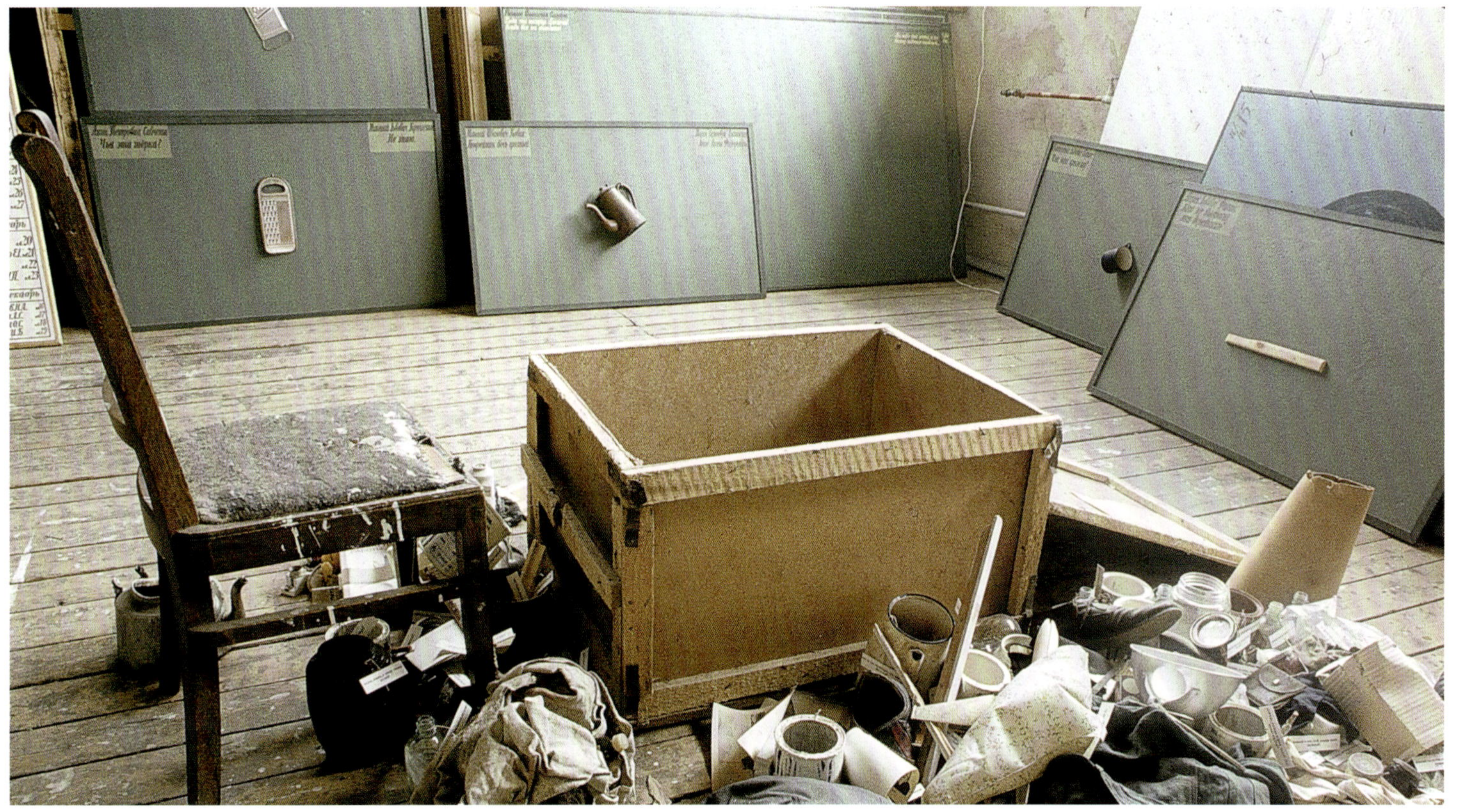

226 Ilya Kabakov, box with garbage in the artist's studio, Moscow, 1986, with (in the background) works from the *Kitchen Series*, 1982.

kind of *faktura* of dystopia, the antithesis of the formalist concept of *faktura* that encoded a utopian consciousness.

Anufriev's visual paradigm of changed Soviet externalities was developed by other artists who similarly rejected the notion of color as an aesthetic component, and conveyed a sense of damage and disintegration on a formal level. Andrei Roiter's canvases have cuts in the shape of old-fashioned radio speakers, which for most Soviet citizens were the mouthpiece of an endless stream of ideological announcements (fig. 227). In other paintings, a green canvas is punctured with holes, signifying the ellipses in any ideological speech. After the first Sotheby's auction in Moscow, in the summer of 1988, Igor Makarevich produced his first green piece, *Sotheby's* (fig. 228), which drew attention to the new commercial status of vanguard art. Painted in dark green impasto, the work can be separated into two parts, both with

suitcase handles, alluding to the fact that vanguard art is made for foreign collectors. The word "Sotheby's" is composed of letters that fell off the facade of the only State bank, *Sberkassa*, which Makarevich picked up. Using these letters to render the name of the Western auction house brought out the contrast between a shattered socialist economy and a prosperous capitalist company. Makarevich's instruction to exhibit *Sotheby's* on an easel was a jab at Russian modernists, on one hand; on the other, the presence of an easel reveals his uneasiness about sacrificing painting to installation art.

Earlier, I discussed how Kabakov and Irina Nakhova in their first installations excluded painting altogether. This changed when both artists started to exhibit in the West and used their paintings from the Moscow period as the structural and discursive driver of their installations (figs. 229, 230). In Kabakov's case, this contributed to a substantial alteration to the context

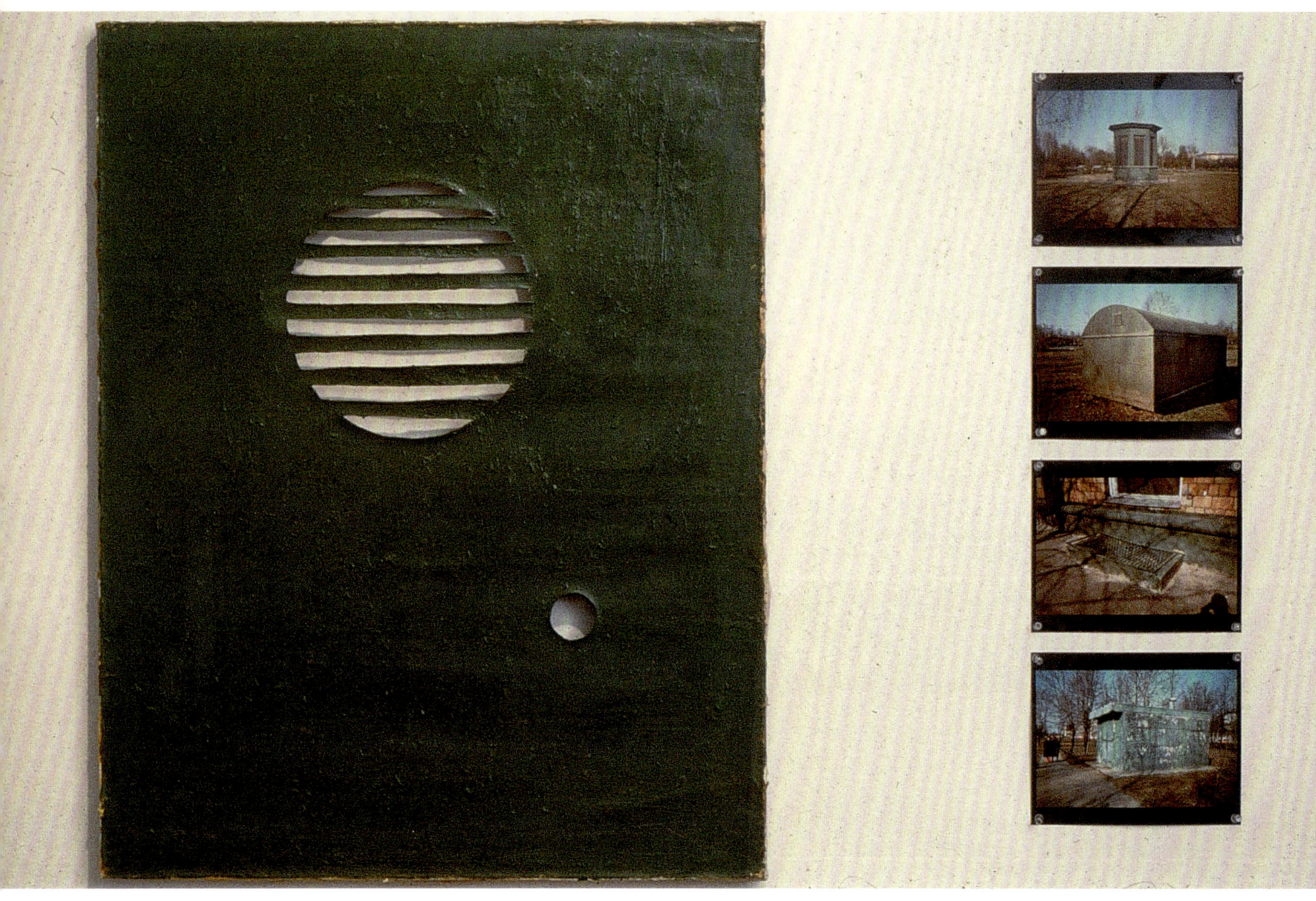

227 Andrei Roiter's installation in *The Green Show*, Exit Art, New York, 1989.

of his two–dimensional art. Those artists who contin-ued to work and exhibit in Moscow during pere-stroika also demonstrated a tendency toward this form of installation art. For example, the group Medical Hermeneutics' *Work* (1989) carries the double meaning of a work of art and the process of con-structing an installation (fig. 231). The same can be said of Makarevich and Elagina's *Children's* (1989) that, like *Work*, began with a wall piece (familiar medium for a Moscow artist) and then was extended into actual space by incorporating installation ele-ments (fig. 232). *Children's* also identified the bank-ruptcy of Soviet utopian projects: universal hygiene, children's welfare, medicine, and equality of the sexes.

The issue of gender equality was particularly reso-nant since, as in the period of the Russian avant-garde, perestroika was full of intellectually vigorous and artistically original female artists. Michel Foucault argued that what is "true" depends on who controls the discourse, and in the 1930s, Stalin's domination of the cultural politics trapped women inside a male "truth." During Socialist Realism, female imagery, like all other represntation, was subjected to the strictest control and stereotyping. Represented primarily as heroines performing for the collective, or as idealized mothers and workers, Socialist Realist women were portrayed as ultimately happy human beings, unfail-ingly ready to serve the state's objectives. Such specific

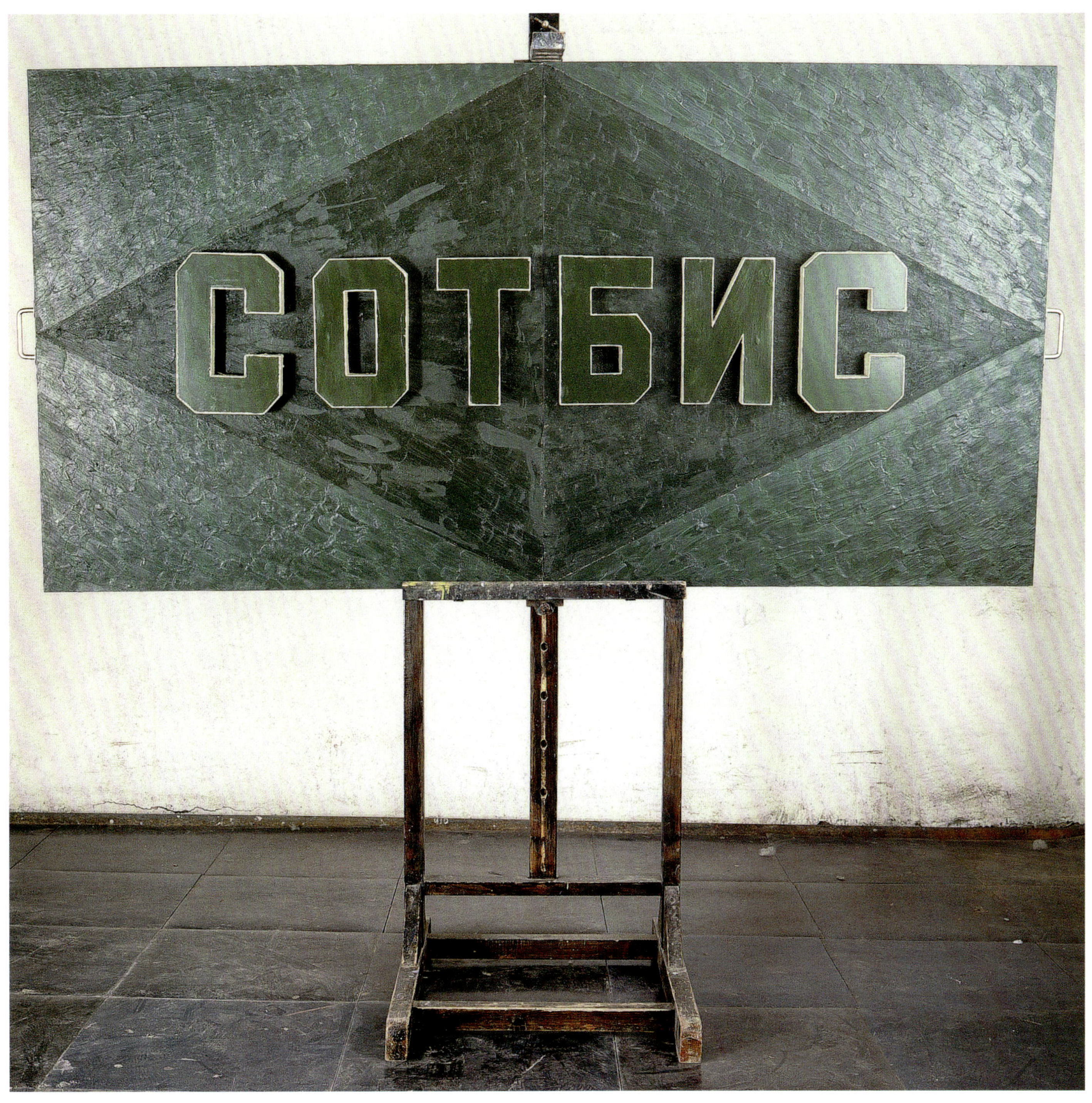

228   Igor Makarevich, *Sotheby's*, 1988. Collection Aleksandr Valger, New York.

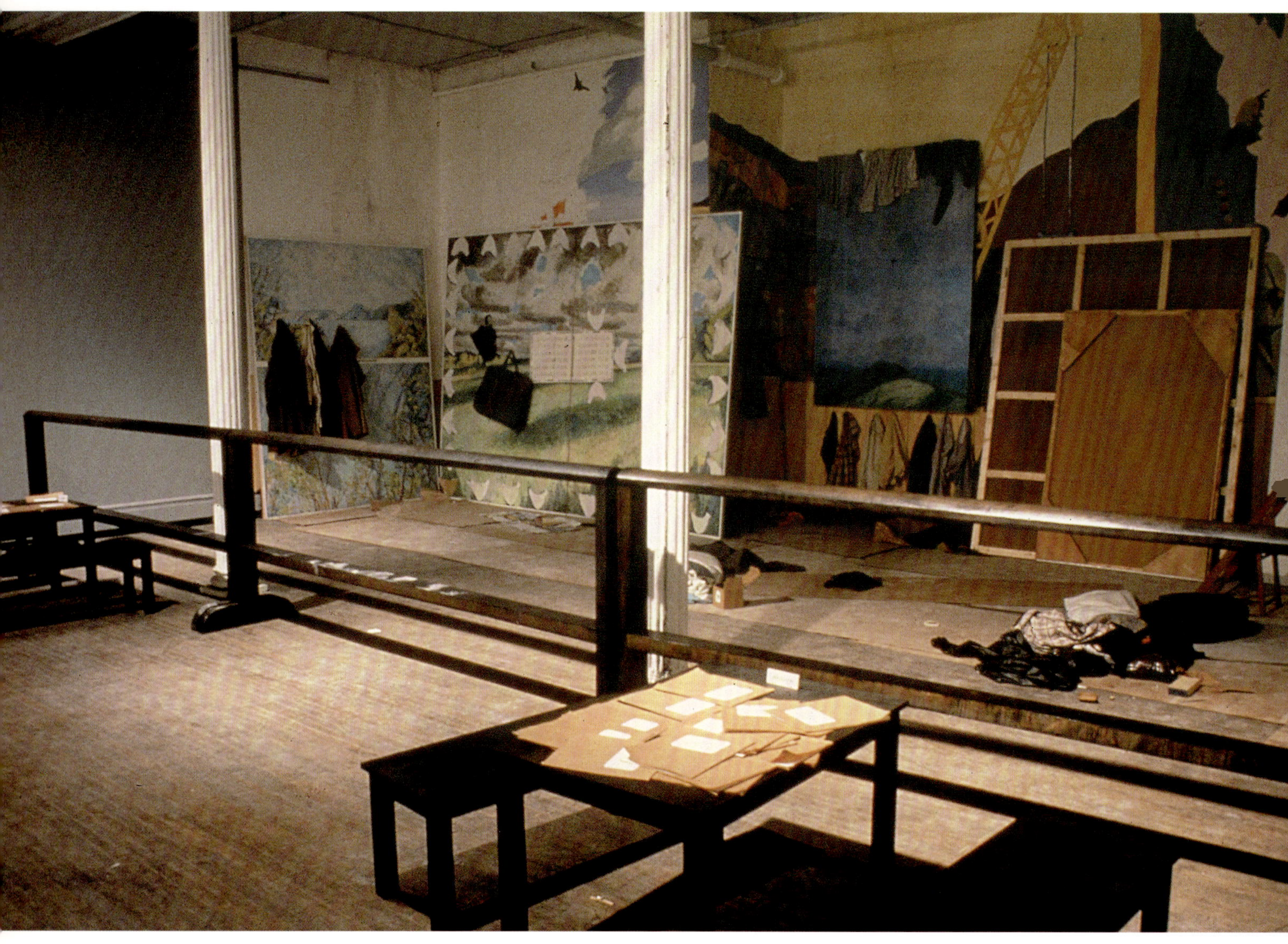

229   Ilya Kabakov, *He Lost His Mind, Undressed, Ran Away Naked*, 1990, at Ronald Feldman Fine Arts, New York.

characterizations of women in mass culture severely restricted their choices in life, forcing them to follow tightly controlled models of female behavior. As a result of this monolithic masculine model of the world, by the time of Khrushchev's thaw, women artists from all art circles had inherited what can be called the patriarchal unconscious. They adhered to the idea that in order to speak they had to assume a masculine position; thus, almost invariably, they met any attempt to analyze their work from a feminist point of view with unconcealed skepticism or indif- ference. Like every other discourse, the feminist one took a new direction during perestroika, largely as a result of the influx of Western literature. A number of artists attempted to unravel the heritage of heroic mass media and communal imagery, and to rethink their meaning and function within the framework of gender politics.

Elagina's installations made of industrial and house- hold paraphernalia asserted that in the Soviet Union the key to women's liberation and equality lay in women's denial of "womanness," and in the commit-

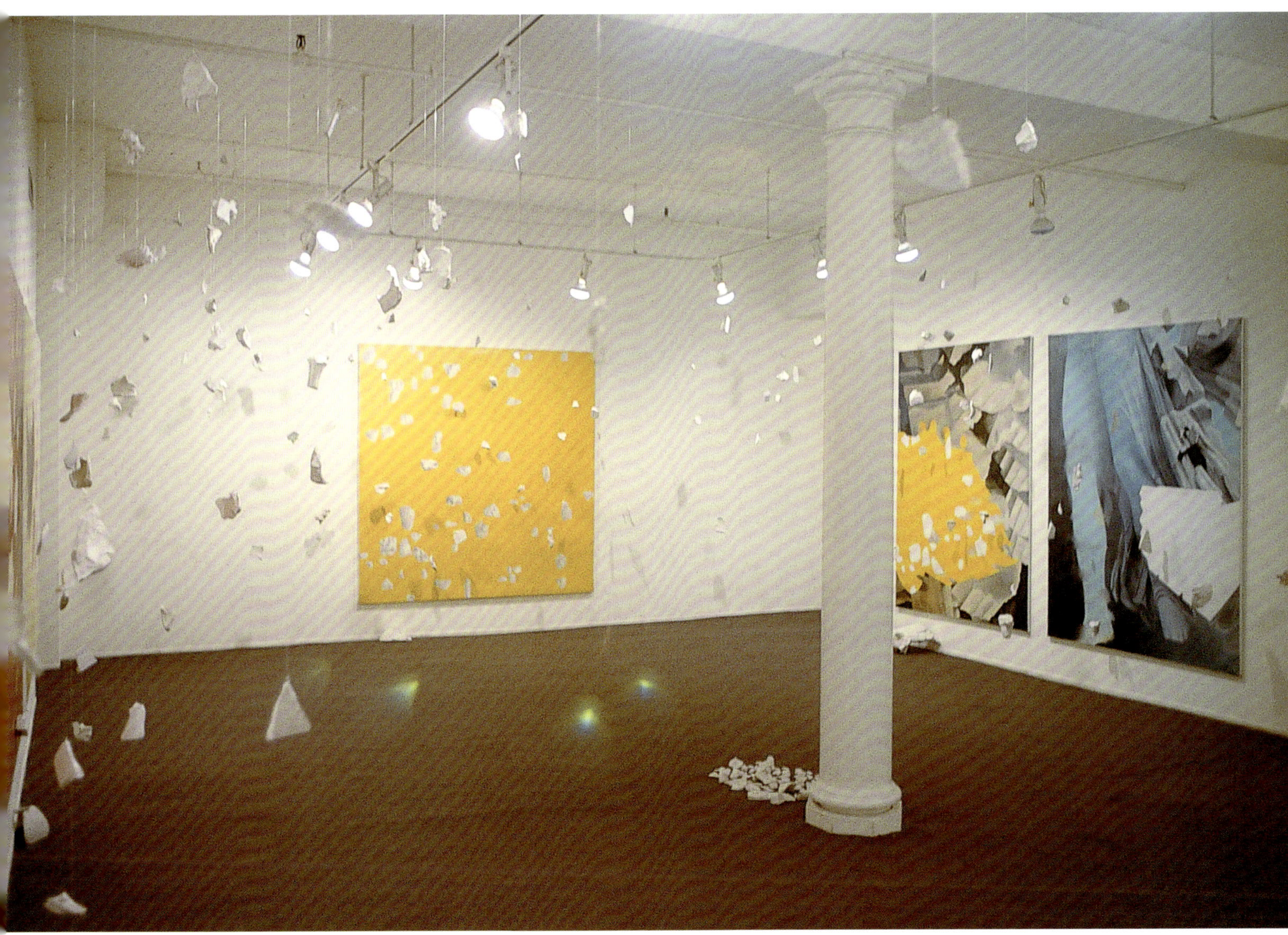

ment to arduous work, both at home and in society. In her optimistic titles she emphasized the gap between the media's hypocritical promotion of women's positive experiences and their chronic lack of everyday necessities. Elagina's *PRE* (1990; fig. 233) expressed this breach by interrupting the adjective *prekrasnoe* (wonderful), and thus signaling the falsehood of this message. A further sense of misrepresentation arises from the color red (included are two red pots placed on a red shelf), a habitual compensator for all ideological gaps and inconsistencies. *PRE* also fits into

the crucial practice for the Russian avant-garde of a play between visual and verbal elements to create shifts in meanings and new modes of visual perception. In *prekrasnoe, krasnoe* (red) follows *pre*, and thus the viewer (albeit only one who reads Russian) first sees three white letters and reads *pre*, and then sees red pots, which in the mind of the viewer complete the word "wonderful," through visual rather than verbal means.

Larisa Rezun who, like Anufriev, came from Odessa to join the Apt Art movement, is drawn to objects

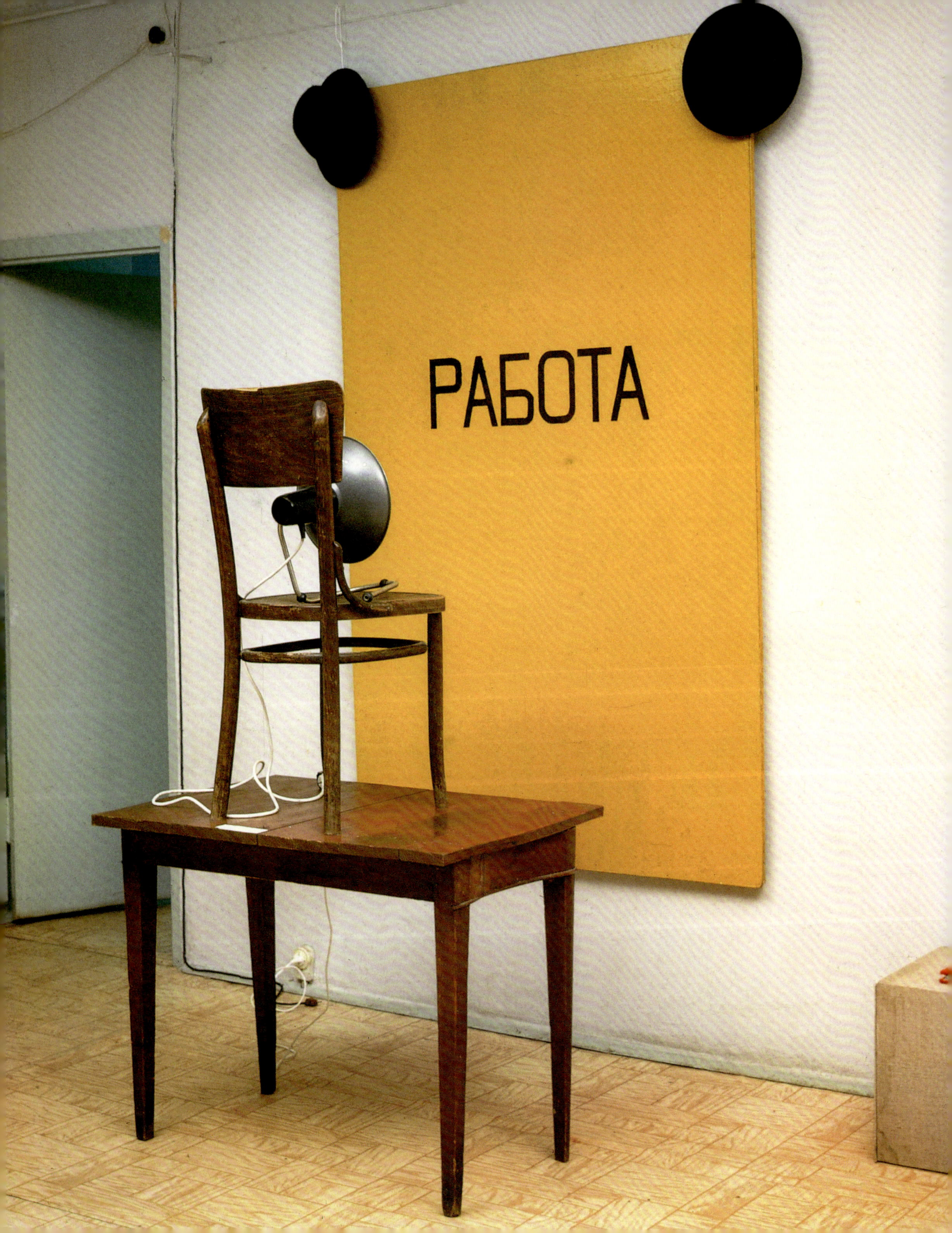
РАБОТА

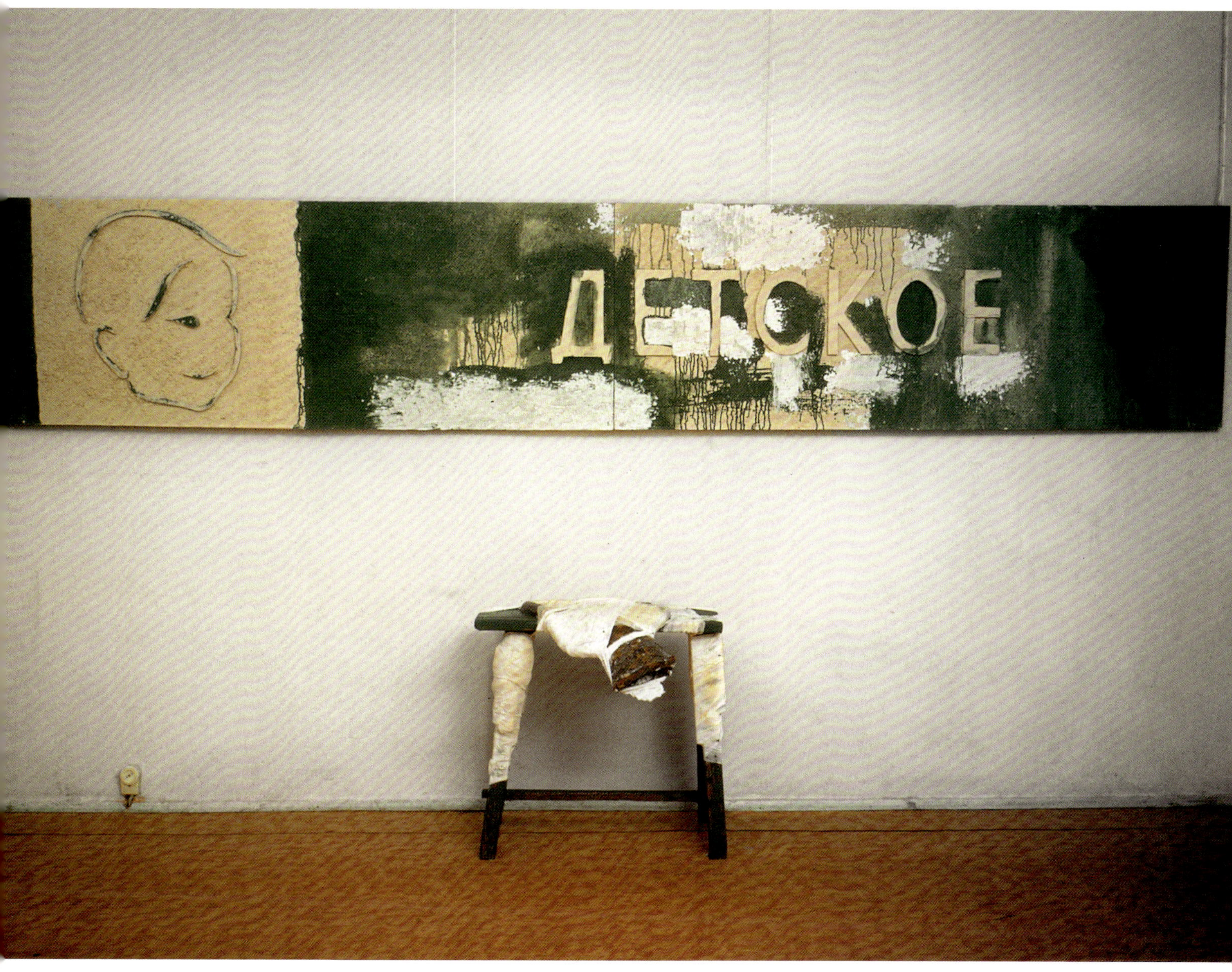

OPPOSITE PAGE 231   Medical Hermeneutics, *Work*, 1989.

ABOVE 232   Elena Elagina and Igor Makarevich, *Children's*, 1989. Stella Art Foundation, Moscow.

taken from the popular culture of her childhood, specifically those found in the decor of the dismal communal apartments of the 1950s and 1960s, including cheap mass-produced carpets, embroideries, and textiles (fig. 234). Placed on the walls of tenants' separate rooms, thus removing them from the commotion of a shared kitchen, these objects came to embody the private fantasies and desires kept away from the omnipresent collectivism. Liudmila Skripkina and Oleg Petrenko (the Peppers), also Odessa members of the Apt Art circle, focused on the cliches of Soviet communal objects. In *Slippers* (1991), the Peppers

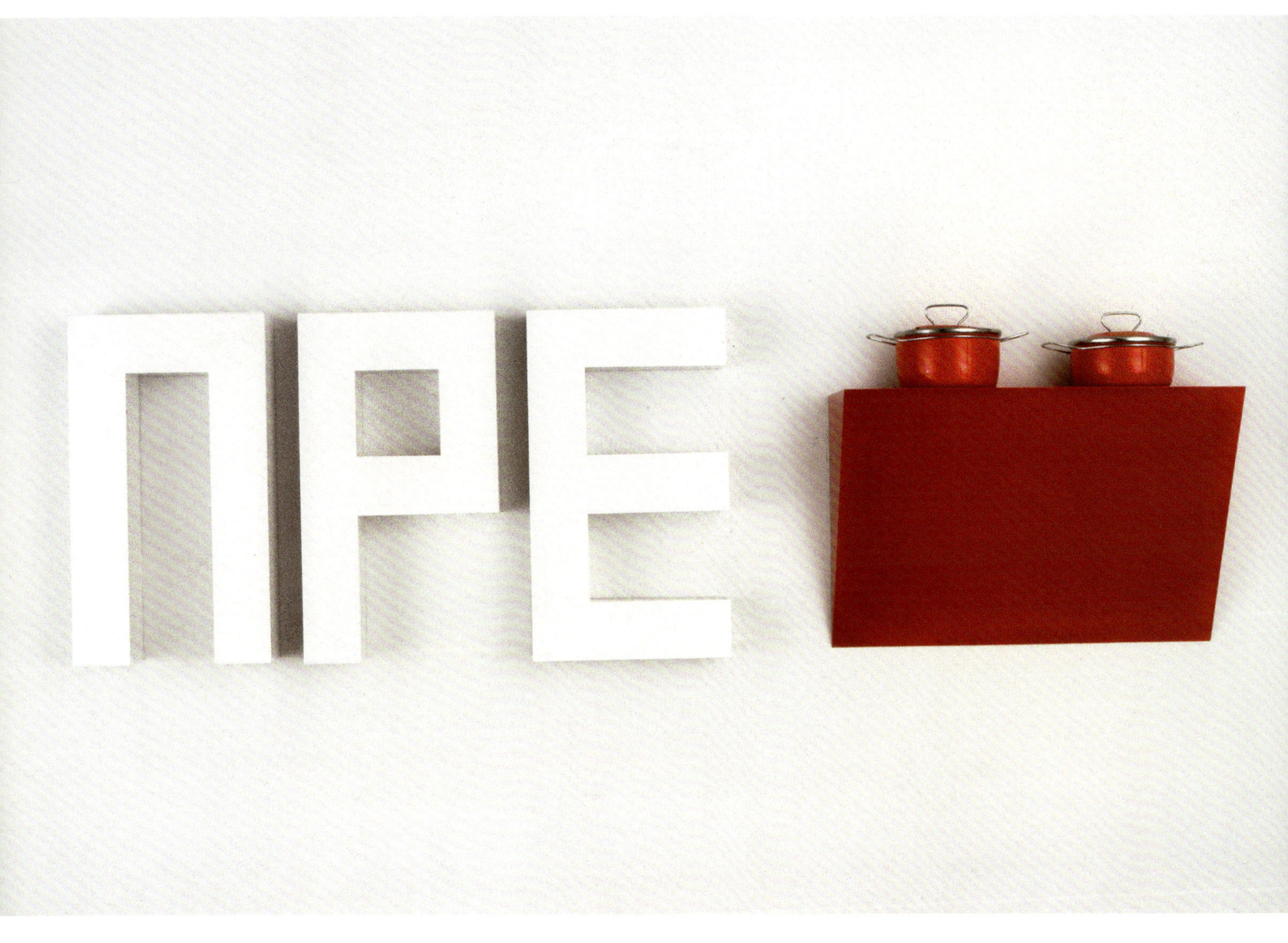

233   Elena Elagina, *PRE*, 1990. Norton and Nancy Dodge Collection of Nonconformist Art from the Soviet Union, Jane Voorhees Zimmerli Art Museum, Rutgers, State University of New Jersey. Collection of the artist, Berlin.

placed two jars of preserved food inside two pairs of slippers, turning these common objects into metaphors for gendered behavior in the communal kitchen (fig. 235). The slippers symbolize men returning from work, only to avoid interaction with neighbors; the jars allude to women returning from work and plunging into the kitchen to realize grand projects of food preservation motivated by fear of food shortages.

Like Elagina, Maria Serebriakova addressed women's everyday burdens. For example, she placed pins over subtle drawings of hands making cookies, which evoke representations of working hands popular in photographs from the era of the first Five-Year Plan. The joyful spirit of labor conveyed in those historical images is turned into a sadomasochistic impression (the pins) of the repetitive rituals of cooking and cleaning in the suffocating space of the communal kitchen (fig. 236). Those kitchens made solidarity among women virtually impossible. Other drawings and collages by Serebriakova advertise "elegant, convenient, useful" objects to Soviet women, projecting

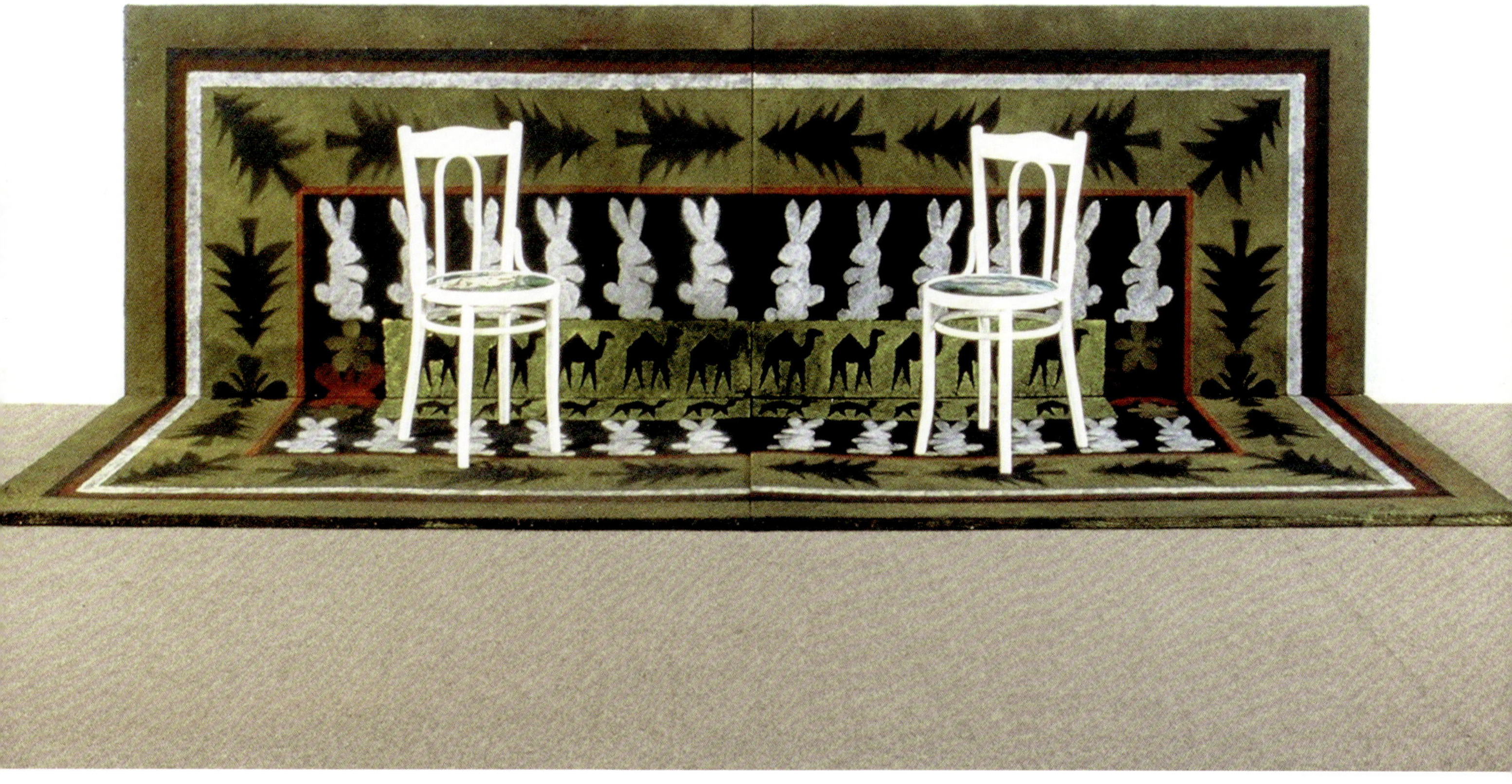

234   Larisa Rezun, *Installation with Two Chairs*, 1989. Collection of the artist, Rotterdam.

the kind of satisfactory consumerism that did not exist before perestroika.

Maria Konstantinova's series of fabric objects provides a feminist critique directed at Russian political and cultural icons. In *Rest in Peace* (fig. 237), she transformed the hard-edged Soviet Red Star into a floppy impotent object, pointing to the end of imperial and militarized Soviet thinking. Kinstantinova's *M.K.K.M.* (fig. 238) replicated in the form of a pillow Malevich's *Black Square*, which Konstantinova like other artists first saw in the 1981 exhibition, and which, as I have noted, generated debates in vanguard art circles. Konstantinova's title displays her initials as the reverse of Malevich's. Through this linguistic play, she marked the space between masculine and feminine discourses. She converted Malevich's austere and provocative canvas into a soft and soothing object, and unknowingly evoked the fact that, before Malevich unveiled Suprematism and *Black Square* at the *0,10* exhibition, he applied Suprematist forms to designs for items such as pillow cases.[13] In other words, prior to Suprematism becoming modernist (read masculine),

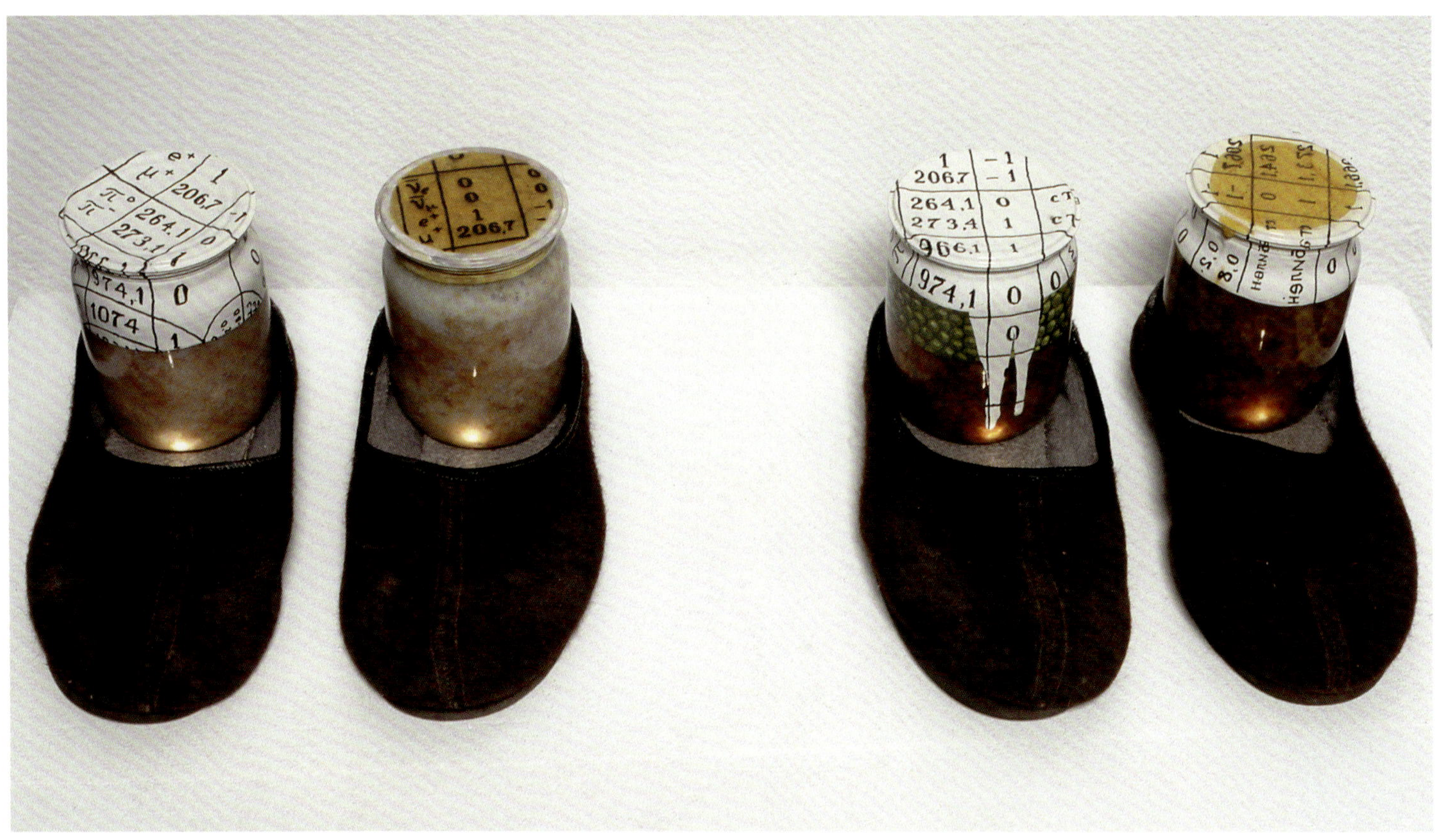

235   Liudmila Skripkina and Oleg Petrenko (the Peppers), *Slippers*, 1991.

it was a feminine weapon of egalitarianism and functionality.

Another form of artistic production that thrived during perestroika was photography. As I have shown in the previous chapters, unauthorized postwar photographic practices were rare, and photography as an independent medium had no discursive trajectory. This is because by the late 1930s there was a sharp turn toward positioning photography as an instrument of political propaganda. The government falsified history with the help of photography, making this medium dubious and artistically unreliable. In its turn, the camera, with its ability to capture everyday events candidly, became, in the eyes of the government, who not long before had urged proletariats to become amateur photographers, a dangerous tool. To control its use, official permissions were required to take pictures in public places, resulting in a significant reduction of the camera's usage. After the implementation of Khrushchev's liberal policies, restrictions on photography were moderated. However, the first generation of post-war modernists could not accept this medium, which for them was a prime suspect in the success of the deceptive political apparatus. When after Khrushchev's deposition it became clear that vanguard art would not become part of official institutions, the camera was the only tool to compensate for this void by documenting the genealogy of the counterculture. Photography's utilitarian role climaxed in 1982, when the members of CAG, together with the Apt Art artists, began to compile a series of folders for the Moscow Archive of New Art (MANI), consisting of photographs and texts that documented the art of this milieu.

First, the 1970s conceptual artists and then, early in the 1980s, Kabakov resuscitated photography's creative potential as a conceptual device as well as a potent readymade. But the medium still awaited rehabilitation

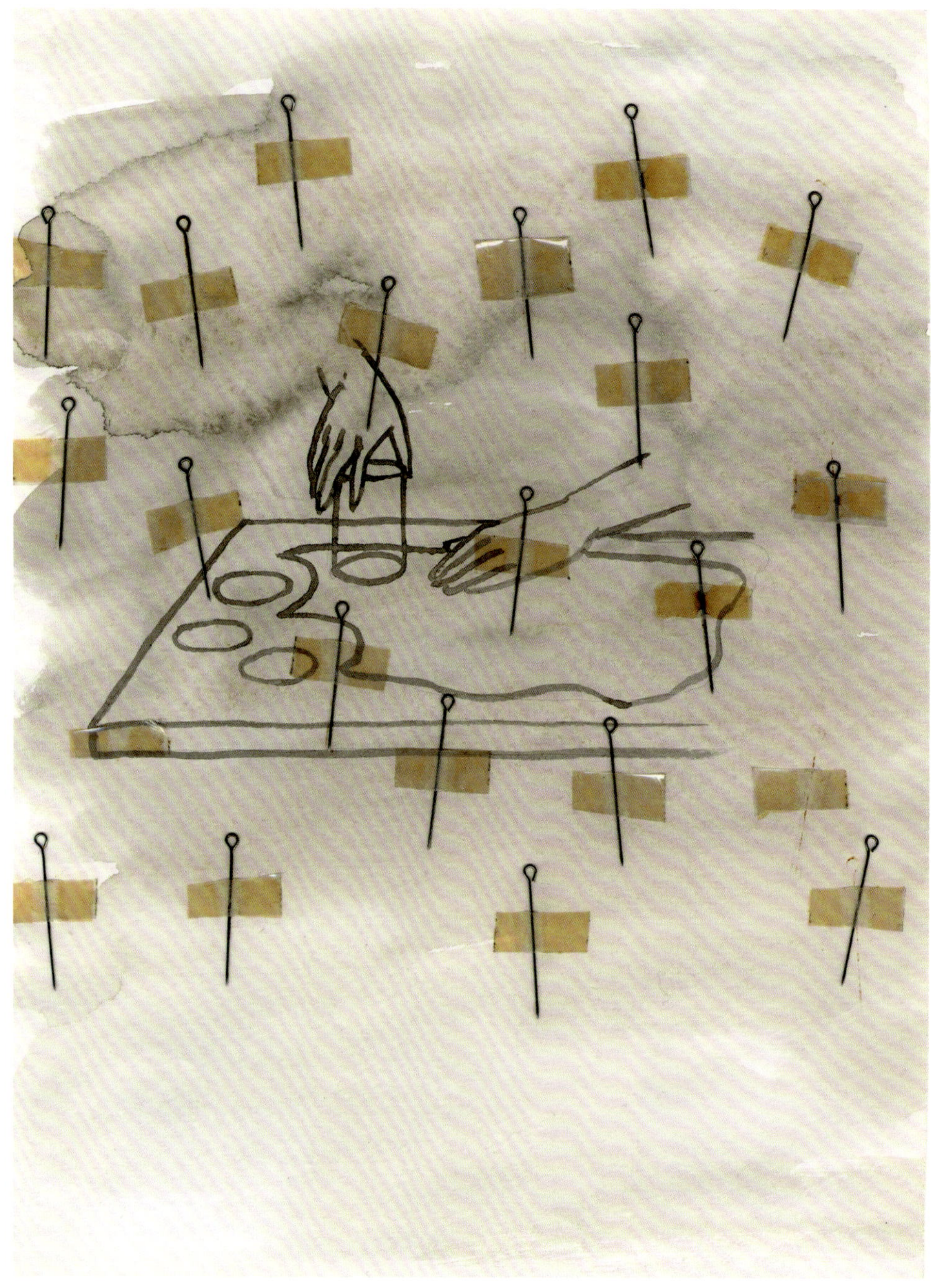

236   Maria Serebriakova, *Untitled*, 1989. Private collection.

as an independent art form. The exhibition, *Possibilities in Photography* (organized in 1981 at the Center for Technical Aesthetics in celebration of the ninetieth anniversary of Aleksandr Rodchenko's birth), marked the beginning of this process on a broader level. While such participants in *Possibilities in Photography* as Vasiliev, Bulatov, and Ivan Chuikov demonstrated photography's role in painting, the Kharkov photographer, Boris Mikhailov, showed his series, *City* (figs. 239–45), in which a dystopian picture of an industrial center sharply contradicted the urban utopia of Rodchenko's "The New Moscow" (1932); this con-

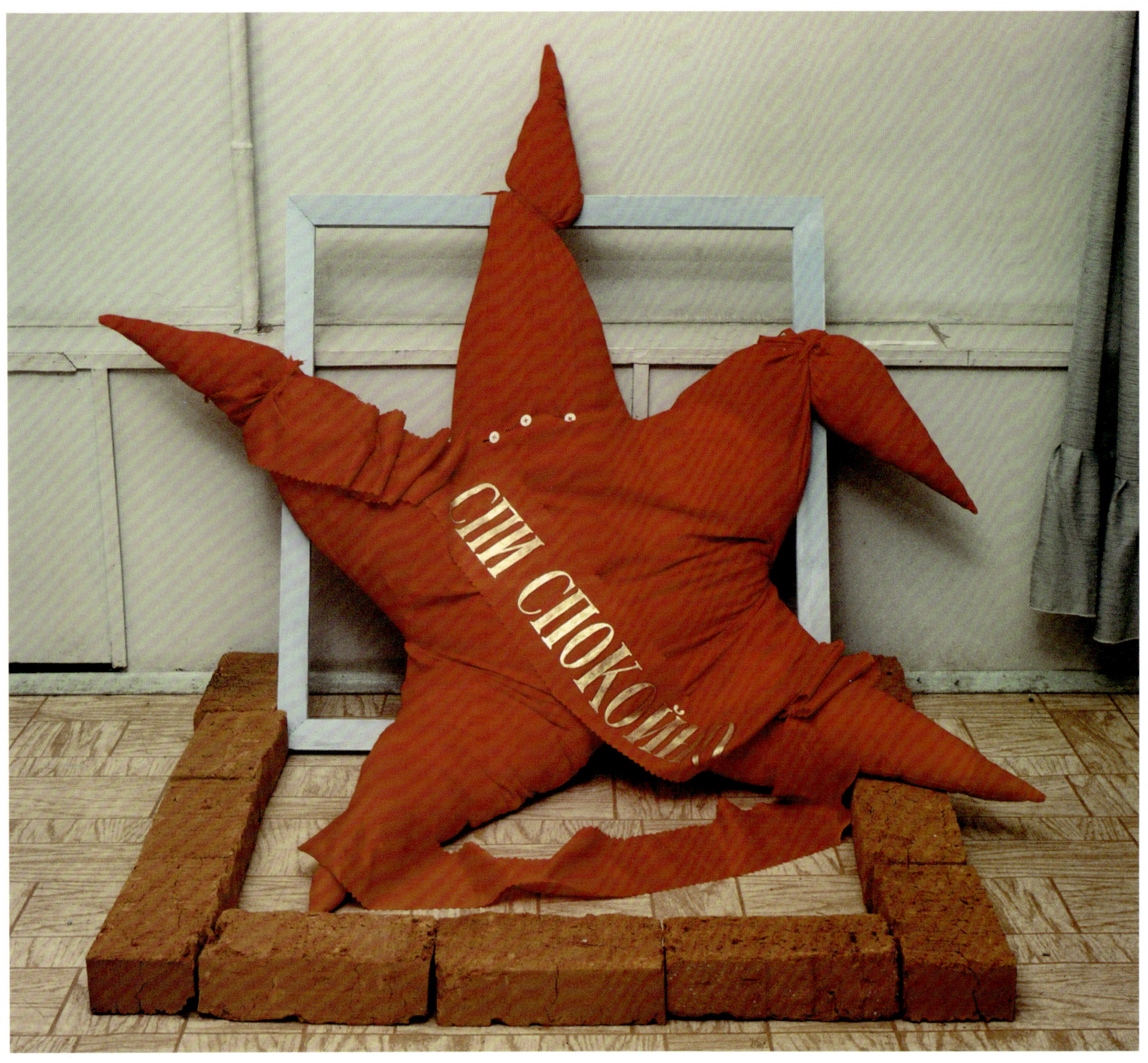

237 Maria Konstantinova, *Rest in Peace*, 1989.

stituted the first discourse between the avant-garde and postwar photographers. Mikhailov, feeling "cut off from all Moscow activities," was eager for a critical interpretation of his work, so he regularly visited Kabakov's studio during trips to Moscow. He has described Kabakov's reaction to his work: "When [Kabakov] looked at the photo, he seemed to enter into it entirely; he perceived and experienced it so vividly that his experience of it was a greater pleasure for me than the very act of creation."[14] And just as Kabakov was fascinated by Mikhailov's experiments in photography, Mikhailov was fascinated by Kabakov's appropriation of official photographs that were empty of originality. Mikhailov explained:

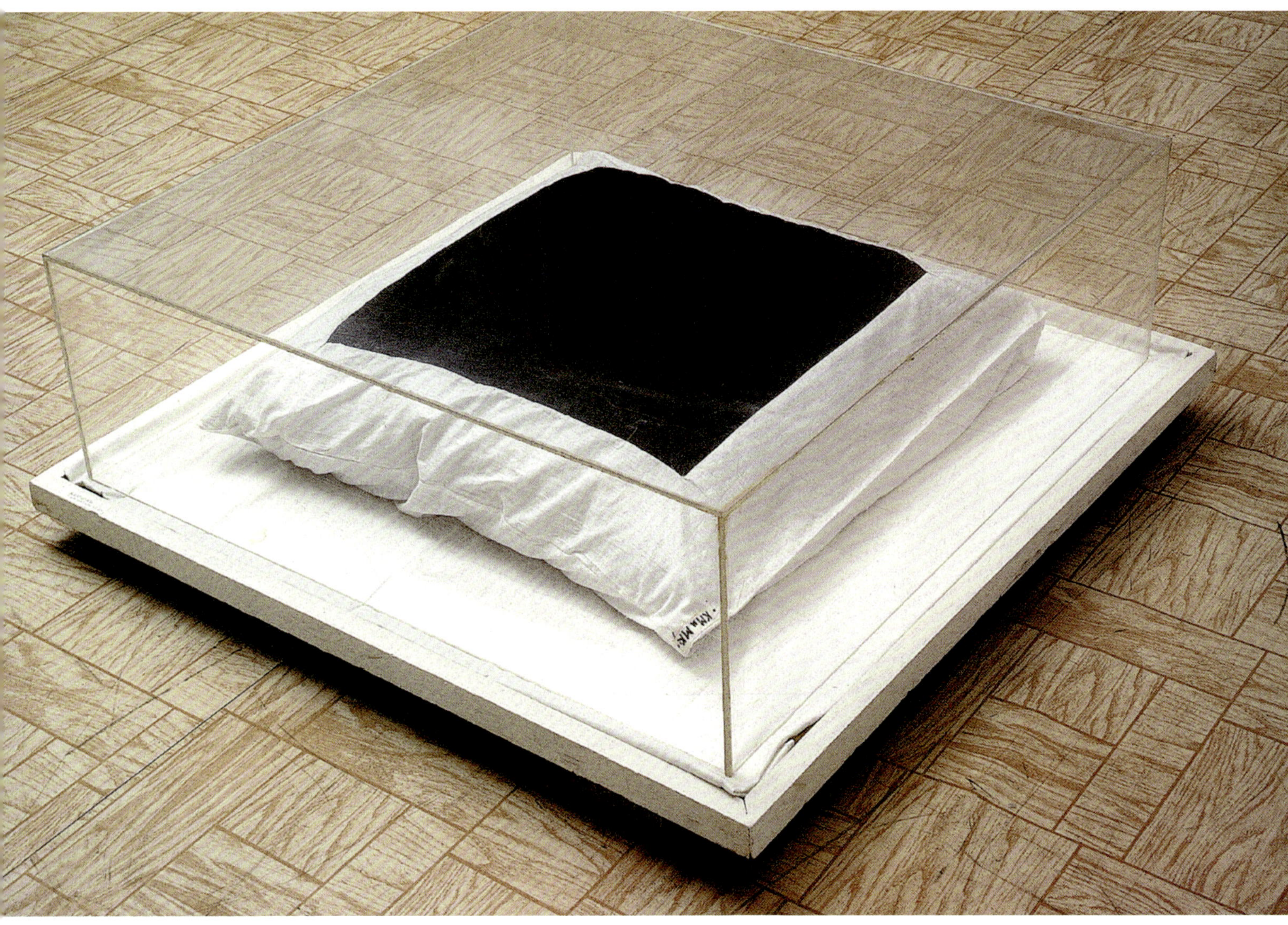

238 Maria Konstantinova, *M.K.K.M*, 1989.

This, for the most part, is not photography, but rather postcards and reproductions, the use of which at that time was the revelation of a new world for me. I have in mind the very idea of using this material, the attitude toward visual representation in general, and toward photography in particular, as some sort of folk production, as well as the attitude toward any style and any iconography as an official, ideological text. Plus, we see the possibility of looking at the entire photographic medium from some different point of view, not just from within.[15]

Before Kabakov's archeological approach to the Soviet archive provided the material for his installations such as *Ship* (fig. 246), he tested it in two-dimensional art in order to redefine the status of the photographic image vis-à-vis painting. In the series *Four Pillars: Production, State, Love, and Art* (fig. 247), Kabakov freed the photograph from being only a referent for a painting or "a painterly photo-picture,"[16] as was the case for some of his works as well as in those of his close friends Bulatov and Vasiliev. Instead, Kabakov demonstrated the photo-

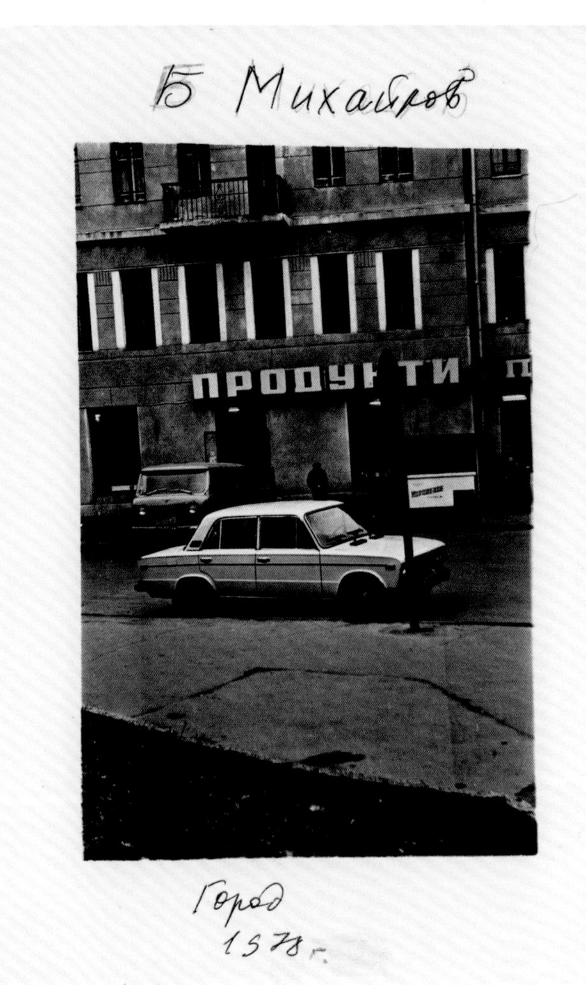

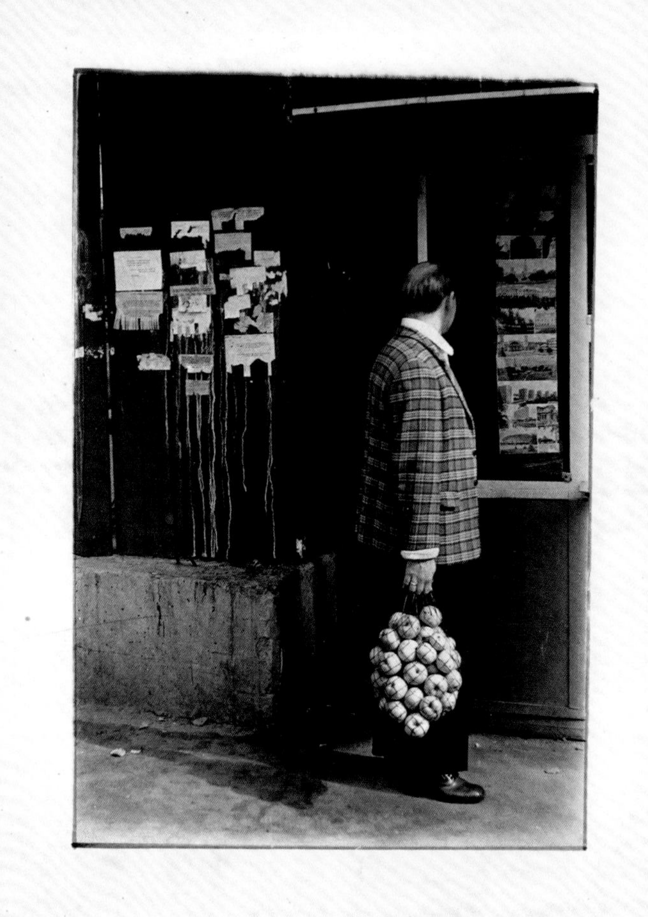

239   Boris Mikhailov, from the series *City*, 1978.

240   Boris Mikhailov, from the series *City*, 1978.

graph's multiplicity, the way it "eliminates the meaning of uniqueness, a quality attributed purely to painting."[17] To illustrate the four topics of the title as the main themes in official representations, Kabakov excavated images from the multiple layers of the years of propaganda. Distributed over four green panels, the archive "emerges in fragments…with greater sharpness, the greater the time that separates [us] from it," to quote Foucault on cultural archives.[18] In the context of this perception, for Kabakov the "unavoidable" presence of this collection of photographs broke "the thread of transcendental teleologies"[19] that had governed underground artists since they manifested themselves in the late 1950s. Kabakov's "rehabilitation" of this material also led to the dissipation of the

"temporal identity" in which, to paraphrase Foucault, Soviet dissident modernists were pleased to situate themselves when they wished to exorcise the discontinuities of official Soviet history.

As the decorations of public spaces deteriorated and then disappeared, the long-awaited opportunity to deal with reality as it was (without government prescriptions) had arrived. A vast number of themes hitherto forbidden to Soviet photographers opened up under perestroika. One could document and publish any of the ills of Soviet society, including crime, alcoholism, prostitution, political corruption, sexual repression, and the ecological disaster; in other words, virtually every subject that Soviet photography, in close collaboration with the official media, had

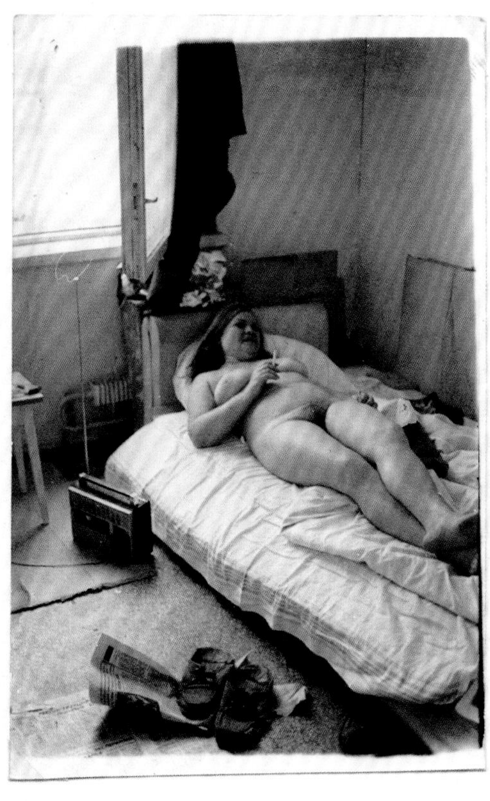

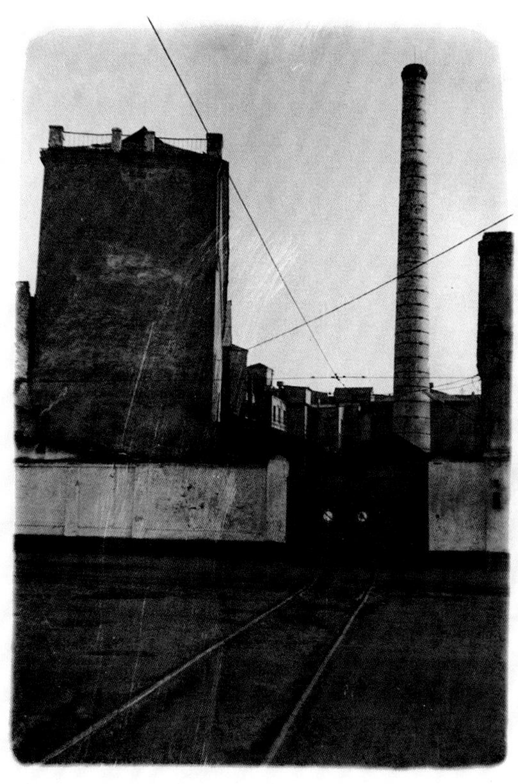

241   Boris Mikhailov, from the series *City*, 1978.

242   Boris Mikhailov, from the series *City*, 1978.

concealed before perestroika. As long as the official media did not relentlessly attack its former boss, the Soviet political establishment, the wide variety of damning material could provide photographers with productive sources for a long time. With all of the enthusiasm that it had exhibited when glorifying the Soviet system, the media now subjected the same system to a degree of subversion impossible to match in individual photographic practices. While this fact by itself did not undermine the importance of those photographers who, alongside the state media, unmasked the regime's prolonged falsehood, it reduced the impact that such photography would otherwise entail. The public, on whose reception this critical practice closely depended, was also saturated by the media's deconstructive campaign. This connection with the suppressed aspects of Soviet history and social life, by means of their explicit and accelerated subversion, made these topics disposable before they had received thorough analysis. In reality, the participants of these denouncing projects were escaping what Foucault called "a *historical a priori*, an *a priori* not of truths that might never be said but the *a priori* of a history that is given, since it is that of things actually said."[20] In other words, for Foucault, history is not "a condition of validity for judgments," an approach taken by many photographers since perestroika, but "a condition of reality for statements." Foucault continues: "It is not a question of rediscovering what might legitimize an assertion, but of

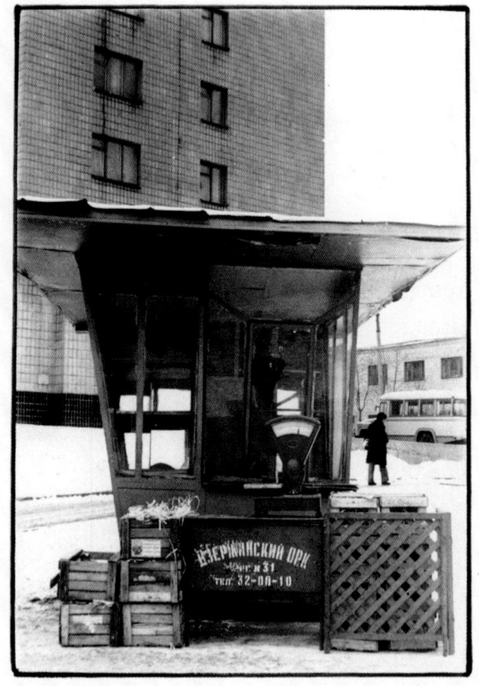

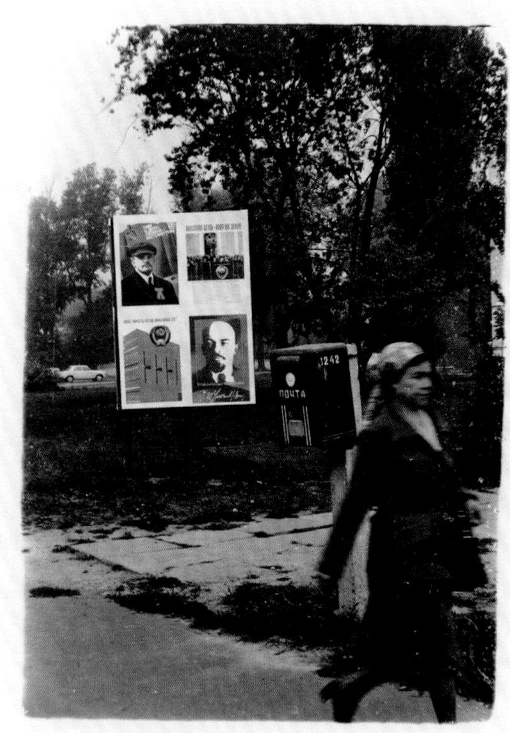

243   Boris Mikhailov, from the series *City*, 1978.

244   Boris Mikhailov, from the series *City*, 1978.

freeing the conditions of emergence of statements [whether events or things], the law of their coexistence with others, the specific form of their mode of being, the principles according to which they survive, become transformed, and disappear."[21]

It is this particular method of locating the material traces left behind by the Soviet empire, and thus to deduce its "historical a priori," that presented an alternative photographic practice. After *Possibilities in Photography*, Vladimir Kuprianov tested photo-readymades in *A Work After Pushkin*, which he first exhibited in the Apt Art gallery (fig. 248).[22] The work is compiled out of sixteen found portraits of Soviet "heroines of labor," each of which Kuprianov captioned with a line from Aleksandr Pushkin's elegy, "Day Has Faded" (*Pogaslo dnevnoe svetilo*). Written

while Pushkin was in exile in 1820, the poem's melancholic content conveys the repressive context in which it was written. In Kuprianov's work, this became an allusion to Andropov's prosecutions of the intelligentsia during his term as KGB chief, as well as when he succeeded Brezhnev at the end of 1982. Another dissonance arises from the association of poetic lines with earthy female workers. It also comes from assigning a male voice and emotions to women. During perestroika, Kuprianov montaged found photographs of workers and peasants into large panels, illustrating on a monumental scale the historical victimization of these two classes (fig. 249). As opposed to the utopian scenes of collective labor best represented in various magazines by the October photographers, Aleksandr Rodchenko and Boris Ignatovich, Kuprianov revisited

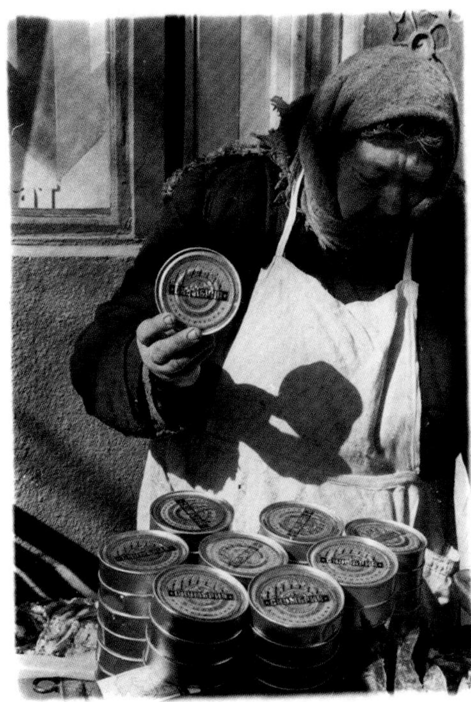

245 Boris Mikhailov, from the series *City*, 1978.

these themes only to certify their bankruptcy. Again, unlike the overt formalism (severe fragmentations, close-ups, and distorted perspectives) of 1920s photography, Kuprianov suppressed his ambitions for formal experimentation.

Aleksei Shulgin took the appropriation of the Soviet photographic archive in a different direction when in the late 1980s he selected and printed images from found negatives of industrial photography (figs. 250, 251). Made by anonymous official photographers, endless rolls of black and white film routinely documented laboring workers, industrial sites, and heavy equipment. Excessive scratching of the negatives marked the uselessness of this material as a factual record in the new era. Shulgin converted this photographic bureaucracy into pictures that mimic the

formal vocabulary of avant-garde photographs. But for him this was neither a formal nor utopian experiment, but an investment of psycho-optics and subjective value judgments into the space of Soviet fabricated objectivity. By calling this series *Others' Photographs*, Shulgin insisted that the medium of photography was the "art of making a choice."[23]

Serebriakova discovered personal photographic archives in a vacant communal apartment that became her studio. Prints abandoned by tenants were piled together, a symbol of de-individualized communal living. Serebriakova chose landscapes from the arsenal of found imagery and obscured or "cured" black and white prints with collage, including pieces of gauze and texts – the visual aid to photography that revealed her interest in Conceptual art (fig. 252). Over one print of a country field (fig. 253), she inscribed in white gouache: "The liar is saying: everything that I assert is a lie," a statement that directly refers to the downfall of photography in the late 1930s. It suggests suspicion of photography as representation in general, and speaks of photography's prolonged subjection to censorship and official accusations that its avant-garde practitioners distorted Soviet reality.

In defense of the work produced in the 1980s in the U.S.A., and based on the appropriation and quotation of photographic images, the art historian Abigail Solomon-Godeau argued that, contrary to the left's criticism of such "work's insularity, its adherence to, or lack of, contestation of the art-world frame, and – more pointedly – its failure to articulate an alternative politics, an alternative vision," art objects of this kind perform "a specifically political function to the extent that they work to actively break down the notion of aesthetic autonomy and to rejoin art and life."[24] If this argument is applied to the photographic work discussed here, somewhat different conclusions may be reached as far as its function is concerned. The difference arises primarily from the fact that, unlike the Western neo-avant-garde, the Soviet vanguard functioned as an *a priori* political phenomenon because, regardless of its often apolitical iconography, officialdom always viewed their work as a political act. But this kind of association with politics was a given rather than a consciously acquired stance, and as such brought about a different concept of

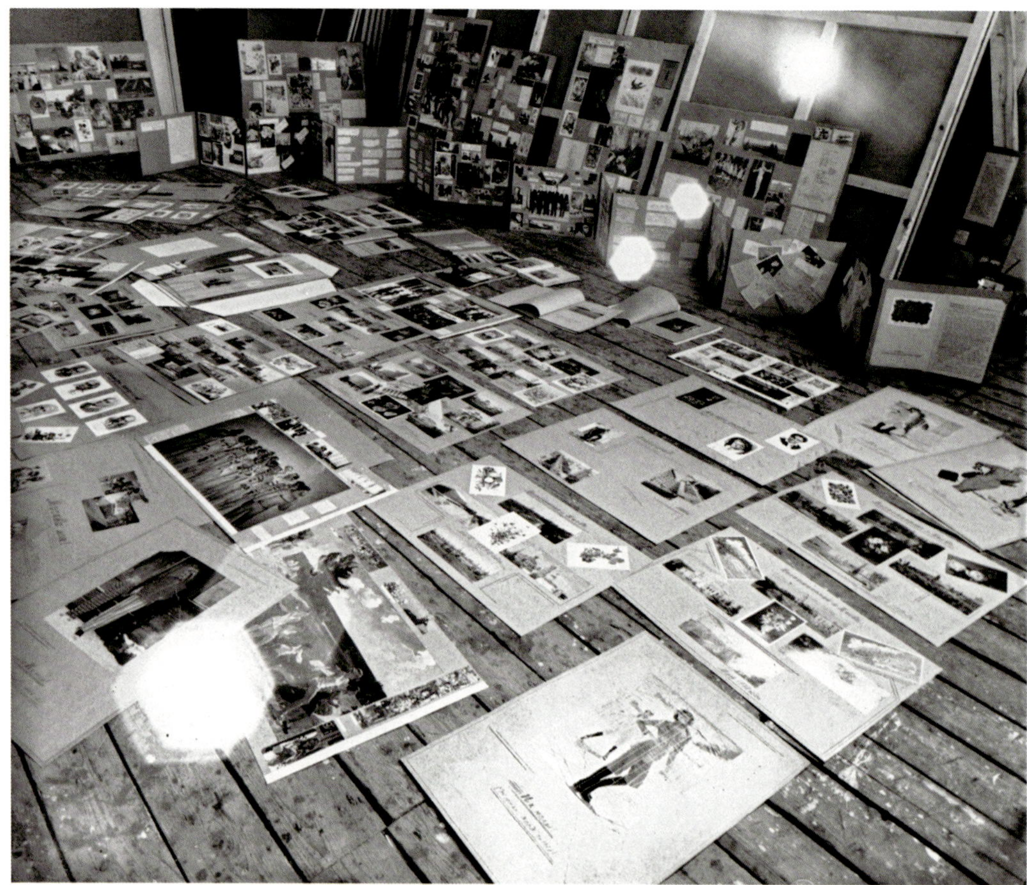

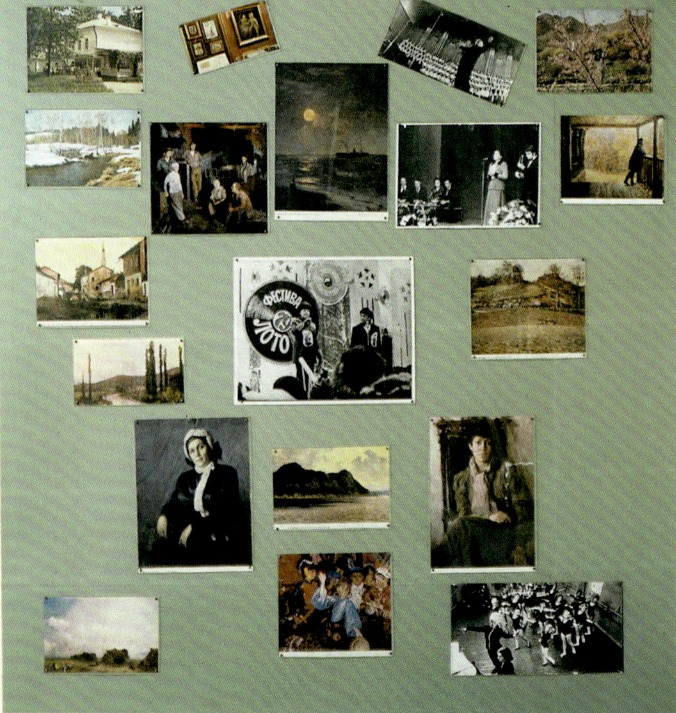

„Повышать роль искусства в воспитании трудящихся, увеличивать сеть клубов, библиотек, Домов культуры".
(Из речи Л.И.Брежнева на апрельском 1979 г. пленуме ЦК)

Как песня, наша жизнь течет
В счастливом братстве всех народов,
Танцует молодость, поет,
Искусство крепнет год от года.

Звучат у нас во всех краях
Они всегда, как братья, вместе-
Живой украинский гопак,
Раздолье нашей русской песни.

Ковров таджикских красота,
Чеканщиков грузинских слава-
Пою вам песню, мастера
Моей страны, моей державы!

Искусство наше, как ручей,
Как руки женщины любимой,
И в этой песне светлый день
Горит огнем неугасимым.

political practice. While Western artists such as Sherry Levine, Richard Prince, and Barbara Kruger borrowed photographic imagery in order to enter one or another political discourse, the Moscow artists appropriated the Soviet photographic archive in order to quit a single political reality. Only after escaping this prison house could a different journey toward a variety of political options become possible.

As I stated at the outset, Khrushchev's thaw and Gorbachev's perestroika had the two most profound impacts on the development of postwar vanguard art. Yet, the difference between the two liberation campaigns was crucial. Khrushchev unlocked the country for foreigners, but preserved restrictions on overseas travel for Soviet citizens; Gorbachev brought down the Iron Curtain alogether. Thus, in the late 1950s, exhibitions of Western art were brought to Moscow, whereas during perestroika, Russian vanguardists traveled abroad for their own exhibitions. This served the older generations of the vanguard well, for – unlike the post-revolutionary avant-gardists, who were ready not only to create a visual language for the Bolshevik epoch, but also to build a new institutional network – the postwar vanguardists saw their institutional future in the West. Furthermore, these older artists were in demand abroad (at least for the period of perestroika), and years of alienation from Soviet institutions made them unprepared (if not unwilling) to reform them. The government's rapid conversion of underground culture into mainstream culture[25] (for profit from sales[26] as well as for international prestige in the sphere of culture) created many opportunities for these artists in the West because, paradoxically, Western institutions were much more willing to embrace Soviet vanguard artists when they were presented through official channels than when they were part of the underground and their works were smuggled out.

Even after such artists as Kabakov, Bulatov, and Vasiliev began exhibiting and living in the West from perestroika onward, they felt they should scrutinize the image of their rapidly changing country. Kabakov,

in installations such as *Ten Characters* at the Feldman gallery in 1988, concentrated on exposing the dystopia and alienation within communal living. He also taught the Western spectator how truly to see Soviet objects, by drawing attention to their high degree of tactility (their *faktura*). Bulatov, for his part, in *Perestroika* (fig. 254), painted in New York, forecasts Gorbachev's political demise as well as the general failure of his rule: like the word "revolution" (present in the earlier canvas *Revolution-Perestroika*), Gorbachev too was removed. In *Sunrise or Sunset* (1989; Ludwig Forum für Internationale Kunst, Ludwig Collection, Aachen), Bulatov expresses the general feeling of uncertainty about the fate of the Soviet Union in the title as well as in his rendering of its state emblem, in place of a sun disk, hanging frozen on the ocean's surface either at the beginning or the end of the daily cycle. While living in New York, Vasiliev commemorated the most dramatic and climactic event associated with the consequences of perestroika – the burning of the Russian White House during the 1993 coup (fig. 255). If Bulatov's *Perestroika* may be called a perestroika flag, Vasiliev's canvas is a marker of the beginning of the post-Soviet era.

Although there was increased demand for Western art institutions to exhibit Russian art, the younger generation was not as eager to take advantage of opportunities to settle in the West. Instead, many of them sought to preserve the collective bond of the underground milieu in Moscow, flocking into a building on Furmanny Lane that became vacant after its communal apartments were emptied and tenants relocated. By doing this they chose to communicate with foreign collectors, dealers, and curators on their own turf (much like in the 1920s). This stance contributed to the preservation of their works' original context. Zakharov described the difference between making art before perestroika in a small and hermetic community with clearly defined social and artistic norms, and no commercial incentive, and making art afterward, when all these characteristics began to crumble:

246   Ilya Kabakov, *The Ship*, the artist's studio, Moscow, 1985.

247   Ilya Kabakov, from the series *Four Pillars: Production, State, Love, and Art*, 1983. Collection Ilya and Emilia Kabakov.

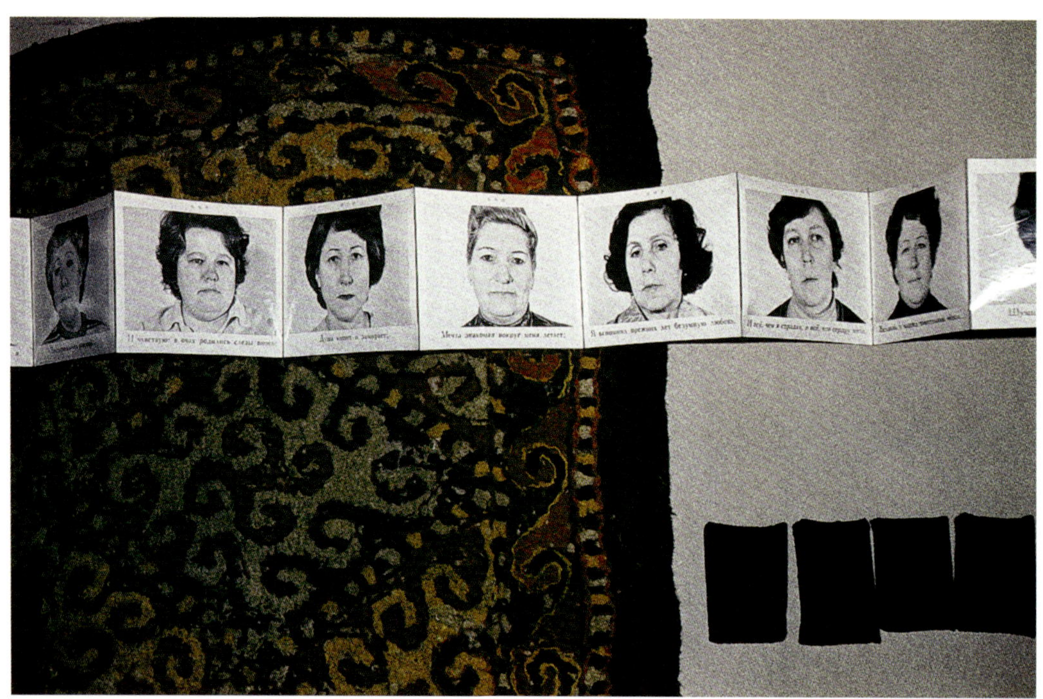

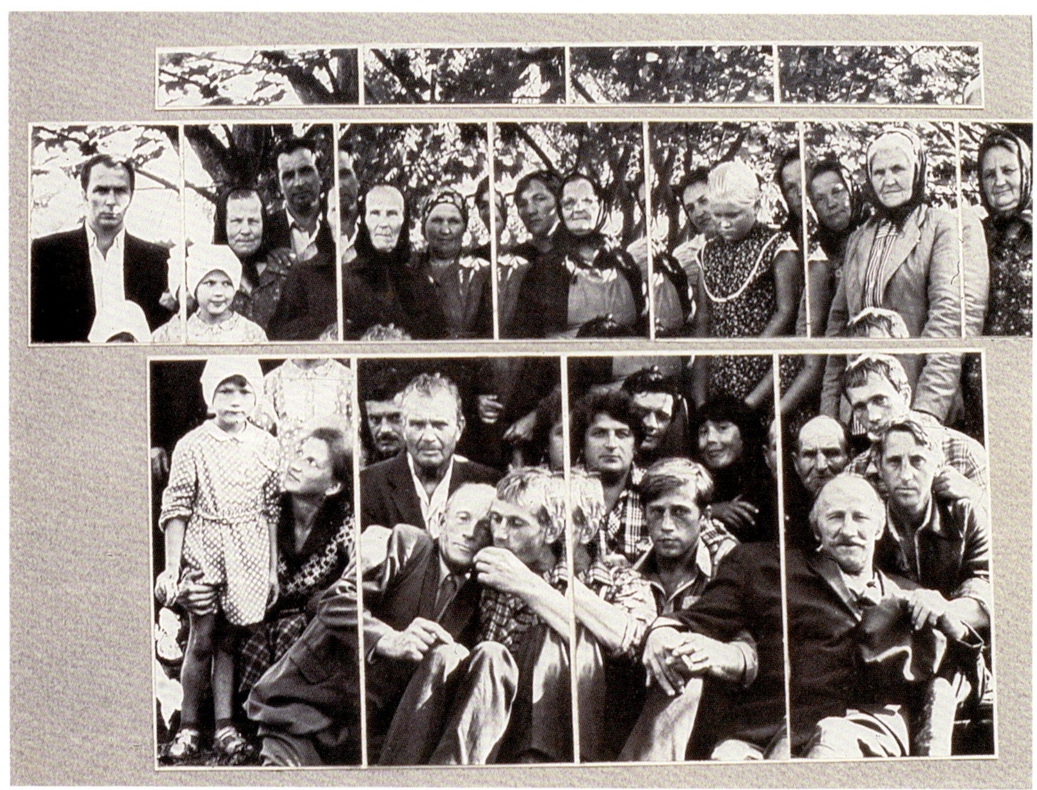

248   Vladimir Kuprianov's *A Work After Pushkin* in the Apt Art gallery's exhibition *Victory Over the Sun*, Moscow, 1983.

249   Vladimir Kuprianov, *Funeral*, 1991. Collection of the artist's estate.

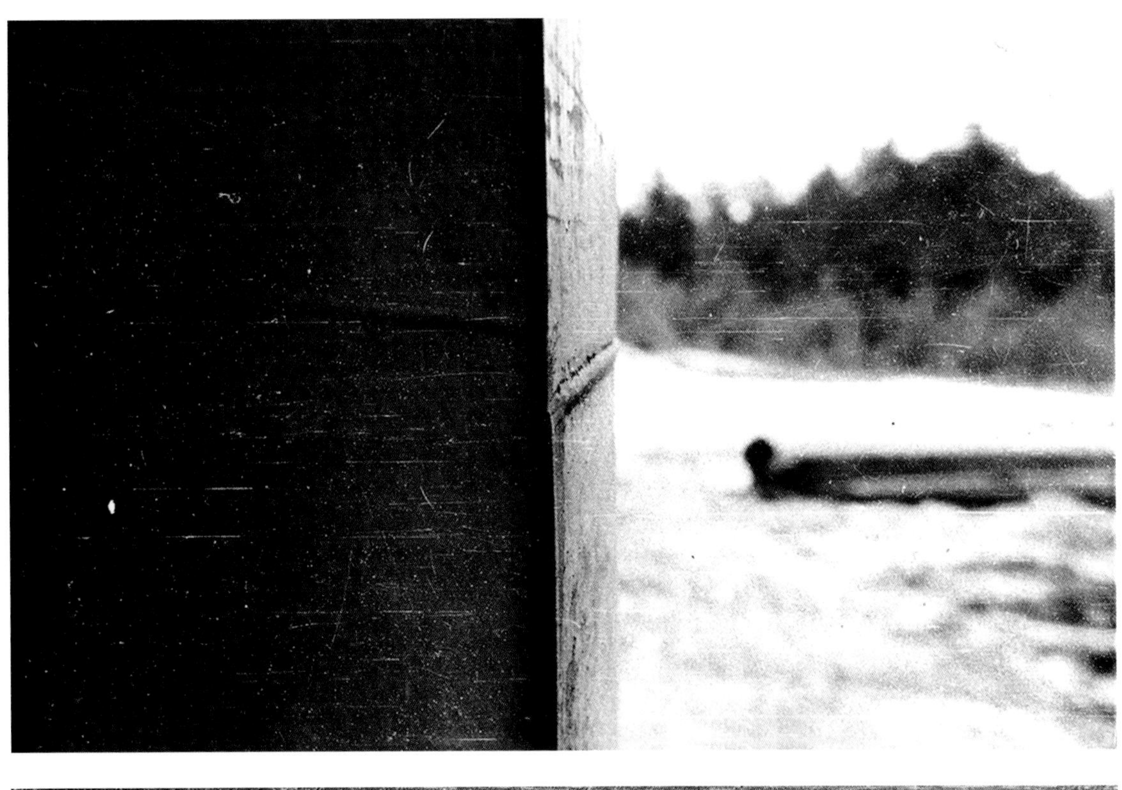

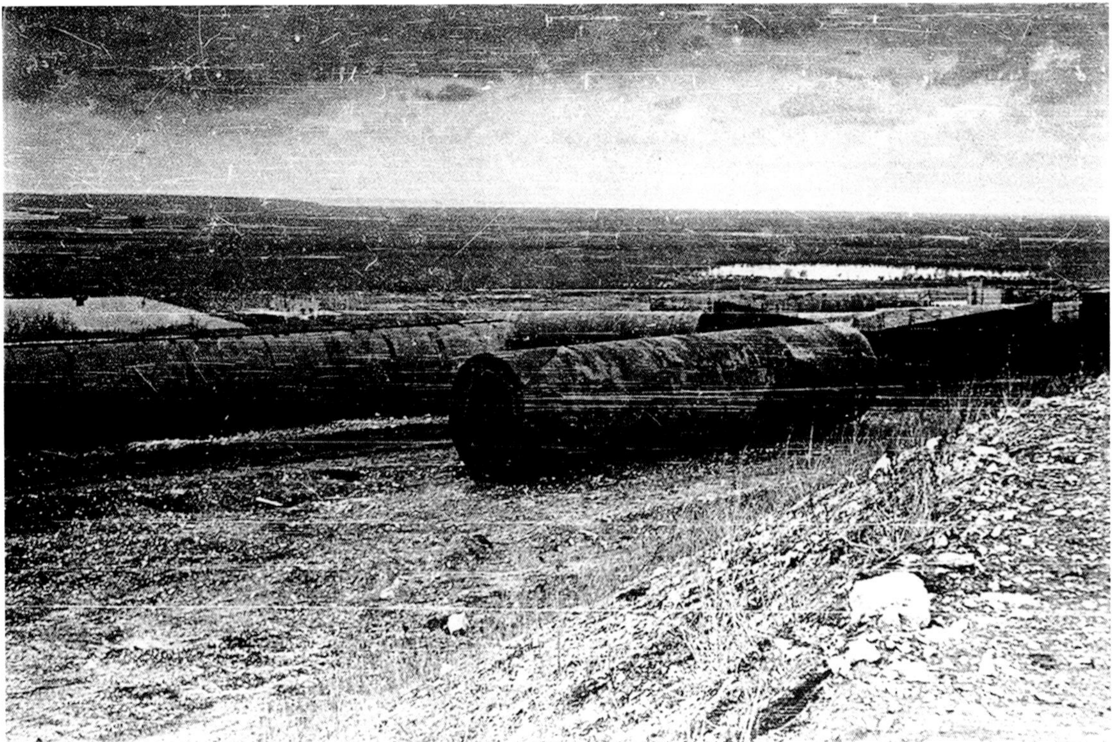

250 & 251   Aleksei Shulgin, from the series *Others' Photographs*, late 1980s.

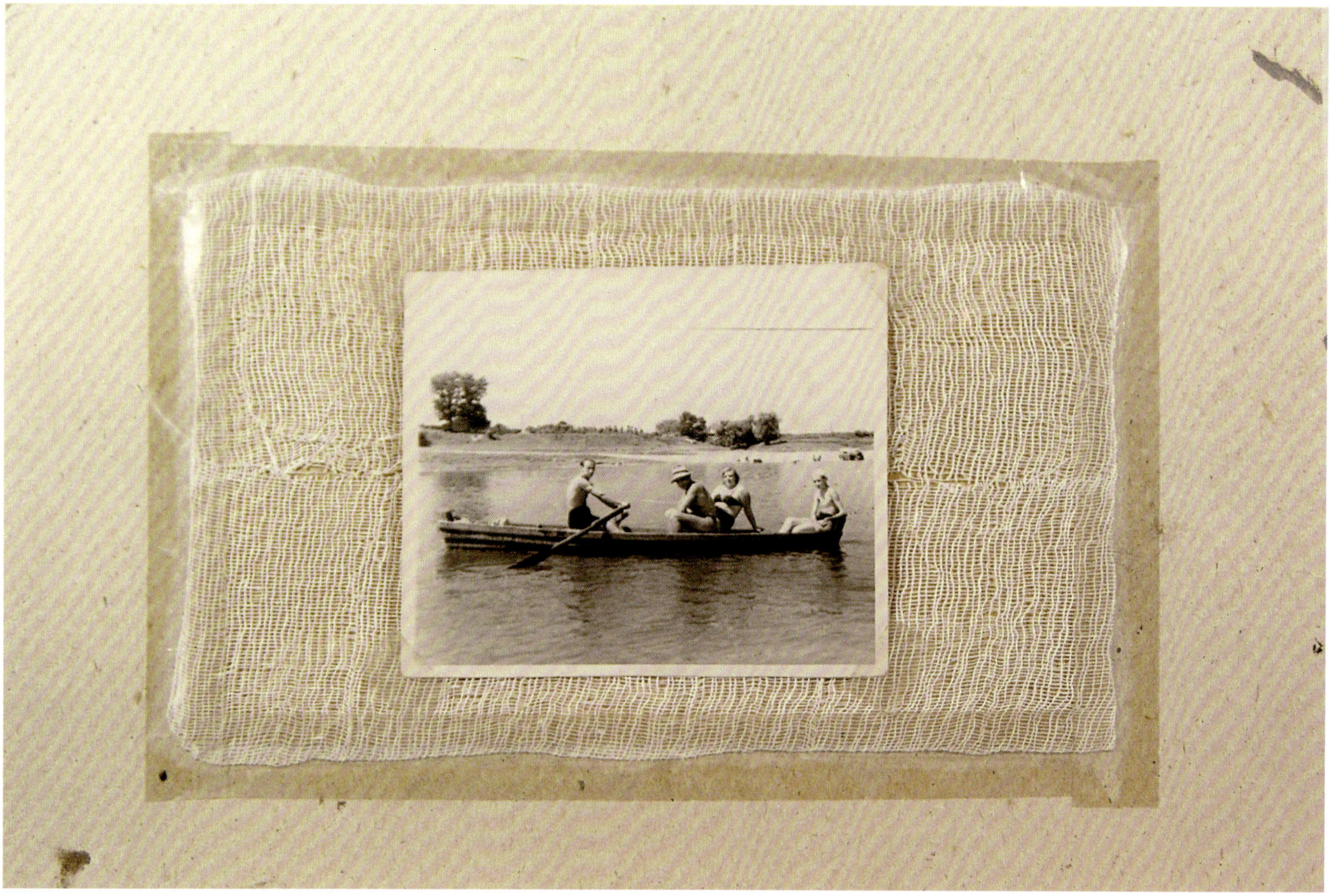

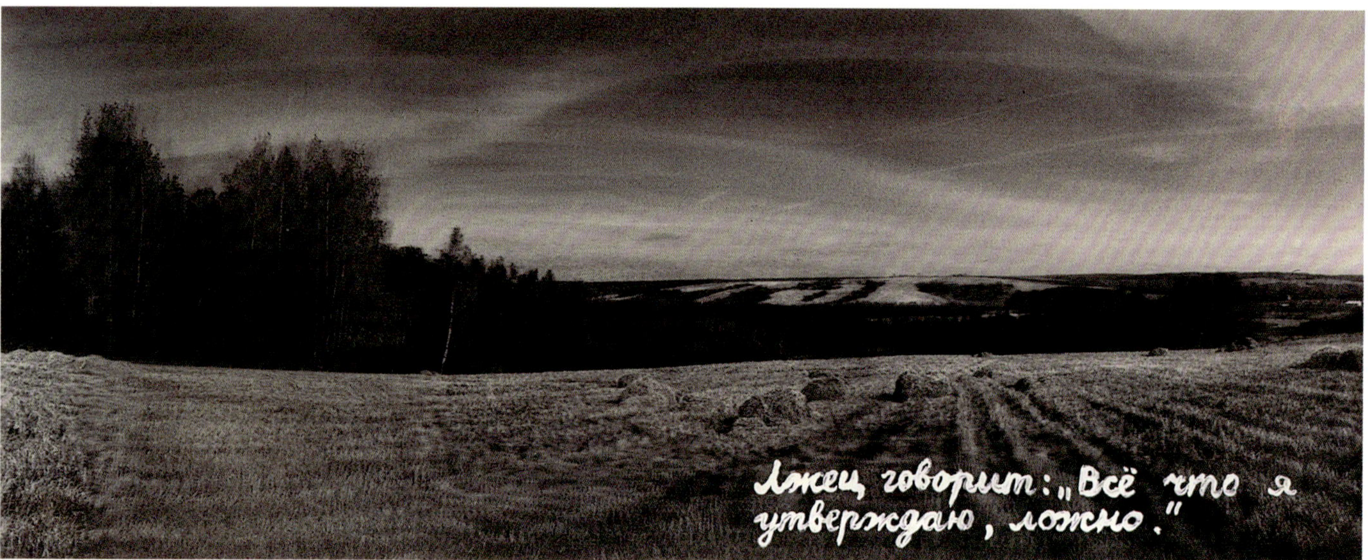

252 & 253   Maria Serebriakova, *Untitled*, 1989. Collection of the artist, Berlin.

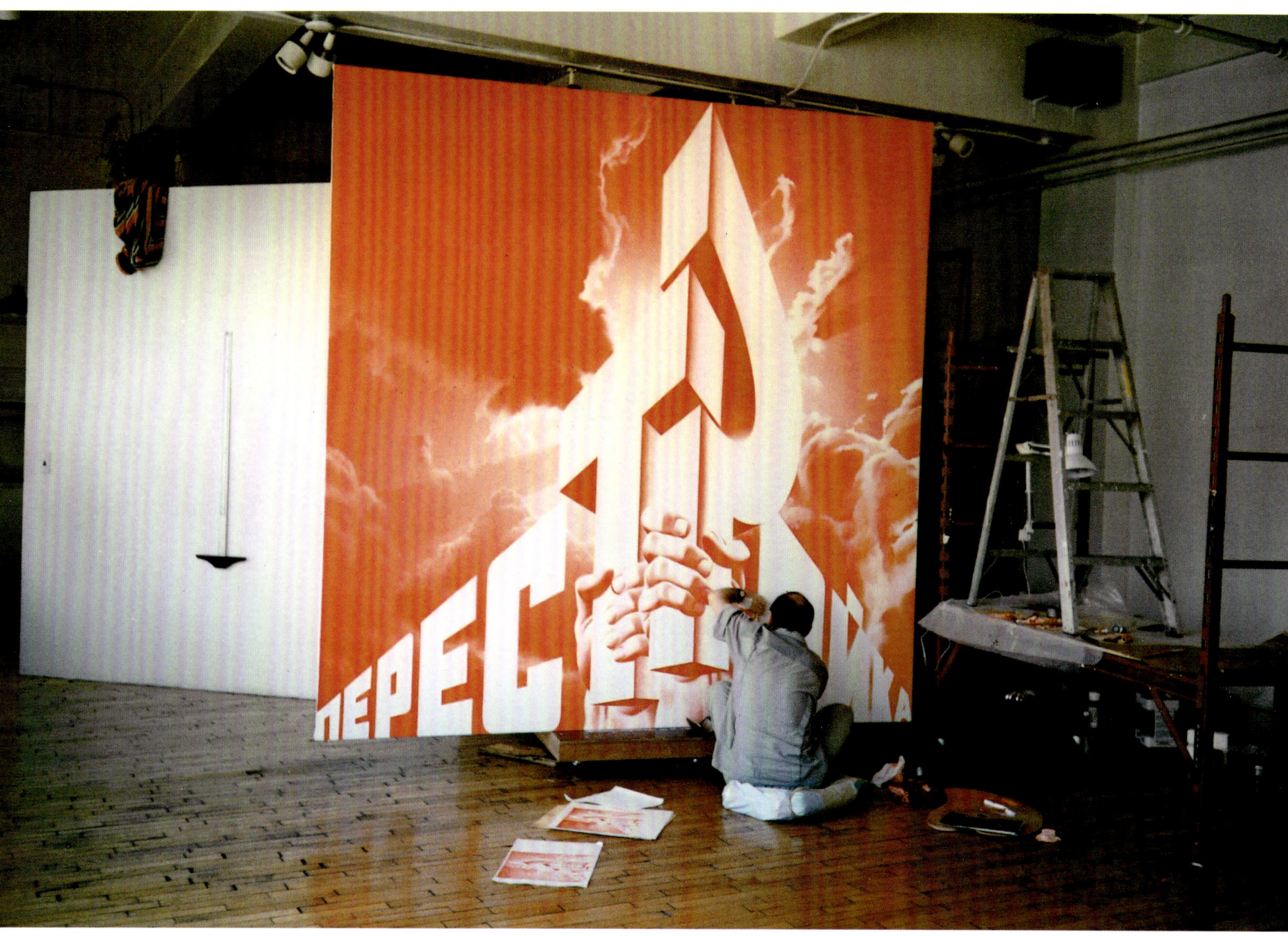

254   Erik Bulatov painting *Perestroika*, in his New York studio, 1989.

The fact is that three years ago [1985] there were only thirty of us in the whole Soviet Union. Now the situation has radically changed. A period of seduction has set in. A mass of new names has appeared: people of a completely different formation…That is, a normal artistic situation has arisen, which for us is not easy to adjust to. In other words, we've entered an age of competition.[27]

The difference is further revealed in Zakharov's own work executed on Furmanny Lane compared with the projects he made during the Apt Art period. For example, the precision of his 1981 photographic series, *I Have Made Enemies*, matched the clear cultural function which it performed: the artist was working out a paradigm of a generational conflict addressed to a specific cultural community. That is why he targeted four artists (everyone in the underground circles knew who these artists were) whom he subjected to a critique, and made his self-portrait central so that from that point onward everyone would recognize him in those circles (figs. 256, 257). In contrast, the ruptured

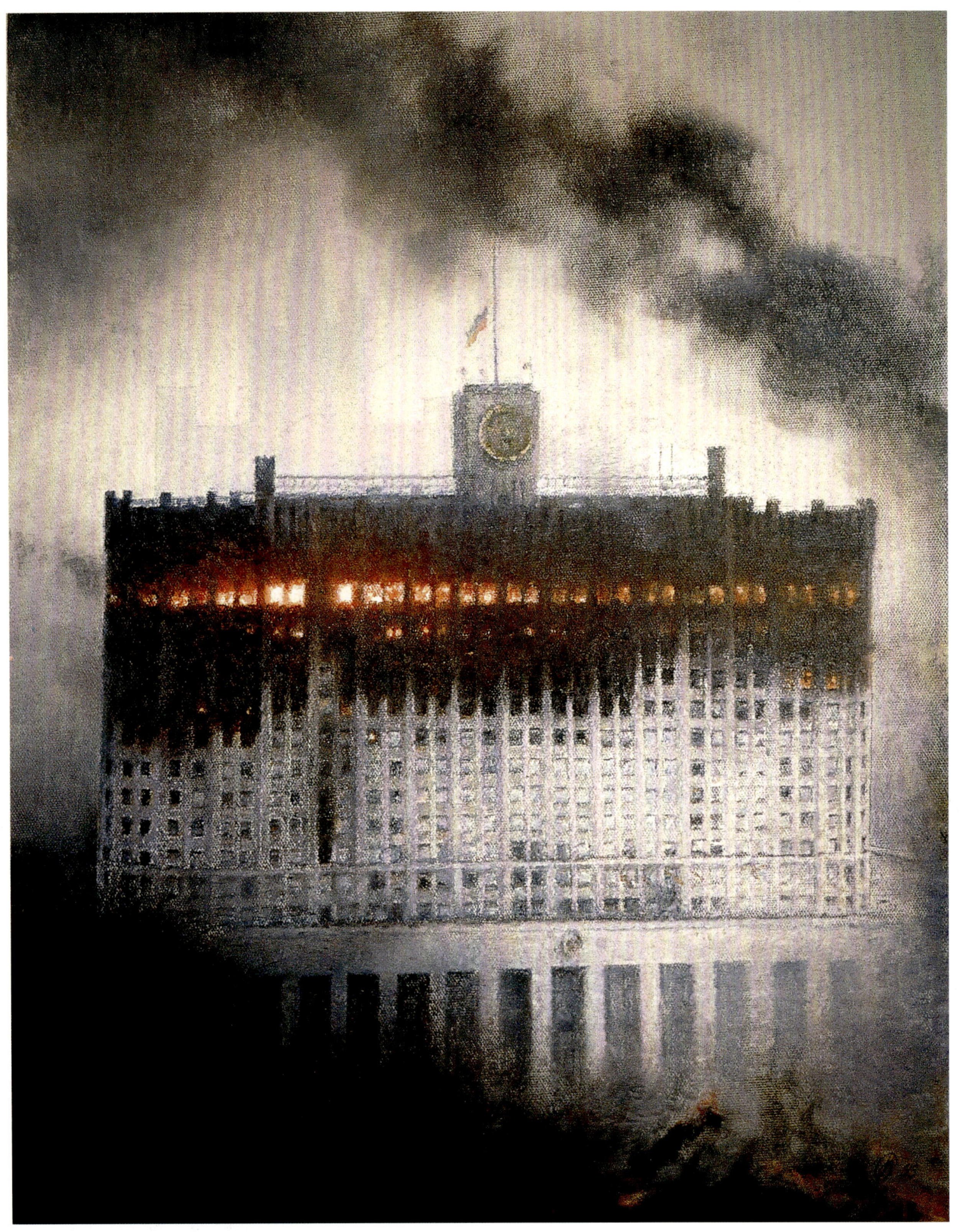

255   Oleg Vasiliev, *Burning White House*, 1993. Private collection.

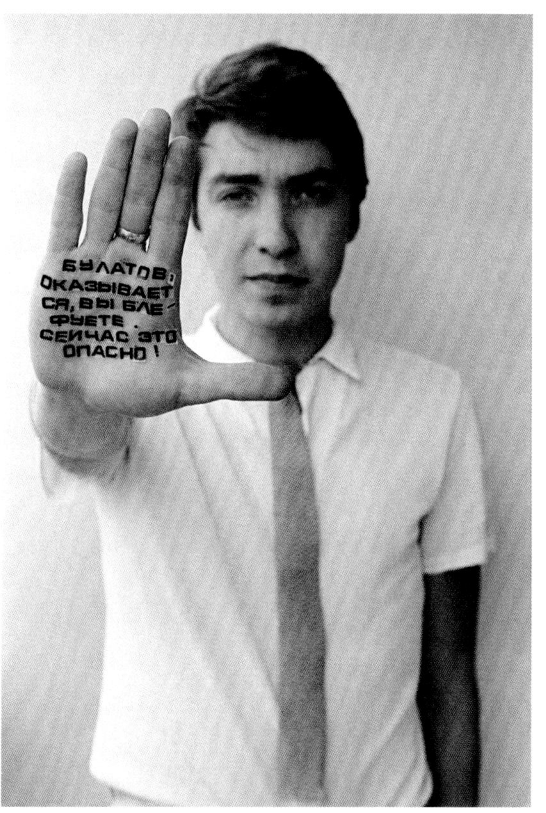

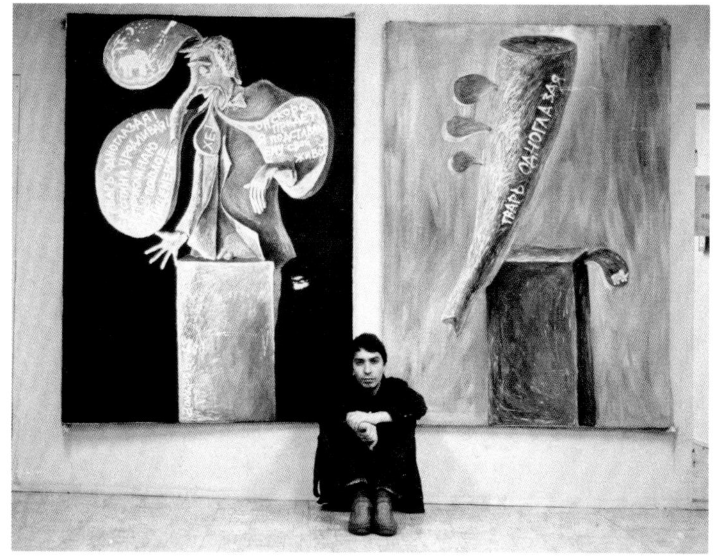

LEFT 256 & 257   Vadim Zakharov, from the series *I Have Made Enemies* (*Bulatov you are bluffing. It's dangerous now*), 1981.

ABOVE 258   Vadim Zakharov next to his paintings, on Furmanny Lane, Moscow, 1989.

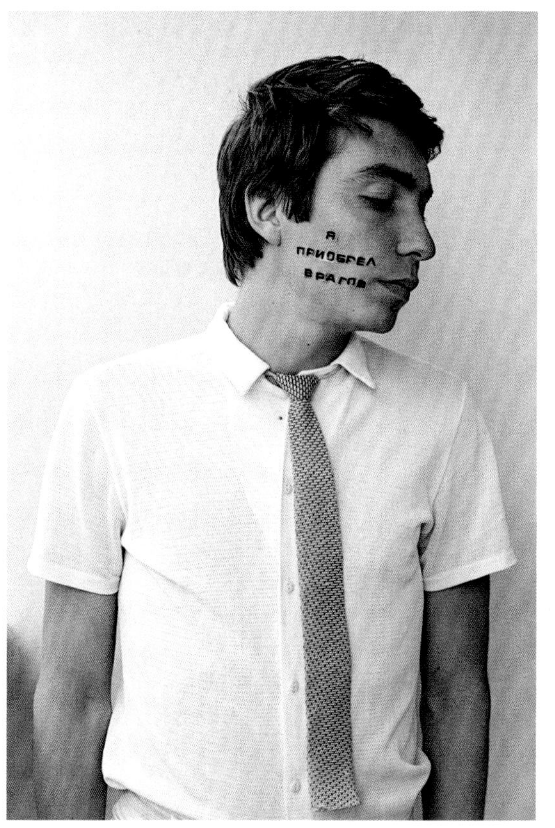

and awkward shapes and ambivalent symbolism of Zakharov's perestroika paintings (a step backward from his earlier ephemeral forms of execution), signaled the signs of a shift from art as a cultural text that takes into account collective references, to what Andrei Monastyrsky called, "an inarticulate chaos of personal psychopathologies"[28] (fig. 258). The rending asunder the veil of *mythos* regarding the West was no doubt a great advantage for Moscow vanguard artists. Whether this significantly narrowed the gap between the two art worlds, and became crucial for the development of the post-Soviet period of Moscow vanguard art, is the subject of another study.

NOTES

INTRODUCTION

1 In 1935, Klutsis began to write a book titled "The Right to an Experiment" (*Pravo na eksperiment*) that was left unfinished owing to his arrest and execution in 1938.

2 *The Collected Essays and Criticism*, ed. John O'Brian, vol. 4 (Chicago: University of Chicago Press, 1986), p. 228.

3 Liubov Popova, quoted in Dmitri V. Sarabianov and Natalia L. Adaskina, *Liubov Popova* (New York: Harry N. Abrams, Inc., 1990), p. 196.

4 Igor Golomstock, "Problems in the Study of Stalinist Culture," in *The Culture of the Stalin Period*, ed. Hans Günther (London: Macmillan, 1990), p. 112.

5 Christina Kiaer, "Lyrical Socialist Realism," *October* no. 147 (Winter 2014), p. 60.

6 I appropriate this term from the chapter "A Modernist Retort," in *Art Since 1900: Modernism, Antimodernism, Postmodernism*, ed. Hal Foster, Rosalind Krauss, Yve-Alain Bois, Benjamin H. D. Buchloh (London and New York: Thames and Hudson, 2005), pp. 284–5, which discusses Western artists' responses to the brutal politics of Europe in the 1930s.

7 Golomstock, "Problems in the Study of Stalinist Culture," p. 110.

1 IN DEFENSE OF NONOBJECTIVE ART

1 Kazimir Malevich in *Malevich o sebe, sovremenniki o Maleviche: pis'ma, dokumenty, vospominaniia, kritika*, ed. I.A. Vakar and T.N. Mikhienko, 2 vols. (Moscow: RA, 2004), vol. 1, p. 33. All translations from Russian sources are mine unless otherwise noted.

2 Katsman believed that Malevich thought of him as a "mediocre artist." In turn, he called Malevich a "useless artist." Ibid., vol. 2, p. 161.

3 Boris Arvatov, *K.S. Malevich: Bog ne skinut (Iskusstvo. Tserkov'. Fabrika)*, Vitebsk, *UNOVIS*, 1922, in "Pechat' i Revolutsiia," Moscow. Kn. 7, pp. 343–4, repr. in ibid., vol. 2, p. 529.

4 On the avant-garde artists' reaction to *Black Square* see "Who is Afraid of *Black Square*?" in Margarita Tupitsyn, *Malevich and Film* (New Haven and London: Yale University Press, 2004), pp. 9–13.

5 Ernst Bloch, *The Utopian Function of Art and Literature*, trans. Jack Zipes and Frank Mecklenburg (Cambridge, Mass.: MIT Press, 1988), p. 106.

6 Ibid.

7 Ibid., p. 107.

8 Katsman, "Pust' otvetiat, zhizn' iskusstva," June 1926, quoted in Vakar and Mikhienko, *Malevich o sebe*, vol. 1, p. 175.

9 Vakar and Mikhienko, *Malevich o sebe*, vol. 2, p. 160 n. 8. Unlike UNOVIS and INKhUK, from the beginning VKhUTEMAS was not homogeneous in its group of teachers, and thus presented a good breeding ground for anti-avant-garde tendencies.

10 Aleksei Gan, A. Morgunov, K. Malevich, "Zadachi iskusstva i rol' dushitelei iskusstva," repr. in *Kazimir Malevich: stat'i*,

manifesty, teoriticheskie sochineniia i drugie raboty. 1913–1929, ed. Aleksandra Shatskikh, 5 vols. (Moscow: Gileia, 1995), vol. 1, pp. 61–2.

11   Malevich, 1920, in Vakar and Mikhienko, *Malevich o sebe*, vol. 1, p. 142.

12   Lenin, 1921, in ibid., vol. 2, p. 160. At the time of this controversy, the nonobjective artists Rodchenko, Popova, and Klutsis taught at VKhUTEMAS.

13   This support from Lunacharsky is also revealed in Malevich's letter to him dated after October 16, 1921 and written from Vitebsk. Malevich had complained that works of "New Art," which the government acquired for museums, were not properly preserved and that this art was criticized in the state newspaper, *Pravda* ("Truth") and artists were called "parasites." Further, Malevich mentioned that the Emergency Commission (CheKa) had tried to arrest him in Vitebsk after he participated in the VKhUTEMAS controversy. Vakar and Mikhienko, *Malevich o sebe*, vol. 1, pp. 149–50. Along with a letter of complaint sent by VKhUTEMAS's conservatives to TSK RKP(b), this tendency to pit state security forces against their aesthetic adversaries laid the foundation for the methods used by this wing for decades in the struggle for cultural power.

14   Lunacharsky, speech to the Third Congress of the Comintern, 1921, not published until 1924 in A.V. Lunacharskii, "Iskusstvo v Moskve," *Iskusstvo i revolutsiia* (Moscow: Novaia Moskva, 1924), p. 98. See also Vakar and Mikhienko, *Malevich o sebe*, vol. 1, p. 150.

15   The 1915 *Exhibition of Paintings of Left-wing Trends* indicates that even before the Revolution nonobjective artists were already endowing this art trend with political connotations. After the Revolution, the avant-gardists reiterated their intention of positioning nonobjectivity as the universal language of Left-wing artists.

16   Lunacharsky, speech to the Third Congress of the Comintern, 1921, not published until 1924 in A.V. Lunacharskii, "Iskusstvo v Moskve," *Iskusstvo i revolutsiia*.

17   Lenin requested 40 million rubles from the Council of People's Commissars (Sovnarkom) to fund this exhibition.

18   For example, one of the exhibition reviewers' concluded: "It seems that for these people, so fatalistically devoted to theories, abstract art has become a dainty dish." Quoted in A.V. Lunacharskii, "Russkaia vystavka v Berline," in *Iskusstvo i revolutsiia*, p. 181. In the painting section, the exhibition included Nathan Altman, Aleksandr Drevin, Aleksandra Exter, Vasily Kandinsky, Konstantin Medunetsky, Aleksandr Rodchenko, Liubov Popova, El Lissitzky, Olga Rozanova, Kazimir Malevich, Ivan Kliun, Gustav Klutsis, Vladimir Tatlin, Vladimir Stenberg, Ivan Puni, and Naum Gabo. In reality, this was a small percentage of 180 participants, and more than 1000 works that were exhibited and executed in "all kinds of different art tendencies." See

Mikhail Lazarev, *David Shterenberg: Khudozhnik i vremia. Put' khudozhnika* (Moscow: Galaktika, 1992), p. 171.

19   Lunacharskii, "Russkaia vystavka v Berline," p. 179.

20   In the beginning, the group called itself the Association of Artists Studying Revolutionary Everyday Life. See *AKhRR: sbornik vospominanii, statei, dokumentov*, ed. I.M. Gronskii and V.N. Perel'man (Moscow: Izobrazitel'noe Iskusstvo, 1973), p. 83.

21   Malevich in his autobiography written in 1933, speaks of "being in love" with the Wanderers early on in his career. In Vakar and Mikhienko, *Malevich o sebe*, vol. 1, p. 32, Katsman himself articulated (to AKhRR's disadvantage) the crucial difference between the Wanderers and AKhRR's objectives when he stated that the former's "favourite hero is a negative personality" because the group "faught against its government...but we live in a wonderful country," that results in the "creation of a positive hero in our art." Katsman's speech at the MOSSKh's discussion on formalism, March 10, 1936, RGALI, fond 990, op. 3, ed.kh.8, 1.79. The avant-garde poet Sergei Gorodetsky, "helped the Wanderers to write their declaration." Gronskii and Perel'man, *AKhRR*, p. 80.

22   E.A. Katsman, "Kak sozdavalas' AKhRR," in Gronskii and Perel'man, *AKhRR*, p. 80.

23   Ibid., p. 81.

24   Ibid.

25   Ibid.

26   Shterenberg in Ibid.

27   Katsman, in Gronskii and Perel'man, *AKhRR*, p. 81.

28   A.V. Lunacharsky, *Rech', proiznessennaia na otkrytii Petrogradskikh gosudarstvennykh svobodnykh khudozhestvenno-uchebnykh masterskikh 10-go oktiabria 1918 g.* (Petrograd: IZO Narkompros, 1918), p. 12.

29   Katsman, in Gronskii and Perel'man, *AKhRR*, p. 82.

30   Manifesto signed by Nikolai Aseev, Boris Arvatov, Osip Brik, Boris Kushner, Vladimir Maiakovskii, Sergei Tret'iakov, Nikolai Chuzhak, "Za chto boretsia Lef?" *Lef* no. 1 (1923), p. 7.

31   Gronskii and Perel'man, *AKhRR*, p. 83. The exhibition was held in a space on Kuznetsky Most, Moscow.

32   Lev Trotskii, "Formal'naia shkola poezii i marksizm," *Pravda* 166 (July 26, 1923), repr. in his *Literatura i revolutsiia* (Moscow: Krasnaia nov'. Glavpolitprosvet, 1923), pp. 130–45. The fact that this article was published in *Pravda* gave the impression that the Party was launching its campaign against formalism.

33   The exhibition took place in the Scientific-technical Club in the House of the Unions. Brandon Taylor has suggested that in Trotsky's *Literature and Revolution*, he criticized AKhRR's portraiture without "nam[ing] names." See Brandon Taylor, "On AKhRR," in *Art of the Soviets: Painting, Sculpture and Architecture in a One-party State, 1917–1992*, ed. Matthew Cullerne Bown and Brandon Taylor (Manchester: Manchester University Press, 1993), pp. 57–8.

34   Gronskii and Perel'man, *AKhRR*, p. 83.

35   Deklaratsiia assotsiatsii khudozhnikov revolutsionnoi Rossii, *AKhRR*, p. 289.

36   A. Nurenberg, review, *Pravda* (July 2, 1922), repr. in ibid., p. 193.

37   Ibid., p. 194.

38   H.H. Arnason, *History of Modern Art: Painting, Sculpture, Architecture* (New York: Harry N. Abrams, 1977), p. 13.

39   Paradoxically, both "left" and AKhRR artists kept calling VKhUTEIN "Academy."

40   Katsman, "Kak sozdavalas' AKhRR," *AKhRR,* p. 88.

41   Ibid., p. 87.

42   After Katsman and Grigoriev left, students stirred up by them wrote many letters with a request to support "the right-wing professors" by firing those who "promote the ruthless line of the futurist movement." Moscow, Russian State Archive of Literature and Art (RGALI), fond 2368, op. 2, ed. kh. 213, l.1.

43   Katsman in Vakar and Mikhienko, *Malevich o sebe*, vol. 2, p. 341, n. 15.

44   Igor Terentiev, letter to Aleksei Kruchenykh, November 21, 1923, in ibid. In collaboration with Malevich, Terentiev wrote "Nonobjectivity," a text that apparently he presented at the meeting with AKhRR; ibid., p. 342 n. 17.

45   Ibid., pp. 126–7.

46   Nikolai Chuzhak, "Ot illuzii k materii," in *Reviziia levogo fronta v sovremennom russkom iskusstve*, ed. V. Pertsov (Moscow: Vserossiiskii Proletkul't, 1925), p. 113.

47   Ibid.

48   Aleksei Gan, "O sovremennykh khudozhestvennykh gruppirovkakh," *Teatral'naiia Moskva* 35 (1922), p. 7.

49   Rosalind E. Krauss, *The Originality of the Avant-garde and Other Modernist Myths* (Cambridge, Mass.: MIT Press, 1985), p. 221.

50   *Veshch-Gegenstand-Objet*, no. 3 (May 1922), Berlin eds. El Lissitzky and Ilya Ehrenburg.

51   Pertsov, *Reviziia levogo fronta*, p. 22.

52   Malevich formulated his concept "to reduce everything to zero" and then "transcend beyond zero" shortly before the opening of *0,10*. In the leaflet distributed during the exhibition, he stated: "I have transformed myself into the zero of forms"; Vakar and Mikhienko, *Malevich o sebe*, vol. 2, p. 109 n. 22. See also Kasimir Malevich, *The World as Objectlessness* (Dessau: Bauhaus-bücher, 1927).

53   Rosalind E. Krauss, *The Picasso Papers* (New York: Farrar, Straus and Giroux, 1998), p. 235.

54   Chuzhak, "Ot illuzii k materii," p. 113.

55   Krauss, *Picasso Papers*, p. 128.

56   Ibid. Among the automated modes of execution of an abstract painting, Krauss also mentions a ruler and a roller, techniques applied by Rodchenko as early as 1916.

57   Aleksei Gan, *Da zdravstvuet demonstratsiia byta!* (Moscow: Goskino, 1923), p. 11.

58   Vakar and Mikhienko, *Malevich o sebe*, vol. 2, p. 25.

59   Boris Arvatov, "Utopiia ili nauka," *Lef* no. 4 (1924), p. 18.

60   K.S. Malevich, "Khudozhniki ob AKhRR" *Zhizn' iskusstva* 6 (1924), repr. in *Kazimir Malevich: stat'i, manifesty, teoreticheskie sochineniia i drugie raboty, 1913–1929*, 2 vols. (Moscow: Gileiia, 1995), vol. 1, p. 277.

61   Ibid.

62   Ibid.

63   Osip Brik, "Formal'nyi method," *Lef* no. 1 (1923), pp. 213–15.

64   Arvatov, "Utopiia ili nauka," pp. 16–21.

65   Ibid., p. 18.

66   Pertsov, *Reviziia levogo fronta*, p. 29.

67   Ibid., pp. 16–17.

68   Gustav Shpet warned against "vulgar nomenclature mixing up metaphysics and mysticism." Gustav Shpet, "Problems of Modern Aesthetics," *Iskusstvo* 1 (1923), p. 98.

69   Chuzhak, "Ot illuzii k materii," p. 137.

70   Ibid., pp. 113–14.

71   Vakar and Mikhienko, *Malevich o sebe*, vol. 2, p. 161.

72   Katsman, "Kak sozdavalas' AKhRR," *AKhRR,* p. 92.

73   A.V. Lunacharskii, "Na vystavkakh," *Izvestiia*, March 24 and 27 (1925), repr. in Gronskii and Perel'man, *AKhRR*, p. 211.

74   Ibid.

75   Ibid., p. 212.

76   "The Immediate Tasks of AKhRR: A Circular to All Branches of AKhRR – An Appeal to All the Artists of the USSR, 1924," letter of May 1924 after their sixth exhibition, *Revolution, Everyday Life, and Labor*, ed. and trans. by John Bowlt, *Russian Art of the Avant-garde: Theory and Criticism, 1902–1934*, (New York: The Viking Press, 1991), pp. 268–71.

77   Lunacharskii, "Na vystavkakh," p. 215.

78   According to Katsman, for their eighth exhibition AKhRR received 70,000 rubles, including money for travel abroad, art materials, and trips around the USSR. Also, the government began a large-scale acquisition of AKhRR's works. Katsman in Vakar and Mikhienko, *Malevich o sebe*, vol. 1, pp. 173–4.

79   For Malevich and his students, GINKhUK, which opened in Petrograd under the auspices of IZO Narkompros in 1923, became an extension of his theoretical and practical work in UNOVIS but from a more scientific angle. As head of the formal-theoretical and practical department, Malevich, along with other GINKhUK artists and critics, was preoccupied with working out a universal art methodology based on nonobjective forms, as well as their application in real life.

80   Kazimir Malevich, letter to F.N. Petrov, July 12, 1925, in Vakar and Mikhienko, *Malevich o sebe*, vol. 1, p. 173. Significantly,

in order to be more persuasive, Malevich defined the Institute's activities as a means "to conquer the West" and argued that if they did not publish the Institute's achievements, Russian critics would later accuse artists of plagiarizing the West. This is exactly what later happened to Rodchenko when the magazine *Soviet Photo* accused him of copying German photographers.

81   G. Serov, "Monastyr' na gossnabzhenii: Otchetnaia vystavka gosudarstvennogo instituta khudozhestvennoi kul'tury," *Leningradskaia Pravda* (June 10, 1926), p. 5.

82   A.V. Lunacharskii, "Diskussiia ob AKhRR," in Gronskii and Perel'man, *AKhRR*, p. 233.

83   Ibid.

84   RGALI, fond 2368, op. 2, ed. kh. 213, l.12a.

85   Ibid., l.60.

86   Katsman, "Kak sozdavalas' AKhRR," *AKhRR*, p. 95.

87   [Vladimir Mayakovsky], "Chitatel'!" *Novyi Lef* no. 1 (1927), p. 1.

88   Boris Arvatov, "Proletariat i levoe iskusstvo," *Vestnik iskusstv* 1 (January 1922), p. 10.

89   Ibid., trans. and repr. in Bowlt, *Russian Art of the Avant-garde*, p. 229. Bowlt states that "*Vestnik iskusstv* [*Art Herald*] was the journal published by the Art Section of Glavpolitprosvet (Central Committee of Political Enlightenment), a department established within Narkompros in November 1920 to take charge of adult education," p. 226. Given this, Arvatov's article demonstrates the high stakes that the government initially had in nonobjective art. Bowlt translated Arvatov's *bespredmetnichestvo* as "abstraction," which I translate as "nonobjectivity" to keep the original usage important for my argument.

90   Boris Arvatov, "Pochemu ne umerla stankovaia kartina," *Novyi Lef* no. 1 (1927), p. 39.

91   Ibid., p. 38. Arvatov noted that left nonobjective ideas found their partial realization in the new architecture.

92   Ibid.

93   Lunacharsky similarly warned AKhRR of "distorting reality" and as a result delivering a "lie." Lunacharskii, "Diskussiia ob AKhRR," p. 230.

94   Osip Brik, "Foto-kadr protiv kartiny," *Sovetskoe foto* 2 (1926), p. 41.

95   Arvatov, "Utopiia ili nauka," p. 18.

96   "October: Association of Artistic Labor Declaration, 1928," in Bowlt, *Russian Art of the Avant-garde*, p. 277.

97   Ibid.

98   Ibid., p. 276.

99   "AKhR: Declaration of the Association of Artists of the Revolution, 1928," in ibid., p. 271.

100   Ibid., pp. 271–2.

101   On February 26, 1928 the whole Politburo headed by Stalin visited the exhibition after which Stalin observed in writing, "I think overall it's good," demonstrating his lack of

interest in visual production other than cinema and forms suitable for effective dissemination in print media. RGALI, fond 2368, op. 1, ed. kh. 3, l.26.

102   On Diego Rivera's time in Moscow see Maria Gogh, "Drawing Between Reportage and Memory: Diego Rivera's Moscow Sketch Book," *October* no. 145 (Fall 2013), pp. 67–9.

103   Lunacharskii, "Diskussiia ob AKhRR," p. 231.

104   As late as 1935 at meetings of the Moscow Regional Union of Soviet Artists (MOSSKh), artists continued "talking about all the painful things that have been building up for a long time, about AKhR, settling scores with the formalists, apologizing for having overestimated Brodsky and Katsman." Valentina Kulagina, diary, December 8, 1935, in Margarita Tupitsyn, *Gustav Klutsis and Valentina Kulagina* (New York: International Center of Photography, and Göttingen: Steidl, 2004), p. 220.

105   A document on this topic states that Brodsky indeed was expelled from AKhRR and accused of a number of wrongdoings. As a result, a special government commission was assembled and cleared him of all accusations. RGALI, fond 2368, op. 2, ed. kh. 213, l.60.

106   AKhRR's "Is Easel Painting Doomed to Die?" was organized by its art history section on March 17, 1930.

107   Kazimir Malevich, letter to N.M. Suetin and B.V. Ender, between February 21 and 28, 1927, in Vakar and Mikhienko, *Malevich o sebe*, vol. 1, p. 183.

108   Right before Malevich departed for Warsaw he wrote: "When the cartoonist Komisarenko comes, I need to make a suprematist film well with him." Ibid.

109   Ibid., p. 185.

110   A.V. Lunacharskii, "Russkie khudozhniki v Berline," *Ogonek* 30 (1927), repr. in Vakar and Mikhienko, *Malevich o sebe*, vol. 2, p. 546.

111   Ibid.

112   Lunacharskii, "Iskusstvo v Moskve," p. 96.

113   Kazimir Malevich, letter to Alexander von Riesen, December 9, 1927, in Vakar and Mikhienko, *Malevich o sebe*, vol. 1, p. 197. The paintings he chose are significant in that their peasant theme was a common one in the formation of early European and Russian modernism; early examples are the representations by Aleksei Venetsianov (in the 1820s) and Jean-François Millet (in the 1850s) of peasants armed with sharp tools of their labor (a sickle and pitchfork) as symbols of anticipated social transformations.

114   Ibid.

115   Charlotte Douglas, "Malevich's Painting: Some Problems of Chronology," in *Soviet Union*, vol. 5, part 2, special issue, ed. John Bowlt and Charlotte Douglas (Tempe: Arizona State University, 1978), pp. 301–10.

116   Ibid. p. 301.

117   Krauss, *Originality of the Avant-garde*, "Grids," p. 9.

118   Ibid.

119   Malevich to Natalia Rafalovich, between January 7 and 14, 1929, in Vakar and Mikhienko, *Malevich o sebe*, vol. 1, p. 258.

120   Feliks Kon, *Krasnaia gazeta*, March 13, 1930, cited in ibid., p. 205.

121   This was a reversal of the Resolution of TsK RKP(b) of June 18, 1925, "On the Politics of the Party in the Field of Literature," which stated that the Party must defend the free competition of the various literary groups.

122   The exhibition *Artists of the RSFSR* opened on November 13, 1932 and included about 2562 paintings and works on paper, 78 sculptures, 184 pieces of porcelain.

123   Nikolai Punin, "Obshchii kharakter vystavki," in *Khudozhniki RSFSR za 15 let, catalog iubileinoi vystavki: zhivopis', grafika i skul'ptura* (Leningrad: Gosudarstvennyi Russkii Muzei, 1932), p. 16. Among the groups mentioned are OST (Society of Easel Painters), 4 Arts, OMKh (Society of Moscow Painters), Makovets (after a hill of that name), and Bytie (Being or Existence).

124   Ibid., p. 18.

125   Igor Grabar', "Prazdnik masterov kisti, karandasha i reztsa," in ibid., p. 12.

126   Kazimir Malevich, letter to Ivan Kliun, December 12, 1932, in Vakar and Mikhienko, *Malevich o sebe*, vol. 1, p. 234. The jury included AKhRR members Bogorodsky, Brodsky, Ioganson, and Perelman; and Punin, Shterenberg, who formally represented the left wing, and Grabar, who was also responsible for installing the exhibition. Some works by nonobjective artists (for example, Rodchenko's) were lost among thousands of delivered objects; Kliun's paintings were recovered by Malevich from storage during the exhibition's installation. Works by Nadezhda Udaltsova and Aleksandr Drevin were included but badly installed. Ibid.

127   Punin, "Obshchii kharakter vystavki," p. 18.

128   Vasilii Rakitin, *Nikolai Mikhailovich Suetin* (Moscow: RA, 1998), p. 162.

129   According to the catalogue, altogether Suetin exhibited seventeen works, including his *Black Square* dated 1932. The State Tretiakov Gallery, which owns the work, has dated it to the early 1920s.

130   Rakitin, *Suetin*, p. 163.

131   The exhibition opened in Moscow's State Museum of History at the end of June 1933.

132   This description of Malevich's and Suetin's installation as a "cabinet of 'nonobjective' art" interestingly correlates with El Lissitzky's *Kabinett der Abstrakten* (Abstract Cabinet), which he came from Moscow to install at *Provinzialmuseum*, Hannover, in 1928.

133   "Khudozhniki RSFSR za 15 let: Iubileinaia vystavka," *Izvestiia* 158 (June 24, 1933), p. 3.

134   Kazimir Malevich, letter to G.N. Petnikov, between July 15 and 28, 1933, in Vakar and Mikhienko, *Malevich o sebe*, vol. 1, p. 239.

135   Malevich, letter to his family, September 14, 1933, in ibid., p. 280.

136   Indeed, two years later, in 1935, Pavlov oversaw Malevich's burial by providing a railway car for the transportation of the artist's coffin from Leningrad to Moscow. Significantly in 1918, Malevich wrote: "[*Black Square*] will be a seal of our time; wherever it's hung, it will not lose its face." "Rodonachalo suprematizma," *Anarchy* 81, 1918.

137   In the Leningrad version of *Artists of the RSFSR of the Last 15 Years*, Tatlin's works never made it from "storage to the exhibition wall," prompting him to grumble, "I attached great importance to *15 Years*... I should have entered the history of art." Aleksandr Drevin defended Tatlin at the expense of Malevich, claiming that in the space that the latter had occupied with his students, one could "hang many good artists," thereby restaging a conflict that had played out between Malevich and Tatlin in *0,10*. Drevin and Tatlin in the "Discussion of the exhibition *Artists of the RSFSR of the Last 15 Years*," MOSSKh, August 12, 1932, RGALI, fond 2943, op. 1, ed.kh. 1128, II. 11, 12.

2   SPECTERS OF FORMALISM

1   Evgenii Katsman, "Sviazan li vkus s mirovozreniem: khudozhniki v gostiakh u genseka," *Nezavisimaia gazeta* 119 (July 4, 1998), p. 16. Paradoxically, many artists including Rodchenko believed that Stalin could personally resolve conflicts between cultural figures.

2   A.K. Lebedev, *A. Gerasimov* (Moscow: Iskusstvo, 1938), p. 28.

3   Katsman, "Sviazan li vkus s mirovozreniem," p. 16. In response the threesome cited the case of Pericles and his democratic rule of Athens and its art. "It was under his leadership that the greatest, unsurpassed masterpieces of art were created. Pericles did not intrude but helped…Comrade Stalin be our Pericles," requested Katsman. Stalin cunningly replied: "Voroshilov is your Pericles…[he] did a lot for artists, did a lot of good, artists owe the most to Voroshilov." Ibid.

4   Katsman mentions a discussion of modernist paintings by Aleksandr Shevchenko and David Shterenberg. Ibid.

5   *O vystavke "Khudozhniki RSFSR za 15 let": Delegatam XVII s'ezda VKP(b)* (Moscow: Vsekokhudozhnik, 1934), p. 4.

6   Ibid., p. 2.

7   Ibid., p. 3.

8   David Shterenberg quoted in M.P. Lazarev, *David Shterenberg: khudozhnik i vremia, put' khudozhnika* (Moscow: Galaktika, 1992), p. 200.

9 Osip Beskin, "Formalizm v zhivopisi," *Iskusstvo* 3 (1933), p. 14.

10 V.N. Perel'man and A.M. Lesuk, *Evgenii Aleksandrovich Katsman* (Moscow: Vsekokhudozhnik, 1935), p. 5.

11 Osip Brik, "Dukh prostokvashi," *Literaturnaia gazeta* (June 26, 1934), p. 4.

12 S. Dinamov, "Advokat formalizma: otvet Briku," *Pravda* 176 (June 28, 1934), p. 4. In his letter to Kliun written on the day of Dinamov's publication, Malevich called it "an unconscious roar of a man unable to explain the New Art," thus joining Brik in a conviction that the Party critics were not able adequately to analyze the avant-garde art; in *Malevich o sebe, sovremenniki o Maleviche: pis'ma, dokumenty, vospominaniia, kritika*, ed. I.A. Vakar and T.N. Mikhienko, 2 vols (Moscow: RA, 2004), vol. 1, p. 251.

13 Andrei Zhdanov, "Speech to the Congress of Soviet Writers," repr. in *Art in Theory: 1900–1990, An Anthology of Changing Ideas*, ed. Charles Harrison and Paul Wood (Oxford: Blackwell, 1992), p. 411.

14 Even during a conversation with Stalin, Katsman described the formalists as people for whom only "particular technical devices are important." Katsman, "Sviazan li vkus s mirovoz-reniem," p. 16.

15 Zhdanov, "Speech," p. 411.

16 The only meaningful and progressive line in Zhdanov's speech was a call for "the principle of equal rights for women"; ibid., p. 410.

17 "From Igor Grabar's Speech," in *Russian Art of the Avant-garde: Theory and Criticism, 1902–1934*, ed. John E. Bowlt (New York: Viking, 1991), p. 295.

18 Zhdanov, "Speech," p. 411.

19 Perhaps this public endorsement of Socialist Realism pushed Grabar to give up his official positions in the late 1930s so that he could demonstrate his distance from Socialist Realism.

20 Igor' Grabar', "Prazdnik masterov kisti, karandasha i reztsa," epigraph to his introduction, in *Khudozhniki RSFSR za 15 let, catalog iubileinoi vystavki: zhivopis, grafika i skul'ptura* (Leningrad: Gosudarstvennyi Russkii Muzei, 1932).

21 "From Igor' Grabar's Speech," p. 295.

22 For example, one of the last known letters written by Malevich, on January 11, 1935, was addressed to Shterenberg, whom Malevich thanks for "caring about him"; in Vakar and Mikhienko, *Malevich o sebe*, vol. 1, pp. 251–2. In 1933 Malevich also wrote a will addressed to MOSSKh, giving instructions on his official burial; ibid., p. 573.

23 I believe that Sergei Gerasimov's namesake, the anti-modernist Aleksandr Gerasimov, was wrongly credited with supporting Impressionism "as late as 1939" in the chapter on Socialist Realism, "1934a," in *Art Since 1900: Modernism, Antimodernism, Postmodernism*, ed. Hal Foster, Rosalind Krauss, Yve-Alain Bois and Benjamin H.D. Buchloh (London and New York: Thames and Hudson, 2005), p. 260.

24 A.V. Lunacharskii, *Ob izobrazitel'nom iskusstve*, v.1–2 (Moscow, 1967), p. 501.

25 Linda Nochlin, *Realism: Style and Civilization* (New York: Penguin, 1972), p. 28. Impressionism played an important role in the formation of Russian modernism and the avant-garde. For example, the connection between Impressionism and non-objectivity had been underscored in the *Fifth State Exhibition: From Impressionism to Nonobjective Art* (1918–19) and then again by the editors of *Lef* magazine in their introduction to the first issue in 1923; "What *Lef* is Fighting For," *Lef* no. 1 (March 1923), p. 1. There, the futurist publication *A Trap for Judges* (in Russian, *Sadok Sudei*, 1910) was described as "the first impressionist flare-up." In fact, the first futurist publication was the volume edited by Nikolai Kulbin, *Studiia Impressionistov* (The Studio of the Impressionists), which, according to Vladimir Markov, was published "about two months before *Sadok Sudei*…[and] can be considered a kind of prologue to the history of Russian futurism." Vladimir Markov, *Russian Futurism: A History* (Berkeley: University of California Press, 1968), p. 6.

26 Nochlin, *Realism*, p. 179.

27 Ibid.

28 Katsman's *Lacemakers from Kaliazin* was exhibited in the eleventh and last AKhRR exhibition, *Art into Masses* (1929).

29 Kazimir Malevich, letter to Ivan Kliun, June 28, 1934, in Vakar and Mikhienko, *Malevich o sebe*, vol. 1, p. 250. Leicist and Leicism were Malevich's neologisms taken from the Leica camera.

30 It was exactly at this time that *The Studio* launched a soft attack on abstract art, praising Soviet government art policies: "Soviet artists are free to devote their energies solely to creative work, unhindered by the same necessity for uncongenial 'plot-boiling' as are their fellows under other systems of government. Intense realism is the keynote of contemporary Russian art." L. de C.-Butcher, "Artist [*sic*] Life in Russia," *The Studio* (March 1934), p. 113.

31 Roger Fry quoted in Linda Nochlin, "The Realist Criminal and the Abstract Law II," *Art in America* 61 (November–December 1973), p. 98.

32 Zhdanov's "Speech to the *Congress of Soviet Writers*," p. 411.

33 Malevich, letter to Kliun, in Vakar and Mikhienko, *Malevich o sebe*, vol. 1, p. 250.

34 See Nochlin, *Realism*, pp. 176–7.

35 It is possible that Malevich was also reacting to campaigns against Impressionism as a neo-Kantian practice that aimed at the "representation of…external, transcendental…empirical reality." Mikhail Lifshits, "Marksizm i iskusstvo," lecture given on May 7, 1933 at the Moscow Club of Artists; RGALI, fond 990, op. 3, ed. kh. 10, l.9.

36 A.V. Lunacharskii, "Zhivopisets schast'ia," introduction to Ambroise Vollard, *Renuar* (Leningrad: Izdatelstvo Leningradskogo Oblastnogo Soiuza Sovetskikh Khudozhnikov, 1934), p. 6.

37 Ibid., p. 11.

38 Igor Golomstock, "Problems in the Study of Stalinist Culture," in *The Culture of the Stalin Period*, ed. Hans Günther (London: Macmillan, 1990), p. 110.

39 Ibid. Studies of Socialist Realism can be divided into several categories. A view of it as part of a totalitarian and oppressive culture is rooted in the dissident tradition of the 1960s and was adopted by the Western scholars of Slavic studies and by a handful of art historians specializing in Russian art. Interpretations created primarily by émigré scholars (with the exception of Igor Golomstock) in the '80s proposed a postmodern recontextualization of official representation. In the post-Soviet period, the museum establishment that remained in power from the Soviet era rehabilitated official production and gave its works the status of "masterpieces" of academic painting.

40 Valentina Kulagina, diary, February 24, 1932, in Margarita Tupitsyn, *Gustav Klutsis and Valentina Kulagina: Photography and Montage After Constructivism* (New York: International Center of Photography and Göttingen: Steidl, 2004), p. 201.

41 Ibid.

42 Ibid., August 26, 1932, p. 205.

43 Ibid., December 10, 1933, p. 210.

44 Ibid., April 17, 1934, p. 215.

45 Ibid., July 26, 1935, pp. 216–17.

46 The same issue of quality applied to painting: for example, in 1935 Kliun said that he remembered Katsman's diploma works for MUZhVZ, which although already "highly naturalist…were executed more meticulously and worked on subtly; now he works crudely and sloppily"; quoted in Vakar and Mikhienko, *Malevich o sebe*, vol. 2, p. 161 n. 14.

47 Valentina Kulagina, diary, May 15, 1940, private archive.

48 Ibid.

49 Ironically, the signing of the Molotov–Ribbentrop (Soviet–German) Nonagression Pact in 1939 turned fascists into the allies of the Soviet Union and made such accusations irrelevant, until Germany invaded Russia in 1941.

50 Klutsis was arrested after he returned from Paris as part of the delegation of designers to the Paris World's Fair, and had already been selected to prepare designs for the New York World's Fair in 1939. In 1938, it was not enough for anti-avant-garde activists to purge institutions: they also had their artist adversaries killed.

51 Kulagina, diary, March 10, 1940, in Tupitsyn, *Klutsis and Kulagina*, pp. 234–5.

52 After Klutsis' arrest in 1938, MOSSKh decided to resettle one room in Kulagina's private apartment. Her "complaint against MOSSKh was heard by the court. The court ruled that the small room should be given back," but later she lost this battle. Kulagina, diary, 14 May, 1938, private archive.

53 See Katsman, "Sviazan li vkus s mirovozreniem," p. 16.

54 Aleksandr Rodchenko, "Manifesto of the Flying Federation of Futurists," diary, May 24, 1939, in *Aleksandr Rodchenko: Experiments for the Future, Diaries, Essays, Letters, and Other Writings*, ed. A.N. Lavrentiev, trans. Jamey Gambrell (New York: Museum of Modern Art, 2005), p. 260.

55 On this period see my "Aleksandr Rodchenko: 'Woman with a Leica' or 'Letters not About Love,'" *History of Photography* 27, no. 2 (Summer 2003), pp. 172–87.

56 Rodchenko, diary, February 4, 1934, in *Rodchenko: Experiments for the Future*, p. 308.

57 Ibid., March 14, 1934, p. 310.

58 Ibid., January 15, 1937, p. 314.

59 Ibid., February 18, 1934, p. 309.

60 Ibid., February 21, 1934, p. 309.

61 Gustave Courbet, letter to Francis Way, 1850, at https://en.wikipedia.org/wiki/Gustave_Courbet, accessed on June 5, 2016.

62 Nochlin, *Realism*, p. 25.

63 Ibid., p. 130.

64 Rodchenko, diary, August 30, 1936, in *Rodchenko: Experiments for the Future*, p. 312.

65 Ibid.

66 Ibid., January 12, 1937, p. 313.

67 Ibid.

68 Ibid., January 15, 1937, p. 314.

69 Ibid., December 7, 1937, p. 316.

70 Ibid., April 2, 1938, p. 317.

71 Rodchenko mentions print sizes as large as 90 × 130 cm.

72 Ibid., May 6, 1938, p. 318.

73 Ibid., May 17, 1938, p. 319.

74 Ibid., September 10, 1938, p. 323.

75 Ibid., May 15, 1938, pp. 317–18. In a postcard to A. Leporskaia, Nikolai Suetin wrote that during his trip to Paris with a delegation to work on the Soviet Pavilion of the Paris World Fair in 1937, he visited Picasso's studio and saw *Guernica*. Rakitin, *Nikolai Mikhailovich Suetin*, p. 179. It is almost certain that he discussed it with Soviet artists working in the pavilion and after he returned to Moscow.

76 Rodchenko, diary, August 18, 1938, in *Rodchenko: Experiments for the Future*, p. 321. In that year Gerasimov painted a large-scale canvas, *Stalin and Voroshilov at the Kremlin* (1938), in which he gave the patron of AKhRR equal standing with Stalin, backed by the Kremlin.

77 K.I. Chukovskii, *Dnevnik 1901–1929* (Moscow: Sovetskii Khudozhnik, 1991), p. 370.

78   In 1939, another prominent Socialist Realist, Aleksandr Laktionov, painted Brodsky impeccably dressed and sitting on an antique chair with a group of antique sculptures in the background. The paradox of the Soviet bourgeois is evident in Brodsky's wearing a medal (Soviet surrogate jewelry) as well as a diamond ring.

79   Isaak Brodskii, letter to the editors, *Krasnaia gazeta*, November 25, 1930, in which he also accuses the Russian Museum of postponing an exhibition of Filonov's paintings. Quoted in Vakar and Mikhienko, *Malevich o sebe*, vol. 2, p. 297 n. 45.

80   Konstantin Rozhdestvenskii, "GINKhUK," quoted in ibid., p. 296.

81   These works by Malevich are not part of Brodsky's museum in St. Petersburg, and their location is unknown.

82   Vakar and Mikhienko, *Malevich o sebe*, vol. 1, p. 239.

83   Ibid., p. 240.

84   Ibid., p. 239.

85   Ibid.

86   Ibid., p. 240.

87   Hans Richter, *Dada: Art and Anti-art* (London: Thames and Hudson, 1965), p. 217. For comparison of the two artists see Charlotte Douglas, *Malevich and De Chirico: Rethinking Malevich* (London: Pindar Press, 2007).

88   Lebedev, *A. Gerasimov*, p. 19.

89   Ibid., p. 26. Gerasimov's paintings of female bathers can be also interpreted as an experiment in the modernist popular theme of female bathers.

90   Gerasimov could have been prompted by the Wanderers falling out of favor with such founding members of AKhRR as Aleksei Volter, who in an article of 1933 for *Iskusstvo* described the Wanderers' 47th exhibition as "*polumernaia* [literally, "half-measure," half-hearted] and cowardly" and the artists as "representatives of a prerevolutionary intelligentsia unable to perceive the ideology of the struggling proletariat." A.A. Volter, "Stat'ia o zadachakh izobrazitel'nogo iskusstva," March 14, 1933, RGALI, fond 990, op. 3, ed. kh. 9, l.5. This proved once again that AKhRR had nothing in common with the Wanderers and initially used them for self-promotion.

91   Aleksandr Gerasimov, letter to Evgenii Katsman and Grigorii Perel'man, August 10, 1934, RGALI, fond 2650, op. 2, ed. kh. 88, l.1.

92   Gerasimov refused to paint from photographs, explaining "for me to paint from photographs, without seeing people, is impossible; photography never fully mirrors a face. In order to paint well one must know a person, to have him in your visual memory." Cited in "I.V. Stalin i K.E. Voroshilov: Aleksandr Gerasimov," at www.tinlib.ru/kulturologija/100_velikih_kartin/p97.php, accessed on June 25, 2016.

93   Golomstock, "Problems in the Study of Stalinist Culture", p. 115.

94   Katsman's studio, undated photograph, RGALI, fond 2368, op. 2, ed. Kr. 240, l.5.

95   See Victor Tupitsyn, *The Museological Unconscious: Communal (Post)Modernism in Russia* (Cambridge, Mass.: MIT Press, 2009), "Susan Buck-Morss in Conversation with Victor Tupitsyn," p. 3. Christina Kiaer, "Lyrical Socialist Realism," *October* no. 147 (Winter 2014), p. 60.

96   See Kulagina, diary, February 27, 1941, private archive.

97   During the war, Kulagina noted: "It's typical to receive two rations. Everyone thinks he 'has a right,' well, as a member of the 'Union,' which means you are a genius and the government must support him, give him a studio space, all kinds of favors, and encouragement"; ibid., December 25, 1943.

98   Rodchenko, "Manifesto of the Flying Federation of Futurists," in *Rodchenko: Experiments for the Future*, p. 263.

99   Kulagina, diary, January 9, 1933, in Tupitsyn, *Klutsis and Kulagina*, p. 206.

100   See Kulagina, diary, February 27, 1941, private archive. Kulagina writes that stores are full of products but there is no money to buy them, yet bureaucrats are all fat and promise much.

101   This challenges the claim that from the middle of the 1930s Aleksandr Gerasimov had become "the omnipresent dictator of Soviet art." Igor Golomstock, *Totalitarnoe iskusstvo* (Moscow: Galart, 1994), p. 102.

102   Kulagina, diary, February 27, 1941, private archive.

103   Ibid., February 5, 1940. Boris Deikin, a member of AKhRR from 1922, attended the class of Abram Arkhipov at MUZhVZ.

104   Ibid., February 10, 1940. By the fall of that year Kulagina reports that "in the food queues there are a lot of harsh and plainly unsatisfied conversations about the Party, government, and general conditions." Ibid., September 12, 1940.

105   See Margarita Tupitsyn, "At the Dawn of Russian Modernism," *Art in America* 10 (October 1997), pp. 96–101. Since the Renaissance, the still life had represented a way of breaking free from prescribed religious themes and canons of execution. Thus, the tulip in the sixteenth century had become the flower of an epoch.

106   Golomstock, "Problems in the Study of Stalinist Culture," p. 114.

107   Malevich, letter to Kliun, June 28, 1934, in Vakar and Mikhienko, *Malevich o sebe*, vol. 1, p. 250.

108   Kulagina wrote: "Malevich was over today. He's gained a lot of weight. Haven't seen him in years. Had outrageous stories to tell about his harassment in Leningrad. He had a very bad time, they wouldn't let him work." Kulagina, diary, May 20, 1933, in Tupitsyn, *Klutsis and Kulagina*, p. 206. While attending Anton Pevsner's classes in VKhUTEMAS in 1921, she "began making Suprematist works," but found this led to work "from

the intellect rather than the heart…it was cold." Kulagina, diary, October 8, 1946, private archive.

109   Kulagina, diary, March 9, 1938, in Tupitsyn, *Klutsis and Kulagina*, p. 230.

110   Ibid. While artists painted idyllic still lifes and landscapes, Soviet industry was destroying nature and the environment. Nature in Russia was violated just like the population.

111   Malevich, letter to Kliun, June 28, 1934, in Vakar and Mikhienko, *Malevich o sebe*, vol. 1, p. 250.

112   Kulagina, diary, March 28, 1940, private archive.

113   Ibid., April 4, 1940.

114   On Klutsis' influence on Kulagina's thinking on painting, see Tupitsyn, *Klutsis and Kulagina*, pp. 170–1.

115   The All-Union Agricultural Exhibition opened in 1939 to commemorate the industrial and agricultural achievements of the first and second Five-Year Plans, and functioned as such until the fall of the Soviet Union in 1991.

116   Kulagina, diary, April 3, 1939, in Tupitsyn, *Klutsis and Kulagina*, p. 233.

117   Kulagina, diary, June 4, 1940, private archive. When Kulagina was expelled from MOSSKh at the end of 1943, she began to look at production art through different eyes, writing that she was able to contribute to it "skill and taste." Ibid., December 14, 1943.

118   Rodchenko writes *pisat'* that, as pointed out earlier, is used for both "writing" and "painting." The translation of this edition of Rodchenko's diaries uses "to write" here although it is not obvious in the Russian original if Rodchenko wanted to imitate van Gogh's letter-writing or his painting. The latter seems more logical for an artist.

119   Rodchenko, diary, May 2, 1939, in *Rodchenko: Experiments for the Future*, pp. 324–5.

120   See Tupitsyn, "Aleksandr Rodchenko: 'Woman with a Leica,'" pp. 172–87.

121   Rodchenko, diary, May 28, 1939, in *Rodchenko: Experiments for the Future*, p. 326. For Zhdanov see n. 13 above.

122   Vladimir Markov points to a close connection in Russian culture between literary impressionism and "ego-futurism." Markov, *Russian Futurism*, p. 6. Some of the "ego-futurists" were influenced by Helena Blavatskaia, Max Stirner, and Henri Bergson. At this point Rodchenko adopts this dissonance paradigm of Russian modernism because it synthesized painting and writing, visual and verbal.

123   Aleksandr Rodchenko, "Rodchenko's System," in *Rodchenko: Experiments for the Future*, p. 84.

124   Rodchenko, diary, January 12, 1940, in Ibid., p. 326.

125   Ibid., June 3, 1940, p. 328.

126   Kulagina, diary, October 15, 1941, private archive.

127   Ibid., October 16, 1941.

128   Ibid., October 17, 1941.

129   Rodchenko, diary, March 3, 1943 in *Rodchenko: Experiments for the Future*, p. 353.

130   Ibid., March 14, 1943, p. 355.

131   Ibid., April 8, 1943, p. 358.

132   Ibid., July 29, 1943, p. 370.

133   Kulagina, diary, June 8, 1943, private archive.

134   Ibid., August 28, 1943.

135   Ibid., June 21, 1943.

136   Briony Fer's description of Jean (Hans) Arp's drawings "L'Air est une racine," published in 1933 in the last number of *Le Surrealisme au service de la révolution*. Briony Fer, *On Abstract Art* (New Haven and London: Yale University Press, 1997), p. 59. Rodchenko's compositions of the early 1940s are similar to these Arp drawings. Further comparison can be made with works by the Abstraction-Création group.

137   Rodchenko, diary, January 15, 1937 in *Rodchenko: Experiments for the Future*, p. 314.

138   Ibid., June 3, 1940, p. 328.

139   Ibid., January 1, 1944, p. 381.

140   Malevich, letter to G.N. Petnikov, July 15–28, 1933, in Vakar and Mikhienko, *Malevich o sebe*, vol. 1, p. 242. Malevich's "duel" with the AKhRR painter Dmitry Toporkov in 1933 (a friend of Katsman and, ironically, Malevich's second brother-in-law from the opposing camp), was over how to paint a landscape, a portrait, and a human figure.

141   Rodchenko, diary, February 12, 1943, in *Rodchenko: Experiments for the Future*, p. 350.

142   Ibid., July 30, 1943, p. 370.

143   Ibid., January 15, 1937, p. 314. For a comparison of Rodchenko's and Jackson Pollock's techniques see Margarita Tupitsyn, *Against Kandinsky* (Ostfildern: Hatje Cantz Verlag, 2006), pp. 152–61.

144   Rodchenko, diary, August 11, 1943, in *Rodchenko: Experiments for the Future*, p. 372.

145   Victor Tupitsyn, *Museological Unconscious*, p. 2.

146   Ibid., p. 297 n. 6.

147   According to Kulagina in 1947, information was streaming to Russia from foreign broadcasts: "we are listening to the BBC, the program from America and England, we hear many sad truths and wonder how we are allowed to listen to such programs" Kulagina, diary, September 4, 1947, private archive.

148   Golomstock, *Totalitarnoe iskusstvo*, p. 140.

149   Evgeny Katsman quoted in Matthew Cullerne Bown, "Aleksandr Gerasimov," in *Art of the Soviets: Painting, Sculpture and Architecture in a One-party State, 1917–1992*, ed. Matthew Cullerne Bown and Brandon Taylor (Manchester: Manchester University Press, 1993), p. 135.

150   Kulagina, diary, August 16, 1948, private archive.

151   G.H. Lewes quoted in Nochlin, *Realism*, p. 35.

152   Rodchenko, diary, August 11, 1947, in *Rodchenko: Experiments for the Future*, p. 407.

153   From Tatlin's speech at the MOSSKh discussion on formalism, March 20, 1936, RGALI, fond 990, op. 3, ed.kh.8, l.97.

154   Malevich, letter to Kliun, June 28, 1934, in Vakar and Mikhienko, *Malevich o sebe*, vol. 1, p. 250.

155   Kulagina, diary, October 21, 1948, private archive. A year earlier, both Deineka and Sergei Gerasimov had exhibited with Aleksandr Gerasimov in Vienna. Perhaps the successful reception of their paintings there resulted in this later harassment.

156   W.E.B. Du Bois, "The Nature of Intellectual Freedom," 1948, in *Marxism and Art*, ed. Maynard Solomon (New York: Vintage Books, 1974), p. 260.

157   Kulagina, diary, March 12, 1949, private archive.

158   Ibid.

159   *Narodnost* was the national principal that culture should be accessible to the masses. It was a prescribed element of Socialist Realism.

160   In 1957, Gerasimov was dismissed from his post as president of the Academy of Arts of the USSR.

3   REINVENTING ABSTRACTION

1   See Matthew Cullerne Bown, "Aleksandr Gerasimov," in *Art of the Soviets: Painting, Sculpture and Architecture in a One-party State, 1917–1992*, ed. Matthew Cullerne Bown and Brandon Taylor (Manchester: Manchester University Press, 1993), p. 135.

2   The academics included Boris Ioganson, at the time the Academy's vice-president, A. Gerasimov, Martiros Sarian, and Sergei Konenkov, all laureates of the Stalin Prize.

3   Pablo Picasso quoted in V. Volovnikov, *O neobyknovennom gode neobyknovennoi epokhi: neizvestnaia istoriia vystavki Pablo Picasso v SSSR v 1956 godu* (Moscow, 2007), pp. 62–3.

4   Il'ia Kabakov, *60–70 …: zapiski o neofitsialnoi zhizni v Moskve* (Vienna: *Wiener Slawistischer* Almanach, *Sonderband* no. 47, 1999), p. 1.

5   Iury Sobolev quoted in *"Drugoe" iskusstvo: Moskva 1956–76. K khronike khudozhestvennoi zhizni*, ed. Irina Alpatova and Leonid Talochkin, 2 vols. (Moscow: SP Interbuk, 1991), vol. 1, p. 24.

6   Kabakov, *60–70*, p. 2.

7   Vladimir Slepian, interview with Pierre Schneider, "I Was an Abstractionist in the USSR: Interview with 'Woks,'" *Artnews* (March 1959), p. 29.

8   In private documents Cordier lists Slepian with his last name but in public ones as "a painter from Leningrad." Galerie Daniel Cordier archive, Bibliothèque Kandinsky, Centre Georges Pompidou, Paris. At the time, Cordier exhibited abstract artists such as Jean (Hans) Arp, Sophie Taeuber-Arp, Piet Mondrian, Claude Viseux, and Jean Dewasne. The last's paintings looked similar to Rodchenko's 1940s compositions. Another early appreciation of Soviet underground art was by the Mexican muralist David Siqueiros, who in the 1930s had a considerable influence on Jackson Pollock and other American artists. As the president of an art competition at the Moscow Youth Festival, Siqueiros awarded a young Moscow artist, Anatoly Zverev, with a gold medal for an expressionist drawing.

9   Slepian, interview with Schneider, "I was an Abstractionist," p. 29.

10   Ibid., p. 62.

11   Harold Rosenberg, "The American Action Painters," *Artnews* 51/8 (December 1952), repr. in Harold Rosenberg, *The Tradition of the New* (New York: Horizon, 1959), pp. 24–5.

12   The Moscow abstract artist Lev Kropivnitsky quoted in Alpatova and Talochkin, *"Drugoe" iskusstva*, vol. 1, p. 33.

13   Iury Zlotnikov quoted in ibid., p. 24.

14   Slepian, interview with Schneider, "I Was an Abstractionist," p. 62.

15   "In Paris; Was Smuggled Out," *Herald Tribune* (October 16, 1957). Although Slepian was at first positively received, he did not become a successful artist in the West. That caused frustration, and shifted his interest to writing. Much later, his text "Fils de Chien" (Son of a Dog), published in *Minuit* 7 (January 1974), received attention from Gilles Deleuze and Félix Guattari in their 1980 *Mille Plateaux*. As they wrote, they provided "a very simplified presentation" of Slepian's text: "I am hungry, always hungry, a man should not be hungry, so I'll have to become a dog – but how? This will not involve imitating a dog, nor an analogy of relations. I must succeed in endowing the parts of my body with relations of speed and slowness that will make it become dog, in an original assemblage proceeding neither by resemblance nor by analogy." *A Thousand Plateaux: Capitalism and Schizophrenia*, trans. Brian Massumi (Minneapolis: University of Minnesota Press, 1987), p. 258. To me, Slepian's image of a dog expressed both his personal feeling of being a poor underdog in the West and the Cold War image of Russia that impacted all emigrants (he first went to Poland in 1958, then to Paris). He is Mother Russia's prodigal son who, unlike the biblical one, cannot return home. This creates both physical suffering (hunger) and a psychological trauma, expressed in the masochistic concept of becoming an animal. In Russia he resolved his frustration with the system by becoming an "underground artist." Given this interpretation, it is logical that Slepian "bases his attempt to become-dog on the idea of tying shoes to his hands using his mouth-muzzle." Ibid. In other words, he demonstrates the impossibility of releasing himself from the status of being a double victim of both Western and Soviet repressive apparatuses.

16   Daniel Cordier quoted in an unidentified press clipping, "From Underground," 1957, Galerie Daniel Cordier archive, Bibliothèque Kandinsky, Centre Georges Pompidou, Paris.

17   Slepian, interview with Schneider, "I Was an Abstractionist," p. 62.

18   Vladimir Nemukhin, "O vremeni i o sebe," in *Vladimir Nemukhin: zhivopis', grafika, skul'ptura, farfor* (Moscow: Bonfi, 2012), p. 18.

19   Pollock, who in his youth was called "a rotten rebel from Russia," studied with the Russian émigré writer and artist Dan Graham (Ivan Dabrowsky) who introduced him to Kandinsky. Given that Thomas Hart Benton, Pollock's teacher at the Art Students League, was "a Paris-trained modernist turned Realist apostate [who] had come to spurn any form of abstraction and all progressive developments abroad," it is possible that Pollock's turn to Abstract Expressionism was a reaction to Benton's conservative realism. See Margarita Tupitsyn, *Against Kandinsky* (Ostfildern: Hatje Cantz Verlag, 2006), pp. 152–6.

20   Also exhibited were works by William Baziotes, Adolph Gottlieb, Robert Motherwell, Mark Rothko, and Bradley Walker Tomlin.

21   Vladimir Nemukhin, "O vremeni i o sebe," in *Vladimir Nemukhin*, p. 18.

22   Slepian, interview with Schneider, "I Was an Abstractionist," p. 28.

23   Lydia Masterkova remembers being excited about its opening. She ran to the address given and considered this event to be a miracle, for all the schools' teachers had been blacklisted as "formalists" and had not been able to find employment. Among the teachers were Malevich's student Petr Sokolov (Nemukhin's teacher), Mikhail Perutsky and Moisei Khazanov (both Masterkova's teachers), A.M. Gliuzkin, and Pavel Kuznetsov. In 1946, Masterkova entered the equally alternative Moscow Art Institute, studying there until it was closed in 1950 for a "left leaning." Lydiia Masterkova, "Avtobiografiia khudozhnitsy L. Masterkovoi," ca. 1969, private collection, pp. 2–3.

24   Ibid., p. 3. I am translating the word *soderzhanie* as "subject matter" rather than "content," following Greenberg's distinction between the two: "Subject matter as distinguished from content: in the sense that every work of art must have content, but that subject matter is something the artist does or does not have in mind when he is actually at work." Clement Greenberg, "Towards a Newer Laocoon," in *Pollock and After: Critical Debate*, ed. Francis Frascina (New York: Harper and Row, 1985), p. 39.

25   The *American National Exhibition* included Blume's 1937 anti-fascist canvas *The Eternal City* and Tanguy's 1954 *Multiplication of Arches*. A free and detailed discussion of the exhibition and ardent criticism of Abstract Expressionism in the official press informed as well as attracted even more artists to this mode of painting. See e.g. V. Kemenev, "Sovremennoe iskusstvo SShA na vystavke v Sokol'nikakh," *Sovetskaia kul'tura* 87, no. 958 (July 16, 1959), unpaginated, which illustrated De Kooning's *Asheville* (1948).

26   Rosalind Krauss, "Early Images Coming Through," in *Abstraction, Gesture, Ecriture: Paintings from the Daros Collection* (Zurich: Alesco AG, 1999), p. 23.

27   *Vladimir Nemukhin*, p. 18.

28   In view of a growing current tendency to elevate Socialist Realist painting to the level of masterpieces, it is appropriate to cite a 1972 interview between Willem de Kooning and Harold Rosenberg. To the latter's question "You think there could be someone like Rubens today?," De Kooning replied: "I would say there is no reason why there couldn't be. George Spaventa and I were open minded, and we thought there was no reason why, after 40 years of power, maybe one or two Russian artists would be gifted in the kind of painting that the Russian government demanded. We went to the Russian exhibition at the New York Coliseum with open minds. It turned out to be terrible painting – awful; the kind of painting done in this country in 1910 for the *Saturday Evening Post*." "Willem de Kooning: A 1972 Interview with Harold Rosenberg," repr. in David Whitney, *De Kooning: A Centennial Exhibition* (New York: Gagosian Gallery, 2004), p. 65.

29   Masterkova, "Avtobiografiia khudozhnitsy," p. 4.

30   Ibid.

31   Mikhail Larionov and Liubov Popova quoted in Benjamin H.D. Buchloh, "From *Faktura* to Factography," *October* no. 30 (Fall 1984), p. 86 n. 6.

32   On this point see "Being-in-Production: The Constructivist Code," in *Rodchenko and Popova: Defining Constructivism*, ed. Margarita Tupitsyn (London: Tate Publishing, 2009), pp. 13–30.

33   Kropivnitsky quoted in Alpatova and Talochkin, *"Drugoe" iskusstvo*, vol. 1, p. 33.

34   Cordier quoted in "From Underground."

35   Vladimir Yankilevsky, "Memoirs of the Manezh Exhibition, 1962," *Zimmerli Journal* 1 (Fall 2003), p. 70.

36   Ibid., p. 73.

37   Ibid.

38   Ibid., p. 74. In the West, Sooster is known primarily for his association with Ilya Kabakov, with whom he shared a studio in the 1960s. He moved to Moscow from Estonia in 1957 after being released from a camp in Karaganda. Sooster reaffirmed "the spirit of free communication" and the tradition of debating that had disappeared from the postwar Moscow art world. That skill came from his association with the Tartu Art Institute before his arrest in 1949, where he regularly engaged in debates, the subjects of which included "the expansion of artistic borders. The role of self in art. The role of one's own vision. The role of deformation. The right to create an image according to your own vision." Reet Varblane, "Ülo Sooster and His Time," in Ilya Kabakov, *On Ülo Sooster's Paintings: Subjective Notes* (Tallinn: Kirjastus "Kunst," 1996), p. 207.

39   Yankilevsky notes that Romm liked his work because it had an obvious relation to his film. Yankilevsky, "Memoirs of the Manezh Exhibition," pp. 71–2.

40   E. Neizvestnyi, "Otkryvat' novoe!," *Iskusstvo* 10 (1962), pp. 9–11.

41   See www.sql.ru/forum/535011/stenogramma-prisutstviy a-n-s-hrushheva-na-vystavke-hudozhnikov-avangardisto v-v-manezhe, accessed on July 30, 2016.

42   Neizvestny quoted in Alpatova and Talochkin, *"Drugoe" iskusstvo*, vol. 1, p. 36.

43   Leonid Ilichev quoted in ibid., p. 105.

44   "Tvorit' dlia naroda-vysshaia tsel' khudozhnika," *Kommunist* no. 1 (1963), quoted in ibid., p. 111.

45   Ibid.

46   See, for example, "Iskusstvo prinadlezhit narodu," *Pravda* (December 3, 1962) in ibid., p. 108.

47   "Tvorit' dlia naroda–vysshaia tsel' khudozhnika," *Kommunist* no. 1, (1963) quoted in ibid., p. 111.

48   Yankilevsky, "Memoirs of the Manezh Exhibition," p. 76. To add to his argument, the *American National Exhibition* was attended by 2.7 million people, prompting many public and private discussions.

49   Ibid.

50   A.K. Lebedev, *Protiv abstraktsionizma v iskusstve* (Moscow: Izdatelstvo Akademii Khudozhestv SSSR, 1963), p. 3. In 1938, Lebedev, whose specialism was nineteenth-century Russian realism, had also published *A. M. Gerasimov: ocherk zhizni i tvorchestva sovetskogo zhivopistsa,*

51   A good example is A. Gulyga's "'Istinnaia' teoriia abstrakt-sionizma," *Iskusstvo* 10 (1962), pp. 71–2, where the author analyzes a recent theory of abstraction in Arnold Gehlen, *Zeit-Bilder: Zur Soziologie und Ästhetik der Modernen Malerei* (Frankfurt-am-Main: Athenäum, 1960). Gehlen's insistence that abstraction performed a purely "optical task" lent credibility to the idea that it was the antithesis of official realism.

52   S.E. Mozhniagun, *Abstraktionizm: razrushenie estetiki* (Moscow: Izdatel'stvo Sotsial'no-ekonomicheskoi Literatury, 1961).

53   Mozhniagun illustrated his text about Malevich with a canvas from the *White on White* series (1918) that belongs to New York's Museum of Modern Art, rather than with a work from a Russian collection, thus underlining the foreignness of suprematism. Ibid., p. 34.

54   Vasily Kandinsky, "Point and Line to Plane," in *Kandinsky: Complete Writings on Art*, ed. Kenneth C. Lindsay and Peter Vergo (New York: Da Capo Press, 1994), p. 578.

55   Nikolai Ladovsky quoted in S.O. Khan-Magomedov, *Osnova, Osa, i gruppy Inkhuka* (Moscow, 1994), p. 15.

56   Maria Gough, "In the Laboratory of Constructivism: Karl Ioganson's Cold Structures," *October* no. 85 (Spring 1998), p. 102.

57   Rosalind Krauss, *Passages in Modern Sculpture* (Cambridge, Mass.: MIT Press, 1977), p. 264.

58   Kandinsky, "Point and Line to Plane," p. 657.

59   Viacheslav Koleichuk, *Kinetizm* (Moscow: Galart, 1994), pp. 51–2.

60   Lev Nusberg, "Some of my thoughts," 1965, Ms., quoted in ibid., p. 49.

61   See V. Kutuzov, "Ploshad' 9 muz," *Sovetskii Soiuz* 12 (1965), pp. 44–5.

62   Koleichuk, *Kinetizm*, p. 52.

63   Kabakov, *60–70*, p. 17.

64   Lee Krasner quoted in Rosalind Krauss, *The Originality of the Avant-garde and Other Modernist Myths* (Cambridge, Mass.: MIT Press, 1985), p. 239.

65   Paul Sjeklocha and Igor Mead, *Unofficial Art in the Soviet Union* (Berkeley: University of California Press, 1967), p. 116.

66   Mikhail Chernyshov, *Moskva, 1961–67* (New York, self published, 1988), pp. 46–7.

67   Mikhail Chernyshov quoted in Alpatova and Talochkin, *"Drugoe" iskusstva*, vol. 1, p. 133.

68   Ibid., p. 131.

69   Ibid.

70   Kabakov, *60–70*, p. 9.

71   Ibid., p. 10.

72   Ibid., p. 16.

73   Varblane, "Ulö Sooster and His Time," p. 207.

74   Kabakov, *60–70*, p. 20.

75   Il'ia Kabakov and Iurii Kuper: *52 dialoga na kommunal'noi kukhne/ Ilya Kabakov and Yuri Kuper 52 entretiens dans la cuisine communautaire* (Marseilles: Ateliers Municipaux d'Artistes, 1992), p. 48.

76   Ibid.

77   Ibid., p. 278.

78   Ibid., p. 280.

79   Ibid., p. 274.

80   Erik Bulatov, "Slovo o kartine," *WAM* (*World Art Museum*) 11 (2004), p. 62.

81   Krauss, *Originality of the Avant-garde*, p. 9.

82   Rosalind Krauss, "On Frontality," in *The Great Decade of American Abstraction: Modernist Art, 1960 to 1970* (Houston, Tex.: Museum of Fine Arts, 1974), p. 89.

83   This was article 129 guaranteeing freedom of speech, the press, assembly and rallies, street processions and demonstrations. Significantly, the Stalin Constitution lasted from 1936 to 1977 when it was replaced by the Brezhnev Constitution to which a paragraph on parasitism was added. It had a direct impact on the life of the unsanctioned cultural milieu forced by the law to be employed.

84   Komar and Melamid, letter to Margarita Tupitsyn, December 1, 2001.

85 John Coplans, "Mel Bochner on Malevich, an Interview," *Artforum* (June 1974), repr. in *Malevich and the American Legacy* (New York: Gagosian Gallery, 2011), p. 60.

86 Ibid. p. 62.

4 DANGEROUS LUNCHEON ON THE GRASS

1 Allan Kaprow, quoted in Robert Storr, "Creativity and Commerce," moderated by Douglas Dreishpoon, *Art in America* (May 2013), p. 70.

2 Linda Nochlin, *Realism: Style and Civilization* (New York: Penguin, 1972), p. 137.

3 Paul Wood, "Introduction," in *The Challenge of the Avant-garde*, ed. Paul Wood (New Haven and London: Yale University Press, 1999), p. 15.

4 Vasily Kandinsky, "Point and Line to Plane," in *Kandinsky: Complete Writings on Art*, ed. Kenneth C. Lindsay and Peter Vergo (New York: Da Capo Press, 1994), p. 538.

5 The script for *The Appearance* set up the structure of every performance by CAG. That included inviting a limited number of people, and thus virtually excluding a random audience; using an open field as the stage for acting out a script written in advance by a single member; and collating the recollections and interpretations of participants. The CAG's founding member, Andrei Monastyrsky, believes that "our actions can be realized as something valuable only in interpretation." Monastyrsky, letter to V. Tupitsyn, March 8, 1979, in Viktor Agamov-Tupitsyn and Andrei Monastyrskii, *Tet-a-Tet: perepiska, dialogi, interpretatsiia, faktografiia*, ed. Margarita Masterkova-Tupitsyna (Vologda: BMK, 2013), p. 52. All CAG's performance scripts can be accessed at http://conceptualism.letov.ru/KD-ACTIONS.htm, accessed August 2, 2016.

6 The founding members' original idea was not to have a formal group but to present each action by listing the author, then the participants' names. This reflected their fluid membership and a broader notion of collective creativity.

7 Monastyrsky to Victor Tupitsyn on a photograph taken by Georgy Kizevalter and inscribed on verso by Monasyrsky. Archive of Margarita and Victor Tupitsyn.

8 In spring 1976, Monastyrsky wrote: "Looks like I have finished with the words in poetry(?)." Monastyrsky, letter to V. Tupitsyn, spring 1976, in Agamov-Tupitsyn and Monastyrskii, *Tet-a-Tet*, p. 13.

9 Monastyrsky in conversation with Viktor Tupitsyn, *"Drugoe" iskusstva: besedy s khudozhnikami, kritikami, filosofami, 1980–1995* (Moscow: Ad Marginem, 1997), p. 224.

10 Roman Jakobson, "On a Generation that Squandered its Poets," *Verbal Arts, Verbal Sign, Verbal Time* (Minneapolis: University of Minnesota Press, 1985), p. 115.

11 Andrei Monastyrskii, ed., *Kollektivnye deistviia: poezdki za gorod* (Moscow: Ad Marginem, 1998), p. 21.

12 Ibid., p. 19.

13 Monastyrsky, letter to V. Tupitsyn, March 8, 1979, in Agamov-Tupitsyn and Monastyrskii, *Tet-a-Tet*, p. 52.

14 Ibid.

15 Monastyrsky, letter to V. Tupitsyn, October 10, 1986, in ibid., p. 208.

16 Monastyrsky, letter to V. Tupitsyn, November 1979, in Margarita Tupitsyna and Viktor Tupitsyn, "Moskva–N'iu Iork," *WAM* (*World Art Museum*) 21 (2006), p. 154.

17 I have asked Monastyrsky whether they used a still camera because they did not have access to a cine camera. He replied that although one could buy an 8 mm cine camera in Russia at that time, he was not then interested in filming CAG actions. Email correspondence, September 17, 2013.

18 Il'ia Kabakov and Iurii Kuper, *52 dialoga na kommunal'noi kukhne*/Ilya Kabakov and Yuri Kuper, *52 Entretiens dans la cuisine communautaire* (Marseilles: Ateliers Municipaux d'Artistes, 1992), p. 256.

19 At the end of the performance of *Pictures*, the participants were asked to display the "pictures" in a vertical position, creating a contrast with the horizontal position in which they had been made.

20 Ilya Kabakov quoted in "Passkaz I. Kabakova (ob aktsii Mesto deistviia)," in Monastyrskii ed., *Kollektivnye deistviia*, p. 66.

21 Kabakov and Kuper, *52 dialoga*, p. 262.

22 Other paintings that Kabakov included in this white group are *Couch-painting* (1967; see fig. 78) and *Berdianskaia Spit* (1970).

23 Il'ia Kabakov, "Mozhno li pisat' na 'belom' slova?" 1983, Ms., Archive of Margarita and Victor Tupitsyn. I have made every effort to find out if this has been published in English, but the artist has been unable to confirm this.

24 Monastyrsky, letter to V. Tupitsyn, September 20, 1980, in Tupitsyna and Tupitsyn, "Moskva–N'iu Iork," p. 172.

25 Kabakov, "Mozhno li pisat' na 'belom' slova?"

26 Kabakov quoted in Monastyrskii ed., *Kollektivnye deistviia*, p. 153.

27 Ibid., p. 154.

28 In his discussion of *At the Edge*, Kabakov mentions Kandinsky as one of the early artists to dismiss classical perspective in his semifigurative works. Of a work that Kabakov identifies as from the "Kremlin" series, dated 1912, he points out: "In the center there is a dot from which a city is blossoming with petals; thus this painting can be rotated this way and that, but buildings would always stick out in different directions." This description would fit Kandinsky's *Moscow I* (1916). Kabakov and Kuper, *52 dialoga*, p. 256.

29 Vasily Kandinsky, "The Great Utopia," in *Kandinsky: Complete Writings*, p. 448.

30 Although the constructivists' program promoted the goal of attaining the unattainable, it is logical that postwar nonconformist artists, who detested Marxist theory as a result of its corruption by the Soviet regime, would adhere to a more universal paradigm of utopia. Like the architects of Zhivskulptarkh, who supported Kandinsky's program, CAG was committed to laboratory creativity, and to correlation with concepts developed in painting. On the difference between constructivist and Kandinsky's utopian models, as well as on collaboration between Kandinsky and the Zhivskulptarkh architects, see Margarita Tupitsyn *Against Kandinsky* (Ostfildern: Hatje Cantz Verlag, 2006), pp. 138–45.

31 Gorkom Grafikov's *Color, Form, and Space* (Tsvet, forma, prostranstvo) took place February 17–28, 1979, and in its emphasis on the formal properties of painting signaled the end of the anti-formalist campaigns I discussed earlier.

32 Monastyrsky, letter to V. Tupitsyn, February 1979, in Tupitsyna and Tupitsyn, "Moskva–N'iu Iork," p. 141.

33 Erik Bulatov, "O kartine," April 11, 1989, Ms., Archive of Margarita and Victor Tupitsyn.

34 See Rosalind Krauss, "The Im/Pulse to See," in *Vision and Visuality*, ed. Hal Foster (Seattle: Bay Press, 1988), p. 52.

35 Ilya Kabakov, videotaped interview with the photographer Sergei Borisov, Moscow, 1986. Courtesy Sergei Borisov.

36 Monastyrsky, letter to V. Tupitsyn, December 14, 1978, in Agamov-Tupitsyn and Monastyrskii, *Tet-a-Tet*, p. 46.

37 Monastyrsky, letter to V. Tupitsyn, March 8, 1979, in ibid., p. 52.

38 Monastyrsky, letter to V. Tupitsyn, Fall 1983, in Tupitsyna and Tupitsyn, "Moskva–N'iu Iork," p. 197.

39 Nochlin, *Realism*, p. 141. Significantly, the only complete version of Monet's *Déjeuner sur l'herbe* is the small painting in the Pushkin State Museum of Fine Arts, Moscow.

40 Erik Bulatov quoted in Monastyrskii ed., *Kollektivnye deistviia*, p. 242.

41 Monastyrsky, letter to V. Tupitsyn, August 15, 1983, in Tupitsyna and Tupitsyn, "Moskva–N'iu Iork," p. 196.

42 Nikita Alekseev, letter to V. Tupitsyn, July 14, 1982, in ibid., p. 222.

43 Nikita Alekseev, "Ne govoria uzh o nebe, oblakakh, solntse, vode, ptitsakh, etc.," June 1983, Ms., Archive of Margarita and Victor Tupitsyn.

44 Nikita Alekseev, text for *Speech*, April 1980, Ms., Archive of Margarita and Victor Tupitsyn.

45 Ibid.

46 Nikita Alekseev, letter to V. Tupitsyn, January 20, 1983, in Tupitsyna and Tupitsyn, "Moskva–N'iu Iork," p. 225. For further discussion of Apt Art see Ch. 5 here and Margarita Tupitsyn "The Decade BC (Before Chernenko) in Contemporary Russian Art," in *Exhibition*, ed. Lucy Steeds (London: Whitechapel Gallery; Cambridge, Mass.: MIT Press, 2014), pp. 194–9, and Margarita Tupitsyn and Victor Tupitsyn, eds., *Anti-shows: APTART, 1982–1984* (London: Afterall, 2017).

47 Alekseev, "Ne govoria uzh o nebe."

48 Monastyrsky, letter to V. Tupitsyn, June 29, 1983, in Agamov-Tupitsyn and Monastyrskii, *Tet-a-Tet*, p. 165.

49 Vladimir Markov, *Printsipy tvorchestva v plasticheskikh iskusstvakh: Faktura* (St. Petersburg: Obshchestvo Khudozhnikov Soiuz Molodezhi, 1914), p. 8.

50 The sixteen artists were Iury Albert, Victor Skersis with Vadim Zakharov (SZ), Natalia Abalakova and Anatoly Zhigalov (Totart), Sven Gundlakh, Sergei and Vladimir Mironenko, Konstantin Zvezdochetov, and Aleksis Kamensky (the Mukhomor group), Andrei Filippov, Andrei Monastyrsky, Mikhail Roshal, Sergei Anufriev, Nikita Alekseev, and Manuel Alkaide (an artist from Cuba).

51 One of the actions, *Exponat* (Artifact), was by Andrei Monastyrsky, once again distinguished by semantic complexities and sound effects insisting on a *faktura* of noise.

52 Alekseev, letter to V. Tupitsyn, June 1, 1983, in Tupitsyna and Tupitsyn, "Moskva–N'iu Iork," p. 227.

53 Sven Gundlakh, "The Show Must Go On," June 1983, Ms., Archive of Margarita and Victor Tupitsyn.

54 Ibid.

5 RAISON D'ETRE OF INSTALLATION ART

1 I. Kabakov and A. Monastyrskii, "Zritel'-Personazh," conversation recorded August 1988, in *Sborniki MANI: moskovskii arkhiv novogo iskusstva* (Vologda: BMK, 2010), p. 497.

2 Ibid., p. 493.

3 In 1984, Komar and Melamid made an exact copy of *Double Self-portrait*, destroyed in *The Bulldozer Exhibition*, for its tenth anniversary. The work illustrated here is the replica.

4 These and other quotations about *Paradise* come from Komar and Melamid's description, Ms., Archive of Margarita and Victor Tupitsyn. It was prepared for me when I was writing "Red Guardians of Tradition: The Performances of Russian Émigré Artists Komar and Melamid," *High Performance* 28 (1984), pp. 41–3, 95.

5 Ibid.

6 Specifically, the style of Jacques Lipchitz and Ernst Neizvestny.

7 Michel Foucault, "Of Other Spaces: Utopias and Heterotopias," http://web.mit.edu/allanmc/www/foucault1.pdf, accessed on August 9, 2016.

8   J. Bakshtein, and A. Monastyrskii, "Vnutri kartiny," conversation recorded on September 11, 1988, first published in *Sborniki MANI*, p. 551.

9   During Monastyrsky's absence, his mother-in-law threw *Pile* into the trash. Had it survived, we would have had not only an early example of Soviet interactive art but also an archeology of bohemian everyday life.

10   Ivan Chuikov in conversation with Victor Tupitsyn, 1988, in Viktor Tupitsyn, *"Drugoe" iskusstva: besedy s khudozhnikami, kritikami, filosofami, 1980–1995* (Moscow: Ad Marginem, 1997), p. 79.

11   See Ivan Chuikov and Mariia Valiaeva, "Interv'iu s khudozhnikom," in *Ivan Chuikov: 1966–1997* (Moscow: State Tretiakov Gallery, 1998), p. 6.

12   Chuikov grew up in a family of official artists. His farther, Semen Chuikov, a laureate of the Stalin Prize who "wrote articles against abstract art." Ibid.

13   Ibid., p. 16.

14   Chuikov quoted in Tupitsyn, *"Drugoe" iskusstva*, p. 77.

15   Rosalind Krauss, *The Originality of the Avant-garde and Other Modernist Myths* (Cambridge, Mass.: MIT Press, 1985), p. 17.

16   Rosalind Krauss, *Bachelors* (Cambridge, Mass.: MIT Press, 1999), p. 65.

17   Igor Makarevich, "Transformation," artist's text, 1978, Ms., Archive of Margarita and Victor Tupitsyn.

18   Ibid.

19   I am adapting Robert Morris's title for his 1961 work, *Box for Standing*. After making "Transformation," Makarevich joined CAG, which might be interpreted as a desire for collective practices after his questioning of extreme individualism in "Transformation."

20   Makarevich, "Transformation."

21   Andrei Monastyrsky, letter to V. Tupitsyn, May 17, 1980, in Viktor Agamov-Tupitsyn and Andrei Monastyrskii, *Tet-a-Tet: perepiska, dialogi, interpretatsiia, faktografiia*, ed. Margarita Masterkova-Tupitsyna (Vologda: BMK, 2013), p. 103.

22   Ibid.

23   Monastyrsky in Bakshtein and Monastyrskii, "Vnutri kartiny," p. 529.

24   Ibid.

25   Mikhail Bakhtin quoted in T. V. Akhutina, "The Theory of Verbal Communication in the Works of M.M. Bakhtin and L.S. Vygotsky," trans. M.E. Sharpe, *Journal of Russian and East European Psychology*, vol. 41, no. 3, pp. 96–114 (May–June 2003), at www2.fcsh.unl.pt/psicolinguistica/docs/3akhutina.pdf, accessed on 22 July 2016.

26   Monastyrsky, letter to V. Tupitsyn, May 17, 1980, in Agamov-Tupitsyn and Monastyrskii, *Tet-a-Tet*, p. 104.

27   Monastyrsky, letter to V. Tupitsyn, February 9, 1981, in ibid., p. 123.

28   Igor Makarevich quoted in R. and V. Gerloviny, "Mukhomory," *A-Ya* 3 (1981), p. 12.

29   Kabakov, "Mozhno li pisat' na 'belom' slova?" 1983, Ms., Archive of Margarita and Victor Tupitsyn.

30   Monastyrsky, letter to V. Tupitsyn, July 19, 1981, in Margarita Tupitsyna and Viktor Tupitsyn, "Moskva–N'iu Iork," *WAM* (*World Art Museum*) 21 (2006), p. 181. I base my description of *Drainage* on Monastyrsky's in this letter.

31   Ibid.

32   Sven Gundlakh, "APTART (Pictures From an Exhibition)," *A-Ya* 5 (1983), p. 5.

33   A. Zhigalov and N. Abalakova, letter to Victor and Margarita Tupitsyn, January 3, 1983, detailing the Apt Art installation, in Tupitsyna and Tupitsyn, "Moskva–N'iu Iork," p. 237.

34   On the checklist, *Novel* is catalogued under Mukhomor, but some sources list it as Zvezdochetov's object.

35   After the two open-air exhibitions *Apt Art in Plein Air* and *Apt Art Behind the Fence* (see Ch. 4), Aptartists returned to Alekseev's apartment for several more events. For in-depth discussion of Apt Art, see Margarita Tupitsyn and Victor Tupitsyn, eds., *Anti-shows: APTART, 1982–1984* (London: Afterall, 2017).

36   Nikita Alekseev, letter to Margarita and Victor Tupitsyn, February 18, 1983, in Tupitsyna and Tupitsyn, "Moskva–N'iu Iork," p. 230.

37   Il'ia Kabakov, "Khudozhnik-personazh," 1985, typescript, Archive of Margarita and Victor Tupitsyn.

38   Ibid.

39   Ibid.

40   See Tony Stooss, ed., *Ilya Kabakov: Installations, 1983–2000*, cat. raisonné (Düsseldorf: Richter, 2003), pp. 54–7. Although Kabakov dates this installation from 1983, the existing photographs show a floor label with the date 1986 and the title *Upward*. Apparently, *Upward* is the original title of this installation, which Kabakov renamed in the West as *Little White Men* when he conceived a different version of it. With no other documentation, it is difficult to be sure about its exact date. It is possible that Kabakov dated *Little White Men* for its year of conception rather than installation.

41   Irina Nakhova quoted in Margarita Tupitsyn, "A Conversation with Irina Nakhova," in Margarita Tupitsyn and Victor Tupitsyn, *Irina Nakhova and Pavel Pepperstein: Moscow Partisan Conceptualism* (London: Orel Art, 2010), p. 21.

42   Irina Nakhova, "Chetyre komnaty," in *Sborniki MANI*, p. 254. According to Nakhova, the dates for all three rooms given here are erroneous and should be 1983–6. Nakhova's email to Margarita Tupitsyn, September 3, 2013.

43   Ibid., p. 254.

44 The *Moskva–Parizh* exhibition in 1981 had included a number of Kandinsky's paintings, such as *Composition No. 6* (1913), which could also have prompted Nakhova to number her *Rooms*.

45 Anatoly Zhigalov and Natalia Abalakova interviewed by Vadim Zakharov for the Moscow Archive of New Art (MANI), 1982, MANI folders, Collection of Elena Kuprina-Liakhovich, Moscow.

46 See Ilya Kabakov, "Not Everyone Will Be Taken into the Future," *A-Ya* 5 (1983), pp. 34–5.

47 Stooss, *Kabakov: Installations*, p. 67.

48 Kabakov in Kabakov and Monastyrskii, "Zritel'-Personazh," p. 514.

49 See my feminist interpretation of Bakshtein's idea of interviewing the male artists in "Unveiling Feminism: Women's Art in the Soviet Union," *Arts* (December 1990), pp. 66.

50 Eduard Gorokhovsky in Joseph Bakshtein, "Interviews with Moscow Artists in *Room No. 2*," in *Irina Nakhova: The Green Pavilion*, ed. Margarita Tupitsyn (Moscow: Stella Art Foundation, 2015), p. 51. Vasiliev in ibid., p. 55.

51 *Sborniki MANI*, p. 279.

52 Gorokhovsky in ibid., p. 51.

53 Erik Bulatov in ibid., p. 55.

54 Ilya Kabakov in ibid., p. 51.

55 In Western literature, the title has been repeatedly translated as *The Man Who Flew into Space from His Apartment*, whereas, in Russian, Kabakov called this installation "Chelovek, kotoryi uletel v kosmos iz svoei komnaty," which refers to a room in a communal apartment.

56 Stooss, *Kabakov: Installations*, p. 96.

57 E. V. Bulatov, "O moem otnoshenii k sotsial'noi real'nosti," April 1984, typescript, Archive of Margarita and Victor Tupitsyn.

58 Stooss, *Kabakov: Installations*, p. 96.

59 Michael Fried, "Art and Objecthood," *Artforum* (Summer 1967), p. 31.

60 Monastyrsky in Bakshtein and Monastyrskii, "Vnutri kartiny," p. 525.

61 Ibid.

62 Kabakov, "Not Everyone Will Be Taken," p. 35.

6 MOSCOW–NEW YORK

1 Victor Skersis, "Instead of an Introduction," in *Donskoi, Roshal', Skersis: The Nest*, ed. Olga Holmogorova (Moscow: Gosudarstvennyi Tsentr Sovremennogo Iskusstva, 2008), p. 8.

2 Ibid. p. 12.

3 See C.S. Pierce, "Logic as Semiotic: The Theory of Signs," *Philosophical Writings of Pierce*, ed. Justus Buchler (New York: Dover Publications, 1966), p. 102.

4 Selection committee comment quoted in Vitaly Komar's email to Margarita Tupitsyn, February 8, 2014.

5 Nikita Alekseev, "Vystavka dostizhenii sovetskogo nonkonformizma," *Vremia novostei*, 178 (September 27, 2005), p. 6.

6 Skersis, "Instead of an Introduction," p. 62.

7 Komar and Melamid, letter to Margarita Tupitsyn, December 1, 2001.

8 Grace Glueck, "Art Smuggled Out of Russia Makes Satiric Show Here," *The New York Times* (February 7, 1976).

9 Vagrich Bakhchanian in conversation with Victor Tupitsyn in *"Drugoe" iskusstva: besedy s khudozhnikami, kritikami, filosofami, 1980–1995* (Moscow: Ad Marginem, 1997), p. 52 (recorded in 1980 in New York).

10 Ibid., p. 54.

11 Ibid.

12 Ibid.

13 Vagrich Bakhchanian and Anatoly Ur, "Joseph Beuys: Art and Politics, Interview," *A-Ya* 2 (1980), p. 56.

14 Ibid.

15 Benjamin H.D. Buchloh, "Beuys: The Twilight of the Idol," *Artforum* 5, 18 (January 1980), pp. 35–43.

16 Olga Holmogorova, "Interview with Mikhail Roshal," in Holmogorova, *Donskoi, Roshal', Skersis*, p. 72.

17 Aleksandr Kosolapov quoted in Grace Glueck, "A Forum for Dissident Art," in *The New York Times* (December 28, 1979).

18 Ibid.

19 Rimma Gerlovina and Valery Gerlovin, letter to Margarita and Victor Tupitsyn, 1980, in Margarita Tupitsyna and Viktor Tupitsyn, "Moskva-N'iu Iork," *WAM* (*World Art Museum*) 21 (2006), p. 218.

20 I curated *Russian New Wave* and became CRACA's curator after its opening. In addition to working with the Norton Dodge Collection, I curated *Vagrich Bakhchanyan: Calendar* (1982), *Henry Khudyakov: Visionary Nonwearables, ESPionage* (May 8–August 15, 1982), *Lydia Masterkova: Striving Upward to the Real* and *What Happened to the Art of the Russian Amazons?* (February 10–April 17, 1983), *Evidence of Things not Seen: Zubkov and the Sterligov Group* (with Charlotte Douglas, April 21–June 30, 1983). In November 1983, CRACA moved to 145 Chambers Street where Victor Tupitsyn and I curated *APTART in Tribeca*. CRACA continued its activities as an informal center for cultural exchange between New York and Moscow until 1998.

21 Lenin to Vladimir Bonch-Bruevich, 1918, quoted in Katharina Hegewisch, "Preface," in *Lenin by Warhol* (Munich: Galerie Bernd Klüser, 1987), p. 67.

22 Aleksandr Kosolapov, "Aleksandr Kosolapov," *A-Ya* no. 2 (1980), p. 34.

23 Rimma Gerlovina and Valery Gerlovin, *Kontsepty* (Vologda: BMK, 2012), p. 53.

24 The replica was made by the sculptor and editor of *A-Ya* magazine, Igor Shelkovsky.

25 Ann Magnuson at the time (1981) was organizing the *Performance Rites* event at PS1 (held April 11–May 2, 1982).

26 According to Vitaly Komar, he and Melamid met Torres in 1978 and it is possible that he saw their preliminary drawings for the painting, *What Is to Be Done?* (1982–3). Both Torres's *What Is to Be Drunk?* and Kosolapov's *Prehistoric Communism* (1981) were included in *Visual Politics* at New York's Alternative Museum (April 17–May 22, 1982). In turn, Komar and Melamid's performance, *Art Belongs to the People*, staged at The Kitchen on March 16, 1984, could have been conceived as a reaction to Torres's installation. See my review, "Vodka and Modernism," *High Performance* 26 (1984), pp. 65–6.

27 This probably arose from their disappointment after failing to organize a group show in Moscow in Melamid's apartment in 1974. As participants started submitting their works, it became clear that their ideas on Sots Art were too diverse to constitute a coherent movement.

28 Komar and Melamid quoted in Robert Hughes, "Through the Ironic Curtain," *Time* 17 (October 25, 1982), p. 73.

29 The exhibition, *Sots Art: Russian Mock-heroic Style*, was curated by me.

30 Eleanor Heartney, "Sots Art," *Art News* (March 1984), p. 113.

31 Ellen Handy, "Sots Art," *Arts Magazine* (March 1984), p. 37.

32 See the chapter "1980–1989" in *Art Since 1900: Modernism, Anti-modernism, Postmodernism*, ed. Hal Foster, Rosalind Krauss, Yves-Alain Bois and Benjamin H.D. Buchloh (London and New York: Thames and Hudson, 2005), pp. 612–16.

33 Slavoj Žižek, *Did Somebody Say Totalitarianism? Five Interventions in the (Mis)use of a Notion* (London: Verso, 2001), p. 102.

34 Jacques Derrida quoted in *A Derrida Reader: Between the Blinds*, ed. Peggy Kamuf (New York: Columbia University Press, 1991), p. viii.

35 Douglas Crimp, Rosalyn Deutsche, and Ewa Lajer-Burcharth, "A Conversation with Krzysztof Wod-iczko," *October* no. 38 (Fall 1986), pp. 45–6. Rosalind Krauss asked me to respond to the criticism of Sots Art in this conversation, but Crimp objected to it appearing in *October*. Instead, with the support of Fredric Jameson, my response was published as "Sots Art: Round Dance Versus Ritual" in *Social Text* 22 (1989), pp. 148–53. Prior to this, Jameson, after receiving the *Sots Art* catalogue, wrote to me: "I can only consider Sots art to be Soviet Post-modernism; it's very exciting and interesting indeed. I was not aware of the existence of this until now, although I see that there have been articles on these very interesting painters already…The entire catalogue was very fascinating and stimulating." Fredric Jameson, letter to Margarita Tupitsyn, June 30, 1986, Archive of Margarita and Victor Tupitsyn.

36 Crimp, Deutsche, and Lajer-Burcharth, "A Conversation with Krzysztof Wodiczko," p. 45.

37 Ibid., p. 46

38 Ibid.

39 Warhol was presented with the photograph of Lenin by the Munich dealer Bernd Klüser, who in turn received it from an Italian friend. The original photograph was taken in 1897 and included Lenin's future revolutionary comrades who later fell out of favor and were cropped. Warhol died the year he finished this series of Lenin's portraits, which were exhibited at the Bernd Klüser Gallery two days after his death.

7 THE WORK OF ART IN THE AGE OF PERESTROIKA

1 The show was the 17th Youth Exhibition on Kuznetsky Bridge (Kuznetsky Most). Although the exhibition included artists from various generations and circles, it also featured such young vanguardists as Iury Albert, Sven Gundlakh, Nikolai Filatov, Vladimir Mironenko, Andrei Roiter, German Vinogradov, and Vadim Zakharov.

2 In this space, Leonid Bazhanov organized a comprehensive exhibition, *Retrospective: 1957–1987*, in Fall 1987. By limiting it to underground art, he was in effect claiming that it was the most important visual art produced in the Soviet Union in the postwar period.

3 Nikita Alekseev, letter from Paris to Victor and Margarita Tupitsyn, April 20, 1987, Archive of Margarita and Victor Tupitsyn. Trans. Todd Bludeau.

4 It was in the Sandunovsky Baths that Sergei Eisenstein shot the missing Black Sea scene for his *Battleship Potemkin* (1925).

5 Among the participants were Monastyrsky, Filippov, Makarevich, Elagina, Albert, Konstantin Zvezdochetov, and Boris Matrosov.

6 Curiously, Aleksandr Gerasimov converted (probably in the 1940s) a steam bath near his private house in Moscow into a living space to which he escaped in order to paint scenes of bathing women.

7 Theodor Adorno in "Something's Missing: A Discussion between Ernst Bloch and Theodor W. Adorno on the Contradictions of Utopian Longing" (1964), in Ernst Bloch, *The Utopian Function and Literature: Selected Essays*, trans. Jack Zipes and Frank Mecklenburg (Cambridge, Mass.: MIT Press, 1989), p. 10.

8 Vitaly Komar, email to Margarita Tupitsyn, May 22, 2014.

9 On the color green in Russian art, see my catalogue, *The Green Show* (New York: Exit Art, 1989).

10 "Board-installations" and "zero objects" are Kabakovs' expressions. See Il'ia Kabakov and Iurii Kuper, *52 dialoga na kommunal'noi kukhne / Ilya Kabakov and Yuri Kuper 52 Entretiens dans la cuisine communautaire* (Marseilles: Ateliers Municipaux d'Artistes, 1992), pp. 312, 324.

11 Ilya Kabakov, "On Emptiness," trans. Clark Troy, in *Between Spring and Summer: Soviet Conceptual Art in the Era of Late Communism*, ed. David Ross (Cambridge, Mass.: MIT Press, 1990), p. 54. The "Kitchen Series" and this text were produced after Kabakov's trip to Czechoslovakia in Spring 1981.

12 Sergei Anufriev quoted in Victor Tupitsyn, "Medical Hermeneutics' Inspection of Inspectors," *Flash Art* (Summer 1989), p. 135. In 1987, Anufriev, together with Peppershtein and Iury Leiderman, formed the group Medical Hermeneutics whose theoretical premise was the "creation of the canon of emptiness."

13 Malevich's designs were shown in the Exhibition of Modern Decorative Art (Verbovka) in November 1915. See Aleksandra Shatskikh, *Black Square: Malevich and the Origin of Suprematism* (New Haven and London: Yale University Press, 2012), pp. 88–9.

14 Boris Mikhailov quoted in Victor Tupitsyn, "Who is Afraid of a 'Bad' Photograph?" in Margarita and Victor Tupitsyn, *Ilya Kabakov and Boris Mikhailov: Verbal Photography and the Moscow Archive of New Art* (Porto: Museu Serralves, 2004), p. 158.

15 Ibid.

16 Leonid Volkov-Lannit, "Fata na foto," *Novyi Lef* no. 11 (1928), p. 34.

17 Mikhailov quoted in V. Tupitsyn, "Who is Afraid of a 'Bad' Photograph?" p. 160.

18 Michel Foucault, *The Archeology of Knowledge and the Discourse on Language*, trans. Alan Sheridan Smith (New York: Pantheon Books, 1972), p. 130.

19 Ibid., p. 131.

20 Ibid., p. 127.

21 Ibid.

22 This series is often dated to 1984, but in a letter of September 12, 1983, Zhigalov mentions this work as in the exhibition *Victory Over the Sun* (September 10–11, 1983). Anatoly Zhigalov, letter to Victor and Margarita Tupitsyn, September 12, 1983, in Margarita Tupitsyna and Viktor Tupitsyn, "Moskva–N'iu-Iork," *WAM* (*World Art Museum*) no. 21 (2006), p. 240.

23 In 1983, at the School gallery in Moscow, Shulgin curated the exhibition, *What Am I? The Art of Making a Choice*, for which he selected photographs by Sergei Leontiev, Igor Mukhin, and Andrei Bezukladnikov. Together with Shulgin, they formed the group Straight Photography.

24 Abigail Solomon-Godeau, "Living with Contradictions: Critical Practices in the Age of Supply-side Aesthetics," in *The Critical Image*, ed. Carol Squiers (Seattle: Bay Press, 1990), p. 64.

25 An ample example of this conversion was Sergei Soloviev's film, *Assa* (1987), in which the film's hero, Bananan, played by the artist and musician Sergei Bugaev (Africa), explains to his girlfriend that the mysterious word "Assa" means "strength and purity," and is associated with underground culture. He brings her to a rented room in a communal apartment where at the entrance hangs Nest's *Iron Curtain*, and where he teaches her how to use Nest's *Communication Tube*. This was the first time that an official filmmaker featured underground culture in a mainstream movie.

26 This is particularly true of Sotheby's auction that took place in Moscow in 1988, which broke record prices for postwar Russian art, including that by Vladimir Nemukhin, Irina Nakhova, Ilya Kabakov, and Vadim Zakharov.

27 Vadim Zakharov quoted in Margarita and Victor Tupitsyn, "The Studios on *Furmanny Lane* in Moscow," *Flash Art* 142 (1988), p. 103.

28 Monastyrsky, letter to V. Tupitsyn, December 12, 1985, in Tupitsyna and Tupitsyn, "Moskva-N'iu Iork," p. 20.

SELECTED BIBLIOGRAPHY

Alpatova, Irina, and Leonid Talochkin, eds. *"Drugoe" iskusstvo, in Moskva 1956-76. K khronike khudozhestvennoi zhizni,* 2 vols. Moscow: SP "Interbuk," 1991.

A-Ya, no. 2 (1980), no. 3 (1981), no. 5 (1983).

Banks, Miranda, ed. *The Aesthetic Arsenal: Socialist Realism Under Stalin.* New York: PS1, 1993.

Berger, John. *Art and Revolution: Neizvestny and the Role of the Artist in the USSR.* New York: Pantheon, 1969.

Bloch, Ernst. *The Utopian Function of Art and Literature,* trans. Jack Zipes and Frank Mecklenburg. Cambridge, Mass.: MIT Press, 1988.

Bois, Yve-Alain. *Painting as Model.* Cambridge, Mass.: MIT Press (October Books), 1993.

Bowlt, John E., ed. and trans. *Russian Art of the Avant-garde: Theory and Criticism, 1902–1934.* Second ed. New York: Thames and Hudson, 1988.

Buchloh, Benjamin H.D. *Formalism and Historicity: Models and Methods in Twentieth-century Art.* Cambridge, Mass.: MIT Press (October Books), 2015.

__________. "From Faktura to Factography." *October* no. 30 (Fall 1984): 83–118.

Chernyshov, Mikhail. *Moskva, 1961–67.* New York: self-published, 1988.

Clark, Katerina. "Engineers of Human Souls in an Age of Industrialization: Changing Models, 1929–1941." In Lewis Siegelbaum and William Rosenberg, eds. *Social Dimensions of Soviet Industrialization.* Bloomington: Indiana University Press, 1993.

Crimp, Douglas. *On the Museum's Ruins.* Cambridge, Mass.: MIT Press, 1993.

Cullerne Bown, Matthew, and Brandon Taylor, eds. *Art of the Soviets: Painting, Sculpture and Architecture in a One-party State, 1917–1992.* Manchester: Manchester University Press, 1993.

Czech, Hans-Jörg and Doll, Nikola, eds. *Kunst und Propaganda im Streit der Nationen, 1930–1945.* Berlin: Deutsches Historisches Museum and Dresden: Sandstein Verlag, 2007.

Dabrowski, Magdalena, Leah Dickerman, and Peter Galassi, eds. *Aleksandr Rodchenko.* New York: The Museum of Modern Art, 1998.

Danilova, Aleksandra, and Elena Kuprina Liakhovich, eds. *Pole deistviia: moskovskaia kontseptualnaia shkola i ee kontekst 70-80-e gody XX veka.* Moscow: Fond Kultury "Ekaterina," 2010.

Dickerman, Leah. "Camera Obscura: Socialist Realism in the Shadow of Photography." *October* no. 93 (Summer 2000): 138–53.

Fitzpatric, Sheila. *The Commissariat of Enlightenment: Soviet Organization of Education and the Arts under Lunacharsky, October 1917–1921.* Cambridge: Cambridge University Press, 1970.

Fore, Devin, ed. "Soviet Factography: A Special Issue." *October* no. 118 (Fall 2006).

Foster, Hal. *The Anti-aesthetic Essays on Postmodern Culture.* Seattle: Bay Press, 1983.

__________. ed. *Vision and Visuality.* Seattle: Bay Press, 1988.

Foucault, Michel. *The Archeology of Knowledge and the Discourse on Language,* trans. Alan Sheridan Smith. New York: Pantheon, 1972.

Francisco Infante: Artifacts. Retrospective. Moscow: National Centre for Contemporary Arts, 2004.

Global Conceptualism: Points of Origin, 1950–1980s. New York: Queens Museum, 1999.

Golomstock, Igor. *Totalitarian Art: In the Soviet Union, the Third Reich, Fascist Italy and the People's Republic of China.* Trans. Robert Chandler. New York: Icon Editions, 1990.

Gough, Maria. *The Artist as Producer: Russian Contructivism in Revolution.* Berkeley and Los Angeles: University of California Press, 2005.

Gray, Camilla. *The Great Experiment: Russian Art, 1863–1922.* London: Thames and Hudson, 1962. Rev. and enlarged ed. Marian Burleigh Motley, under the title *The Russian Experiment in Art, 1863–1922.* New York: Thames and Hudson, 1986. New York, Harry N. Abrams, 1962.

The Great Decade of American Abstraction: Modernist Art, 1960 to 1970, Houston: Museum of Fine Arts, 1974.

The Great Utopia: The Russian and Soviet Avant-garde, 1915–1932. New York: Solomon R. Guggenheim Museum, 1992.

Gronsky, I. M., and V. N. Perelman, ed. *AKhRR: sbornik vospominanii, statei, dokumentov.* Moscow: Izobrazitelnoe Iskusstvo, 1973.

Groys, Boris, David A. Ross, and Iwona Blazwick. *Ilia Kabakov.* London: Phaidon Press Limited, 1998.

Harrison, Charles, and Paul Wood, eds. *Art in Theory: 1900–1990, An Anthology of Changing Ideas.* Oxford: Blackwell, 1992.

Holmogorova, Olga, ed. *Donskoi, Roshal, Skersis: The Nest.* Moscow: Gosudarstvennyi Tsentr Sovremennogo Iskusstva, 2008.

Ivan Chuikov: *1966–1997.* Moscow: State Tretiakov Gallery, 1998.

Jackson, Matthew Jesse. *The Experimental Group: Ilya Kabakov, Moscow Conceptualism, Soviet Avant-guards.* Chicago: University of Chicago Press, 2010.

Jacob, John, P. ed. *The Missing Picture: Alternative Contemporary Photography from the Soviet Union.* Cambridge. Mass: MIT List Visual Arts Center, 1990.

Jameson, Fredric. *The Prison-house of Language: A Critical Account of Structuralism and Russian Formalism,* Princeton: Princeton University Press, 1972.

__________. *The Political Unconscious: Narrative as a Socially Symbolic Act.* Ithaca, N.Y.: Cornell University Press, 1981.

Kabakov, Ilia, "60–70 . . .: zapiski o neofitsialnoi zhizni v Moskve, Vienna: Wiener Slawistischer." Almanach, *Sonderband* no. 47, 1999.

__________. and Yurii Kuper. *52 dialoga na kommunal'noi kukhne / Ilya Kabakov and Yuri Kuper, 52 entretiens dans la cuisine communautaire.* Marseilles: Ateliers Municipaux d'Artistes, 1992.

Kalinsky, Yelena. *Collective Actions: Audience Recollections From the First Years, 1976-1981.* Chicago: Soberscove Press, 2012.

Kiaer, Christina. *Imagine No Possessions: The Socialist Objects of Russian Constructivism.* Cambridge, Mass.: MIT Press, 2005.

__________. "Lyrical Socialist Realism." *October* no. 147 (Winter 2014): 56–77.

Kizevalter, Georgy, ed. *Perelomnye vosmidesiatye v neofitsialnom iskusstve SSSR.* Moscow: Novoe Literaturnoe Obozrenie, 2014.

Koleichuk, Viacheslav. *Kinetizm.* Moscow: Galart, 1994.

Krauss, Rosalind E. *The Originality of the Avant-garde and Other Modernist Myths.* Cambridge, Mass.: MIT Press, 1985.

Kurchanova, Natasha. "Osip Brik and the Avant-garde," *October* no.134 (Fall 2010): 52–73.

Landau, Ellen G. ed. *Reading Abstract Expressionism: Context and Critique.* New Haven and London: Yale University Press, 2005.

Lavrentiev, Aleksandr N, ed. *Aleksandr Rodchenko: Experiments for the Future, Diaries, Essays, Letters, and Other Writings.* Trans. Jamey Gambrell. New York: Museum of Modern Art, 2005.

Lazarev, Mikhail. *David Shterenberg: khudozhnik i vremia. Put khudozhnika.* Moscow: Galaktika, 1992.

Leonid Sokov: Sculptures, Paintings, Objects, Installations, Documents, and Articles. St. Petersburg: The State Russian Museum, 2001.

Lingwood, James, ed. *Erik Bulatov. Moscow.* London: Institute of Contemporary Art and Zurich: Parkett, 1989.

Lissitzky-Kuppers, Sophie, ed. *El Lissitzky: Life, Letters, Texts.* London: Thames and Hudson, 1968.

Lodder, Christina. *Russian Constructivism.* New Haven and London: Yale University Press, 1985.

Malevich and the American Legacy. New York: Gagosian Gallery, 2011.

Manner, Boris, ed. *Igor Makarevich and Elena Elagina: In Situ*. Moscow: Stella Art Foundation and Vienna: Kunsthistorisches Museum, 2009.

Masterkova-Tupitsyna, Margarita, ed. *Viktor Agamov-Tupitsyn and Andrei Monastyrskii, Tet-a-Tet: perepiska, dialogi, interpretatsiia, faktografiia*. Vologda: BMK, 2013.

Monastyrsky, Andrei, ed. *Kollektivnye deistviia: poezdki za gorod*. Moscow: Ad Marginem, 1998.

Natalia Abalakova and Anatoly Zhigalov, TOTART: Chetyre kolonny bditelnosti. Moscow: Maier, 2012.

Neumaier, Diane, ed. *Beyond Memory: Soviet Nonconformist Photography and Photo-related Works of Art*. New Brunswick: Rutgers University Press, 2014.

Nochlin, Linda. *Realism: Style and Civilization*. New York: Penguin, 1972.

Obukhova, Aleksandra, ed. *Group SZ: Victor Skersis and Vadim Zakharov. Collaboration*. Moscow: E.K. ArtBureau, Art Projects Foundation, ArtChronica, 2004.

__________. *Mukhomor*. Vologda: BMK, 2010.

Osborne, Peter. "The Kabakov Effect: 'Moscow Conceptualism' in the History of Contemporary Art." *Afterall* no. 42 (Autumn/Winter 2016): 111–17.

Pertsov, Viktor, ed. *Reviziia levogo fronta v sovremennom russkom iskusstve*. Moscow: Vserossiiskii Proletkult, 1925.

Rakitin, Vasilii. *Nikolai Mikhailovich Suetin*. Moscow: RA, 1998.

Ratcliff, Carter. *Komar and Melamid*. New York: Abbeville Press, 1992.

Roberts, John. *Revolutionary Time and the Avant-garde*. London and New York: Verso, 2015

Ross, David, ed. *Between Spring and Summer: Soviet Conceptual Art in the Era of Late Communism*. Cambridge, Mass.: MIT Press, 1990.

Rudenstine, Angelica Zander. *Russian Avant-garde: The George Costakis Collection*. New York: Harry N. Abrams, Inc., 1981.

Sborniki. *MANI: moskovskii arkhiv novogo iskusstva*. Vologda: BMK, 2010.

Sjeklocha, Paul, and Igor Mead. *Unofficial Art in the Soviet Union*. Berkeley: University of California Press, 1967.

Slavoj Žižek. *Did Somebody Say Totalitarianism: Five Interventions in the (Mis)Use of a Notion*. London and New York: Verso, 2001.

Solomon, Maynard, ed. *Marxism and Art*. New York: Vintage Books, 1974.

Spieker, Sven. *The Big Archive: Art from Bureaucracy*. Cambridge, Mass.: MIT Press, 2008.

Squiers, Carol, ed. *The Critical Image*. Seattle: Bay Press, 1990.

Stahel, Urs, ed. *Boris Mikhailov: A Retrospective*. Zurich: Scalo and Winterthur: Fotomuseum, 2003.

Stooss, Tony, ed. *Ilya Kabakov: Installations, 1983–2000*, cat. Raisonné. Düsseldorf: Richter, 2003.

Tupitsyn, Margarita. *Gustav Klutsis and Valentina Kulagina: Photography and Montage After Constructivism*. New York: International Center of Photography and Göttingen: Steidl, 2004.

__________. *Sots Art*. New York: The New Museum of Contemporary Art, 1986.

Tupitsyn, Margarita, and Victor Tupitsyn, eds. *Anti-shows: APT ART, 1982–1984*. London: Afterall, 2017.

Tupitsyn, Victor. *The Museological Unconscious: Communal (Post)Modernism in Russia*. Cambridge, Mass.: MIT Press, 2012.

Vakar, Irina., and Tatiana Mikhienko. *Malevich o sebe, sovremenniki o Maleviche: pisma, dokumenty, vospominaniia, kritika*. 2 vols. Moscow: RA, 2004.

Vladimir Nemukhin: zhivopis, grafika, skulptura, farfor. Moscow: Bonfi, 2012.

Volovnikov, V. *O neobyknovennom gode neobyknovennoi epokhi: neizvestnaia istoriia vystavki Pablo Picasso v SSSR v 1956 godu*. Moscow, 2007.

Wallis, Brian, ed. *Art After Modernism: Rethinking Representation*. New York: The New Museum of Contemporary Art and Boston: David R. Godine, Publisher, Inc., 1984.

Fer, Briony. *On Abstract Art*. New Haven and London: Yale University Press, 1997.

Wood, Paul, ed. *The Challenge of the Avant-garde*. New Haven and London: Yale University Press, 1999.

Yankilevsky, Vladimir. *Anatomy of Feelings*. Paris: Somogy Éditions d'Art and London: Aktis Gallery, 2009.

Zhadova, Larissa A. *Malevich: Suprematism and Revolution in Russian Art, 1910–1930*. Trans. Alexander Lieven. New York: Thames and Hudson, 1982.

ILLUSTRATION CREDITS

In most cases illustrative material has been provided by the owners or custodians of the works. Those for which further credit is due are listed below. Note that photographs of works reproduced in this book have in many instances been provided by the artists to the author before the artworks entered museum and other collections.

Photograph © Archives Nakov, Paris: 3; El Lissitzky © [2017] Artists Rights Society (ARS), New York / VG Bild-Kunst, Bonn: 4; Gustav Klutsis © [2017] Artists Rights Society (ARS), New York / VG Bild-Kunst, Bonn: 5, 8, 24, 26, 27; © 2016, State Russian Museum, St. Petersburg: 14, 16, 17, 19, 20, 21; © 2016 State Tretiakov Gallery, Moscow: 15, 18, 22, 23, 44; Valentina Kulagina © [2017] Artists Rights Society (ARS), New York / VG Bild-Kunst, Bonn: 25, 29, 33, 34, 35, 36, 37; Photo courtesy of A. Rodchenko and V. Stepanova Archive, Moscow: 30, 39, 42; Photo by Vadim Kovrigin, courtesy of A. Rodchenko and V. Stepanova Archive, Moscow: 40; Bibliothèque Kandinsky, Centre Georges Pompidou, Paris: 47, 48; Photograph courtesy of Irina Alpatova, Moscow: 49, 50, 57; Photograph © Heirs of Valery Gende-Rote: 51; Photograph courtesy of the artist's estate [Vladimir Nemukhin]: 53, 54; Courtesy of the Tsukanov Family Foundation, London: 55, 56; Photograph courtesy of the artist [Vladimir Yankilevsky]: 58, 60, 134, 158; Photograph Aleksandr Ustinov, courtesy of Irina Alpatova, Moscow: 59; Photograph courtesy of the artist [Ernst Neizvestny]: 62, 63; Photograph courtesy of the artist

[Lev Nussberg]: 65; Photograph courtesy of the artist [Francisco Infante]: 66, 67, 71, 88; Photograph courtesy of Viacheslav Koleichuk: 68; Photograph courtesy of the artist [Mikhail Chernyshov]: 72, 73; Photograph courtesy of the artist [Mikhail Roginsky]: 74, 75; Courtesy of the artist. Ilya Kabakov © [2017] Artists Rights Society (ARS), New York / VG Bild-Kunst, Bonn: 76, 77, 78, 113, 155, 156, 167, 191, 226, 229, 247; Photograph courtesy of the artist [Erik Bulatov]: 79, 80, 81, 94, 95, 119, 123, 135, 168, 220; Courtesy of the artists [Vitaly Komar and Aleksandr Melamid]: 82, 83, 84, 85, 86, 87, 97, 137, 138, 139, 140, 172; Photograph courtesy of the artists [Francisco Infante and Nona Gorunova]: 89, 90; Photograph Valentin Serov: 100, 101, 102, 103, 104; Photograph Georgy Kizevalter: 106, 107, 108, 110, 150, 159, 246; Photograph courtesy of the artist [Andrei Monastyrsky]: 109, 141, 148; Photograph Nikita Alekseev: 111; Photograph Igor Makarevich, courtesy of Igor Makarevich: 112, 116, 117, 118, 120, 121, 122, 124, 136, 145, 146, 149, 157, 165, 166, 187, 190, 214; Photograph Andrei Abramov: 114; Photograph courtesy of the artist [Sergei Mironenko]: 130, 221; Photograph courtesy of the artist [Vadim Zakharov]: 131, 256, 257; Photograph Igor Palmin, courtesy of Igor Palmin: 132, 133, 194; Photograph courtesy of the artist [Ivan Chuikov]: 142, 143, 144; Igor Makarevich. Photograph Valentin Serov: 147; Photograph Rimma Solod, courtesy of Vladimir Yankilevsky: 161; Photo courtesy of Sabine Hänsgen: 162; Photograph courtesy of the artist

[Anatoly Zhigalov]: 163; Photograph courtesy of Stella Art Foundation, Moscow: 164; Photograph Anatoly Gritsuk, courtesy of the artist [Irina Nakhova]: 169, 170, 171; Photograph courtesy of Victor Skersis: 173, 174, 175; Photograph courtesy of Ronald Feldman Fine Arts, New York: 176, 200; Photograph courtesy of the artists [Andy Warhol with Aleksandr Melamid and Vitaly Komar] / ARS: 177; Photograph courtesy of the artist's estate [Vagrich Bakhchanyan]: 179, 180, 181; Photograph courtesy of the artist [Natalia Abalakova]: 184; Aleksandr Kosolapov © [2017] Artists Rights Society (ARS), New York / VG Bild-Kunst, Bonn: 185; Photograph courtesy of the artist [Valery Gerlovin]: 192; Photograph D. James Dee, courtesy of Ronald Feldman Fine Arts, New York: 201, 202, 222; Photograph courtesy of the artist [Oleg Vasiliev]: 210; Photograph courtesy of the artist [Elena Elagina]: 233; Photograph Dennis Cowley, courtesy of Ronald Feldman Fine Arts, New York: 235; Photograph courtesy of the artist [Maria Konstantinova]: 237, 238; Photograph courtesy of the artist. Boris Mikhailov © [2017] Artists Rights Society (ARS), New York / VG Bild-Kunst, Bonn: 239, 240, 241, 242, 243, 244, 245; Photograph courtesy of the artist [Aleksei Shulgin]: 250, 251.